Social Psychology

EIGHTH EDITION

Saul Kassin
Williams College

Steven Fein
Williams College

Hazel Rose Markus
Stanford University

Prepared by

Steven Fein

Bryan L. Bonner

Revised by

Samuel R. Sommers
Tufts University

WADSWORTH
CENGAGE Learning

Australia • Brazil • Japan • Korea • Mexico • Singapore • Spain • United Kingdom • United States

ISBN-13: 978-0-8400-3173-0
ISBN-10: 0-8400-3173-4

Wadsworth
20 Davis Drive
Belmont, CA 94002-3098
USA

Cengage Learning is a leading provider of customized learning solutions with office locations around the globe, including Singapore, the United Kingdom, Australia, Mexico, Brazil, and Japan. Locate your local office at: **www.cengage.com/global**

Cengage Learning products are represented in Canada by Nelson Education, Ltd.

To learn more about Wadsworth, visit **www.cengage.com/wadsworth**

Purchase any of our products at your local college store or at our preferred online store **www.CengageBrain.com**

For product information and technology assistance, contact us at
**Cengage Learning Customer & Sales Support,
1-800-354-9706**

For permission to use material from this text or product, submit all requests online at **www.cengage.com/permissions**
Further permissions questions can be emailed to
permissionrequest@cengage.com

READ IMPORTANT LICENSE INFORMATION

Printed in the United States of America
1 2 3 4 5 6 7 14 13 12 11 10

Instructor's Resource Manual Contents

Test Bank Contents

To the Instructor

INSTRUCTOR'S RESOURCE MANUAL

This manual, accompanying *Social Psychology*, Eighth Edition, by Saul Kassin, Steven Fein, and Hazel Rose Markus is designed to meet the needs of a variety of instructors — from graduate teaching assistants to experienced professors of social psychology. The manual includes a wide range of lecture and discussion topics and classroom activities (many new to this edition) that can be used in classes of all sizes. In conjunction with these topics and activities are dozens of handouts that can be used to make the material come alive for students and enable instructors to conduct a variety of ambitious and memorable exercises in and out of class.

Learning about social psychology should be an enjoyable experience for students, and teaching it should be an enjoyable experience for instructors. The material is relevant to so much of our lives and observations. This manual is designed to help instructors take advantage of this fact by challenging their students to think critically about the issues, to become engaged in a way that should make them learn and remember the material much better, and to maximize the extent to which they find the issues applicable to their lives.

ORGANIZATION OF THe MANUAL

Learning Objectives

The first section lists the learning objectives for the chapter. The objectives provide a means for the instructor to ensure that all relevant issues have been reviewed. These objectives are used in the *Test Bank* to help instructors choose representative test questions. They are also used in the *Study Guide* to guide students toward a better understanding of the most important material in each textbook chapter. Students should be encouraged to review these learning objectives when studying.

Detailed Chapter Outline

These outlines, which are more detailed than the outlines at the beginning of each chapter of the textbook, are designed to help instructors prepare their lectures for each chapter.

Lecture and Discussion Ideas

Each chapter contains numerous thought-provoking and practical ideas for topics to use in lectures and/or to bring up for discussion. These are designed to encourage students to apply their knowledge of social psychology beyond the textbook and the classroom. Many of these ideas concern applications of theories, principles, and empirical findings to issues outside the laboratory. We also include suggestions of ways to integrate into class discussions particularly "hot" and controversial issues such as pornography, terrorism, and ethics. Moreover, we suggest other possible resources to be used to stimulate students' thinking about the issues raised in the chapter--such as books, articles, films, song lyrics, and internet discussion groups or websites. Finally, for topics that cross over between chapters we have included suggestions for tying these themes together.

Classroom Activities

These activities will encourage students to think and become excited about social psychology in ways that no other method of teaching can. Many of them are likely to be highlights of the course for the students--because they are enjoyable, vivid, and memorable, and because they make the theoretical concepts and empirical findings come alive.

The activity suggestions offered in this manual are quite comprehensive. We have included such a diverse set of ideas, methods, and procedures that we think that any instructor should be able to find at least one or two (and perhaps ten or twelve) very appropriate activities for every chapter. We have asked our colleagues around the country to identify those issues in social psychology for which they have had the most difficult time finding compelling activities, and we have responded by including a particularly large number of activities for these issues. Thus, for example, Chapter 2 of the textbook covers methodological issues--which are extremely important for the rest of the course but present a challenge to instructors about how to make this material come alive in the classroom. We have included 13 very detailed activities, along with almost thirty pages of handouts, to help instructors meet this challenge.

Each activity is accompanied by a "What if this bombs?" section, which is designed to alleviate instructors' fears about conducting a demonstration that might not work. Ways to avoid and recover from "bombs" are suggested so that any contingency will seem expected and so that you can make each and every activity a successful and productive one.

Most of these activities are designed to be run in class. Some are designed to be run outside of class. In general, it is preferable to conduct these activities *before* the students have read the corresponding textbook chapter. When this is a particularly important issue, we make note of it in our discussion of the activity.

Multimedia Resources

Encompassing both classic and contemporary material, a number of videotapes are described in each chapter that can help illustrate important points and facilitate discussion about the relevant issues from the chapter. Source information is provided for each. In addition, we have included information about computer programs and simulations, blogs and other websites, etc., that may be used to engage students ... the material.

Handouts

We have constructed an extremely large and detailed set of handouts to be used in conjunction with some of the lecture and discussion ideas and many of the classroom activities. Instructors will not need to search the literature for particularly relevant scales or to create sets of questions or manipulations in order to conduct exercises and activities; these are included in the manual.

Some of these handouts have titles that make them easily identifiable (e.g., "Instructions for the Confederate"), but many do not because the titles would reveal to the students what the activity is about before they should realize this (e.g., "Hostility Toward Women" scale). To identify the handouts, refer to their numbers (and letters, if applicable). For example, "Handout 12.4a" refers to the 4th classroom activity in Chapter 12, and it is version "a" for this activity. There are also versions "b," "c," and "d" for this activity. Similarly, "Handout 4.15e" is the "e" version of the 15th activity included in Chapter 4.

TEST BANK

This *Test Bank* accompanies the Eigth Edition of *Social Psychology* by Saul Kassin, Steven Fein and Hazel Rose Markus. It contains over 1700 multiple-choice and 70 essay questions with sample answers. These multiple-choice and essay questions have been designed to give instructors flexibility in their test construction. For all of the major points, several questions are offered so that instructors can easily construct alternative versions of quizzes and exams for different sections of a course or for different semesters. In addition, we have designed questions that vary in difficulty and style.

The newly added questions reflect changes in the textbook, and include a greater number of conceptual questions that challenge the student to integrate different ideas and to give rigorous thought to the implications of the findings described in the textbook. Within each chapter, there is a fairly even mix of items that test students' knowledge of factual information, their ability to show conceptual understanding of social psychological ideas, and their ease in applying this knowledge to practical situations or problems. Useful information about each question is indicated in the left-hand margin, such as in the following example:

    Ans: a

    p. 164

    LO1, F

The first entry specifies the correct answer for the question. The second entry identifies the page(s) in the text where the information needed to answer the question can be found. The sequence of questions follows the order in which the information is presented in the text. The third entry identifies which of several learning objectives the item addresses. The learning objectives are found in both the *Instructor's Resource Manual* and the student *Study Guide* that accompany the text. **LO1**, for example, indicates that the question is most relevant to the first learning objective of the chapter. Students are encouraged in the *Study Guide* to use these learning objectives to help organize and understand the principal ideas of each chapter. The last entry designates whether the item assesses students' knowledge of facts (**F**), their conceptual knowledge (**C**), or their ability to apply this information to practical situations (**A**).

By systematically choosing items according to learning objectives, an instructor can ensure that a test assesses the *breadth* of students' understanding of course material. By varying the proportion of items that are factual, conceptual, or applied, the instructor can manipulate the extent to which the test assesses the *depth* of the students' understanding. The variety and number of multiple-choice questions should provide instructors with a wide range of choices for test construction, but instructors should keep in mind the potential problems of using multiple questions about a similar issue on the same test. For example, one question might ask the student to identify a particular concept based on its definition or description. A subsequent question might identify this particular concept and ask the student to apply it to some practical problem. If these two items are used on the same test, particularly if they are presented in close proximity to each other, students may be able to answer the first question by reading the second question. We have put these kinds of overlapping questions near each other in the *Test Bank* so that they will be easy to spot, giving instructors the opportunity to select which items are most appropriate for any one particular test and to save other items for alternative or subsequent tests.

The essay questions share a common goal of requiring students to demonstrate thoughtful understanding of the important issues raised in the textbook rather than rote memorization. Each essay question is followed by a sample essay that can be used as a standard or guide for the instructor to use when evaluating the students' answers.

This test bank is also available in Examview for Windows and Macintosh computers. The easy-to-use software allows instructors to edit and scramble questions, add their own material, and generate exams.

CHAPTER 1

What is Social Psychology?

LEARNING OBJECTIVES: GUIDELINES FOR STUDY

You should be able to do each of the following by the conclusion of Chapter 1.

1. Define social psychology. Identify the kinds of questions that social psychologists try to answer. (*pp. 5-7*)

2. Explain how social psychology differs from sociology and other fields of psychology. Assess the limitations of the following statement: *all social psychological findings are simply common sense.* (*pp. 9-12*)

3. Describe the early origins of social psychology and the state of the field up until 1950. Identify when the field of social psychology became a distinct field of study, the various founders of the field, and the historical event that inspired interest in and shaped the field of social psychology. Explain the contributions made by Allport, Sherif, and Lewin. (*pp. 13-15*)

4. Describe the state of social psychology from the 1960s to the mid-1970s, from the mid-70s to the 1990s, and in the present, new century. Explain the various ways in which contemporary social psychology can be referred to as "pluralistic." (*pp. 15-16*)

5. Distinguish between different perspectives social psychologists use to understand human behavior. Define social cognition. Summarize the increasing effort in social psychology to develop an international and multicultural perspective. (*pp. 17-19*)

6. Explain how social psychology incorporates biological, evolutionary, and sociocultural perspectives of human behavior. Describe the role of new technologies such as PET and fMRI in the investigation of social behavior. (*pp. 18-21*)

DETAILED CHAPTER OUTLINE

I.   What is Social Psychology?
   A.   Defining Social Psychology
      1.   Scientific study
      2.   How individuals think, feel, and behave
      3.   A social context
   B.   Social Psychological questions and Applications
   C.   The Power of the Social Context: An Example of a Social Psychology Experiment
   D.   Social Psychology and Related Fields: Distinctions and Intersections
      1.   Social psychology and sociology
      2.   Social psychology and clinical psychology
      3.   Social psychology and personality psychology
      4.   Social psychology and cognitive psychology
   E.   Social Psychology and Common Sense
II. From Past to Present: A Brief History of Social Psychology
   A.   The Birth and Infancy of Social Psychology: 1880s–1920s
   B.   A Call to Action: 1930s–1950s
      1.   Muzafer Sherif
      2.   Kurt Lewin

            a)   social perception
            b)   the interactionist perspective
            c)   applications of social psychology

    C.   Confidence and Crisis: 1960s–Mid-1970s
        1.   Stanley Milgram's research on obedience
        2.   Critiques of experiments
    D.   An Era of Pluralism: Mid-1970s–1990s
        1.   "Hot" versus "cold" perspectives
        2.   Social cognition
        3.   International and cultural perspectives

III. Social Psychology in a New Century
    A.   Integration of Emotion, Motivation, and Cognition
    B.   Biological and Evolutionary Perspectives
        1.   Behavioral genetics
        2.   Evolutionary psychology
    C.   Cultural Perspectives
        1.   Cross-cultural research
        2.   Multi-cultural research
    D.   New Technologies

LECTURE AND DISCUSSION IDEAS

Idea 1.   Defining Social Psychology

Read to the class the definition of social psychology that is presented in the textbook: "Social psychology is the scientific study of how individuals think, feel, and behave in a social context." Divide this definition into different parts, and ask the students to explain what they think each part means in the context of defining the field. These parts could consist of "scientific study," "how individuals think, feel, and behave," etc. First, ask the students what it means to study something in a "scientific" way. Refer to the discussion of this topic in the textbook in Chapter 1 and throughout Chapter 2. Second, what is the significance of the word "individuals" in the definition of social psychology? (This raises the issue of the level of analysis used in the field.) See the discussion of this in the textbook; for example, sociology tends to have a "group" level of analysis whereas social psychology tends to focus on individuals. Third, ask the students to consider what "social context" means. Ask them for examples from their own lives in which they've felt a social context impacted their behavior.

Distinguish social psychology from sociology and other fields within psychology (such as cognitive and personality), and from common sense or intuition. You might want to use Table 1.2 from the textbook to guide this discussion.

All of these questions should get students to think about the kinds of issues that will be covered in the course, which should serve both as a preview of the material to be covered and as a way to get students to better understand what social psychology is and is not.

One alternative method of raising these issues is to ask the students to write down their own guesses as to what social psychology really is *before* you read the definition to them. This would only work well if the students have not read Chapter 1 already. After they come up with their own definitions, you can start a discussion of how their definitions differ from each other's and from the book's, and why.

Related to this lecture/discussion idea are the second and third Classroom Activities. These activities concern the similarities and distinctions between social psychology and some related fields. (In each chapter of this *Instructor's Resource Manual*, the Classroom Activities follow the Lecture and Discussion Ideas.)

Idea 2.   Becoming a Social Psychologist

Students often find it very interesting to learn why and how their instructors first became interested in their fields. Tell students what first attracted you to social psychology and how your initial interests evolved into your present interests and position (if you are not a social psychologist, explain why you were interested in teaching social psychology).

One way to get students excited about social psychology is to show them how some famous social psychologists first got excited about it themselves. The book, *Social Psychologists: Research Adventures*, can be an excellent resource here. A number of social psychologists talk in engaging, informal ways about what got them interested in the research that they do and how they do this research. The topics range from love to prejudice, aggression to helping, including applied areas such as law and health. Consider summarizing some of these stories to the students during the first classes or assigning part of the book for the students to read.

Brannigan, G. G., & Merrens, M. R. (1995). Social psychologists: Research adventures. New York: McGraw-Hill.

Idea 3.   Relevance of Social Psychology to a Variety of Careers

Most students will not become social psychologists. However, it should become clear to them as they read the textbook and come to class that social psychology training is relevant to a huge variety of careers. Instruct your students to consider this as they read about each new topic in the course. Discuss some of the jobs for which social psychology training can be particularly appropriate. Within the academic community, these range from other positions within a psychology department, such as industrial/organizational psychology, and other academic positions, such as in business schools, law schools, communications departments, political science departments, sociology departments, public health departments, and women's studies departments. There are even more numerous non-academic avenues, such as in marketing, advertising, sales, organizational consulting, human resource management, mass media, jury consulting, the military, government agencies (such as the National Science Foundation, the Federal Judiciary Center, and the Centers for Disease Control), political consulting, opinion polling, etc. Discuss how social psychological training can be so valuable for any executive, investor, or person who needs to make decisions about how to manage groups of people, how to predict how others will behave or react, and how to avoid many of the biases that impair people's ability to make accurate, rational decisions.

A great resource on the Internet for information about careers relevant to psychology, as well as a host of related issues, is Scott Plous's website at: http://www.socialpsychology.org/career.htm.

As a way of illustrating why social psychological training can be so valuable for so many types of occupations, go over each textbook chapter with the students and ask them to imagine the relevance of the topics listed in the chapter preview or outline for as many different kinds of jobs as they can imagine. Another way to do this is to choose a job such as in sales or marketing. Choose a topic or two from each of several chapters and discuss how understanding these issues would help someone in this field. For example, discuss how understanding research design and opinion polling (Ch. 2), self-monitoring (Ch. 3), shortcuts and biases in how people form impressions of others (Ch. 4), stereotypes (Ch. 5), theories of persuasion (Ch. 6), compliance techniques (Ch. 7), negotiation (Ch. 8), etc. would be extremely valuable to someone in sales or marketing.

Consider telling the students about the results of a study by Lehman, Lempert, and Nisbett (1988) that examined the effects of graduate training in various fields, including psychology, on the use of rules of inductive reasoning—which are crucial for effective decision making and evaluation. The participants in this study were graduate students in psychology, chemistry, law, and medicine at the University of Michigan. Lehman and colleagues found that of these different types of graduate training, the psychology training had the most dramatic and positive effect on the students' reasoning abilities, concerning both material with scientific content and material with everyday-life content. This study is referred to in Chapter 2 of the textbook.

Lehman, D. R., Lempert, R. O., & Nisbett, R. E. (1988). The effects of graduate training on reasoning: Formal discipline and thinking about everyday-life events. American Psychologist, 43, 431-442.

Idea 4.   Placing Social Psychology in its Historical Context

Discuss the history of social psychology based on the review in Chapter 1. One interesting point of discussion could be connecting how issues that were salient in the world at various points of time during the twentieth century influenced what issues were being researched in social psychology at the time. The easiest place to start this discussion would be the 1930s and 1940s, around the time of World War II. Ask the students to imagine what types of questions the war raised about humanity. Then review the kinds of social psychological research that became popular during and after this period, including research on stereotypes and prejudice, aggression, attitudes and persuasion, conformity, and obedience (see the discussion of this era in the textbook). You can also discuss how the social upheaval of the 1960s and early 1970s led to the period marked both by confidence and crisis in the field.

As we are now in a new century, it might be appropriate to ask the students to consider the social issues that were most pressing at the turn of the twentieth century, and now at the start of the 21st. Have the students consider how events in the world a century ago might have influenced the first social psychological research by Triplett (1897–1898). This research examined the performance of the individual in the presence of other people. Did this interest reflect concerns in the industrialized world as it approached the turn of the century? What do the students think are the big issues a century later, at the beginning of the new millennium? What impact might these issues have on the social psychology research of the next decade or two?

Triplett, N. (1897-1898). The dynamogenic factors in pacemaking and competition. American Journal of Psychology, 9, 507-533.

Idea 5.   Using the Social Psychology Classroom as a Laboratory

In chapters 12, 13, and 14 of the textbook, the authors apply the principles of social psychology to law (Ch. 12), business (Ch. 13), and health (Ch. 14). Randolph Smith (2005) proposes applying social psychology concepts to an additional domain, the classroom. He discusses how teaching students (and teachers) to recognize certain social psychological concepts in their classroom behavior might help them to avoid negative tendencies, nurture positive ones, and see an improvement in their overall ability to make wise decisions. The following topics are encountered in the classroom:

Self-handicapping. Self-handicapping has to do with sabotaging or undermining one's own performance in order to have a ready excuse in case of failure. That such behavior occurs in the classroom was supported by several research studies. Specifically, it was found that high self-handicappers tend to procrastinate when it comes to studying for tests, spend less time studying, and consequently receive lower grades. Randolph says that students self-handicap because not doing so and failing in spite of hard work would make them feel incompetent or stupid. So, self-handicapping protects their self-esteem. Moreover, he says that faculty members are also often guilty of self-handicapping by procrastination when it comes to preparing lectures, polishing conference papers, or submitting grant applications.

Self-serving bias. The self-serving bias is the tendency to attribute success to our own efforts or talents and failure to outside forces that are not under our control. In one study, pairs of students were engaged in a teaching/learning situation. When the learners received false feedback about their performance with a grade of 90 or 50 percent, they justified the 90 by extolling to their own ability and excused the 50 by blaming the teacher. When students do not assume responsibility for failures, they have no reason to try a different behavior, such as studying more effectively. A follow-up study demonstrated a similar tendency among instructors. When asked to think of a recent course where they gave a student an A or an F, instructors took credit for students' successes and distanced themselves from the failures by blaming the students. Like self-handicapping, the self-serving bias helps both students and teachers to maintain high self-esteem.

Belief perseverance. Belief perseverance is the tendency to maintain beliefs in the face of contradictory evidence. When psychology students were given a 60-item test of "common misconceptions about psychology," they tended on the average to agree with 20% of those false beliefs. That was true even for students who had taken 5 psychology courses. The belief perseverance began to wane significantly only for those who had taken at least 6 classes. Some instructors, says Randolph, despair that they're unable to change the beliefs about psychology that students bring to class. By thinking that, the instructors, too, are manifesting belief perseverance.

Fundamental attribution error. The fundamental attribution error is the tendency to emphasize personal factors and downplay the situation when it comes to explaining other people's behavior. In one study, where students read pro-Castro and anti-Castro essays written by people who either chose the position or were assigned to it, the students attributed characteristics to the writers based solely on the content of the essays. A similar result was found when students were asked to rate professors' hypothetical lectures on the topic of biological influences on intelligence: again, the students ignored the situation and focused only on the lectures and concluded that the professors were racist and sexist. Likewise, similar attributional biases were found in elementary school teachers. At the beginning of the year, they were asked to rank students based on academic potential. Several months later, they were asked to list reasons for students' successes and failures. When students were successful, teachers made internal attributions for those they had ranked high and external attributions for those they had ranked low (e.g., He succeeded because he's smart, and she succeeded because her older sister tutored her). When the students failed, the pattern was reversed (e.g., He failed because his parents got a divorce, and she failed because she is not very smart). According to Randolph, students believe that professors are what they teach and teachers believe that students are what grades they earn. Both need to learn to consider more than just personal factors.

Social categorization. Social categorization involves the process of sorting people into groups according to certain characteristics. That inevitably leads to seeing some people as belonging to an ingroup and all others as members of outgroups. In one study involving social categorization, students were divided into two groups based on the flip of a coin. When asked to rate each other on eight personality characteristics, they showed a clear ingroup bias, in that they tended to rate those not in their group much lower. When there are outgroups and ingroups there is inevitably an outgroup homogeneity bias. That refers to seeing variability in our own group but perceiving all those in the other group to be similar. This effect was demonstrated when students and elderly people who were asked to rate hypothetical students and hypothetical elderly people on eight attributes. Each group gave less variable ratings to the other group than to their peers. Randolph states that social categorization is responsible for students and teachers adopting an "us versus them" mentality. He quotes colleagues who complain, "They're all so lazy," and he wonders what students feel about all professors.

Overjustification effect. The overjustification effect occurs when a person is rewarded for doing something that was rewarding in itself. As a result, the activity loses its intrinsic value. Randolph says that the study of psychology carries intrinsic value for students until they are made to study it for grades. He cites a study where undergraduates who liked solving puzzles were paid to do so and were subsequently less interested in the activity. In a similar vein, Randolph mentions how he used to belong to a faculty reading group, where members would get together monthly and discuss a book. At the end of each meeting, the leader of the group would introduce the next selection. After a while, says

Randolph, the professors began to sound just like the students. Instead of looking forward to future reading, they griped about how many pages were in the book and how the print was too small. Citing a study where the influence of the overjustification effect was mitigated by stressing intrinsic motivation, Randolph calls on teachers to stop teaching social psychology as if it were a dry, boring subject. Instead, he says, teachers must understand that social psychology is inherently interesting to students, in that it satisfies their curiosity about how others behave. With creative teaching, he believes that students can again realize how much they enjoy learning all about it.

Smith, R. (2005). The classroom as a social psychology laboratory. Journal of Social and Clinical Psychology, 24, 1, 62-71.

Idea 6.   Hidden-Camera "Experiments" in the Media

In addition to spotlighting actual social psychological research, prime-time TV news magazine shows also frequently do their own brand of research in which they use hidden cameras to observe and record instances of bias and discrimination. Showing one of these stories may be an especially provocative way of introducing the students to several issues relevant to the course. For example, show students one of the following segments from ABC News programs *Prime Time Live* or *20/20*: a story illustrating racial discrimination, called "True Colors"; a story illustrating sexism, called "The Fairer Sex?"; a story illustrating age discrimination, called "Age & Attitudes"; or a story illustrating how people are treated differently as a function of how physically attractive they are, called "The Ugly Truth." Each of these stories includes vivid, compelling, and sometimes infuriating footage. The students will be engrossed. The focus of each of these stories—racism, sexism, physical appearance, etc.—will be covered in the course. In addition, these stories raise issues about research methods, such as how to make observations of people's behavior, the use of covert techniques, the discrepancy between self-reports (in which people claim to not be prejudiced) and actual behavior, and the scientific method. This last issue is one that the students often don't realize, but it is very important to discuss. The news programs may report only those incidents that make for the most interesting, easy-to-tell story. These incidents may not be representative of all that their hidden cameras saw, and the validity may be suspect. Contrast these standards with the standards that social psychologists must adhere to in their own research. Finally, any discussion of hidden-camera observations should include a discussion of ethics. Is it ethical to secretly videotape people? Under what conditions is or isn't it appropriate? Does the greater good of illustrating the presence of discrimination outweigh the invasion of privacy and deception that are likely to be involved? Consider also discussing the role of values here. Do the values of the people at the TV networks influence which kinds of stories they are most likely to pursue? Would they be as quick to air and promote stories about discrimination, for example, that might be considered "politically incorrect," or that might annoy financially powerful sponsors of the networks? *Should* values play an important role in these programs? What about in social psychological research? There is no consensus of opinion on this issue within the field, so there is unlikely to be much consensus among your students, but it could make for interesting and thought-provoking discussion.

All above referenced videos are listed in the multimedia resources section of Chapter 5 in this manual.

Idea 7.   Cultural Perspectives

Social psychologists today are considering the role of culture in their research more than ever before. Discuss this emerging theme in social psychology, and ask the students to consider the challenges and importance of doing research in ways that take into account cultural similarities and differences. Discuss any one classic experiment in social psychology, and ask the class to speculate about whether or not they think the results are likely to be culturally specific or universal. Have the students justify their guesses. Research on conformity or obedience might be particularly good to use as an example. Preview a classic study (such as Asch's line-judgment research or Milgram's research on obedience;

see Chapter 7), and ask the students to imagine whether similar or different results would apply in a variety of other countries. Ask the students to explain their responses. Why do they predict similar or different results? On a more general level, ask the students to indicate what they think of when they hear the word "conformity" or that someone acted in a conforming way. What are the connotations? Most students will probably indicate negative connotations, such as people being "spineless" or "wishy-washy" or untrue to their "selves." Point out to the class that these may be very Western, individualistic perspectives. In more collectivistic cultures, conforming to the norms of others is often seen much more positively, as adopting the role that is appropriate in a particular situation. People from such cultures are less likely to worry about being true to their one core "self" and instead see their selves as fluid and multi-faceted. For more information about this see Chapters 3 and 7 of the textbook.

This discussion will not only preview some of the cross-cultural research discussed in the course, but should also be used to make a general point about the influence of socio-cultural contexts on individuals' thoughts, feelings, and behaviors. This point lies at the heart of social psychology.

Idea 8. Using Neuroimaging to Test Social Psychological Constructs

As the text mentions, there are researchers who are interested in bridging neuroscience and social psychology. One technique that is fueling this research is the fMRI, or functional magnetic resonance imaging. The fMRI is a non-invasive, relatively inexpensive method that can be used with healthy brains and that allows researchers to localize neural activity that is associated with mental activity. It does this by measuring blood flow. It's based on the assumption that neural activity creates an increased demand for oxygen at the active region, which is met by an increase of blood shunted to the region. The technology identifies which particular structures of the brain are associated with specific psychological functions.

Students might be interested in learning how one social psychological construct, social exclusion, was studied using the neuroimaging technique of fMRI.

The researchers (Eisenberger, Lieberman & Williams, 2003) hypothesized that social exclusion produces an emotional pain (caused by hurt feelings) that is analogous to physical pain, and that, therefore, both events would be experienced in the same neural structures of the brain.

Participants were scanned by fMRI while they played a virtual ball-tossing game ("Cyberball"), with two other "players." In reality, there were no other players. They were only playing with a preset computer. There were three groups of participants. One group watched the other "players" play but its members were unable to join in because of what they were told were "technical problems." A second group was allowed to join the play. Members of the third group, the experimental one, received seven tosses and were then shut out of the game (for the next 45). Afterwards, members of the group were asked to fill out questionnaires to assess their emotional distress as a consequence of being excluded from the game.

The scans revealed patterns of activation that were similar to those that had been reported in studies of physical pain. Namely, that the anterior cingulate cortex (ACC) was more active during exclusion than during inclusion and correlated positively with levels of self-reported distress. The ACC is the part of the brain that is normally activated by physical pain and serves notice that "something is wrong." Another area of the brain, the right ventral prefrontal cortex (RVPFC), was also active during exclusion and correlated positively with self-reported distress. The RVPFC has been implicated in the regulation or inhibition of pain messages. Its heightened activation signals that the brain is acting to alleviate pain. The researchers concluded that the social pain of exclusion is neurologically similar to physical pain, which is why we feel the pain when we lose someone that we love.

Eisenberger, N. I., Lieberman, M. D., & Williams, K. D. (2003). Does rejection hurt? An fMRI study of social exclusion. Science, 302, 290-292.

Willingham, D. T., & Dunn, E. W. (2003). What neuroimaging and brain localization can do, cannot do, and should not do for social psychology. Journal of Personality and Social Psychology, 85, 662-671.

Idea 9.   Doing Research on the Internet

The Internet presents social psychologists with unique research opportunities. In their article, "Plan 9 from outer space," authors McKenna and Bargh (2000) elaborate on some of the advantages and methodological specifics of doing research online.

The obvious advantage of online naturalistic studies is that they can be done unobtrusively by observing chat room responses or newsgroup posts. Data collection is simplified by using searchable archives such as Dejanews (http://www.dejanews.com/), which contains hundreds of thousands of newsgroups' posted messages going back to 1995. Worldwide populations are available for study. And an anonymity factor allows people to let down their guard and express, to a greater degree, uncensored emotions and thoughts. Although, the same lessened control could also mean that communication is more affected by temporary states, such as mood, emotion, or experiences.

The main advantage to doing surveys on the Internet is that participants are easier and less costly to recruit. However, population parameters need to be carefully defined. Users of the various communication venues (e.g., newsgroups, chat rooms, and multi-user dungeons) are very different from each other. Moreover, cross-cultural samples may not be representative of the general population of their respective countries.

Each communication venue has its own specific methodological requirements. Newsgroups are easily accessible but it's necessary to choose one whose postings are not mostly cross-posts and spam. Chat rooms and multi-user dungeons require an access program, users are not identified by e-mail addresses, and postings take place in real time. That means that the population varies by age and nationality according to the time of day.

Experimental studies can be conducted online, as well, with all the advantages of offline experiments (like random assignment and control of extraneous variables). Any manipulation that is conducted in real life experiments can be duplicated with persons in the laboratory who have separate direct connections to the Internet.

However, there are some special risks and safeguards inherent in doing experimental research online. These were summarized, as follows, in a recent article in American Psychologist (Kraut, Olson, Banaji, Bruckman, Cohen, & Couper, 2004). In addition to the aforementioned generalizability problem, the sample may also be biased because of self-selection and the high dropout rate of online research. Moreover, data collection is problematic because the online researcher has less control than he would in the lab. For example, it's more difficult to verify identity, age, and gender online. It's also less obvious when intervention is called for due to undesirable effects on participants. Moreover, the anonymous nature of the Internet permits those who are so inclined to submit multiple responses.

Then there is the possibility that the researcher will not be able to appropriately debrief those who drop out, especially in studies that use deception. As a result, a participant may leave a study upset at discovering some "truth" about him or her self, which in reality is not true. There is also the potential for harm to participants if the group in which they participate is somehow damaged by the research study. For example, group members occasionally become disenchanted with being observed and break up a support group.

In closing, the authors offer the following advice to those who wish to conduct online research: be on guard for potentially biased samples, start with a small pilot project to screen for potential problems, distinguish between private and public online behavior, take special precautions to keep out minors without parental consents, and if the potential risk to participants is high, don't use the Internet.

Ask your students if any of them ever participated in online research and if they felt the experience was positive. If they've also participated in offline research, ask them to compare the two in terms of procedure (i.e., consent, data collection, and debriefing).

Kraut, R., Olson, J., Banaji, M., Bruckman, A., Cohen, J., & Couper, M. (2004). Psychological research online: Report of Board of Scientific Affairs' Advisory Group on the Conduct of Research on the Internet. American Psychologist, 59, 105-117.

McKenna, K. Y. A., & Bargh, J. A. (2000). Plan 9 from cyberspace: The implications of the Internet for personality and social psychology. Personality and Social Psychology Review, 4, Issue 1.

Idea 10.   Articles from the Book of Readings

Available with the textbook is *Readings in Social Psychology: The Art and Science of Research*, which features original classic and contemporary articles reporting social psychological research. For the first class or two, a classic article that could spark great interest in the course and good discussion is Rosenthal and Jacobson's (1968) article on the self-fulfilling prophecy in the classroom, entitled, "Teacher Expectations for the Disadvantaged." Similarly, discussing Milgram's (1963) classic, "Behavioral Study of Obedience," could be a great way to kick off the class.

Idea 11.   The Society of Personality and Social Psychology: Becoming a Member and Getting Lecture and Discussion Ideas through its e-Mail Lists

The Society of Personality and Social Psychology (SPSP) is the largest organization of social and personality psychologists in the world. Membership in SPSP is open to students as well as professionals – anyone interested in personality and social psychology is welcome to join. We strongly encourage you consider joining; the benefits are great and the costs are low. You might also encourage your students join as well.

The benefits of SPSP membership include publications, annual conference events, public interest activities, and support for student education and research. At no additional cost beyond the annual membership fee, SPSP members receive subscriptions to the following three publications: (1) *Personality and Social Psychology Bulletin*; (2) *Personality and Social Psychology Review*; and (3) *Dialogue* (the Society's semi-annual newsletter). The cost of membership is $38 for those who have earned a doctorate or $25 for undergraduate students, graduate students, or retired faculty. For more information, check out the SPSP webpage (http://www.spsp.org/), or contact Dr. David Dunning, the Executive Officer of SPSP (Department of Psychology, Cornell University, Ithaca, NY 14850; dad6@cornell.edu).

Another benefit of SPSP membership is that you can join an e-mail group that facilitates communication among the many members. The social and personality psychologists in this group discuss topical and classic issues in the field, and this list can be a very valuable resource from which to get ideas for lecture and discussion in your class. You don't have to say a word if you don't want to; just sit back and read the many e-mails that come through this list, and you'll see discussions and debates about many different issues, such as the ethics of particular lines of research, the public policy implications of some research findings, or how to get students interested in a particular topic. In addition to these discussion ideas, you will also see announcements of conferences, jobs, new books, etc. If you're interested, contact Dr. Kathryn Quina by e-mailing kquina@uri.edu.

You can learn about some other relevant e-mail groups at the following address: http://www.spsp.org/email.htm

CLASSROOM ACTIVITIES

Note: Most of the classroom activities we include here could also be used in conjunction with Chapter 2 because both chapters introduce the students to the field of social psychology, although Chapter 2 focuses specifically on research methods. In addition, many of the ideas offered in Chapter 2 of this manual could be great for the first day or two of the course, as additional ways to introduce social psychology.

Activity 1. Intuitions About Social Psychology

This activity can serve as an engaging preview of the kinds of questions that will be addressed in the course. In addition, it can illustrate how much of social psychology might seem intuitive or commonsensical—*after* one learns the findings. Because common sense and intuition can be used to explain even contradictory principles or findings, there is a tendency among many students to think that what they are learning in the course is obvious. This activity, as well as the next one, can be used to illustrate how this is more a result of hindsight than a real problem.

Handout 1.1a contains 40 statements concerning social psychological phenomena from every chapter of the textbook. Some of these statements are true, others are false. Distribute copies of the handout to students and ask them to read each statement, to write a "T" or "F" in the first blank line before each statement to indicate whether they think that statement is true or false, and then to write a number from 1 to 7 in the second blank line to indicate the degree to which they are confident in the answer they gave for that statement.

The correct answer for some of these statements is likely to be consistent with most people's intuitions, for other items it is likely to be counter-intuitive, and for still other items it is unclear which response is warranted by intuition. The correct answer for each statement is given below (in parentheses next to each answer is the number of the relevant textbook chapter for that statement).

T (Ch. 1)	T (Ch. 6)	T (Ch. 9)	F (Ch. 11)
T (Ch. 2)	F (Ch. 6)	T (Ch. 9)	F (Ch. 11)
F (Ch. 3)	F (Ch. 7)	T (Ch. 9)	F (Ch. 12)
F (Ch. 3)	T (Ch. 7)	T (Ch. 9)	T (Ch. 12)
T (Ch. 3)	T (Ch. 7)	F (Ch. 9)	F (Ch. 12)
T (Ch. 4)	F (Ch. 7)	F (Ch. 10)	F (Ch. 12)
T (Ch. 4)	T (Ch. 7)	F (Ch. 10)	F (Ch. 13)
F (Ch. 4)	F (Ch. 8)	T (Ch. 11)	F (Ch. 13)
F (Ch. 5)	T (Ch. 8)	T (Ch. 11)	T (Ch. 14)
T (Ch. 5)	F (Ch. 8)	T (Ch. 11)	F (Ch. 14)

Handout 1.1b is a similar questionnaire, but it contains only twenty items and thus can be used instead of Handout 1.1a if time is short in class. Most, but not all, of the items in Handout 1.1b are different from those in Handout 1.1a. The correct answers and relevant chapter numbers for these statements are listed below:

F (Ch. 1)	F (Ch. 5)	F (Ch. 8)	F (Ch. 11)
T (Ch. 2)	F (Ch. 5)	F (Ch. 9)	F (Ch. 12)
F (Ch. 3)	F (Ch. 6)	F (Ch. 9)	F (Ch. 12)
T (Ch. 4)	T (Ch. 7)	T (Ch. 10)	F (Ch. 13)
F (Ch. 4)	T (Ch. 7)	T (Ch. 11)	T (Ch. 14)

When the students have completed the questionnaires, either (a) collect them and calculate for each statement what proportion of the students got the answer correct, or (b) read each question to the students and ask them to raise their hands if they said "true," and try to get a sense of what proportion of students gave the correct responses. Discuss several of these items, and ask some of the students to explain their responses. If you collect their questionnaires, calculate the average degree of confidence that students had in their correct and incorrect answers. It would be particularly interesting to demonstrate that students were no less confident on average in their incorrect answers than in their correct answers. You also might look to see if there are gender differences in confidence, particularly because men tend to report higher levels of confidence than do women -- this could lead to another interesting topic of discussion.

As you discuss the various items, you can begin to preview the course and get students thinking in social psychological terms. Provide explanations to students for some of the answers, but also encourage the students to think on their own by asking them to try to come up with their own explanations during the course of the term.

An important point to make with this activity is the value of social psychology's emphasis on empirical research and the scientific method. As this questionnaire should illustrate, intuition and common sense are correct some of the time, incorrect some of the time, and irrelevant or too ambiguous to be useful most of the time. Rather than relying on introspection and unsystematic observation, social psychologists use scientific methods to test their hypotheses. This is part of the fun, and the challenge, of being a social psychologist. Encourage students to see the creativity, as well as the scientific rigor, involved in the studies they will be learning during the course.

We know of other versions of this activity in which all of the answers are counter-intuitive or all are false. That is not the case with this exercise, in part because such questionnaires are vulnerable to response biases and suspicion. For example, if all of the answers are counter-intuitive, students may figure this out as they go through the activity, or they may be rewarded for simply being biased toward counter-intuitive responses. These are methodological flaws that might be worth discussing as you go over the results of the questionnaire. Moreover, it is misleading to suggest that all, most, or even just the most interesting social psychological findings are counter-intuitive. The point is that intuition alone is not likely to lead one to make accurate, valid predictions. Rather, empirical research using the principles of the scientific method is necessary.

Consider giving the same questionnaire to the students at the end of the course. At the end of the course, their answers should be much more accurate. Compare their pre- and post-course performances to illustrate to the students how much they learned in the course.

♦*What if this bombs?* This activity is fairly bombproof. Because the variety of statements on the questionnaire provides a good preview of the kinds of issues that the course will cover, this activity is bombproof as a way to introduce the field of social psychology to your students. The statements concern issues that are interesting and representative, and every student should be enthusiastic at the prospect of learning more about at least some of the important points. The only way that this activity could bomb is if you introduce this activity as one that is designed to show that much of social psychology is counter-intuitive. Although it is very unlikely, it certainly is possible that many of the students in a class will give the correct response to most of the statements, and that their reported confidence will predict their accuracy. Thus, if you introduce the activity as one that should demonstrate how counter-intuitive most of social psychology is, and you later reveal that most of the students knew the correct answers, the value of the activity will be undermined (and you will have a small "bomb" on your hands).

Therefore, you should introduce the activity simply as a way to preview some of the topics that will be covered in the course, and explain that you are interested in the students' intuitions about these topics. If the results of the questionnaire reveal that the students were not particularly good at distinguishing accurately between true and false statements, and that their reported confidence did not predict their accuracy, *then* you can make the additional points about the shortcomings of intuition, the tendency to see these points in hindsight as not surprising even though they really are, etc. Even if the students' intuitions do lead them to give the correct responses, emphasize the point that intuition alone should not be trusted and that only through empirical research that uses the principles of the scientific method can we know which of our intuitions are accurate and which are not.

Activity 2. Distinguishing Social Psychology from Personality Psychology

Handout 1.2 contains brief descriptions of the behaviors of four fictitious individuals in the same set of four situations. Distribute copies of the handout to the students, or make a transparency from the handout and show it to the class. Use this handout to illustrate the different perspectives that a personality psychologist and a social psychologist might take in analyzing the information given.

The personality perspective emphasizes the cross-situational consistency within the individuals. For example, across the four different situations, Karen seems to be extroverted and likes to talk a lot, Jessica is more withdrawn and apparently unhappy, Arnold (who is meant to be a parody of the movie image of Arnold Schwarzenegger) has violent thoughts and tendencies, and Bob seems rather non-descript. This perspective -- focusing on the personal characteristics and dispositions of individuals -- is one that people often take when observing others and trying to explain their behavior (see Chapter 3).

The social psychological perspective, on the other hand, looks for consistency across different individuals within particular situations. That is, the social psychologist would be especially interested in examining why particular situational factors influence most people in a similar way. Therefore, a social psychologist might note that when these individuals heard bad news about the economy, they all responded by doing something rather negative. More strikingly, when they heard a sudden loud noise, three of the four individuals responded in the same way. These similar effects across individuals suggest that there may be a phenomenon of interest to social psychologists (for relevant explanations of this phenomenon, see the textbook discussions concerning social comparison theory [Ch. 3], the link between fear or stress and the desire to affiliate [Ch. 9], and intervening in an emergency [Ch. 10]).

Note that Arnold's reactions to these situations are not very similar to those of the other individuals. This illustrates an important point. There are some exceptions to virtually any rule, or, in this case, to any social psychological principle. The social psychological principles that will be discussed throughout the course may apply to most people, or to most people within particular cultures or categories, but no social psychologist would expect that *everyone's* behavior will be entirely consistent with the principles. In this case, Arnold may be better served by a clinical psychological approach than by a personality or social psychological approach.

After distinguishing the social from the personality perspective, inform the students that the distinction you illustrated was a simplified version of reality. In truth, many social psychologists are interested in _both_ individual differences _and_ the effects of situational factors. As Chapter 1 explains, these intersections have been quite fruitful in generating theory and research. You can trace the roots of this _interactionist perspective_ to Kurt Lewin's work in the 1930s and 1940s. Moreover, you can also call attention to other ways in which social psychology is linked to other fields within and beyond psychology, such as social cognition, social development, political psychology, organizational behavior, and human resource management.

> ◗*What if this bombs?* This activity should be relatively bombproof. Students should find the activity interesting, and, as long as they put some effort into the task, it should serve as a good introduction to the distinction between social and personality psychology.

Activity 3. Social Psychology and Related Fields: Distinctions and Intersections

This activity is related to the second lecture/discussion idea described earlier in this chapter. The activity is designed to get the students to understand what it means to think like a social psychologist, as well as to get them to see the links between social psychology and other fields. It is designed also to give the students the experience of doing some library research and summarizing the results of one or more studies.

Assign the students to find relevant, recent journal articles that report empirical research that bridges social psychology with one other field, either within psychology (such as personality, clinical, cognitive, developmental, organizational, health, biological, educational, etc.) or outside of psychology (sociology, biology, economics, etc.). You might want to assign one or two of these topics to some students, a different one or two to a different set of students, and so on. Use your judgment about what constraints to use, such as requiring that the research be no more than one year old. Lecture and Discussion Idea 2 lists the titles of some journals that are particularly appropriate outlets for such research. Consider explaining how to do a literature search on an electronic database, such as _PsycLit_. Using multiple keywords on such databases (such as "'social psychology' and 'sociology'"), students can quickly get information about numerous journal articles that might be appropriate and interesting for this assignment.

Tell the students that the articles they find should be interesting and understandable to them, and that they clearly should be relevant to social psychology but also applicable to the other field. The students should summarize the article(s), including stating the purpose of the research, how the research was conducted, what the researchers found, and what the implications of these findings are. These summaries should be fairly brief, but they should capture the gist of the article(s). Finally, the students should explain how this research was social psychological (using the definition of social psychology presented in Chapter 1), as well as how it is applicable to the other field(s).

> ◗*What if this bombs?* The only way this activity can bomb is if the students do not complete the assignment. Use your judgment about how much the students realistically can accomplish as your prepare this activity. How accessible are the journals for these students? Will they be able to use an electronic database? Should they work individually or in teams? Most students should have little trouble finding and summarizing one article, and letting them work in small groups should make the activity even easier (and possibly more fun) for them. If you fear that your students might not have the time or ability to do this, consider giving the students a specific article that you've found that bridges social psychology with another field and simply require the students to read the article and discuss it in class.

Activity 4. A First-Day Demonstration that Uses Deception to Introduce Course Content

LoSchiavo, Buckingham, and Yurak (2002) describe how they've used the following procedure on the first day to introduce social psychology content and get students excited about the study of social psychology.

Prior to the first class meeting, you need to engage the services of a confederate, someone who is older than the students and who might impress them as being an instructor. (The authors used a graduate student in their studies.) The confederate needs to come in on the first day dressed as a professor and introduce him or herself with the following script:

> Hi everyone. My name is _____. We have a lot that we need to do today and we're pressed for time, so let's get started right away. The first thing I need you to do is complete this Student Information Sheet.

At this point, the confederate distributes Handout 1.4, which is only identified as "Student Information Sheet." The handout requests students to provide personal data such as their names, addresses, phone numbers, dates of birth, social security numbers, and driver's license numbers. The confederate responds to all questions by saying, "We'll get to that soon, but first, please fill out the information sheet."

When everyone is done, the confederate collects the forms and says, "Now I need you all to stand up and face the back of the room." In order to get everyone to comply, he repeats, "Go ahead, everyone face the back of the room." When everyone has complied, the confederate says that he left something in his office by mistake and that they should remain quiet and continue standing until he comes back. He never returns to the room.

Three minutes after he leaves, you, the actual instructor, walk in. You say, "Sorry I'm late," and take notice of the students who are likely to be standing and facing the wall. The authors say that each of four times that they have conducted the demonstration, the ensuing dialogue was basically as follows:

Instructor: Why are you all facing the back of the room?

Class: That guy told us to.

Instructor: What guy?

Class: Some guy told us to fill out a form and then stand up.

Instructor: What was the guy's name?

Class: He said his name was _____.

Instructor: I don't know any _____. You filled out a form?

Class: Yes. A student information sheet.

Instructor: What kind of information did you provide?

Class: Name, address, telephone number, date of birth, social security number, driver's license number.

Instructor: What? You gave a complete stranger all of that information?

Class: Uh, yes.

Instructor: Why would you provide personal information to a stranger?

At this point, list all their answers to the final question on the board. They will now begin to realize that they were participating in a demonstration. Confirm their suspicions by admitting that you had arranged for the confederate to come to class.

You can now proceed to lecture on social psychological explanations for why the students obeyed the stranger. Augment the lecture with real-life examples. The following topics can be used:

Stereotypes. The confederate fit the students' idea of what a professor looks like. He was older, dressed well, and acted as if he was in charge.

Obedience to perceived authority. Because the confederate appeared to be a professor, he was viewed as a legitimate authority figure. At this point, you could briefly describe Milgram's obedience studies.

Conformity. The authors found that if people were slow to respond to fill out the form or stand up, the group pressured them to do so. This is an opening to a discussion about the relative strength of situational factors above personality factors in determining behavior.

Mindlessness. Mindlessness occurs when persons are not paying attention or giving careful thought to what they are doing when they act automatically. Explain that usually individuals are rewarded for being obedient by their teachers, parents, and bosses. Moreover, conforming, or doing the same as everyone else, leads to social acceptance. Therefore, people are prone to mindless conformity and obedience. At this point, you could discuss studies that would be considered unethical by today's standards (For example, Zimbardo's Stanford prison study and Milgram's obedience studies).

According to the authors, the possibility of bad feelings between students and professor was addressed by surveys where students reported that they were not at all upset, angry, anxious, embarrassed, nervous, or resentful after the demonstration.

💣 ***What if this bombs?*** The main purpose of the demonstration is to introduce social psychological concepts in a way that is sure to capture students' attention. As long as students obey the confederate, they are sure to be interested in an explanation for their behavior. Even in the unlikely event that students choose to disobey the confederate, you could still describe what happened in the original studies and discuss why those students obeyed. Then ask your students to explain why they behaved differently. Their personal involvement should be enough to guarantee that they will be curious to learn more about the lecture topics.

LoSchiavo, F.M., Buckingham, J.T., & Yurak, T.J. (2002). First-Day Demonstration for Social Psychology Courses. Teaching of Psychology, 29, 3, 216-219.

Activity 5. Finding Relevant Examples from the Media

One of the things that students often find so interesting about social psychology is how relevant it is to issues that are part of their everyday lives. To encourage students to think this way, and to facilitate discussion and participation in class throughout the course, consider giving the students an assignment that requires them to come to class with examples from the media.

Incidents in the world outside the psychology laboratory can help illustrate social psychological principles in a very compelling, memorable way. Students find it very rewarding when they realize that they can use what they've learned from social psychology to help understand some event or behavior that they observed or that is presented in the media. For example, students may read about an incident in which someone was attacked in front of witnesses who did not intervene to help the victim. They may see news clips of a prominent trial or listen to the explanations given by jurors as to why they found the defendant guilty or innocent. They may read a newspaper article about vandalism or rioting at particular concerts or sports events. They may see advertisements that make claims about the effectiveness or superiority of various products. They may watch a debate between political candidates. They may read a magazine article about racism on campus. The may view a celebrity trying to backtrack on a racist comment that they now claim was inadvertent.

To help ensure that each of these events can serve as potential material for informative and engaging discussion, require students to bring to class, on a regular basis, relevant examples from the media. These can be summaries or tapes of things they saw on television or heard on the radio, copies of newspaper or magazine articles or of materials from the Internet, etc. Students could be required to turn in a particular number of these examples during the course or to turn them in on a regular basis, such as once a week, once for every chapter of the textbook, once for each of the four major sections of the textbook, etc. You can arrange this by topic, such as requiring students to bring in a "pop" psychology article about the self-concept that appears in popular magazines (Ch. 3), an advertisement that uses the principles of attribution theory (Ch. 4), an article or report about prejudice (Ch. 5), etc. You can have the students look throughout the course for advertisements that make potentially invalid claims or for media reports that summarize social psychology research.

Each week or so, mention some of the examples that the students found. Depending on the time you have, you can use these examples to spark good class discussion or as fresh material in a lecture. By mentioning these in class, the students will consistently see the relevance of the course material to things they see in the media, and they will feel proud to contribute to the class discussion or the lectures.

> ⚫*What if this bombs?* The only way that this activity could bomb is if students don't do the assignment. You can try to avoid this problem by being enthusiastic about the material, explaining the purpose of the assignment, and, perhaps, grading their contributions. You should also have ready some examples that *you've* found from the media to make relevant points. (Almost any advertisement would work. Also, special science sections of the *New York Times*, and magazines like *Time*, *Newsweek*, etc., can be good sources of material.) If possible, return the materials to all the students (including those whose materials you did not mention in class) with some brief feedback, mostly encouraging, about their materials.

Activity 6. Student-Generated Ideas for Discussion

One way to encourage students to do the reading and think about the course material in an active way throughout the course is to require them to write questions that they think would be good for discussion. One extra advantage of this activity is that it gives students who are intimidated or otherwise reluctant to speak out in class the chance to raise issues that might not get addressed adequately in class. Moreover, this will give you the chance to see what questions and issues are of interest or concern to the students.

The students' ideas should be clearly articulated and written down to be turned in to you in advance of the class. As with Activity 5, you can choose to require students to turn in a particular number of these ideas during the course or to turn them in on a regular basis, such as once a week, once for every chapter of the textbook, once for each of the four major sections of the textbook, etc.

Bring up these ideas for discussion as often as you can. If the class is not very big, try to mention at least one idea from every student. If possible, return the written ideas to the students, and provide them with encouraging feedback. When you discuss their ideas in class, you might want to mention the name of the student who suggested it, but we recommend *against* this because students might feel too inhibited to submit ideas if they think that their names will be mentioned in association with them, and if their ideas do not elicit any discussion or are mocked in some way, they might feel very embarrassed. So we recommend mentioning their ideas but not their names.

🔴*What if this bombs?* Although in general this activity will not bomb (as long as the students do the assignment), there is a real possibility that some of the students' ideas would not lead to good discussion. For example, some ideas might be irrelevant to the course or specific assignment. Other ideas might be too obvious, obscure, controversial, or poorly worded. You can minimize these problems by having students turn in their materials before the class at which they will be discussed, giving you the chance to examine the materials first and select materials that are relevant, interesting, and safe for discussion, and you can re-word or otherwise modify the ideas to make them more likely to engage the students. By selecting only a sample of the materials or questions to include in class discussion, you can highlight those that should be most interesting and that fit best with the points you wish to make. Even so, occasionally one of these ideas will fall flat. In this case, you need to use your judgment about why it didn't work. If possible, say something like, "That's a really interesting question, but we'd need a lot more time to address it adequately at this point. It's something that you should all think about, but for now, let's move on to...." Other ways to deflect discussion away from an idea that hasn't caught on is to say that the field needs more research to address this issue, or that you'll probably be getting back to this issue later in the course.

Activity 7. Scales and Questionnaires to Be Used in Future Classes

One useful activity that can be conducted during the first class or two is to have students complete some of the scales or other questionnaires to which you will be referring in classes or activities later in the course. Thus, before the students will have had a chance to read about these issues and therefore become biased, suspicious, or too well informed, you could give out questionnaires designed to measure their levels of self-esteem (Chs. 2 and 3), self-monitoring (Ch. 3), attributional complexity (Ch. 4), modern racism (Ch. 5), feelings of passionate love (Ch. 9), hostility toward women (Ch. 11), etc., and then refer back to these when you get to the relevant section of the course. After reading in Chapter 6 about the role of the need for cognition in persuasion, for example, the students will be interested to learn where they stand on this dimension, and you could refer back to the questionnaire they had completed several weeks before. You could give them their scores, and the class average, and then discuss with them the relevance of these scales and how the students feel about their scores (were they surprised? relieved? disappointed? why?).

The advantage of having students complete these questionnaires during the first class or two is not only that they will be more naive at this point in the course, which typically is ideal for these scales and questionnaires, but also because the questions should pique the students' interest. They will wonder what these questionnaires are designed to measure or address, and they will be curious to learn about the social psychological concepts and applications that are relevant to them.

You might consider going over one or more of these questionnaires and asking students to speculate about what their purposes are. This could be a fun activity for the students, and it encourages them to think psychologically. It also can make them more interested in these topics when they read about them later in the course.

🔴*What if this bombs?* There really is nothing to bomb here. Depending on which questionnaires you choose, and how long they are, some students might be bored with this activity, although most typically find it interesting. Just emphasize that the relevance of these questionnaires will be made clear in subsequent classes.

Activity 8. Role-Playing some of the Classics

One way to excite students about the subject of social psychology is to introduce them to some of the classic experiments in the field. In small groups (of 4–6 students), students are assigned to one of the experiments. They then read the article describing the study and prepare a skit reenacting the experiment to be performed at the next class session, complete with appropriate props, with group members playing the parts of the experimenter and the participants (and confederates, if there are any).

You could ask students to research some of the studies that are listed in **Handout 1.8**, for this activity. Or, you can choose from your favorite classics (Classic studies can be found in: *Readings in Social Psychology: The Art and Science of Research,* which is available with the textbook, Ellyson & Halberstadt's *Explorations in Social Psychology: Readings and Research,* and T. F. Pettijohn's *Sources: Notable Selections in Social Psychology.*). One way to assign the experiments is to prepare small pieces of paper, each with the title of the study and its author(s) and have a member of each group draw one study out of a paper bag.

> *What if this bombs?* There is no bombing potential. Students usually enjoy acting in a group and the material is certain to engage the rest of the class. As the term goes on, an extra bonus will be that you will be able to count on group members to elaborate on the text's treatment of the classic studies that they dramatized.

Ellyson, S. J., & Halberstadt, A. G. (Eds.). (1995). Explorations in social psychology: Readings and research. New York: McGraw-Hill.

Pettijohn, T. F. (Ed.). (1994). Sources: Notable selections in social psychology. New York: McGraw-Hill/Dushkin.

Activity 9. Checking Out Social Psychologists' Webpages

One way for students to get a quick glimpse of what social psychologists do and think about is to have the students read the webpages of several social psychologists. This could be done as an in-class activity if you have the technology in your classroom to use one or more computers to access the web and to display the information in such a way that all the students can read it (such as on a big screen, or if each student or small group of students can have their own monitor). If this is impossible, then this activity can be done as an assignment that students complete outside of class.

Instruct the students to find webpages for some number of social psychologists—a half dozen, for example. If you are doing this as a classroom activity in which only you have access to a computer, then you would select the pages yourself, possibly while soliciting suggestions from the students of ways to proceed. There are a few different ways for you or the students to find the webpages.

One way is to use a list of social psychologists and their webpages, such as the list maintained by Scott Plous of Wesleyan University (http://www.socialpsychology.org/). A similar list can be accessed at: http://www.psych-central.com/professor.htm. The students can use lists such as this one and arbitrarily select some number of social psychologists to read about.

Another approach is to use a search engine to look for the home pages of particular universities or colleges, and to go from there to find the faculty who teach social psychology courses. For example, you might do a search for University of X, then select the most relevant-looking option such as "Departments," and then select "Psychology," and then "Faculty," and then look at the faculty research descriptions for social psychology interests. Schools vary considerably in how their pages are set up, but it's usually pretty easy to find the social psychology faculty, if the school has any.

A third approach is to search by the names of particular social psychologists. Have the students skim through the textbook and select the names of a few social psychologists mentioned there, perhaps one per chapter or section of the book. Not all of the social psychologists mentioned will have a webpage (indeed, several people whom students select might not be alive today), but it shouldn't take many tries to find several who do have webpages.

Once the pages are found, students should peruse the page and any links from the page, and they should take note of the kinds of questions that the social psychologists are interested in. Individuals' webpages vary dramatically in how much information they have, how personal they are, and so forth, but often one can learn a good deal about the research and interests of the person. Ask the students to summarize what they've learned about the social psychologists whose pages they read.

This activity need not be limited to the first days of the course. As each chapter of the textbook is covered, consider having the students search the Internet for information about one or more of the researchers discussed in this chapter.

What if this bombs? The only potential problems with this activity concern the ability of the students to search the Internet. If you do this as an in-class activity, the only real potential for a bomb is if your computer crashes or it takes too long to load the websites. In this case, blame the school, the Internet, Bill Gates, and whoever else comes to mind—the students will more than understand—and turn the in-class activity into a take-home assignment. You might also consider "priming the pump" by providing the students with a few examples of faculty websites that you consider especially interesting.

Activity 10. An Example of Cross-Cultural Research

Bernard Carducci (2003) presents an interesting example of a cross-cultural comparison that involves the study of personal ads.

The individualistic culture is represented by the following two ads (from the San Francisco Chronicle):

> 28 SWM, 6'1", 160 lbs. Handsome, artistic, ambitious, seeks attractive WF, 24–29, for friendship, romance, and permanent partnership.

> Very attractive, independent SWF, 29, 5'6" 110 lbs., love fine dining, the theater, gardening, and quiet evenings at home. In search of handsome SWM 28–34 with similar interests.

On the same day, two ads representing a collectivist culture, appeared in the India Tribune (a California newspaper with a readership of immigrants from India):

> Gujarati Vaishnav parents invite correspondence from never married Gujarati well settled, preferably green card holder from respectable family for green card holder daughter 29 years, 5'4", good looking, doing CPA.

> Gujarati Brahmin family invites correspondence from a well cultured, beautiful Gujarati girl for 29 years, 5'8", 145 lbs. Handsome looking, well settled boy.

Carducci points out that the first two ads reflect the individualistic perspective, focusing on the uniqueness of the individual and emphasizing personal qualities and interests. In contrast, the second set of ads reflects the collectivist perspective by emphasizing group membership. For example, it places the name of the family instead of the individual in the ad, it indicates the region from whence they came, and the caste of the family.

Distribute **Handout 1.10** to your students and initiate a discussion using the following questions:

1. In which culture would you expect a greater degree of happiness? Why? (Diener, Diener, & Diener, 1995)

2. In which culture would you expect a higher degree of crime rate? Why? (Triandis, 1994)

3. How might students in such cultures react differently to personal success and failure? (Lee & Seligman, 1997)

4.   How and why might individuals in these two cultures have different orientations to dealing with time? What would be an easy way to examine cross-cultural comparisons to time orientation? (Levine & Bartlett, 1984)

What if this bombs? This activity is bombproof. It is sure to provoke an interesting discussion.

Carducci, B.J. Looking for love: A cross-cultural perspective teaching module. Poster Presentation at the Annual Meeting of the American Psychological Association. Toronto: 2003.

Diener, E., Diener, M., & Diener, C. (1995). Factors predicting the subjective well-being of nations. Journal of Personality and Social Psychology, 69, 851-864.

Lee, Y., & Seligman, M.E.P. (1997). Are Americans more optimistic than the Chinese? Personality and Social Psychology Bulletin, 23, 32-40.

Levine, R.V., & Bartlett, K. (1984). Pace of life, punctuality, and coronary heart disease in six countries. Journal of Cross-Cultural Psychology, 15, 233-255.

Triandis, H.C. (1994). Culture and Social Behavior. New York: McGraw-Hill, Inc.

MULTIMEDIA RESOURCES

Video

Age & Attitudes. This ABC News *Prime Time Live* special report uses hidden cameras to get a peek at how older workers are discriminated against on the job market. A team of discrimination testers reveals some of the obstacles faced by talented, motivated people because of age discrimination, which some experts say is often harder to detect than race or gender bias. This video could be used with Lecture/Discussion Idea 6. (1994, 16 min.) Available from corVision Media (800-537-3130).

Candid Camera Classics for Social Psychology. Uses classic footage from Candid Camera to illustrate such concepts as conformity, obedience, helping behavior, power of suggestion, and sex roles. (1994, 60 min.) Available from McGraw-Hill Media Solutions (708-223-2506).

Dreamworlds. Using clips from more than 165 music videos, this explicit program explores the impact of seeing objectified images of women and sexual violence on viewers' thoughts and behaviors. This could be a provocative introduction to the course by challenging students to think about how these images, which most of them will have taken for granted, can have very serious social psychological implications and consequences. For mature audiences -- some of the footage is explicit. (1995, 56 min.) Available from Insight Media (800-233-9910).

The Fairer Sex? This ABC News *Prime Time Live* special report features remarkable hidden-camera footage of gender discrimination in a variety of settings, from a job interview to a car dealership. This is a fast-paced, provocative, and well-produced story, sure to captivate the students. This video could be used with Lecture/Discussion Idea 6. (1993, 16 min.) Available from corVision Media (800-537-3130).

Invitation to Social Psychology. This video introduces students to the field of social psychology. Stanley Milgram discusses affiliation, attribution theory, cognitive dissonance, conformity, and aggression. The video includes reenactments of several classic studies, such as Asch's experiments on conformity, the aggression and social learning theory research of Bandura and Walters, Milgram's research on obedience, and Zimbardo's prison simulation study. (1975, 25 min.) Available from Insight Media (800-233-9910).

The Power of the Situation. Uses some classic social psychological studies to introduce the field, including studies by Lewin, Asch, and Milgram. These studies illustrate the central concept of social psychology: Situational factors can exert powerful influence over human behavior. This selection is part of the *Discovering Psychology* series (Updated edition). (2001, 30 min.) Available from Annenberg/CPB Collection (800-532-7637).

The Social Animal. Investigates some of the ways in which people are influenced and changed by social factors. Demonstrates the effects of group pressures to conform and the consequences of publicly stating ideas contrary to one's private belief. Shows the nature of the bargaining process. Presents simulations of classic social psychological studies by Asch, Festinger, Deutsch, and Schacter. Very dated, but therein lies its charm, along with the charisma of some of these groundbreaking social psychologists. (1963, 29 min.) Available from Iowa Films, Media Library, University of Iowa, Iowa City, IA 52242.

Socialization. The focus of this video is on how individuals' personalities are influenced profoundly by the socio-cultural context in which they develop. It explores gender socialization, the social and cultural aspects of emotion and emotional expression, and the nature-nurture debate. It includes footage from the United States and the former Soviet Union to show the contrast in social settings. This video could be used as a way to introduce students to the power of the situation, a core issue in the field. (1991, 30 min.) Available from Insight Media (800-233-9910).

Social Psychology. Introduces the field by discussing a variety of programs of research, including research on stereotypes and prejudice, attribution theory, ingroup/outgroup differences, and the power of social roles. Phil Zimbardo's prison study is described and analyzed; discussing Zimbardo's study in the context of Chapter 1 could be a good way to facilitate discussions of ethics. (1990, 30 min.) Available from Insight Media (800-233-9910).

True Colors. This was the first of several ABC News *Prime Time Live* special reports using hidden cameras to illustrate how prevalent and debilitating discrimination is in society today. In this startling exposé, we see two friends virtually identical in all respects but one -- John is white, Glen is black. We see how differently the two are treated in a variety of settings, such as interviewing for a job, looking for housing, browsing in a store, trying to hail a cab. This is a truly powerful and memorable story. This video could be used with Lecture/Discussion Idea 6. (1991, 19 min.) Available from corVision Media (800-537-3130).

The Ugly Truth. This ABC News *20/20* story focuses on "lookism," demonstrating how widespread is the discrimination faced by people as a function of their looks. From the opening images of two women—one average looking, one very attractive—seeking roadside assistance for their car, we see how differently people are treated based on their physical appearance. This story illustrates how lookism affects people's ability to get jobs, the pay they receive for their jobs, how much your students may like you, etc. This video could be used with Lecture/Discussion Idea 6. (1991, 19 min.) Available from corVision Media (800-537-3130).

Women Seen on Television. Like the video, *Dreamworlds*, described above, this video can be used to show students how images they see on television can have profound social psychological consequences. This video is briefer and less explicit than the *Dreamworlds* video, and it focuses on the depiction of women in the media more generally, rather than specifically on music videos. (1991, 11 min.) Available from Insight Media (800-233-9910).

Writing for the Social Sciences. If you are planning to have the students write research reports, you might consider this video, which uses lively examples to illustrate how to write for the social sciences. (1991, 30 min.) Available from Insight Media (800-233-9910).

Internet

Websites offer a large variety of relevant information and resources, including discussion groups, reference information, electronic refereed journals, etc. Given the "wild frontier" nature of the Internet, it is always possible that sites will be moved or withdrawn with little notice; thus, our listing is current only as of this writing. Nevertheless, these are some of the Internet resources that we think you might find helpful and interesting for yourself, or that you might want to pass on to your students to get them excited about surfing the net for social psychological material.

BBC Science and Nature Homepage. At this site, students can participate in surveys and take tests in areas such as facial perception, morality, interpersonal attraction, career decisions, and adultery. Visit the site at: http://www.bbc.co.uk/science/humanbody/mind/index_surveys.shtml.

Current Research in Social Psychology. Current Research in Social Psychology (CRISP) is a peer reviewed, electronic journal covering all aspects of social psychology. Publication is sponsored by the Center for the Study of Group Processes at the University of Iowa which provides free access to its contents. Visit this site at http://www.uiowa.edu/~grpproc/crisp/crisp.html.

Encyclopedia of Psychology. This site supports more than two thousand psychology-related links broken up into several helpful categories. This site is not specific to social psychology but many of the links are relevant to this class. Visit this site at http://www.psychology.org/

Hanover College Home Page. An ambitious, impressive list of Internet sites and resources relevant to psychology is the webpage of Hanover College (http://psych.hanover.edu/), which was created by Dr. John H. Krantz (krantzj@hanover.edu). Due to the extensive references listed at this site, you would be well advised simply to give students the address of the Hanover page and let them explore from there.

Psybersite. Psybersite is a gateway to web tutorials on a variety of topics in the field of psychology. All of the educational modules available here have been created by advanced undergraduate and graduate students at Miami University. This site has selections such as "social psychology in the news," "social psychology in humor," "physical attraction," and so forth. Visit this site at: http://www.units.muohio.edu/psybersite/

PSYC. Psyc is short for Psycoloquy, a refereed electronic journal sponsored by the American Psychological Association. It offers refereed articles/brief reports along with commentary and responses. The intent is to provide rapid international/interdisciplinary peer feedback in all areas of psychology and related fields (e.g., biobehavioral, cognitive, neural, and social). Psycoloquy can be accessed at http://psycprints.ecs.soton.ac.uk/

PE, or psych. Experiments, is an online cognitive and social psychology laboratory site run by the University of Mississippi, that invites students to participate in interactive experiments. At this time, the experiments include: Be a Juror, Facial Recognition, Self-reference, and Social Balance. The site can be visited at: http://psychexps.olemiss.edu/index.html.

PSYCGRAD or Psychology Graduate Students Discussion Group. Its main purpose is to provide a medium through which graduate students in the field of psychology can communicate. Conversation topics are limited to those relevant to being a graduate student in psychology. Views, debate, conference information, technique sharing, job announcements, and more are available. An electronic journal PSYGRD-J is also available. E-mail address: LISTSERV@ACADVM1.UOTTAWA.CA

PSYCINFO LIST. Provides tips and techniques used to search the psychological research literature. E-mail address: PSYCINFO@LISTS.APA.ORG

Psychology Matters. This is a web-based compendium of psychological research that is run by the APA. It includes research studies pertaining to many social psychological topics such as consumerism, gender, health, law and justice, aggression, and workplace and industry. Visit this site at: http://www.psychologymatters.org.

Psychology Online Resource Central. This site presents dozens of different categories of psychology related links including: "APA writing links," "career center," "conventions," "discussion and news groups," "graduate school info," "interactive websites," "library links," "online journals," "online surveys," "psychology departments on the web," "psychology store," "psychology students home pages," "professors' home pages," "research links," and many more. Visit this site at:

http://www.psych-central.com/

Psychology Virtual Library. This site provides a very useful research tool and resource for both students and instructors alike. This virtual library is a virtual cornucopia of online psychological information. Visit this site at: http://www.dialogical.net/psychology/index.html.

Social Cognition Paper Archive and Information Center. Several types of information are available on this site, including preprints or abstracts of papers or presentations and links to information about active researchers in the area of social cognition (the intersection of social psychology and cognitive psychology). Visit this site at: http://www.indiana.edu/~soccog/scarch.html.

A Sociological Social Psychology. This is a very interesting site that focuses on the intersection of sociology and psychology. This site has both original material and links other similarly oriented sites. Visit this site at http://www.trinity.edu/~mkearl/socpsy.html.

TIPS (Teaching In Psychology). All aspects of teaching in psychology are covered here. Though the psychological sciences are the primary content focus, membership is open to all who share an interest in exchanging ideas and information about teaching. Discussion of teaching experiences, exchanges of teaching demonstrations, reviews of teaching materials, and the sharing of teaching materials are all welcome. E-mail address: LISTSERV@FRE.FSU.UMD.EDU

Today in the History of Psychology. This site provides an interesting glimpse into the history of psychology. The information here isn't specific to social psychology but much of it is relevant to the area. Visit this site at http://www.cwu.edu/~warren/today.html.

Computer Programs

Anxiety and Personality Questionnaires. Administers questionnaires on state anxiety, trait anxiety, test anxiety, the Thayer affect adjective checklist, the self-consciousness scale, and others. Instruction booklet included. This can be used during discussion of measurement issues, such as the use of self-reports. (Macintosh.) Available from the Educational Psychology Department, University of Calgary, AL T2N 1N4.

Laboratory in Social Psychology. Demonstrates classic laboratory experiments in social psychology. (DOS.) Available from the Academic Computing Center, University of Wisconsin, 1210 W. Dayton Street, Madison, WI 53706.

HANDOUT 1.1A INTUITIONS ABOUT SOCIAL PSYCHOLOGY

For each statement, please indicate whether you think it is true or false by printing the letter **T** or **F** in the first space in front of it. In the second space in front of each statement, write a number from **1** (<u>not at all confident</u>) to **7** (<u>very confident</u>) to indicate the degree to which you feel confident in your true/false answer for that statement.

1. _____ _____ The pain of social rejection is felt in the same area of the brain as physical pain.

2. _____ _____ A survey of about 1,000 people can be used to accurately predict about the entire US population.

3. _____ _____ Older people are more likely to spontaneously recall negative life events than are younger people.

4. _____ _____ Promising, and delivering, rewards to people for doing an enjoyable activity should, in the long run, make them enjoy the activity even more.

5. _____ _____ People are disproportionately more likely to marry others with similar first or last names.

6. _____ _____ Focusing on a person's voice is a better way to detect whether someone is telling a lie than is focusing on the person's face.

7. _____ _____ People are quicker to spot an angry face in a crowd than a happy face.

8. _____ _____ Information has a greater impact when it's presented at the end of a sequence rather than at the beginning.

9. _____ _____ Older people find it easier to suppress stereotypes than do younger people.

10. _____ _____ Gender stereotypes become activated as soon as parents meet their newborns babies.

11. _____ _____ If people tell a lie for money, they are more likely to come to believe the lie if they are paid a small rather than a large amount of money for telling the lie.

12. _____ _____ When it comes to influencing customers' intentions to buy products, the physical looks of a salesperson have no effect.

13. _____ _____ A person is more likely to be influenced by the unanimous opinion of one six-person group than by that same opinion voiced by two three-person groups.

14. _____ _____ Asking people to give you 26 cents is likely to be more profitable than asking people to give you a quarter.

15. _____ _____ Once people have rejected a large request, they become more likely to agree to a smaller request.

16. _____ _____ Majorities have a greater influence on us when it comes to questions involving opinion, whereas minorities have a greater influence when it comes to questions of fact.

17. _____ _____ When told by an experimenter in a psychology experiment to administer severe, very painful electric shocks to another person, more than 50% of American female and male participants obeyed.

18. _____ _____ Group discussions tend to make group members feel less strongly about their initial attitudes, even if most people in the group have similar attitudes at the beginning of the discussion.

19. _____ _____ Simply having other people around tends to make individuals perform better on easy tasks.

20. _____ _____ Brainstorming groups produce a greater number of useful ideas than do brainstorming individuals.

21. _____ _____ Physically attractive individuals are usually seen as less intelligent than physically unattractive individuals.

22. _____ _____ Women tend to value and seek economic status in a mate more than men do.

23. _____ _____ The more often that people are exposed to a neutral stimulus, the more positively they evaluate that stimulus.

24. _____ _____ Women's sexual orientation is more flexible and open than that of men.

25. _____ _____ The "Seven-year itch" does not occur to most married couples.

26. _____ _____ People in a sad mood are less likely to help others than are people in a neutral mood.

27. _____ _____ People in a happy mood are less likely to help others than are people in a neutral mood.

28. _____ _____ Individualism is associated with a greater degree of charitable giving and voluntarism than collectivism.

29. _____ _____ People are more likely to be aggressive when it's hot outside than when it's cool.

30. _____ _____ Exposure to aggressive models in the media increases aggressive behavior among viewers of the aggression.

31. _____ _____ Boys are more likely than girls to harm another person intentionally.

32. _____ _____ Husband-to-wife violence is much more common than wife-to-husband violence.

33. _____ _____ When witnesses are identifying suspects from photographs, those who take their time are more likely to be accurate than those who make snap decisions.

34. _____ _____ Jurors who support the death penalty are more likely to find a defendant guilty than jurors who do not believe in the death penalty.

35. _____ _____ When a jury is equally divided after the initial vote, its consequent deliberations are likely to lead to a guilty verdict.

36. _____ _____ The jury foreperson tends to have much more influence on the jury's verdict than does anyone else in the jury.

37. _____ _____ Most men would rather work for a male boss and most women would rather work for a female boss.

38. _____ _____ When deciding whether or not to continue to invest money into a project that is failing, your decision is most likely to be a wise one if you focus on how much money you have already invested in the project.

39. _____ _____ Unrealistic optimism is associated with health and well-being.

40. _____ _____ Americans are happier now than they were fifty years ago.

HANDOUT 1.1B INTUITIONS ABOUT SOCIAL PSYCHOLOGY

For each statement, please indicate whether you think it is true or false by printing the letter **T** or **F** in the first space in front of it. In the second space in front of each statement, write a number from **1** (<u>not at all confident</u>) to **7** (<u>very confident</u>) to indicate the degree to which you feel confident in your true/false answer for that statement.

1. ____ ____ Social psychologists often use a random sample of participants in their experiments.

2. ____ ____ A well-designed survey that uses only about a thousand people randomly selected from a population of millions can accurately represent the opinions of the general population.

3. ____ ____ Humans are the only species who can recognize themselves when looking in a mirror.

4. ____ ____ People are better able to identify emotions on the faces of others who share their ethnic background than on those who do not.

5. ____ ____ People are more likely to touch others when they are dominant to them than when they are subordinate to them.

6. ____ ____ One of the best ways to avoid being influenced by stereotypes about an outgroup is to simply suppress all such thoughts.

7. ____ ____ People tend to see the members of other groups as more different from each other than they see the members of their own groups.

8. ____ ____ The persuasive impact of a message given by a credible communicator tends to *increase* over time, whereas the persuasive impact of a message given by a non-credible communicator tends to *decrease* over time.

9. ____ ____ People are just as likely today to conform today as they were 20 or 30 years ago.

10. ____ ____ When told by an experimenter in a psychology experiment to administer severe, very painful electric shocks to another person, more than 50% of American women and men obeyed.

11. ____ ____ People usually work harder when working together on a task with others than they do when working alone.

12. ____ ____ The loneliest people in the United States are older adults.

13. ____ ____ "Opposites attract" is more accurate than "Birds of a feather flock together."

14. ____ ____ When someone is in an accident or otherwise needs help, he or she has a better chance of getting help if only one other person is present than if several are present.

15. ____ ____ Cultures of honor promote violent behavior.

16. ____ ____ Watching a very violent film or television show allows people to release their aggressions in a safe way, making them less likely to aggress themselves.

17. ____ ____ For maximal accuracy, it's better to let eyewitnesses who are identifying suspects to view many photographs all at once, rather than one at a time.

18. ____ ____ Eyewitnesses are better able to accurately identify a criminal if they saw a weapon at the scene of the crime than if they did not.

19. ____ ____ On the job, when asked to complete self-evaluations, women rate themselves higher than men, and subordinates rate themselves higher than managers.

20. ____ ____ Sharing personal secrets with a supportive listener is good for the teller's health.

HANDOUT 1.2 DISTINGUISHING SOCIAL PSYCHOLOGY FROM PERSONALITY PSYCHOLOGY

Below are brief descriptions of the behaviors of four different individuals in the same set of four situations.

Bob. When Bob sees an acquaintance as he is walking down Main Street, he waves hello. When he returns to his dorm, he reads in the newspaper some very troubling information about the economy, and he yells at his roommate about something. The next day, as he is waiting to take a midterm exam, he reads a sports magazine. In another class later that day, he hears a sudden, very loud but unidentifiable noise, and he looks at the other people in the class.

Karen. When Karen sees an acquaintance as she is walking down Main Street, she crosses the street and converses with her. When she returns to her dorm, she reads in the newspaper some very troubling information about the economy, and she rants and raves about politicians. The next day, as she is waiting to take a midterm exam, she talks to her friends at length about how she is worried about failing (even though she always gets good grades). In another class later that day, she hears a sudden, very loud but unidentifiable noise, and she looks at the other people in the class.

Jessica. When Jessica sees an acquaintance as she is walking down Main Street, she ignores this person. When she returns to her dorm, she reads in the newspaper some very troubling information about the economy, curses "those foreigners," and gets rather angry. The next day, as she is waiting to take a midterm exam, she quietly reads her notes, not engaging in conversation. In another class later that day, she hears a sudden, very loud but unidentifiable noise, and she looks at the other people in the class.

Arnold. When Arnold sees an acquaintance as he is walking down Main Street, he thinks of four different ways he could kill him from where he is standing. When he returns to his dorm, he reads in the newspaper some very troubling information about the economy, and he begins to make plans to start a bloody revolution. The next day, as he is waiting to take a midterm exam, he sharpens his hunting knife. In another class later that day, he hears a sudden, very loud but unidentifiable noise, and he jumps up, says "Hasta la vista, baby; I'll be back," and runs out of the room.

STUDENT INFORMATION SHEET

Name _____

Address _____

Phone Number _____

Date of Birth _____

Social Security Number _____

Driver's License Number _____

HANDOUT 1.8 ROLE-PLAYING SOME OF THE CLASSICS

1. Allport, G. W., & Postman, L. J. (1947). *The psychology of rumor*. New York: Holt.

2. Asch, S. (1951). Effects of group pressure upon the modification and distortion of judgments. In H. Guetzkow (Ed.), *Groups, leadership, and men*. Pittsburgh, PA: Carnegie Press.

3. Berkowitz, L., & LePage, A. (1967). Weapons as aggression-eliciting stimuli. *Journal of Personality and Social Psychology, 7*, 202-207.

4. Darley, J. M., & Batson, C. D. (1973). From Jerusalem to Jericho: A study of situational and dispositional variables in helping behavior. *Journal of Personality and Social Psychology, 27*, 100-108.

5. Festinger, L., & Carlsmith, J. M. (1959). Cognitive consequences of forced compliance. *Journal of Abnormal and Social Psychology, 58*, 203-210.

6. Latane, B., & Darley, J. M. (1968). Group inhibition of bystander intervention. *Journal of Personality and Social Psychology, 10*, 215-221.

7. Loftus, E. F., & Palmer, J. C. (1974). Reconstruction of automobile destruction: An example of the interaction between language and memory. *Journal of Verbal Learning and Verbal Behavior, 13*, 585-589.

8. Rosenthal, R., & Jacobson, L. (1968). *Pygmalion in the classroom: Teacher expectation and pupils' intellectual development*. New York: Holt, Rinehart, and Winston.

9. Milgram, S. (1963). Behavioral study of obedience. *Journal of Abnormal Psychology, 67*, 371-378.

10. Schachter, S. (1959). The psychology of affiliation: *Experimental studies of the sources of gregariousness*. Stanford, CA: Stanford University Press.

11. Triplett, N. (1897-1898). The dynamogenic factors in pacemaking and competition. *American Journal of Psychology, 9*, 507-533.

HANDOUT 1.10 AN EXAMPLE OF A CROSS-CULTURAL COMPARISON

The following two ads are from the San Francisco Chronicle:

> 28 SWM, 6'1", 160 lbs. Handsome, artistic, ambitious, seeks attractive WF, 24–29, for friendship, romance, and permanent partnership.

> Very attractive, independent SWF, 29, 5'6" 110 lbs., love fine dining, the theater, gardening, and quiet evenings at home. In search of handsome SWM 28–34 with similar interests.

These two ads appeared on the same day in the India Tribune (a California newspaper with a readership of immigrants from India):

> Gujarati Vaishnav parents invite correspondence from never married Gujarati well settled, preferably green card holder from respectable family for green card holder daughter 29 years, 5'4", good looking, doing CPA.

> Gujarati Brahmin family invites correspondence from a well cultured, beautiful Gujarati girl for 29 years, 5'8", 145 lbs. Handsome looking, well settled boy.

CHAPTER 2

Doing Social Psychology Research

LEARNING OBJECTIVES: GUIDELINES FOR STUDY

You should be able to do each of the following by the conclusion of Chapter 2.

1. Describe the process of generating research ideas in social psychology, searching the relevant literature, and developing hypotheses. Understand the differences between applied and basic research. (*pp. 27-30*)

2. Distinguish between hypotheses and theories, between conceptual variables and operational definitions. (*pp. 30-31*)

3. Explain self-report and observational research practices, including the advantages and disadvantages of each. (*pp. 31-33*)

4. Understand the usefulness of traditional research methodologies such as archival studies and surveys, as well as explain the potential contributions of new technologies to contemporary social psychology research. (*pp. 33-36*)

5. Contrast correlational research with descriptive research. Define the correlation coefficient, and explain what it means to say that two variables are negatively correlated, positively correlated, or uncorrelated. Summarize the advantages and one major disadvantage of correlational research designs. (*pp. 36-39*)

6. Explain the importance of control and random assignment in experimental research. Differentiate random sampling from random assignment, as well as an independent variable from a dependent variable. (*pp. 39-42*)

7. Explain the importance of the following terms with regard to experimental research design: statistical significance, internal validity, and external validity. (*pp. 43-45*)

8. Discuss the function of ethics in social psychological research, including the use of deception and confederates. Describe the roles of institutional review boards, informed consent, and debriefing in protecting the welfare of human participants. Summarize the competing points of view about the role of values in science. (*pp. 48-50*)

DETAILED CHAPTER OUTLINE

I.   Why Should You Learn About Research Methods?
II. Developing Ideas: Beginning the Research Process
    A.   Asking Questions
    B.   Searching the Literature
    C.   Hypotheses and Theories
    D.   Basic and Applied Research
III. Refining Ideas: Defining and Measuring Social Psychological Variables
    A.   Conceptual Variables and Operational Definitions: From the Abstract to the Specific
    B.   Measuring Variables: Using Self-Reports, Observations, and Technology

IV.   Testing Ideas: Research Designs
    A.   Descriptive Research: Discovering Trends and Tendencies
       1.   Observational studies
       2.   Archival studies
       3.   Surveys
    B.   Correlational Research: Looking for Associations
       1.   Correlation coefficient
       2.   Advantages and disadvantages of correlational research
    C.   Experiments: Looking for Cause and Effect
       1.   Random sampling versus random assignment
       2.   Laboratory and field experiments
       3.   Independent and dependent variables
       4.   Subject variables
       5.   Statistical significance
       6.   Internal validity: Did the independent variable cause the effect?
          a)   control groups
          b)   experimenter expectancy effects
       7.   External validity: Do the results generalize?
          a)   representative versus convenience samples
          b)   mundane realism
          c)   experimental realism
          d)   deception
          e)   confederates
    D.   Meta-Analysis: Combining Results across Studies
    E.   Culture and Research Methods
V.   Ethics and Values in Social Psychology
    A.   Institutional Review Boards and Informed Consent: Protecting Research Participants
    B.   Debriefing: Telling All
    C.   Values and Science: Points of View

LECTURE AND DISCUSSION IDEAS

Idea 1.   Common Sense and the Empirical Approach

This Lecture/Discussion Idea could also be used for Chapter 1.

An effective demonstration of how social psychology differs from simple observations of people and why the scientific approach is so valuable to the field is to demonstrate the shortcomings of common sense and intuition. Some of the ideas presented in Chapter 1 of this manual are relevant to this goal. One point emphasized in Chapter 2 of the textbook is that common sense and personal intuitions can be too contradictory or vague to be of much use in *predicting* many social psychological phenomena, although they are easy to apply in hindsight after one has observed or learned about the phenomena in question.

Discuss why introspection is an inherently flawed method of learning social psychological truths, and introduce the students to some of the ways that people's perceptions and attributions are biased (such as from Chapters 3, 4, and 5). Explain how people's perceptions of the same behavior or stimulus can vary dramatically from person to person — perhaps due to different expectations, moods, motives, cultural backgrounds, etc. Given these influences, inferences based on nonsystematic observations can be particularly misleading.

Handout 2.L/D.1a contains pairs of common-sense principles, or aphorisms. Within each pair, either aphorism has a great deal of intuitive appeal. Indeed, if social psychological studies came to the conclusion consistent with *either* principle within a pair, most people would find the results to be unsurprising and might even disparage social psychology as nothing more than common sense. The punch line is, of course, that the two principles within each pair contradict each other. Which is true? Only through careful, systematic research that is consistent with the principles of the scientific method can we begin to answer that question (or, more accurately, to address the question of under what conditions is one or the other more likely to be true).

Handout 2.L/D.1b contains similar pairs of contradictory principles, but these are phrased more as research questions than aphorisms. Use these as a preview of things to come in the course, to get students enthusiastic about the material they will be encountering.

NOTE: If you conduct Classroom Activity 1 of this chapter, these activities should be conducted *before* you begin this discussion of common sense and the empirical approach.

Idea 2.   Correlations and Experiments

Discuss the advantages and disadvantages of correlational research and of experiments. Ask students to think of some variables that should be positively correlated with each other, negatively correlated with each other, or not correlated with each other. Emphasize why one should not infer causality on the basis of a correlation. Describe some correlations between pairs of variables, such as the amount of a child's exposure to violent television and the child's tendency to behave aggressively, and ask students to speculate about what other factors could explain these relationships (e.g., children who watch a lot of violent television may lack parental supervision, and this lack of supervision may be an important cause of the child's aggressive behavior). For some of these correlations, ask students to think of how experiments could be designed to begin to test some of the causal relationships about which the students speculated.

Idea 3.   Searching the Literature

Helping your students learn how to find journal articles and conduct library research can enable your class to have access to a wealth of information, make the students more self-sufficient, and allow you to give more ambitious assignments. Many students have not been exposed to research articles before and need to begin at the basics, so explain to the class what it means for research to get published and what the differences are between journals (in which scholars submit original material that gets judged by other scholars in the field), books, and popular press outlets that report research findings. Describe some of the different journals in the field, and what a journal article typically is like (the intended audiences; the various sections of a paper — abstract, introduction, method, results, discussion, references; the use of statistics; what it means to have "significant" results). In the introduction of the book of readings, *Readings in Social Psychology: The Art and Science of Research*, that accompanies the textbook, we offer some advice for students about how to read journal articles; you might consider assigning students to read that.

Once the students have some understanding of what is meant by "the literature," next explain to them how to search this literature. If the students have access to electronic databases such as *PsycInfo*, either demonstrate to the class how to use these databases or inform them about how they can learn about these, such as through a local librarian. Also mention the advantages and disadvantages of Google searches and websites like Wikipedia.

Idea 4.   Evaluating Research

Have your students read one or a few original, empirical journal articles concerning some social psychological issue(s). You can choose one or more articles from *Readings in Social Psychology: The Art and Science of Research*, which is available with the textbook, or from recent issues of journals such as *Personality and Social Psychology Bulletin* or *Journal of Applied Social Psychology*. In class, ask the students to summarize the main points of the articles. Ask them to articulate the hypotheses that were tested, why and how the researchers tested these hypotheses, and what the results suggested about these hypotheses. Discuss with the students the implications of the research. These discussions can give students experience in synthesizing and articulating the important issues from a research paper. At first, this will probably be much more difficult than students expected. If you encourage students to discern the important points and summarize these studies in their own words, they should begin to develop a much better understanding of the language and value of research.

Discuss methodological issues such as random assignment and experimental control, internal and external validity, experimenter expectancy effects, and mundane and experimental realism, and ask the students to critique the research reported in the article(s) with these concepts in mind. Discuss the advantages and disadvantages of different kinds of self-report and observational measures, and ask the students to comment on the kinds of measures used in this research.

When telling students how to read journal articles, you might want to refer to the introduction to *Readings in Social Psychology: The Art and Science of Research*, in which we explain to students how to read journal articles for the first time. This would also be a good time to tell students whether you expect them to read the articles in a different manner or at a different level than that suggested in this introduction.

For more advanced groups of students, consider giving them a peek into how social psychologists critique each other's research. This could help the students develop the kind of critical thinking that can be such a valuable tool for them to have. Although there are many forums for this kind of thing, two of the most appropriate are the journals *Psychological Inquiry* and *American Psychologist*. Each issue of *Psychological Inquiry* features one or more target articles, followed by a number of subsequent articles that comment on the target article(s). These commentaries sometimes lead to heated debate, and sometimes not, but they can serve as a great example for your students about how scholars read each other's work with a critical eye. *American Psychologist* sometimes includes debates and commentary on important, contemporary research topics as well. Neither journal is strictly a social psychological journal, so only some of the articles will be relevant to your course.

Idea 5.   Web-Based Research

How does Internet-based research differ from that of the traditional psychological laboratory? What kinds of questions are being addressed on the Internet and what methods are used to answer them? Are there any disadvantages to doing such studies online?

In an article reviewing all APA journal articles published between 2003–2004, the authors (Skitka & Sargis, 2006) found that three approaches to research were being used on the internet:

Translational: This is when traditional research methods and questions are adapted to the Internet. For example, one such study adapted Milgram's "lost letter" technique. When the technique is implemented offline, a large number of unmailed letters are dispersed in various places in city streets. The letters are enclosed in envelopes that are addressed and stamped, but not yet posted. When a person comes across one of these letters, he has the option of mailing it, disregarding it, or actively destroying it. The focus of the technique is to note how many letters get mailed, a rate that varies according to the name of the organization printed on the envelope.

An online version of the technique was used by researchers who wanted to explore whether people would be more likely to respond to lost e-mail messages if the writer was a member of an ingroup or an outgroup and if the message expressed a primary or secondary emotion (Primary emotions are those that are common to both humans and animals, such as fear, anger, or surprise, whereas secondary emotions are those that are uniquely human, such as disillusion, hope, and admiration.). Instead of letters, they "erroneously" sent 400 professors at a Belgian university an e-mail with the writer identified either as a researcher from the same university (ingroup) or a different university (outgroup). They also calculated a solidarity index based on whether the explanatory note accompanying the forwarded e-mail contained more formal or informal pronouns. The only effect found was that forwarded messages expressed greater solidarity when the original writer was a member of the ingroup (same university) and when the e-mail expressed a secondary, rather than primary emotion.

In another translational study, researchers sought to locate 500 participants for a survey involving the use of anabolic steroids. Participants were recruited through postings in five anabolic steroid discussion boards. This study highlights how the Web facilitates access to specialized populations and how sensitive subjects can be approached with higher response rates because of the anonymity provided by the Internet.

The authors found that most Web-based studies were translational; asking the same type of questions and using the same methods as do offline studies. The Internet was used in these cases because it offered an easier way to recruit participants and collect data.

Phenomenological: This is when a study addresses an online behavior. Specifically, phenomenological studies focus on how thoughts, feelings, and behavior are affected by the Internet. The authors note that the online psychological environment differs in four ways from the offline psychological environment. First, in real-life encounters, we're used to inferring a great deal of information based on appearances. On the Internet, however, these physical cues are absent. Second, in real-life, we interact only with those who are near, whereas on the Web physical distance is not a barrier. Third, in real-life encounters, we have less choice as to when or where to respond. And fourth, in Internet conversations there is less of a chance to discern emotions, as there are no auditory cues (from tone of voice), and no visual cues (from body language or facial expression).

One phenomenological study sought to assess whether reading blogs, or online journals, creates a sense of community. The researcher used the Julie/Julia blog that was posted by a young woman who documented her year-long progress at working through every recipe of *Julia Child's Mastering the Art of French Cooking*. It was found that active participation, via the posting of comments, did contribute to a sense of community.

In another study, researchers investigated the connection between hours spent online and psychological well-being. Results indicated an initial short-term deleterious effect where loneliness increased. After a while, however, higher levels of use were actually associated with greater social support and less incidence of depression than lower levels of use. The one negative effect found to persist with higher levels of Internet use was that early adolescents who used instant messaging were more likely to show social anxiety and loneliness in school.

Phenomenological research was also used for studies on the following topics: cyber-ostracism, effectiveness of online therapies, e-mail as a tool for improving smoking cessation, and quality of emotional support of online breast cancer support groups.

Novel: This is when the method used was created solely for Web-based research. For example, researchers staged an online auction on a German auction site for the purpose of examining ethnic discrimination among bidders. Accordingly, they offered comparable items for sale with the sellers' names varied by ethnicity. They found that sellers with Turkish names (a minority in Germany) took longer to receive winning bids than did those with German surnames.

Another novel study explored the accuracy of inferences made about the personalities of owners of personal websites. Website owners and two close associates (supplied by them) were asked to complete personality inventories about the website owner. These were then compared with personality assessments made by strangers who only looked at the websites. Results indicated that there was a high level of agreement across judges on four of the Big Five dimensions (all but agreeableness).

Ask students to think about what might be some potential weaknesses in web-based studies like these. The authors state the following concerns: First, there's the fact that Web users, like college students, may not be representative of the general population. Web users tend to be younger, wealthier, and better educated. They've also been shown to be more trusting and to have larger social networks.

Second, it's easier to turn down or ignore an e-mail request for a survey than an in-person or telephone appeal. Accordingly, the non-response rates are higher for Internet-based research with only 10 percent of those approached by e-mail responding to survey questions. However, it remains unclear whether such a low response rate affects the validity of the data.

Third, there are certain technical constraints. For example, depending on how they access the Internet, which browser they use, and what computers they own, some people may not have the ability to load pages as quickly as others. Moreover, it's impossible to touch, taste, or smell over the Internet.

And fourth, there's the problem with lack of control. In a lab, the environment is controlled so that everyone is subject to manipulation under similar conditions, but in a Web study, the environment can vary. For example, some participants might be alone, whereas others might be in the company of many others.

Skitka, L.J. & Sargis, E.G. (2006). The Internet as psychological laboratory. Annual Review of Psychology, 57, 529-555.

Idea 6.   Converging Research Methods

Students are likely to overestimate the value that social psychologists place on individual studies. Explain the critical importance to the field of converging evidence to support a particular finding, hypothesis, or theory. It's especially impressive when evidence collected from a variety of research perspectives and paradigms all converge to support a particular point. Because laboratory experiments, field studies, correlational research, and archival research have their own advantages and disadvantages, evidence that is consistent across these different approaches is quite compelling.

An effect found in a laboratory experiment, for example, can be very important, but, depending on the issue being studied, one might wonder whether evidence that is consistent with this finding could be found also in more naturalistic, but less controlled, contexts. On the other hand, finding evidence in naturalistic contexts in which many extraneous variables cannot be controlled often leads to the question of whether the evidence could be found under more precise conditions, such as in a laboratory experiment.

Compare and contrast the advantages and disadvantages associated with laboratory experiments, with field experiments, and with correlational research. Ask students how researchers can maximize the advantages of these different types of research. Discuss how researchers sometimes go back and forth from the laboratory to the field to obtain converging evidence to support a particular theory or set of hypotheses, or to revise them to make them more generalizable. You might also introduce the concept of computer-simulated studies in this regard.

A specific example. As a specific point of discussion, you can focus on one particular issue and ask students to devise ways in which this issue can be researched from different approaches so that the disadvantages of each specific approach can be overcome by the advantages of the others. For example, you can discuss the issue of heat and aggression, which is discussed in Chapter 11. Ask the students for ideas about how to test the hypothesis that "people are more aggressive when the ambient temperature is hot." Have them make specific suggestions about correlations to examine, and then discuss the shortcomings of each suggestion and the need for converging evidence.

For instance, one correlation that might be (and has been) examined is the number of violent crimes reported in a particular city on each day of a particular year, and the maximum temperature in that city for each of those days. Ask the students to discuss the kind of correlation that would be expected if the hypothesis is true, and ask them to offer alternative explanations for such a correlation. Suggest that perhaps there were more violent crimes during the hottest days because these days were in the summer when there are more people outside and when most students are not in school. What other correlations could be examined that do not have these problems? One suggestion would be to look at the same period of time (e.g., summer), but to compare across different cities that have different temperatures (e.g., San Francisco vs. Dallas). This would avoid some of the problems of the previous correlational study, but it would be open to a new set of alternative explanations, and so on. After discussing different correlational studies, then discuss different laboratory experiments. In the lab, the measures of aggression tend to be much less naturalistic, but it would be possible to test for cause-and-effect relationships between heat and aggression.

The point is that if evidence found across a variety of empirical approaches is consistent with the hypothesis that "people are more aggressive when the ambient temperature is hot," or, more strongly, that heat causes aggression, then we can have much more confidence in this hypothesis than if the evidence stemmed from only one type of research.

Idea 7.   Ethical Issues in Social Psychological Research

Discuss the issue of ethics in social psychological research. Begin broadly, with a general discussion of what it means for research to be ethical or unethical. Next, focus on some specific research practices, such as deception. Finally, focus on some specific studies, both real and hypothetical, and ask students to discuss their ethics. To make this even more dramatic, consider showing some of the video, *Obedience*, which depicts Stanley Milgram's classic research on destructive obedience (see Chapter 7), and have students debate the ethics of this study. (We suggest that you show only enough of the video to give students a topic for debate; we recommend that you show the video in its entirety when discussing Chapter 7.) Explain to the students the valuable contribution that this research made to our understanding of humanity, and how most people never would have guessed that ordinary people are so vulnerable to conformity and obedience; but explain also how stressful the situation was for the research participants and how they did not consent to be in the kind of situation in which they found themselves. Ask the students whether the scientific merit, or the potential societal contribution, of research should be a factor in determining whether or not the research meets ethical standards.

Review the American Psychological Association's *Ethical Principles of Psychologists and a Code of Conduct* (1992), which can be obtained free of charge (800-374-2721).

Consider using **Handout 2.L/D.7** to help facilitate discussion. This handout briefly describes a number of specific research procedures and asks students to evaluate whether or not they are ethical. There are likely to be strong differences of opinion about some of these procedures and a lot of consensus about others. Ask students to try to articulate a code or system of ethics on the basis of their responses.

CLASSROOM ACTIVITIES

Note: Several of the classroom activities we include here could also be used in conjunction with Chapter 1 as a way of introducing the class to the field and methods of social psychology. In addition, many of the ideas offered in Chapter 1 of this manual could work wonderfully in association with this chapter, so we recommend that you consider the ideas presented there as well.

Activity 1. Explaining Research Findings: "Hindsight Is 20-20"

This activity is designed to illustrate the value of conducting empirical research in order to understand social psychological issues rather than relying on intuitions, introspection, or unsystematic observations. This is an important point in Chapter 2, as well as in the entire field of social psychology. By illustrating this point, you can reduce the likelihood that students will dismiss the research findings they learn about during the course as trivially obvious. This activity can also illustrate important points such as the hindsight bias (Ch. 3) and the confirmation bias (Ch. 4), and it can be used further to highlight one or more interesting research findings in order to pique students' interest in things to come in the course.

Handouts 2.1a through **2.1h** contain four matched pairs of summaries of "research findings" in social psychology. Within each pair (e.g., 2.1a and 2.1b is one pair; 2.1c and 2.1d is another), one of the summaries does accurately reflect the gist of the research in the field concerning a particular issue, and the other summary presents the <u>opposite</u> finding. More specifically:

Handout **2.1a** presents a summary that concludes that people tend to be attracted to others who are similar to them on a variety of dimensions. The research does indeed support this conclusion (see Chapter 9). Handout **2.1b**, on the other hand, presents a fictitious summary of the opposite point: that people tend to be attracted to others who are very <u>dissimilar</u> to them.

Handout **2.1c** concludes that the key to increasing people's true, intrinsic interest in a task is to encourage them to do the task with incentives that they feel are rewarding and worthwhile. The actual research in social psychology is <u>inconsistent</u> with this point. Rather, the research is consistent with the conclusion of Handout **2.1d**, which states that such incentives can undermine people's enjoyment of and internal interest in a task (see Chapters 3 and 13).

Handout **2.1e** concludes that people who are in a happy and cheerful mood are more likely to help a stranger who needs help than are people who are in a neutral mood. The actual research does support this conclusion (see Chapter 10). Handout **2.1f**, on the other hand, presents fictitious research indicating that people in a happy mood are less likely to help.

Finally, Handout **2.1g** presents the wrong conclusion, and Handout **2.1h** presents the accurate conclusion about the social psychological research on ingroup favoritism in the minimal groups paradigm (see Chapter 5).

<u>**Introducing the activity**</u>. Tell the students that you are interested in seeing how well they can "think like a social psychologist." Explain that there are various ways to explain or interpret any research finding but that many of these ways are not truly social psychological explanations. For example, they may emphasize clinical or personality factors rather than social ones. Explain that you will be presenting the students with some research findings (or, if you present only one, say that you will be presenting them with <u>a</u> research finding) and that you want them to explain the reasons underlying these findings.

For each pair of handouts, each student should receive only one of the pair; no student should receive both handouts of a particular pair. Students should not realize until the end of the activity that the research summaries may be bogus, or that other students are reading the opposite summaries. Rather, they should be led to believe that these are real summaries of the relevant research. We have included four pairs of handouts for this activity; feel free to use as many or as few pairs as you feel is appropriate. Each student may receive more than one handout, but again you should be sure that no student receives both handouts from any one pair, and that each student receives a mix of handouts such that at least one is accurate and one is bogus.

Results and discussion. You can either (a) collect the handouts, analyze the results, and discuss the results and the points made below in the next class, or (b) immediately begin a rough "analysis" of the results by discussing the activity with the students as soon as they've completed the handouts. If you take the former approach, calculate the average "surprise" ratings that the students gave for each handout, and see how the averages compare within each pair of handouts. Were the students very surprised by the bogus results? To the extent that they were not, you could explain how this demonstrates the hindsight bias. Also, select a few of the students' written explanations for either accurate or bogus research findings, and point out to the class how it is possible to come up with compelling explanations for either the real findings or their opposites. This would demonstrate powerfully the hindsight bias and the necessity of conducting objective empirical research to test our hypotheses and theories.

If you take the second approach and want to analyze and discuss the results of this activity immediately (or if you first analyze the results on your own and then come to class with the results, you can begin your discussion of them in this way), begin by asking the students how surprising they thought the research findings were. For example, ask for a show of hands to indicate how many students thought that the research findings about Interpersonal Attraction were very surprising, and how many thought they were not surprising. Do not reveal that there were two different versions of these findings; to accomplish this, be sure to be vague in your descriptions of the handouts (as in saying only "Interpersonal Attraction" to describe the first pair of handouts). Then do the same for the other handout topics that you used (i.e., "Motivation," "Mood and Helping," and "Us vs. Them"). Keep track of how many students did and did not feel that the results were surprising.

Next, ask only the students who had Handout 2.1a to indicate whether or not they were surprised by the results, followed by those students who had Handout 2.1b, and so on. Don't indicate to the students how these versions differed from each other. Record the numbers of students from each version who were and were not surprised. An ideal result would be if there is little difference between the versions. That is, if the conclusion that opposites attract (2.1b) and the conclusion that people are attracted to similar others (2.1a) are found to be unsurprising by the same number of students, you will have demonstrated the hindsight bias quite convincingly. Even if there is a difference in these ratings, however, it is likely that the absolute levels of reported surprise will be low for both versions within a pair, thereby also illustrating the hindsight effect quite well.

After asking the students how surprised they were, ask various students to explain the research findings. At this point, the students will begin to realize that you had given them opposite summaries. Have the students from the different conditions debate each other about which finding within a pair makes more sense, and why. This is likely to generate some good discussion, and to increase the students' interest in learning what the research really has to say about these issues. Therefore, this activity can serve as a good way of introducing the course.

If it has not been made clear by now, be sure to explain to the class how the competing versions of the handouts differed from each other, and discuss the extent to which students were or were not surprised by the findings. If most students were not surprised by the findings, ask them to explain why students were not surprised by either of two contradictory results. Ask the class to explain why several students were able to come up with intuitively compelling explanations for bogus results; discuss the implications of this with the class. Explain how this should make it clear why empirical research that uses the principles of the scientific method (Ch. 2) is so necessary. Explain the hindsight bias (Ch. 3), which is the tendency, once an event has occurred, to overestimate the ability to have foreseen this outcome; and the confirmation bias (Ch. 4), which is the tendency to seek, interpret, and create information that verifies existing beliefs. Explain how these biases can make students of social psychology think that many of the research findings they will learn appear to be obvious in hindsight -- this not only can make the course seem less interesting but also can lead to confusion when it comes time to be tested on the material in quizzes and exams. Tell the students that you hope as they read about various theories and research findings during the course they will always try to imagine alternative explanations and think about ways of testing these explanations, as well as to try to explain why the opposite results might have been found, and why they weren't.

> ● *What if this bombs?*   You are unlikely to bomb with this activity if you do not "hype" the activity too much or in too specific a way. Even if the students who read the bogus summaries are much more surprised by the findings than are the students who read the accurate summaries, you can make the points described above as long as *some* of the students are able to come up with explanations that would support opposite sets of results. Even in the unlikely event that no students could offer good explanations for the bogus results, *you* could offer some (e.g., it is commonly believed that opposites attract [as is evident in most romantic comedies in television and in the movies]; both behaviorism and common sense emphasize how rewards make us like the things with which we associate those rewards; people in a happy mood might not want to risk ruining their good mood by getting involved in someone else's problems, or they may be too distracted or self-satisfied to do so — indeed, these are real limitations of the good mood effect on helping [see Table 10.4 in the textbook]; unless there is competition or conflict between groups, there is no rational justification for favoring certain people over others simply because of an obviously arbitrary criterion). Once these explanations are discussed, you should point out to the class that because it is easy to come up with intuitively appealing explanations for competing results, it should be clear that there is an important need to conduct good research instead of relying on intuition and common sense. Instructors who are very nervous about using an in-class activity because of the potential of a bomb may be advised to collect the students' handouts and analyze them outside of class, and then they can have more control over the discussion and select to read to the class only those completed handouts that best demonstrate the hindsight bias.

Activity 2. Testing the Hypothesis that Class Participation Will Kill You

Bernardo Carducci (1990) developed a very creative, effective icebreaker that is designed both to encourage class participation (particularly in large classes—the kinds of classes in which students often are too intimidated to raise questions or points for discussion) and to introduce some basic points about research methods. The present activity is an expanded version of Carducci's activity. We have reworked the details of the activity considerably in order to illustrate additional methodological points and to provide more material for discussion, but we have tried to retain the basic point and the lighthearted flavor of Carducci's activity.

Carducci writes, "On the basis of the irrational belief held by many students that speaking up in class will 'kill' them, this demonstration uses a very simple pretest-posttest design to test in a rational manner this irrational belief right before the students' eyes."

Our expansion of this activity allows for a more complete experimental design to "test" the same irrational belief.

Random sampling and random assignment. The first step is to randomly select a sample of the students from the class. This sample will be divided into two conditions. The size of the sample depends on the size of the class and how much class time you want to devote to this activity. Half of the sample will be asked to say a few (brief) things to rest of the class, so budget your time accordingly. In our own classes, we typically select about 20 students, assigning 10 to each condition. (In small classes, all of the students could be included in the activity, in which case you would ignore random sampling and need only to randomly assign each student to one of the two conditions.)

How you do your random sampling is another issue. One way is to select students in advance of the class. If there is time, however, it is ideal to do the random sampling in front of the students so that they can see how it works. You can accomplish this by having students pick up a small piece of paper as they enter the class. Each piece will have one number on it, ranging from 1 to the maximum number of students you expect to be at class. (This is also an easy way to check to see how many students attended the class.) When you are ready to begin the activity, use a random number table or a computer program's random number generator to select the sample. Call out the numbers and ask the students whose numbers are called to stand. When the sample has been selected, point out why this constitutes a random sample of students from the overall population of students in the class.

Next, assign each student to either the <u>Treatment</u> or <u>Control</u> condition by flipping a coin (or, to encourage more class participation, ask the students who are seated closest to the students who are standing to flip a coin and assign that student to the condition). Have the selected students write down whether they have been assigned to the Treatment or Control condition, and have them return to their seats. Point out how this constitutes random assignment to conditions. This would be a good time to explain to the students the purposes of random sampling and random assignment, and how they differ from, for example, convenience sampling or self-selection to conditions.

State the hypotheses. Explain the importance of class participation and discuss how everyone benefits if students remain involved and inquisitive throughout the course. Explain also that you understand that some students may be afraid to speak out in class. State that while you can sympathize with their concerns, you will demonstrate scientifically for them that they should not be afraid. Then, write on the board, or use **Handout 2.2a** to make a transparency to be shown to the students, "HYPOTHESIS 1: Class participation will kill you." Below this, write (or show via overhead) "HYPOTHESIS 2: Class participation will <u>not</u> kill you." Announce to the class that you will be testing these rival hypotheses, and that you are so confident in Hypothesis 2 that you are willing to bet their (the students') lives on it. (To add some more humor to this, you may want to announce something like, "Of course, I could be wrong, so those of you in the Treatment condition may want to hug your neighbors goodbye, providing it's okay with them.")

Hand out the pre-treatment questionnaire. Distribute copies of the <u>top</u> half of **Handout 2.2b** to the students in both conditions. This handout simply asks the students to record their name and condition, and to indicate if they are alive or dead.

The treatment: Class participation. Ask the students in the class who are not in either condition to help you come up with three or four questions that the students in the Treatment condition should answer in front of the class. Explain that these questions should be innocuous—questions that they themselves would be willing to answer. You may suggest questions concerning their name, hometown, intended major, why they're taking this course, and their favorite soup. Explain that the act of answering these questions will signify "class participation" for purposes of testing the rival hypotheses. (If you want to go into more depth about issues of methodology, this would be a good time to discuss the issue of why and how researchers operationally define, or create an empirical realization of, their independent variables.) Once you and the class have come up with the set of questions, have each student in the Treatment condition stand up and answer these questions in front of the class. You may consider asking each of these students a lighthearted follow-up question or two, to begin to establish the norm of give-and-take (i.e., a conversation) between you and the students.

Students in the Control condition should not be asked to say anything in front of the class.

Hand out the post-treatment questionnaire. Distribute copies of the <u>bottom</u> half of Handout 2.2b to the students in both conditions. These questions are identical to those asked on the Pre-Treatment Questionnaire.

Discussion of dependent measures. Explain to the students that the dependent variable in this study is whether or not the participants were killed during the experiment. Explain the purpose of the pre- and post-treatment questionnaires. Tell the students that these are self-report measures. Explain that self-reports are very frequently used in social psychology but that there are other ways of measuring dependent variables. You may refer to Chapter 2 of the textbook for a discussion of these issues. Ask the students to help you come up with an <u>observational</u> measure to determine if the participants were killed during the experiment. (Again, if you want to go into more depth about issues of methodology, this would be a good time to discuss the issue of why and how researchers operationally define, or create an empirical realization of, their dependent variables.) When you have selected a technique, conduct your observation of the participants to determine that each is, indeed, alive. You might want to bring a mirror to class, to hold under a participant's nose to see if they fog it up. Consider bringing some other amusing props for this task.

Report the results. Collect the questionnaires and report to the class each of the following: (a) the number of students in each condition, (b) the number of students in each condition who reported themselves as alive in the Pre-Treatment Questionnaire, (c) the number of students in each condition who reported themselves as alive in the Post-Treatment Questionnaire, and (d) the number of students in each condition who were observed to be alive based on the observational measure.

General discussion. The results should indicate that the second hypothesis—that class participation will <u>not</u> kill you—was supported by the data. The observational measure should reveal that none of the students were killed in either condition. Because some students may try to be funny, some may indicate in their questionnaires that they are not alive. If this is the case, explain to the rest of the class how this illustrates an important problem with self-report measures and why using multiple methods, such as observational measures along with self-reports, can be so valuable. Explain also that researchers may use self-report questionnaires differently than the research participants anticipate. Researchers may use questions that are written in such a way that they can infer if participants are lying or giving misleading information, or the critical questions are embedded within a larger set of questions that are irrelevant to the focus of the research, so that the participants will be less on their guard when responding to the critical questions. Illustrate this more sophisticated approach to using self-reports by announcing that you will ignore <u>what</u> the students wrote on their questionnaires and instead focus on whether or not they wrote <u>anything</u>— using the criterion that if they wrote anything, they must have been alive. (If, on the other hand, none of the students reports that he or she is not alive, ask the class to imagine that someone did report himself or herself as dead, and discuss these same issues with them.)

Ask the students to explain why a control (non-treatment) condition was included in the study. Ask the students to explain the advantage of conducting an experiment to test the rival hypotheses rather than simply observing whether the students who volunteer to participate during the first few classes are killed during class (i.e., discuss the issue of self-selection to conditions as a threat to internal validity, keeping in mind that the students who choose to participate may be importantly different [e.g., less nervous?] than the students who choose not to participate). If you haven't already done this, discuss the purpose of random assignment.

Ask the students to speculate about what alternative explanations they could offer, and how they could test them, if somebody in the study had, indeed, died. This should lead to a discussion of the importance of random assignment, control conditions, and statistical analyses.

Finally, point out that all of the students who were not part of the experiment but who participated in class by suggesting various ideas also did not die from their participation, adding converging evidence supporting the hypothesis that class participation will not kill you.

What if this bombs? This activity is fairly bombproof. Even in the unlikely event that the students do not find the activity to be fun and amusing, thereby negating the value of the activity as an icebreaker, the activity does raise several important methodological issues that are covered in Chapter 2 and that will remain relevant throughout the course. The only way, then, that the activity could really bomb is if someone does, in fact, die. Of course, a death in class would put a damper on any activity, and, from a purely methodological standpoint, a number of important issues about the laws of probability and inferential statistics could be raised to illustrate that the death does not confirm the first hypothesis.

More seriously, if you are at all concerned with using words like "kill" and "dead" as part of this activity, you could substitute other hypotheses, such as that class participation will (or will not) cause students to be laughed out of the classroom, spontaneously combust, or experience some other unpleasant outcome.

Carducci, B. J. (1990). Will class participation "kill" you? Refuting a common irrational belief by teaching research methods In V. P. Makosky, C. C. Sileo, L. G. Whittemore, C. P. Landry, & M. L. Skutley (Eds.), Activities Handbook for the Teaching of Psychology (Vol. 3, pp. 203-205). Washington, DC: American Psychological Association.

Activity 3. The Importance of Random Assignment

This activity is designed to illustrate how random assignment serves the valuable function of being "the great equalizer" that allows one to infer cause-and-effect relationships between independent and dependent variables in an experiment. As Chapter 2 explains, random assignment is one of the two defining features of an experiment (the other feature being experimental control). This activity is designed to be an easy way to demonstrate the importance of random assignment, as well as its effectiveness. Though especially well suited for large classes, it can work with any size class.

This activity can be done in many different ways. The key features of the activity are the following:

First, describe an experiment (either a real one or a hypothetical one) that has two different conditions. Summarize the results (again, either real results or hypothetical results) of the experiment, ensuring that they are simple to understand, and that there is a significant difference between the two conditions on the dependent variable of interest. You could use the "experiment" described in the previous Classroom Activity as an example.

Then, ask the students if they can infer from these results that the manipulation of the independent variable (i.e., the difference in treatment between the two conditions) caused the difference found on the dependent variable. Ask the students what other factors could explain the difference.

Inevitably, some students will raise alternative explanations concerning individual differences between the participants in the two conditions that could account for the results. What these students fail to understand is that random assignment should have made it very unlikely that such differences could have existed between the conditions. That is, random assignment should have ensured that, on average, there were no pre-existing differences between the participants as a function of condition. After raising this issue with the students, tell them that you understand that it can be a difficult concept to grasp immediately, and that to help them see the function of random assignment, you will conduct a demonstration.

Then, randomly assign the class (or a sample from the class) to two different conditions, such as by a flip of the coin.

Finally, compare the students in one condition with those in the other condition on a number of dimensions, such as sex, age, political affiliation or orientation, height, attitude about some campus issue, number of math classes taken, whether they would prefer soup or salad if they were offered it right then, etc.

That is the basic outline of the activity. What experiment(s) you choose to describe in order to introduce the concept of random assignment, how many students you assign to each condition, and how and on what variables you measure the students in the two conditions are up to you. In the paragraphs below, we offer three specific suggestions.

Version 1. One version of this activity is based on an activity proposed by David Watson (1990). This activity requires no calculations (i.e., you do not need to calculate and compare the average questionnaire responses between the two conditions), and it can provide a visual demonstration of the effectiveness of random assignment. To begin this activity, tell the students that you think that you have devised a new way of coaching basketball that will enable you to train a team to be winners. (To add some humor here, you can briefly explain your new method, although this is not at all necessary. You can choose something absurd, like having the players each construct a shrine worshipping you, or playing Britney Spears music constantly.) Say to the students that, being trained in social psychology, you recognize the need to demonstrate empirically that your method of coaching really is superior. Explain that the best way to test your idea is to run an experiment in which one team will be trained by your new method and another team will be trained by the traditional methods. Each team will then play in a tournament, and, if your method really is superior, the team coached by it should do better in the tournament.

Ask the students if there is anything wrong with this experiment. Some students will probably say that the teams might be different to begin with -- i.e., <u>before</u> the different training methods are used. If, for example, the team coached by your new method is a better team to begin with, then it would not be clear if its success is due to your methods or if it was due to the fact that it is the better team. (In the unlikely event that no student raises this point, then you should raise it as a potential problem.) Ask the students if they can think of any specific, easy-to-measure individual differences that might exist between the players on the two teams that would likely have an important effect on their basketball success. Some student should (or, if not, you should) suggest that height makes a big difference and that the teams might differ on this dimension. How can you make it unlikely that the teams would differ on height? Explain that random assignment should solve this problem. Tell the students that you will form two basketball teams from the students who are in class, and that you will randomly assign them to one of the two teams.

Watson suggests that instructors use only one sex in order to reduce some of the variation in height. You might consider using only women first, and then using only men in a replication of the demonstration.

Select about two dozen students to be in the experiment. Randomly assign them to either Team A or Team B by flipping a coin. Ask the students to stand on different sides of the room as they are assigned to their teams. When the students have all been assigned, have the students in Team A come to the front of the class, and line them up from tallest to shortest. Then, have the students in Team B line up behind them (or, we suggest, have them line up facing Team A in close proximity, to make it seem more like two teams about to face each other in battle), also from tallest to shortest. If the random assignment is successful, all of the students in the class should see that the two teams do not differ much in height.

Version 2. A second version of this activity is to randomly assign all of the students in the class to either of two conditions, call these conditions Team A and Team B, and distribute copies of **Handout 2.3** to the students. This handout asks the students to indicate the team to which they have been assigned and to answer a series of questions about themselves. Collect the completed handouts, separate them by condition, and compare the responses as a function of condition. Report to the class at least some, and ideally all, of these comparisons. The two groups should have similar averages on all of these dimensions.

Version 3. You could also do a combination of these two versions of the activity. That is, set the demonstration up as an experiment to test your new method of coaching basketball, and do the activity as described above, including lining up the two teams and comparing their heights. But then ask the students in the class why you couldn't simply divide the group into two teams by matching them for height. That is, rather than randomly assigning them to the conditions, why not assign the two tallest students to opposite teams, the next two tallest to opposite teams, and so on? You should explain that the problem with doing this is that there are numerous other dimensions on which these two teams might differ, and just because you rule out height does not mean that the other differences no longer exist. Explain that the value of random assignment is that it should equalize all of these other dimensions, as well as all the dimensions that you cannot even think of but that do exist.

To see if random assignment did indeed equalize the two teams on a variety of dimensions, distribute copies of **Handout 2.3** to them, and compare the averages as a function of team. If random assignment worked, the two teams should have similar averages.

> ●*What if this bombs?* The laws of probability suggest that it is very unlikely for random assignment to fail to sufficiently equalize the two conditions if your sample (class) size is sufficiently large. Be sure to explain to the students that the two conditions do not have to have the exact same averages on height, etc. -- that some variation is inevitable. The students should be made to recognize that the variation within a condition is (or should be) greater than the variation between the two conditions. If, however, the difference between the two conditions seems more than trivially small, you should treat this not as a failure but as an opportunity to say a bit more about methodological issues. To do this, simply explain that with the relatively small numbers of students involved in this demonstration, some variation is not terribly surprising. Explain that with large samples, the averages are much more likely to be equal and reliable (of course, if the sample you used was very large, then skip this point and go to the next one). In addition, and perhaps more important, explain that the field of social psychology rarely puts much stock in the results of any one experiment. Tell the students that social psychology research proceeds cautiously, that typically it is only after several studies have shown similar findings that social psychologists are satisfied that a particular cause-and-effect relationship has been demonstrated adequately.

> At this point, you could try the demonstration again, counting on the laws of probability to hold true for you this second time, and/or you could go into a bit more detail about probability and the benefits of replication. That is, you can explain the notion of statistical significance (which is explained in Chapter 2), and how the standard that the field has set for accepting a finding as statistically significant is if the statistics indicate that the odds are less than 1 in 20 that the results occurred by chance alone. Point out that if the results of one study are statistically significant, and if these results are replicated and statistically significant in a second study, our confidence in the finding increases dramatically.

Watson, D. L. (1990). A neat little demonstration of the benefits of random assignment of subjects in an experiment. In V. P. Makosky, C. C. Sileo, L. G. Whittemore, C. P. Landry, & M. L. Skutley (Eds.), <u>Activities Handbook for the Teaching of Psychology</u> (Vol. 3, pp. 3-4). Washington, DC: American Psychological Association.

Activity 4. Designing a Questionnaire

This activity is designed to give students experience in writing questions for research participants to answer—and in critiquing those questions. This can be a fun exercise for the students, but it should also demonstrate very effectively that it can be quite a challenge to create a set of questions in a way that elicits unbiased, unambiguous, and meaningful data. There is no better way to show students the many obstacles and pitfalls that people face when designing questionnaires and surveys, and it should give the class a better sense of why they should think about the methodology of a non-scientific poll or survey before taking the results at face value. The activity is also good at getting students to appreciate the challenge of operationally defining the variables that they wish to investigate. In addition to these perks, this activity can also be used as a springboard into discussing measurement devices such as Likert scales that play a central role in the assessment of attitudes.

Choose a topic. Either present students with a topic or set of topics that will be the focus of their questionnaires, or ask the students to make their own suggestions. The topic should be something that clearly is relevant to social psychology, is of interest to most students, is not unethical to pursue, and can elicit quantifiable data. The advantages of having the students make suggestions for the topic are that the students would be more involved and committed to the activity, they would choose something of interest to them, and they would be forced to think of how their abstract ideas can be turned into a concrete set of questions. The disadvantages of this are that it takes up more class time (which may not be a disadvantage if you have time to spare) and that some of the students' ideas will be inappropriate or otherwise difficult to pursue.

Give the assignment. This activity can be done either in class or as a take-home assignment. If it is done in class, you should have students work on it in small groups; if the activity is done outside of class, students can do this either individually or in small groups. Have the students develop a brief questionnaire designed to investigate the topic that was selected for this activity. Tell the students that they should construct the questionnaire as if they really were going to distribute it to people outside of the class. (Indeed, to make this an even more ambitious activity, you could have the students actually conduct a survey, collect the data, and interpret the findings together in class. This would, of course, require much more time and work, and you might need to get your survey approved by an ethics board, but the payoff could be high because students find such an activity to be very engaging and memorable.)

Emphasize to the students that the questionnaire should include instructions that are clear and not likely to bias the results. Explain that subtle changes in the wording and the order of the questions can make a big difference in the responses that participants give. Instruct the students to write questions in such a way that the potential responses to these questions can be quantified easily. In addition to writing the questions, the students should be required to describe how they would collect their data. That is, tell the students to indicate who their participants would be and, specifically, how they would recruit them (you might want to tell the students to imagine that they have no money, or have only some specific amount of money, to pay people to participate in the survey).

If the students work on this activity in class, give them a few minutes to get started with the assignment and then go around the room and observe the various small-group discussions. Probe each group with questions such as, "How are you going to measure that?" or, "Is there a way to have the respondents answer this question along some scale rather than in an open-ended format?" Key concepts to discuss with the students as they are working on the activity are the wording of questions, the order of questions, the response options given to respondents, the difficulty of analyzing open-ended responses, and how they would interpret various responses to the questions. Compliment the students for any good questions they've created, and try to spread enthusiasm for the task.

Evaluate the questionnaires. Collect the various questionnaires. We recommend that you do not evaluate the questionnaires immediately in class but rather take the time outside of class to evaluate them more carefully, after which you can report on them at the next class. Examine each questionnaire and identify mistakes or other problems that you can discuss in class to illustrate some important points. For example, students often word questions in such a way that their meanings are ambiguous, and thus the responses to these questions may be impossible to interpret. Students often have one particular meaning in mind, and they fail to recognize that other meanings are plausible. Another common problem is that instructions or response scales tend to be confusing. A third common problem concerns the framing of a question; for example, a question can be introduced in such a way that there seems to be a clearly preferred response, or the questions are ordered in ways that may seem to alter their meaning. See Chapter 2 of the textbook for a discussion of some of these and related problems. Also, identify particularly good questions. Bring to class examples of the problems you noted, as well as examples of good questions, and discuss these with the class. Be careful not to embarrass students by seeming to ridicule them or by taking more bad examples from any one student or group of students than from others.

Also, evaluate and critique the sampling procedures suggested by the students. Are they likely to be biased? For example, will some of these procedures lead to a disproportionate number of respondents who are of relatively high socioeconomic status, or who are particularly interested or experienced in the topic, or unusually friendly? Even a practice such as picking phone numbers at random from the phone book can lead to a number of biases (it will exclude people who don't have phone service or whose numbers are unlisted; depending on the time of day in which the calls are made, some types of people may be more or less likely to be home than others; the first person who answers the phone in a house may tend to be one kind of person, such as a teenager, more than another, such as a busy young parent). Discuss a procedure that is so commonly used in television, radio, newspapers, and now even the Internet: inviting people to call or mail in their responses to some question that is presented in the program, newspaper, or Internet site. The kinds of people who are likely to respond in such cases— especially when responding costs them money, as when they must indicate their response by calling a number that is not toll-free—are probably different from the rest of the population in a variety of important ways.

Explain to the students that the mistakes they made in their questionnaires are very typical of people who have not been trained in this field. Point out that these are the kinds of problems that can be found in the majority of surveys that are conducted in the real world — because most of these studies are not done in scientific ways. It would be ideal to bring to class some examples from these real-world surveys, such as those described in advertisements, on tabloid news shows that feature call-in polls, etc. The point is not that surveys are therefore meaningless or too difficult to conduct well. Rather, the point is that being trained to design such research is necessary, and that because we are all exposed to a great deal of information based on survey questionnaire results, we should think critically about alternative explanations for these results and, when possible, examine the methods used to collect the data.

It is quite likely that several of the questions that students wrote turned out to be much more ambiguous than the students had realized. Use these examples to illustrate an important social psychological point about how different perceivers may interpret the same stimulus very differently from each other, and that any one perceiver may interpret the same stimulus differently at different points in time because of differences in expectations, contexts, moods, and so on. This will be an important point throughout the course. Explain that because of the great potential for ambiguity and misunderstanding, researchers are advised to test their surveys and questionnaires with people who are similar to those who will be asked to participate in the actual surveys or studies. The data from such "pilot tests" serve as trial runs that allow the researchers to see how their questions and other materials are interpreted. Researchers often interview the pilot test participants about their perceptions, and these interviews can be very constructive for the researchers.

Explain also that writing these kinds of questions is not limited to designing surveys. Most experiments also include sets of questions asked of participants. More generally, the challenge of going from abstract, broadly defined ideas that researchers would like to study to creating a specific set of clear, unambiguous, unbiased, easily quantifiable measures is a critical step in all social psychological research. And it is a step, or, more accurately, a long series of steps, that can be challenging, frustrating, and likely to require compromises. On the other hand, this process can be interesting and rewarding because of this challenge—that is, it requires creativity and thoughtfulness. It requires the ability to put oneself into the minds of potential respondents and to be able to anticipate the meaningfulness of the variety of responses that the questions are likely to elicit.

A specific example. One of the present authors conducted this exercise with his students a few years ago, and Handout 2.4 presents examples of questions that some of these students submitted, along with some of the critiques of the wording of these questions that were discussed in the next class. You can use this handout as an example to help guide you, or you can distribute copies of the handout to students so that they can see some problematic questions.

The topic of this survey was selected by the students. They wanted to focus on "dating on campus," and they were particularly interested in learning how prevalent dating was on campus (and to compare the prevalence across different categories of students, such as athletes and non-athletes, first-year students and seniors, etc.), what attributes were most important in choosing whom to date, and what students did on dates. (Of course, due to issues of sensitivity, instructors must be careful to make sure that students do not offend each other or that the task does not become too puerile.) The questions on Handout 2.4 are real questions submitted by students for this activity.

> *What if this bombs?* This activity is fairly bombproof. It is almost certain that there will be questionnaires submitted that can be used as examples of methodological problems that would be worthy of discussion. Particularly if you give yourself time to read through the questionnaires and summarize good, but sensitive, critiques that you can explain in the next class, you should be able to make several important points. Even if all the students submit excellent questionnaires, you should be able to make this activity a success by explaining to the students what they did right. Students do not mind hearing compliments from their instructor, and you can still point out how the majority of surveys and questionnaires that are used in the real world are very unsound. The only real chance for this activity to bomb at all is if the students perceive you to be ridiculing their efforts when you offer your critiques. You can avoid this by being sensitive to this issue, pointing out how pervasive such errors are in the real world, and discussing how this can serve as a valuable learning experience for them.

Activity 5. Demonstrating the Social Desirability Bias in Surveys

The social desirability bias refers to the tendency to overreport socially desirable behaviors and underreport socially undesirable behaviors in surveys. This bias remains a source of error in much survey research. Randall A. Gordon (1987) presents a technique for demonstrating the bias in the classroom. In his demonstration, students were given two forms of a survey about their dental habits. The questions on the two forms were identical, but the instructions accompanying the surveys differed. The standard instructions merely asked students to respond to the questions without signing their name on the form. The more elaborate instructions stressed the anonymity of the data, referred to the task as contributing valuable information, and urged the participants to provide accurate answers. Consequently, subjects who received the elaborate instructions reported substantially lower rates of dental checkups and other dental health care behavior than those who received the standard instructions (who demonstrated the bias by overreporting this socially desired behavior).

This activity uses the same method to demonstrate the bias in connection with the use of cell phones while driving. Because using a cell phone while driving is considered to be a socially undesirable behavior, it is expected that students receiving the standard instructions will underreport the behavior (thus demonstrating the bias), whereas students who receive the elaborated instructions will tend to be more accurate.

The two versions of the survey are **Handout 2.5S** (which has the standard instructions) and **Handout 2.5E** (which has the elaborate instructions). The standard instructions of handout 2.5S are expected to show the bias of underreporting the behavior. The more elaborate instructions of Handout 2.5E are expected to elicit truthful responses. Moreover, to add to their impact, the elaborated instructions start out with the statement that "Cell phones have recently been singled out as the most common cause of car crashes" (Insurance Information Institute, November, 2006).

Tell the students that you would like them to participate in a short survey on cell phone usage. Without letting on that there are two forms, distribute one form to half the students and the other form to the other half. Allow them 5 minutes to complete the forms and collect both, keeping the two forms separate.

To tabulate the results, draw two columns on the chalkboard, with one labeled "Standard Instructions" (Handout 2.5S), and the other labeled "Elaborate Instructions" (Handout 2.5E). Explain to the class that the survey questions were framed so that (a) answers are more socially desirable — lowest usage of cell phones while driving and (c) answers are least socially desirable — highest usage of cell phones while driving. Tally the number of (a), (b), and (c) answers to each question separately for each form. Now assign a value of 1 to each (a) answer, a value of 2 to each (b) answer, and a value of 3 to each (c) answer, and add up the totals. You should have two separate totals, one for Handout 2.5S and one for Handout 2.5E.

The social desirability bias will be demonstrated if the answers for those responding to Handout 2.5E show a higher use of cell phones while driving (a higher total elicited by more elaborate instructions) than the answers of those responding to Handout 2.5S (who are expected to underreport this socially undesirable behavior, which should result in a lower total).

Begin a discussion of the results by disclosing the two different types of instructions that accompanied the forms. Ask your students to analyze which elements of the elaborated instructions elicited higher rates of disclosure. What do they think motivated those who reported higher as opposed to lower rates of usage?

> ●*What if this bombs?* The more elaborate instructions should elicit more accurate responses and therefore expose a social desirability bias in those who received the standard instructions. If that does not happen, present the results of Gordon's article and ask the class to propose possible reasons for failure to demonstrate the bias in this case. One reason might be that your students are not using their cell phones while driving. However, that would make them the exception: According to the 2005 National Occupant Protection Use Survey (NOPUS), at any given daylight moment, there are 974,000 drivers in the US who are holding a phone up to their ear. That's 6 percent of all drivers, but 10 percent of drivers between the ages of 16–24.

Gordon, R.A. (1987). Social desirability bias: A demonstration and technique for its reduction. Teaching of Psychology, 14, 1, pp. 40-42.

Facts about cell phones and vehicular accidents can be accessed at the website of the Insurance Information Institute at: http://www.iii.org/media/hottopics/insurance/cellphones/

The 2005 National Occupant Protection Use Survey (NOPUS), which is conducted by the National Center for Statistics and Analysis, can be viewed at: www-nrd.nhtsa.dot.gov/pdf/nrd-30/NCSA/RNotes/2005/809967.pdf.

Activity 6. Operationalizing Variables

One of the most challenging, and fun, aspects of designing research is trying to take abstract, conceptual variables and make them concrete and specific so that they can be manipulated or measured. This process of creating operational definitions of the variables in the study is a critically important step in any research project. There typically are many different ways of operationalizing (coming up with operational definitions for) variables in social psychology research. See the discussion of this in Chapter 2 of the textbook.

You can have students do this activity either individually or in groups (the latter typically is more fun for the students, but the slower students might sit back and let the faster ones in the group dominate). Either make a transparency of **Handout 2.6**, or distribute copies of it to the class. The handout includes several conceptual variables that need to be operationally defined for a study. For example, the handout describes how one team of researchers is interested in correlating how much people like their romantic partner with how much they love them. At a conceptual level, we know what it means to "like" someone and what it means to "love" them. But how, exactly, does one measure this? There are many, many different, valid (and invalid) ways to do this—which one(s) should you choose?

Have the students come up with operational definitions for the variables and report them to the class. Compare the different ideas that the various students proposed for the same conceptual variables. Then discuss the construct validity — the extent to which the measures really do measure the variables they were designed to measure and the manipulations really do manipulate the variables they were designed to manipulate — of the various operational definitions. Discuss how one might test the construct validity of these operational definitions.

Point out the advantages of using multiple methods and gathering converging evidence to be more confident in the construct validity. This is an important methodological point. Students often demonstrate little patience when it comes to research — they want the study they design or read about to answer the research questions definitively. It rarely happens that way. Multiple studies with different methodologies are typically necessary before we can draw confident conclusions from the results. Even then, it is likely that future research will refine and modify these conclusions.

> *What if this bombs?* This activity cannot bomb. Different students (or different groups of students) will come up with different ways of operationalizing these variables, so that guarantees some interesting things to talk about. Discuss the advantages and disadvantages of the various ideas, how you could try to test their validity, how you could actually conduct these studies pragmatically (would it require too many participants or too high a budget?), what their predictions of the results would be, and so on.

Activity 7. Designing an Experiment

Working together to design an experiment can be a very enjoyable and educational experience for students. It can provide them with a much greater appreciation for the art and science of taking abstract ideas and turning them into a concrete experiment. It can also help them understand important issues such as independent and dependent variables, internal and external validity, experimental and mundane realism, the use of deception, and concerns about ethics and values.

There are many different ways of conducting an activity such as this. You can give the students a specific or general topic and have them design an experiment to address the issue, or you can have the class decide together about an issue to examine. You can have all of the students work on the same topic together, or have them all work on the same topic but in small groups. We recommend that there should be some collaborative component. Students tend to get more out of the activity if they are working in small groups, rather than either individually or in very large groups in which only a few students get to participate actively.

You can get ideas for the topic to be studied from a number of sources, such as by skimming the textbook, opening up a journal such as *Personality and Social Psychology Bulletin* and trying to conduct a study related to one in the journal, or testing one of the ideas in **Handout 2.6**. One example, based on one of the ideas in Handout 2.6, is described in detail below.

A specific example. One example of a general topic that can be assigned to students is the issue of the effects of media depictions of violence on people's attitudes or behaviors. You can ask students about the controversy concerning violence on television, in movies, or in music lyrics or videos. You can steer the discussion so that it begins to focus on, for example, the effects of sexist or violent lyrics in contemporary popular music on people's attitudes or behaviors. If there seems to be general interest in this issue, ask the students to suggest specific hypotheses that could be tested in an experiment. When some hypotheses have been suggested, such as "Exposure to sexist lyrics will (will not) increase people's hostility toward members of the opposite sex," divide the class into small groups and have them design an experiment to test this hypothesis (or a pair of competing hypotheses).

Instruct the students to write a specific, detailed summary of their experiment. Tell them to identify the independent and dependent variables. We advise that you limit the experiments to one or two independent variables, and one or two dependent variables. Instruct the students to be very specific about how the independent variable(s) will be manipulated and how the dependent variable(s) will be measured. As the students work on their designs, go around the room to the various groups and listen to their discussion. Be both encouraging and critical. If you see that they have not included an appropriate control or comparison group, be sure to explain to them how the internal validity of the study would be questionable without it.

Evaluate the designs. When the students have completed the assignment, evaluate the experiments on a number of dimensions. Consider using the questions on **Handout 2.7** as a guide for these evaluations, or distribute copies of the handout to the students for their own evaluations. Consider having the students see copies of each other's experimental design summaries, or have members of each group present an oral description of their designs to the rest of the class. The students could then evaluate each other's ideas. Students can use Handout 2.7 as a guide with which to evaluate their classmates' designs.

Be sure to emphasize how challenging it is to create a well-designed experiment, that it takes training and experience. Discuss with the students how working on and thinking about experimental designs can prove to be very valuable in helping them develop critical thinking skills that will serve them well for the rest of the course. That is, by thinking in depth about how an experiment can be designed to test a particular hypothesis; how variables can be defined, manipulated, and measured; how alternative explanations might be ruled out by particular combinations of variables, students should develop skills that will allow them to better understand and evaluate the research about which they will be reading during the course, and, more generally, they should become more sophisticated consumers of information about research findings to which they will be exposed in the media and in their jobs in the future.

Note also that this activity should illustrate that no one particular experiment can address adequately the general issues that inspired the research in the first place. The different groups of students will come up with a variety of experimental designs; point out that many of these ideas could contribute something different to the attempt to better understand the social psychological phenomenon in question. Discuss how this is the way the field progresses -- that evidence from a variety of different studies and paradigms can converge to give us a more complete and reliable understanding.

Hypothetical results. To make this an even more ambitious activity, you might consider giving each group of students hypothetical results and have them interpret the results in terms of main effects, interactions, and overall implications. Create patterns of results that are interesting and that are consistent with some social psychological principle(s). If possible, create results that suggest at least one main effect and at least one interaction. This can be a very valuable exercise to students, helping them develop a skill that would serve them well as they read about and try to understand the numerous research findings with which they will be confronted in, and beyond, this course.

> *What if this bombs?* This activity is bombproof. No matter how good or bad the ideas submitted by the students are, the process of trying to design an experiment and receiving feedback about their own and other students' attempts will be very educational, and it should give the class a better appreciation and understanding of the methodological paradigm that dominates social psychology (i.e., the experiment). As with the previous activity, the only potential for a problem is if the instructor gives feedback to the students in such a way that they feel that they are being ridiculed or that their efforts were futile. Be sensitive to this issue, and try to encourage the students to use the same kinds of critical analysis when they learn about experiments during the course.

Activity 8. Conducting an Experiment

Like Activity 7 (Designing an Experiment), this activity can be fun and educational for students. Even more than designing an experiment, actually <u>conducting</u> an experiment can be a compelling and memorable exercise for students.

The same kinds of skills can be developed and points made in this activity as in the previous activity. Indeed, Activities 7 and 8 can be combined so that students conduct the studies after they design them. Of course, students will be able to create more ambitious and complex designs if they don't actually have to conduct the experiment. The designs of any experiments that they will actually conduct must be fairly simple. The experiments should be quick to run and should not require a great deal of resources (such as money or confederates). Moreover, for ethical reasons, it probably would not be a good idea to have these students conduct experiments that involve much deception or that concern sensitive, personal issues.

One possibility is to have students design an ambitious study as part of Activity 6, but then they could apply the knowledge they gained from that experience to this activity, in which they help design a more limited experiment that they actually have the time and ability to conduct.

We recommend that you have all of the students in class work on the same experiment, rather than dividing the students into small groups and having them conduct separate experiments, so that they will be better able to collect enough data. Another advantage of this approach is that you can spend more time in class discussing this one experiment and its implications.

Evaluating the experiment before it is conducted. You can use **Handout 2.7** with this activity as well as with Activity 7. The design of the experiment should be discussed and critiqued at length before the experiment is conducted. This will give you and the students a chance to make any changes to the design before it is too late. Since the ethics of the experiment should also be discussed before the experiment is conducted, you will probably need to submit a description of the experiment to an ethics board for approval before it is conducted.

The students should be given very clear, explicit instructions about the procedure and debriefing. They should practice conducting the study with their fellow students or with friends of theirs who will not be in the actual experiment. If there is time, it would be ideal if the class has a chance to meet and re-evaluate the procedures after everyone has had a chance to run a few practice sessions. If the experiment is a simple field study in which there is very little for the students to actually do (as in the "Smiling" study described below), then there would be much less need for such rehearsals.

Evaluating the experiment after it is conducted. From the beginning of this project, you should emphasize that the success or failure of this activity does not rest on what kinds of results the study produces. Explain that it often takes researchers months and even years to design, fine-tune, pre-test, revise, and conduct experiments, and so the students should not be disappointed if a hastily conceived and conducted experiment does not yield interesting data. The point of the activity is to get some experience designing and conducting the experiment. Although it would be great to get results that are consistent with predictions or that clearly are interesting, it can also be a fun and meaningful experience if the results are "mush." Explain that experiments that do not yield good results can be very informative. It can be very helpful to speculate about why they got results that they did -- new ideas about the design or the hypotheses can emerge from such speculations. Depending on the results, ask the students for suggestions about how subsequent experiments could be designed to rule out potential alternative explanations, address additional issues raised by the study, improve the chances of yielding data consistent with the hypothesis, and/or provide a better test of a revised hypothesis.

A specific example. Jon Grahe, Kipling Williams, and Verlin Hinsz (2000) describe a field experiment on smiling that is simple and interesting enough to work well for this activity. Conducting this experiment will allow students to gain a better understanding of such methodological issues as random assignment, equalizing the strength of manipulations, and experimenter bias.

The basic hypothesis of the experiment is that people are more likely to reciprocate smiles than frowns. The experiment is a replication of a study by Hinsz and Tomhave (1991). In that study, students went to public places and presented a smile, a frown, or a neutral face to strangers. They found that more than half the people (52.6 percent) returned the smile but very few (4.6 percent) frowned back.

You could start by familiarizing students with the Hinsz and Tomhave (1991) study. Explain that the experiment will be done in pairs with one student displaying the facial expression and the other recording the result.

Random assignment is achieved by having students write "smile" on six slips of paper and "frown" on another six. Then, the displayers will draw a slip at a time, at random, to determine which facial expression to present.

In order to equalize the manipulation strength, students need to practice creating consistent facial expressions. The authors present the following as their operational definition of a smile: "The eyes wide open, the forehead is not creased, and the corners of the mouth pulled back and turned up." While smiling, students were asked to imagine that they were with a good friend that they enjoyed being with very much. For a consistent frown, the authors used the following operational definition: "Eyes are focused, the forehead is creased, and the corners of the mouth are pulled back and turned down." While frowning, students were asked to imagine being with a close friend and that something very bad happened to that friend.

The authors had students practice their facial expressions in pairs until they were fairly certain that their strength matched, so that the frowns were as likely to be labeled as such as were the smiles.

To reduce experimenter bias, the students practiced working with another pair (who acted as passersby) to achieve standardization in their coding of the reciprocal expression. While the student acting as experimenter presented a facial expression (randomly drawn and not shared with anyone else), the student acting as recorder walked 1.5 meters behind. When the experimenter made eye contact, he/she signaled the recorder with a behind-the-back gesture that the passersby should be counted as a participant. In this way, students learned that it was important to keep the recorder from knowing which stimulus (smile or frown) was being presented, so as to avoid an interpretation bias as to which expression was being returned.

After students have practiced their expressions and are confident as to their ability to accurately code the response, have them pick a public location with high pedestrian traffic, such as a mall, a park, or the college campus. Instruct them to go out in pairs with one acting as the displayer and the other as a recorder and to pick a dozen subjects who are by themselves.

If you are also interested in having students explore the effect of the sex variable, tell students to make note of the sex of the displayer and to choose six males and six females as participants, with three of each receiving frowns and three of each receiving smiles.

When the data have been collected, analyze the main effect by calculating the number and the percentage of strangers in each condition who smiled in response to a smile and the number and percentage of those who frowned in response to a frown.

To look at the effect of the sex variable, do these calculations separately for male subjects in each condition (smile versus frown), in response to male or female displayers and for female subjects in each condition (smile versus frown) in response to male or female displayers. Present a table of percentages to the students, and look for differences between conditions, between male and female strangers, and between male and female experimenters, as well as for interactions among these variables (e.g., are male strangers more likely to respond with a smile than female strangers to a female experimenter who is smiling?) The Hinsz and Tomhave study did demonstrate such sex effects.

Ask your students to offer interpretations of the results. Explain the difference between main effects and interactions, which is discussed briefly in Chapter 2. Ask the students to suggest some theoretical reasons to account for any differences that you found between or among conditions. Ask for alternative explanations and for suggestions for follow-up studies that might answer some of the questions raised by the study. Ask the students to discuss anything that they learned about experimentation by having participated in the running of the study.

What if this bombs? Even though the authors report that this effect was reliably replicated many times, there is always the chance that your students will fail to find differences between conditions. This is no reason for the activity itself to bomb, however. You should make it very clear to the students before they conduct the experiment that there is a possibility that the study will not work—that is, there might be no consistent differences between conditions or the results might be the opposite of what was predicted. Emphasize that such failures are an important part of the process by which researchers develop, revise, and strengthen their theories and hypotheses. Emphasize also that researchers typically take much more time to design their experiments and to create and test their materials, and so the researchers' chances for success are greater.

The key is that, both before and after the students conduct the experiment, you explain to them that the purpose of the activity is to give them direct experience with the challenge of conducting an experiment. Inform them that what you want them to get out of the activity is a better understanding not necessarily of the phenomenon being studied but of the process of conducting an experiment, including how to take abstract ideas and turn them into specific independent variables that can be manipulated and controlled and dependent variables that can be measured, how to try to rule out alternative explanations, how to assess the internal and external validity of an experiment, etc.

One problem with null results in an activity like this is that students are deprived of the chance to practice interpreting, or making sense out of, a pattern of potentially interesting results. Therefore, if the results of their experiment are not interesting, present the students with a set of fake results that you create. (Present these results after you discuss the real results, and tell the students that the second set of results is hypothetical.) Create results that are interesting and consistent with some social psychological principle or finding. If there were two or more independent variables, it might be ideal to create results that suggest an interaction between independent variables. By giving students these results, you can help them begin to develop the skill of summarizing and understanding a set of research results, which should prove valuable during the rest of the course as they read about numerous research findings.

Grahe, J.E, Williams, K.D., & Verlin, B. (2000). Teaching experimental methods while bringing smiles to your students. Teaching of Psychology, 27, 2, 108-111.

Hinsz, V.B. & Tomhave, J.A. (1991). Smile and (half) the world smiles with you, frown and you frown alone. Personality and Social Psychology Bulletin, 17, 586-592.

Activity 9. Using Jelly Beans to Teach Methodology Concepts

Hank Rothgerber and Eric Day Anthony (1999) created this simple activity that will allow you to demonstrate several methodological concepts, such as random assignment, interpreting main effects and interactions, and generating alternative explanations.

Before the lesson, you will need to obtain one jelly bean for each student, in two flavors, one a typical sweet, fruity one (the authors recommend cherry), the other a more unusual one (the authors recommend buttered popcorn or cappuccino). Place each of the jelly beans in its own envelope. In half the envelopes containing cherry jelly beans and in half the envelopes containing the buttered popcorn jelly beans, insert a piece of paper that identifies the flavor. In the rest of the envelopes place a piece of paper with an identifying mark (for example, C for cherry and B for buttered popcorn) so that you'll know who received which unidentified flavor. Place all the envelopes in a box.

In class, explain that you are conducting a taste test. Randomly assign the students to one of the four conditions: (e.g., cherry identified, cherry unidentified, buttered popcorn identified, and buttered popcorn, unidentified) by calling each one up in turn to choose an envelope. Ask the students to refrain from opening, talking about, or smelling their envelopes. When everyone has an envelope, instruct them to open the envelopes and silently read the information contained inside, if any. Next, tell them to eat the jelly bean.

Now ask the students to indicate on the sheet that came in the envelope, how much the taste of the jelly bean met their expectations, on a scale of 1 to 5, with 1 being "very little" and 5 being "very much." Collect the papers and compute the mean for each condition.

Before presenting the results, explain that perception is influenced not only by physical sensation but also by prior knowledge or expectations. In this case, the expectation for a jelly bean is that it would taste sweet and fruity. Therefore, those who had the cherry flavored jelly bean were likely to have thought that it met their expectations more than those who tasted a salty (i.e., buttered popcorn) or bitter jelly bean (i.e., cappuccino).

Explain that some students were told the flavor beforehand. Accordingly, those students should have had different expectations and less reliance on the general idea of what a jelly bean should taste like than students who did not know the flavor they were about to taste. That difference should have been especially noticeable for those who tasted the buttered popcorn (or any other unusual flavor).

Explain that the design of the experiment is a 2 x 2 between-subjects design. Draw the following table on the board:

	Prior information	No prior information
Cherry		
Popcorn		

Ask students if they know how they were placed in each condition. Have someone explain why the method of random assignment is so important. For example, what if all the female students were given one flavor and all the males another? What if those who were familiar with unusual jelly bean flavors were given buttered popcorn and all the others were given cherry? How would those situations impact the results? Next, ask students how they think the prior information might have influenced the results? Have them phrase their predictions in terms of main effects and interactions. They should realize that there are two main effects (cherry flavor will meet expectations more than buttered popcorn, and taste expectations will be met to a greater extent for those given prior information), and one interaction (prior information will lead to a greater degree of meeting expectations when the flavor is unusual, but not when the flavor is typical).

Place the computed means for the class in a table, as in the following hypothetical example:

Prior information	No prior information	Main effect--flavor
Cherry	4.20	4.00	4.10
Popcorn	3.80	2.00	2.90
Main information	4.00	3.00	

effect-

You might also graph the results as follows:

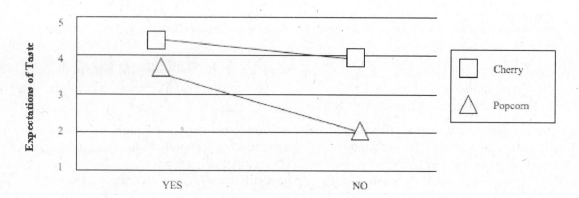

After plugging in the figures in the table and graphing the results, ask students to explain what the results mean. Were the initial hypotheses supported?

Then present the results along these lines: As you can see in the table and graph, the main effect of flavor is indicated, in that, overall, the cherry flavor led to higher expectations than the buttered popcorn flavor. Likewise, the main effect of prior information is indicated, in that, overall, when prior information was included, expectations were more closely matched than when there was no prior information. The interaction between flavor and prior information, as depicted in the graph, is indicated in that providing information as to the flavor of the jelly bean beforehand led to a higher degree of meeting expectations for the buttered popcorn flavor (from M=2.00 to M=3.80) than for the cherry flavor (from M=4.00 to M=4.20). In general, the effect of providing information on taste expectations is influenced by the flavor of the jelly bean. When the flavor is typical, prior information has little effect; however, when the flavor is unusual, prior information leads to a much higher degree of matching expectations.

Finally, ask students to generate possible alternative explanations for the results. For example, an alternative explanation might be that receiving any kind of prior information makes a person more likely to say that a product has met his or her expectations in order to show that the information was of use.

What if this bombs? This activity is relatively bombproof. Even in the unlikely event that your results do not support the hypotheses, students will still gain a better understanding of the methodological concepts involved. The authors do bring up one possible hitch: some jelly beans are made with gelatin, which comes from animals, and may therefore be unacceptable to strict vegetarians and students who follow a Kosher diet.

Rothgerber, H. & Day, E.A. (1999). Using jelly beans to teach some concepts in research methodology. In L.T. Benjamin, B.F. Nodine, R.M. Ernst, & C.B. Broeker (Eds.), Activities Handbook for the Teaching of Psychology (Vol. 4, pp. 69-73). Washington, DC: A.P.A.

Activity 10. Evaluating Research Claims Made in the Media

This activity is designed to encourage students to think more critically and less mindlessly when they are exposed to advertisements or other attempts at persuasion; accordingly, this activity can be a preview of Chapter 7 (or it can be used in conjunction with Chapter 7).

We are all exposed to numerous advertisements that feature impressive claims about the effectiveness or superiority of a particular product. In addition, politicians, salespeople, spokespersons, and many others often make strong claims about some point without having the data (or at least any unbiased data) to back up these claims. Bring to class some examples of these kinds of claims, and have students do likewise.

One common problem with research reported in advertising or the media is that it is not clear if there was an appropriate control or comparison group used in the study. For example, you might find a report about an effective weight-loss product that claims that people who use this product lose X number of pounds on average. Does the report mention anything about a control group? That is, was there a group of participants who went through similar experiences and were told the same things as the participants in the treatment group, but who received a placebo treatment rather than the real thing? If not, it's possible that the weight loss experienced by the participants in the treatment condition might have been due to any of a number of factors not directly related to the treatment, such as their positive expectations, the amount of money or effort they committed to the treatment, etc.

It's a good idea to collect such advertisements or reports in the media whenever you see them and store them for future use in this class. Bring one or a few examples to class, and distribute copies to all the students. If possible, have them form small groups and discuss the material. Is the validity of the claim questionable? How should the claim be tested further? What are its implications? You should include at least one ad or report that is not flawed, and inform the students that this is the case (but don't identify which ones are OK and which ones aren't) so that the students cannot (or should not) assume that everything they see is discernibly problematic. You want them to be skeptical consumers of information, but you don't want them simply to dismiss everything they encounter as flawed.

Encourage (or require) the students to collect examples of ads or reports that are flawed or suspect methodologically and bring them to you. Having them look for such examples will probably have more long-term impact on the way the students process such information from the media than simply having them evaluate the materials you bring to class.

What if this bombs? If the students themselves don't bring in good material, you can avoid a bomb here by bringing in good material yourself. It is relatively easy to find such material. The evaluation of the material is a bombproof exercise: If the students don't see the methodological problems in the ads or reports, then this provides you with the chance to teach the students how to look for them. If they do see the problems, then you can point out how they can use this type of thinking to be much more sophisticated consumers of information than are most people. Although the discussion of all this in class may or may not be exciting, it will be educational.

Activity 11. Conducting an Empirical Study to Test Some Claim from an Advertisement

This activity takes the previous one to the next step, and it can be a fun and memorable way for students to become familiar with methodological issues and gain first-hand experience conducting research. Rather than just discuss the validity of some claim from an advertisement or some report in the media, you can actually test it empirically.

Choose one advertisement (or similar claim from some other source) whose claim can be tested empirically in a simple study. For example, can you replicate the finding that X% of people in a blind taste test prefer Brand A over Brand B? Have the students conduct such a test, being sure to counterbalance the labels and positions of the two products.

The value of this activity stems not from whether the results support the advertisement claim but rather from getting the students to think critically about the claim, thereby helping them learn about methodological issues such as manipulating and measuring variables, using appropriate control groups, etc. This should help the students get a better sense of the importance of well-designed studies. Thus, we recommend that you let the students try to come up with the design and materials, under your guidance, rather than that you give the students a design and have them simply conduct the study. The trial-and-error process that they experience as they try to find a testable hypothesis and try to determine how many conditions they need in the study can be very educational for them.

What if this bombs? There is little chance of this activity bombing. Be sure to have a study in mind when you introduce this activity; that way, if the students can't come up with one on their own, you can give them your idea. The students should be interested in the results—whether or not they are consistent with the claim made in the advertisement, so there is no potential for the activity to bomb based on the results found.

Activity 12. Evaluating the Internal Validity and Conclusions of Research

Being able to assess the internal validity of an experiment and to think of alternative explanations for some research finding is a very valuable skill to have. The media are replete with examples of misinterpretations of research findings. The results of many flawed studies have been believed and have received a great deal of press attention, and even attention in professional journals, without any awareness that the studies are flawed and the results are not necessarily to be trusted (and should thus be viewed with a high degree of skepticism). This activity is designed to encourage students to think critically about research findings.

Give students examples of research in which the methodology is flawed or the conclusions are unjustified. These can be hypothetical studies that you construct and/or examples found in the popular press or other sources. Have the students evaluate these research designs or conclusions in small groups or individually. If you give the students several examples, it would be a good idea to include one or more examples of research whose methodology does not appear to be flawed and whose conclusions seem justified, so that students learn that being overly critical and resistant can be a problem just as mindlessness can be.

Handouts 2.12a-e Provide five examples that can be used in this activity. Each page contains a separate example, so you can choose to use either some or all of these. Distribute copies to the students and instruct them to evaluate each study carefully. Instruct the students to explain their answers, and tell them that if they believe that there are alternative explanations for the results, they should explain how subsequent studies could rule out these alternative explanations.

Discuss the methodological issues raised in Chapter 2, such as experimental control, random assignment, construct validity, internal validity, external validity, experimental realism, mundane realism, etc.

Example #1. The first example (2.12a) is called "Taste Test." The principal flaw in this study is that there was no counterbalancing of the labels and positioning of the two drinks. That is, people may have preferred Diet Duff's versus Diet Smash because the former was on the right and/or because it was labeled "M." Thus, the internal validity of the study must be called into question. The study could be improved by having each drink placed on the left side half of the time and on the right side half of the time, and each drink labeled "Q" half the time and "M" half the time (indeed, it really is not necessary to label the cups with any letter—the participants could simply indicate that they prefer the cup on the left or right). Another potential problem is experimenter bias. If people from Diet Duff's (or people hired by them) ran the test, their hopes about the outcome of the test might have influenced the participants in subtle but significant ways. The best way to minimize this potential problem is to have the person who interacts with the participants not know which drink was in which cup until <u>after</u> the participant makes his or her selection. One final point is that the difference between 105 people selecting Diet Duff's and 84 people selecting Diet Smash (ignoring the 11 participants who could not indicate a preference) is not statistically significant. Therefore, the preference for Diet Duff's may have been due to chance. (Although most students would not be expected to know this, this last point is important to discuss because the students will be exposed to claims such as those of Diet Duff's, and they should develop a healthy skepticism about the reliability of results such as these.)

Example #2. The second example (2.12b) is called "Political Attitudes." The internal validity of this study is called into question because there was no random assignment to condition. It is not clear if the political attitudes of the liberals and conservatives became less extreme because of the role playing or if some other factor caused the moderation. For example, some news event that occurred between the first and second parts of the study may have caused most people, not just the people in the study, to adopt more moderate attitudes. Another possibility is that these results could be explained by the statistical concept known as regression to the mean. The easiest way to explain this concept is with an example. Imagine having students roll two dice. You select the student who rolled the highest number — 12 — and the one who rolled the lowest number — 2. Have these students roll again. The odds are very high that the person who rolled a 12 will now roll something lower this time, and the odds are equally high that the person who rolled a 2 will roll something higher this time. Because you should expect that any particular roll will be around the expected average, or mean, anyone who rolled above the mean one toss would have a better-than-even chance of getting a lower score the next time, and anyone who rolls below the mean would have a better-than-even chance of getting a lower score the next time. Next, apply this logic to the political attitudes study: To the extent that people's reported attitudes may have been, in part, randomly determined, those who reported particularly extreme attitudes at Time 1 would be expected to give more moderate responses at Time 2 that were closer to the overall average, whether or not they participated in any role playing or other treatment. Thus, the design of this study does not allow one to rule out the possibility that their political attitudes fluctuated randomly.

This study would be improved if the extreme conservatives and extreme liberals were randomly assigned to one of two or more conditions. In one condition, the participants would do the role playing. A different set of participants, however, would not be given any treatment. In yet another condition, participants might be given some other treatment that has nothing to do with role playing. If after the four weeks the participants who did the role playing show less extreme attitudes than do the participants in the other conditions, this would suggest that role playing had the intended effect (although there would be no direct evidence to support the conclusion that role playing made the participants "more understanding of the other side").

Example #3. The third example (2.12c) is called "Cheating and Mirrors." Like the previous example, the internal validity of this study is called into question because of a lack of random assignment. In this study, participants were not randomly assigned to cheat or not to cheat; rather, they "self-selected," or were put into the different conditions on the basis of their own behavior. Thus, it is very possible (and likely) that the kinds of children who would cheat at this game tend to be different from the kinds of children who would not cheat at it. Because of this, the difference in the levels of optimism displayed in the essays of the children who cheated versus those who did not cheat may have nothing to do with guilt but may instead reflect the differences between the kinds of children who cheat and those who don't. For example, the children who cheated at this game may have needed the money more than did the other children, and this greater need for money may have been the cause of their relative pessimism. Moreover, if the children who did not cheat were placed in front of a mirror after an incident in which they <u>did</u> cheat, the presence of the mirror might have a significant effect on them. In the absence of random assignment, then, it is impossible to know how to account for the results of the study.

Example #4. The fourth example (2.12d), entitled "Fear and Affiliation," is based on Stanley Schachter's (1959) experiment. Although students may recognize alternative explanations about the process by which the fear in this study led to the desire to affiliate, or may question its external validity (e.g., would the same results be found in a situation in which fear was manipulated differently?; would male participants show the same effects as female participants?); there are no serious threats to internal validity. The participants were assigned randomly to conditions, and the experimenter had control over the procedures. The one potential problem that would be serious, however, concerns experimenter bias. That is, the experimenter's behavior toward the participants may be subtly different as a function of condition (such as when the participants are given the choice about where to sit and wait for the study to begin). This is a very real possibility. The way to avoid this is to have the experimenter give the participants written instructions that include the choice of where to sit or to have the experimenter explain that he or she has to set things up and then have a second experimenter, who is not aware of the conditions to which each participant was assigned, escort the participants away from the first experimenter and deliver the information about the different waiting rooms.

Example #5. The fifth example (2.12e) is entitled "Staring." It is based on a study by Ellsworth, Carlsmith, & Henson (1972), but we have ruined the internal validity of their study by creating a very serious confound. In our version of this study, the experimenter does not randomly assign the "participants" (i.e., the drivers) to conditions. Rather, the assignment is very non-random: The first 250 cars (and drivers) are put in the control condition, and the next 250 are put in the staring condition. There could be many reasons why the latter 250 cars sped away more quickly than the first 250, such as the time of day, different weather conditions, different traffic conditions, etc. Another potential problem is that the experimenter may bias the results through subtle changes in how the dependent variable is measured. That is, the recording of how many seconds it takes for each of 500 cars to cross an intersection is subject to error, and this error may, in part, be influenced systematically by whether or not the experimenter had just been staring at the car. For example, the experimenter may be quicker to start the stopwatch when the light turns green if she had been staring at the car than if she had not.

After they've evaluated the study, ask the students to assess its internal validity if the experimenter chose randomly whether or not to stare at the drivers (and if the dependent variable was recorded by someone else who was not aware of the condition). In this improved study, there might be a number of competing explanations as to <u>why</u> the staring caused the drivers to go faster relative to the non-staring condition, and whether the effect would generalize, but there should be no question that the manipulation of staring was indeed the cause of the difference found.

  What if this bombs? This activity is bombproof. The task of evaluating research and looking for alternative explanations is very educational; if you are enthusiastic about the task and explain its relevance for the course and beyond, the students should find it enjoyable and interesting. If students find the examples to be very easy, then you can compliment them on their skills and be sure to point out how valuable these skills will be. Be sure to challenge the class to think of ways to rule out the alternative explanations that they identified. If the students find the examples very difficult, explain that you expected them to have difficulty with the examples because these are the kinds of research findings that mislead most people. Show the students why the studies are flawed, and work together on designing studies that would have the potential to rule out the alternative explanations.

Ellsworth, P. C., Carlsmith, J. M., & Henson, A. (1972). The stare as a stimulus to flight in human subjects: A series of field experiments. Journal of Personality and Social Psychology, 21, 302-311.

Schachter, S. (1959). The psychology of affiliation: Experimental studies of the sources of gregariousness. Stanford, CA: Stanford University Press.

Activity 13. Putting It All Together: Evaluating a Research Article

This activity is designed to address many of the issues raised in Chapter 2 all in one activity. The idea of this activity is simple: The students read a journal article reporting an experiment, and they discuss the article in terms of a number of issues from the chapter. The simplicity of the idea, however, should not mask the fact that this can be a difficult exercise: Depending on the article(s) chosen, students may have a difficult time reading and understanding the material. Journal articles are written in a style with which most students are unfamiliar, and their intended audience often is other researchers rather than undergraduate students.

You can either assign the research article(s) or have the students choose them. The advantage of the former approach is that you can choose wisely -- articles that are easy to understand, well written, relevant to issues you plan to focus on in the course -- and you won't have to read as many articles yourself. The advantages of having students choose their own are that it gives them the chance to gain more experience searching the literature and that they get to choose an article that is of interest to them.

One good, easy place to find articles that could work well here is in the book of readings associated with the textbook—*Readings in Social Psychology: The Art and Science of Research*. Be sure to encourage students to read the introduction of this book before they read the articles because it provides some helpful hints for reading articles. Among the journals that might feature articles at the appropriate level are *Personality and Social Psychology Bulletin*, *Journal of Applied Social Psychology*, and *Basic and Applied Social Psychology*.

Distribute copies of **Handout 2.13** to the students for them to use in their evaluation of the article they read. If the article reports more than one experiment, you can tell the students to discuss only one of the experiments.

What if this bombs? As with most of the other activities in this chapter, there really is no chance for this to bomb. Some students may find this activity very difficult, but you can use that difficulty to motivate them to learn the material in Chapter 2. Be sure to explain to the students how difficult it often is to understand research articles, and impress upon them the fact that the target audience for these articles typically consists of trained professionals.

MULTIMEDIA RESOURCES

Video

Against All Odds: Inside Statistics. Uses creative examples and illustrations to explain important methodological and statistical issues, such as confounds, random assignment, experimenter expectancy effects, probability, hypothesis testing, etc. This series is divided into 26 programs. (1989, 30 min. program.) Available from Annenberg/CPB Collection (800-532-7637).

Experimental Design. Distinguishes between observational studies and experiments, teaching basic principles of experimental design. This video covers issues such as sampling, replication, and the question of causation. (1989, 2 parts, 30 min. each) Available from Insight Media (800-233-9910).

Experiments in Human Behavior. Illustrates how psychological experiments are designed, using examples from classic social psychological research on important topics such as obedience to authority, prisoner/guard relationships, cult behavior, and alcohol consumption. Discusses critical methodological issues. Although the visual component of this video isn't dynamic (because of the use of still images), the examples are compelling. (1985, 35 min.) Available from Insight Media (800-233-9910).

Inferential Statistics: Hypothesis Testing: Rats, Robots, and Roller Skates. Illustrates basic principles of research with humorous sketches. Covers such topics as hypothesis testing, random assignment, control groups, and statistical inference. (1976, 28 min.) Available from John Wiley & Sons, Inc., 605 Third Ave., New York, NY 10016.

Methodology: The Psychologist and the Experiment. Explores methods and basic rules common to research by documenting Stanley Schachter's "fear and affiliation" experiments and Austin Riesen's visual motor coordination development experiments. Includes interviews with both researchers, live action sequences, and graphic animation. Riesen's research is, of course, less relevant to social psychology; thus, consider showing only the discussion of Schachter's research on the video. (1975, 31 min.) Available from the Bureau of Audio Visual Instruction, University of Wisconsin at Madison, PO Box 2093, Madison, WI 53701-2093; or from Insight Media (800-233-9910).

Observation. This video shows techniques for observing children, which can be an engaging way to get students to consider the issues of observing behavior and measuring variables that are discussed in Chapter 2. (1993, 38 min.) Available from Insight Media (800-233-9910).

The Power of the Situation. Uses some classic social psychological studies to introduce the field, including studies by Lewin, Asch, and Milgram. These studies illustrate the central concept of social psychology: Situational factors can exert powerful influence over human behavior. By focusing on specific experiments, this video can be used as a way to discuss research methods, while at the same time previewing some of the classic findings in the field. This is part of the *Discovering Psychology* series (Updated edition). (2001, 30 min.) Available from Annenberg/CPB Collection (800-532-7637).

Research Methods for the Social Sciences. Introduces research methods, explaining how to gather and interpret data. This video illustrates different types of experimental designs and discusses when each is most appropriate, and considers the use of control and experimental groups. (1995, 33 min.) Available from Insight Media (800-233-9910).

Social Psychology. Introduces the field by discussing a variety of programs of research, including research on stereotypes and prejudice, attribution theory, ingroup/outgroup differences, and the power of social roles. Zimbardo's prison study is described and analyzed; discussing Zimbardo's study in the context of Chapter 2 could be an excellent way to facilitate discussions of methodology and, in particular, ethics. (1990, 30 min.) Available from Insight Media (800-233-9910).

The Scientific Method. This video traces the evolution of the scientific method and shows the three-step process of observing, developing a hypothesis, and testing it through experimentation. (1988, 23 min.) Available from Insight Media (800-233-9910).

Statistics and Psychology. This video demonstrates the use of statistics to test the relationship between experimental data and reported historical findings. (1994, 25 min.) Available from Insight Media (800-233-9910).

Why Use Statistics? A four-part series that highlights the relevance of statistics and teaches students some basic statistical concepts and methods. The videos illustrate relevant situations across a broad range of subject areas. (20-25 min. per part) Available from Films for the Humanities and Sciences (800-257-5126).

Writing for the Social Sciences. If you are planning to have the students write research reports, you might consider this video, which uses lively examples to illustrate how to write for the social sciences. (1991, 30 min.) Available from Insight Media (800-233-9910).

Internet

Social Psychology Network. Scott Plous maintains this extremely impressive site. It is the largest social psychology database on the Internet (http://www.socialpsychology.org/). It has more than 3,500 links to psychology-related resources, including professional organizations, conferences, discussion groups, Ph.D. programs, research groups, online social psychology studies, and so on. There is also a list of the home pages and e-mail addresses of more than 400 social psychologists. This network of sites can be a great place for students to browse for research ideas and discussions of methodological and ethical issues.

CD-ROMs and Computer Programs

Electronic Companion in Statistics. Allows users to study a variety of topics in statistics, such as normal distributions, correlations, and the analysis of variance. Uses animation, colorful interactive artwork, video segments, and narration. Students can access topic reviews, quizzes, and a dictionary of terms. (1997, Mac/Windows CD-ROM) Available from Insight Media (800-233-9910).

Laboratory in Social Psychology. This computer program demonstrates classic laboratory experiments in social psychology. (DOS.) Available from the Academic Computing Center, University of Wisconsin, 1210 W. Dayton Street, Madison, WI 53706.

MacLaboratory for Psychology Research. This CD-ROM allows users to design and conduct research projects. Students can create computer-presented questionnaires, record participants' reaction time in responding to questions or stimuli, and import movie clips and simulations into an experiment. (1994, Macintosh CD-ROM). Available from Insight Media (800-233-9910).

Books

Aronson, E., Ellsworth, P. C., Carlsmith, J. M., & Gonzales, M. H. (1990). <u>Methods of Research in Social Psychology</u>. New York: McGraw-Hill. This book can be a valuable resource for providing instructors with background and ideas in preparation for covering Chapter 2 of the textbook.

Gilbert, D. T., Fiske, S. T., & Lindzey, G. (Eds.) (1998). <u>The handbook of social psychology</u> (4th ed.). New York: McGraw-Hill. As noted in Chapter 1 of this Instructor's Resource Manual, this book is a comprehensive volume of chapters written by eminent social psychologists about a wide range of topics, including the history of the field, research methods, and most of the major research areas in the field. There are four chapters relevant to research methods: Experimentation in Social Psychology (which we recommend most highly for purposes of connecting to Chapter 2 of the textbook); Survey Methods; Measurement; and Data Analysis in Social Psychology.

HANDOUT 2.L/D.1a COMMON SENSE AND THE EMPIRICAL APPROACH

Absence makes the heart grow fonder

vs.

Out of sight, out of mind

Many hands make light the work

vs.

Too many cooks spoil the broth

A bird in the hand is worth two in the bush

vs.

Patience is a virtue

He who hesitates is lost

vs.

Look before you leap

HANDOUT 2.L/D.1b COMMON SENSE AND THE EMPIRICAL APPROACH

Seeing violence on TV provides a release and thus reduces real violence

vs.

Seeing violence on TV leads to more real violence

People learn to like things for which they are rewarded

vs.

Being rewarded for something reduces intrinsic enjoyment

When trying to persuade someone to your point of view, you would be more effective to acknowledge the competing point of view

vs.

When trying to persuade someone to your point of view, you would be more effective not to acknowledge the competing point of view

It is better to go first in a debate than last

vs.

It is better to go last in a debate than first

HANDOUT 2.L/D.7 ETHICAL ISSUES

Imagine that various researchers are planning to conduct research in which they follow the procedures listed below. For each proposed procedure, indicate whether you would approve or reject the study on the basis of ethical issues. If you would approve, write "OK" in the space before the procedure; if you would disapprove, write "NO" in the space.

_____ 1. Conduct a survey that asks parents their opinion of sex education in schools.

_____ 2. Use students' test scores and grade-point averages to predict success in future scholastic endeavors.

_____ 3. Randomly assign some but not all minority students to an experimental program that is designed to help improve graduation rates.

_____ 4. Instruct participants to say insulting things to another participant as this other participant tries to complete a task.

_____ 5. Select a group of adults who answer an advertisement about an experiment concerning a weight-loss program, and randomly assign half of them to a "mental exercise" condition that the researchers predict will lead to weight loss and assign the other half to a control condition that the researchers predict will lead to no weight change.

_____ 6. Present male and female college students with pornographic materials, and measure their physiological arousal in response to these materials.

_____ 7. Conduct a survey in which college students are asked if they have ever contemplated suicide.

_____ 8. Recruit adults to participate in a two-week study of prison life, and inform them that some participants will be prisoners in a makeshift prison for two weeks in the psychology department building and that other participants will be the prison guards; then randomly assign a sample of the adults who volunteered for the study to either the "prisoner" condition or the "guard" condition, put the "prisoners" in their cells and let the "guards" begin to guard them, and record what happens.

_____ 9. With the parents' permission but without the children's awareness, videotape nursery school children playing games of "pretend."

_____ 10 Have participants hear what sounds like someone falling and yelling in pain in another room while they are filling out a questionnaire.

_____ 11 Conduct an experiment in which some participants "overhear" another participant, who is actually a confederate, say something negative about them.

_____ 12 Conduct a survey that asks about sexual fantasies and practices.

_____ 13 Ask newlywed couples to discuss how conflicts begin and get resolved in their relationship.

HANDOUT 2.1a EXPLAINING RESEARCH FINDINGS

Interpersonal Attraction

Using laboratory experiments, field studies, and correlational research, social psychologists have found that people are more attracted to others who are similar rather than dissimilar to them. The importance of similarity holds true for many different dimensions: geographic background, socioeconomic status, political orientation, a host of attitudes, and even physical attractiveness. Moreover, people's attraction to similar others is not simply an American phenomenon -- the importance of similarity to attraction has been found in a number of cross-cultural studies as well.

What social psychological reasons do you think could help explain this finding? In the space below, list the reasons you can think of.

How surprising do you personally think this finding is? (Please circle one.)

1	2	3	4	5	6	7
not at all surprising					very surprising	

HANDOUT 2.1b EXPLAINING RESEARCH FINDINGS

Interpersonal Attraction

Using laboratory experiments, field studies, and correlational research, social psychologists have found that people are more attracted to others who are different from them than to others who are similar. Indeed, people seem to be particularly attracted to others whose geographic background, socioeconomic status, political orientation, attitudes, and even physical attractiveness are rather opposite their own. People who like to be controlling, for example, are attracted to those who are submissive, and vice versa. Social psychologists call this phenomenon "complementarity" — meaning that people are attracted to others whose traits complement their own, so that together they form a well-balanced pair. Moreover, people's attraction to dissimilar others is not simply an American phenomenon — the importance of complementarity to attraction has been found in a number of cross-cultural studies as well.

What social psychological reasons do you think could help explain this finding? In the space below, list the reasons you can think of.

How surprising do you personally think this finding is? (Please circle one.)

1	2	3	4	5	6	7
not at all surprising					very surprising	

HANDOUT 2.1c EXPLAINING RESEARCH FINDINGS

Motivation

Teachers, coaches, and employers have all struggled with the challenge of keeping their students, players, and workers truly interested in their tasks. Social psychologists have examined this issue in a variety of ways over the years. Many studies have found that offers of financial or other incentives are the best way to increase interest in a task. Indeed, recent research suggests that any factors that are perceived to be very rewarding will serve as important enticements to perform the activity, thus, in turn, increasing people's enjoyment and interest in the task. Rewarding factors include not only financial incentives but other kinds of rewards, such as the promise of increased status, symbolic gestures, etc. The key to increasing people's true, internal interest in a task is to offer incentives that they feel are rewarding and worthwhile.

What <u>social psychological</u> reasons do you think could help explain this finding? In the space below, list the reasons you can think of.

How <u>surprising</u> do you personally think this finding is? (Please circle one.)

1	2	3	4	5	6	7
not at all surprising					very surprising	

HANDOUT 2.1d EXPLAINING RESEARCH FINDINGS

Motivation

Teachers, coaches, and employers have all struggled with the challenge of keeping their students, players, and workers truly interested in their tasks. Social psychologists have examined this issue in a variety of ways over the years. Many studies have found that offers of financial or other incentives make people <u>lose</u> interest in a task. That is, after getting paid to do a task that they already enjoyed, the people would want to do the task subsequently only if they were going to get paid. Otherwise, they would no longer have any interest in doing the task. Indeed, recent research suggests that financial incentives are not the only incentives that undermine internal interest in tasks. These studies have found that any factors that are perceived to be very rewarding enticements to perform the activity will be likely to undermine people's enjoyment and interest in the task. The key point is that getting people to do a task by offering incentives that they feel are rewarding and worthwhile can backfire on teachers, coaches, employers, etc., by undermining the very motivation that they wish to encourage.

What <u>social psychological</u> reasons do you think could help explain this finding? In the space below, list the reasons you can think of.

How <u>surprising</u> do you personally think this finding is? (Please circle one.)

1	2	3	4	5	6	7
not at all surprising					very surprising	

HANDOUT 2.1e EXPLAINING RESEARCH FINDINGS

Mood and Helping

If you ever find yourself suddenly needing assistance, would you be better off if someone who is in a happy, cheerful mood comes along or if someone who is in a more neutral mood comes along? Social psychological research has found that people who are in good moods are significantly more likely to help a stranger than are people in neutral moods. Researchers in some very creative studies have put people in a good mood through a variety of procedures, such as by rigging a situation in which they find money, or by supplying them with candy, and then putting them in a situation in which they encounter a stranger who needs help. Across a variety of manipulations and settings, the research reliably finds that people in a happy and cheerful mood are more likely to help the stranger than are people in a neutral mood.

What social psychological reasons do you think could help explain this finding? In the space below, list the reasons you can think of.

How surprising do you personally think this finding is? (Please circle one.)

1	2	3	4	5	6	7
not at all surprising					very surprising	

HANDOUT 2.1f EXPLAINING RESEARCH FINDINGS

Mood and Helping

If you ever find yourself suddenly needing assistance, would you be better off if someone who is in a happy, cheerful mood comes along or if someone who is in a more neutral mood comes along? Social psychological research has found that people who are in good moods are significantly less likely to help a stranger than are people in neutral moods. Researchers in some very creative studies have put people in a good mood through a variety of procedures, such as by rigging a situation in which they find money, or by supplying them with candy, and then putting them in a situation in which they encounter a stranger who needs help. Across a variety of manipulations and settings, the research reliably finds that people who are in a happy and cheerful mood are more likely to ignore the stranger and refrain from helping than are people who are in a neutral mood.

What <u>social psychological</u> reasons do you think could help explain this finding? In the space below, list the reasons you can think of.

How <u>surprising</u> do you personally think this finding is? (Please circle one.)

1   2   3   4   5   6   7

not at all surprising   very surprising

HANDOUT 2.1g EXPLAINING RESEARCH FINDINGS

"Us vs. Them"

Do people have a very strong "Us vs. Them" mentality that can be aroused at the drop of a hat? That is the question asked by a number of social psychologists in North America and Western Europe. They designed and conducted experiments in which participants were divided into two groups in any of several ways, and then gave the participants in these groups the chance to show either fairness or favoritism toward one or the other group. These studies have found that an "Us vs. Them" mentality is not so easily activated. When participants are divided into two groups by a seemingly arbitrary criterion, such as the flip of a coin, and when the two groups are not in direct competition with each other, the participants do <u>not</u> show a favoritism for their own group. These studies have found that favoritism for one's own group is likely to be found only when there is a history of conflict between the two groups, or if the two groups currently are competing for valuable resources, such as money, power, or status.

What <u>social psychological</u> reasons do you think could help explain this finding? In the space below, list the reasons you can think of.

How <u>surprising</u> do you personally think this finding is? (Please circle one.)

1	2	3	4	5	6	7
not at all surprising					very surprising	

HANDOUT 2.1h EXPLAINING RESEARCH FINDINGS

"Us vs. Them"

Do people have a very strong "Us vs. Them" mentality that can be aroused at the drop of a hat? That is the question asked by a number of social psychologists in North America and Western Europe. They designed and conducted experiments in which participants were divided into two groups in any of several ways, and then gave the participants in these groups the chance to show either fairness or favoritism toward one or the other group. These studies have found that an "Us vs. Them" mentality can be activated quite easily. When participants are divided into two groups by a seemingly arbitrary criterion, such as the flip of a coin, and when the two groups are not in direct competition with each other, the participants <u>do</u> show a favoritism for their own group. These studies have found that favoritism for one's own group is likely to be found between groups as soon as there is a division formed between one's own group and another group—even when there is no history of conflict between the two groups, nor any competition between the two groups for valuable resources, such as money, power, or status.

What <u>social psychological</u> reasons do you think could help explain this finding? In the space below, list the reasons you can think of.

How <u>surprising</u> do you personally think this finding is? (Please circle one.)

1	2	3	4	5	6	7
not at all surprising					very surprising	

HANDOUT 2.2a RIVAL HYPOTHESES

HYPOTHESIS 1: Class participation will kill you.

HYPOTHESIS 2: Class participation will **not** kill you.

HANDOUT 2.2b QUESTIONNAIRES

Pre-Treatment Questionnaire

Your name: _____

Please respond to each of the following questions by circling the appropriate answer:

To which condition were you assigned?	Control	Treatment
Are you currently alive or dead?	Alive	Dead

****

Post-Treatment Questionnaire

Your name: _____

Please respond to each of the following questions by circling the appropriate answer:

To which condition were you assigned?	Control	Treatment
Are you currently alive or dead?	Alive	Dead

HANDOUT 2.3 RANDOM ASSIGNMENT

To what team were you assigned? (Circle one.)   TEAM A   TEAM B

What sex are you? (Circle one.)   FEMALE   MALE

What is your age in years? _____ years old

What is your height in inches? _____ inches

How politically liberal or conservative are you? (Circle one.)

1	2	3	4	5	6	7	8	9
very liberal							very conservative	

How much experience do you have playing basketball? (Circle one.)

1	2	3	4	5	6	7	8	9
very little							very much	

How much experience do you have playing the piano? (Circle one.)

1	2	3	4	5	6	7	8	9
very little							very much	

How many siblings do you have? _____

If you were offered soup or salad right now, which would you choose? _____

HANDOUT 2.4 DESIGNING A QUESTIONNAIRE: SOME WORDING PROBLEMS

Below are some examples of the problems that a group of students ran into when they were trying to come up with the wording of questions for a questionnaire. The students wanted to focus on "dating on campus," and they were particularly interested in learning how prevalent dating was on campus (and in comparing the prevalence across different categories of students, such as athletes and non-athletes, first-year students and seniors, etc.), which attributes were most important in choosing whom to date, and what students did on dates.

Several students wanted to ask questions about the respondents' sexual activities on a first date. Although they all had virtually the same thing in mind, these students used a variety of different terms, including: "sexual relations," "sexual relationship," "sexual encounter," "sexually active," "sex," and "hooking up."

For example, one student asked, "On how many first dates have you had sexual relations?" Another student asked, "How important is it to have a sexual encounter on a first date?" Another student asked, "How often have you hooked up with someone after a party?" Different respondents may or may not have different things in mind when answering any one of these questions, and the same respondent may or may not have different things in mind when answering more than one of these questions.

****

Below are some specific questions in quotation marks, followed by some critiques. As you read the questions, and before you read the critiques, try to think for yourself what might be ambiguous about their wording. Also, note that these critiques are not exhaustive; you should be able to think of other critiques for several of these questions.

"On average, how many times a month do you engage in sexual relations?"

- Sexual relations can be an ambiguous term.

- Does this mean how many specific <u>experiences</u>, or with how many different <u>people</u>? That is, if a respondent has had sexual relations multiple times with the same partner, does this count as one time, or does each time count? Also, does more than one such activity on a given day count as one or more than one?

"Please rate the importance of the following characteristics in choosing a partner for a romantic relationship (1=lowest, 5=highest)."

- Importance to whom? That is, should the respondent answer this in terms of how much he or she values these characteristics, how important he or she thinks that most people find these characteristics to be, how much impact these characteristics have on choices even if people don't consciously realize it at the time, etc.?

"How important is it for you to have a mate who is athletic?"

- What exactly is meant by "mate"?

- Does this mean generally athletic, or athletic during "mating"?

"Are you in a monogamous sexual relationship?"

- Would a "no" response to this mean that the respondent is not in a sexual relationship, or that he or she is in a sexual relationship that is not monogamous?

"How many relationships have you had in the last year?"

- What is meant by "relationships"?

"How many dates have you had in the last year?"

- Does date refer to the person or the activity?

"Do you use alcohol to justify your actions on a date?"

- The socially desirable way to answer this question seems obvious.

- What is meant by "justify"?

- Justify to whom?

- If the respondent had done this once, should he or she say "yes," or does this question ask (particularly because it is written in the present tense) whether the respondent does this consistently, or currently?

"How important is each of the following to you in choosing a partner to date?" [Following this question is a list of specific features, such as "eyes," "hair," "legs," etc.]

- Although most respondents would know what is meant by this question, one could interpret it to mean something like, "How important is it that a partner has eyes, or hair, or legs, etc.?" as opposed to, "How important is the perceived attractiveness of these features in choosing a partner?"

HANDOUT 2.5S CELL PHONE USAGE SURVEY

Please answer the following survey questions regarding your cell phone usage by circling the appropriate response choice. Please do not write your name on this sheet. Thank you for your participation.

Your age _____   Your sex _____

1. When you receive a telephone call while driving, do you

    a. Always pull over and stop before taking the call

    b. Sometimes take the call while driving and at other times pull over and stop

    c. Always take the call while continuing to drive

2. How often do you find yourself initiating a cell-phone call while driving?

    a. Rarely

    b. Occasionally

    c. Very often

3. How often do you receive text messages while driving?

    a. Rarely

    b. Occasionally

    c. Very often

4. How often do you send text messages while driving?

    a. Rarely

    b. Occasionally

    c. Very often

5. Do you think there should be tougher cell-phone laws or tougher enforcement of existing cell-phone laws?

    a. Definitely yes

    b. Not sure

    c. Definitely not

HANDOUT 2.5E CELL PHONE USAGE SURVEY

There are now over 224 million cell-phone users in the US, and recently cell phones were singled out as the most common cause of car crashes. Psychologists have been working in conjunction with the government and insurance companies to record the demographics of drivers who use cell phones and to investigate the degree of hazard that such devices present on the roads. You can contribute to this effort by answering the following survey questions regarding your own cell-phone usage as honestly and accurately as possible. Please do not write your name on this sheet, as we are not interested in individual responses, only in the behavior of people in general. Thank you for your participation.

Your age ____   Your sex ____

1.   When you receive a telephone call while driving, do you

   a.   Always take the call while continuing to drive

   b.   Sometimes take the call while driving and at other times pull over and stop

   c.   Always pull over and stop before taking the call

2.   How often do you find yourself initiating a cell-phone call while driving?

   a.   Rarely

   b.   Occasionally

   c.   Very often

3.   How often do you receive text messages while driving?

   a.   Rarely

   b.   Occasionally

   c.   Very often

4.   How often do you send text messages while driving?

   a.   Rarely

   b.   Occasionally

   c.   Very often

5.   Do you think there should be tougher cell-phone laws or tougher enforcement of existing cell-phone laws?

   a.   Definitely yes

   b.   Not sure

   c.   Definitely not

HANDOUT 2.6 OPERATIONALIZING VARIABLES

Research Idea #1: A social psychologist was interested in whether people are more likely to exhibit conformity when they are in situations that make them feel nervous and unsure of themselves.

Research Idea #2: People who are involved in an intimate relationship may experience distinct, although related, feelings of liking for each other and love for each other. It is possible to like someone and not love them, of course, but it is also possible to love someone but not like them all that much (think of a couple that fights a great deal but can't think of life without the other person, or siblings who don't get along but feel a sense of familial love). A group of researchers wanted to examine the degree to which one's liking for his or her partner was correlated with his or her love for that partner, and whether this correlation would be higher or lower for women's feelings about their partner than for men's.

Research Idea #3: Are people more or less creative in their work if they are pressured to be creative?

Research Idea #4: A researcher speculated that people may be more prejudiced in their judgments of individuals of a different race if they (that is, the people making the judgments) are in a bad mood than if they are in a good mood.

Research Idea #5: A social psychologist hypothesized that exposing children to violent television shows would make them behave more aggressively.

HANDOUT 2.7 DESIGNING AN EXPERIMENT

On a separate piece of paper, complete the following assignment.

1. How many independent variables are there in your study?

2. For each independent variable, do each of the following: (a) describe it, including how many different levels of the variable there will be (e.g., you may have an independent variable concerning exposure to different television programs, and you may have three different versions of this variable: dramas with violence, dramas without violence, and comedies; this would count as <u>one</u> independent variable, with <u>three</u> levels), (b) describe how you intend to manipulate the variable and (c) explain why this independent variable is included in the design, and why each level of this variable is included.

3. Describe your dependent variable(s), including how each will be measured.

4. How many different conditions will there be in this experiment?

5. How will you assign participants to the different conditions?

6. What hypothesis or hypotheses will you be testing with this experiment? Describe the kinds of results that would support the hypothesis (or that would support one but not the other hypothesis).

7. What alternative explanations might there be for the results you described in the previous question? How can these be tested in subsequent experiments?

8. Evaluate the internal validity and external validity of the experiment and the construct validity of the variables.

9. Evaluate the experimental realism and mundane realism of the experiment.

10. Evaluate the ethics of conducting this experiment. Are there any reasons to be concerned about the welfare of the participants?

HANDOUT 2.12a EVALUATING RESEARCH

For each of the studies described below, what conclusions can be reached? Are the researchers' conclusions valid? Why or why not? What alternative explanations, if any, can there be for the research findings? Is the study high or low in internal validity? If you think there are problems with the study or the conclusions reached, how can the study be improved so that there are no flaws or so that alternative explanations can be ruled out? (Note: Some of these studies may not have any serious methodological flaws or alternative explanations.)

In addition to addressing these issues, evaluate each study in terms of its experimental realism, mundane realism, and ethics.

Taste Test

The owners of a soft-drink company believed that its product, Diet Duff's, was better than its more popular competitor, Diet Smash. They decided to run a "blind taste test" in which individuals would taste some of each product without knowing which cup contained which drink. Two hundred randomly selected men and women from three different communities participated in the test. Each participant was seated at a table. A cup on the person's left was labeled "Q" and contained six ounces of Diet Smash. A cup on the person's right was labeled "M" and contained six ounces of Diet Duff's. The participants, of course, were not told which drink was in which cup. Half of the time the participants were told to try the cup on the left first, and half of the time they were told to try the cup on the right first. The drinks in both cups were equally fresh and cold.

The results supported Diet Duff's hopes: Diet Duff's was preferred by 105 people, Diet Smash was preferred by 84 people, and 11 people could not indicate a preference between the two drinks. Diet Duff's began an advertisement campaign stating that in a blind taste test, more people preferred Diet Duff's than Diet Smash.

HANDOUT 2.12b EVALUATING RESEARCH

For each of the studies described below, what conclusions can be reached? Are the researchers' conclusions valid? Why or why not? What alternative explanations, if any, can there be for the research findings? Is the study high or low in internal validity? If you think there are problems with the study or the conclusions reached, how can the study be improved so that there are no flaws or so that alternative explanations can be ruled out? (Note: Some of these studies may not have any serious methodological flaws or alternative explanations.)

In addition to addressing these issues, evaluate each study in terms of its experimental realism, mundane realism, and ethics.

Political Attitudes

Some researchers were concerned with what they believed to be an increasing polarization in the political attitudes of Americans. They wondered if people who are extreme conservatives and people who are extreme liberals might become less extreme if they could spend some time imagining themselves taking the opposite position. They speculated that such role playing might enable people to understand arguments they had previously refused to consider and to empathize with the fears and hopes of people they had previously rejected as ignorant or selfish.

To test this idea the researchers asked 500 adults to complete a questionnaire that measured their political attitudes. From this group, they then selected 60 people who scored very high on conservatism and 60 people who scored very high on liberalism to participate in the role-playing tasks. One of these tasks consisted of asking the conservatives to write a good, logical, and impassioned essay arguing in favor of some liberal policies, and asking the liberals to do the same for some conservative policies. Four weeks later, these 120 participants were given the same questionnaire that they had been given initially. The researchers found that, on average, the conservatives had become more liberal and the liberals had become more conservative. The researchers concluded that role playing causes extreme conservatives and liberals to become more moderate in their positions and more understanding of the other side.

HANDOUT 2.12c EVALUATING RESEARCH

For each of the studies described below, what conclusions can be reached? Are the researchers' conclusions valid? Why or why not? What alternative explanations, if any, can there be for the research findings? Is the study high or low in internal validity? If you think there are problems with the study or the conclusions reached, how can the study be improved so that there are no flaws or so that alternative explanations can be ruled out? (Note: Some of these studies may not have any serious methodological flaws or alternative explanations.)

In addition to addressing these issues, evaluate each study in terms of its experimental realism, mundane realism, and ethics.

Cheating and Mirrors

Some researchers interested in studying the effects of self-awareness on guilt and optimism were aware of previous studies that had found that placing participants in front of a mirror made the participants more self-focused -- that is, more likely to think about, or be affected by, their own personal attitudes, norms, and standards. Thus, they decided to examine the effects of placing a mirror in front of participants who have just done or not done something that was morally wrong. Specifically, they wanted to see whether the presence of the mirror would make participants who have just done something wrong feel more guilty about what they have done, and whether this guilt would affect their thoughts about their future.

To investigate this notion, the researchers took a random sample of children from a junior high school and placed each alone in a room with no mirror. The child was given a game to play in the room. All children were told that if they won the game, they would receive some money. The researchers rigged this game so that the children had an easy opportunity to cheat. Using hidden cameras, they were able to record which children cheated. In this study, about 50% of the children cheated. After the game was over, the researchers put the children into another room. For half of the children, a large mirror was in the room with them; for the other half, no such mirror was present. The researchers asked the children to write an essay about their futures. The dependent variable was how optimistic their essays were.

The researchers found that the children who had cheated wrote essays that were less optimistic about their future than were the essays written by the other children. They also found, however, that the presence or absence of a mirror had no effect on these essays. The researchers concluded that cheating does make children feel more guilty, and therefore less optimistic about their future, but that self-awareness does not make this effect any stronger.

HANDOUT 2.12d EVALUATING RESEARCH

For each of the studies described below, what conclusions can be reached? Are the researchers' conclusions valid? Why or why not? What alternative explanations, if any, can there be for the research findings? Is the study high or low in internal validity? If you think there are problems with the study or the conclusions reached, how can the study be improved so that there are no flaws or so that alternative explanations can be ruled out? (Note: Some of these studies may not have any serious methodological flaws or alternative explanations.)

In addition to addressing these issues, evaluate each study in terms of its experimental realism, mundane realism, and ethics.

Fear and Affiliation

A researcher conducted a study designed to investigate whether people who are experiencing fear prefer to be alone or with other people. The participants (who were all women) were randomly assigned to one of two conditions. In the "Fear" condition, the participants arrived at a lab and were greeted by a serious-looking experimenter who was dressed in a white lab coat, had a stethoscope visible in his pocket, and was standing in front of an array of elaborate-looking electrical equipment. He introduced himself as Dr. Gregor Zilstein. He said slowly:

What we will ask each of you to do is very simple. We would like to give each of you a series of electrical shocks. Now, I feel I must be completely honest with you and tell you exactly what you are in for. These shocks will hurt, they will be painful. As you can guess, it is necessary that our shocks be intense. What we will do is put an electrode on your hand, hook you into an apparatus such as this, give you a series of shocks, and take various measures.... Again, I do want to be honest with you and tell you that these shocks will be quite painful but, of course, they will do no permanent damage.

In the "No Fear" condition, the participants arrived at the lab and were greeted by Dr. Zilstein, but the electrical equipment was not displayed and Dr. Zilstein exhibited a much more pleasant, comforting demeanor. He said:

What we will ask each of you to do is very simple. We would like to give each of you a series of very mild electrical shocks. I assure you that what you will feel will not in any way be painful. It will resemble more a tickle than anything unpleasant. We will put an electrode on your hand, give you a series of very mild shocks and measure such things as your pulse rate -- which I am sure you are all familiar with from visits to your family doctor.

In both conditions Dr. Zilstein added:

Before we begin with the shocking proper there will be about a 10-minute delay while we get this room in order. We have several pieces of equipment to bring in and get set up.... Here is what we will ask you to do for this 10-minute period of waiting. We have on this floor a number of additional rooms so that each of you, if you would like, can wait alone in your own room. These rooms are comfortable and spacious; they all have armchairs and there are books and magazines in each room. It did occur to us, however, that some of you might want to wait for these 10 minutes together with some of the other girls here. If you would prefer this, of course, just let us know. We'll take one of the empty classrooms on the floor and you can wait together with some of the other girls there.

The participants then stated whether they preferred waiting alone or waiting with others or had no preference. The researcher found that participants who were in the "Fear" condition were much more likely to prefer to wait with other people than to wait alone, whereas the participants in the "No Fear" condition showed no clear preference. The researcher concluded that fear led to the desire to affiliate.

HANDOUT 2.12e EVALUATING RESEARCH

For each of the studies described below, what conclusions can be reached? Are the researchers' conclusions valid? Why or why not? What alternative explanations, if any, can there be for the research findings? Is the study high or low in internal validity? If you think there are problems with the study or the conclusions reached, how can the study be improved so that there are no flaws or so that alternative explanations can be ruled out? (Note: Some of these studies may not have any serious methodological flaws or alternative explanations.)

In addition to addressing these issues, evaluate each study in terms of its experimental realism, mundane realism, and ethics.

Staring

A researcher was interested in the effects of staring. She hypothesized that people become uncomfortable when someone stares at them, and that they will try to escape the situation as quickly as possible. To test this idea she bought a stopwatch and stood at a randomly selected street corner in Santa Barbara, California. She wanted to see if cars that are stopped at a red light would speed away faster when the light turned green if the driver had been stared at while waiting for the light than if he or she had not been stared at. To get a reliable baseline for average speed of crossing an intersection, she recorded the average number of seconds it took 250 cars (each of which was the first car at the red light) to cross the intersection after the light turned green. For the next 250 cars (again, each of which was first at the light), she stared directly at the driver, without wavering. She discovered that drivers who had been stared at crossed the intersection significantly faster than did drivers who had not been stared at. She concluded that staring causes people to drive away faster than they would normally.

HANDOUT 2.13 EVALUATING A RESEARCH ARTICLE

On a separate piece of paper, complete the following assignment.

1. Look toward the back of the article and see the References section. See how other journal articles are cited. Using the same format, write down the citation for the article you read, indicating the author(s), year of publication, title of the article, name of journal, volume number of journal, and page numbers of the article.

2. For each independent variable, do each of the following: (a) describe it, including how many different levels of the variable there were (e.g., there may be an independent variable concerning exposure to different television programs, and there may be three different versions of this variable: dramas with violence, dramas without violence, and comedies; this would count as <u>one</u> independent variable, with <u>three</u> levels), (b) describe how the variable was manipulated—that is, what was the operational definition of the variable, and (c) discuss what you think of its construct validity.

3. Describe the dependent variable(s), including how each was measured and what you think of its construct validity.

4. How did the authors get participants for this study? Was there random sampling in this study? Was there random assignment in this study?

5. What hypothesis or hypotheses were the authors testing with this experiment? Describe the results of the experiment (in your own words, not the jargon used in the article) and whether or not they supported the hypotheses.

6. What alternative explanations might there be for the results you described in the previous question? How can these be tested in subsequent experiments?

7. Evaluate the internal validity and external validity of the experiment.

8. Evaluate the experimental realism and mundane realism of the experiment.

9. Evaluate the ethics of conducting this experiment. Should there have been any reasons to be concerned about the welfare of the participants?

10. Did you find this article to be interesting? What did *you* learn from it?

CHAPTER 3

The Social Self

LEARNING OBJECTIVES: GUIDELINES FOR STUDY

You should be able to do each of the following by the conclusion of Chapter 3.

1. Explain the idea of the self-concept and how it relates to the ways in which we attend to, interpret, and remember the world around us. Understand the ways in which studying the brain can shed light on the nature of the self-concept. (*pp. 56-57*)

2. Explain what is meant by describing the self as "relational." Discuss the social factors that contribute to the self-concept. (*pp. 60-64*)

3. Discuss the limitations of introspection when it comes to achieving self-insight. Explain the relevance of affective forecasting to this issue. (*pp. 58-60*)

4. Describe self-perception theory, and explain how it can be applied to human emotion, behavior, and motivation. Define the overjustification effect and discuss the relationship between intrinsic and extrinsic motivation. (*pp. 60-64*)

5. Explain social comparison theory, identifying when people tend to engage in social comparison and with whom they tend to compare themselves. Explain the two-factor theory of emotion and its relevance to social comparison theory. (*pp. 64-67*)

6. Discuss autobiographical memories and explain how they are influenced by our self-concept. (*pp. 67-69*)

7. Describe the influences of gender, race, and culture on our understanding of self. (*pp. 69-72*)

8. Define self-esteem. Explain the basis for the claim that people have a "need for self-esteem." Discuss the potential costs associated with the pursuit of self-esteem. (*pp. 72-74*)

9. Explain how self-discrepancy theory accounts for the general level of and changes in people's self-esteem, and impacts emotional states such as shame, guilt, and anxiety. (*pp. 75-76*)

10. Identify different types of self-focusing situations and personality types. Explain the self-awareness "trap."(*pp. 76-79*)

11. Explain the limitations of self-regulation. Explain what is meant by "ironic processes of self-control" and how this concept relates to self-regulation. (*pp. 79-82*)

12. Identify four ways that people strive for self-enhancement (i.e., positive illusions) and discuss the implications of self-enhancement for mental health and the perception of reality. Discuss the debate regarding whether or not such self-enhancement is adaptive. (*pp. 82-89*)

13. Compare and contrast strategic self-presentation and self-verification. (*pp. 90-93*)

14. Describe the differences between people who are high and low in self-monitoring. Explain how both of these strategies can be useful. (*pp. 93-95*)

DETAILED CHAPTER OUTLINE

I.   The Self-Concept
   A.   Rudiments of the Self-Concept
      1.   Is the self specially represented in the brain?
      2.   Do nonhuman animals show self-recognition?
      3.   What makes the self a social concept?
   B.   Introspection
      1.   Introspection and accuracy of self-knowledge
      2.   The durability bias in affective forecasting
      3.   Introspection and cognitive resources
   C.   Perceptions of Our Own Behavior
      1.   Self-perceptions of emotion
         a)   facial feedback hypothesis
         b)   body posture and emotion
      2.   Self-perceptions of motivation
         a)   the overjustification effect
         b)   motivational orientation
   D.   Influences of Other People
      1.   Social comparison theory
      2.   Two-factor theory of emotion
   E.   Autobiographical Memories
      1.   Flashbulb memories
      2.   Egocentric bias
   F.   Culture and the Self Concept
      1.   Individualism and collectivism (as well as dialecticism)
      2.   Conceptions of self
II. Self-Esteem
   A.   The Need for Self-Esteem
      1.   Social basis of the need for self-esteem
      2.   Terror management theory of self-esteem
      3.   Self-esteem and its life consequences
      4.   Self-esteem and ethnicity
   B.   Self-Discrepancy Theory
   C.   The Self-Awareness Trap
      1.   Self-awareness theory
      2.   Self-awareness and alcohol consumption
      3.   Private self-consciousness
      4.   Public self-consciousness
   D.   Self-Regulation and Its Limits
      1.   Self-regulation fatigue
      2.   The paradoxical, or ironic, effects of self-control
   E.   Ironic Mental Processes
   F.   Mechanisms of Self-Enhancement
      1.   Implicit egotism
      2.   Self-serving cognitions
      3.   Self-handicapping
      4.   Basking in the glory of others
      5.   Downward social comparisons
   G.   Are Positive Illusions Adaptive?
   H.   Cultural Influences on Self-Esteem

III. Self-Presentation
    A.   Strategic Self-Presentation
    B.   Self-Verification
    C.   Individual Differences in Self-Monitoring
IV. Epilogue: The Multi-faceted Self

LECTURE AND DISCUSSION IDEAS

Idea 1.   Flashbulb Memories

Most of your students are likely to have vivid memories of certain shocking events that have happened in recent history. You might ask them if they can remember and recount the details of Lady Diana's fatal car crash (1997), the September 11 attacks on the World Trade Center and the Pentagon (2001), the space shuttle Columbia tragedy (2003), or the death of a celebrity they cared about (perhaps Michael Jackson; 2009). Many students will have vivid detailed recollections of these events, particularly if they told others about these events. Discussion of these phenomena can address the question of why these memories are so potent and vivid. One account suggests that it is the emotional significance of the event (Bohannon, 1988). A different account suggests that it is confidence in the memory that increases with this type of event (Weaver, 1993). Students should have fairly consistent, detailed, and confident accounts of these events. You might compare these accounts with student accounts of something that happened earlier in the class. Typically, you should see more detailed and more confident accounts for the flashbulb memories than for the recent but more mundane memories. This naturally poses the question, why are our memories and introspections better for some events than for others? This topic can be used as a springboard into issues such as introspection, self-knowledge, and self-perception.

Bohannon, J. N. (1988). Flashbulb memories for the space shuttle disaster: A tale of two theories. Cognition, 29, 179-196.

Weaver, C. A. (1993). Do you need a "flash" to form a flashbulb memory? Journal of Experimental Psychology General, 122, 39-46.

Idea 2.   Rewards and the Overjustification Effect

Two meta-analytic literature reviews (Cameron & Pierce, 1994 and Eisenberger & Cameron, 1996) have argued that rewards rarely undermine intrinsic motivation as is suggested by the overjustification effect. These reviews argue that rewards only lead to an overjustification effect in very specific circumstances that can be easily avoided. This has sparked a heated debate in the field. Others (Lepper, 1998; Sansone & Harackiewicz, 1998) have provided sharp criticism of these literature reviews. They argue that the reviews were done poorly and did not take into consideration important theoretical variables that have been identified by previous research. In addition to addressing a fundamental issue in human motivation, discussing these issues would provide an example of how science is always in the process of developing and testing ideas. There is not simply a set of facts that must be learned, rather our understanding of psychology is a dynamic process of testing ideas.

Cameron, J., & Pierce, W. D. (1994). Reinforcement, reward, and intrinsic motivation: A meta-analysis. Review of Educational Research, 64, 363-423.

Eisenberger, R., & Cameron, J. (1996). Detrimental effects of reward: Reality or myth? American Psychologist, 74, 704-714.

Lepper, M. R. (1998). A whole much less than the sum of its parts. <u>American Psychologist, 53</u>, 675-676.

Sansone, C., & Harackiewicz, J. M. (1998). "Reality" is complicated. <u>American Psychologist, 53</u>, 673-674.

Idea 3.   Culture and the Self-Concept

The research on culture and the self-concept is a quickly growing aspect of the field, but one that your students are unlikely to have considered. Ask your students to generate how they think their culture has affected their self-concept. Most students (in Western cultures) will probably have a hard time recognizing how their culture has shaped their self-concept. Note to students that this is exactly what would be expected in an independent, individualistic culture. In this sort of culture, people believe that they shape their own destiny. You might also have students reflect on variations within their own culture. Are some people more individualistic than others? Are people more collectivistic in some situations than in others?

Idea 4.   Trendy Names and Self-Perception

The *Psychology Today* (2004) article, "Hello My Name is Unique," discusses the relationship between self-perception and first names.

These days, more parents are giving their children unusual names in the belief that the perfect name can affect a child's destiny. Kent Evans, a psychology professor at Bellevue University in Nebraska, credits the trend to our strip-mall culture, claiming that it fosters the desire to distinguish one's child from the crowd. Evans says that unusual names reflect parents' high hopes and signal to the world that their child is special. He adds that this belief is not corroborated by research, which has found no correlation between a given name and academic or social achievement.

Moreover, an unusual name has the disadvantage of either making a child stand out too much, or of not allowing him or her to fit in. In fact, some early archival studies have even shown a correlation between having unique or peculiar first names and higher rates of emotional disturbance (Ellis & Beechley, 1954 and Hartman, Nicolay, & Hurley, 1968).

In today's culture, however, where unusual names have become commonplace, the negative impact of having a unique name is lessened. Accordingly, a recent study (Christopher, 1998), has found that uncommon names are judged even more favorably than familiar names, at least in the context of personal ads.

There is also the matter of matching a name to a child's personality. A child will be unhappy and feel alienated if his or her given name does not echo his or her self-perception. In fact, the child's attitude toward the name is in itself a gauge of self-esteem.

The *Psychology Today* article presents the views of several individuals who discuss how their self-perception interacts with their name. Ask your students to add their own thoughts on the subject.

Another interesting trend mentioned in the same article that students might want to discuss is that parents have been increasingly naming their babies after possessions, such as cars, perfumes, electronic devices, and designers. What effect might being named after a material object have on a child's self-perception?

Christopher, A.N. (1998). The Psychology of Names: An Empirical reexamination. <u>Journal of Applied Social Psychology, 28</u>, 13, 1173-1195.

Ellis, A. & Beechley, R.M. (1954). Emotional disturbance in children with peculiar given names. <u>Journal of Genetic Psychology, 85</u>, 337-339.

Flora, C. (Mar./Apr., 2004). Hello my name is Unique. <u>Psychology Today</u>, Vol. <u>37</u>, p. 44.

Hartman, A.A., Nicolay, R.C., & Hurley, J. (1968). Unique personal name as a social adjustment factor. <u>Journal of Social Psychology, 75</u>, 107-110.

Idea 5.   The Terror Management Theory of Self-Esteem and its Implications

According to terror management theory, the knowledge that we are fated to die encourages us to search for meaning in our lives by endorsing a worldview (religious, cultural, or ethnic) and thus to bolster our self-esteem. Although the theory was first proposed in 1986, it has become particularly relevant in the wake of the terrorist attacks of 9/11/01, which have made people more aware of their mortality. Many studies have since been carried out to test the theory and its implications.

You might wish to elaborate on the text discussion of terror management theory by acquainting students with some of the research methods used by proponents of the theory and their subsequent findings.

Usually, these studies involve a manipulation intended to produce mortality salience, or an awareness of death. Some studies accomplish that by interviewing participants in the vicinity of a funeral parlor. Others do so by asking participants to complete word stems that are related to death (e.g., cof___, gr___, or cor___— coffin, grave, and corpse) or simply by having participants answer questions about the process of dying.

In various studies, after being reminded of death, participants were found to express a desire to distance themselves from animals (Goldenberg, et. al., 2005), to seek close, committed relationships (Florian, Mikulincer, & Hirschberger, 2002), and to have offspring (Wisman & Goldenberg, 2005). Others (Landau, et. al., 2006) reacted negatively to modern art after such manipulation.

Ask your students to discuss how terror management theory might account for all those reactions. Additionally, how would the theory explain the prosocial behaviors (donations, empathy, and help for victims' families) and anti-Muslim feelings that predominated after 9/11. What are some other implications of the theory? How might intimations of mortality affect feelings of prejudice, sexual behavior, aggressive tendencies, and the type of leaders one is likely to endorse?

Florian, V., Mikulincer, M. & Hirschberger, G. (2002). The anxiety-buffering function of close relationships: Evidence that relationship commitment acts as a terror management mechanism. Journal of Personality and Social Psychology, 82, 4, 527-542.

Goldenberg, J., Pyszczynski, Greenberg, J., Solomon, S., Kluck, B., & Cornwell, R. (2001). I am not an animal: Mortality salience, disgust, and the denial of human creatureliness. Journal of Experimental Psychology: General, 130, 3, 427-435.

Landau, M.J., Greenberg, J., Solomon, S., Pyszczynski, T. & Martens, A. (2006). Windows into nothingness: Terror management, meaninglessness, and negative reactions to modern art. Journal of Personality and Social Psychology, 90, 6, 879-892.

Wisman, A., & Goldenberg, J. (2005). From the grave to the cradle: Evidence that mortality salience engenders a desire for offspring. Journal of Personality and Social Psychology, 89, 1, 46-61.

Idea 6.   Shyness, the Hyperculture, and Coping Strategies

Surveys show that over the last decade and a half, the incidence of shyness in this country has risen from 40% to 48%. You might wish to discuss the connection between the rise in shyness and the current culture.

Writing in *Psychology Today* (2000), Philip Carducci states that one reason for the exacerbation of shyness in our society is the phenomenon termed hyperculture—the speeding up of everyday life by technological innovations such as the Internet, cell phones, e-mail and beepers.

According to Carducci, one critical feature of shyness is slowness to warm up. Shy people need more time to warm up to people, to face new situations, and to make progress toward intimate relationships.

Shy people are therefore understandably having a more difficult time in this speeded-up culture. Moreover, to get noticed in the hyperculture, it is necessary to raise the volume, to stand out from the crowd, to be an intense personality. This also puts shy people at a disadvantage. Then, too, there's the fact that the hyperculture has caused people to become more distant, rude, and exclusive. People today are less likely to practice civility in face-to-face interactions, as good manners are deemed irrelevant or incidental in voicemail, e-mail, and text messaging. With rudeness, there is more aggression being released, and those who are least assertive or shy are most likely to be on the receiving end of mistreatment and to further withdraw from social interactions.

The article discusses strategies that shy people use to cope in this hyperculture. Some are dysfunctional. For example, some shy people become "liquid" extraverts, turning to drugs or alcohol to remove their inhibitions. Others retreat to cyberspace, where they either misrepresent themselves in order to attract others or they become more alienated by reading endless information and avoiding people altogether.

Then there are those who Carducci calls the successfully shy. These are the people who acknowledge that they have a problem in social situations and take steps to try to overcome it. Instead of being self-conscious, they attempt to focus on other people. They force themselves to become better listeners. They plan ahead for what they can contribute to a conversation. They arrive early at social gatherings to allow themselves time to warm up to the situation. In general, instead of remaining in their own shells, they get involved in the lives of others.

An accompanying piece at the end of the article details the eight habits of highly popular people that anyone can master to become more socially successful.

Carducci, B. (Jan./Feb., 2000) Shyness: The new solution. Psychology Today, 33, 1, 38-46.

Idea 7.   Self-Enhancement and Mental Health

Taylor & Brown (1988) have argued that self-enhancing cognitions lead to mental health. In the strong form of this argument they suggest that even if self-enhancing cognitions are illusions and irrational they can foster mental health. This analysis suggests one intriguing function of self-enhancing biases. Yet this position is in conflict with many basic psychological theories that suggest that rationality and veridical perception of oneself and others is a crowning feature of mental health. This basic controversy can lead to some interesting questions. Is it good to have a positive yet erroneous view of oneself? Will this have costs in the future? Can you have a view of the self that is too positive? How about too accurate?

Taylor, S. E., & Brown, J. D. (1988). Illusion and well-being: A social psychological perspective on mental health. Psychological Bulletin, 103, 193-210.

Idea 8.   Self-Presentation Online

Self-presentation has to do with the way we package ourselves for others to see. This topic is especially relevant now with the popularity of personal web pages, social networking sites, and web logs.

One study (Marcus, Machilek, & Schütz, 2006) investigating personal web sites found that visiting a well-designed personal web page for just 5 minutes allowed for meaningful inferences about the owner's personality, at least as they corresponded to self-reported traits. So, such sites allow individuals to project an image of their selves that is "read" by others.

Self-presentation looms even larger in social networking sites. These are online communities where individuals manipulate their self image as they communicate and share information with others, such as MySpace, Facebook, and Twitter.

According to the text, there are two types of self-presentation: strategic and verification. In strategic self-presentation, an individual contrives to shape an identity in such a way as to gain an advantage with others for purposes of being liked or to be seen as competent. In verification self-presentation, the goal is to be viewed by others in accordance with how the individual sees him or her self.

Ask students to discuss the form of self-presentation that is predominant in personal web pages, social networking sites, and blogs. Also, which type of self-presentation do they think is most evident in the home videos posted on YouTube?

Discuss some of the positive and negative aspects associated with such sites. For example, on the plus side, when social networking sites require students to create profiles that highlight their talents and interests, they are helping them to forge their self-identity. Moreover, such sites help students to find others who share sometimes quirky interests and these niche relationships can lead to feelings of acceptance and a sense of belonging. Do your students see any other advantages to being connected to others in this fashion? In the future, might this type of social networking become a springboard to professional networking?

To explore possible problems with this form of social networking, ask students how they infer whether or not online portraits are accurate. Do these sites encourage the posting of information that is dishonest or inappropriate in a quest for popularity? Is there a tendency to disclose more information online than one would in real-life interactions? What are some clues that they use in real life to judge the genuineness of self-presentations that are lacking online?

Andrews, M. (2006). Decoding MySpace. U.S. News and World Reports, 141, 10, 46-60.

Bugeja, M. (2006). Facing the Facebook. The Chronicle of Higher Education, 52, 21, C1-C4.

Marcus, B., Machilek, F., & Schutz, A. (2006). Personality in cyberspace: Personal web sites as media for personality expressions and impressions. Journal of Personality and Social Psychology, 90, 6, 1014-1031.

Idea 9.   Apes and Self-Concept Formation and Apes and Sign Language

Gallup's (1977) research on self-image recognition in some primates poses some interesting questions about the ways that apes and humans do or do not differ. Many students will assume that animals are "just different from people." This research and research on language acquisition among apes (see Gibson, 1994; and Sevcik & Savage-Rumbaugh, 1994 for recent summaries of this research) challenge some of these basic assumptions. If apes can form a self-concept and use language, what makes them different from humans?

Gallup, G. G., Jr. (1977). Self-recognition in primates: A comparative approach to the bidirectional properties of consciousness. American Psychologist, 32, 329-337.

Gibson, K. R. (1994). Continuity theories of human language origins versus the Lieberman model. Language and Communication, 14, 97-114.

Sevcik, R. A., & Savage-Rumbaugh, E. S. (1994). Language comprehension and use by great apes. Language and Communication, 14, 37-58.

CLASSROOM ACTIVITIES

Activity 1. The Name Letter Effect and the Birth Date Effect

The name letter effect (NLE) is the tendency for people to prefer the letters in their own name. The effect was first demonstrated by Nuttin (1985), who attributed the phenomenon to "mere belongingness of self," a positive, unconscious bias that people exhibit in favor of stimuli that are associated with their self. This bias is so strong that people have been found to prefer brand name products that begin with the same letter as their first or last name, and to disproportionately choose an occupation that matches one of their initials and even to marry someone who shares their first or last initial (Flora, 2006).

But it's not only the letters in one's name that are so favored. A similar effect, dubbed the "mere ownership effect," and described as an example of implicit egotism, was found for the date of one's birth, as well (Kitayama & Karasawa, 1997).

Handout 3.1 will allow your students to simultaneously test themselves for the name letter effect and the birth date effect. Plan on doing this activity before students have read about the name letter effect in the text. The handout presents a random listing of letters and numbers and asks students to evaluate them on a scale of 1 to 5, with 1 being "not at all beautiful" and 5 being "extremely beautiful." Following the Nuttin (1985) paradigm, the task is described as an aesthetic exercise and students are encouraged to use their intuitive feelings, as opposed to rational thought.

Distribute the handouts face-down. Explain that they will have only three minutes to quickly evaluate letters and numbers on their aesthetic value. Encourage them to use only their intuitive feelings, as opposed to thinking about what it is that makes the stimuli more or less attractive.

After three minutes, ask them to put down their pens and briefly discuss how people display a positive bias for self-associated stimuli, such as the letters in their names and the date of their birth. Have them examine the lists and circle the letters in their first name and last names. They should then compare the scores for those letters with the scores received by other letters (not numbers). If the name letter effect is demonstrated, the letters in their names will have been scored higher. The effect should especially hold for the first letter in their first name.

Next, have them circle their birth date number. That score should be higher than that of other numbers. If it is, then they will have demonstrated the birth date effect.

For a more precise measure, students can figure out the average score per letter for letters not in their name (first or last) and compare that to the average score per letter in their name (first and last). The same procedure can be done for the birth dates.

●*What if this bombs?* If the effect is not demonstrated for most students, discuss how thinking about a process that is usually unconscious and spontaneous can interfere with the process. Introduce the distinction between implicit self-esteem (under which such effects are activated) and explicit self-esteem, which involves conscious self-evaluation and is not required for these effects.

Flora, C. (2006). My dear namesake. Psychology Today, 39, 4, 26.

Kitayama, S., & Karasawa, M. (1997). Implicit self-esteem in Japan: Name letters and birthday numbers. Personality and Social Psychology Bulletin, 23, 736-742.

Nuttin, J. (1985). Narcissism beyond Gestalt and awareness: The name letter effect. European Journal of Social Psychology, 15, 353-361.

Activity 2. Self-Reference Effect

The self-reference effect (SRE) is the facilitation of memory that occurs when people relate information to their self-concept when processing information. This activity should provide a demonstration of the SRE. Randomly give students either **Handout 3.2a** or **Handout 3.2b**. Ask students to read through the list of activities following the directions for the task. After doing something else for about twenty minutes, ask the students to take out a blank piece of paper and write down as many of the activities as they can remember. Students who had Handout 3.2a -- who processed the information in a self-relevant fashion -- should remember more of the activities. This demonstration shows the power of the self-concept in organizing our memories.

> 💣*What if this bombs?* The self-relevant processing should increase the details of the memories as well. Students given Handout 3.2a should have more complete descriptions of the activities. If the expected results do not occur, you may wish to emphasize that, given the probabilistic nature of empirical science, occasion replication failures can be expected to happen even when the effect of interest is generally valid.

Activity 3. The Facial Feedback Hypothesis

The facial feedback hypothesis states that changes in facial expression can trigger corresponding emotional experiences. This exercise is an adaptation of the experiment (Laird, 1974) that first tested the hypothesis. The exercise requires students to rate two cartoons from the next chapter of the textbook. But, if preferred, any two other cartoons may be used. The cartoons can also be projected and shown on a screen to the whole class at once. The activity is best done before students have read the chapter.

Introduce the activity by telling the class that they will be taking part in an experiment on the activity of facial muscles. Divide them into two groups. On command, have one group practice smiling and have the other group practice frowning.

Tell them that you will be asking them to look at two cartoons and rate them, on a scale of 1 to 10, 1 being "not funny at all" and 10 being "hilarious." Ask them to form their respective facial expression as they open their textbooks and turn to a cartoon in the book (have one picked out before class), look at it, write down their rating, and relax. Then, with their faces forming their assigned expression again, ask them to open the textbooks and turn to another cartoon in the book (again, have one picked out before class), look at it, write down their rating of it, and relax their facial expressions.

Tally the results on the board. If the experiment worked, then the smiling group should have a higher total rating (found the cartoons funnier) than the frowning group.

> 💣*What if this bombs?* This should work. However, if it does not, you might discuss how the activity diverged from Laird's study. Perhaps students did not hold their facial expressions throughout. Another possibility is that the use of only two cartoons was insufficient to produce the effect. In the original experiment, Laird used a series of cartoons.

Laird, J. (1974). Self-attribution of emotion: The effects of expressive behavior on the quality of emotional experience. Journal of Personality and Social Psychology, 29, 475-486.

Activity 4. BIRGing

Basking in reflected glory (BIRGing) is displayed when an individual takes pride in the achievement of the groups with which he or she is associated. Cialdini and his colleagues (1976) have shown that college students BIRG after their college teams win major sporting events. This activity can replicate this classic study. Have students count the number of people wearing sweatshirts and hats from your college or university on a typical day that isn't right after a major sporting event. Then have students count the number of people wearing these items the day after a significant sporting contest. The outcome of the contest should dramatically affect the number of people wearing these articles of clothing. After a win people tend to "bask in reflected glory": WE won the game. After a loss people tend to distance themselves from the team: THEY got clobbered. This basic self-enhancing bias is usually reflected in the wearing of school colors. You might do a similar demonstration using the wearing of clothing from fraternities and sororities. Members of these groups tend to wear their colors more after significant group events.

> 💣 *What if this bombs?* If the sports event does not yield results, try the same task with fraternities and sororities. If the specific measures do not show evidence of BIRGing, an interesting discussion of the phenomenon should still be possible because virtually all students can think of examples in which they have BIRGed. Ask the students to discuss these instances, and see if there are any interesting patterns to the responses (e.g., are there gender differences, differences as a function of class year, etc.?).

Cialdini, R. B., Borden, R. J., Thorne, A., Walker, M. R., Freeman, S., & Sloan, L. R. (1976). Basking in reflected glory: Three (football) field studies. Journal of Personality and Social Psychology, 34, 463-476.

Activity 5. The Twenty Statements Test

Trafimow and his colleagues (1991) have used a measure developed by Kuhn & McPartland (1954) to examine cultural differences in the self-concept. This measure simply asks participants to complete twenty statements that begin with "I am." They found that North American students tended to describe themselves with trait descriptions whereas Chinese students tended to identify themselves by group affiliations. You might want to have your students complete this measure by having them write twenty sentences that each begin with "I am." Afterward, have students count the number of trait descriptions and group affiliation descriptions they made. Point out that there might be a subtle effect of culture on how they described themselves.

> 💣 *What if this bombs?* This exercise should be relatively bombproof. The finding that North Americans tend to describe themselves in trait terms on the instrument appears to be quite strong. If, however, students do not complete the exercise this way, it should still provide an interesting way for students to examine how they think about themselves, and discussion of this process should prove fruitful.

Kuhn, M. H., & McPartland, T. (1954). An empirical investigation of self-attitudes. American Sociological Review, 19, 58-76.

Trafimow, D., Triandis, H. C., & Goto, S. G. (1991). Some tests of the distinction between private and collective self. Journal of Personality and Social Psychology, 60, 649-655.

Activity 6. Ironic Effects of Self-Control

This activity seeks to replicate a study by Wegner and his colleagues (1997). In this experiment they had people hold a pendulum (a crystalline pendant suspended by a fishing line) over two intersecting axes that form a grid. Some people were told to hold the pendulum still. Others were told to hold it still but to be sure to keep the pendulum from swinging horizontally on the axes. They found that people had a hard time holding the pendulum steady, but when told to not let it swing horizontally this is exactly the way the pendulum was likely to swing. This effect was especially pronounced when students were distracted by counting backwards from 1000 by 7's.

In replicating this experiment the most difficult part is finding a good pendulum. The object you use for the pendulum should be fairly heavy and symmetrical, and you should suspend it from as thin a piece of string as you can find. Of course if you can get your hands on a ready-made pendulum, this would be best. The authors have found that a good makeshift pendulum can be made by tying a piece of string to a key. Once you have the pendulum made, have several students try to hold it steady over the center of an axis. They should have trouble doing so. Next have other students try, but tell them not to let it swing left to right. As they hold the pendulum, it should start to swing from left to right. If they are able to keep it from swinging left to right, say that you are going to make the task a little harder. Now have them count backwards from 1000 by 7's while keeping the pendulum from swinging left to right. Let a number of students try this to show how difficult the task is.

It is important to note how this activity demonstrates the ironic effects of self-control. Explain how trying not to do something requires that you think of doing it and then try to suppress these actions. Note that the effect occurs when this suppression goes awry. This happens on demanding or stressful tasks. The pendulum task is such a demanding task.

The general principle behind this experiment can also be illustrated without the aid of the pendulum. Simply have your students concentrate on some facet of their sensory input that they are not used to focusing on. For example, have them concentrate for a several moments on the sensation of their feet inside their shoes, the position of their tongue in their mouth, or something similar. Once they have this clearly in their minds, tell them to dismiss these thoughts entirely and not to think about their feet or their tongues for the rest of class. The typical result of this is that the students are unable to shift their attention completely away from these thoughts however hard they try and will squirm for the rest of the class hour (for this reason you might want to consider doing this activity near the end of class).

What if this bombs? This activity is relatively bombproof. The effect is quite strong and reliable. If one student fails to show the effect, testing it with several students will virtually guarantee that a number of them show the effect.

Wegner, D. M., Ansfield, M., & Pilloff, D. (1998). The putt and the pendulum: Ironic effects of the mental control of action. Psychological Science, 9, 196-199.

Activity 7. Self-Serving Cognitions

The text describes self-serving cognitions, whereby people tend to take credit for successes and distance themselves from failures. David Dunn (1989) notes that students have difficulty recognizing this attributional bias in their own behavior. In order to illustrate this self-serving bias, Dunn suggests the following exercise:

At the end of the class period prior to the one in which you will discuss self-serving cognitions, tell the students that you intend to focus on the self-concept in the next class. Then ask them to take out a blank sheet of paper and, without putting their name on it, to draw a line down the middle. Tell them to label one column "strengths" and the other "weaknesses" and then to list their strengths and weaknesses. Collect the sheets and, before the next class, compute the mean number of weaknesses and strengths. There will likely be more strengths than weaknesses. This can be used to generate a discussion of this self-serving bias including the processes that contribute to its occurrence and its potential for positive and negative effects on behavior.

What if this bombs? This activity is probably bombproof. As the text states, the bias has been demonstrated by people with high and low self-esteem, in public and in private, and by those who are attempting to be honest as well as by those who are trying to make a good impression.

Dunn, D.S. (1989). Demonstrating a self-serving bias. Teaching of Psychology, 16, 21-22.

MULTIMEDIA RESOURCES

Video

The Galatea Effect. The film presents the concept titled the Galatea effect which describes the confidence that comes from high personal expectations. It suggests that this concept is important for improved productivity. (1986, 28 min.) Available from CRM/McGraw-Hill Films, 2233 Faraday Avenue, Carlsbad, CA 92008.

The Inner Woman: The Question of Self-Concept. Judith Bardwick, psychologist and author of publications about female psychology and physiology, explores the reasons why increasing numbers of women seek counseling and therapy, and why traditional therapeutic approaches are failing. One of the concepts that emerges is that because women's options have increased, so has the conflict and resulting stress engendered by the necessity of making choices. Produced by WXYZ, Detroit. (1975, 29 min.) Available from the Pennsylvania State University, Audio-Visual Services, University Park, PA 16802 (800-826-0132).

Judging Emotional Behavior. This film shows subjects' responses to emotion-eliciting information. The audience interacts with the film by judging subjects' emotions and then assessing the accuracy of their judgments. The difference in judging our own and others' emotions can be emphasized by this film. (1976, 24 min.) Available from the Indiana University Audio-Visual Center, Bloomington, IN 47401.

The Self. This program explores the emotional and motivational consequences of beliefs about oneself. (1990, 30 min.) Available from Insight Media (800-233-9910).

Internet

International Society for Self and Identity. The International Society for Self and Identity (ISSI) is a scholarly association dedicated to promoting the scientific study of the human self. Visit this site at http://www.psych.neu.edu/ISSI/socinfo.htm.

Self-Efficacy Information. This is a great resource for information on self-efficacy with a focus on the life and work of Albert Bandura. Visit this site at http://www.des.emory.edu/mfp/self-efficacy.html.

The Shyness Reading List. The books and articles listed at this site are all related to the concept of shyness. This list is maintained by The Shyness Institute, a non-profit research institution dedicated to research regarding shyness, social phobia, and related anxiety disorders. Visit this site at http://www.shyness.com/shyness-reading-list.html.

Computer Programs

Social Cognition: A Computer Simulation. This program provides a demonstration of the self-reference effect. Four different experiments with various memory measures are available. Available from ABi, 2124 Kittendge, Suite 215, Berkeley, CA 94704.

HANDOUT 3.1   AESTHETIC JUDGMENTS OF SIMPLE STIMULI

Below are a list of letters and numbers. Please evaluate them on a 5-point scale (1=not at all beautiful, 5=extremely beautiful) according to your positive or negative feelings. Do not hesitate or ponder their shape or meaning. Rely only on your first intuitive reactions. Work as quickly as you can. Don't think abut the task, just try to feel how attractive or unattractive each one feels to you.

Stimulus	Rating	Stimulus	Rating	Stimulus	Rating
B	____	7	____	5	____
X	____	28	____	30	____
14	____	Q	____	16	____
J	____	10	____	M	____
1	____	31	____	25	____
40	____	2	____	W	____
23	____	G	____	Z	____
26	____	U	____	24	____
H	____	8	____	V	____
36	____	P	____	S	____
3	____	19	____	E	____
33	____	18	____	27	____
C	____	L	____	20	____
F	____	12	____	9	____
6	____	4	____	29	____
Y	____	15	____	R	____
11	____	T	____	32	____
21	____	17	____	22	____
N	____	K	____	37	____
39	____	O	____	I	____
34	____	13	____	D	____
38	____	A	____	35	____

HANDOUT 3.2a

As you read the following list of activities, try to imagine yourself engaging in each of them.

1.   Buying an ice cream cone on a hot summer day.

2.   Walking to class on a very windy day.

3.   Being followed by a stranger on a dark street.

4.   Stepping into a mud puddle on a rainy day.

5.   Calling a friend in the middle of the night.

6.   Waking up late for an exam.

7.   Eating at a nice restaurant.

8.   Driving over a bridge.

9.   Shopping for a friend's birthday present.

10.   Coming home late after studying in the library.

HANDOUT 3.2b

As you read the following list of activities, try to remember as many of them as possible.

1. Buying an ice cream cone on a hot summer day.

2. Walking to class on a very windy day.

3. Being followed by a stranger on a dark street.

4. Stepping into a mud puddle on a rainy day.

5. Calling a friend in the middle of the night.

6. Waking up late for an exam.

7. Eating at a nice restaurant.

8. Driving over a bridge.

9. Shopping for a friend's birthday present.

10. Coming home late after studying in the library.

CHAPTER 4

Perceiving Persons

LEARNING OBJECTIVES: GUIDELINES FOR STUDY

You should be able to do each of the following by the conclusion of Chapter 4.

1. Explain the importance of first impressions in social perception. Consider the cues (facial features, name, style of dress) that contribute to these snap judgments. (*pp. 102-104*)

2. Explain the function of scripts in social perception. Discuss the expectations and beliefs people tend to have with regard to "mind perception" as well. (*pp. 105*)

3. Explain the role of nonverbal cues in social perception. Summarize the research concerning perception of angry faces. Discuss the roles of other nonverbal cues, including body language, eye contact, and touch. Discuss the role of cultural norms in evaluating nonverbal behavior. (*pp. 105-110*)

4. Describe people's ability to detect deception. Contrast the channels of communication that are most likely to reveal that someone is lying with the channels that perceivers typically try to use to detect deception. (*pp. 110-112*)

5. Define what is meant by attribution. Distinguish between personal and situational attributions. Summarize Jones's correspondent inference theory and Kelley's covariation theory. (*pp. 113-116*)

6. Describe cognitive heuristics in general and the availability heuristic in particular. Explain the relationship between the availability heuristic, the false-consensus effect, and the base-rate fallacy. (*pp. 116-118*)

7. Define counterfactual thinking and identify when it is likely to occur. (*pp. 118*)

8. Define the fundamental attribution error and describe the factors that make this error more or less likely to occur. Compare the fundamental attribution error with the actor-observer effect, and discuss the two explanations for the actor-observer effect. Understand the role of culture in the attribution process. (*pp. 119-121*)

9. Explain how attribution biases may stem from motivational factors, such as the desire to take more credit for success than for failure. Define what is meant by the "belief in a just world," and identify the factors that lead to defensive attributions. (*pp. 123-126*)

10. Explain the summation and averaging models of impression formation. Explain the role of perceiver characteristics (including the effects of individual differences, priming, and mood) and of target characteristics (including the trait negativity bias) on impression formation. (*pp. 126-129*)

11. Explain how people's implicit personality theories affect their impressions of other people. Describe the effects of central traits and the primacy effect on these impressions. Identify two explanations for the primacy effect. (*pp. 130-132*)

12. Define confirmation bias. Describe how belief perseverance, confirmatory hypothesis testing, and the self-fulfilling prophecy can each contribute to this bias. Discuss the relationship between confirmation bias and belief perseverance. (*pp. 132-138*)

13.   Describe generally how people fare as social perceivers listing reasons for being both optimistic
      and pessimistic regarding people's competence as social perceivers. (*pp. 138-139*)

DETAILED CHAPTER OUTLINE

I.   Observation: The Elements of Social Perception
      A.   Persons: Judging a Book by Its Cover
            1.   First impressions
            2.   Baby-faced vs. mature features
      B.   Situations: The Scripts of Life
      C.   Behavioral Evidence
            1.   Dividing up the stream of human behavior
            2.   Mind perception
            3.   Nonverbal behavior
                  a)   perceiving emotions
                  b)   body language
                  c)   eye contact
                  d)   touch
                  e)   cultural differences
            4.   Distinguishing truth from deception
II.   Attribution: From Elements to Dispositions
      A.   Attribution Theories
            1.   Jones's correspondent inference theory
                  a)   choice
                  b)   expectedness
                  c)   intended effects or consequences
            2.   Kelley's covariation theory
                  a)   the covariation principle
                  b)   consensus
                  c)   distinctiveness
                  d)   consistency
      B.   Attribution Biases
            1.   Cognitive heuristics
                  a)   the availability heuristic
                  b)   the false-consensus effect
                  c)   the base-rate fallacy
                  d)   counterfactual thinking
            2.   The fundamental attribution error
                  a)   demonstrations of the error
                  b)   explanations for the error: the two-step model, cultural differences
      C.   Culture and Attribution
      D.   Motivational biases
            1.   Self-serving attributions
                  a)   ideological motives
                  b)   the belief in a just world
III. Integration: From Dispositions to Impressions
      A.   Information Integration: The Arithmetic
            1.   Impression formation
            2.   Information integration theory
      B.   Deviations from the Arithmetic
            1.   Perceiver characteristics

2. Priming effects
3. Target characteristics
    a) five factors of personality
    b) trait negativity bias
4. Implicit personality theories
    a) networks of assumptions
    b) central traits
5. The primacy effect
    a) attention
    b) need for closure
    c) the change-of-meaning hypothesis
IV. Confirmation Biases: From Impressions to Reality
   A. Perseverance of Beliefs
       1. Impact of expectations
       2. Belief perseverance
   B. Confirmatory Hypothesis Testing
   C. The Self-Fulfilling Prophecy
       1. *Pygmalion in the Classroom*
       2. Accuracy of expectations
       3. Causes of the self-fulfilling prophecy
       4. Limits to the self-fulfilling prophecy
V. Social Perception: The Bottom Line

LECTURE AND DISCUSSION IDEAS

Idea 1.   Judging Books by Their Covers

Ask the students how many of them make snap judgments of others. If many students raise their hands, ask them to describe how they do this. What cues do they use to make these judgments? How accurate do they tend to be (and how do they know if they are accurate)? How would they feel if others judged them in these ways? If very few students raise their hands (which is probably what will happen), ask them if they infer anything about people based on…

- their clothes. What if the person is dressed all in black? Leather? Bright colors? Expensive suit? Clothes that are seven years out of fashion?

- their hairstyle.

- body piercings.

- whether they smile or sneer.

- their physical attractiveness.

- the physical attractiveness of the other people they're with.

- their posture.

After discussing these, ask the class for suggestions of other cues that seem to signal things about the personalities of the individuals.

Idea 2.   Identifying Emotions and Autism

As the text states, just about everyone in the world knows how to read the six basic primary emotions in others' faces. It is an automatic ability that we take for granted. (In Activity 3 of this chapter, students get a chance to see how well they "read faces.") There is, however, one exception to this universality: Individuals who have autistic disorder are unable to read emotions in faces. They remain unaware when others are delighted, bored, irritated, or enraged with them.

To help them, two computer scientists at MIT have created what they call the Emotional-Social Intelligence Prosthesis. The device consists of a small camera, mounted on eyeglasses or on a cap, which photographs the facial expression of the person the autistic individual is interacting with. The system tracks movements of facial features and classifies them according to the coding system developed by Paul Ekman. Then it compares them with a second taxonomy of emotional states developed by Simon Baron-Cohen, an autism researcher. All this happens in an instant, resulting in the computer sending a whispered message to the wearer about how the other person is feeling.

The system is currently being tested with teens who have high-functioning autism and Asperger's syndrome (a variant of autism, where language development is normal but social interaction and non-verbal communication is impaired). There is also a second version of the device that photographs the user's face to let him know what emotion he is sending out and so perhaps to change it to a more appropriate expression.

The technology is still being developed and is not yet being marketed. Currently, its accuracy rate is only 65 percent. Eventually, however, the inventors hope to not only help autistic individuals but also to create a parallel device that would aid ordinary people who have difficulty judging when they've droned on too long and are boring others, or when they are monopolizing the conversation. Ask students to speculate on whether or not there would be a demand for such a device.

Schuessler, J. (2006). The social-cue reader. The New York Times Magazine, Dec. 10, 74.

Idea 3.   Nonverbal Communication: The power of Touch

The text notes that touch is a very powerful form of nonverbal behavior. Students would likely be interested in a study (Hubbard, Tsuji, Williams, and Seatriz, 2003) that linked touch with the amount of tips that people left in a bar and a restaurant. Apparently, waiters and waitresses who touched patrons lightly on the shoulder received larger tips than did those who did not touch the patrons. Moreover, in the bar setting, the tips were greater when the waiter or waitress was of the opposite sex than the patron.

Ask students to speculate on the reasons that touch brought about an increase in tips. Also, why did gender make a difference in the bar setting but not in the restaurant (where tips were larger for the waiters and waitresses who touched regardless of gender)?

Hubbard, A. S. E., Tsuji, A. A., Williams, C., & Seatriz, V. (2003). Effects of touch on gratuities received in same-gender and cross-gender dyads. Journal of Applied Social Psychology, 33, 2427-2438.

Idea 4.   Correspondent Inference Theory and Covariation Theory

Jones's correspondent inference theory and Kelley's covariation theory are both important models of the attribution process, and students often have difficulty understanding these models. It is important, therefore, to help the students understand the specific concepts relevant to these models. Give the students practice with concrete examples of each concept. To illustrate the correspondent inference theory, give the class examples of behaviors that vary on each of the three relevant dimensions: degree of choice that the actor had, the expectedness of the behavior, and the intended effects of the behavior. By going through several examples, the students should come to realize that they do indeed have a good intuitive understanding of the logic underlying this model. Similarly, students should realize that they understand the logic underlying Kelley's covariation principle (see the Multimedia Resources section below for information about a video concerning Kelley's model). Provide the class with examples of actors' behaviors that vary in terms of consensus, consistency, and distinctiveness. Ask some students to come up with other examples. When the students have become familiar with the theories, then discuss the biases that reflect deviations from these theories, such as the fundamental attribution error and the base-rate fallacy.

Idea 5.   The Base-Rate Fallacy

The base-rate fallacy has to do with the tendency to ignore or distort statistical information and instead base decisions on less predictive, but often more dramatic, information.

For example, if students hear that an identification test has a 90 percent accuracy rate, they might assume that because it is a large percentage, the test is very reliable. Instead of considering the 10 percent of false negatives (people who should be identified but won't be) or the 10 percent of false positives (people who should not be identified but will be), they focus on the fact that the test is able to identify 90 percent of the targets. A concrete demonstration will help them to better understand the base-rate fallacy and why such a test, that appears to be highly reliable, is not really.

Tell them to suppose that the principal of a large school, with a 5,000 student body population, has decided to institute random drug testing. To do that, the administration has acquired a urine testing kit that has a 90 percent accuracy rate. Suppose also that 50 students are using drugs on the first day of testing. The test will accurately identify 90 percent of them, or 45 students. Only 10 percent, or 5 drug users, will not be identified. That does not sound too bad.

However, at the same time, this test will falsely identify 10 percent of the remaining 4,950 non-users, or 495 innocent students, as using drugs. Therefore, of the 540 students accused of using drugs (45 guilty + 495 innocent), only 12 percent really are, and the 90 percent accuracy figure is very misleading and not at all acceptable.

Challenge students to determine what the rates of identification would be with a 99 percent accuracy rate. They'll see that although it sounds virtually error-proof, and is sure to identify almost all the guilty students (99 percent of 50= 49.5), it still would lead to a 49.5 false positive rate (1 percent of the 4,950 innocent students = 49.5) or almost 50 falsely accused students. That means that out of 100 accused students, only half would actually be guilty.

Idea 6.   The Fundamental Attribution Error and the Passage of Time

Social perception is a two-step process. The first step involves forming a quick impression of others, which usually focuses on personal attributions (hence, the fundamental attribution error). The second is a slower, conscious attempt to factor in the elements of the situation as part of the explanation. Accordingly, it's logical to expect the fundamental attribution error to diminish over time, as distance from an event makes personal characteristics less salient and situational influences become clearer.

A recent study (Truchot, Maure and Patte, 2003) provided evidence for the hypothesis that the fundamental attribution error diminishes over time. The study took place in France, where firemen, besides putting out fires, are called on to respond to any situation where there might be public casualties. As such, they occasionally tend to be victims of verbal and even physical assaults. Eighty firemen who experienced such attacks were divided into two groups, those who had been attacked within the last three months, and those who had been attacked more than three months ago. Then they were asked to make attributions regarding their attackers. The finding was that the recent attacks were more likely to be attributed internally (intentions or personality), whereas the less recent attacks were more likely to be attributed externally (daily circumstances or social climate).

Ask your students to comment on the implication of the finding that the fundamental attribution error diminishes over time. For example, what are the implications for criminals whose trials are delayed? Can they think of other implications (e.g., in the area of disciplining children or marital disagreements)?

Truchot, D., Maure, G. & Patte, S. (2003). Do attributions change over time when the actor's behavior is hedonically relevant to the perceiver? Journal of Social Psychology, 143, 202-209.

Idea 7.   Attribution Biases and Protecting the Self

Integrating aspects of Chapter 3 with the discussions of attribution biases in Chapter 4 can provide students with a deeper understanding both of the self-concept and of attribution processes. Discuss how attribution biases can enhance and protect one's self-concept. For example, does the tendency for people to attribute their own behavior to situational factors tend to make them feel blameless for their negative behaviors? The media provide lots of examples of this, as politicians, athletes, criminals, celebrities, and others are often quoted making external attributions for their failures or poor judgment. Keep a file of such examples and bring some to class.

Discuss how different patterns of attributions can affect self-esteem. Some patterns should enhance self-esteem, while others could be associated with depression. Ask for some volunteers to discuss how they make attributions for their successes or failures in various domains (e.g., academic, social, athletic). Discuss the role of attribution in self-handicapping. Try to get some volunteers to discuss instances in which they've self-handicapped; ask these students to describe whether this was a conscious process or not, and what the outcome of it was.

Students often fail to recognize that there are both cognitive and motivational factors that contribute to attribution biases. Explain and clarify this for them. For example, discuss how the false-consensus effect may be due to cognitive factors (e.g., the availability heuristic) and motivational, self-protection factors (e.g., not wanting to appear to deviate from the group norm).

Idea 8.   Rosenhan's "On Being Sane in Insane Places": Demonstrating Confirmation and Attribution Biases

David Rosenhan's (1973) article, "On Being Sane in Insane Places," is a classic demonstration of confirmation and attribution biases. This article concerns a demonstration in which normal, sane individuals got themselves admitted to a number of mental hospitals by complaining of auditory hallucinations and, once admitted, proceeded to act perfectly normally. Despite the fact that these individuals (called pseudopatients) behaved normally once admitted, the staff at these hospitals continued for various amounts of time to think that the pseudopatients were mentally ill, and they interpreted many of the pseudopatients' innocuous behaviors or life experiences as confirmation of their alleged psychopathology.

Assign Rosenhan's (1973) article, "On Being Sane in Insane Places," to the class. Students invariably find this a fascinating, as well as disturbing, reading. It most clearly, and vividly, demonstrates the influence of expectations and labels on social perception and illustrates the confirmation bias, and, to some extent, the change-of-meaning hypothesis. It also suggests how self-fulfilling prophecies might develop on the basis of these expectations. (For an even more contemporary example of the same phenomenon Rosenhan studied, you could also include clips from the 2008 Clint Eastwood movie *Changeling*, starting Angelina Jolie as a 1920's mother of a missing boy who finds out the hard way how powerful self-fulfilling prophecies of mental illness can be.)

In addition to discussing these topics, ask the class to point out examples of the fundamental attribution error being committed by people described in the article. There are several examples described in which the pseudopatients' behavior was caused by the situation they were in and yet was interpreted by the staff as reflecting characteristics of their psychopathology. For example, the absence of activities or diversions in the hospital created a great sense of boredom, causing many of the pseudopatients to pace back and forth down the hallways or to take notes. Rather than attributing these behaviors to the patients' external environment, the staff tended to attribute these behaviors to their psychopathologies. The difference between the staff members' interpretations of the pseudopatients' behaviors and the pseudopatients' own interpretations of these behaviors provides an excellent illustration of the actor-observer effect.

Rosenhan, D. L. (1973). On being sane in insane places. Science, 179, 250-258.

CLASSROOM ACTIVITIES

Activity 1. Social Perception and Nonverbal Communication

Mark Costanzo and Dane Archer (1991) have designed a very engaging task that provides an excellent introduction to social perception in general and to nonverbal communication in particular. It can be used before or after the students have read Chapter 4.

Costanzo and Archer developed what they call the Interpersonal Perception Task (IPT). As they describe it, "The IPT contains 30 brief scenes, each 30 to 60 seconds in length. Each scene is paired with a question that has two or three possible answers—this gives the viewer a chance to 'decode' something important about the people he or she has just seen. For example, the viewer may see a woman talking on the telephone; the viewer is asked whether the woman is talking to her mother, a close female friend, or her boyfriend.... In each scene of the IPT, there is an objectively correct answer to the question asked...." Students enjoy the challenge of trying to use verbal and nonverbal cues to answer these questions.

The IPT-15, a shorter version that contains 15 of the scenes, is available from Berkeley Media LLC, 2600 Tenth St., Suite 626,, Berkeley, CA 94710, (510) 486-9944, or info@berkeleymedia.com. The IPT materials include the videotape and a guide to the IPT that contains detailed instructions, background information, explanations of correct answers, a bibliography, and the questionnaire to be copied and distributed to students.

Distribute copies of the questionnaire, and show them the 15 scenes, asking students to circle what they think is the correct answer after each scene. Students invariably find this task fun, interesting, and challenging. After the task is complete, go over the correct answers with the students, asking those who did and did not get the correct answer to explain their guesses. Discuss what kinds of cues do, and do not, lead to the greatest accuracy.

●*What if this bombs?* This activity is bombproof; it cannot fail. Students enjoy trying to succeed at the task, and they are very interested in learning their scores and seeing how their performance compares to their classmates'. The guide to the task provides more than enough information for the instructor to use in discussion.

Costanzo, M., & Archer, D. (1991). A method for teaching about verbal and nonverbal communication. Teaching of Psychology, 18, 223-236.

Activity 2. Perceiving Emotions from Faces

In their book *Unmasking the Face*, Ekman and Friesen (1975) include pictures of a number of faces, each expressing one or more of the following six emotions: anger, disgust, fear, happiness, sadness, and surprise. Show several or all of the pictures to the class, and have the students guess which emotion(s) is (are) expressed in each person's face. Ekman and Friesen explain how to use and code these pictures.

Compare the students' perceptions with the correct answers. Which students were most accurate? Ask students to explain the strategies they used. Compare these with the ones suggested by Ekman and Friesen. For which emotions was there the most or least consensus? Have the students discuss why these emotions did or did not elicit consensus.

> 💣 *What if this bombs?* This is a fun activity that cannot bomb. Any pattern of results (e.g., whether or not there is a lot of consensus, whether or not students are accurate in their perceptions) should lead to interesting discussion.

Ekman, P., & Friesen, W. (1975). <u>Unmasking the face</u>. Englewood Cliffs, NJ: Prentice Hall.

Activity 3. Detection of Deception

This exercise is designed to familiarize students with the research and issues concerning how people attempt to distinguish truth from deception, and how this often differs from how they <u>should</u> attempt to do this. It is also relevant to the issue of nonverbal behavior.

<u>Preparation</u>. Ask for volunteers to serve as target persons and ask each of them to come to the next class prepared to speak in front of the class briefly about their background. These students should describe where they are from, what their parents and siblings are like, what their parents do or did for a living, and what they (the students) and their hometown friends used to do for fun. Instruct half the students to tell the truth about all details, and instruct the other half to lie about many of the details. The fabricated stories should be no more or less interesting than the true stories, so you should either check and edit all of the stories before they are presented to the class or pair students together and have one student prepare a true story about his or her background that the other student learns, such that both students later tell the same story in front of the class.

These students should be told that the other students in the class will be asked to determine who is telling the truth and who is lying. It is important that the students be motivated to try to appear to be telling the truth, so perhaps offer a prize for the students who are most successful in coming across as believable.

<u>Presenting the stories</u>. When the students have prepared their stories, present them to the class in random order, and tell the rest of the class that some of these students are telling the truth and that others are lying about many details, and that their task is to distinguish which students are doing which. This activity can be done in a few different ways. One way is to do this exercise before the students have read Chapter 4 and leave the students to their own devices about how to try to detect deception. Another way is to run through only half of the stories before they read Chapter 4, and the rest after they read it, and then compare their performance as a function of having read this material. That is, are they better able to distinguish truth from deception after having read about this research?

A third way to run this activity is to do it before the students have read the chapter, but give each student one of three handouts. These handouts differ in the instructions given to the students, either suggesting no specific strategies (**Handout 4.3a**), emphasizing facial cues (**Handout 4.3b**), or emphasizing body movements and voice (**Handout 4.3c**). Research suggests that body movements and the voice offer the most reliable cues for detecting deception, although perceivers are less likely to focus on these spontaneously.

<u>Dependent measures and discussion</u>. After each speaker tells his or her story, have the rest of the students indicate whether or not that person was telling the truth. You may wish to have the students also indicate their degree of confidence in each judgment, such as on a 7-point scale. Students should disqualify themselves from making judgments about speakers with whom they are familiar enough to know their background. When all the speakers have presented their stories, inform the rest of the class which of the speakers told the truth and which did not, and ask the students to calculate what percentage

of their guesses were accurate. If Handouts 4.4a, b, and c are used, determine if there is a difference in accuracy as a function of condition. Ask students who did very well, and other students who did not do very well, to discuss how they made their judgments. Was confidence correlated with accuracy? Was there a lot of consensus about particular targets? If so, why?

> ● *What if this bombs?* This exercise should be fun and interesting for all students, so it cannot bomb. If there are no differences in performance as a function of the handouts, the instructor should explain that the voice and body cues that typically "leak out" when someone is lying are most likely to be evident if the person is truly motivated to deceive others successfully. In this class activity, the motivation for successful deception may have been too weak for these cues to emerge. In addition, since most students are nervous speaking in front of their class, even those telling the truth may have been revealing cues consistent with deception, causing students who were looking for the "right" cues to falsely accuse people of lying. In any case, the students should enjoy comparing their performances with each other and discussing the relevant issues.

Activity 4. Application of Attribution Models

This activity is designed to heighten students' interest in attribution theory and to stimulate a better appreciation of how the logic underlying attribution models is applied outside the psychology laboratory. The activity should be conducted after the students have read the section of Chapter 4 concerned with attribution.

Ask the class to look for examples of advertisements that illustrate the logic underlying Jones's correspondent inference theory and Kelley's covariation theory, each of which is described in Chapter 4. For example, how do advertisers try to discourage the audience from discounting a spokesperson's appeal for a product in light of the fact that the audience assumes that the spokesperson is getting paid for making the appeal? Can the students find ads that emphasize the distinctiveness of the person using a product, or the degree of choice the person had? Do any ads emphasize how unexpected the behavior was, or how much consensus there was?

The students should write down a description of the ad and an explanation of how it uses the logic of attribution theory. In class, the students should discuss which specific principles the ads illustrate, and how effective they think each ad is in utilizing these principles.

> ● *What if this bombs?* As long as the students follow through on this activity, it cannot bomb. Some ads chosen by the students may not fit well with attribution theories and thus be inappropriate for this activity. But the instructor should also bring to class ads that he or she has selected, just in case the students do not select enough interesting or appropriate ads.

Activity 5. Attributions and Cross-Cultural Dialogues

The text reviews research that shows the effects of culture on how people make attributions or interpret others' behavior. In order to demonstrate these cultural differences in social perception, consider using Craig Storti's book *Cross-Cultural Dialogues* (1994). The book is a collection of brief conversations, each one taking place between an American and someone from a different (mostly collectivist) culture. Each dialogue is like a riddle, challenging students to figure out what cultural norms are causing the two people to misunderstand each other. After role-playing and discussing some of the dialogues, you might want to divide students into small groups and have them develop their own dialogues.

> ●*What if this bombs?* There is nothing here that could bomb. The dialogues are short and challenging, and the explanations of the cultural norms that are causing the problems are informative. Students will likely enjoy the exercise.

Storti, C. (1994). Cross-Cultural Dialogues. Yarmouth, Maine: Intercultural Press.

Activity 6. The Availability Heuristic

The availability heuristic is the tendency to judge a probability or make an estimate based on how easily a subject comes to mind. The role of familiarity in shaping availability and therefore influencing decisions is demonstrated in **Handout 4.6**. The handout presents students with pairs of cities and asks them to guess which of the two cities has a population that is approximately twice as large as the other. Although, in each case, the less familiar city will have the larger population, students are more likely to choose the familiar city.

Population Figures (As of January 1st, 2006)

Rio de Janeiro, Brazil (6,211,000) vs. Buenos Aires, Argentina (11,595,183)

Baghdad, Iraq (5,948,800) vs. Seoul, South Korea (10,409,345)

Los Angeles, California (3,900,700) vs. Kinsasha, Democratic Republic of the Congo (8,096,254)

Berlin, Germany (3,387,300) vs. Lima, Peru (7,857,121)

Madrid, Spain (3,290,900) vs. Tehran, Iran (7,160,094)

Montreal, Canada (3,263,800) vs. Bogota, Columbia (7,235,084)

Chicago, Illinois (2,888,200) vs. Bangkok, Thailand (4,935,988)

Rome, Italy (2,453,100) vs. Santiago, Chile (4,893,495)

Paris, France (2,107,600) vs. Sydney, Australia (4,444,513)

Houston, Texas (2,071,800) vs. Wuhan, China (4,236,023)

Philadelphia, Pennsylvania (1,483,000) vs. Omdurman, Sudan (2,970,099)

Tijuana, Mexico (1,313,800) vs. Addis Ababa, Ethiopia (2,823,167)

San Diego, California (1,290,000) vs. Kiev, Ukraine (2,491,404)

Dallas, Texas (1,234,400) vs. Giza, Egypt (2,468,625)

> **What if this bombs?** The activity has the potential of bombing only if your students are particularly knowledgeable in population statistics. Otherwise, they'll probably be fooled into picking at least some of the more familiar (but less populated) alternatives.

All population figures are from http://www.world-gazetteer.com/home.htm.

Activity 7. Counterfactual Thinking and the First Instinct Fallacy

Counterfactual thinking is the tendency to think about what might have been. The text cites a study by Kruger, Miller, and Wirtz (2005), which found that students were more likely to engage in counterfactual thinking after changing a correct test answer to an incorrect one than after failing to change an incorrect answer. This happens partly because changing a correct answer to an incorrect one results in more frustration and regret and is therefore a more memorable event.

Consequently, these more available memories lead students to develop the "first instinct fallacy," the belief that first instinct answers are more likely to be right than second thought answers. Many studies have shown that this belief is false, in that, statistically, the majority of such changes are from incorrect to correct.

Handout **4.7a** is a 10-question multiple-choice test, based on the first chapter of the text, which will allow your students to partially duplicate the Kruger, Miller, and Wirtz study.

Explain to the students that you'd like to do an experiment involving counterfactual thinking. Distribute handout 4.7a and read the instructions out loud. Allow students five minutes to answer the questions, then say, "Pens down."

Now distribute Handout **4.7b**. Ask students to copy their first instinct answers from 4.7a onto 4.7b. Now allow them two minutes more to give each question a second thought and change it if it seems incorrect or leave it alone if it seems to be right.

As you read off the correct answers to the test, ask them to grade Handout 4.7a. Then read the answers a second time in order for them to grade Handout 4.7b.

The correct answers are as follows:

1. a   6. d

2. a   7. d

3. d   8. b

4. b   9. b

5. d   10. c

If more students were helped by changing their first instinct responses (if the score on 4.7b is greater than that of 4.7a), then you will have shown that sticking with one's first instinct on a test is not a good strategy and changing it is.

> **What if this bombs?** Statistically, this should work. However, it is entirely possible that more students will hurt their scores by changing their answers. In that case, present the findings of the Kruger, Miller, and Wirtz study and ask students to think of possible explanations for why their results deviated (Were the questions too easy? Were they too hard? Was the sample of questions too small?) Also, remind them that a statistical advantage does not mean that the effect will occur every time.

Kruger, J., Wirtz, D., & Miller, D. T. (2005). Counterfactual thinking and the first instinct fallacy. Journal of Personality and Social Psychology, 88, 5, 725-735.

Activity 8. The Fundamental Attribution Error: The Quiz Show

This exercise is designed to illustrate the fundamental attribution error by using a procedure based on the "quiz show" study of Ross and colleagues (1977), which is discussed in Chapter 4.

Procedure. This activity should be performed before the students have read Chapter 4. First, ask for two volunteers for a demonstration. The two volunteers should not know each other well. Explain that you are going to simulate a quiz show by having one participant play the role of quiz master and the other play the role of contestant. In front of the whole class, flip a coin to determine which student plays which role. Instruct the quiz master to come up with five challenging questions from his or her store of general knowledge. Take the quiz master to another room, or to the hallway outside the room, to work on the questions. When the quiz master is out of the room, emphasize to this student that he or she should make the questions very difficult (if you do not remind quiz masters about this, they may be overly polite and write easy questions). After about five to ten minutes, begin the show, with the remainder of the class participating as the studio audience. Instruct the quiz master to ask the first question. The contestant should be given about ten seconds to answer. The quiz master should then announce whether the contestant's answer was correct or not (if the contestant does not offer an answer in the allotted time, it should be considered a wrong answer). If the answer is incorrect, the quiz master should give the correct answer. The procedure should continue until all five questions have been completed.

The quiz master should ask questions that most students would not be able to answer correctly. Thus, the contestant should get most of the questions wrong. After the quiz, distribute **Handout 4.8a** to all of the students in the audience, **Handout 4.8b** to the quiz master, and **Handout 4.8c** to the contestant. Instruct the class to answer the questions on the handouts as honestly and quickly as they can, without looking at anyone else's responses.

Results. The handouts contain filler items to distract from the main purpose of this demonstration. The critical measures are the ratings of general knowledge. Calculate the average ratings that the audience members give concerning the general knowledge of (a) the quiz master, (b) the contestant, and (c) themselves, and also record the ratings given by the quiz master and the contestant of themselves and of each other. On average, students almost always rate the quiz master as having greater general knowledge than they rate the contestant, and often they rate the quiz master as having greater general knowledge than they rate themselves.

Discussion. To the extent that students rate the quiz master as possessing more general knowledge than the contestant, the fundamental attribution error is suggested. Based on the logic of attribution models, it should be clear to all the students that the assignment of roles was determined randomly, and that the situation was designed so that the quiz master would have a huge advantage over the contestant by being able to write questions concerning issues about which he or she was an expert. However, as Ross and his colleagues (1977) found in a study that many others have since replicated, people tend to underutilize the information about the situational determinants of the performance when making their ratings. To demonstrate that this is indeed an error, the instructor, after collecting the students' handout responses, could switch the roles of the quiz master and contestant, and demonstrate that the latter can just as easily come up with questions to stump the former.

What if this bombs? This is a very robust phenomenon. Indeed, one of the textbook authors has successfully demonstrated this phenomenon in class more than two dozen times without a failure. One way it could fail to work, however, is if the quiz master asks questions that are too easy, so be sure to encourage the quiz master to write very difficult questions that are likely to stump the contestant. (Yet the questions should not be so obscure that it is immediately obvious to everyone that they were impossible to answer.)

In the unlikely event that although the contestant does fail to answer the questions, the ratings do not reflect the fundamental attribution error, emphasize to the students that most naive participants in this kind of study, those who have not taken a social psychology course, tend to be insensitive to the kind of information that they (the students in your class) were able to take into account. In this way, the instructor can use the findings to demonstrate the difference between the successful use of the logic of attribution models (which most of them demonstrated) and the fundamental attribution error (which most people not in a social psychology class tend to demonstrate). Indeed, if the demonstration fails to replicate the fundamental attribution error, and you use the explanation we've just suggested, you may succeed in making the fundamental attribution error seem to your class to be a more powerful and surprising, albeit less robust, effect than it otherwise might have appeared. The key here is that having gone through the activity, the students will come to a better understanding of what the fundamental attribution error is and how research has demonstrated it. It therefore is not essential that the students themselves fall prey to the bias in this activity. If they do commit the bias (as they typically do in this demonstration), so much the better.

Ross, L. D., Amabile, T. M., & Steinmetz, J. L. (1977). Social roles, social control, and biases in social-perception processes. Journal of Personality and Social Psychology, 35, 485-494.

Activity 9. Impression Formation: Summation vs. Averaging Models

How do people integrate the various traits they have learned about a person to form a coherent, overall impression of the person? Chapter 4 discusses the process of impression formation, which is the process by which people integrate information about a person to form a coherent impression. The textbook identifies two competing models of impression formation: *the summation model* and *the averaging model*. These models offer competing predictions in situations in which perceivers learn a trait about a person that is positive but not as positive as most of the other traits they know about the person. This activity is designed to contrast these models.

Handout 4.9a and **Handout 4.9b** are designed to look like a form completed by a professor concerning a student. Handout 4.9a includes a list of four traits that the professor chose to describe this student. These four traits were selected because they were rated very positively by the students in Anderson's (1968) study, which is described in Chapter 4. Handout 4.9b includes the same information, except that a fifth trait ("inoffensive") is added. This fifth trait, although rated positively by the students in Anderson's (1968) study, was rated less positively than any of the other four traits. The summation model and the averaging model offer different predictions about the impact that this fifth trait should have on students' overall impressions of this person. According to the summation model, students should have a more positive overall impression of the student described because the fifth trait is positive. According to the averaging model, students should have a more negative overall impression of the student described because the fifth trait lowers the overall average of the set of traits.

Distribute copies of Handout 4.9a to half the class and copies of Handout 4.9b to the other half. Tell the students to complete the scale at the bottom of the handout to indicate their overall impression of the student. Collect the completed handouts and compare the average rating given of the student in Handout 4.9a with the average rating of the student in Handout 4.9b. If the overall impression is more positive among students who received Handout 4.9a than among students who received Handout 4.9b, the results will have supported the summation model. If the opposite occurs, the results will have supported the averaging model.

Discuss the results with the class. What implications do they have for someone who is writing a letter of recommendation or applying for a job? Discuss the general issue of impression formation, as well as the specific issues of the summation, averaging, and weighted averaging models and information integration theory. Point out to the class that Norman Anderson concluded from his research that people tend to use a weighted average when integrating information about others. Explain what this means and what the implications are. Discuss whether or not the results of this activity were consistent with this idea, and speculate about why they were or were not.

> 💣 *What if this bombs?* Because this exercise tests two models that make opposite predictions, this exercise is virtually bombproof—either way, one of the models will be supported. If the means are virtually identical between the two conditions, ask the students why this might have been the case. Among the reasons you could suggest to explain this are that the students did not pay close attention to the words, some students thought "inoffensive" was positive and others negative, and some students tend to follow a summation model and others an averaging model.

Anderson, N. H. (1968). Likableness of 555 personality-trait words. <u>Journal of Personality and Social Psychology</u>, <u>9</u>, 272-279.

Activity 10. Priming: Raising the Tide

This exercise, based on a study by Nisbett and Wilson (1977), is designed to provide a simple demonstration of the effects of priming. It can be done before or after the students have read Chapter 4.

In this exercise, students are asked to memorize a list of words, many of which are relevant to the word "tide." Later, in an ostensibly unrelated and unimportant task, these students are asked to name the first brand of laundry detergent that comes to mind. A large percentage of the students will probably mention the brand *Tide*, even though many of these students use some other brand of detergent. The words in the list should prime the students to think of *Tide*. (Some students may be primed to think of the detergent named *Surf* instead, thus also demonstrating priming; this is much less likely, however, because *Surf* is not a well-known detergent.)

Procedure. Tell the students that you are giving them a test of their memory. Read the following instructions to the class: "I am going to read to you a list of words to memorize. You may use any strategy you want except for writing the words down. After reading the list of words to you twice, I will ask you to think about something else, and then we will do a test of recall."

Read the following words at a brisk pace: **ocean, moon, tree, building, chair, salt, sand, surf, fire.**

Repeat the list at the same pace. Then tell the students, "Now, as a distractor task, I'm going to read some things to you, and I want you to write down the first thing that comes to mind for each." Then, read the following, leaving time for the students to write something down for each:

- A brand of coffee

- A musical group or singer

- A brand of laundry detergent

- An athletic event

After going through this list, ask the students to write down all of the words that they can remember from the original list of nine words, in any order. Go over the list with them and ask how many got all of them right, how many got all but one, etc.

As if it were a tangential point, tell the students that you also want to see what they wrote down during the distractor task. Ask for a show of hands to indicate how many of the students gave particular responses to "A brand of coffee." That is, ask the students, "How many of you said *Taster's Choice*? How many of you said *Starbucks*? and so forth. Do the same for the musical group or singer.

There should be a wide range of responses to these questions. Next, ask the students, "For the laundry detergent, how many of you said *Fresh Start*? How many said *Cheer*? How many said *Tide*? A large proportion of the students should raise their hands when you say *Tide*. Students usually find this very amusing, and several of them will realize that the words from the list served to prime the word "tide." Be sure to ask also how many students wrote *Surf*, particularly because it was one of the words in the original list (given the greater popularity of *Tide*, however, students will more likely refer to it than to *Surf*). Ask the students who said *Tide* to stand up. Ask all of those who regularly use *Tide* to return to their seats. There should still be a number of students standing. Ask them why they chose this brand if they don't use it regularly.

The instructor may wish to run a proper control group to test this priming effect more carefully, although it is not necessary to illustrate the point of priming. For this control condition, a separate group of students would have to be read a different list of words, and none of these words could be related to the words "tide" or "surf." Compare the proportion of students in each condition who do and do not write *Tide* or *Surf*; there should be a smaller proportion in the control condition.

Recently, one of us conducted this activity and discovered an interesting additional effect: An unusually large number of responses concerning a musical group or singer were names of bands that had an ocean-like theme, such as "The Beach Boys" and "Phish." Try to identify these kinds of effects, too—although they are relatively rare.

🔆 *What if this bombs?* We have done this exercise every year for several years, and it has never failed. If you run a control condition and find no difference between it and the priming condition described here, it could be because *Tide* is such a popular brand of detergent among your students that there was no room for a priming effect to be evident (for example, if 90% of the students in the control condition say *Tide*, there is no room for the priming effect to increase such a huge percentage). If this is the case, it would be easy to explain such results. Be prepared to describe the Higgins, Rholes, and Jones (1977) study, which is summarized in Chapter 4, to provide students with an example of a successful demonstration of the priming effect.

Higgins, E. T., Rholes, C. R., & Jones, C. R. (1977). Category accessibility and impression formation. Journal of Experimental Social Psychology, 13, 141-154.

Nisbett, R. E., & Wilson, T. D. (1977). Telling more than we know: Verbal reports on mental processes. Psychological Review, 84, 231-259.

Activity 11. Central Traits and Impression Formation

An important point from Chapter 4 is that people form impressions of each other in dynamic, complex ways. When people learn a set of traits about another person, each trait is not a static piece of data but rather is integrated into the context of other information, often changing meaning dramatically as a function of this context. Solomon Asch (1946) was the first to examine this issue extensively. In addition to demonstrating the primacy effect and advancing the change-of-meaning hypothesis (see Activity 15 below), Asch discovered the presence of what he called *central traits*, which, as the textbook explains, "exert a powerful influence on overall impressions."

This activity is based on Asch's pioneering research and is designed to demonstrate the power of the central traits *warm* and *cold* in affecting the impressions people form of others. You can distribute copies of the handouts that are described below, or you can make transparencies from these handouts and discuss this exercise with the class rather than demonstrating it. (The phenomenon is so robust that even discussing it without having the students do the exercise should be enough to make students appreciate the power of central traits; however, having students complete the exercise should be a more impressive illustration. If you choose to have the students do the exercise, the students should complete it before they read Chapter 4.)

Handout 4.11 includes a list of trait words that describe a hypothetical target person. Note that the middle trait is *warm*. **Handout 4.11b** includes the identical list, except that the trait *warm* is changed to *cold*. It should be easy to see from these two lists how one's overall impression of the person would change dramatically as a function of this one difference. Distribute copies of Handout 4.11a to half the class, and Handout 4.11b to the other half. When the students have completed the questions on the handout, collect the handouts and compare the impressions of the person as a function of the *warm/cold* difference. Compare their responses on questions 5a through 5f; for which traits is there a dramatic difference in students' responses as a function of the central trait? Why are some of the traits on this list more affected by the central traits than others? (For example, the last two may be less affected than the first four.)

Points of discussion include what other traits may be central traits, the potential impact of central traits on confirmatory hypothesis testing, more general issues about implicit personality theories, and whether race, sex, sexual orientation, or other category-level information can have similar effects as central traits.

Handout 4.11c is included as a baseline condition against which the instructor can compare the *warm/cold* conditions. This handout includes the same list as the others, except that the central trait has been deleted. This third handout can be included in larger classes, but using only Handouts 4.12a and b can be sufficient to demonstrate the effect.

Handout 4.11d and **Handout 4.11e** are also included as a pair of comparison conditions that instructors with large classes might want to use in addition to Handouts 4.11a and b (and, possibly, c). Each student should get only one of the four (or five) handouts. Handouts 4.11d and 4.11e contain the same lists as Handouts 4.11a and 4.11b, except that the central traits of *warm* and *cold* have been changed to *polite* and *blunt*, respectively. Because these latter traits are not central traits, the differences between the inferences made in these two conditions should be less pronounced, although they should make some difference in the impressions that the students form.

> *What if this bombs?* This is a very robust phenomenon, so the activity is extremely unlikely to fail, particularly if the students do not read the chapter beforehand. However, in the unlikely event that the manipulation of *warm/cold* does not have much effect, you should explain to the class that in real-world situations, people do not learn information about others in list form like this, and that the effect can be much more powerful when the information is learned in a more subtle, naturalistic way. Ask students to suggest what traits they think tend to exert particularly powerful effects on their impressions. You could frame this question such as, "If you could choose to learn one trait about a potential date, what would it be?" In this way, you divert attention away from the actual results of the demonstration and focus on the issue behind it—the role of central traits in impression formation.

Asch, S. E. (1946). Forming impressions of personality. Journal of Abnormal and Social Psychology, 41, 258-290.

Activity 12. The Primacy Effect

Research on the primacy effect has demonstrated how powerful first impressions can be. Asch's (1946) paradigm of presenting lists of trait words in different orders can serve as a very simple, but rather elegant, way of demonstrating this point. It also can spark discussions about impression formation in general, as well as about more specific issues such as information integration theory, the role of attention, the change-of-meaning hypothesis, and the confirmation bias.

In **Handout 4.12a** Students are asked to see themselves as interviewers of two people that they are considering for jobs as counselors at a summer camp. They are asked to make a hiring judgment based on five phrases that describe each candidate's character. In each case, the positive traits are mentioned first, and are then followed by more negative traits. **Handout 4.12b** is identical except that, in the phrases that describe each of the candidates, the order of traits is reversed, with the more negative qualities mentioned first.

This demonstration should be conducted before the students have read Chapter 4. Distribute copies of the handouts to the class, with half receiving Handout 4.12a and the other half receiving Handout 4.12b. After the students have completed the handouts, calculate the total ratings for Penelope for Handout 4.4a and compare it with the total ratings for Penelope for handout 4.12b. Repeat for Derek. If the students who received Handout 4.12a formed a more positive impression of the candidates than did the students who received Handout 4.12b, then you have succeeded in demonstrating the primacy effect.

> *What if this bombs?* This activity is unlikely to fail, particularly if the students have not read the chapter. If the data does not support the effect, use a similar explanation as suggested in the previous activity: Explain to the students that in real-world situations, people do not learn information about others in list form like this, and that the effect can be much more powerful when the information is learned in a more naturalistic way.

Activity 13. Confirmatory Hypothesis Testing

Mark Snyder and William Swann (1978) found that when participants were given the opportunity to interview another participant to test a particular hypothesis about the other participant's personality, they tended to ask questions that were biased toward eliciting confirmation of the hypothesis. Thus, if they thought the person they'd be interviewing was introverted, they chose to ask this person introversion-oriented questions that would tend to elicit introverted-sounding responses. The present exercise is designed to illustrate the effects of this kind of biased hypothesis testing. In addition, it is designed to illustrate the fundamental attribution error.

Overview. In this activity, half the students are instructed to answer the kind of biased questions that participants in the Snyder and Swann (1978) study chose to ask other participants. The other half of the participants are then given these responses and asked to judge how introverted or extroverted the students who wrote them are. Students who respond to extroversion-oriented questions should be judged as more extroverted than students who respond to introversion-oriented questions. This difference may emerge even if the students who judge these responses are aware of the questions that elicited them. That is, although these judges should be able to see that the questions were biased toward eliciting a particular type of response, they may fail to take that into sufficient account when making their judgment, thereby demonstrating the fundamental attribution error.

Handouts. Half the class should be designated as "responders" who respond to a series of questions about themselves, and the other half should be designated as "judges" who judge the personality of one of the responders. Each of the responders should receive one of the following handouts: 4.13a, 4.13b, 4.13c, or 4.13d. Handout 4.13a contains extroversion-oriented questions (questions 2, 3, and 5) and is designed so that the judges will see the questions along with the responders' responses. Handout 4.13b contains the same extroversion-oriented questions, but the students are asked to answer these questions on a separate piece of paper; the judges see only the answers, not the questions that elicited the answers. Handout 4.13c contains introversion-oriented questions (questions 2, 3, and 5) and is designed so that the judges will see the questions along with the responders' responses. Handout 4.13d contains the same introversion-oriented questions, but the students are asked to answer these questions on a separate piece of paper; again, the judges see only the answers, not the questions that elicited the answers.

Collect the completed handouts (be sure that the students with Handouts 4.13b and 4.13d turn in only their answer sheets, not the questions), mix them up, and give each judge one of the completed handouts. In addition, each judge should receive a copy of Handout 4.13e. Be sure to remind the judges to write the number of the handout that was completed by the responder they are judging.

Results. When the judges have completed Handout 4.13e, collect all the handouts. Examine the judges' ratings given on Handout 4.13e. Compare the judges' ratings of the responders' extroversion-introversion as a function of which of the four handouts (a, b, c, or d) the judges had been given to evaluate. First, compare the judgments made of responders who had been given Handouts 4.13b and 4.13d. The former should be rated as much more extroverted than the latter. This would illustrate the potential biasing effects of confirmatory hypothesis testing.

Next, compare the judgments made of responders who had been given Handouts 4.13a and 4.13c. Does the difference continue to emerge? To the extent that it does, this would illustrate both the powerful effect of confirmatory hypothesis testing and the fundamental attribution error. Ignore the judges' ratings of the responders' intelligence; it was included only as a distractor. The judges' ratings of the respondents' likeability and popularity, on the other hand, might yield interesting results.

What if this bombs? Instructors should not fear trying this demonstration because even if it fails, (a) students, by seeing examples of biased questions, gain a better insight into what is meant by biased hypothesis testing, and (b) the failure to find any strong differences as a function of the questions can be explained easily. To explain null results, the instructor should point out that

Snyder and Swann's participants asked a greater number of biased questions than were given to the students in this exercise, and thus the effect would be weaker in this classroom activity. The instructor should also point out that the effect of these biased questions would probably have been much stronger if the judges had been given a hypothesis to test about the responders that was consistent with these biased questions. That is, if a judge had <u>expected</u> the responder to be extroverted, and <u>then</u> saw the responder's answers to extroversion-oriented questions, the judge would have been more likely to infer that he or she indeed was extroverted.

Snyder, M., & Swann, W. B., Jr. (1978). Behavioral confirmation in social interaction: From social perception to social reality. <u>Journal of Personality and Social Psychology</u>, <u>36</u>, 1202-1212.

Activity 14. Demonstrating the Self-Fulfilling Prophecy

Michelle Hebl and Eden King created an amusing interactive demonstration of the self-fulfilling prophecy that can easily be used in class. The only materials necessary are five baseball caps with labels stuck on the front reading: "very attractive," "annoying," "good leader," "lazy," and "funny."

After a brief description of the self-fulfilling prophecy, and a warning that this activity might be somewhat embarrassing, five volunteers are solicited to blindly choose hats, which are then placed on their heads without allowing them to see the labels (Before class, the labels may be covered with construction paper pieces that are easily removed after the caps are placed on the heads).

The volunteers are then instructed to treat each other in accordance with the information on the hats while working together on a series of tasks. The tasks used in the original study are as follows: a) naming a new school mascot, b) determining the three best reasons for being a psychology major, c) deciding on the distance between two major buildings on the college campus, and d) lining up in the order of their likeability as a function of their interactions with the other volunteers.

When the tasks are completed, the volunteers are asked to state whether they think their hat labels are positive or negative, if they know exactly what they are, and how they came up with their answers.

Finally, the rest of the class is asked to point out specific examples of the self-fulfilling prophecy that occurred during the demonstration.

> 💣 *What if this bombs?* This is a fun and interesting way to demonstrate how self-fulfilling prophecies can occur. However, the authors warn that some students may not take the tasks seriously enough because of the self-consciousness involved in being in front of the class. To prevent that from happening, they propose that the exercise be carried out in small groups.

Hebl, Michelle R., & King, Eden B. (2004). You are what you wear: An interactive demonstration of the self-fulfilling prophecy. <u>Teaching of Psychology</u>, <u>31</u>, 4, 260-262.

Activity 15. The Wasson Task

Another way to illustrate the principle of confirmatory hypothesis testing is to show your students the Wasson task. To do this, tell the students that you have a rule governing numbers in mind and they are going to guess the rule. Give them the numbers "2," "4," and "6" as three numbers that fit your rule and let them guess what the rule is and choose another number to test it. The actual rule is "increasing numbers" but they will almost always choose "increasing <u>even</u> numbers" (an embedded or "incorrectly-too-specific" answer) and will choose the number "8" to test their hypothesis. This choice demonstrates the bias to test positively and, with embedded answers like this one, never leads to the correct solution.

> 💣 *What if this bombs?* This is a very robust effect and is unlikely to fail. You can increase the probability of this demonstration working by giving them a longer initial series of even numbers before asking them to guess the rule but this is not usually necessary.

Wasson, P. C. (1960). On the failure to eliminate hypotheses in a conceptual task. Quarterly Journal of Experimental Psychology, 12, 129-140.

MULTIMEDIA RESOURCES

Video

Attribution Motives. This film explains attributional concepts and the way in which causality is determined. (1975, 22 min.) Available from University Films of Canada, 7 Hayden Street, Toronto, Ontario, Canada M4Y 2P2.

Communication: The Nonverbal Agenda. In this film Raymond Birdwhistell describes how nonverbal messages, communicated through posture, gesture, and expression, can be interpreted in terms of meaning. (1974, 30 min.) Available from the Pennsylvania State University, Audio-Visual Services, University Park, PA 16802 (800-826-0132).

Constructing Social Reality. This tape which is part of the *Discovering Psychology* series, explains how understanding the psychological processes that govern our·behavior may help us deal with society. The tape also includes "The Power of the Situation," which illustrates how situational forces can affect beliefs and behavior. (1990, 2 parts, 30 min. each) Available from Insight Media (1-800-233-9910).

Eye of the Beholder. Illustrates how ambiguous social reality can be for perceivers, and emphasizes the roles of social psychological factors such as the actor-observer difference and confirmation biases in perceivers' interpretations of that reality. The fact that this film is quite dated adds to its entertainment value without detracting from its educational value, particularly if the instructor prompts students to take a tongue-in-cheek perspective while watching. (1958, 25 min.) Available from Stuart Reynolds Productions, 9465 Wilshire Blvd., Beverly Hills, CA 90212.

Impression Formation and Interpersonal Attraction. This film demonstrates the importance of first impressions, central traits, and implicit personality theories as they relate to person perception. (1975, 27 min.) Available from University Films of Canada, 7 Hayden Street, Toronto, Ontario, Canada M4Y 2P2.

The Interpersonal Perception Task-15. Contains 15 brief scenes showing various common social interactions, each followed by a multiple-choice question relating to the nature of the interaction or the status of the people involved. The tape comes with a printed copy of the questions and the correct answers. An essential exercise for psychology classes and all students of social behavior. (1993, 20 min.) Available from Berkeley Media LLC (510-486-9900).

Judgment and Decision Making. This film examines some of the biases and heuristics that influence perception, judgment, decision making, and behavior. Tversky and Kahneman are interviewed and illustrate the availability and representativeness heuristics. (1989, 30 min.) Available from the Annenberg/CPB Project, Intellimation, P.O. Box 1922, Santa Barbara, CA 93116.

Kelley's Model of Causal Attribution. Explains Kelley's model of causal attribution by illustrating the effects of consistency, consensus, and distinctiveness to explain why a man trips over his partner's feet in a dance class. (1989, 20 min.) Available from the Office of Research and Sponsored Programs, Ball State University (317-285-1600).

Nonverbal Communication. Researchers in the field of nonverbal communication are interviewed in this film, hosted by Stanley Milgram. Areas covered include interpersonal distance, eye contact, posture, and gesture. Gender differences in perceiving and understanding nonverbal behavior are also discussed. (1975, 24 min.) Available from Insight Media (1-800-233-9910).

Paralanguage and Proxemics. This film shows how voice quality, rate and volume of speech, word emphasis, inflection, and tone can change the meaning of words. It also examines spatial relationships in various communication systems. (1986, 28 min.) Available from Insight Media (1-800-233-9910).

Productivity and the Self-Fulfilling Prophecy: The Pygmalion Effect. This film presents examples of several situations showing how people's expectations influence others' behavior. (1975, 28 min.) Available from CRM-McGraw-Hill, Box 641, Del Mar, CA 90214.

What do you see? Giving Stereotypes a Second Look. Addressing different motivations for stereotyping, this video presents a group of students sharing their experiences with stereotyping. (1999, 28 min) Available from Insight Media (1-800-233-9910).

Internet

"Baby Face" Nelson. This FBI site provides an interesting look into the life of one of the most famous "baby-faced" lawbreakers of all time. Visit this site at: http://www.fbi.gov/libref/historic/famcases/babyface/babyface.htm.

Spot the fake smiles. This BBC science site presents video clips, based on the research of Paul Ekman, that challenge visitors to test their ability to tell a genuine smile from a fake one. Visit this site at: http://www.bbc.co.uk/science/humanbody/mind/surveys/smiles/

Exploring Nonverbal Communication. At this site, run by the University of California at Santa Cruz, students can test their ability to read nonverbal communication by taking a self-test version of the IPT. Visit the site at: http://nonverbal.ucsc.edu/ipt.html.

HANDOUT 4.3a DETECTION OF DECEPTION

You will be seeing some students talk a little about their background, concerning such details as where they are from, what their parents and siblings are like, what their parents do or did for a living, and what they (the students) and their friends used to do for fun. Some of the students will be telling the truth about their background, and others will be lying about many of the details they give. Your task is to try to distinguish the students who are telling the truth from those who are lying. You should use whatever strategy feels best to you to make your judgments, but please try to do your best.

If you know any of the students well enough to be sure whether or not they are lying, you should make a note of that when reporting your judgments.

HANDOUT 4.3b DETECTION OF DECEPTION

You will be seeing some students talk a little about their background, concerning such details as where they are from, what their parents and siblings are like, what their parents do or did for a living, and what they (the students) and their friends used to do for fun. Some of the students will be telling the truth about their background, and others will be lying about many of the details they give. Your task is to try to distinguish the students who are telling the truth from those who are lying. Please try to do your best. When you are watching the students make their presentations, pay special attention to their faces. Do they look very serious? Are their eyes moving more than usual? Are they or are they not making eye contact with the audience?

If you know any of the students well enough to be sure whether or not they are lying, you should make a note of that when reporting your judgments.

HANDOUT 4.3c DETECTION OF DECEPTION

You will be seeing some students talk a little about their background, concerning such details as where they are from, what their parents and siblings are like, what their parents do or did for a living, and what they (the students) and their friends used to do for fun. Some of the students will be telling the truth about their background, and others will be lying about many of the details they give. Your task is to try to distinguish the students who are telling the truth from those who are lying. Please try to do your best. When you are watching the students make their presentations, pay special attention to their body movements and their voices. Try to ignore their faces and the content of what they're saying and pay more attention to the following: Are their hands and feet fidgety? Do they seem to restlessly shift their posture more than usual? Do their voices rise in pitch? Is there an increase in speech hesitations? The more of these questions to which the answer is "yes," the more likely it is that the person is lying.

If you know any of the students well enough to be sure whether or not they are lying, you should make a note of that when reporting your judgments.

HANDOUT 4.6

For each of the following pairs of cities, circle the city in each pair that has double the population of the other:

1. Rio de Janeiro, Brazil & Buenos Aires, Argentina

2. Baghdad, Iraq & Seoul, South Korea

3. Los Angeles, California & Kinsasha, Democratic Republic of the Congo

4. Berlin, Germany & Lima, Peru

5. Madrid, Spain & Tehran, Iran

6. Montreal, Canada & Bogota, Columbia

7. Chicago, Illinois & Bangkok, Thailand

8. Rome, Italy & Santiago, Chile

9. Paris, France & Sydney, Australia

10. Houston, Texas & Wuhan, China

11. Philadelphia, Pennsylvania & Omdurman, Sudan

12. Tijuana, Mexico & Addis Ababa, Ethiopia

13. San Diego, California & Kiev, Ukraine

14. Dallas, Texas & Giza, Egypt

HANDOUT 4.7a TEST

For each question in this test, select the correct answer. If you're not sure, go with your first instinct. Once you've written an answer, don't give it a second thought.

1.   Recent research has found that social rejection and physical pain both produce activity in which part(s) of the brain?

    a.   Anterior cingulate cortex
    b.   Locus coeruleus
    c.   Reticular formation
    d.   Suprachiasmatic Nuclei

My answer is _____.

2.   When young people were asked to imagine living a day in the life of a particular older man, their ratings of the elderly

    a.   became more positive.
    b.   demonstrated greater ageism.
    c.   remained unchanged.
    d.   were reinforced.

My answer is _____.

3.   The first published research article in social psychology was authored by

    a.   Floyd Allport
    b.   Gordon Allport
    c.   Muzafer Sherif
    d.   Norman Triplett

My answer is _____.

4.   The interactionist perspective is associated with which of the following:

    a.   Edward Ross
    b.   Kurt Lewin
    c.   Max Ringelmann
    d.   William McDougall

My answer is _____.

5.   Max Ringelmann's 1913 research involved which of the following:

    a.   Bicycles
    b.   Eating habits
    c.   Prejudice
    d.   Rope pulling

My answer is _____.

6.   In the study where students watched a 1984 debate between Ronald Reagan and Walter Mondale, with or without funny one-liners, which of the following was TRUE:

   a.   Students who saw the tape without the one-liners rated Reagan more negatively than those who saw the tape with the one-liners but with the audience reactions edited out.
   b.   Students who saw the entire unedited tape rated Reagan more negatively than those who saw the tape without the one-liners.
   c.   Students who saw the tape with one-liners but with the audience reactions edited out rated Reagan more positively than those who saw the entire unedited tape.
   d.   Students who saw the entire tape rated Reagan more positively than students who saw the tape with the one-liners but with the audience reactions edited out.

My answer is ____.

7.   When Japanese and Canadian participants were asked to write brief descriptions of themselves, the Canadians tended to describe themselves _____, whereas the Japanese tended to describe themselves _____.

   a.   in balanced terms; negatively
   b.   in balanced terms; positively
   c.   negatively; in balanced terms
   d.   positively; in balanced terms

My answer is ____.

8.   Which of the following is a TRUE finding of social psychology research:

   a.   Attractive people tend to be seen as less intelligent than unattractive individuals.
   b.   People merely have to imagine being criticized by others to feel a decline in their self-esteem.
   c.   Playing violent video games is cathartic in that it allows for the release of aggression and makes it less likely that people will act violently against others.
   d.   The more reward a person receives for doing an activity, the more the person will come to like the activity.

My answer is ____.

9.   One difference between social psychologists and sociologists is that social psychologists are more likely to

   a.   focus on the group rather than on the individual.
   b.   conduct experiments.
   c.   study such societal variables as social class.
   d.   publish articles in scholarly journals.

My answer is ____.

10.   One of the important theories introduced by Leon Festinger concerned

   a.   individuals' vulnerability to the commands of authority.
   b.   the willingness of people to conform to a wrong majority.
   c.   the tendency of people to learn about themselves through comparison with others.
   d.   the kinds of leaders who elicit the best work from their employees.

My answer is ____.

HANDOUT 4.7b TEST

Quickly go over each question and answer. If your original answer seems correct, leave it alone. If you think another answer is correct, cross out your first instinct answer and write down your second thought.

1.   Recent research has found that social rejection and physical pain both produce activity in which part(s) of the brain?
    a.   Anterior cingulate cortex
    b.   Locus coeruleus
    c.   Reticular formation
    d.   Suprachiasmatic Nuclei

My answer is ____.   On second thought, my answer is _____.

2.   When young people were asked to imagine living a day in the life of a particular older man, their ratings of the elderly
    a.   became more positive.
    b.   demonstrated greater ageism.
    c.   remained unchanged.
    d.   were reinforced.

My answer is ____.   On second thought, my answer is _____.

3.   The first published research article in social psychology was authored by
    a.   Floyd Allport
    b.   Gordon Allport
    c.   Muzafer Sherif
    d.   Norman Triplett

My answer is ____.   On second thought, my answer is _____.

4.   The interactionist perspective is associated with which of the following:
    a.   Edward Ross
    b.   Kurt Lewin
    c.   Max Ringelmann
    d.   William McDougall

My answer is ____.   On second thought, my answer is _____.

5.   Max Ringelmann's 1913 research involved which of the following:
    a.   Bicycles
    b.   Eating habits
    c.   Prejudice
    d.   Rope pulling

My answer is ____.   On second thought, my answer is _____.

6. In the study where students watched a 1984 debate between Ronald Reagan and Walter Mondale, with or without funny one-liners, which of the following was TRUE:
    a. Students who saw the tape without the one-liners rated Reagan more negatively than those who saw the tape with the one-liners but with the audience reactions edited out.
    b. Students who saw the entire unedited tape rated Reagan more negatively than those who saw the tape without the one-liners.
    c. Students who saw the tape with one-liners but with the audience reactions edited out rated Reagan more positively than those who saw the entire unedited tape.
    d. Students who saw the entire tape rated Reagan more positively than students who saw the tape with the one-liners but with the audience reactions edited out.

My answer is ____.   On second thought, my answer is _____.

7. When Japanese and Canadian participants were asked to write brief descriptions of themselves, the Canadians tended to describe themselves _____, whereas the Japanese tended to describe themselves _____.
    a. in balanced terms; negatively
    b. in balanced terms; positively
    c. negatively; in balanced terms
    d. positively; in balanced terms

My answer is ____.   On second thought, my answer is _____.

8. Which of the following is a TRUE finding of social psychology research:
    a. Attractive people tend to be seen as less intelligent than unattractive individuals.
    b. People merely have to imagine being criticized by others to feel a decline in their self-esteem.
    c. Playing violent video games is cathartic in that it allows for the release of aggression and makes it less likely that people will act violently against others.
    d. The more reward a person receives for doing an activity, the more the person will come to like the activity.

My answer is ____.   On second thought, my answer is _____.

9. One difference between social psychologists and sociologists is that social psychologists are more likely to
    a. focus on the group rather than on the individual.
    b. conduct experiments.
    c. study such societal variables as social class.
    d. publish articles in scholarly journals.

My answer is ____.   On second thought, my answer is _____.

10. One of the important theories introduced by Leon Festinger concerned
    a. individuals' vulnerability to the commands of authority.
    b. the willingness of people to conform to a wrong majority.
    c. the tendency of people to learn about themselves through comparison with others.
    d. the kinds of leaders who elicit the best work from their employees.

My answer is ____.   On second thought, my answer is _____.

HANDOUT 4.8a QUIZ SHOW (AUDIENCE MEMBER)

*Please rate the quiz master, the contestant, and yourself on each of the following scales, relative to the average student on campus. (For each scale, circle a number from 1 to 10, where 1 = **much lower than average** and 10 = **much higher than average**.)*

QUIZ MASTER:

Friendliness	1	2	3	4	5	6	7	8	9	10
General Knowledge	1	2	3	4	5	6	7	8	9	10
Nervousness	1	2	3	4	5	6	7	8	9	10

CONTESTANT:

Friendliness	1	2	3	4	5	6	7	8	9	10
General Knowledge	1	2	3	4	5	6	7	8	9	10
Nervousness	1	2	3	4	5	6	7	8	9	10

YOURSELF:

Friendliness	1	2	3	4	5	6	7	8	9	10
General Knowledge	1	2	3	4	5	6	7	8	9	10
Nervousness	1	2	3	4	5	6	7	8	9	10

HANDOUT 4.8b QUIZ SHOW (QUIZ MASTER)

*Please rate the contestant and yourself on each of the following scales, relative to the average student on campus. (For each scale, circle a number from 1 to 10, where 1 = **much lower than average** and 10 = **much higher than average**.)*

CONTESTANT:

Friendliness	1	2	3	4	5	6	7	8	9	10
General Knowledge	1	2	3	4	5	6	7	8	9	10
Nervousness	1	2	3	4	5	6	7	8	9	10

YOURSELF:

Friendliness	1	2	3	4	5	6	7	8	9	10
General Knowledge	1	2	3	4	5	6	7	8	9	10
Nervousness	1	2	3	4	5	6	7	8	9	10

HANDOUT 4.8c QUIZ SHOW (CONTESTANT)

*Please rate the quiz master and yourself on each of the following scales, relative to the average student on campus. (For each scale, circle a number from 1 to 10, where 1 = **much lower than average** and 10 = **much higher than average**.)*

QUIZ MASTER:

Friendliness	1	2	3	4	5	6	7	8	9	10
General Knowledge	1	2	3	4	5	6	7	8	9	10
Nervousness	1	2	3	4	5	6	7	8	9	10

YOURSELF:

Friendliness	1	2	3	4	5	6	7	8	9	10
General Knowledge	1	2	3	4	5	6	7	8	9	10
Nervousness	1	2	3	4	5	6	7	8	9	10

HANDOUT 4.9A RECOMMENDATION FORM

Dear Professor: A student has applied for a summer job with the Conference Office to help with a number of conferences that we will host this summer. Whenever a student applies for one of these jobs, we ask the student's professors for a brief assessment of that student's qualities. As we get closer to making our final hiring decisions, we will ask some of these professors to write a more detailed letter about the student. For this first round, however, all we ask you to do is answer the following questions on this form and send it back to us within three weeks. Thank you in advance for your help.

Student's Name: __Thomas A. Brady__

Your Name: Dr. Robert H. Taylor

Your Title: Associate Professor

Your Department: Romance Languages

How long, and in what capacity, have you known the applicant?

Tom was a student in my Intermediate Spanish (RLSP 105) course two years ago, and is currently a student in my Art, Film, and Literature of the Spanish Civil War (RLSP 331) course.

Do you know anything about this student's non-academic work habits? If so, please elaborate.

I am not familiar with Tom's non-academic work habits; I can comment only on Tom's work in my classes.

Please list a few traits, or personal characteristics, which you think accurately describe this student:

Tom seems to me to be sincere, self-disciplined, happy, and productive.

****

Based on what the professor wrote about Thomas Brady, how positive or negative is your overall impression of this student?

1	2	3	4	5	6	7	8
very negative							very positive

HANDOUT 4.9B RECOMMENDATION FORM

Dear Professor: A student has applied for a summer job with the Conference Office to help with a number of conferences that we will host this summer. Whenever a student applies for one of these jobs, we ask the student's professors for a brief assessment of that student's qualities. As we get closer to making our final hiring decisions, we will ask some of these professors to write a more detailed letter about the student. For this first round, however, all we ask you to do is answer the following questions on this form and send it back to us within three weeks. Thank you in advance for your help.

Student's Name: **Thomas A. Brady**

Your Name: Dr. Robert H. Taylor

Your Title: Associate Professor

Your Department: Romance Languages

How long, and in what capacity, have you known the applicant:

Tom was a student in my Intermediate Spanish (RLSP 105) course two years ago, and is currently a student in my Art, Film, and Literature of the Spanish Civil War (RLSP 331) course.

Do you know anything about this student's non-academic work habits? If so, please elaborate.

I am not familiar with Tom's non-academic work habits; I can comment only on Tom's work in my classes.

Please list a few traits, or personal characteristics, that you think accurately describe this student:

Tom seems to me to be sincere, self-disciplined, happy, inoffensive, and productive.

****

Based on what the professor wrote about Thomas Brady, how positive or negative is your overall impression of this student?

1	2	3	4	5	6	7	8
very negative							very positive

HANDOUT 4.11A FORMING IMPRESSIONS

Imagine an individual who has the following set of traits or characteristics. As you learn of these traits, try to form a complete impression of this person.

This individual is:

intelligent

skillful

industrious

warm

determined

practical

cautious

1.   What is your overall impression of this individual?

1	2	3	4	5	6	7
very unfavorable					very favorable	

2.   How likable or unlikable do you think this person would be?

1	2	3	4	5	6	7
very likable					very unlikable	

3.   In your own words, what do you think is meant by "determined" as a description of this individual?

4.   In your own words, what do you think is meant by "cautious" as a description of this individual?

5.   For each of the following traits, please indicate whether or not you think the trait probably describes this individual accurately by circling either "YES" or "NO":

A.   generous   YES   NO
B.   wise   YES   NO
C.   happy   YES   NO
D.   good-natured   YES   NO
E.   reliable   YES   NO
F.   important   YES   NO

HANDOUT 4.11B FORMING IMPRESSIONS

Imagine an individual who has the following set of traits or characteristics. As you learn of these traits, try to form a complete impression of this person.

This individual is:

intelligent

skillful

industrious

cold

determined

practical

cautious

1. What is your overall impression of this individual?

1	2	3	4	5	6	7
very unfavorable					very favorable	

2. How likable or unlikable do you think this person would be?

1	2	3	4	5	6	7
very likable					very unlikable	

3. In your own words, what do you think is meant by "determined" as a description of this individual?

4. In your own words, what do you think is meant by "cautious" as a description of this individual?

5. For each of the following traits, please indicate whether or not you think the trait probably describes this individual accurately by circling either "YES" or "NO":

A.	generous	YES	NO
B.	wise	YES	NO
C.	happy	YES	NO
D.	good-natured	YES	NO
E.	reliable	YES	NO
F.	important	YES	NO

HANDOUT 4.11C FORMING IMPRESSIONS

Imagine an individual who has the following set of traits or characteristics. As you learn of these traits, try to form a complete impression of this person.

This individual is:

intelligent

skillful

industrious

determined

practical

cautious

1.   What is your overall impression of this individual?

1	2	3	4	5	6	7
very unfavorable					very favorable	

2.   How likable or unlikable do you think this person would be?

1	2	3	4	5	6	7
very likable					very unlikable	

3.   In your own words, what do you think is meant by "determined" as a description of this individual?

4.   In your own words, what do you think is meant by "cautious" as a description of this individual?

5.   For each of the following traits, please indicate whether or not you think the trait probably describes this individual accurately by circling either "YES" or "NO":

   A.   generous   YES   NO
   B.   wise   YES   NO
   C.   happy   YES   NO
   D.   good-natured   YES   NO
   E.   reliable   YES   NO
   F.   important   YES   NO

HANDOUT 4.11d FORMING IMPRESSIONS

Imagine an individual who has the following set of traits or characteristics. As you learn of these traits, try to form a complete impression of this person.

This individual is:

intelligent

skillful

industrious

polite

determined

practical

cautious

1. What is your overall impression of this individual?

    1   2   3   4   5   6   7
    very unfavorable   very favorable

2. How likable or unlikable do you think this person would be?

    1   2   3   4   5   6   7
    very likable   very unlikable

3. In your own words, what do you think is meant by "determined" as a description of this individual?

4. In your own words, what do you think is meant by "cautious" as a description of this individual?

5. For each of the following traits, please indicate whether or not you think the trait probably describes this individual accurately by circling either "YES" or "NO":

    A. generous   YES   NO
    B. wise   YES   NO
    C. happy   YES   NO
    D. good-natured   YES   NO
    E. reliable   YES   NO
    F. important   YES   NO

HANDOUT 4.11e FORMING IMPRESSIONS

Imagine an individual who has the following set of traits or characteristics. As you learn of these traits, try to form a complete impression of this person.

This individual is:

intelligent

skillful

industrious

blunt

determined

practical

cautious

1.   What is your overall impression of this individual?

1	2	3	4	5	6	7
very unfavorable					very favorable	

2.   How likable or unlikable do you think this person would be?

1	2	3	4	5	6	7
very likable					very unlikable	

3.   In your own words, what do you think is meant by "determined" as a description of this individual?

4.   In your own words, what do you think is meant by "cautious" as a description of this individual?

5.   For each of the following traits, please indicate whether or not you think the trait probably describes this individual accurately by circling either "YES" or "NO":

   A.   generous   YES   NO
   B.   wise   YES   NO
   C.   happy   YES   NO
   D.   good-natured   YES   NO
   E.   reliable   YES   NO
   F.   important   YES   NO

HANDOUT 4.12A

You have just interviewed two candidates for the position of counselor in a summer camp. As you read your notes from each of the interviews, you need to make a decision as to whether or not you would recommend that the camp hire the person.

Penelope Bates

Penelope is intelligent. She is also kind and loves children. She is a skilled tennis player. She is emotional and high-strung. She is talkative, stubborn, and somewhat sloppy.

My recommendation regarding hiring her as a counselor:

1	2	3	4	5
definitely do not hire	leaning toward not	neutral	leaning toward hiring	definitely hire

Derek Lee

Derek is a natural leader. He is athletic and loves kids. He is self-assured and somewhat arrogant. He has an offbeat sense of humor. He is egotistical, cynical, and impatient.

My recommendation regarding hiring him as a counselor:

1	2	3	4	5
definitely do not hire	leaning toward not	neutral	leaning toward hiring	definitely hire

HANDOUT 4.12B

You have just interviewed two candidates for the position of counselor in a summer camp. As you read your notes from each of the interviews, you need to make a decision as to whether or not you would recommend that the camp hire the person.

Penelope Bates

Penelope is talkative, stubborn, and somewhat sloppy. She is emotional and high-strung. She is a skilled tennis player. She is also kind and loves children. She is intelligent.

My recommendation regarding hiring her as a counselor:

1	2	3	4	5
definitely do not hire	leaning toward not	neutral	leaning toward hiring	definitely hire

Derek Lee

Derek is egotistical, cynical, and impatient. He has an offbeat sense of humor. He is athletic and loves kids. He is self-assured and somewhat arrogant. He is a natural leader.

My recommendation regarding hiring him as a counselor:

1	2	3	4	5
definitely do not hire	leaning toward not	neutral	leaning toward hiring	definitely hire

HANDOUT 4.13A RESPONDER QUESTIONS

Please answer each of the following questions in the spaces provided. Please answer these questions honestly. Do not write your name anywhere on this page; your responses will be read by another student.

1. What are two or three of your favorite movies of all time?

2. What would you do if you wanted to liven things up at a party?

3. What kinds of settings or situations do you seek out if you want to meet new people?

4. If you had to donate some money to a charity, which charity would you choose and why?

5. In which situations are you most talkative? What is it about these situations that makes you like to talk?

HANDOUT 4.13B RESPONDER QUESTIONS

Please answer each of the following questions on a separate piece of paper. Do not repeat the questions on this other sheet of paper; simply write the <u>number</u> of each question, followed by the answer. Please do, however, write "Handout 4.16b" on the top-right corner of the page. When you are asked to turn in your handouts, turn in the page with the answers, not this page with the questions.

Please answer these questions honestly. Do not write your name anywhere on the paper with your answers; your responses will be read by another student.

Please limit your responses to just a few sentences each.

1.   What are two or three of your favorite movies of all time?

2.   What would you do if you wanted to liven things up at a party?

3.   What kinds of settings or situations do you seek out if you want to meet new people?

4.   If you had to donate some money to a charity, which charity would you choose and why?

5.   In which situations are you most talkative? What is it about these situations that makes you like to talk?

HANDOUT 4.13C RESPONDER QUESTIONS

Please answer each of the following questions in the spaces provided. Please answer these questions honestly. Do not write your name anywhere on this page; your responses will be read by another student.

1.   What are two or three of your favorite movies of all time?

2.   In what situations do you wish you could be more outgoing?

3.   What factors make it hard for you to really open up to people?

4.   If you had to donate some money to a charity, which charity would you choose and why?

5.   What things do you dislike about loud parties?

HANDOUT 4.13D RESPONDER QUESTIONS

Please answer each of the following questions on a separate piece of paper. Do not repeat the questions on this other sheet of paper; simply write the <u>number</u> of each question, followed by the answer. Please do, however, write "Handout 4.16d" on the top-right corner of the page. When you are asked to turn in your handouts, turn in the page with the answers, not this page with the questions.

Please answer these questions honestly. Do not write your name anywhere on the paper with your answers; your responses will be read by another student.

Please limit your responses to just a few sentences each.

1.   What are two or three of your favorite movies of all time?

2.   In what situations do you wish you could be more outgoing?

3.   What factors make it hard for you to really open up to people?

4.   If you had to donate some money to a charity, which charity would you choose and why?

5.   What things do you dislike about loud parties?

HANDOUT 4.13E JUDGE'S FORM

Handout #:_____

On the line above, print the number and letter of the handout that was completed by the person whom you are judging.

In this task, we would like you to judge the other student on a few traits. The first trait concerns how extroverted or introverted you think the student really is. Below are definitions of what is meant by these two traits:

Extroverts *are typically outgoing, sociable, energetic, confident, talkative, and enthusiastic. Generally confident and relaxed in social situations, this type of person rarely has trouble making conversation with others. This type of person also makes friends easily and is usually able to make a favorable impression on others quickly.*

Introverts *are typically shy, timid, reserved, quiet, distant, and retiring. This type of person usually prefers to read a book or have a serious discussion with a close friend rather than attend loud and large social gatherings. Often this type of person seems awkward and ill at ease in social situations.*

Please rate the other student along the following dimensions. For each question, circle one number to indicate your judgment.

1. How extroverted or introverted do you think this student is?

    1   2   3   4   5   6   7   8
    very extroverted   very introverted

2. How intelligent do you think this student is?

    1   2   3   4   5   6   7   8
    not at all intelligent   very intelligent

3. How much do you think you would like this student?

    1   2   3   4   5   6   7   8
      very little   very much

4. How popular do you think this student is?

    1   2   3   4   5   6   7   8
    not at all popular   very popular

CHAPTER 5

Stereotypes, Prejudice, and Discrimination

LEARNING OBJECTIVES: GUIDELINES FOR STUDY

You should be able to do each of the following by the conclusion of Chapter 5.

1. Define and distinguish the concepts of stereotyping, prejudice, and discrimination. Explain what is meant by modern and implicit racism and explain how each is measured empirically (*pp. 147-148*)

2. Discuss recent psychological findings regarding the processes of interracial perception and interaction. (*pp. 148-154*)

3. Discuss the role of ambivalent sexism and double standards when it comes to understanding discrimination based on gender. (*pp. 155-158*)

4. Explain how prejudice differs from stereotyping. Describe the significance of realistic conflict theory—as well as the Robbers Cave study—for understanding prejudice. (*pp. 160-162*)

5. Explain social identity theory and how it accounts for ingroup favoritism. Discuss cultural differences in social identity processes, as well as the role of ideology when it comes to understanding prejudice. (*pp. 162-165*)

6. Discuss the role of cultural factors in social identity and prejudice. Explain how individual motives affect issues related to prejudice and status. (*pp. 164-165*)

7. Explain the different ways in which stereotypes form. Describe the human tendencies towards social categorization, dehumanization, and the formation of ingroup/outgroup distinctions, and discuss the repercussions of these tendencies. (*pp. 166-169*)

8. Describe the ways in which stereotypes are perpetuated, including illusory correlation, attributional processes, subtyping, and confirmation bias. (*pp. 169-172*)

9. Examine the impact of socialization and social role theory on the development of gender stereotypes. Discuss the stereotype content model (*pp. 172-178*)

10. Identify factors that can impact whether or not stereotypes influence social judgment. Discuss the question of whether stereotyping is automatic or intentional, and consider the implications of this issue for real-world events, such as the police shooting of Amadou Diallo. (*pp. 178-186*)

11. Describe the effects of discrimination from the target's perspective. Explain the concept of stereotype threat, including the reasons it happens and its range of consequences. Consider the different situations likely to elicit stereotype threat, and the different populations susceptible to stereotype-threat effects. (*pp. 186-192*)

12. Explain the contact hypothesis and the conditions that enable intergroup contact to reduce prejudice. Describe the jigsaw classroom and how it can reduce prejudice. (*pp. 192-196*)

DETAILED CHAPTER OUTLINE

I. The Nature of the Problem
  A. Persistence and Change
  B. Defining our Terms
    1. Stereotyping, Prejudice, & Discrimination
    2. Ingroups & Outgroups
    3. Racism
      a) modern racism
      b) implicit racism
      c) interracial perceptions
      d) interracial interactions
    4. Sexism
      a) ambivalent sexism
      b) double standards and sexism
II. Causes of the Problem: Intergroup and Motivational Factors
  A. Intergroup Conflict
    1. Robbers Cave: Setting the stage
    2. Realistic conflict theory
  B. Social Identity Theory
    1. Basic predictions
      a) threats to one's self-esteem heighten the need for ingroup favoritism
      b) expressions of ingroup favoritism enhance one's self-esteem
    2. Situational and individual differences
    3. Culture and social identity
  C. Implicit Theories and Ideologies
    1. Social dominance orientation
    2. System justification
III. Causes of the Problem: Cognitive and Cultural Factors
  A. Social Categorization
  B. Ingroups versus Outgroups
    1. Outgroup homogeneity
    2. Dehumanization
  C. How Stereotypes Survive and Self-Perpetuate
    1. Illusory correlations
    2. Attributions
    3. Subtyping
    4. Confirmation biases and self-fulfilling prophecies
    5. Stereotype accuracy?
  D Stereotype Formation
    1. Culture and socialization
    2. Gender and Social Role Theory
    3. Stereotype Content Model
  C. Is Stereotyping Inevitable? Automatic versus Intentional Processes
    1. Stereotypes as (sometimes) automatic
    2. Motivation: Fueling activation or putting on the brakes
    3. Exerting control: The need for cognitive resources
    4. Automaticity versus control: Additional factors
    5. "41 Shots" Revisited

LECTURE AND DISCUSSION IDEAS

Idea 1.   Homegrown Stereotypes

The text's discussion of stereotypes pertains to the ways that ingroup members think about outgroup members. The discussion can be extended to include another type of stereotype—the "homegrown" stereotype. Homegrown stereotypes reflect the beliefs that people hold about their own ingroup. For example, in one survey, college students were asked how comfortable they felt about college drinking practices and how comfortable the rest of the students on campus felt about it. Students consistently thought that most students were fairly comfortable with the amount of drinking that was going on (the homegrown stereotype), even though they themselves were less comfortable with it. In this case, the homegrown stereotype is combined with pluralistic ignorance; most of the students who were surveyed believed that they themselves were less comfortable with drinking behaviors than were the rest of the students.

In a second example, the members of a religious community were strictly forbidden from card playing, drinking, and smoking. However, even though most members of the community believed that everyone else supported these church bans (the homegrown stereotype), in private, in the company of the researcher, most played cards, smoked, and drank. They too were demonstrating pluralistic ignorance.

Homegrown stereotypes are not always accompanied by pluralistic ignorance. In the wake of the September 11, 2001, attacks many Americans took to flying the flag. This was done as an expression of patriotic self-presentation directed at the ingroup, which gave rise to the homegrown stereotype that Americans are a patriotic group. This is how most homegrown stereotypes come to be. Self-presentations that are enacted by most group members are assumed to be the values that apply to the entire group. This kind of self-stereotyping is most likely to happen when conditions heighten the salience of group identity, as happened on September 11, 2001.

Ingroup members tend to present themselves differently to each other than they do to outgroup members. For example, a teacher presents herself one way to students, but another way when she relaxes in the company of other teachers in the staff lounge. Neither presentation is necessarily an authentic one, reflecting the private self. However, the way that she presents herself to other teachers is more likely to conform to a homegrown stereotype of what teachers are like.

Self-presentations that reflect homegrown stereotypes usually include some degree of outgroup antagonism. For example, teachers in one high-school setting strongly believed that the majority of teachers distrusted pupils and considered it necessary to focus on maintaining order and strict discipline in the school, even though they themselves did not harbor such an anti-student sentiment. The homegrown stereotype was supported by the views that teachers expressed publicly to each other. The same outgroup antagonism was evident in a survey of prison guards and prisoners. Everyone surveyed overestimated the harshness of their own group's attitude toward the other group. Both prisoners and guards tended to see their groups as hostile and unsympathetic to the other group, even though they themselves held a more moderated private view.

Self-presentations also produce homegrown stereotypes when they're motivated by a desire to be seen as loyal to one's ingroup and its values. For example, nurses, who stereotypically present a facade of professionalism, calmness, and competence often cover up feelings of anxiety and stress because they feel that expressing such feelings would deviate from the way that nurses are supposed to behave.

What the homegrown stereotype says about group members depends not only on the way that individual members present themselves, but also on who is doing the presentation. Some group members are more vocal, public, and expressive than are others. They are likely to be the people who hold the most prototypical views. For example, in a school with an extreme liberal reputation, it is the conspicuous, extreme liberal minority that defines the homegrown stereotype, not the less extreme majority.

Homegrown stereotypes are generally accurate in the sense that they accurately reflect how group members want to present themselves publicly, even if they are inaccurate insofar as members' private self-ratings. People are better at convincing others of what they are like than at convincing themselves.

Ask students to compare homegrown and outgroup stereotypes. How do they differ in terms of origin, the mechanisms that perpetuate them, and the functions that they serve? What are some homegrown stereotypes that they have discerned in their own groups? Might those homegrown stereotypes be reflecting pluralistic ignorance? How would they find out?

Prentice, D. A., & Miller, D. T. (2002). The emergence of homegrown stereotypes. American Psychologist, 57, 352-359.

Idea 2. Social Identity and College Rivalries

Many colleges and universities have a rival that they love to hate. If you are at such a school, talking about this rivalry can provide an excellent way to introduce social identity theory. Why do students at your school assume that students at the other school have a number of negative qualities? Why do students at your school love to heckle the other team at basketball or football games? Social identity theory (Tajfel, 1982) suggests that we favor our own group to elevate the status of our own group and that elevating the status of our group can enhance our own self-esteem. In the case of college rivalries, basking in reflected glory (Cialdini & colleagues, 1976) is one example of this effect.

Cialdini, R. B., Borden, R. J., Thorne, A., Walker, M. R., Freeman, S., & Sloan, L. R. (1976). Basking in reflected glory: Three (football) field studies. Journal of Personality and Social Psychology, 34, 366-375.

Tajfel, H. (Ed.). (1982). Social identity and intergroup relations. London: Cambridge University Press.

Idea 3. Sexism and Barbie Dolls

Several years ago Mattel came out with a version of their famous Barbie doll that said, "Math class is tough" (many reports stated the quote as "Math is hard," but same idea). You might ask your students to come up with other examples of media portrayals of women in ways that are sexist. It should not take long to come up with a list of ways that women are portrayed in the media that help perpetuate stereotypes. You might ask students, "What impact do these images in the media have on your lives and on your views of women?" Although students can easily come up with sexist examples from the media, most will think that these examples are unlikely to affect them. Ask students to think critically about this belief that they are unaffected by these images. Is this just another example of the self-serving biases described in Chapter 3? Ask students to think of ways that they can minimize the impact of such images.

One appropriate study you may cite in conjunction with the topic was conducted by Davies, Spencer, and Steele (2005). The researchers found that exposing participants to gender-stereotypic television commercials resulted in women being less likely to choose to be leaders on an ensuing task. In the second part of the study, the researchers were able to defuse the effects of the gender stereotypic commercials by assigning some female participants to read a modified description of the leadership task that included research findings showing that men and women were equally capable in performing such tasks.

Davies, P.G., Spencer, S.J., & Steele, C.M. (2005). Clearing the air: Identity safety moderates the effects of stereotype threat on women's leadership aspirations. Journal of Personality and Social Psychology, 88, 2, 276-287.

Idea 4.   Two Examples of Social Role Theory at Work

According to social role theory, differences between men and women are based on behavioral differences that are mistakenly attributed to gender differences, when in fact they are due to social roles. To enhance students' understanding of the theory, you might want to discuss the following two studies that are based on the theory.

The first study examines how social role theory contributes to gender stereotypes in the area of gender differences in mathematics (Nosek, Banaji, and Greenwald, 2002). The researchers argued that the dual observation that men like to study math more than women do and that men tend to outperform women at math is not a function of real gender differences. Rather, it is the result of the interaction of the male or female's social role identity and related experiences.

Using implicit measures of math attitude, math-identity, math-gender stereotypes, and gender identity, the researchers found that strength of male identity was positively correlated with liking for math and math identity, but that strength of female identity was negatively correlated with liking for math and math identity. The authors concluded that being categorized at birth as male or female produces identification with one's social group and that this identity shapes and is shaped by experiences that are expected of one's social group. From such experiences, flow preferences (such as a like or dislike for math) and abilities (such as doing well or poorly in math) that can enhance or limit the individual.

In another study of social role theory, Yoder, Hogue, Newman, Metz, and LaVigne (2002) explored how gender-role expectations could lead to gender differences in door-holding behavior in certain contexts. The researchers unobtrusively observed college-age male-female pairs (where one opened a door for the other) at sixteen different locations. Some were everyday locations, such as fast-food restaurants, a mall, and university buildings. Others were dating venues, such as skating rinks and sit-down restaurants. They found that in everyday locations, women were more likely to hold the doors open for men than vice versa (55.2% versus 44.8%). They noted that earlier studies had found a much smaller percentage of women holding doors for men. They interpret these findings to mean that door holding, which used to have a connotation of chivalry (a masculine domain), has become associated with politeness or even caregiving (both of which are feminine domains).

But in the dating contexts, the figures changed, with two thirds of males holding the doors for the females. The inconsistency across contexts led the researchers to conclude that in dating situations, door holding reflects benevolent sexism. In essence, males are appearing to be kind but are really conveying a message of male dominance and female weakness.

Nosek, B. A., Mahzarin, R. B., and Greenwald, A. G. (2002). Math = male, me = female, therefore math γ me. Journal of Personality and Social Psychology, 83, 44-59.

Yoder, J. D., Hogue, M., Newman, R., Metz, L., and LaVigne, T. (2002). Exploring moderators of gender differences: Contextual differences in door-holding behavior. Journal of Applied Social Psychology, 32, 1682-1686.

Idea 5.   Racism on College Campuses

In discussing racism, many students may think of it as a problem of the past or as a problem that isn't seen in their environment. Yet there have been many incidents of racism on college campuses recently. The film *Racism 101* documents a number of these incidents. You might ask students to think of examples from your own campus where racism of both the blatant and modern forms can be seen. Many students will be surprised by the extent to which racism is a feature of their own environment.

Idea 6.   The Nature and Prevalence of Hate Groups

What constitutes a hate group? The Southern Poverty Law Center, which attempts to track such groups, has identified more than 500 different active hate groups. This number has increased in recent years, with a pronounced spike in hate group activity reported in the immediate wake of Barack Obama's election in November 2008. You might ask your students to try to explain this increase. Is it due to economics? Increased racial and religious tension? Is it an artifact of watching for these groups more vigilantly? Although a conclusive answer is unlikely, this is a timely topic that should interest your students.

Not all of these groups have been named without controversy. The Nation of Islam, a prominent African-American group that organized the "million man march" and which is led by Minister Louis Farrakhan, has also been listed as a hate group by the Southern Poverty Law Center. You might challenge your students to try to define a hate group. You can also visit the web site of the Southern Poverty Law Center at http://www.splcenter.org/

Idea 7.   Disparagement Humor and Prejudice

In disparagement humor, a specific group is denigrated, belittled, or insulted. The target can be a race, a sex, a religion, an ethnicity, or an age group. The joke is conveyed through the use of negative stereotypes. Students can probably name several comedians and radio talk-show hosts who have used this type of humor. They are also likely to be familiar with the bigoted Archie Bunker character in the TV sitcom *All in the Family,* the four foul-mouthed, wildly politically incorrect third-graders featured in Comedy Central's *South Park* cartoon, and with actor Sacha Baron Cohen's portrayal of a fictional lecherous, anti-Semitic and racist Kazakh journalist in *Borat: Cultural Learnings of America for Make Benefit Glorious Nation of Kazakhstan.*

Ask your students to speculate on the effects of such humor. Do they think that this type of humor is a positive indication of how far we have come as a society that we are now able to make fun of the absurd stereotypical beliefs of the past? Do characters like Borat appear so foolish that they cause prejudiced individuals to reject their prejudiced beliefs? Or, do they see negative social consequences to this type of humor? Do the media legitimatize these stereotypes? Does exposure to this sort of humor create a norm of tolerance that allows for the degradation of others and serves to perpetuate prejudice?

In *Jokes and their Relation to the Unconscious* (1905/1991), Freud said that jokes allow us to express aggressive feelings in a socially approved way. So, people enjoy a disparaging joke because it allows them to express feelings of hate that they normally keep to themselves. If Freud was right and jokes are expressions of our hidden aggressive desires, is it good or bad to express such desires? Does having a safe outlet for blowing off steam allow us to go out into the world and behave decently toward others? Or does it expand the boundaries of appropriate conduct and increase the likelihood that such stereotypes will be activated and applied in our next encounter with a member of the target group?

Do your students think that disparaging humor has a different effect on those who are high in prejudice as opposed to those who are low in prejudice? Would one group find disparaging humor more amusing? Do prejudiced people laugh at and enjoy these kinds of jokes because they affirm their stereotypes? Or would those high in prejudice sense that they themselves are the butt of the jokes and avoid such humor? Why would people who are without any prejudice, or a need to vent aggressive impulses, find such jokes to be funny at all?

And does it matter who delivers the joke? Are racist, Black target jokes harmless if delivered by a Black person? Are jokes that reinforce anti-Semitic stereotypes benign when told by a Jewish comedian?

You might also ask students to consider "equal opportunity bigots" like Archie Bunker and Borat who insult almost everyone. Are they so over the top that no one could possibly take them seriously?

You might wish to introduce some pertinent research findings. For example, one study (Hobden & Olson, 1994) found that reciting jokes that made fun of lawyers led participants to have a more negative attitude toward lawyers. Another study (Ford, 1997) found that Whites who viewed skits that disparaged Blacks were more likely later to make stereotyped judgments concerning a Black target than participants who watched a neutral skit. And a third study (Thomas and Esses, 2004) found that men who scored high in hostile sexism were more likely than men who scored low on the scale to appreciate the humor in jokes that disparaged women.

Ford, T.E. (1997). Effects of stereotypical television portrayals of African-Americans on person perception. Social Psychology Quarterly, 60, 266-278.

Freud, S. (1905/1991). Jokes and their Relation to the Unconscious. Harmondsworth: Penguin.

Hobden, K.L. & Olson, J.M. (1994). From jest to antipathy: Disparagement humor as a source of dissonance-motivated attitude change. Basic & Applied Social Psychology, 15, 3, 239-249.

Thomas, C.A. & Esses, V.M. (2004). Individual differences in reactions to sexist humor. Group Processes & Intergroup Relations, 7, 1, 89-100.

Idea 8.   Stereotype Threat

The text reports research on stereotype threat (Spencer, Steele, & Quinn, 1999; Steele, 1997; Steele & Aronson, 1995) that examines how concerns about being stereotyped can affect the academic performance of women and African-Americans. Although this research has focused on these groups, this perspective suggests that stereotype threat can occur in many other settings and to many other groups of people. Elderly people may feel stereotype threat when asked to perform a memory task. European-American students may feel stereotype threat on the basketball court when competing with African-Americans. Men might feel stereotype threat when they attend a baby shower or are asked to hold a baby. Ask your students to think of a time when they might have felt stereotype threat—the sense that others might be evaluating them stereotypically.

Spencer, S. J., Steele, C. M., & Quinn, D. M. (1999). Stereotype threat and women's math performance. Journal of Experimental Social Psychology, 35, 4-29.

Steele, C. M. (1997). A threat in the air: How stereotypes shape intellectual identity and performance. American Psychologist, 52, 613-629.

Steele, C.M., & Aronson, J. (1995). Stereotype threat and the intellectual test performance of African-Americans. Journal of Personality and Social Psychology, 69, 797-811.

CLASSROOM ACTIVITIES

Activity 1. Stereotypes and Prejudice

This activity introduces students to the topic of stereotyping and prejudice by demonstrating their own stereotyping of two groups: the elderly and the disabled. It's best to have students complete the handouts before they've read the chapter.

Without explanation, other than telling them not to put their name on it, distribute **Handout 5.1a**, **Handout 5.1b**, and **Handout 5.1c** to all students, so that each one-third of the class receives a different handout (without their knowing that the handouts differ).

The handouts vary as follows: Handout 5.1a concerns a 28-year-old female who tells the police that she has seen a Bigfoot-like creature. Handout 5.1b is identical, except that the woman's age is now 73. Handout 5.1c also concerns a woman who reports seeing a Bigfoot-like creature, but this time the handout does not state the woman's age, but describes her as sitting in a wheelchair. In each case, students are asked to make a judgment as to the credibility of the woman.

After collecting the handouts. Sort them separately. Then, tally the results on the board as follows:

	Handout 5.1a	Handout 5.1b	Handout 5.1c
may have seen Bigfoot			
probably saw unusual natural phenomenon			
probably imagined			
probably made it up			

Generally, the students view the younger woman as more credible than either the older woman or the disabled one. This provides a good lead into a discussion of stereotypes, and how and why they form.

What if this bombs? This activity is usually bombproof. Either way, it should lead to an interesting discussion. If students display stereotyping, as expected, they might attempt to justify their views, which would lead to a discussion on the accuracy of stereotypes. In the unlikely event that students do not show evidence of stereotyping, this too could lead to a good discussion about why the class deviated from the expected stereotypical responses.

Activity 2. An Exercise about Sexism

Today's undergraduates might think that sexism is a problem of past generations and that women today have the same opportunities and expectations as do men. This activity might shake those beliefs. Do the exercise before discussing sexism in class.

Ask your students to list all the reasons they can think of for why they might want to be the opposite sex and, when they are finished, to list all the reasons they can think of for wanting to be the sex they are. The exercise is done anonymously, with students indicating only whether they are male or female. When they are finished with the second list, have them count the number of items on each list and write the total at the bottom of the respective page. Collect the lists. Write the totals on the board under four headings: males being female, females being male, males being male, and females being female. Compute the mean for each column (if it is a large class, simply examine one-third or one-half of the responses).

Generally, females are able to think of more reasons to want to be male than males can think of to want to be female. As for wanting to be one's own gender, the difference between males and females will also provide provocative material for a discussion. Samples of the lists' contents can also be shared with the class at this time, or they could be summarized at the next class session.

● *What if this bombs?* The exercise could bomb if there are no gender differences in the lengths of the lists. In that case, you can note that much progress has been made in the area of sex discrimination. As mentioned in the text, women are no longer devalued, as they were not so long ago when Philip Goldberg (1968) found that even women were prejudiced against women. Moreover, if there are no findings of sexism in class, students can weigh in on whether the class findings reflect the state of sexism in society at large.

Bronstein, P.A., & Quina, K. (Eds.), (1988). Teaching a Psychology of People: Resources for Gender and Sociocultural Awareness. Washington, D.C.: American Psychological Association.

Goldberg, P. (1968). Are women prejudiced against women? Transaction, 5, 28-30.

Activity 3. "The Breakfast Club," Stereotyping, and the Contact Hypothesis

Writing in Teaching of Psychology, Andrew Christopher and colleagues (2004) suggest using the film *The Breakfast Club* (Tanen & Hughes, 1985), or selected clips from it, to illustrate concepts related to prejudice, stereotypes, discrimination, and especially the contact hypothesis.

The 92-minute film depicts five high school students who have been assigned to spend a Saturday together in detention. Each of the five students fits a common teen stereotype: there's an "athlete," a "brain," a "princess," a "criminal," and a "basketcase." In the beginning, it's apparent that the five have nothing in common. As the day progresses, however, the power of the stereotypes wanes as the five begin to relate to each other as unique, complex individuals.

The authors recommend showing the entire film as a good demonstration of the contact hypothesis. They show how scenes from the movie match the following five conditions that are necessary for the contact hypothesis to effectively reduce prejudice.

First, outgroup members must display behaviors and traits that challenge the negative stereotypes associated with their group. In the movie, all five characters do so: Brian (the "brain") has smoked marijuana, failed an easy class, and carries a pornographic picture in his wallet. Andy (the "athlete") has allowed his father to control his life. Alison (the "basketcase") actually desires the company of others. Claire (the "princess") smoked marijuana and has parents who fight a lot. And John (the "criminal") willingly takes responsibility for the others when they skip out of detention showing that he is unselfish.

Second, local authorities and norms must support the contact. In the movie, all the students were thrown together and treated as a group by the principal, Mr. Vernon.

Third, contact must be among individuals of equal status. In the movie, Mr. Vernon establishes their equal status by letting the students know that none of them is deserving of special treatment. Later on in the movie, the characters begin to see that they are alike in many ways.

Fourth, the contact needs to occur at the individual level, a condition that is met because the students are not members of a group as long as they're in detention. They eventually come to treat each other as individuals.

Fifth and last is the condition that members of the groups must work together toward a common goal. In the movie, the goal becomes making Mr. Vernon aware of his prejudicial stereotypical attitude toward all the students.

You might wish to distribute **Handout 5.3** to your students to complete after viewing the film. The handout asks them to describe the scenes that exemplify various topics related to prejudice and stereotyping. This should facilitate a post-film discussion of the issues. One line of discussion can explore how the movie would have differed had the cast been more racially diverse (It was purported to take place in an all-White school).

For instructors who do not wish to spend class time on the entire film, the authors suggest the following clips with their respective quotes as good illustrations of some of the concepts covered in this chapter:

Discrimination: Mr. Vernon calls on Andy (the "athlete") to prop open the door and criticizes him when he can't: "I expected a little more from a varsity letterman." (Clip begins at 0:10.27 and lasts 4.00 minutes)

Prejudice: Andy tells John he is worthless: "You know, Bender, you don't even count. If you disappeared forever it wouldn't make a difference." (Clip begins at 0:11.28 and lasts 3.53 minutes)

Ingroup Favoritism: Students degrade each others' social groups: "I knew you had to be smart to be a, a wrestler." (Same clip as # 2)

Outgroup homogeneity: Claire (the "princess") and John differentiate between social and academic clubs: "Academic clubs aren't the same as other kinds of clubs." (Same clip as # 2)

Fundamental attribution error: Students express their impressions of students who belong to different social groups: "Only burners like you get high." (Same clip as # 2)

Stigmatized targets: Brian (the "brain") implies he and Claire have had sex to avoid confirming that all smart kids are virgins: "It's only because I didn't want her to know I was a virgin, okay?" (Clip begins at 0:35.20 and lasts 1.40 minutes)

Illusory correlation: Brian pulls out his lunch, in which all of the food groups are represented: "Did your mom marry Mr. Rogers?" (Clip begins at 0:39.20 and lasts 3.55 minutes)

Stereotyping: John provides his impersonation of Brian's family life: "Here's my impression of life at Big Bri's house." (Same clip as # 7)

Subtyping: Claire discusses how, when the students return to school on Monday, they will not be able to associate with other members of each student's group: "If Brian came walking up to you in the hall on Monday…you'd say 'hi' to him then cut him all up so your friends wouldn't think that you really liked him." (Clip begins at 1:06.29 and lasts 22.37 minutes)

Realistic conflict theory: John reveals his jealousy of Claire's life: "Don't you ever, ever, compare yourself to me. You got everything, and I got (nothing)." (Same clip as # 9)

The contact hypothesis: Students discuss how they share similar relationships with their parents: "I think your old man and my old man should get together and go bowling." (Same clip as # 9)

 What if this bombs? There is little chance of bombing as students are likely to enjoy viewing the movie or clips and to gain a better understanding of stereotyping, prejudice, and the contact hypothesis as a result.

Christopher, A.N., Walter, J.L., Marek, P. & Koenig, C.S. (2004). Using a "new classic" film to teach about stereotyping and prejudice. Teaching of Psychology, 31, 3, 199-202.

Tanen, N. (producer) & Hughes, J. (producer and director). (1985). The Breakfast Club. Hollywood, CA: Universal City Studios. This movie is available at: http://homevideo.universal studios.com/catalog/catalog_content.html.

Activity 4. The Implicit Association Test

In order to explore the stereotypes and prejudices that exist below our conscious awareness, Greenwald and his colleagues (1998) have developed a covert measure of people's attitudes that utilizes a reaction time procedure. When taking this test, an attitude is paired with pleasant and later with unpleasant words. If people's reaction time in recognizing a word is facilitated when it is paired with a pleasant word compared to when it is paired with an unpleasant word, then a positive implicit attitude is inferred. If people's reaction time in recognizing a word is facilitated when it is paired with an unpleasant word compared to when it is paired with a pleasant word, then a negative implicit attitude is inferred. Greenwald has used this task to measure implicit cognitions about a number of different constructs, including attitudes, stereotypes, and evaluative judgments.

If you have the facilities, you could use the program that Greenwald and his colleagues have developed to test implicit attitudes. They call this the Implicit Association Test. The test can be taken online at: http://implicit.harvard.edu/implicit/

You may also wish to acquaint your students with some of the controversy regarding what the Implicit Association Test actually measures. The topic was addressed by Bruce Bower in an article for Science News (2006).

Bower reports that critics have questioned the validity of the test. They claimed that IAT scores are meaningless because they are not applicable to real-world behaviors. For example, a racial IAT score of 1.3 indicates a strong unconscious bias against Blacks, but it's not clear how a person with that score would differ from one with a 1.0 score when it comes to making hiring decisions. A related problem involves the poorly defined range of scores that the test encompasses. So, it remains unknown whether a person whose score suggests an anti-Black bias regards Blacks and Whites positively, only whites more so; regards blacks and whites negatively, only whites more so; or regards Blacks negatively and Whites positively.

In a similar vein, a second line of criticism of the test's validity asserts that the test is actually measuring one's familiarity with one's own ingroup, not antipathy toward an outgroup. For example, in one study, British subjects easily associated any British citizens, from the Queen Mother to a British mass murderer, with pleasant words, whereas an array of foreigners that included Albert Einstein were more easily linked to unpleasant words. The linking of racial groups to "pleasant" and "unpleasant" labels might also be simply tapping into familiarity with how the media portrays these cultural groups. Still other critics suggest that it can take longer to react to black faces and names because those stimuli give rise to feelings of compassion and guilt over African-Americans' history, not because of unconscious hostility.

Finally, there is the fact that after one or two administrations, people find it easy to fake their scores so as to appear to be totally without prejudice. In one study, after German subjects took the test that assessed their implicit attitudes toward Turks, they were asked to take the test a second time and fake their responses. Experts studying the results found it impossible to tell which tests were the first administrations and which were the second tests that had been purposefully faked.

🔴*What if this bombs?* This activity should be relatively bombproof. Students should find it enjoyable to test their implicit cognitions using this procedure.

Bower, B. 2006. The bias finders. Science News, 169, 16, 250-253.

Greenwald, A. G., McGhee, D. E., Schwartz, L.K. (1998). Measuring individual differences in implicit cognition: The implicit association test. Journal of Personality and Social Psychology, 75, 1464-1480.

MULTIMEDIA RESOURCES

Video

Age & Attitudes. This ABC News *Prime Time Live* special report uses hidden cameras to get a peek at how older workers are discriminated against on the job market. A team of discrimination testers reveals some of the obstacles faced by talented, motivated people because of age discrimination, which some experts say is often harder to detect than race or gender bias. (1994, 16 min.) Available from corVision Media (800-537-3130).

Anti-Gay Hate Crime. This video chronicles the disturbing rise in anti-gay hate crimes. It tours the Christian Right's anti-gay factions and interview experts who speculate on why these crimes have escalated. (1999, 50 min) Available from Insight Media (800-233-9910).

A Question of Fairness. This video of an *NBC Dateline* special report presents opinions from both sides in the affirmative action controversy at the University of Michigan. (2003, 1 hour) Available from Burrelle's Transcripts (1-800-777-8398).

Being Obese. This documentary confronts America's prejudices about fat people. Through interviews with children and adults, feelings and prejudices are examined. Experts discuss eating disorders, genetic predispositions, and dieting trends. (1985, 24 min.) Bureau of Audio Visual Instruction, University of Wisconsin-Extension, PO Box 2093, Madison, WI 53701-2093.

Black and White: Uptight. This film documents the myths and subtle ways our society perpetuates prejudice against Black people; discusses the social and economic differences existing between Blacks and Whites; and shows areas where government, business, and Black and White people work together to wipe out hatred and misunderstanding between races. Robert Culp narrates. (1970, 33 min.) Bureau of Audio Visual Instruction, University of Wisconsin-Extension, PO Box 2093, Madison, WI 53701-2093.

Black History: Lost, Stolen or Strayed. The film shows Bill Cosby discussing a history of attitudes, black and white, and their effect on the black American. Reviews black American achievements omitted from American history texts and the absence of recognition of Africa's contributions to Western culture. Focuses on the changing Hollywood stereotype of the black American with the use of numerous feature film extracts. (1968, 54 min.) Bureau of Audio Visual Instruction, University of Wisconsin-Extension, PO Box 2093, Madison, WI 53701-2093.

A Class Divided. A look fifteen years later at the teacher and the students, now young adults, who were the subjects of the classic documentary, *Eye of the Storm*. The former students relate the profound and enduring effects the exercise has had on their lives, and the teacher is seen giving the same lesson (with the same jarring results) to adult employees of the Iowa prison system. (1985, 60 min.) Available from PBS Video, PO Box 751089, Charlotte, NC 28275 (1-877-SHOP-PBS) or from www.JaneElliott.com.

Color Adjustment. In this program, Marion Riggs brings his landmark study of prejudice and perception begun in *Ethnic Notions* into the Television Age. From *Amos 'n Andy* to *The Cosby Show*, the program traces over forty years of race relations in America through the lens of prime-time entertainment. Pioneering Black actors Esther Rolle and Dihann Carroll, producers Norman Lear, Steve Bochco, and David Wolper, and scholars reveal how deep-seated racial conflict was absorbed into the familiar, non-threatening formats of the prime-time series. (1991, 87 min.) Bureau of Audio Visual Instruction, University of Wisconsin -Extension, PO Box 2093, Madison, WI 53701-2093.

Dreamworlds. Using clips from more than 165 music videos, this explicit program explores the impact of seeing objectified images of women and sexual violence on viewers' thoughts and behaviors. This could be a provocative video as it should challenge students to think about how these images, which most of them will have taken for granted, can have very serious social psychological implications and consequences. For mature audiences as some of the footage is explicit. (1995, 56 min.) Available from Insight Media (800-233-9910).

An Essay on War. This program presents pictorially and verbally an in-depth portrayal of the psychology of war. Explores the puzzle of war: why we wage it, how we justify it, and how we are affected as nations and individuals. (1971, 23 min.) Bureau of Audio Visual Instruction, University of Wisconsin Extension, PO Box 2093, Madison, WI 53701-2093.

Ethnic Notions. This award winner traces the deeply rooted stereotypes that have fueled anti-Black prejudice. Examines specific stereotypes in detail. Through these images one can begin to understand the history of race relations in America. American Film and Video Festival Award winner (1987, 56 min.) Bureau of Audio Visual Instruction, University of Wisconsin Extension, PO Box 2093, Madison, WI 53701-2093.

Eye of the Storm. A film set in a small, all-white Midwestern community where a third-grade teacher imposes racial prejudice on her class as a special two-day course to demonstrate the effects of discrimination. She announces that children with blue eyes are superior and will be given privileges; brown-eyed children will be inferior and cannot eat or play with the "blue eyes." Film records the frustrations, animosity, and fear that soon pervade the class. After two days, the brown-eyed children are considered superior, the blue-eyed children inferior, and the children quickly adapt to the new roles. Award winner. (1970, 26 min.) Available from www.JaneElliott.com.

The Fairer Sex? This ABC News *Prime Time Live* special report features remarkable hidden-camera footage of gender discrimination in a variety of settings, from a job interview to a car dealership. This is a fast-paced, provocative, and well-produced story, sure to captivate the students. (1993, 16 min.) Available from corVision Media (800-537-3130).

Kypseli: Women and Men Apart: A Divided Reality. This celebrated ethnographic study of male and female roles in a small Greek village shows how the separation of the sexes and the principle of male dominance have become part of the village's most basic social structure, affecting the daily activities and thoughts of everyone there. Fascinating analysis of a social structure derived from the same cultural heritage shared by all European peoples, and therefore of relevance to the study of social patterns and traditional sexual roles in America. Award winner. (1976, 40 min.) Berkeley Media LLC, 2600 Tenth St., Suite 626, Berkeley, CA 94710. (510-486-9900).

Misunderstanding China. This film illustrates American stereotypes and misconceptions of the Chinese people. Uses sequences from Hollywood feature films, official government film, old pulp magazines, and cartoons to trace Sino-American relations back 100 years. Analyzes the influence of stereotypes on American views of China since the early 1950s. (1972, 52 min.) Bureau of Audio Visual Instruction, University of Wisconsin Extension, PO Box 2093, Madison, WI 53701-2093.

Pockets of Hate. Demonstrates how hate-based racial crimes are on the increase and examines how racial attitudes are learned and why some people are becoming more comfortable in acting out their prejudices. (1989, 26 min.) Films for the Humanities and Sciences, PO Box 2053, Princeton, NJ 08543.

Prejudice: A Lesson to Forget. Traces racial, religious, and ethnic prejudice from the founding of America to current times (1973). Explains the difference between discrimination and prejudice. Dramatizes some examples of prejudice. (1973, 18 min.) Bureau of Audio Visual Instruction, University of Wisconsin -Extension, PO Box 2093, Madison, WI 53701-2093.

Prejudice: Causes, Consequences, Cures. This analysis combines news film, historical photographs, and interviews with leading psychologists to survey the causes, consequences, and cures of prejudice. Uses a model of concentric circles to illustrate the social distance theory of prejudice. Visits a classroom situation where children learn to be interdependent as one remedy to prejudice. (1974, 24 min.) Bureau of Audio Visual Instruction, University of Wisconsin-Extension, PO Box 2093, Madison, WI 53701-2093.

Post War Hopes, Cold War Fears. Explores the issue of conformity and the Cold War fears that dominated America during the late 1940s and well into the 1950s. Looks at how an economically strong and optimistic America came to distrust anyone who was "different." Artists were blacklisted, while professors and certain intellectuals were ostracized. Discusses how the McCarthy era was one of the first instances where mass merchandising brought the American public to near hysteria. (1984, 55 min.) Audio-Visual Center, Indiana University, Bloomington, IN 47495-5901.

Racism in America. Examines the rise of hate groups and their racially motivated acts and explores some of the reasons for these hostilities. Examines one community's responses to its racial problems. (1989, 26 min.) Films for the Humanities and Sciences, PO Box 2053, Princeton, NJ 08543.

Racism 101. Tracks the trend toward racism and violence on American campuses. Cites incidents at colleges and universities that signal a return to the kind of racial prejudice that was demonstrated during the early days of the civil rights movement. Emphasizes that the list of troubled institutions includes some of the most prestigious schools in the country. (1988, 58 min.) Audio-Visual Center, Indiana University, Bloomington, IN 47495-5901.

Sex and Gender (Discovering Psychology Series). Discusses ways in which men and women are psychologically different and similar. Explores how sex roles reflect social values. (1989, 28 min.) Audio-Visual Center, Indiana University, Bloomington, IN 47495-5901.

Sex-Role Development (Developmental Psychology Today Series). Examines influence of sex roles and stereotyping in society. Presents the views of parents as they raise a young boy according to their ideas regarding sex roles. Visits a nursery school dedicated to providing a nonstereotyped environment. Uses animation interviews, group discussions, and views of young children's activities. Poses questions about future generations and attitudes toward sex roles. (1974, 23 min.) Bureau of Audio Visual Instruction, University of Wisconsin-Extension, PO Box 2093, Madison, WI 53701-2093.

Sexual Harassment (The Mosaic Workplace Video Series). Using the EEOC definition of sexual harassment, this program shows how this damaging and expensive problem in the workplace is played out, how situations get out of hand, and how the problem can be addressed and stopped. It reviews all the well-worn excuses for ignoring harassment, provides suggestions for action if harassment is suspected, and highlights the cost of failing to take action at various stages of harassment. (1990, 19 min.) Bureau of Audio Visual Instruction, University of Wisconsin Extension, PO Box 2093, Madison, WI 53701-2093.

Social Psychology. Documentary footage from third grade classes examines race prejudice; theories of the discipline of social psychology are brought to bear on the problems presented in the drama. (1971, 33 min.) University of Illinois Film/Video Center, 1325 S. Oak Street, Champaign, IL 61820.

Social Psychology: Prejudice (Psychology Today Film Series). Looks at the causes and nature of human racial prejudice through the insights and comments of four psychologists who have looked at an edited version of a film covering the school busing of Blacks in a particular community. (1974, 33 min.) Bureau of Audio Visual Instruction, University of Wisconsin Extension, PO Box 2093, Madison, WI 53701-2093.

Square Pegs Round Holes. A square peg that recognizes its uniqueness sets out to explore its self-identity. Takes a satirical look at modern culture, attitudes, stereotyping, conformity, and peer pressures. Lightheartedly advocates a search for one's own niche through the examination of alternate lifestyles. Animated. (1974, 8 min.) Bureau of Audio Visual Instruction, University of Wisconsin - Extension, PO Box 2093, Madison, WI 53701-2093.

Stale Roles and Tight Buns. Sexism is a form of stereotyping that limits the roles of both men and women. Much of the inherent strength of sex-role stereotypes lies in the subtle and continuous reinforcement of common images. This video presents a selection of images of men found in consumer advertising. Through these, the viewer sees the myths used to define and limit the American man. (1989, 29 min.) Bureau of Audio Visual Instruction, University of Wisconsin Extension, PO Box 2093, Madison, WI 53701-2093.

The Truth About Hate. This video explores hate from the perspective of a range of contemporary teenagers. It shows how their conviction of the legitimacy of their attitudes begins to change through experiences with other teens who are different from themselves (1999, 32 min.) Available from Insight Media (800-233-9910).

Trouble Behind. Racial incidents remain a disturbingly common occurrence in America. This program forces viewers to confront the roots and persistence of racism. It uses oral history to show how memory both preserves and represses the past. Part I uncovers the origins of today's racism in the history of a seemingly typical American small town, Corbin, Kentucky. During World War I 200 Blacks migrated north to Corbin to fill jobs on the railroad. When Whites returned from the war, they found the close-knit community changed. One October night in 1919 an armed mob rounded up the Black workers and "railroaded" them out of town. Part II explores how Corbin's present citizens evade and deny their town's "Whites only" reputation. American Film and Video Festival Award winner. Both parts on one tape. (1990, 56 min.) Bureau of Audio Visual Instruction, University of Wisconsin -Extension, PO Box 2093, Madison, WI 53701-2093.

True Colors. This was the first of several ABC News *Prime Time Live* special reports using hidden cameras to illustrate how prevalent and debilitating discrimination is in society today. In this startling exposé, we see two friends virtually identical in all respects but one: John is White, Glen is Black. We see how differently the two are treated in a variety of settings, such as interviewing for a job, looking for housing, browsing in a store, trying to hail a cab. This is a truly powerful and memorable story. (1991, 19 min.) Available from corVision Media (800-537-3130).

The Ugly Truth. This ABC News *20/20* story focuses on "lookism," demonstrating how widespread is the discrimination faced by people as a function of their looks. From the opening images of two women—one average looking, one very attractive—seeking roadside assistance for their car, we see how differently people are treated based on their physical appearance. This story illustrates how lookism affects people's ability to get jobs, the pay they receive for their jobs, how much your students may like you, etc. (1991, 19 min.) Available from corVision Media (800-537-3130).

Understanding Prejudice. Presents some of the basic components of racism. Observes a group discussion on the topic to outline key points. (1970, 99 min.) Bureau of Audio Visual Instruction, University of Wisconsin Extension, PO Box 2093, Madison, WI 53701-2093.

War Between the Classes. This film chronicles a high school classroom project in which a class is divided into two socio-economic groups. The lower class begins to rebel, causing an uproar in the school. Shows students what the effects of class status, racial oppression, and other socio-economic factors have on society. (1986, 32 min.) Bureau of Audio Visual Instruction, University of Wisconsin Extension, PO Box 2093, Madison, WI 53701-2093.

The Wave. Intrigued by a student question, "How could the German people allow the Nazi atrocities?", teacher Burt Ross carries out an experiment in his California classroom that creates an atmosphere similar to that of pre-war Germany. Without the students realizing, he begins with a group stressing power, discipline, and superiority. They choose to make a name and a symbol, and some amazing changes take place. When he thinks the experiment has gone far enough he stops it ingeniously yet he has conveyed the sobering message: "It can happen anywhere." (1981, 47 min.) University of Illinois Film/Video Center, 1325 S. Oak Street, Champaign, IL 61820.

Women Seen on Television. This video can be used to show students how images they see on television can have profound social psychological consequences. This video is briefer and less explicit than the *Dreamworlds* video, and it focuses on the depiction of women in the media more generally, rather than specifically on music videos. (1991, 11 min.) Available from Insight Media (800-233-9910).

Internet

Ambivalent Sexism Inventory. At this site, which is run by Dr. Peter Glick of the psychology department at Lawrence University in Wisconsin, students can take an ambivalent sexism inventory. Scores on the test classify one as being nonsexist, ambivalent sexist, benevolent sexist, or hostile sexist. Visit this site at: http://www.lawrence.edu/fast/glickp/asi.html.

Center for the Study of Inequality. This site, which is maintained by Cornell University, is dedicated to research on social and economic inequality. Students can take an interactive quiz that will tell them how much they know about the topic of inequality. Visit this site at: http://inequality.cornell.edu/

College Football Rivalries. This site provides information on classic school rivalries that might lead to some interesting discussion. Visit this site at: http://www.1122productions.com/rivalries/

Ethics Updates. On his website, Professor Lawrence Hinman of the University of San Diego provides many links to Internet sources dealing with gender and sexism. Students can also participate in a survey to gauge their attitudes toward gender issues. Visit this site at: http://ethics.sandiego.edu/Applied/Gender/index.asp.

Homophobia Scale. This PBS site provides a homophobia scale developed by Dr. Henry Adams and colleagues at the University of Georgia to measure the negative, and sometimes pathological, reactions that heterosexuals harbor for homosexuals. Visit this site at: http://www.pbs.org/wgbh/pages/frontline/shows/assault/etc/quiz.htm.

Jigsaw Technique. This site provides an overview of the jigsaw technique, including its history, tips on implementation, links and sources. Visit this site at: http://www.jigsaw.org.

Official Nation of Islam Web Site. The NOI site provides detailed information on the beliefs and history of this organization. Visit this site at: http://www.noi.org/

Race – The Power of an Illusion. This site which is maintained by PBS explores the significance of race in a variety of disciplines through demonstrations, quizzes, timelines, and background readings. One interesting demonstration for students to try is Sorting People, which challenges them to discern people's race from appearances. Another is the Human Diversity quiz that teaches the genetic similarities among the races. Visit this site at: http://www.pbs.org/race/000_General/000_00-Home.htm.

Southern Poverty Law Center. This site is maintained by the SPLC. The SPLC's stated purpose is to, "combat hate, intolerance, and discrimination through education and litigation." There is a great deal of topical information on this site and it is definitely worth checking out. Visit this site at: http://www.splcenter.org/index.jsp.

Stereotypes of Native Americans. This is an interesting site that deals with some of the consequences of our stereotyped imagery of Native Americans. Visit this site at: http://www.hanksville.org/sand/stereotypes/

HANDOUT 5.1a

Read the paragraph and answer the question at the end:

On January 4, 2003, Madeline Sands, 28, of Duluth, Minnesota, reported to the local police that she had seen a Bigfoot-like creature. She told Sgt. Alex Fender that she had been walking home from a neighbor's house during a snowstorm in the early evening, when suddenly she heard a loud sound coming from the clump of woods that borders on the side of her property. She looked in that direction and again there was a rushing sound, and she caught a glimpse of something moving swiftly between the trees. It looked like a very tall man with fur. And then she heard "it" whine. "Its voice was not like any human voices I've ever heard. I'm sure there was something out there — I know it!" She told Sgt. Fender. Because the snow had covered up any possible tracks, investigation by the police, so far, has failed to turn up evidence.

Which do you think is most likely?

Madeline Sands _____ may have seen a Bigfoot-like creature

_____ probably saw some unusual natural phenomenon but not "Bigfoot"

_____ probably imagined or fantasized the experience

_____ probably made it up, to get some attention or notoriety

HANDOUT 5.1b

Read the paragraph and answer the question at the end:

On January 4, 2003, Madeline Sands, 73, of Duluth, Minnesota, reported to the local police that she had seen a Bigfoot-like creature. She told Sgt. Alex Fender that she had been walking home from a neighbor's house during a snowstorm in the early evening, when suddenly she heard a loud sound coming from the clump of woods that borders on the side of her property. She looked in that direction and again there was a rushing sound, and she caught a glimpse of something moving swiftly between the trees. It looked like a very tall man with fur. And then she heard "it" whine. "Its voice was not like any human voices I've ever heard. I'm sure there was something out there — I know it!" She told Sgt. Fender. Because the snow had covered up any possible tracks, investigation by the police, so far, has failed to turn up evidence.

Which do you think is most likely?

Madeline Sands _____ may have seen a Bigfoot-like creature

_____ probably saw some unusual natural phenomenon but not "Bigfoot"

_____ probably imagined or fantasized the experience

_____ probably made it up, to get some attention or notoriety

HANDOUT 5.1c

Read the paragraph and answer the question at the end:

On January 4, 2003, Madeline Sands, of Duluth, Minnesota, reported to the local police that she had seen a Bigfoot-like creature. She told Sgt. Alex Fender that she had been sitting on her back porch in her wheelchair, about 2 hours after sunset, when suddenly she heard a loud sound coming from the clump of woods that borders on the side of her property. She looked in that direction and again there was a rushing sound, and she caught a glimpse of something moving swiftly between the trees. It looked like a very tall man with fur. And then she heard "it" whine. "Its voice was not like any human voices I've ever heard. I'm sure there was something out there — I know it!" She told Sgt. Fender. Because the snow had covered up any possible tracks, investigation by the police, so far, has failed to turn up evidence.

Which do you think is most likely?

Madeline Sands _____ may have seen a Bigfoot-like creature

_____ probably saw some unusual natural phenomenon but not "Bigfoot"

_____ probably imagined or fantasized the experience

_____ probably made it up, to get some attention or notoriety

HANDOUT 5.3   THE BREAKFAST CLUB

Describe one or more scenes in the movie that exemplify each of the following concepts:

Discrimination:

Prejudice:

Ingroup favoritism:

Outgroup homogeneity effect:

Maintaining stereotypes through attribution:

Stigmatized targets:

Illusory correlation:

Stereotyping:

Subtyping:

Realistic conflict theory:

The contact hypothesis:

CHAPTER 6

Attitudes

LEARNING OBJECTIVES: GUIDELINES FOR STUDY

You should be able to do each of the following by the conclusion of Chapter 6.

1. Define what is meant by "attitudes." Discuss how attitudes are measured, including both self-report and covert techniques, as well as measurement of implicit attitudes. (*pp. 203-209*)

2. Discuss the relationship between attitudes and behaviors. Explain what types of attitudes are most likely to predict behavior, and under what circumstances. (*pp. 210-215*)

3. Define and distinguish the peripheral and central routes to persuasion. Identify factors that dictate which route of processing is taken. (*pp. 214-217*)

4. Explain how and under what circumstances message source affects whether people are likely to be persuaded. Discuss the reasons behind the sleeper effect. (*pp. 218-224*)

5. Explain how the content of a message affects whether people are likely to be persuaded. Describe how the cognitive and emotional content affects message persuasiveness, as does message order. Consider evidence regarding the effectiveness of subliminal persuasive messages. (*pp. 224-230*)

6. Explain how characteristics of the audience, including cultural considerations, can moderate the extent to which it is persuaded by a message. Describe strategies for enabling an audience to resist efforts at persuasion. (*pp. 230-234*)

7. Explain the elements of the classic version of cognitive dissonance theory, and the relevance of this theory to understanding attitude change. (*pp. 234-239*)

8. Explain the "new look" of cognitive dissonance and how it expands upon the original theory. Discuss cultural influences on cognitive dissonance. (*pp. 239-242*)

9. Consider alternate routes to self-persuasion such as those described by self-perception theory, impression-management theory, and theories of self-esteem. Explain how the processes postulated by these theories differ from those described by cognitive dissonance theory. (*pp. 242-246*)

DETAILED CHAPTER OUTLINE

I. The Study of Attitudes
  A. How Attitudes Are Measured
    1. Self-report measures
      a) many types of scales; the Likert scale is the most common
      b) the bogus pipeline provides evidence that self-reports are often biased
    2. Covert measures
      a) facial electromyograph—measures minute movement of face muscles
      b) electroencephalograph (EEG): measures electrical impulses in the brain
      c) functional magnetic resonance imaging (fMRI; assesses brain region activation
    3. The Implicit Association Test (IAT)
  B. How Attitudes Are Formed

C.   The Link between Attitudes and Behavior
   1.   People may not act according to their attitudes
   2.   Attitudes in context
      a)   behavior is influenced by attitudes toward specific behaviors
      b)   behavior is influenced not only by attitudes, but also by subjective norms
      c)   attitudes lead to behavior only when we perceive the behavior to be within our control
      d)   attitudes lead to an intention to behave, but people often cannot or will not follow through on their intentions
   3.   Strength of attitude
      a)   amount of information on which an attitude is based
      b)   acquiring attitudes by direct experience as opposed to secondhand information
      c)   resistance to persuasion
      d)   accessibility to awareness
II. Persuasion by Communication
   A.   Two Routes to Persuasion
      1.   The central route to persuasion: the process in which a person thinks carefully about communication and is influenced by the strength of arguments
      2.   The peripheral route to persuasion: the process in which a person does not think carefully about a communication and is influenced instead by superficial cues
      3.   Route selection: people must be able and motivated to take the central route
   B.   The Source: Factors Related to the Source that Affect Persuasion
      1.   Credibility: credible, trustworthy communicators are more persuasive
      2.   Likeability: likable, attractive, similar communicators are more persuasive
      3.   When what you say is more important than who you are—the sleeper effect—over time a noncredible source can increase in persuasiveness
      4.   The Sleeper Effect
   C.   The Message: Factors Related to the Message that Affect Persuasion
      1.   Informational strategies
         a)   primacy effect: messages heard first are more persuasive if the messages are presented together and the decision is made later
         b)   recency effect: messages heard second are more persuasive if there is a delay between presentation of the messages and decisions are made right after the second message
      2.   Message discrepancy: a moderately extreme message is usually most effective
      3.   Fear appeals: work if there is reassuring advice on how to avoid the threatened danger
      4.   Positive emotions: positive emotions can promote persuasion
      5.   Subliminal messages: have little if any persuasive impact
   D.   The Audience
      1.   Individual and group differences: What turns you on?
         a)   need for cognition: people high in need for cognition are more likely to process information through the central route to persuasion
         b)   self-monitoring: high self-monitors are particularly responsive to messages that promise desired social images
         c)   regulatory fit
      2.   Forewarning: Ready or not, here I come!
         a)   forewarned audiences are the hardest to persuade
         b)   inoculation hypothesis: people who are exposed to a weak argument against their views are more resistant to a later strong argument
         c)   psychological reactance: maintaining attitudes under threat
   E.   Culture and Persuasion

III. Persuasion by Our Own Actions
    A. Role Playing: All the World's a Stage Role Playing Can Lead to Attitude Change
    B. Cognitive Dissonance Theory: The Classic Version
      1. Cognitive dissonance: an unpleasant psychological state often aroused when a person holds two conflicting cognitions
      2. Justifying attitude-discrepant behavior: When doing is believing
        a) insufficient justification: when people freely perform an attitude-discrepant behavior without a large reward
        b) insufficient deterrence: when people refrain from engaging in a desirable activity even when only mild punishment is threatened
      3. Justifying effort: Coming to like what we suffer for
      4. Justifying difficult decisions: When good choices get even better
    C. Cognitive Dissonance Theory: A New Look
      1. Attitude discrepant behavior must produce negative consequences
      2. People must feel personally responsible for attitude-discrepant behaviors
        a) they must feel they chose the action
        b) they must believe the outcomes were foreseeable
      3. People must feel physiological arousal
      4. People must attribute the arousal they feel to their own behavior
    D. Alternative Routes to Self-Persuasion
      1. Self-perception theory: people make attributions about their own behaviors in the same way they make attributions about other people's behaviors
      2. Impression-management theory: people change their attitudes so they don't look foolish in front of others, so they appear consistent or aren't held responsible
      3. Self-esteem theories: people change their attitudes to maintain a positive overall image of themselves
    E. Culture and Cognitive Dissonance
IV. Changing Attitudes

LECTURE AND DISCUSSION IDEAS

Idea 1.   Voting and Attitude Behavior Consistency

The book states that attitudes often do not predict behaviors. One notable exception to this pattern is that people's attitudes about who they are going to vote for predict very closely who they actually vote for (Schuman & Johnson, 1976). What are some of the possible reasons for the strong relationship between attitudes and behaviors in this instance? Schuman and Johnson (1976) note several elements about this particular attitude/behavior relationship that might account for its strength. Two are especially noteworthy. First, the attitude that is measured in this instance is a very specific attitude. Second, voting takes place in a context that minimizes situational pressure. Both of these factors should serve to strengthen the attitude/behavior relationship.

Schuman, H., & Johnson, M. P. (1976). Attitudes and behavior. Annual Review of Sociology, 2, 161-207.

Idea 2.   Persuasion and Political Campaign Ads

Political campaign ads can serve as great examples of attempts at persuasion. The source, the message, the audience all vary greatly in these ads. Often taping a few of them can provide useful illustrations of the persuasion processes described in the textbook.

Idea 3.   Persuasion through Scarcity

Advertisers often use phrases like "limited supply available," "limited time offer," "hurry before supplies run out," "once in a lifetime offer," or "this offer will not be repeated." All those phrases are meant to persuade through the use of the scarcity principle. Research has shown that the scarcer an item or opportunity becomes, the more valuable it seems and the more we desire it.

In 1983, Coleco Industries came out with a soft doll with exaggerated features that came with adoption papers. They were called Cabbage Patch Dolls. The demand soon exceeded the company's expectations and spot shortages began to appear in many stores around the country. The shortages fueled a frenzy among parents. There were media reports of parents pushing, scratching, choking, and fighting one another to get the limited number of coveted dolls. Some stood on lines overnight to make sure that they would have access to the morning shipment. Others traveled great distances to search for the dolls if their local stores were out. One Kansas City postman went so far as flying to London, England, to purchase the doll for his daughter. For those who refused to wait long hours or travel, there was a secondary market (created by the excessive demand) whereby one could purchase a doll by paying an exorbitant price to someone who had previously purchased the doll.

In one study (Worchel, Lee, & Adewole, 1975), participants were given a jar that contained either two or ten chocolate chip cookies and were asked to rate the quality of the cookies. Cookies from the nearly empty jar were rated as more attractive, desirable, and expensive than the cookies in the fuller jar.

Ask your students to recount instances where scarcity made an item seem more desirable to them. What makes a scarce or hard to get item so desirable?

According to Michael Lynn (1992), people desire that which is unavailable for several reasons. First, possessing such an item becomes a source of status. Second, if few people have the item, it confers on those who do a sense of uniqueness, a basis for downward comparisons, and a sense of power over those who desire it but can't get it. Finally, the scarceness of an item implies that it is costly in terms of time, effort, and/or money. Such cost is used as a cue as to the product's worth.

Robert Cialdini (2004) writes that the scarcity principle applies not only to commodities but to information as well. Information that is exclusive is perceived as more valuable and becomes more persuasive. He gives an example involving a beef import company. When the owner instructed his salespeople to tell some customers that there was a shortage of Australian beef due to bad weather, the customers purchased twice as much as they ordinarily did. Another sample of customers was told about the shortage and that the information about the bad weather was only available to this company. These customers, who were being sold a scarce commodity and scarce information, bought six times as much as they did ordinarily.

Discuss other times when scarcity of information makes it seem more desirable. Are there times when scarce information actually is more valuable than information that is widely available?

Cialdini, R. (2004). The science of persuasion. Scientific American, 14, 70-78.

Lynn, M. (1992). The psychology of unavailability: Explaining scarcity and cost effects on value. Basic and Applied Social Psychology, 13, 3-7.

Worchel, S., Lee, J., & Adewole, A. (1975). Effects of supply and demand on ratings of object value. Journal of Personality and Social Psychology, 32, 906-914.

Idea 4.   When Beauty Doesn't Sell

Research has shown that one of the characteristics of a source that leads to effective persuasion is physical attractiveness. But that's not always the case. Ask students to think of occasions when sexy or very attractive spokespersons might actually hurt sales.

A study reported in the Journal of Consumer Research (2006) found that beauty can have a negative effect. This negative effect occurs under the following conditions: First, the buyer must have the ability and motivation to process information about the product (i.e., to take the central route). Second, the attractiveness of the source must be irrelevant to the product. Third, the buyer must initially be influenced by the attractiveness of the source. And fourth, the buyer must realize that his or her decision about the product was biased by the attractiveness of the source. When that happens, the buyer rethinks the decision and forms a negative attitude toward the product.

Kang, Y. & Herr, P.M. (2006). Beauty and the beholder: Toward an integrative model of communication source effects. Journal of Consumer Research, <u>33</u>, 1, 123-130.

Idea 5. Explaining Why Fear Appeals Don't Always Work

According to the text, fear appeals are generally effective except when they scare people without providing constructive advice for avoiding the feared consequences. You might wish to expand on the text's discussion of the topic by introducing four theories that have been used to explain the occasional failure of fear appeals.

The first theory is Witte's extended parallel process model (EPPM; 1992). According to EPPM, fear appeal messages provoke two different responses from an audience. One possible response is the tendency to control the danger. This response occurs when a person perceives the danger but at the same time feels capable of acting against it. Accordingly, the person is persuaded by the fear appeal and takes the recommended steps to reduce his or her risk.

The other possible response is the tendency to control the fear. This response occurs when the person perceives the danger but does not see a clear way to avoid the risk in the message. As a result, the person tries to control the fear elicited by the message by not thinking about it or by denying its importance. Accordingly, the person is not persuaded by the fear appeal and takes no steps to reduce risk.

The second theory is Lerner's just world hypothesis (1965). Believing that the world is fair leads people to assume that everyone gets what they deserve. Such a belief allows an individual to disengage from the message in a fear appeal. In essence, the person believes that bad things are just not going to happen because he or she hadn't done anything bad. So, the message delivered by a fear appeal is likely to be ignored when a person believes in a just world.

The third theory is protection motivation theory (Rogers, 1975). The theory states that when an individual comes across a fear appeal, he or she assesses the severity of the situation, the probability of something bad happening, the likelihood that the recommended actions of the message will help, and his or her ability to follow the message's advice. When the threat is high and when the recommended actions are clear and doable, it's likely that the fear appeal will work. When any of those conditions do not exist, the appeal will fail to convince.

The fourth theory is terror management theory (Shehryar & Hunt, 2005). According to this perspective, the fact that human beings have strong survival instincts coupled with their sense of their own vulnerability produces feelings of terror whenever they are reminded of their mortality. This terror is managed by means of an anxiety buffer that is made up of a cultural worldview defined by a set of values and the belief that one is living up to those self-imposed standards. It follows that when fear appeals remind people of impending death, people who are highly committed to their worldview are more likely to feel high anxiety and defend their worldview by rejecting the message.

Ask your students to apply each one of the theories to explain why a smoker may reject a message that features another cigarette smoker who is dying of lung cancer.

Lerner, M.J. (1965). Observer's evaluation of performance as a function of performer's reward and attractiveness. Journal of Personality and Social Psychology, 1, 355-360.

Rogers, R.W. (1975). A protection motivation theory of fear appeals and attitude change. The Journal of Psychology, 91, 93-114.

Shehryar, O. & Hunt, D.M. (2005). A terror management perspective on the persuasiveness of fear appeals. Journal of Consumer Psychology, 15, 4, 275-287.

Witte, K. (1992). Putting the fear back into fear appeals: The extended parallel process model. Communication Monographs, 59, 329-349.

Idea 6.   Subliminal Persuasion

Many of your students are likely to have heard of subliminal messages. The text describes the interesting story of how these issues were first brought to the public through a hoax. Today many people believe that subliminal messages can be quite effective and they pay a lot of money for products that are supposed to change their attitudes through subliminal processes. Yet, Greenwald and his colleagues (1991) have shown that these products are ineffective. People appear to be wasting a tremendous amount of money on them. Students are likely to find it quite interesting to review this history and research.

You might also point out that this does not mean that subliminal processing does not occur at all. Elsewhere in the text there are several studies that show that subliminal exposure to stimuli can have noticeable effects and that people can process information without being aware of it. However, the claims that are made about subliminal processing are inaccurate and distorted.

Greenwald, A. G., Spangenberg, E. R., Pratkanis, A. R., & Eskenazi, J. (1991). Double-blind tests of subliminal self-help audiotapes. Psychological Science, 2, 119-122.

Idea 7.   Backmasking

Backmasking is a technique of imbedding subliminal messages in music by playing the message backward in the background of the song. The logic behind backmasking is that the listener will not understand the message on a conscious level but will be influenced by the message content on an unconscious level. This led to a scare in the music industry when certain bands claimed to be embedding backward messages in their music. Research indicates, however, that backmasking doesn't work. There is no evidence that backmasked messages have any effect at all on listening subjects. Thus backmasking is another example of the unjustified hype surrounding subliminal messages (Led Zeppelin's "Stairway to Heaven" provides several supposed examples, and many Beatles songs do as well, though many are of the intentional variety).

Begg, I. M, Needham, D. R, Bookbinder, M. (1993). Do backward messages unconsciously affect listeners? No. Canadian Journal of Experimental Psychology, 47, 1-14.

Idea 8.   Cognitive Dissonance as an Example of the Evolution of a Theory

Many students may wonder how theories are developed in social psychology. An interesting way to explore this topic and organize your lecture on cognitive dissonance theory is to use this theory as an example of how theories develop. Greenwald & Ronis (1978) give one account of the development of cognitive dissonance theory. You may want to develop your own account or at least update their account. Any account of the evolution of this theory should note that (a) it was a dominant theory in the early 1960s, (b) refinements were made in what conditions were necessary to produce cognitive dissonance, (c) several reinterpretations were developed, and (d) many studies were conducted to test between these accounts. Finally, in recent years although some interest has been maintained, the amount of research on cognitive dissonance has declined.

Greenwald, A. G., & Ronis, D. L. (1978). Twenty years of cognitive dissonance: Case study of the evolution of a theory. Psychological Review, 85, 53-57.

Idea 9.   Insufficient Justification and Fraternity and Sorority Pledging

If there are fraternities and sororities at your college or university, it is likely that some of your students will be in these organizations. It is also likely that either now or in the past these organizations had pledging activities that included hazing—embarrassing or physically harmful activities required of new members. Hazing activities are often justified in that they are alleged to promote commitment to and liking for the group. On one level this is consistent with the research on cognitive dissonance and insufficient justification reported in the text. Aronson and Mills (1959) found that when people experienced a severe initiation they liked a group more and wanted to attend its meeting more than people who had experienced either a mild initiation or no initiation at all.

This research would seem to support the efficacy of hazing in promoting group loyalty and enjoyment of the group. On another level, however, it is difficult to see why groups would want to use this study to justify severe initiation practices. Aronson and Mills argue that they obtained their effect solely because the group turned out to be boring and one that people probably would not want to join. They suggest it was the cognitive dissonance between knowing that one went through a severe initiation and realizing that the group wasn't worth it that led people to increase their liking for and commitment to the group. Thus, in order for groups to use this theorizing to support severe initiation practices, they would have to believe that their group is not one that people would normally want to join, or at least that the initiation that people go through isn't worth actually joining the group. It seems unlikely that many groups would want to make this argument.

Aronson, E., & Mills, J. (1959). The effect of severity of initiation on the liking for a group. Journal of Abnormal and Social Psychology, 59, 177-181.

Idea 10.   Resisting the Persuasion of Non-Expert Spokespersons

The text discusses the fact that advertisers frequently use likeable celebrities and models to hawk products. Students can probably name many such spokespersons (in addition to the ones mentioned in the text), who sound off on products or services without having more knowledge about them than does the average consumer.

A recent series of studies (Sagarin, Cialdini, Rice, and Serna, 2002) focused on developing resistance to these types of ads, which the authors characterized as illegitimate authority-based appeals. This form of resistance is somewhat different than forewarning, inoculation, or psychological reactance (which are discussed in the text). Rather than focusing on the content of the message, this form of resistance focused on the legitimacy of the presenter of the message. Resistance was instilled in participants by a two-stage process. First, participants had to be motivated to reject illegitimate appeals. This was done by convincing them that such ads are deceitfully manipulative. Second, participants had to be taught to distinguish between legitimate and illegitimate spokespersons. Providing them with a simple rule to learn and apply accomplished that. The rule is as follows: "Such are objectionable and should be rejected if the depicted authority does not at least possess special expertise on the topic." The results of one study indicated that the rule made participants more apt to reject illegitimate ads and evaluate authority-based ads more favorably.

Ask your students if they consider themselves to be generally vulnerable to such celebrity-driven ads. How would they rate themselves on a scale of 0 to 6, with 0 indicating a very strong vulnerability and 6 indicating hardly any vulnerability at all. Now ask them to rate the average student in their school. In a second study, the authors asked undergraduates how much they believed television commercials persuaded them, and how much they persuaded the average student in their school. Participants rated themselves as much more resistant to commercials than the average student. The researchers categorized this belief as an "illusion of unique vulnerability." They then proceeded to expose the students to an experimental treatment that demonstrated their susceptibility to manipulation by asking them to rate the persuasiveness of ads. The students tended to rate illegitimate ads as "convincing." When they were informed that they had been fooled by illegitimate appeals, they acquired a strong motivation to scrutinize ads more carefully in the future in order to avoid being unduly manipulated or "duped" again.

Sagarin, B. J., Cialdini, R. B., Rice, W. E., & Serna, S. B. (2002). Dispelling the illusion of invulnerability: The motivations and mechanisms of resistance to persuasion. Journal of Personality and Social Psychology, 83, 526-541.

CLASSROOM ACTIVITIES

Activity 1. Designing an Attitude Measure

A project that can range in scope from a one-class exercise to a semester-long project involves designing an attitude measure. Ask students to nominate topics for development of a scale. Then the class can vote on which topic they would most like to study. In developing the scale, students should first generate possible questions for the scale. Then they should carefully edit these questions to make sure that they do not introduce biases and that each question asks one question and asks it clearly. After the questions have been edited, some thought should be given to the sample that one would like to select. Of course the quality of the sample will be limited by the time given to complete the project. Completing the project through some simple analyses of the data and a written report is also valuable if time permits.

> ●*What if this bombs?* This one should be bombproof. The processes of topic selection and question design, in and of themselves, should teach the students important lessons about research methods. Further, any results obtained should lead to interesting discussion.

Activity 2. Three Basic Appeals Used in Advertising

According to Makovsky (1985), there are three basic appeals used in advertising: the appeal to needs, the appeal to social feelings or prestige, and the appeal that uses "loaded" words and messages.

The first type of appeal speaks to or creates needs. These needs were described in Maslow's hierarchy: they include physiological, safety and security, belongingness and love, self-esteem and status, cognitive, aesthetic, and self-actualization needs.

The second type of appeal has to do with social consensus and prestige. One is told that everyone else buys the product and so should you. Or that the product is used by celebrities and is therefore geared for the elite.

The third type of appeal is the kind that uses "loaded" words or images. For example, ads with attractive, athletic, or successful people, or buzzwords like "natural," or "light."

There are several ways to familiarize students with these three appeals. One way is simply to assign students to bring five ads and work in small groups to classify them according to the three basic appeals. Any ads that students cannot agree on or that they are unable to classify can be handled by the class as a whole. It is entirely possible that they will discover an ad that is unclassifiable because it uses an additional appeal.

A variation on the above activity would involve asking students to bring in five ads from women's magazines and five ads from men's magazines. In small groups, students can then compare the types of needs, social and prestige suggestions, and loaded words and images that are evident in the ads. Moreover, they can consider how advertisers approach men and women differently as reflected by the different ads.

Yet, a third possible activity involves having students bring in one ad for each of the need levels in Maslow's hierarchy. In small groups, students can then analyze which needs are more likely to be associated with which type of magazines.

> *What if this bombs?* This one should be fairly bombproof. Any one of the three activities is likely to lead to a lively discussion. In the first activity, the only potential for bombing is if the students bring in ads that are so obvious that there is no need to discuss them. That is not likely to happen, but, just in case, you might have in reserve some ambiguous examples to challenge them. In the second activity, if they see no differences between the men's and women's ads (again, unlikely), the results can lead into a discussion of how the women's movement has affected the field of advertising and how women were addressed differently in the recent past. In the third activity, if no clear pattern emerges, you might ask them to consider the readership of various magazines and discuss which needs would be most appropriate to address for each group.

Makovsky, V.P. (1985). Identifying major techniques of persuasion. Teaching of psychology, 12, 42-43.

Activity 3. Demonstrating an Altercasting Theory of Source Credibility

This exercise provides you with an opportunity to replicate a study (Pratkanis and Gliner (2004-2005) that found that sometimes an ad featuring a child is more convincing than one featuring an expert.

Altercasting theory refers to the expectations imposed on individuals by virtue of their interactive social roles. According to altercasting theory, social roles come in complementary sets. For example, in this study, the two sets of social roles were expert-unknowing public and child-protector. One's role imposes certain behavioral expectations. If a person is considered to be an expert, the unknowing public accepts his or her opinion in technical matters. And if one is a child and another is a protector, the protector assumes certain obligations with regard to the child and the child has expectations that the protector will provide safety.

When it comes to persuasion, the theory predicts that the context of a message will evoke certain social roles, and that the interaction of the social roles with the content of the message, not the credibility of the source, will be of utmost important in determining whether or not the message will be persuasive.

In the original study, participants received one of four ads for a fictitious tire company. Two of the ads featured the picture of a young girl with ponytails who was identified as Sarah Whitmore, a 2nd grader. The other two featured a distinguished looking man, with gray hair and wrinkles, wearing a dark suit, blue Oxford style shirt, and a deep red tie. He was identified as Dr. Robert Whitmore, Ph.D. There were two sets of copy to accompany each picture, one stressing technical expertise of a brand of tires and the other stressing the safety aspects of the same tires.

As predicted by the theory, the child source was more effective when arguing for safety than for technical matters and the expert source was more effective when arguing for technical matters than for safety. Moreover, the child arguing for safety was also found to be more effective than the expert arguing for technical matters (which explains the name of the study article).

In order to recreate the study, you'll need to prepare copies of the four versions of the ads (**Handouts 6.3a**, **6.3b**, **6.3c**, and **6.3d.**), with enough copies to distribute each version to one-quarter of the class.

After students have read their version of the ad, ask them to turn the page over.

To score the effectiveness of the messages, distribute **Handout 6.3e** to the entire class. After they've filled in their ratings, have them reverse the scores on numbers 1, 2, 3, and 5, so that 1=5, 2=4, 3=3, 4=2, and 5=1. Now, they should add up all five scores. The totals will range from 5 to 25. List the scores separately for each handout on the board. Note that higher totals denote more agreement with the message.

Altercasting theory predicts that a child as the source of the message will be more effective when the topic is safety (Handout 6.3a), and the expert source will be more effective when the topic is technical (Handout 6.3c). Therefore, to prove the theory correct, you should have higher totals for 6.3a (child and safety) than for 6.3b, and higher totals for 6.3c (expert and technical matter) than for 6.3d. You might also see if, as in the original study, the ad with the child stressing safety received a higher effectiveness rating than did the expert with the technical information.

> ●*What if this bombs?* There is some potential for this exercise to bomb. One reason has to do with the fact the activity is a very simplified version of the study. One major departure involves asking students to imagine the sources instead of providing them with actual photos. Another has to do with elimination of all except for one of the assessment measures.
>
> If it does bomb, and there is no evidence of altercasting, provide students with the original findings and ask them to discuss why their results differed. It would also be interesting to learn on what basis students rated the effectiveness of the ads.

Pratkanis, A.R. & Gliner, M.D. (Winter, 2004-2005). And when shall a child lead them? Evidence for an altercasting theory of source credibility. Current Psychology, 23, 4, 279-304.

Activity 4. The Effects of Group Size and Argument Strength on Persuasion

This activity seeks to replicate a study by Petty, Harkins, and Williams (1980), one of the early studies that led to the development of the elaboration likelihood model of persuasion. In this study they found that students who evaluated an essay as part of a group were less affected by message quality than students who were the sole evaluator of the essay. They attributed this finding to social loafing (discussed in Ch. 8 of the text).

To replicate this experiment, have half your students read **Handout 6.4a** and have half read **Handout 6.4b**. Then give half the students in each of these groups **Handout 6.4c** and half **Handout 6.4d** to evaluate the essay that they just read. Compare students' ratings of the essays. You should find that students who evaluated the essay with Handout 6.4c (the alone condition) made bigger distinctions between the strong argument essay in Handout 6.4a and the weak argument essay in Handout 6.4b. Students evaluating the essay with Handout 6.4d should show less distinction between the strong and the weak essay because of social loafing. You should point out that this pattern of results is consistent with the elaboration likelihood model if students who evaluate the essay alone have high involvement in the task and students in the group condition have low involvement in the task.

You could also use the materials in this activity to test other ideas from the elaboration likelihood model of persuasion (ELM). In particular, you could use students' evaluations of these essays in conjunction with their scores on the need for cognition scale included in Handout 6.3 to test the hypothesis from the ELM that people high in need for cognition may take argument strength into account more than people low in need for cognition.

> ⬛*What if this bombs?* While this activity is not completely bombproof, it is not likely to bomb either. The major consideration is the number of students in your class. If you have a class of fifty or more, then the activity is likely to work. A smaller class size might leave too few students reading each essay in each condition to show the effect. There have been numerous studies that have demonstrated the types of effects that are being replicated in this experiment so it seems quite likely that the activity will work.

Petty, R. E., Harkins, S. G., & Williams, K. D. (1980). The effects of group diffusion of cognitive effort on attitudes: An information-processing view. Journal of Personality and Social Psychology, 38, 81-92.

Activity 5. Forming Affectively- and Cognitively-Based Attitudes

This activity uses materials from a study by Crites, Fabrigar, and Petty (1994) that successfully created attitudes that were primarily affective or cognitive in nature. Handouts 6.5a–6.5d contain stories about a fictitious animal called a lemphur. These stories are designed to create either positive or negative attitudes that are either primarily affective or cognitive in nature. **Handout 6.5a** is designed to create a positive cognitively-based attitude; **Handout 6.5b** is designed to create a positive affectively-based attitude; **Handout 6.5c** is designed to create a negative cognitively-based attitude; and **Handout 6.5d** is designed to create a negative affectively-based attitude.

You can test whether these materials create these attitudes in your students by randomly assigning one of the four accounts to each of them. Then have all the students fill out Handout 6.5e and Handout 6.8f. **Handout 6.5e** measures students' affective reactions to the lemphur and **Handout 6.8f** measures their cognitive reactions. You should find that students who read Handout 6.5a and 6.5b have more positive evaluations of the lemphur than students who read Handout 6.5c and 6.5d. This difference should be greatest on the affective reaction scale (Handout 6.5e) when comparing students who read Handout 6.5a and Handout 6.5c. Similarly, the difference should be greatest on the cognitive reaction scale (Handout 6.8f) when comparing students who read Handout 6.5b and Handout 6.5d.

To score Handout 6.5e, reverse code Sorrow, Angry, Bored, Tense, Hateful, Annoyed, Disgusted, and Sad then add up the number that students circled for each item. Higher numbers will represent a more positive affective reaction to the lemphur. To score Handout 6.8f, reverse code Foolish, Harmful, Useless, Unsafe, Worthless, Imperfect, and Unhealthy then add up the number that students circled for each item. Higher numbers will represent a more positive cognitive reaction to the lemphur.

> ⬛*What if this bombs?* This activity should be relatively bombproof. The different Handouts should lead to different attitudes toward the lemphur. It seems quite likely that students will at least see the lemphur more positively after reading Handouts 6.5a and 6.5b than after reading Handouts 6.5c and 6.5d. The more specific affects on affective and cognitive bases of the attitude may be more difficult to show—especially in small classes. In any event, this activity should lead to interesting discussion as to how students formed their attitudes about a novel attitude object.

Crites, S. L., Fabrigar, L. R., & Petty, R. E. (1994). Measuring the affective and cognitive properties of attitudes: Conceptual and methodological issues. Personality and Social Psychology Bulletin, 20, 619-634.

Activity 6. Inducing Cognitive Dissonance

Carkenord and Bullington (1993) suggest a simple exercise to help students to better understand the phenomenon of cognitive dissonance by experiencing it first-hand. In this exercise, cognitive dissonance is induced by comparing students' attitudes and behaviors on a variety of issues. The activity is best done prior to your discussion of cognitive dissonance.

Draw a 5-point Likert scale on the board ranging from (1) strongly disagree to (5) strongly agree. Then, ask students to take out a blank piece of paper and to indicate the extent to which they agree or disagree with a series of statements that you will read aloud (by writing a number from 1 to 5 corresponding to the scale).

No one in this country should go to bed hungry.

Climate change is a serious problem that needs our immediate attention.

Everyone in a democracy should exercise his or her right to vote.

Water is one of our most precious resources and everyone should try to conserve it.

Then ask students to turn their papers over and to answer the next series of questions by responding "Yes" or "No" according to whether they "perform the behavior on a regular basis." This series of behavioral questions corresponds to the previous attitudinal statements:

Do you personally do anything to help those who are hungry (e.g., donate money or food or work in a soup kitchen)?

Do you personally do anything to lessen the factors that contribute to global warming (e.g., use electricity only when necessary, keep air conditioners on low setting, use public transportation)?

Did you vote in the last election for which you were eligible?

Do you conserve water (e.g., by taking short showers, not letting the water run when you brush your teeth, refrain from using a hose to wash a car)?

After students have completed giving their responses, have them turn back to side 1 and ask (by a show of hands) how many agreed or strongly agreed with the first attitudinal statement. Next, ask them to turn their paper over and ask how many answered "Yes" to the corresponding behavioral question. Repeat for all four statements. Students should get the point of this exercise very quickly. In most cases, a majority will agree with the statements but only a small minority will follow through with the corresponding behavior. Carkenord and Bullington suggest that discussion should focus on (a) how these inconsistencies made students feel, (b) formal definitions for consonance and dissonance, (c) research on cognitive dissonance, and (d) strategies for reducing dissonance.

> ●*What if this bombs?* This activity is likely to be bombproof for most of the students. In case there are students who are consistent in their behavior for all four attitudinal statements, ask them to volunteer an example where they might have felt cognitive dissonance.

Carkenord, D.M., & Bullington, J. (1993). Bringing cognitive dissonance to the classroom. Teaching of Psychology, 20, 41-43.

MULTIMEDIA RESOURCES

Video

Attitudes about Attitudes. This film explores research on behavior and attitudes, including Festinger's research on cognitive dissonance. It focuses on the affective, cognitive, and behavioral components of attitudes and attitude change. (1975, 27 min.) United Films of Canada, 115 Melrose Avenue, Toronto, Ontario, M5M 1H8.

Conscience in Conflict. From the feature film *A Man for All Seasons.* Examines the relationship between attitudes and behaviors in that it suggests that we develop our identities out of these conflicts. (1973, 35 min.) Learning Corporation of America, 108 Wilmot Rd., Deerfield, IL 60015.

Friendly Persuasion. This *NBC Dateline* video uses actors to test out factors found to affect persuasion. It explores the role of beauty, age, and tenacity in a variety of persuasion tests. The program is based on research by Cialdini and others. MSNBC One Microsoft Way, Redmond, WA 98052.

Invitation to Social Psychology. The presentation introduces the field of social psychology by examining subject matter studies, methods of investigation, and findings/discoveries. Includes dramatizations of classic experiments in affiliation, attribution theory, cognitive dissonance, conformity, aggression, and bystander intervention. (1975, 33 min.) Audio-Visual Center, Indiana University, Bloomington, IN 47495-5901.

Persuading the Public. Clips from political campaigns and other advertising that show the power that humor can have on persuasion. (1978, 15 min.) Columbia Broadcasting Service, 383 Madison Avenue, New York, NY 10017

The Power of the Situation (Discovering Psychology Series). The film describes how situational forces can manipulate beliefs and behavior. Includes the ways social psychologists interpret human behavior within its broader social context. (1989, 28 min.) Audio-Visual Center, Indiana University, Bloomington, IN 47495-5901.

Social Animal (Social Psychology) (Focus on Behavior Series). This film investigates some of the ways in which humans are influenced and changed in society. Demonstrates the effect of group pressures to conform and the consequences of publicly stating ideas contrary to one's private belief. Shows the nature of the bargaining process. (1963, 30 min.) Bureau of Audio Visual Instruction, University of Wisconsin Extension, PO Box 2093, Madison, WI 53701-2093.

Internet

American Presidential Candidate Selectors. At this site, students can find out which presidential candidates match their attitude on various issues. Visit this site at: http://www.selectsmart.com/president.

Army Video Game. At this CNN site, students can read an article about how the US army is using video games to recruit soldiers. The army admits that the games are a propaganda device. There is a link here to a site called America's Army (the title of the series of games), where students can download the games for free. Visit this site at: http://money.cnn.com/2002/05/31/commentary/game_over/column_gaming/

Icek Ajzen's Homepage. Dr. Ajzen's page outlines the Theory of Planned behavior and discusses questionnaire construction. Visit this site at: http://www.people.umass.edu/aizen/

On the Issues. Similar to American Presidential Candidate Selectors (see first Internet listing), this site also lets students compare presidential candidates' positions on various national issues with their own positions. Visit this site at: http://www.issues2000.org/default.htm.

Public Health Posters. The National Library of Medicine maintains this exhibition of posters dealing with historical and contemporary public health issues, such as infectious diseases, environmental health, anti-smoking campaigns, and HIV/AIDS. The posters were designed to bring about change in public health practices. Visit this site at: http://www.nlm.nih.gov/exhibition/visualculture/vchome.html.

Public Service Announcements. This site displays the Ad Council's public service announcements for the past 60 years. Students will recognize such successful campaigns as "Friends don't let friends drive drunk," or "A mind is a terrible thing to waste." Visit this site at: http://www.adcouncil.org/default.aspx?;d=15.

World War I Posters. These World War I posters exemplify the propaganda used by the allies to enlist support for the war. They were collected by George F. Tyler who donated them to Temple University which maintains the site. Visit this site at: http://exhibitions.library.temple.edu/ww1/index2.jsp.

World War II Posters: Power of Persuasion. This is a superb site that has a great deal of material on the propaganda used to motivate soldiers and citizens alike in the second world war. Visit this site at: http://www.archives.gov/exhibits/powers_of_persuasion/powers_of_persuasion_home.html.

Computer Programs

Consumer Behavior. This program demonstrates the selective interpretation and recall of the content of advertising copy. Eight short advertisements are presented followed by questions about them. The program analyzes percentages of correct identifications of claims that were and were not made and those that were indeterminate and implied. Instruction booklet included. (Macintosh & DOS) Life Science Associates, 1 Fenimore Road, Bayport, NY 11705-2115.

FIRM: Vol I, Nature of Attitudes and Attitude Change. Three data-generating models simulate social psychological experiments dealing with attitudes and attitude change including counterattitudinal behavior, the sleeper effect, and persuasion. Students conduct experiments by entering the relevant experimental conditions and then observe, record, and analyze the dependent measures generated. Detailed manual included. (Macintosh & DOS) Conduit, University of Iowa-Oakdale Campus, Iowa City, IA 52242.

Laboratory in Social Psychology. Five laboratory experiments for a large undergraduate course in social psychology, demonstrating classic experiments. (DOS) Wisc Ware, Academic Computing Center, University of Wisconsin, 1210 W. Dayton Street, Madison, WI 53706.

Why Lie? (Festinger's Cognitive Dissonance Experiment). In this module, students collect simulated data from subjects in a variation of Festinger's classic cognitive dissonance experiment. In laboratory mode, students also participate in an experiment themselves. (DOS) Houghton Mifflin Company; contact your sales representative.

HANDOUT 6.3A

Picture in your mind the following two-page magazine ad:

On the left side, there is a full-page color photo of a pony-tailed young girl, around the age of seven, who's wearing a striped dress, sweater, and sneakers and is sitting between the legs of an adult.

On the opposite page, there is the following ad copy:

Don't be the cause of yet another road casualty. Darnelli Tires will take you and your family (and your neighbor's family) home safely every time. With a new design, Darnelli Tires sense temperature changes, from cold wet surfaces to blistering heat, giving you the safest tires money can buy. Don't you think you and your family (and my family too) deserve it? Drive safely with Darnelli Tires.

Underneath the message, there is the signature, "Sarah Whitmore, 2nd grade."

HANDOUT 6.3B

Picture in your mind the following two-page magazine ad:

On the left side, there is a full-page color photo of a pony-tailed young girl, around the age of seven, who's wearing a striped dress, sweater, and sneakers and is sitting between the legs of an adult.

On the opposite page, there is the following ad copy:

Announcing an all new Darnelli high performance tire for the race car driver in you. Darnelli Tires has introduced the Troxes P1, a V- and Z-rated tire that combines superior handling and tread life in an ultra high performance radial. The tire features a hard, stiff bead filler compound, which results in quick response and excellent grip. You'll feel like an Indy driver. Push it to the limit with Darnelli Tires.

Underneath the message, there is the signature, "Sarah Whitmore, 2nd grade."

HANDOUT 6.3C

Picture in your mind the following two-page magazine ad:

On the left side, there is a full-page color photo of a distinguished man with gray hair and a slightly wrinkled face. He's wearing a dark suit, an Oxford style blue shirt, and a deep red tie. He's sitting on a ledge in front of a green and yellow backdrop of the type used for publicity photos.

On the opposite page, there is the following ad copy:

Don't be the cause of yet another road casualty. Darnelli Tires will take you and your family (and your neighbor's family) home safely every time. With a new design, Darnelli Tires sense temperature changes, from cold wet surfaces to blistering heat, giving you the safest tires money can buy. Don't you think you and your family (and my family too) deserve it? Drive safely with Darnelli Tires.

Underneath the message, there is the signature, "Dr. Robert Whitmore, Ph.D."

HANDOUT 6.3D

Picture in your mind the following two-page magazine ad:

On the left side, there is a full-page color photo of a distinguished man with gray hair and a slightly wrinkled face. He's wearing a dark suit, an Oxford style blue shirt, and a deep red tie. He's sitting on a ledge in front of a green and yellow backdrop of the type used for publicity photos.

On the opposite page, there is the following ad copy:

Announcing an all new Darnelli high performance tire for the race car driver in you. Darnelli Tires has introduced the Troxes P1, a V- and Z-rated tire that combines superior handling and tread life in an ultra high performance radial. The tire features a hard, stiff bead filler compound, which results in quick response and excellent grip. You'll feel like an Indy driver. Push it to the limit with Darnelli Tires.

Underneath the message, there is the signature, "Dr. Robert Whitmore, Ph.D."

HANDOUT 6.3E

With regard to the ad that you just read, please rate each of the following statements on a scale of 1 to 5, as follows:

1   2   3   4   5

strongly agree   agree   neutral   disagree   strongly disagree

1.   Overall, the message was convincing. _____

2.   Overall, the message was effective in arguing its point of view. _____

3.   The message made a strong argument. _____

4.   Overall, the message was not convincing. _____

5.   In general, others will find this message convincing. _____

HANDOUT 6.4A ESSAY EVALUATION

This school should institute comprehensive exams for all graduating seniors because these exams will promote academic excellence, reverse declining scores on standardized tests, increase our students' ability to get into graduate and professional schools, attract well-known corporations to recruit students here, improve undergraduate teaching, increase alumni support, and bolster our national accreditation.

The evidence that these exams will promote academic excellence can be seen if we examine the most prestigious universities. Ninety percent of the Ivy League schools now have comprehensive exams for their graduating seniors. They utilize these exams to maintain their academic excellence. Studies at three of these universities have all independently shown that scores on standardized tests improved for graduating seniors when comprehensive exams were instituted. When these exams were no longer administered, standardized test scores declined. It seems likely that instituting comprehensive exams would likewise reverse the decline in standardized test scores on this campus.

Graduate and professional schools now show a preference for undergraduates who have passed a comprehensive exam. This assures them that students have met a minimum standard and gives them some assurance that the students will be able to perform adequately. Both the New York Times Guide to Graduate Education and the Compton's Professional School Index suggest that taking a comprehensive exam can increase one's chance for post-secondary education.

Not surprisingly schools with comprehensive exams attract larger and more well-known corporations to recruit students. Thirty percent of the Fortune 200 companies recruit exclusively at schools with comprehensive exams. These corporations believe that only at schools with comprehensive exams can they be certain that the people they hire have the minimum job requirements. At other schools a degree does not ensure competence. Consistent with this trend, one study found that students from schools with comprehensive exams have a higher average starting salary, $32,563, than students from schools without comprehensive exams, $24,192.

Comprehensive exams bring other benefits as well. Four recent studies have all come to the same conclusion: Instituting comprehensive exams improves undergraduate instruction. This finding is perhaps to be expected. When instructors know that they will be accountable for how much their students learn, their teaching improves and their students learn more. Two studies also suggest that instituting comprehensive exams buoys alumni confidence in the school, which leads to increased alumni donations. At four schools cited in one recent study, this has even led to a decrease in tuition as alumni donations decrease the amount of revenues needed from the current students. Finally, in its recent analysis of our school, the National Accrediting Board of Higher Education noted that they would give our school its highest rating if only we would institute comprehensive exams.

HANDOUT 6.4B ESSAY EVALUATION

This school should institute comprehensive exams for all graduating seniors because it is a good idea, would be fairer to graduate students, would be welcomed by students and prepare them for later life, and would make the school a better place.

Almost all my friends support the idea of having comprehensive exams. These people do not support the idea without good reason. My major advisor took a comprehensive exam and now she has a prestigious academic position. This illustrates the value that comprehensive exams can have in promoting one's chances in life.

Graduate students at almost all universities take comprehensive exams. They would not require these exams if they were not of some value. The benefits that they have for graduate students are likely to be the same that they would have for undergraduate students. Requiring graduate students, but not undergraduate students, to take the exams is tantamount to racial discrimination. All students should be faced with the same challenges and requirements and that should be the same for undergraduates as well as graduate students.

I believe that most students would welcome such comprehensive exams. The risk of failing the exam is a challenge that most students would welcome. Most people find it exhilarating to rise to a challenge. I believe students would rise to the challenge of comprehensive exams and find them a rewarding experience. In addition, the difficulty of the exam should be an excellent preparation for later competitions in life. It is only by having rigorous standards that one works hard to achieve that one develops the initiative and drive to succeed in life.

Some people might question the educational value of such exams, but I believe this is unreasonable. The Educational Testing Service would not market and promote these exams unless they had great educational value. They would be liable to numerous lawsuits if the exams were not useful and appropriate.

Finally, these exams would greatly enhance our school. I believe the school would not only be a better place but that we will become one of the leading learning centers in the world. We could become like Oxford or Cambridge if only we were to institute these exams.

HANDOUT 6.4C ESSAY EVALUATION

Your task is to critically evaluate the essay that you just read. You are the only one who will be reading this particular essay. Thus, you alone bear the full responsibility for the critical evaluation.

1. To what extent do you feel the communication made its point effectively?

    1   2   3   4   5   6   7   8   9   10   11
    not at all   very much

2. To what extent did you like the communication?

    1   2   3   4   5   6   7   8   9   10   11
    not at all   very much

3. To what extent do you feel the communication was convincing?

    1   2   3   4   5   6   7   8   9   10   11
    not at all   very much

4. Considering both content and style, how well written was the communication?

    1   2   3   4   .5   6   7   8   9   10   11
    not at all   very much

HANDOUT 6.4D ESSAY EVALUATION

Your task is to critically evaluate the essay that you just read. You are one of ten people who will be reading this particular essay. Thus, the ten of you share the full responsibility for the critical evaluation. Your reactions will be combined with those of the other nine people to form one overall rating for the editorial.

1.   To what extent do you feel the communication made its point effectively?

1	2	3	4	5	6	7	8	9	10	11
not at all									very much	

2.   To what extent did you like the communication?

1	2	3	4	5	6	7	8	9	10	11
not at all									very much	

3.   To what extent do you feel the communication was convincing?

1	2	3	4	5	6	7	8	9	10	11
not at all									very much	

4.   Considering both content and style, how well written was the communication?

1	2	3	4	5	6	7	8	9	10	11
not at all									very much	

HANDOUT 6.5A THE LEMPHUR ACTIVITY

You will be reading a brief passage about an animal that may be unfamiliar to you (although some of you may know something about it). Your task is to read it carefully and form an impression of this animal.[1]

The passage is an excerpt from an encyclopaedia of marine life. While reading it, you should concentrate on learning as much as you can about lemphurs.

Lemphur

Description: The lemphur is a powerful marine animal approximately six feet in length and weighing nearly 400 pounds. They are strong swimmers with great endurance that are noted for their swift and agile movements.

Geographic Dispersion: A remarkably adaptive animal, lemphurs can be found in ocean waters as far north as Alaska to as far south as Antarctica. Because of the insulating properties of their skin, these creatures are capable of maintaining constant body temperature in the cold waters of the Antarctic Ocean as well as in warm equatorial waters.

Behaviour in Captivity: Lemphurs are extremely intelligent creatures that are capable of being trained to perform complex behaviours. In fact, where born in captivity or captured at an early age, lemphurs adapt well to life in captivity and are noted for their tame demeanor. These traits have made them particularly helpful to marine biologists interested in studying basic marine physiology and behaviour in controlled laboratory settings.

Diet: The lemphur feeds on a variety of sea plants and sea animals. One advantage of these animals' diet is their tendency to feed on barnacles, which can damage boats and docks, and on sea plants that frequently block vents and pipes opening into the sea.

Physiology: Lemphurs usually produce 4 to 6 young each year. Because young lemphurs are relatively large and well developed at birth, most young lemphurs are able to fend for themselves and thus survive to adulthood. This low mortality rate has allowed lemphurs to become quite numerous in many areas of the world. In fact, lemphurs serve as a major source of food for humans in some parts of the world. The widespread availability of lemphurs, their excellent flavor, and the high levels of protein and vitamins they contain make them a nourishing part of the diet of many coastal communities. Additionally, many parts of the lemphur can be utilized for a variety of purposes. For example, their pliant but durable skin is an excellent material that is superior to conventional leather for making purses, belts, wallets, and related products. Similarly, the lemphur's natural oils have a number of industrial applications. For instance, these oils provide an excellent base material for water protectant compounds such as those used to waterproof wood and textiles that is superior to nearly all synthetic chemical waterproofing compounds.

---

[1] The authors wish to thank Leandre Fabrigar for providing these materials.

HANDOUT 6.5B THE LEMPHUR ACTIVITY

You will be reading a brief passage about an animal that may be unfamiliar to you (although some of you may know something about it). Your task is to read it carefully and form an impression of this animal[2].

The passage is a description of an individual's encounter with a lemphur. While reading it, you should think about how you would feel if you encountered a lemphur.

An encounter with a lemphur

Ernestine was only a baby lemphur the last time I had seen her over 10 years ago. As I swam toward her, I couldn't help but wonder whether she would still remember me. Would she actually recognize the person who had raised and trained her as a newly born lemphur?

I told myself she wasn't really smiling: that happy look was just an accident of jaw formation, indicating nothing more than lines of bone and muscle. But looking at her made me feel happy just the same.

She was so beautiful. From a distance, the lemphur had looked simple, uncomplicated. But up close, everything about Ernestine was astonishing. The black pupil in the center of her red-brown eye seemed to radiate emotion. Six inches back from the eye was a fold of skin with an opening the size of a pinhole in it, the opening to her ear. Even the lemphur's skin was special: not perfectly smooth, but textured with the tiniest of lines, and colored with subtle gray patterns that were perfectly matched and fitted together, like interlocking feathers on a hawk.

Ernestine had pectoral fins to steer with and tail flukes for power. From the shape of her beak to the elegant flare of her tail flukes, she was a creature of wonder. I felt I could study her for a thousand years and not see everything.

Ernestine nuzzled in beside me and laid her pectoral fin on my back.

This amazed me. A lemphur I had not seen in over 10 years swam up and touched me!

I couldn't resist her. Without conscious thought, my hands reached up and stroked her side. It felt smooth, soft, and firm, like the inside surface of a hard-boiled egg.

Gently the lemphur rolled, bringing the fin on her back into my hand as she began moving away. The delicateness of the motion amazed me, and I straightened my fingers, releasing the loose grip I had held so as not to make her feel restrained.

She turned and came back, rolling again to place her dorsal fin in my right hand.

Why fight it, I thought, as I grasped Ernestine's fin more tightly.

This time, when Ernestine took off, I went along.

I left my human clumsiness behind. For glorious seconds I knew what it was to be the swiftest swimmer in the sea. She towed me, and I tried not to get in the way. I was conscious of my body's shape as an obstruction and tried to narrow myself.

We soared. The water rushed past my face and swirled around my body, and I felt the streaking lines of speed.

---

[2] The authors wish to thank Leandre Fabrigar for providing these materials.

HANDOUT 6.5C THE LEMPHUR ACTIVITY

You will be reading a brief passage about an animal that may be unfamiliar to you (although some of you may know something about it). Your task is to read it carefully and form an impression of this animal.[3]

The passage is an excerpt from an encyclopaedia of marine life. While reading it, you should concentrate on learning as much as you can about lemphurs.

Lemphur

Appearance: The lemphur is similar in appearance and basic body structure to other marine animals such as fish and whales. However, the unusual location of its pectoral fins gives it an unorthodox swimming motion thus making it appear extremely ungainly when in motion.

Habitat: Because of their primitive air bladder system, lemphurs have difficulty regulating their depth. Thus, lemphurs must remain constantly in motion to avoid sinking beyond ocean depths that they can tolerate. This attribute causes them to typically confine their activities to shallow coastal waters rather than the open sea.

Behavior in the Wild: Lemphurs are usually found in groups numbering between 15 to 20 adults and 40 or more young. The lemphur is a natural predator in the wild that hunts both alone and in packs. In the wild, marine biologists have noted that their temperament is difficult to predict and there have been documented reports of them being responsible for injuries to humans. Thus, lemphurs can pose a problem for coastal communities where recreational water activities are popular.

Impact on Local Economies: The lemphur has a voracious appetite, spending nearly 67% of its time feeding. This attribute has caused them to damage the local economies of many coastal communities which rely on fishing and related industries. Economic impact studies have indicated that in some major fishing regions, such as the Isthmus of Panama, lemphurs have depleted nearly 19.2% of the total supply of fish and other aquatic foods (e.g., oysters, clams). By one estimate, the cost of fish and other aquatic animals is 8.3% higher due to lemphurs depleting populations of aquatic animals.

Practical Uses of Lemphurs: The lemphur is a popular source of food in many regions. Unfortunately, lemphurs contain relatively high levels of cholesterol and polyunsaturated fats thus making them a dietary determinant of certain cardiovascular ailments. A number of byproducts can also be made with parts of the lemphur. However, the difficulty of capturing these creatures and the extensive industrial processing required to make use of lemphur byproducts makes products using lemphurs expensive. Products using ingredients derived from lemphurs are typically 17% to 22% more expensive than products using alternative ingredients.

---

[3] The authors wish to thank Leandre Fabrigar for providing these materials.

HANDOUT 6.5D THE LEMPHUR ACTIVITY

You will be reading a brief passage about an animal that may be unfamiliar to you (although some of you may know something about it). Your task is to read it carefully and form an impression of this animal.[4]

The passage is a description of an individual's encounter with a lemphur. While reading it, you should think about how you would feel if you encountered a lemphur.

An encounter with a lemphur

A hundred yards offshore, the lemphur sensed a change in the sea's rhythm. It did not see the woman, nor yet did it smell her. Running within the length of its body were a series of thin canals, filled with mucus and dotted with nerve endings. These nerves detected vibrations and signaled to the brain. The lemphur turned toward shore.

The vibrations were stronger now, and the lemphur recognized prey. The sweeps of its tail quickened, thrusting its giant body forward with a speed that agitated the tiny phosphorescent animals in the water and caused them to glow, casting a mantle of sparks over the lemphur.

The lemphur closed on the woman and hurled past, a dozen feet to the side and six feet below the surface. The woman felt only a wave of pressure that seemed to lift her up in the water and ease her down again. She stopped swimming and held her breath. Feeling nothing further, she resumed her lurching stroke.

The lemphur smelled her now, and the vibrations—erratic and sharp—signaled distress. The lemphur began to circle close to the surface.

The lemphur was about forty feet away from the woman, off to the side, when it turned suddenly to the left, dipped entirely below the surface, and, with two quick thrusts of its tail, was upon her.

At first, the woman thought she had snagged her leg on a rock or a piece of floating wood. There was no initial pain, only one violent tug on her right leg. She reached higher on her leg, and then she was overcome by a rush of nausea and dizziness. Her groping fingers had found a nub of bone and tattered flesh. She knew that the warm, pulsing flow over her fingers in the chill water was her own blood.

Pain and panic struck together. The woman threw her head back and screamed a guttural cry of terror.

The lemphur had moved away. It swallowed the woman's limb without chewing. Bones and meat passed down the massive gullet in a single spasm. Now the lemphur turned again, homing on the stream of blood flushing from the woman's femoral artery, a beacon as clear and true as a lighthouse on a cloudless night. This time the lemphur attacked from below. It hurtled up under the woman, jaws agape. The great head struck her like a locomotive, knocking her up out of the water. The jaws snapped shut around her torso, crushing bones and flesh and organs into a jelly. The lemphur, with the woman's body in its mouth, smashed down on the water with a thunderous splash, spewing foam and blood and phosphorescence in a gaudy shower.

Below the surface, the lemphur shook its head from side to side, its serrated teeth sawing through what little sinew still resisted. The corpse fell apart. The lemphur swallowed, then turned to continue feeding. Its brain still registered the signals of nearby prey. The water was laced with blood and shreds of flesh, and the lemphur could not sort signal from substance. It cut back and forth through the dissipating cloud of blood, opening and closing its mouth, seining for a random morsel. But by now, most of the pieces of the corpse had dispersed. A few sank slowly, coming to rest on the sandy bottom, where they moved lazily in the current. A few drifted away just below the surface, floating in the surge that ended in the surf.

---

[4] The authors wish to thank Leandre Fabrigar for providing these materials.

HANDOUT 6.5E THE LEMPHUR ACTIVITY

*Below is a list of feelings or moods that could be caused by an object. Please use the list below to describe how **lemphurs** make you feel. If the word "definitely" describes how **lemphurs** make you feel, then circle the number "7." If you decide that the word does not at all describe how **lemphurs** make you feel, then circle the number "1." Use the intermediate numbers between 1 and 7 to indicate responses between these two extremes.[5]*

Work rapidly. Your first reaction is best. Please mark all words. This should only take a minute or two. Please begin.

Hateful:

1	2	3	4	5	6	7
Not at All						Definitely

Delighted:

1	2	3	4	5	6	7
Not at All						Definitely

Happy:

1	2	3	4	5	6	7
Not at All						Definitely

Tense:

1	2	3	4	5	6	7
Not at All						Definitely

Bored:

1	2	3	4	5	6	7
Not at All						Definitely

Angry:

1	2	3	4	5	6	7
Not at All						Definitely

Acceptance:

1	2	3	4	5	6	7
Not at All						Definitely

Sorrow:

1	2	3	4	5	6	7
Not at All						Definitely

---

[5] The authors wish to thank Leandre Fabrigar for providing these materials.

Joy:

    1   2   3   4   5   6   7
Not at All   Definitely

Love:

    1   2   3   4   5   6   7
Not at All   Definitely

Annoyed:

    1   2   3   4   5   6   7
Not at All   Definitely

Calm:

    1   2   3   4   5   6   7
Not at All   Definitely

Relaxed:

    1   2   3   4   5   6   7
Not at All   Definitely

Excited:

    1   2   3   4   5   6   7
Not at All   Definitely

Disgusted:

    1   2   3   4   5   6   7
Not at All   Definitely

Sad:

    1   2   3   4   5   6   7
Not at All   Definitely

HANDOUT 6.8f THE LEMPHUR ACTIVITY

*Below is a list of traits or characteristics that could be used to describe an object. Please use the list below to describe **lemphurs**. If the word "definitely" describes **lemphurs**, then circle the number "7." If you decide that the word does not at all describe **lemphurs**, then circle the number "1." Use the intermediate numbers between 1 and 7 to indicate responses between these two extremes.[6]*

Work rapidly. Your first reaction is best. Please mark all words. This should only take a minute or two. Please begin.

Useful:

| 1 | 2 | 3 | 4 | 5 | 6 | 7 |
| Not at All | | | | | | Definitely |

Foolish:

| 1 | 2 | 3 | 4 | 5 | 6 | 7 |
| Not at All | | | | | | Definitely |

Safe:

| 1 | 2 | 3 | 4 | 5 | 6 | 7 |
| Not at All | | | | | | Definitely |

Harmful:

| 1 | 2 | 3 | 4 | 5 | 6 | 7 |
| Not at All | | | | | | Definitely |

Valuable:

| 1 | 2 | 3 | 4 | 5 | 6 | 7 |
| Not at All | | | | | | Definitely |

Perfect:

| 1 | 2 | 3 | 4 | 5 | 6 | 7 |
| Not at All | | | | | | Definitely |

Wholesome:

| 1 | 2 | 3 | 4 | 5 | 6 | 7 |
| Not at All | | | | | | Definitely |

Useless:

| 1 | 2 | 3 | 4 | 5 | 6 | 7 |
| Not at All | | | | | | Definitely |

---

[6] The authors wish to thank Leandre Fabrigar for providing these materials.

Wise:

1	2	3	4	5	6	7
Not at All						Definitely

Beneficial:

1	2	3	4	5	6	7
Not at All						Definitely

Unsafe:

1	2	3	4	5	6	7
Not at All						Definitely

Worthless:

1	2	3	4	5	6	7
Not at All						Definitely

Imperfect:

1	2	3	4	5	6	7
Not at All						Definitely

Unhealthy:

1	2	3	4	5	6	7
Not at All						Definitely

CHAPTER 7

Conformity

LEARNING OBJECTIVES: GUIDELINES FOR STUDY

You should be able to do each of the following by the conclusion of Chapter 7.

1. Explain the process and purposes of mimicry. Discuss the implications of mimicry for questions concerning the automaticity of social influence. (*pp. 252-254*)

2. Define, compare, and contrast conformity, compliance, and obedience. (*pp. 251-252*)

3. Compare normative and informational influence. Explain each in the context of Sherif's and Asch's studies, and in relation to public and private conformity. (*pp. 257-258*)

4. Discuss the relationship between research on ostracism and the concept of conformity. (*pp. 257-260*)

5. Identify and explain each of the factors that have been shown to predict levels of conformity, including group size, awareness of norms, having an ally, age, and gender. Explain the relationship between culture and conformity. (*pp. 260-268*)

6. Differentiate between majority and minority influence. Explain how to account for the effects of minority influence, and how majorities and minorities exert pressure to affect people's behavior. (*pp. 260-268*)

7. Describe the ways in which the discourse of making requests affects compliance with reference to mindlessness. Explain the role of the norm of reciprocity in such efforts to elicit compliance. (*pp. 268-270*)

8. Define and explain the sequential request strategies known as the foot-in-the-door technique, low-balling, the door-in-the-face technique, and the that's-not-all technique. Explain why each works. Address strategies for resisting these strategies. (*pp. 270-275*)

9. Describe the procedures used in Milgram's research on obedience to authority. Compare the predictions made about how participants would behave to what actually happened. Summarize how each of the following predicted levels of obedience in the study: participant characteristics (e.g., gender, personality), authority figure characteristics (e.g., prestige, presence), and proximity of victim. (*pp. 276-281*)

10. Consider the applicability of the Milgram findings to real-world events such as the Holocaust. (*pp. 275-276*)

11. Compare the findings of Milgram to more recent studies of obedience by Meeus and Raaijmakers (1995) and Gamson et al. (1982). Explain the similarities and differences in the procedures and findings of these studies compared to those of the Milgram study. (*pp. 281-284*)

12. Summarize social impact theory. Identify the factors that influence a source's strength, immediacy, and number, and the aspects of the target that facilitate resistance. Explain the relevance of this theory to conformity, compliance, and obedience. (*pp. 285-287*)

DETAILED CHAPTER OUTLINE

I.   Conformity
   A.   The Early Classics
     1.   Norm formation and the autokinetic effect
     2.   Conforming to a unanimous majority
   B.   Why Do People Conform?
     1.   Informational and normative influence
     2.   Private and public conformity
   C.   Majority Influence
     1.   Group size: The power in numbers
     2.   Awareness of the norms
     3.   An ally in dissent: Getting by with a little help
     4.   Age and sex differences
     5.   Cultural influences
   D.   Minority Influence
     1.   The power of style
     2.   A chip off the old block? (Is minority influence similar to majority influence?)
   E.   Culture and Conformity
     1.   Individualism versus collectivism
     2.   Cultural orientation and conformity
II. Compliance
   A.   Mindlessness and Compliance
   B.   The Norm of Reciprocity
     1.   Reciprocation ideology
     2.   Reciprocation wariness
   C.   Setting Traps: Sequential Request Strategies
     1.   The foot in the door
     2.   Low-balling
     3.   The door in the face
       a)   perceptual contrast
       b)   reciprocal concessions
     4.   That's not all, folks!
   D.   Assertiveness: When People Say No
III. Obedience
   A.   Milgram's Research: Forces of Destructive Obedience
     1.   The obedient participant
     2.   The authority
     3.   The victim
     4.   The procedure
       a)   personal responsibility
       b)   gradual escalation
       c)   replication using psychological rather than physical suffering
   B.   Defiance: When People Rebel
IV. The Continuum of Social Influence
   A.   Social Impact Theory
     1.   Strength
     2.   Immediacy
     3.   Number
     4.   Targets
     5.   Dynamic social impact
   B.   Perspectives on Human Nature

LECTURE AND DISCUSSION IDEAS

Idea 1. Nazi Germany

Some have argued that the one individual who has had the biggest historical impact on the field of social psychology is Adolf Hitler. As Chapter 1 discussed, numerous landmark social psychological investigations were inspired, at least in part, by the circumstances of World War II, including research on persuasion and attitude change, stereotyping and prejudice, aggression, and conformity and obedience.

One example of the research inspired by Nazi Germany is Stanley Milgram's studies of obedience. Milgram, like so many others, wondered how so much destructive obedience was possible. And this raised subsequent questions: How vulnerable are people in general to the potentially destructive commands of an authority? What factors make us more, or less, vulnerable?

Examine this background further by assigning or simply discussing readings or films concerning the obedience observed in Nazi Germany. Particularly relevant to Milgram's research is the case of Adolf Eichmann. As is discussed in Chapter 7, Eichmann, one of the most notorious of the Nazi war criminals, was described by his interrogator as "utterly ordinary" (Arendt, 1963; Lifton, 1986; Von Lang & Sibyll, 1983). Assign excerpts from one or more of these cited sources. Discuss the implications of cases like Eichmann's for a social psychological understanding of obedience. Consider showing excerpts from the award-winning 1993 film *Schindler's List* as well.

Discuss how some of the same underlying processes can be observed in numerous dramatic as well as mundane examples since the 1940s. Some of the dramatic examples are mentioned in the textbook or in the Lecture and Discussion Ideas to follow. Another dramatic illustration can be found in the film *The Wave* (see Multimedia Resources below), in which a high-school teacher uses his authority to create a fascistic group of students, demonstrating how vulnerable we all are to some of the underlying forces that helped make possible the obedience found in Nazi Germany. Particularly relevant and powerful is the scene toward the end of the film in which the teacher stuns the students by revealing the identity of the person responsible for this movement to be Hitler. Consider asking the students to come up with their own examples of instances in the news or in their own lives in which people obeyed almost blindly the commands of an authority.

Arendt, H. (1963). Eichmann in Jerusalem: A report on the banality of evil. New York: Viking.

Lifton, R. J. (1986). The Nazi doctors: Medical killing and the psychology of genocide. New York: Basic Books.

Von Lang, J., & Sibyll, C. (Eds.). (1983). Eichmann interrogated (R. Manheim, trans.). New York: Farrar, Straus, & Giroux.

Idea 2. Jonestown

Assign readings concerning the development and self-destruction of the community organized by Jim Jones known as "Jonestown." Jones was an extremely charismatic man who was able to use numerous techniques of social influence to his advantage. He was a minister who built a small following into a national organization of churches, called the Peoples Temple. Jones elicited a tremendous degree of commitment from his followers, to the point where they gave all of their money and property to him. When the government began questioning various financial aspects of the empire that Jones was building, he brought his congregation to the isolated reaches of Guyana, South America, where he established the community bearing his name. Eventually, a congressman from California flew to Jonestown to investigate reports of U.S. citizens being held against their will in this community, and he and several others were killed by Jones's aides. Jones then explained to the members of the community that they would soon be under attack by outside forces, and that the only honorable solution for them would be to commit mass suicide. Most of the people there followed Jones's orders and drank the poison Jones offered them (indeed, there were many instances in which parents gave their children the poison before taking it themselves), although some were killed by Jones's assistants. More than 900 people died in this 1978 tragedy. When news of this tragedy spread, people around the world were shocked at the level of obedience shown by the hundreds of people who followed Jones.

There are a number of important social psychological points that can be made concerning the Jonestown tragedy, such as:

- Discuss the various types of power that Jones was able to develop, and how he developed them.

- Discuss examples of strong informational influence and normative influence in Jonestown.

- Compare the isolation of Jonestown with the situation faced by participants in Sherif's study concerning the autokinetic effect.

- Examine how the processes underlying important compliance techniques, such as the foot-in-the-door technique and the norm of reciprocity, were influential in Jonestown.

- Compare the authority of Jones with that of the experimenter in Milgram's research.

- Discuss how social impact theory could be used to explain what happened in Jonestown.

Other relevant concepts from the textbook that can be integrated into this discussion include social comparison theory (Ch. 3), attribution (Ch. 4), self-fulfilling prophecies (Ch. 4), persuasion (Ch. 6—e.g., one-sided messages, the role of fear, persuasion via the peripheral route), cognitive dissonance (Ch. 6), groupthink (Ch. 8), group polarization (Ch. 8), pluralistic ignorance (Ch. 10), the sunk cost principle (Ch. 13), and leadership (Ch. 13).

There are several readings and films concerning Jonestown. We have found that assigning excerpts from the book *Awake in a Nightmare: Jonestown, the Only Eyewitness Account*, by Feinsod (1981), is particularly effective. It is based on the vivid account of a survivor of Jonestown. Unlike some of the more explicitly psychological treatments of the story, this book simply relates the experiences and observations of Odell Rhodes, who was initially swept up by the charisma and apparent expertise of Jim Jones, went to Jonestown, and began to observe Jones and his followers spiral out of control. Students can be challenged to think for themselves in applying relevant social psychological concepts and principles to this reading. An alternative approach is to assign a reading that does much of this thinking for the students, such as Osherow's (1984) informative social psychological analysis of Jonestown. See the Multimedia Resources section below for video ideas concerning Jonestown.

Feinsod, E. (1981). Awake in a nightmare: Jonestown, the only eyewitness account. New York: Norton.

Osherow, N. (1984). Making sense of the nonsensical: An analysis of Jonestown. In E. Aronson (Ed.), Readings about the social animal (Fourth Edition, pp. 68-86). New York: W. H. Freeman.

Idea 3.   The My Lai Massacre

The event that has come to be known as the My Lai massacre during the Vietnam War can serve as a powerful case study of conformity and obedience, as well as of aggression (see Ch. 11). In this incident, a platoon of U.S. soldiers brutally killed an entire village of innocent men, women, and children in the village known to Americans as My Lai. These men had been given orders to destroy what they believed to be an enemy stronghold, but it soon became clear that the U.S. soldiers had received the wrong information and were killing defenseless civilians. Despite this realization, the killing and brutality continued. You can assign and discuss excerpts from R. Hammer's (1970) book, *One Morning in the War*, to help students appreciate the scope and consequences of conformity and obedience (as well as aggression) in this incident. Hammer's book provides a detailed account of what led up to the massacre and what happened during the massacre itself.

Discuss the roles of informational and normative influence in the tragedy. Point out examples of public and private conformity. Discuss what factors made the soldiers so vulnerable to conformity and obedience pressures. Discuss how some of the processes of self-perception and self-presentation that underlie various compliance techniques (such as the foot-in-the-door technique) may also have played an important role in Vietnam in general and My Lai in particular. Discuss the argument made by Lt. Calley and others who participated in the killing that they were just following orders and should therefore not be held responsible for their actions, and have students debate the issue of whether they should have been punished for their actions. On the one hand, students should see how the explanation of "just following orders" has been used to justify awful actions throughout history, as in Nazi Germany. On the other hand, students should recognize the pressures of war and understand how the military cannot be effective if orders are questioned. Consider showing excerpts from two relevant videos, *Remember My Lai* and *Disobeying Orders* (see the Multimedia Resources section), to add some provocative material to this discussion.

Integrate into the discussion of My Lai concepts from other chapters in the textbook, such as aggression (Ch. 11—e.g., frustration-aggression, displacement of aggression and scapegoating, aggression cues, heat, arousal, excitation transfer, reinforcement, and modeling), self-awareness (Ch. 3), expectations (Ch. 4), attribution (Ch. 4), stereotypes and prejudice (Ch. 5), cognitive dissonance (Ch. 6), group processes (Ch. 8), bystander intervention (Ch. 10), leadership (Ch. 13), and stress (Ch. 14). An excerpt from the popular film directed by Oliver Stone, *Platoon*, can provide a vivid fictional depiction of this kind of massacre. The film *Saving Private Ryan* shows some related kinds of behavior by American troops in World War II.

Hammer, R. (1970). <u>One morning in the war: The tragedy at Son My</u>. New York: Coward-McCann.

Idea 4.   Conformity Across Cultures

Discuss the differences between individualistic and collectivistic cultural orientations. Contrast the connotations of "conformity" in the United States—with its history of valuing "rugged individualism"—with those in collectivistic cultures, such as in many parts of Asia and Africa. In Korea, for example, the word "conformity" is understood to mean maturity and inner strength. Ask the students to explain how conformity can be construed to mean qualities such as maturity and inner strength, sensitivity, flexibility, and a willingness to put aside selfish concerns for the good of the group.

Assign or summarize readings that examine cross-cultural differences that are relevant to the issues of group norms and conformity. Kim and Markus (1999) propose that East Asians conform because conforming makes them feel connected to others in their culture, a desirable outcome. In contrast, they say, Americans view conformity in terms of relinquishing control and being pushed around, a negative outcome. In a series of studies they found that East Asians preferred nonunique abstract figures, whereas Americans preferred unique ones; that East Asians, when shown four orange pens and one green one, chose an orange one, whereas Americans chose the only green one; and that Korean magazine ads were more likely to use a conformity appeal with statements like, "Seven out of ten people use this…", whereas American magazine ads were more likely to use a uniqueness appeal with statements like, "Choose your own view…"

Markus and Kitayama (1991) contrast a maxim familiar to many Americans, "It's the squeaky wheel that gets the grease," with a maxim more familiar to peoples in Asia (such as Japan and China), "The nail that sticks up shall be hammered down." Discuss the implications of these differences for the issues raised in Chapter 7. In what ways should the social psychological principles underlying concepts such as public versus private conformity be similar or different across cultures? Would the two-step compliance techniques be more or less likely to work in collectivistic cultures than in individualistic cultures?

In one recent study, Petrova, Cialdini, & Sills (2007) found that US participants were less likely than Asians to comply with an initial, modest request. But that those (US participants) who chose to comply were more likely than their Asian counterparts to show consistency by agreeing to a subsequent, larger request. How would your students explain that finding?

And would they expect the obedience levels found in Milgram's research in this country to have been much higher in collectivistic settings? What if the participants were children? Shanab and Yahya (1977) found a 73 percent rate of obedience in a study that duplicated Milgram's procedure but used 6- to 16-year-old Jordanian children.

Also, consider the implications of these cross-cultural differences for how people perceive those whose behaviors are or are not consistent with group norms. Discuss how interactions between individuals from different cultural backgrounds may be affected by different conceptions of and attitudes about conforming to group norms.

Kim, H., & Markus, H.R. (1999). Deviance or uniqueness, harmony, or conformity? A cultural analysis. Journal of Personality & Social Psychology, 77, 4, 785-800.

Markus, H.R., & Kitayama, S. (1991). Cultural variation in the self-concept. In J. Strauss and G. R. Goethals (Eds.), The self: Interdisciplinary approaches (pp. 18-48). New York: Springer-Verlag.

Petrova, P.K., Cialdini, R.B., & Sills, S.J. (2007). Consistency-based compliance across cultures. Journal of Experimental Social Psychology, 43, 1, 104-111.

Shanab, M.E. & Yahya, K.A. (1977). A behavioral study of obedience in children. Journal of Personality and Social Psychology, 35, 530-536.

Idea 5.   Informational and Normative Influence

In Chapter 7, informational influence is defined as "influence that produces conformity when a person believes others are correct in their judgments." Normative influence is defined as "influence that produces conformity when a person fears the negative social consequences of appearing deviant." Distinguishing these two types of social influence is important for a better understanding of how and why conformity should be strong or weak in various situations. Discuss these two types of influence and ask students to provide examples from their own lives that illustrate these phenomena. Bring to class your own examples. Ask the class to discuss when they feel particularly vulnerable to each type of influence. Discuss various research findings about conformity in the textbook and have the students analyze the extent to which either or both of these types of influence played an important role. If you discuss some of the historical examples mentioned in the previous lecture/discussion ideas, such as the Jonestown mass suicide or the My Lai massacre, discuss the roles of informational and normative influence. For example, Jim Jones was able to exert a tremendous amount of informational influence on his followers through "miraculous" demonstrations of his knowledge and expertise (often through trickery). Moreover, by cutting off his followers from the rest of the world and from dissenting opinions, he was able to create a situation in which his followers were very vulnerable to informational influence from each other. In addition, by creating a strong, pervasive sense of group identity, such as by fostering "us against the world" thinking, Jones was able to create a situation in which his followers would feel tremendous normative pressure to behave and think as everyone else in the group did.

Consider discussing the potential roles of informational and normative influence in relation to topics from other chapters, such as social comparison theory (Ch. 3), stereotyping (Ch. 5), persuasion (Ch. 6), group processes such as group polarization or groupthink (Ch. 8), helping in emergency situations (Ch. 10), jury decision making (Ch. 12), and economic decision making (Ch. 13). This would both emphasize the importance and ubiquity of these types of influence but also help the students see and think beyond chapter divisions, encouraging them to process the information in the textbook at a deeper level. Also discuss some situations in which informational and normative types of influence may work against each other, as is suggested by the dual-process perspective concerning minority influence.

Idea 6.   Minority Influence

Discuss the ways in which minorities can use the knowledge derived from research on minority influence to increase their influence in society. Examine Moscovici's model of minority influence, presented in the text, in terms of its applicability to various social movements, such as those concerning civil rights, protests against wars, etc. Consider showing the classic film *Twelve Angry Men*, which depicts a lone juror (played by Henry Fonda) struggling against the pressure put on him by the other eleven jurors to change his vote so they could reach a unanimous verdict, but one by one he convinced his fellow jurors to reconsider their position (this movie is discussed briefly in Ch. 12); discuss the potential role of minority influence in juries.

Contrast the single-process and dual-process accounts of majority and minority influence. Why, according to the dual-process approach, do minorities elicit conformity through informational influence whereas majorities do so through normative influence? Why is "style" so important in minority influence, according to Moscovici? Ask students to discuss their own experiences, either as the minority in a group or as observers of a vocal minority in a group. In these experiences, what factors increased or decreased the likelihood that the minority position would have an impact on the majority? Was much normative pressure exerted to keep the minority from defecting to the majority position?

Idea 7.   Pervasive Pressures to Conform: The Influences of Peers and the Media

The fear of embarrassment caused by deviating from a (perceived) group norm can be very powerful among college students. Discuss with the class some of the sources and consequences of conformity pressures. Two pervasive and influential sources with which most college students are familiar are peers and the media. Discuss each of these factors as they affect private as well as public conformity.

It is difficult to overestimate the extent to which peers exert conformity and compliance pressures on each other. These pressures can be very specific and explicit, as when children pressure other children to engage in particular acts of mischief, or they can be fairly subtle, as when an individual is pressured to avoid achieving more than his or her friends. Styles of dress and appearance, ways of presenting one's personality to others, various attitudes and ways of speaking are just a few of the countless dimensions on which peers exert social influence.

More subtle than peer pressure, but not necessarily less pervasive or powerful, are the influences of media depictions of people in television shows, films, advertising, news programs, etc. We are exposed to images from the media throughout our lives, in doses too staggering to comprehend. These images both reflect and help shape various norms and standards. Sometimes intentionally, sometimes unintentionally, the media present messages of what are taken to be the normative ways for people of particular generations or categories to look, think, and behave.

To help create a meaningful discussion of these issues, consider assigning or summarizing the articles by Jennings (Walstedt) and colleagues (1980) and Geis and colleagues (1984). These researchers have conducted experiments concerning the effects of television commercials on women's likelihood of conforming, as well as on their self-confidence and career aspirations. Students tend to find these articles thought provoking. If some students suggest alternative explanations for the results of these studies, you should encourage this kind of critical thinking and challenge the students to think of methods of testing these issues in ways that would be less subject to such alternative explanations. More important, the articles raise important and interesting questions about the effects of advertising and whether or not advertisers should be held responsible for these effects. The film *Still Killing Us Softly*, which has been suggested for other chapters (e.g., Chapters 4 and 11), raises similar questions in a very powerful way.

Crandall's (1988) article, "Social Contagion of Binge Eating," is also very thought provoking and relevant to students' lives and to the issues raised in Chapter 7. Crandall's research examines the extent to which binge eating in college sororities may result, in part, from social influence pressures that the students exert on each other. Eating disorders are all too prevalent on college campuses, and students should be particularly interested in this topic. Crandall's article has the added benefit of offering a review of some of the relevant literature on norms in groups, social impact theory, and related topics.

Crandall, C. S. (1988). Social contagion of binge eating. Journal of Personality and Social Psychology, 55, 588-598.

Geis, F. L., Brown, V., Jennings (Walstedt), J., & Porter, N. (1984). TV commercials as achievement scripts for women. Sex Roles, 10, 513-525.

Jennings (Walstedt), J., Geis, F. L., & Brown, V. (1980). Influence of television commercials on women's self-confidence and independent judgment. Journal of Personality and Social Psychology, 38, 203-210.

Idea 8.   The Norm of Reciprocity

The norm of reciprocity is the social rule that says that we should treat others as they have treated us. The text describes several research studies that have shown how this norm can be used to trap people into compliance (e.g., Regan, 1971, Greenberg and Westcott, 1983, Rind and Strohmetz, 2001).

In an amusing application of the norm, which is not mentioned in the text, Kunz and Woolcott (1976) sent out Christmas cards to a large number of total strangers. Twenty percent of the recipients felt obligated enough to send back cards to people they did not know. When the title Dr. was added in front of the sender's name, the percentage was even higher. In a more outrageous application of the norm, on a whim, a young man sent a wedding invitation to the Sultan of Brunei (whom he'd never met), and the Sultan sent his regrets and an extremely generous check.

There are many other times when the norm of reciprocity comes into play outside of the research lab. For example, the Hare Krishnas give out flowers and charities send out address labels in the hope of getting a contribution; stores give out calendars and food samples; health clubs offer free workouts; real-estate firms offer free appraisals; and wineries give visitors free tastes of wine. All of these techniques increase compliance by spurring interest in the product as well as by activating the norm of reciprocity.

Ask students if they can think of other examples of the norm of reciprocity. When have they been on the receiving end? Did they feel obligated to reciprocate? Did they ever take advantage of the norm themselves to get others to comply?

Greenberg, M. S., & Westcott, D. R. (1983). Indebtedness as a mediator of reactions to aid. In J. D. Fisher, A. Nadler, & B. M. DePaulo (Eds.), New Directions in Helping: Vol. 1. Recipient Reactions to Aid. New York: Academic Press.

Regan, D. (1971). Effects of a favor and liking on compliance. Journal of Experimental Social Psychology, 7, 627-639.

Rind, B. & Strohmetz, D. (2001). Effect on restaurant tipping of presenting restaurant customers with an interesting task and of reciprocity. Journal of Applied Social Psychology, 31, 1379-1385.

Idea 9.   Six Factors in Compliance

According to Robert Cialdini (2004), the reciprocity norm is only one of six tendencies that incline people to say "yes" to a request. Writing in Scientific American, Cialdini elaborates on five additional psychological factors that lead to compliance. (Some of these factors are also covered in Chapter 6 of the text, as characteristics of the source and message that increase persuasion.)

First, there is consistency. Most individuals do not wish to be seen as hypocrites; they are strongly motivated to appear and to be consistent in their attitudes and behaviors. If they make a commitment, they want to follow through on it. So, for example, to increase contributions to the handicapped, one researcher elicited people's signatures on a petition supporting the handicapped two weeks prior to asking them for donations. In this case, consistency was established via the foot-in-the-door technique.

The second tendency is the need for social validation. The larger the number of people that are involved in an action, the more that action becomes socially validated and therefore an example for others to follow. If we hear that all our neighbors signed a petition for the building of a new school, we are much more likely to sign on it too. That's partly why the term "best seller" has a powerful influence on our buying habits: We think, "If everyone else is buying it, it must be good."

The third factor is liking. We tend to say "yes" to those we like and we especially like our friends. That's the logic used by Tupperware and several other companies whose sales are made exclusively at "home parties" where friends are gathered together to buy the products from the friend who hosts the "party."

Liking is not limited to those we know. We can also feel a liking for strangers. We are particularly inclined to like attractive people. That's why one study found that good looking political candidates received more votes than less attractive candidates.

We also tend to like those who appear similar to us in some way. In one study, where donations were solicited on a college campus, simply having the solicitor say the phrase "I'm a student too" resulted in a doubling of the contributions.

Another way that strangers can warm their way into our hearts is by complimenting us. We like those who seem to like us, whether their compliments are genuine or not. In the same vein, we like those who appear to fight on our behalf. So, automobile sales managers frequently play the role of "villains," so that their salespersons can appear to be siding with the customer.

Authority is the fourth element in compliance. That's why, when people watch a commercial, they are more easily persuaded when the person touting the benefits of some product is a doctor, even if the doctor is only an actor with a white coat.

The last factor is scarcity. Things become more valuable to us if we perceive that they are scarce. That's why the terms "one-of-a-kind" and "for a limited time only" are so often used by advertisers.

Students can probably provide many more examples where advertisers make use of these factors to induce compliance. You might also ask them to think about how each of these tendencies to comply is adaptive from an evolutionary point of view; how they have helped human beings to best survive within a social milieu throughout their history.

Cialdini, R.B. (2004) The science of persuasion. Scientific American, 14, 1, 70-77.

Idea 10.   Putting Compliance techniques to a Good Use

Ask students to imagine that they are troubled that a good friend is a very heavy smoker. In small groups, have them discuss how they could use compliance strategies, such as the foot-in-the-door technique, low-balling, the door-in-the-face technique, the norm of reciprocity, and exploitations of mindlessness to get their friend to quit smoking. Let each group share some of their ideas with the rest of the class.

Discuss how several processes seem to underlie most of these strategies. For example, self-presentation concerns can play important roles in all of the compliance techniques mentioned above. Another self-related process—self-perception—plays a critical role in the success of the foot-in-the-door technique. Assimilation and contrast effects are evident in several techniques, such as low-balling and the door-in-the-face technique.

Discuss the ways in which commitment breeds further commitment. Examples can be seen in studies of the foot-in-the-door technique and low-balling, but also in Milgram's research on obedience (i.e., by gradually escalating the voltage, the participants make a long series of commitments, none much greater than the previous one); in events such as those in Jonestown and My Lai; in some cognitive dissonance manifestations, such as effort justification (Ch. 6); and in the sunk cost trap (Ch. 13).

Finally, discuss the role of awareness and knowledge of these traps in people's ability to resist them. This is a nice point about the power of education: The more the students learn about these phenomena, the less vulnerable they should be to them.

Idea 11. Two Additional Compliance Techniques

Students might be intrigued to learn about two additional compliance techniques that are not mentioned in the text. The first is called the pique technique. According to the pique technique, a subject is more likely to comply with a request that he or she would normally turn down automatically, if that mindless refusal is interrupted and the subject's curiosity is piqued by a strange or unusual request.

In the study that introduced the technique (Santos, Leve, & Pratkanis, 1994), it was found that subjects were significantly more likely to comply with panhandlers' quirky requests (for 17 or 37 cents) than with the more ordinary ones (a quarter or any change).

Ask your students if they have ever been on the giving or receiving end of the pique technique. Possible milieus for the technique include telemarketing, trick or treating, fund-raising, magazine advertising, or any other circumstance where one person is mindlessly set to say "No" and another is trying to forestall the refusal with an intriguing departure from the expected request.

Discuss what makes the technique work. What is it about having our curiosity piqued that makes us more likely to comply? According to the authors, the technique works because it interrupts mindless refusal and gets a person to think. Increased thought about an appeal then leads to increased liking for the person making the appeal, which increases the likelihood of compliance.

The second technique is called the "but you are free of" technique. This is a compliance procedure whereby the subject is asked to do something and is then immediately told, "But you are free to accept or refuse."

In one study (Guéguen & Pascual, 2005), subjects were more likely to agree to respond to a survey when they were told that were free to refuse than when they were just asked to respond to the survey. In earlier studies, the technique was found to be effective in increasing the amount of charitable donations and number of visits to a humanitarian website.

Ask students to discuss why such a request would increase compliance. The authors theorize that the phrase "but you are free to accept or refuse" makes people feel more personally involved in the task at hand. It also activates a feeling of freedom, and knowing that they have a choice makes people more amenable to going along with a request.

Guéguen, N., & Pascual, A. (2005). Improving the response rate to a street survey: An evaluation of the "But you are free to accept or refuse" technique. The Psychological Record, 55, 297-303.

Santos, M. D., Leve, C., & Pratkanis, A. R. (1994). Hey buddy, can you spare seventeen cents? Mindful persuasion and the pique technique. Journal of Applied Social Psychology, 24, 755-764.

Idea 12.   Disobedience on a Personal Level

According to the text, disobedience that is not criminal but *is* morally, politically, or religiously motivated is always a collective act. Do your students agree with the statement? Have there been times when they or someone they know chose to individually disobey a law that they felt was morally, politically, or religiously unjust?

Other than criminal, political, religious, or moral, what other motives might there be for disobeying laws? Ask students if they ever personally disobeyed laws regarding minor transgressions, such as speed limits or parking. To what do they attribute their disobedience of such laws? Are the reasons external (e.g., thought they could get away with it)? Or internal (e.g., thought the law was unreasonable)? One study (Sanderson & Darley, 2002) found that people were likely to *obey* such laws for both external and internal reasons (i.e., fear of getting caught and respect for the law).

Recent efforts to decrease drug use by increasing penalties for the possession and sales of narcotics have been largely unsuccessful, at least in part because people feel that such laws are illegitimate and therefore disobey them. How do students feel about recent laws concerning seat belt use, cell phone use, or smoking? When should the government criminalize such behaviors and when should they leave such decisions up to individuals? Do they ever disobey such laws and to what do they attribute such disobedience? Are there other behaviors that they feel should not come under government regulation?

Sanderson, C. A., & Darley, J. M. (2002). "I am moral, but you are deterred": Differential attributions about why people obey the law. Journal of Applied Social Psychology, 32, 375-405.

Idea 13. Milgram's Research on Obedience to Authority

We have five words of advice to all instructors of social psychology courses: Show the Milgram film, *Obedience*. Viewing this film (see Multimedia Resources below), which documents Milgram's classic studies of obedience in the early 1960s, is one of the most powerful, memorable experiences that students will ever have in the classroom. After showing the film, have the students read the original article Milgram published about this research; this article is included in *Readings in Social Psychology: The Art and Science of Research*, the book of readings that is available with the textbook.

You may consider warning the students before you show the film that it may be stressful for some students to watch. During the film, take note of students' reactions. Is there much laughter, particularly early in the film? Do the students seem to sympathize with the participants? After the film, discuss their reactions. If some students laughed, why did they laugh? Could it have been for similar reasons as many of the participants in Milgram's research?

Discuss what factors did and did not significantly affect the levels of obedience observed in this research. Naive viewers always assume that personality differences must account for most of the variance in determining who obeyed and who didn't; emphasize to them that such differences had little effect relative to situational factors. Discuss social impact theory and how it can explain the effects of the various manipulations used.

Ask the class if the obedience observed in Milgram's research was a function of the culture and time in which the research took place. Point out how there might be greater obedience in cultures that are more collectivistic in orientation, and note more recent studies and events that illustrate very high levels of obedience. Discuss how the experimenter in Milgram's studies had relatively little power compared to people in many other situations, such as government officials, some teachers, parents, some peers, doctors, judges, the police, etc. Discuss the five types of power that are identified in Lecture and Discussion Idea 15, and ask the students which of these types of power was exerted by the experimenter. If you discuss Jonestown, explain that the power of Milgram's experimenter paled in comparison to that of Jim Jones.

Ask students if they think that they might have shown full obedience if they had been participants in this research. Very few students believe that they would have. Explain how this is likely to reflect the fundamental attribution error (Ch. 4). From the perspective of a distant observer, it is impossible to appreciate how powerful the situational pressure was on the participants, and therefore we tend to attribute the participants' behaviors to their dispositions rather than to the situation. Consider assigning articles by Bierbrauer (1979) or Safer (1980) on this point. To help facilitate discussion consider conducting Activity 8.

Discuss the debriefing used by Milgram to try to alleviate the strain that participants were under and to make them feel less awful about what they had learned about themselves (see the next Lecture and Discussion Idea below).

Finally, discuss the irony of the fact that conformity can help individuals resist obedience. That is, participants in Milgram's research were much less likely to obey the experimenter's commands if they first witnessed others resist the experimenter. Explain how this is consistent with social impact theory.

Bierbrauer, G. (1979). Why did he do it? Attribution of obedience and the phenomenon of dispositional bias. European Journal of Social Psychology, 9, 67-84.

Safer, M. A. (1980). Attributing evil to the subject, not the situation. Personality and Social Psychology Bulletin, 6, 205-209.

Idea 14.   Discussing the Ethics of Milgram's Research on Obedience to Authority

After reading and discussing Milgram's studies on obedience, have the class consider the ethical implications of the research. Discuss the criticism that Milgram received for conducting the research and have students debate the issue of the scientific value of the research versus experimenters' ethical responsibilities to participants. Consider assigning or summarizing Baumrind's (1964) article critiquing the ethics of Milgram's research. Ask the students to imagine that they were on a review board that had to decide whether Milgram's research could be conducted. How would they make their decisions? Explain to the students that the APA guidelines on the treatment of human participants were developed after Milgram's research and that, given these guidelines, Milgram's research would probably not be allowed to be conducted today.

Baumrind, D. (1964). Some thoughts on ethics of research: After reading Milgram's "Behavioral study of obedience." American Psychologist, 19, 421-423.

Idea 15.   Five Types of Power

French and Raven (1959) identified five types of power. Distinguishing among these five types can be very useful in understanding how and when obedience and compliance are likely to be produced. Compare the bases from which the experimenter in Milgram's research derived power with the bases from which doctors, politicians, military officers, and leaders like Jim Jones do so; such a comparison can be used to illustrate why the results of Milgram's research may underestimate, rather than overestimate, people's susceptibility to obedience in the face of a powerful authority.

The five types of power are:

(1) **Coercive power**. Coercive power concerns the potential to deliver threats and punishment. Majorities may have coercive power. The military and police have coercive power. Parents have coercive power over their children. Teachers have some coercive power over their students. Jim Jones began to rely heavily on his coercive power toward the end of the Jonestown experience. The experimenter in Milgram's research had very little, if any, coercive power.

(2) **Reward power**. Reward power concerns the potential to deliver positive reinforcement. Teachers, parents, employers, and wealthy individuals are among those who derive power from the ability to give rewards. As Jim Jones began to recruit individuals for his Peoples Temple and persuade them to join him in going to South America, he used reward power extensively. The experimenter in Milgram's research had very little, if any, reward power. The participants received their payment whether or not they obeyed the experimenter.

(3) **Expert power**. Expert power is derived from a reputation for being very knowledgeable about a particular issue or area of concern. Doctors have expert power in their areas of specialization. Teachers and researchers may have expert power in their areas of study. Through his demonstrations and lectures, Jim Jones established expert power early on, and he used this power throughout the history of Jonestown, including at the ultimate moment when he convinced his followers that suicide was the only honorable response to their situation. To the participants in Milgram's research, the experimenter probably had some degree of expert power, especially when the study was demonstrated at the prestigious Yale University laboratories.

(4) **Legitimate power**. Legitimate power is derived from a particular role or position that one has. This power is usually limited to a particular domain in which one has a position of authority. Teachers have legitimate power over their students in the classroom, but not outside of school. A judge derives a great deal of legitimate power from the courtroom, but the power does not go with the judge when he or she leaves the court. As the man responsible for the Peoples Church and for the community named after him, Jim Jones had a great deal of legitimate power in Jonestown. The experimenter in Milgram's research had legitimate power in the context of the experiment.

(5) **Referent power**. Referent power is derived from being admired and liked, even revered. A celebrity may have a great deal of power over fans because they admire him or her so much. A role model may be able to exert a considerable amount of social influence over those who look up to him or her. Jim Jones, who was called "Dad" by his followers, had a tremendous degree of referent power among his followers. The experimenter in Milgram's research had no referent power.

French, J. R. P., Jr., & Raven, B. H. (1959). The bases of social power. In D. Cartwright (Ed.), Studies in social power (pp. 150-167). Ann Arbor: University of Michigan Press.

Idea 16.   Social Influence in Psychotherapy and Criminal Investigations

A very provocative and controversial issue that you might consider raising concerns how therapists, counselors, police detectives, and others may—intentionally or not—use their power and social influence to change the beliefs or behaviors of vulnerable individuals in subtle but very powerful ways, possibly to the point where such individuals develop false memories or believe that they have particular psychopathologies. This is a very controversial and sensitive issue that you should handle with great care, but it raises some fascinating questions about social influence, power, compliance, conformity, and social impact theory, as well as about memory and confessions (Ch. 12), self-perception (Ch. 3 & Ch. 6), cognitive dissonance (Ch. 6), and the power of expectations and self-fulfilling prophecies (Ch. 4 & Ch. 5). Because some of these issues are raised in Chapter 12 concerning both criminal confessions and witnesses' memories, you might consider waiting until students read that chapter before you hold this discussion, but these issues clearly are relevant to Chapter 7 as well.

To get this discussion started, assign or summarize some of the following readings: Loftus's (1993) article, "The Reality of Repressed Memories," which argues that most (and perhaps all) "recovered" memories (i.e., memories of events that allegedly were repressed from consciousness for many years and are then recalled many years after the events in question, either through therapy or by exposure to some triggering cue or event) are not real memories but rather are constructed at the time of "recall" and often stem from the suggestions made by a therapist or other people.

Spanos's (1994) article, "Multiple Identity Enactments and Multiple Personality Disorder: A Sociocognitive Perspective," which makes a similar point about multiple personality disorder—that is, that the increased prevalence of this disorder may be a function of the suggestions of therapists, the media, and others. Like the Loftus article, the Spanos article suggests that the dramatic symptoms experienced by many individuals may be due to processes of social influence, such as conformity and compliance.

Wright's (1994) book, *Remembering Satan*, which details the infamous 1993 case involving Paul Ingram and his family in Olympia, Washington. Paul was accused of and confessed to a series of horrific crimes against his wife and children involving, among other things, Satanic ritual abuse. Wright's fascinating and disturbing book provides gripping details about the case and suggests that much, and perhaps all, of what Paul remembered about these incidents was due to his desire to obey the investigators and comply with the wishes of those around him.

Any of these sources can be used to make a point about the potential of conformity, compliance, and obedience to alter people's memories and self-concepts. Each of these readings, however, is open to criticism and debate. It is important to discuss with the class the other side of these issues—that is, that the prevalence of actual physical and sexual abuse is shockingly high, that students should be wary of the tendency to "blame the victim," and that a backlash may emerge against victims and survivors who call attention to these experiences. The point you should make is not that social influence does or doesn't explain the majority of cases involving recovered memory or multiple personality disorder, but rather that the power of conformity, compliance, and obedience can be so great that such consequences are possible.

For an opposite take on the issue, refer to a study by Bernstein, Laney, Morris, and Loftus (2005) on how false beliefs can be implanted to benefit individuals who are trying to lose weight. This study details how participants were led to develop the false memory that strawberry ice cream made them ill when they were children. Afterwards, the participants manifested food avoidance to strawberry ice cream.

Bernstein, D.M, Laney, C., Morris, E.K., & Loftus, E.L. (2005). False beliefs about fattening foods can have healthy consequences. Proceedings of the National Academy of Sciences of the United States of America; 9/27/2005, 102, 39, 13724-13731.

Loftus, E. (1993). The reality of repressed memories. American Psychologist, 48(5), 518-537.

Spanos, N. (1994). Multiple identity enactments and multiple personality disorder: A sociocognitive perspective. Psychological Bulletin, 116 , 143-165.

Wright, L. (1994). Remembering Satan. New York: Knopf.

Idea 17.   The Stanford University Prison Simulation

One of the most controversial studies ever conducted in social psychology was that of Philip Zimbardo and his colleagues (Haney et al., 1973; Zimbardo et al., 1973) in which a prison experience was simulated. A mock prison was established in the basement of the psychology department building at Stanford University, and a group of young men volunteered to participate in a two-week study of prison life. The participants were divided randomly into groups of either "prisoners" or "guards."

The study is described in Chapter 12 of the textbook. Although it can be discussed in the context of the prison experience (Ch. 12) or group dynamics (Ch. 8), perhaps the most dramatic lesson of the research concerns the shocking levels of conformity and obedience observed. A group of normal, healthy young men conformed to the roles that were assigned them, and they in turn influenced each other to the point where the guards became more and more hostile and sadistic and the prisoners became more and more compliant and weak.

Discuss the factors that led to these results. Discuss the implications of the study in terms of conformity to group norms, and to roles dictated by one's job or status. You may find it particularly effective to show the film of this study (see Multimedia Resources below), or excerpts from this film, after showing and discussing the film of Milgram's research on obedience. The transition from the early-1960s crew cuts and displays of respect for authority seen in the Milgram film to the early 1970s long hair and vulgarity is jarring, but the persistence of social influence seen across these studies seems all the more powerful and dramatic as a result.

Any discussion of the Stanford Prison study should include a discussion of the ethics of the research. Whereas the ethics of Milgram's research are debatable, most social psychologists consider the Stanford study to be unacceptable according to current ethical standards in research. The study should have been terminated much sooner than it was, given the behaviors and emotions displayed by the participants. Zimbardo makes an important point about how the researchers themselves got caught up in their own roles and failed to appreciate that their "prison" was not a prison but part of a research study, thereby letting the study go on longer than it should have.

Haney, C., Banks, W. C., & Zimbardo, P. G. (1973). Interpersonal dynamics in a simulated prison. International Journal of Criminology and Penology, 1, 69-97.

Zimbardo, P. G., Banks, W. C., Haney, C., & Jaffe, D. (1973, April 8). The mind is a formidable jailer: A Pirandellian prison. New York Times Magazine, pp. 38-60.

CLASSROOM ACTIVITIES

Activity 1. The Fate of the Deviant

To better understand why people are so likely to conform, one must appreciate what happens to individuals who deviate from a group norm. The present activity is designed to examine this issue, as well as to illustrate some of the dynamics of groups and communication. This activity can be conducted in the context of both Chapter 8 (Group Processes) and Chapter 7.

Background. This activity is based on a study by Schachter (1951) in which groups of participants discussed the case of a juvenile delinquent named Johnny Rocco. The group read about Johnny's family history and delinquent behaviors, and they discussed what would be the best way to encourage Johnny to become an upstanding young adult. The groups consisted of naive participants and three confederates. One of the confederates (the deviant) consistently disagreed with the group's opinion about how to handle Johnny. For example, if the majority of the group advocated a very supportive, warm environment for Johnny, the deviant argued that such an environment would only make it easier for Johnny to continue to misbehave and that what Johnny really needed was an environment in which he would be quickly and sternly punished for any and all transgressions. Another confederate (the slider) began by disagreeing with the group consensus but then gradually came around to the majority, eventually fully supporting the majority opinion. A third confederate (the mode) voiced the majority opinion throughout.

Schachter found that the groups tended to try to reach consensus right away, and that they devoted a lot of their energy to trying to persuade the deviant to change his opinion. After a while, when it was clear the deviant would not yield, the other group members tended to ignore and reject him, in essence re-forming the group so as to exclude this deviant. When the groups were asked to assign group members to various jobs, the deviant consistently was given the worst job. It is important to note that the groups were not instructed to reach unanimity; rather, the groups seemed to spontaneously adopt this as a necessary goal. It is also interesting to note that the groups tended to like the slider quite a bit. Rather than perceiving him to be "wishy-washy" or "spineless," the groups tended to see the slider as someone who was smart and mature enough to recognize the superiority of the majority's opinion.

Overall procedure. The goal of this activity is to have students participate in or observe groups discussing an issue. Within these groups, one of the group members is actually a confederate who consistently deviates from the majority opinion. Depending on time, class size, and logistics, there are many different ways to conduct this activity. In addition, there are many different kinds of "dependent measures" that can be used.

We suggest that the groups should consist of six students, one of whom is a confederate playing the role of the deviant. You or an assistant should play the role of the moderator of the group. Ideally, the students in the group should not know each other well. It is particularly important that the confederate should not be known well by the other students in the group. The confederate should be shown all the materials in advance of the class and given time to prepare to play the role of the deviant. You may consider having a second confederate in these groups play the role of the slider, although this is not necessary for the activity.

The individuals in the group should be seated in a semicircle. The deviant should always sit in a seat that is one seat away from either end of the semicircle. The group should read the brief (fictitious) case history of the juvenile delinquent (we have changed the name from Johnny Rocco to Bobby James and we have changed several of the details to make them seem more contemporary). This case history can be found in **Handout 7.1a**; distribute copies of this handout to the group members. After the group members read the case, the moderator should go around the semi-circle and ask each member of the group to state his or her name and to indicate which of several "treatments" for Bobby he or she would recommend from the kindness-punishment scale. This scale can be found in **Handout 7.1b**; distribute copies of this handout to the group members. The moderator should call on students one at a time around the semi-circle so that the deviant is called next-to-last.

Most of the students who read this case chose a treatment for Bobby that is closer to the "kindness" end of the scale than to the "punishment" end. The modal responses tend to be items #3 or #4 on Handout 7.1b. The deviant should take the opinion most deviant from the rest of the group. Typically, this means the most extreme "strong discipline" approach. (If the average response is midpoint position #4, the deviant should take position #7.) See **Handout 7.1c** for some instructions you can give to the confederate a few days before the activity to help him or her prepare for this role. Except at the very beginning of the activity, the confederate should not initiate discussion but should instead respond when he or she is brought into the discussion.

Let the discussion run for 7–10 minutes. The moderator should begin the discussion by asking the group to discuss the case and the best way to handle Bobby, and then, unless it is absolutely necessary, the moderator should not say a word until it is time to end the discussion. At the end of the discussion, the group members should be given another copy of Handout 7.1b and be asked once again to indicate which treatment for Bobby they would recommend. After they have completed this task, you may want to distribute copies of **Handout 7.1d** to the group members. This handout asks the group members to evaluate the discussion and each other on several dimensions.

Logistics. In addition to having groups discuss the case, you should have other students observe the groups and take notes of communication patterns, changes of opinion, etc. This you can do by using one-way mirrors or by videotaping the group discussion (you should make the discussants aware that they are being, or will be, observed by the other students). You can also consider having the group simply discuss the case in front of the room, but this can be a bit intimidating to the group members, some of whom may try to "perform" for their live audience. Another decision to make is how many group discussions you will conduct. You may have one group discuss the case and the rest of the students in class observe, or you may have several groups discuss the case separately, along with several groups of students observing these groups. This latter approach would probably require that the activity be done outside of class time as a special "lab." We have used this latter approach many times and it has worked quite well.

For purposes of clarity, we assume that you will take the simplest approach: Have six students (including one confederate) discuss the case while the rest of the class observes.

Observations. Even if the group will be discussing the case in front of the rest of the class, in the same room as everyone else, have the group first read about the case in another room or in the hallway outside of your classroom. While these students are outside the classroom, explain to the rest of the class what this activity is all about. Describe the Bobby James case to them briefly, distribute copies of the kindness-punishment scale (Handout 7.1b), and tell them about the confederate. Tell the students who the confederate is and instruct them to watch the other group members' reactions to this confederate when the confederate first offers his or her opinion about how best to handle Bobby. Tell them to watch the dynamics of the group. That is, do the other group members ignore and reject the confederate? Do they spend a lot of time trying to change the confederate's mind? How much informational and normative influence do the group members try to use on the confederate? How uncomfortable does the confederate seem? Do the individuals become locked into their original opinions, or do they show some flexibility? Does anyone offer an opinion at the end of the discussion that deviated from her or his initial opinion?

Assign each observer the task of observing one discussant; the observer should count the number of times this individual speaks in the group. These observations should be split between the first half of the discussion and the second half of the discussion. Unless you have a very small class, there will be multiple observers for each discussant. There are likely to be discrepancies among the observers about how many times a particular discussant spoke (e.g., does "Yeah" count as one?) so take the average from among the observers in these cases (and you can make a point about the importance of using multiple observers and trying to achieve interrater reliability—see Ch. 2). If the group discussion takes place right in front of the observers, tell the observers not to laugh, make any noises, or in any way distract the group members or tip them off as to what is going on—particularly concerning the presence of a confederate. Finally, tell the observers that the entire class, including the discussion group members, will talk about what happened in the discussion at the conclusion of the exercise. Instruct the observers to discuss their observations honestly—except that they should not say anything indicating that the deviant was a confederate until you reveal this.

Post-discussion discussion. When the group has finished its discussion and completed the questionnaire (Handout 7.1d), have the discussants sit with the rest of the class and begin a general discussion of the group dynamics observed. Ask the observers to note anything they thought was interesting or noteworthy about the discussion or the group dynamics. Ask the discussants to indicate how they felt the discussion went and whether or not they found anything interesting in the process or content of the discussion. While this is going on, look at the responses given by the discussants on Handout 7.1d, and calculate the proportion of the group members (excluding the confederate) who picked the confederate as the least likeable group member. Also note which jobs they selected for the confederate and which types of movies they thought the confederate would favor.

Chart the amount of time that the confederate talked during the first and second halves of the discussion. One typical result is that the confederate speaks a lot during the first half of the discussion because so much attention is directed toward the confederate, but then speaks much less during the second half of the discussion when the others begin to ignore the confederate. This does not always happen, however. We have seen many instances in which the other students never stop pressuring the confederate during the discussion, and we have seen a few instances in which the group rejects the confederate quite early in the discussion and ignores him or her throughout. Ask both the observers and the discussants to comment on what happened in this particular instance.

Report the results of the questionnaire. Did the group members tend to dislike the confederate? Did they tend to assign the confederate jobs that would require little interaction with other people? What types of movies did they think the confederate would like? Are there any interesting patterns in these inferences and evaluations? (Because of ethical considerations, don't reveal the responses made about any of the other discussants.)

To the extent that the group had "ganged up" on the confederate, ask them why they did this and how they felt during it. Ask them why they tried to reach a consensus *even though they had never been instructed to do so*. If the group members did not spend much time trying to persuade the confederate, ask them why they did not. If not revealed yet, tell the group members about the confederate. Be sure to emphasize that the confederate had been coached about what to say and how to say it, and that the rest of the students should not commit the fundamental attribution error (Ch. 4) and infer that the confederate believes anything he or she said while playing the role of the deviant. Explain Schachter's (1951) study and its results. Compare the results of Schachter's study with the results of this activity.

We often find that when the discussants initially offer their opinions about how to handle Bobby, they tend to be fairly unsure of themselves. After all, they have just finished reading the case and had virtually no time to consider the various options. And yet, after ten minutes of discussion, few students change their opinions (that is, as long as their initial opinions were close to the majority opinions). If this happens in your class, ask the discussants and observers to speculate about why it happened. Discuss psychological reactance and ask the class to consider whether it played a role. Similarly, discuss the power of making a public commitment to a position, and how it plays a role in many important phenomena, such as in cognitive dissonance (Ch. 6), continuing to invest resources in a failing course of action (Ch. 8 and Ch. 13), and in two-step compliance techniques such as the foot-in-the-door (this chapter [Ch. 7]). Also, we have observed that very few groups discuss ways of handling Bobby other than those mentioned on the kindness-punishment scale. The discussants are not told that they have to stick to this scale when discussing the case, and yet almost all do. This is another example of a norm that develops quickly and has a great deal of influence on the discussants.

Discuss how the conformity pressures exerted on a deviant in a real group situation are often much greater than those observed in this activity because real groups would be more motivated to achieve consensus (so that the groups could function more smoothly in general), they would be less inhibited (because they would not be observed by a psychology class), the groups would probably have more cohesiveness, and the decisions would have more importance to them. With this in mind, ask the students to discuss how difficult it can be to deviate from a group norm. Ask them to discuss the potential benefits of having a "devil's advocate" in any group (see the discussion of groupthink in Ch. 8), and have them discuss why groups fail to take advantage of these potential benefits because of the pressures they put on such individuals.

●*What if this bombs?* This activity is fairly bombproof because of the many interesting points to discuss, as indicated above. Even if the questionnaire results are not interesting, and even if the group dynamics do not replicate Schachter's findings, you can discuss any of a number of fascinating points. For example, ask the confederate to discuss how it felt when he or she deviated from the majority. What different techniques did the discussants use to try to persuade each other? If the discussants were very polite to each other and did not try to exert any informational or normative influence, ask them (and the observers) why this was so. Discuss whether particular norms were established early in the discussion about how the discussion should proceed. We often find this to be a particularly interesting phenomenon: Some groups begin by attacking each other, and the discussion remains heated throughout. Other groups begin by being very non-confrontational, and the discussants remain polite throughout—sometimes running out of things to discuss after only a few minutes. It seems that the one or two people who first speak in the discussion can set the tone for the rest of the discussion. This could be an interesting point to make. As we noted above, another norm that is established early on concerns whether or not the group restricts itself to the kindness-punishment scale. In any case, caution the class against inferring too much from a non-replication of Schachter's findings because in this activity there was only one group observed.

The most difficult type of "bomb" to defuse in this activity would be if there is no consensus to begin with, so that there is no consensus against which the confederate can deviate. We recommend that you simply let the discussion begin anyway (with the confederate advocating position #7) and sit back and see what happens. Does the group try to form a norm during the discussion or not? If so, then you can discuss this process and relate it easily to the issues raised in Chapter 7. If not, ask the class to discuss why this was the case, and explain the factors that make it more likely that conformity pressures would arise, such as if the group had higher status, if there were greater cohesiveness, if the group members believed they would be meeting several times rather than just once, if the consequences of their decisions were greater, and so on. In this way, the activity can provide a valuable lesson about the factors that are relevant in determining the extent to which conformity pressures are likely to emerge in groups.

Schachter, S. (1951). Deviation, rejection, and communication. <u>Journal of Abnormal and Social Psychology</u>, <u>46</u>, 190-207.

Activity 2. Compliance Experiment

This simple activity provides a test of the effectiveness of the foot-in-the-door and door-in-the-face techniques. The students will be the experimenters and use these compliance techniques on students outside the class. This activity can be conducted before or after the students have read Chapter 7.

Depending on the size of the class and the size of the campus, you should have each student in class approach (outside of class) either one or three same-sex students whom he or she does not know well. If the class size is large and the number of students on campus is small, you should have each student approach only one person; otherwise, have the students approach three other students.

Distribute copies of **Handout 7.2a**, **Handout 7.2b**, and **Handout 7.2c** to the students. If your students will be collecting data from only one student each, then distribute the handouts randomly so that each of your students receives only one handout. If your students will be collecting data from three other students each, then each of your students should receive one copy of each handout. Explain that they are to approach one (or three) student(s) from outside the class whom they do not know, and that they are to follow carefully the instructions on the handout(s). Tell them to return the completed handouts at the next class.

Handout 7.2a is for the <u>control</u> condition. The students in this condition are simply to ask another student if he or she would be willing to volunteer for an experiment. **Handout 7.2b** concerns the <u>foot-in-the-door</u> technique; before asking the student if he or she would be willing to volunteer for an experiment, they are to ask the student to answer a couple of questions. **Handout 7.2c** is for the <u>door-in-the-face</u> condition; before asking the student if he or she would be willing to volunteer for an experiment, they are to ask the student if he or she would be willing to volunteer for an experiment that would require a large amount of time. In this latter condition, the respondents are expected to reject the first request, after which they are asked to respond to the "real" request.

<u>**Results and discussion**</u>. The prediction is that a higher proportion of students will comply with the request to volunteer for the study in the foot-in-the-door and the door-in-the-face conditions than in the control condition. In the years in which we have conducted this exercise, the door-in-the-face condition has always elicited much more compliance than the control condition, and the foot-in-the-door condition has often, although not always, elicited about as much compliance as the door-in-the-face condition. Our experience was echoed by a recent study (Rodafinos, Vucevic, & Sideridis, 2005) that compared the effectiveness of the two techniques, and found that the door-in-the-face technique produced significantly more compliance than did either the foot-in-the-door technique or a control condition.

Calculate the proportion of respondents in each condition who did and did not comply with the request to volunteer for the experiment. Also calculate these proportions separately for men and women (we have found that female respondents approached by female students tend to be more likely to comply with the request than are male respondents approached by male students).

Discuss the results with the class. Did either or both of these two-step compliance techniques elicit more compliance than the control condition? Why or why not? Discuss the psychological processes underlying the effectiveness of these techniques. In this exercise, self-presentation concerns may be greater than in some experiments that have investigated these techniques because the person who made the initial request (either the first couple of questions in the foot-in-the-door condition or the large request in the door-in-the-face condition) was the same person who made the second request. In some experiments testing the foot-in-the-door technique, for example, the experimenters were different, and time had passed between the first and second request; in these experiments, the foot-in-the-door technique tends to be very effective, suggesting that self-perception processes may play a critical role in the success of the technique. In the present activity, however, the role of self-perception processes may have been relatively weak due to the kinds of questions initially asked. Discuss the roles of perceptual contrast and reciprocal concessions in the door-in-the-face technique.

> ✹ *What if this bombs?* Although there's a very good chance that at least one of the two compliance techniques will work, it is possible that neither technique will elicit more compliance than the control condition. This could result if the compliance in the control condition was particularly great. If this is the case, it is easy to explain the results. That is, explain that there was a *ceiling effect*; in other words, there was too little room for the effectiveness of the compliance techniques to be measured—either because the students they approached were too nice or because the experimenters were too attractive or likeable for the respondents to reject (your students should appreciate the latter interpretation); in this event, plan to alter the compliance request the next time you conduct the study on this campus. On the other hand, if the compliance rates across conditions are very low, explain that the request may have been too high and that a more reasonable request would have been better able to capture the differences between conditions.
>
> In any case, if the results are not impressive, emphasize to students that there probably were sampling biases, lack of random assignment to conditions, and other biases. Potential sources of random error or systematic bias include the following: Your students may have tended to approach other students who seemed particularly nice; the differences among the experimenters' interpersonal styles, attractiveness, choice of respondents, etc., may have been too great, thus overwhelming the differences between the conditions; your students' expectations about the responders' reactions may have affected their reactions.
>
> After offering these explanations, discuss the results of studies that have illustrated the effectiveness of each technique, and focus on a discussion of why these techniques often work.

Rodafinos, A., Vucevic, A., & Sideridis, G.D. (2005). The effectiveness of compliance techniques: Foot in the door versus door in the face. The Journal of Social Psychology, 145, 2, 237-239.

Activity 3. Norm Formation in Judgments of an Ambiguous Stimulus

This simple activity is designed to conceptually replicate the classic research by Sherif (1936) concerning norm formation in groups. In this activity, present students with ambiguous stimuli, and have them judge the stimuli privately, without anyone in the group discussing or revealing their estimates, or publicly, with everyone in the group announcing their estimates to the others. The prediction is that there should be much more variability in the students' private judgments than in their public judgments. Ideally, you should conduct the activity before the students read Chapter 7.

Background. In his classic research on norm formation in groups, Sherif exposed participants to a very ambiguous stimulus and asked them to make judgments about the stimulus. As is discussed in the textbook, the stimulus in Sherif's research was a point of light that seemed to move in an otherwise pitch-black room. From the perspective of the participants, the degree to which the light moved was extremely ambiguous. Sherif found that when participants gave their estimates orally in small groups, the groups formed a norm in these estimates to which most of the participants conformed. That is, there was a great deal of variability when participants made their estimates privately, and much greater consensus when they made them in the groups.

General procedure. This activity can be done in a few different ways. The most ambitious procedure would be to divide the class into two groups, and separate the groups so that they cannot hear each other (e.g., put one-half of the students in a different room). Have one group do the task in the private condition, and the other in the public condition (between-subjects procedure). If this is not practical, however, then have all the students participate in both conditions, one after the other (within-subjects procedure). Each of these procedures is explained below.

Between-subjects procedure. Present the same stimulus to both groups (see below for a discussion of the stimuli that can be used). One group of students should be told to take out a blank piece of paper and write their judgments on the paper, without discussing their judgments with each other. In order to increase the chances of collecting some interesting data, consider repeating the procedure with a different stimulus. The other group of students should be asked to give their estimates out loud, one by one, as you record them. Here, too, consider repeating the procedure with a different stimulus.

Within-subjects procedure. The activity may have the best chance of yielding significant results if the private condition is conducted first and the public one next. Thus, give the students the instructions for the private condition (i.e., tell the students to take out a blank piece of paper and write their judgment on the paper, without discussing their judgments with each other), and present the stimulus to them. Then, tell the students that for the next task they should not write down their judgments but will instead be asked to state their judgments orally. Then, present the second stimulus. Ask several students, one at a time, to indicate their judgments. After about a dozen or more students have indicated their judgments, have the remaining students write down their judgments.

One potential problem with this within-subjects procedure is that students may begin to suspect when you switch from a private judgment to a public one that you are interested in conformity. If you believe that your students are likely to think this way, consider conducting these two judgment tasks in the opposite order. If you do this, be sure that the two stimuli are very different from each other so that there are no lingering effects from the first judgment task.

Stimuli to be judged. Any perceptual judgment that is very ambiguous without a proper frame of reference (as in Sherif's study) will do. For example, you could bring in a large jar of peanuts or jellybeans, or show a figure consisting of hundreds of dots, and ask the students to estimate the number of peanuts, jelly beans, or dots there are. Or you can videotape the side of the road as you drive past (obviously, the same person should not be driving and shooting the camera, so you'll need assistance with this one) going at least 30 miles per hour, play the tape, and ask the students to estimate how many miles per hour you were traveling. Montgomery and Enzie's (1971) research suggests that judgments of time intervals work well for this activity. That is, tell the students something like, "I'm going to try a little exercise here. Everyone please close your eyes and leave them closed until I tell you otherwise." Take note of exactly when you give this request, and wait for everyone to close their eyes. Then continue, "I'd like you to visualize the following things as clearly as you can, without opening your eyes." Then list a series of items—any will do. After some specific interval of time (e.g., 37 seconds), tell the students to open their eyes. Then ask the students to estimate the amount of time that passed between the point when you told them to close their eyes and the point when you told them to open them.

If you conduct this activity using a within-subjects procedure, there will be two stimuli to be judged. Either you can use similar (even identical) stimuli for the two tasks (e.g., two dot-estimation tasks, with a fairly similar number of dots in both tasks), or you can use very different tasks (e.g., a dot-estimation task and a time interval estimation). Each approach has its advantages and disadvantages. One advantage of using similar stimuli is that the difficulty of the judgment should be fairly constant, and so differences in the variability of the responses are more likely to be a function of the condition (private vs. public) than of the different stimuli presented. A disadvantage of this approach is that the first judgment may affect the second judgment. Thus, it is up to you.

We personally offer the following recommendations. First, if you conduct the private condition first and the public one second, use similar stimuli for both. Second, if you use the time interval estimation for both, do the procedure a bit differently than the way stated above. That is, tell the students that you are going to ask them to judge an interval of time. Tell them when the interval begins and when it ends, and be sure to tell them not to count to themselves (tell them also not to look at their watches or a clock). It would be ideal to distract them with an activity (such as a memory task) during the time interval so that they cannot count how much time has elapsed. Third, if you do the public condition first and the private condition second, use two very different judgment tasks. This latter approach may be the overall best choice, given its simplicity and low-risk.

Results and discussion. Compare the amount of variability in the students' estimates in the private condition and the public condition. If there is less variability in the public condition, then the results conceptually replicate Sherif's. Another interesting pattern of data to look for concerns the estimates given by students in the public condition who were not called on to give their estimates orally. If you had these students write down their estimates after they had heard the other students' estimates, examine whether their estimates tended to be consistent with the estimates given orally. If they were, this would illustrate the role of informational influence independent of normative influence in this situation.

Discuss the general issue of how norms form in groups. Ask the students to speculate on how the processes of norm formation might be different depending on the task in which the group is involved. Discuss the roles of informational influence and normative influence. Ask the students to consider how the activity would have been different if the stimulus were not so ambiguous—that is, if it were more like the task faced by the participants in Asch's (1951) classic research on conformity and independence.

💣 *What if this bombs?* If the results are not consistent with predictions, ask the students if any of them experienced reactance and, therefore, purposely resisted being influenced by the estimates given by others. Ask the students if any felt that they were influenced by the estimates given by others. Discuss how both of these reactions are examples of social influence, albeit in opposite ways. If you used the within-subjects procedure, point out the flaws in this procedure and explain how a between-subjects procedure would be a better way to examine conformity in this kind of study if you could get a large enough sample of participants. Ask the students what factors would have made them more vulnerable to conformity in the public condition, such as a more difficult judgment task, a greater motivation for accuracy or for fitting in with the others, if they had been making these judgments in a setting other than a social psychology class, etc. In this way, the activity can be used as a starting point for a good discussion of the variables that are important to conformity and group norm formation, even if the results are not supportive.

Montgomery, R. L., & Enzie, R. F. (1971). Social influence and the estimation of time. Psychonomic Science, 22, 77-78.

Activity 4. Observing Norms for a Day

This activity is designed to help students think about the prevalence of norms in their everyday lives, and it can be used as a starting point for a discussion about the types of norms that groups form and the various pressures to conform to these norms that the students face every day.

Have the students keep notes for a day about the norms of behavior that they observe around them. This can be done in a fairly unstructured way: for instance, simply instructing the students to have a notebook with them from morning until night for one day and to record in the notebook any and all observations of group norms, pressures to conform, compliance requests, etc. Give the students examples of some norms—perhaps from your own observations that morning or the previous day. Have the students bring their notebooks to class, and either collect them and examine them for interesting examples, patterns, contrasts, etc., or simply have the students discuss some of these norms and observations in class.

In addition, or instead, consider having students use **Handouts 7.4a-d**. Each handout asks students to note whether they observe particular kinds of norms at various points in their day. Distribute copies of the handouts to the students. Consider having the handouts folded and stapled or taped and telling the students not to open or read the handouts until first thing in the morning of the day in which they are to make their observations. Tell them to follow the instructions and to explain their responses. That is, if the handout asks whether they observed a particular norm of behavior in a particular setting, the students should not simply respond, "Yes," but should instead explain these observations. As with the notebooks, you may want to collect the completed handouts and examine them or simply have the students discuss some of these in class.

How much similarity is there among the various students' observations? That is, did they detect the same norms? Did some students perceive norms that seemed to contradict those perceived by others? Have students describe some of these norms in more detail, and ask them to imagine what it would be like to violate them. What would make them more or less likely to resist normative influence and deviate from some widely accepted norms? Ask students to discuss their experiences with conforming to some of these norms despite feeling that the norms were wrong or inappropriate. Also ask them to discuss their experiences with resisting some norms.

 What if this bombs? This activity cannot bomb. It should elicit some interesting observations and facilitate the beginning of a discussion about norms and conformity. To increase the chances that students will understand how to make their observations, give them some examples from your own observations in your dealings with colleagues or from your memories of being a student. If you are worried that your students will be shy or hesitant about mentioning their observations in class, have them turn in their observations and choose an interesting mix to report to the class.

Activity 5. Violating Norms

This activity is designed to help students think about conformity by making them experience, firsthand, what happens when they violate simple, taken-for-granted norms. This activity can be conducted before or after the students have read Chapter 7.

The instructions to be given to the students for this exercise can be found in **Handout 7.5**. Either distribute copies of this handout to the students or read the instructions to them. When the students come to the next class after having violated their norms, either collect their notes and read some anonymous highlights to the class (if you plan to read their notes, you should tell the students this in advance, and give the students the option of indicating on their notes that they don't want you to read them to the class), or ask the students to read their notes to the class. Discuss the kinds of norms that were violated. How did students choose the norms that they violated? Why did they select those and not others? Did the students deviate from particular norms in a moderate way, or did they go out on a limb and act fairly wildly? Why? How did the students feel before, during, and after their norm violations? Did these reactions vary as a function of the types of norms violated, or as a function of the personalities of the students? What reactions did others have? Did friends react differently from strangers? Do the students now have a better sense of what it feels like to stand out from the crowd in violation of an accepted norm?

> **What if this bombs?** As long as the students follow the instructions (and you should caution them again about not doing anything that will get them into trouble), this activity cannot bomb. No matter what the students' reactions or observations are, an interesting discussion should ensue. If the students remark that violating these norms did not seem to be that big a deal, ask them why this was so, and try to get a sense of whether their norm violations were particularly innocuous. If they were, ask the students why they resisted choosing norm violations that would make them stand out more.

Activity 6. Private or Public Conformity?

According to the text, private conformity involves true acceptance or conversion, whereas public conformity refers to a superficial change of behavior. The difference between the two being that the behavioral change noted in private conformity continues long after others are not there to observe it.

Handout 7.6 asks students to decide if an event constitutes private or public conformity, or a combination of both. After students complete the handout individually, follow with a class discussion to reach consensus.

> **What if this bombs?** This activity is bombproof. Some of the examples are clear-cut in their display of private or public conformity. Others are more complex and will likely stimulate a discussion.

Activity 7. Sequential Request Strategies

Handout 7.7 asks students to identify the sequential request strategy that is being used in various scenarios from among these four strategies that are discussed in the text:

> Foot in the door — where a small request is followed by a much larger one (Items 3 and 6)

> Low-balling — where a secured agreement is followed by an enlarged request by revealing hidden costs (Items 1 and 7)

> Door in the face — where a rejected very large request is followed by a more reasonable one (Items 5 and 8)

That's not all — where a somewhat inflated request is immediately followed by a decrease in the size of the request through an offer of a discount or bonus (Items 2 and 4)

🔥 *What if this bombs?* This activity is bombproof and presents an opportunity to stress the similarities and differences between foot in the door and low-balling, and door in the face and that's not all.

Activity 8. Predictions and Inferences about Milgram's Obedience Research

This activity is designed to get students thinking about Milgram's research, to help them appreciate how surprising the results were, and to help raise points for discussion concerning the power of the situation and the fundamental attribution error. This activity must be done <u>before</u> students have read Chapter 7 or learned about Milgram's research. If many of the students have learned about Milgram's research already, such as in a previous course, we recommend that you do not conduct this activity.

<u>Procedure</u>. Show the beginning of the film *Obedience*, which illustrates Milgram's classic research on obedience to authority. Show the film up to the point where the procedure has been explained fully and the first participant shown in the film has refused to continue with the experiment. At this point, stop the film and distribute copies of Table 7.4 from the text. This table lists the learner's protests in the experiment as a function of the level of shock. Explain to the students how after 330 volts the learner would fall completely silent and not respond. Then, distribute copies of **Handout 7.8a** to the students. This handout asks the students to make predictions about the results of the study depicted up to that point in the film. Ask the students to complete the handout. When they have completed it, show the rest of the film. At the conclusion of the film, distribute copies of **Handout 7.8b**. This handout asks the students to make inferences about the participants in the research, and to indicate their perspective concerning its ethics.

<u>Discussion</u>. Discuss the students' predictions about the results. What were the average predictions? To what degree did the students underestimate the level of obedience found in the research? Calculate the averages separately for those who had heard of or read about this research and those who had not. How accurate were the former students? How accurate were the latter? Examine the averages for the questions on Handout 7.8b. Having learned that most of the participants obeyed the commands of the experimenter to the point of thinking that they might be doing great physical harm to the "learner," do the students appreciate the power of the situation enough that they admit that they might have done the same thing? Few students do. Discuss this phenomenon with them. Explain the role of the fundamental attribution error in these judgments. (As stated in Lecture/Discussion Idea 13, the fundamental attribution error helps explain how observers of this research fail to appreciate how powerful the situational pressures on the participants were, so they tend to attribute the participants' behaviors to their dispositions rather than to the situation. Consider assigning or summarizing articles by Bierbrauer [1979] or Safer [1980] on this point—see Lecture/Discussion Idea 13.) Did the students tend to think that their classmates were more likely to obey than they themselves were? In this way, did the students all rate themselves as better than average?

Distribute copies of Table 7.4 from the textbook. Begin a discussion of why there was so much obedience in the study and what factors caused the levels of obedience to increase or decrease. Discuss the issues raised in Lecture/Discussion Idea 13.

🔥 *What if this bombs?* As long as the students are not familiar with the Milgram research when they do this exercise, this activity is virtually bombproof (you might want to ask for a show of hands to see how many of your students are familiar with Milgram's work before you do this activity). It would be just short of miraculous if naive students predict accurately the levels of obedience found in Milgram's study. It is also quite implausible that a large proportion of the students would indicate that they probably would have obeyed all the way in the study. If the students are indeed accurate in their predictions and indicate that they would have obeyed the experimenter's commands, ask the students why they made these predictions and inferences. Compliment your students on being better judges of human nature than the psychiatrists whom Milgram had originally asked to make such predictions—their average prediction was that only about one in a thousand participants would obey all the way—and for being better judges than the thousands of individuals who have made similar inferences since that time. If your students were being serious with their responses, then their responses reflect an uncanny appreciation of the power of the situation and of people's vulnerability to conformity and obedience. Take advantage of this by having the students discuss the issue. The reason this would not be a "bomb" is that you should have a terrific discussion about this issue, and you will not have to work to convince the students of the validity of the points that Milgram's research makes.

Activity 9. Conformity and Compliance in Advertising

To help students recognize the ubiquity of normative and informational influences, have the students evaluate advertising—on television, in newspapers and magazines, or both—in terms of what kinds of social influence are implicit or explicit. That is, are ads designed to make people feel deviant simply because they are not consuming a particular product? Are slogans such as Nike's "Just do it" designed to make people feel guilty or embarrassed for not taking the challenge? When and how do ads use high-status or attractive people to produce conformity pressures? When and how do ads use people who look or seem similar to their audience to produce conformity pressures? When and how do ads try to use reactance to their advantage? What ads use compliance techniques such as the "that's-not-all" technique? What ads exploit the norm of reciprocity, mindlessness, etc.?

Have the students bring to class at least one copy of a print ad or description of a TV ad concerning conformity and at least one concerning compliance. Discuss what these ads illustrate about the issues raised in Chapter 7. To what extent do the students think that the people who made the ads used conformity or compliance pressures intentionally? How effective do the students think these techniques would be, and why? How easy was it to find such ads (i.e., how prevalent are they)?

What if this bombs? This activity is bombproof. There is an inexhaustible supply of appropriate ads, and students should find this activity interesting and somewhat eye-opening. To get the discussion rolling, you might consider bringing in and discussing examples that you found.

Activity 10. Strategies to Elicit or Resist Conformity and Compliance: Role Playing

If you have students who like to perform, you might consider this activity, which can be conducted before or after the students have read Chapter 7. Ask for volunteers to act out how they would behave in various situations involving conformity and compliance. **Handout 7.10** lists a half-dozen different scenarios. Select a scenario, and have each volunteer or group of volunteers (depending on the scenario) come to the front of the class and play their role. Have the observers (i.e., the rest of the class) take notes about the kinds of strategies used by the volunteers. If the class has read Chapter 7, ask the students to examine whether the strategies involve normative influence, informational influence, the norm of reciprocity, low-balling, etc. After the role playing has been completed, discuss the students' observations, as well as the volunteers' decisions about how to act, and ask the volunteers to describe how they felt playing their roles. Discuss the probable effectiveness of these different strategies, and explain what variables would make these strategies more or less likely to be effective.

🎇 *What if this bombs?* As long as you have the volunteers to do this activity, it is fairly bombproof. The role playing should be amusing as well as educational, and it should be very effective in facilitating discussion. The only potential problem is if volunteers freeze and cannot act out their parts. If you are concerned about this possibility, assign small groups of students for each scenario, tell the group what the scenario is and give them a few minutes to discuss their strategies and to choose a confident person or persons from the group to act them out.

Activity 11. Demonstrations of Obedience in Class

Two ideas for activities designed to demonstrate how students are willing to obey seemingly irrational commands by an instructor are detailed in the *Activities Handbook for the Teaching of Psychology*. The first of these was proposed by Hunter (1981). In this exercise, the instructor (preferably a guest instructor) should begin class by giving the students a series of instructions to change seats, stand up, raise hands, etc. The goal of the activity is to demonstrate to students that they were willing to obey a series of increasingly bizarre commands because of the authority they ascribed to the instructor. This can be a good starting point for a discussion of research findings such as Milgram's. Hunter details points for discussion, including the ethics of this activity.

Lutsky (1987) presents another demonstration designed to illustrate the power of conformity and obedience. The gist of this activity is that you should ask the students to write a paper about conformity and obedience (Lutsky suggests that the paper be about Jonestown), and that during the class in which the papers are due, you should tell the students to take out their papers and rip them up. Four confederates should at this point rip up what appear to be their papers. If other students follow suit, you should take note of this but then quickly tell the students to stop, and then distribute tape to allow the students to repair their torn papers. Ask the students how many were about to rip up their papers, how many were considering it, and how many were sure that they would not have ripped up their papers. Lutsky reports that when he used this exercise in his class, a majority (64%) of the naive students did or were just about to rip up their papers when he yelled "Stop" to bring the activity to an end. Like Hunter (1981), Lutsky details points for discussion—including ethics, among others.

We (the authors of this manual) are somewhat less comfortable doing either of these exercises in our own classes, primarily out of concern about the potential ill-will caused by these kinds of manipulations of students during class; but we know of others who have tried one or the other of these exercises quite successfully.

🎇 *What if this bombs?* If the students resist the commands of the instructor, all is not lost because this result would be an interesting point of departure for a discussion about factors that make people more or less susceptible to obedience and conformity. What pressures were the students feeling, and what gave them the courage to defy the commands? What kinds of changes to the procedure might have made them obey? Would they have obeyed similar commands from a different kind of instructor (e.g., older, colder, someone from a different course [who would not be as much under suspicion that they might be running an "experiment" on them], etc.)?

Hunter, W. J. (1981). Obedience to authority. In L. T. Benjamin, Jr., & K. D. Lowman (Eds.), Activities handbook for the teaching of psychology (Vol. 1, pp. 149-150). Washington, DC: American Psychological Association.

Lutsky, N. (1987). Inducing academic suicide: A demonstration of social influence. In V. P. Makosky, L. G. Whittemore, & A. M. Rogers (Eds.), Activities handbook for the teaching of psychology (Vol. 2, pp. 123-126). Washington, DC: American Psychological Association.

Activity 12. Studies in Obedience

Milgram completed his obedience studies in 1962. They are considered to be the "best-known and most widely-discussed work in the social sciences" (Blass, 1999). However, even though they gave rise to many replications and variations on the original paradigm, they did not inspire much in the way of original research on the topic of obedience. You might ask your students to explain why they think that was so. Was obedience a "hot" topic that was suitable at one point in history and became irrelevant over time or was the topic simply too difficult to address without violating the newly instituted ethical standards?

One exception, a variant of which is mentioned in the text, was a study done by Meeus & Raaijmakers (1986). The study involved participants who obeyed an order to make a job applicant nervous and disturb him with negative remarks like, "Your answer to number 14 was totally wrong again," or "This job is much too difficult for you according to the test." Most did this despite feeling uncomfortable with the knowledge that they were causing him to fail the test and remain unemployed.

Another study (Hofling and others, 1966), which was inspired by Milgram's work, involved hospital nurses who proved to be overly obedient. When instructed by a voice on the phone, impersonating a doctor, to administer an overdose of an unauthorized and unknown drug to patients without discussing the matter with anyone else, most had to be stopped from complying at the door to the patient's room.

Ask your students to discuss whether these two studies are more or less ethical than Milgram's studies.

Divide the class into small groups of 4–6 and challenge each of them to come up with a possible research design for an experiment on the topic of obedience. Have one representative from each group present their research proposal. Let the rest of the class discuss the relevance and feasibility of each study and any ethical concerns.

What if this bombs? There is a chance that this will bomb if students cannot come up with any ideas. You might then encourage them to start by thinking of the kinds of relationships or situations where one would expect to see obedience. If necessary, give them a few specific examples (e.g., teachers and pupils, traffic cops and drivers, lifeguards and swimmers, librarians and patrons; or reality television applicants or game show contestants and any person employed on the show). It's more likely that they will come up with inadequate designs than with none at all. In that case, the activity will have been worthwhile as students will learn from discussing the studies' flaws.

Blass, T. (1999). The Milgram paradigm after 35 years: Some things we now know about obedience to authority. Journal of Applied Social Psychology, 29, 5, 955-959.

Hofling, C.K., Brotzman, E., Dairymple, S., Graves, N., & Pierce, C.M. (1966). An experimental study in nurse-physician relationships. Journal of Nervous and Mental Disease, 143, 171-180.

Meeus, W.H.J., & Raaijmakers, Q.A.W. (1986). Administrative obedience: Carrying out orders to use psychological-administrative violence. European Journal of Social Psychology, 16, 311-324.

MULTIMEDIA RESOURCES

Video

Biography: Charles Manson: Journey Into Evil. This video goes in depth on Charles Manson and, among other things, how he used different methods to maintain control over the members of his "family." (50 min.) Available from Arts and Entertainment Biography. http://store.aetv.com/cgi-bin/ae.storefront/

Captive Minds: Hypnosis and Beyond. This video illustrates how cults and Marines produce obedience and loyalty. It examines factors such as isolation, distraction, physical activity, deindividuation, etc. (1985, 55 min.) Available from Insight Media (1-800-233-9910).

Conformity and Independence. This film includes analyses of classic research on conformity and independence, including the ground-breaking research of Sherif, Asch, Crutchfield, Milgram, and Moscovici. (1975, 26 min.) Available from Pennsylvania State University, Audio-Visual Services, University Park, PA 16802 (800-826-0132).

Conformity, Obedience, and Dissent. This video examines research concerning why people conform, obey, and dissent in various social situations. The studies covered include Asch's research on conformity and independence, Milgram's research on obedience, research on styles of leadership and styles of dissent, and research on groupthink. (1990, 30 min.) Available from Insight Media (800-233-9910).

Disobeying Orders. This video examines resistance among soldiers during the Vietnam War and thus provides an excellent counterpoint to the video *Remember My Lai*, or to Lecture and Discussion Idea 3 of this chapter. It illustrates the extremely difficult situation faced by soldiers who were caught between their duty as obedient soldiers and their own personal sense of right and wrong. (1990, 29 min.) Available from Filmmakers Library, 124 East 40th Street, Suite 901, New York, NY 10016.

Face the Rear / Don't Eat Light / Don't Walk on the Black Squares. These segments from the original *Candid Camera* show offer amusing and memorable examples of everyday people conforming to group norms or obeying ridiculous commands. (1962, 1963, 1964; 5 min. total) Available from McGraw-Hill Media Solutions (708-223-2506).

Group Pressures. This video describes Asch's classic study of conformity, as well as other laboratory and field research concerning conformity. (1975, 25 min.) Available from University Films of Canada, 7 Hayden Street, Suite 305, Toronto, Ontario, Canada M4Y 2P2.

Guyana Tragedy: The Story of Jim Jones. This television miniseries dramatizes the story of Jim Jones and his Peoples Temple. The whole miniseries is too long to show in class, but excerpts can work well to illustrate the ways in which Jones elicited conformity and obedience that eventually led to the deaths of more than 900 people. (1980, 190 min.) Available from Videocassette X, 13418 Wyondotte St., N. Hollywood, CA 91605 (800-350-1931).

The Heaven's Gate Cult: The Thin Line Between Faith and Reason. This ABC *Nightline* program, hosted by Ted Koppel, uses the 1997 mass suicide of the members of the Heaven's Gate cult as a starting point for a discussion among prominent scholars about cults. (1998, 20 min.) Available from Films for the Humanities (800-257-5126).

The Lottery. A classic short film based on Shirley Jackson's story about a bizarre and memorable instance of conformity in a small town. (1969, 18 min.) Available from Encyclopedia Britannica, Educational Corporation, 310 South Michigan Avenue, Chicago, IL 60604.

Obedience. This classic film describes Milgram's studies of obedience to authority. Milgram narrates the film, which provides a powerful depiction of the difficult situation faced by the subjects. In addition to illustrating the research, Milgram emphasizes the real-world applicability of the findings. (1969, 50 min.) Available from Pennsylvania State University, Audio-Visual Services, University Park, PA 16802 (800-826-0132).

The People of the Peoples Temple. This video examines Jim Jones and his Peoples Temple; it includes some footage of Jones and his followers, and commentary by Philip Zimbardo. This video would be excellent to use in conjunction with Lecture and Discussion Idea 2 of this chapter. (1979, 24 min.) Available from Pennsylvania State University, Audio-Visual Services, University Park, PA 16802 (800-826-0132).

The Power of the Situation. This film uses some classic social psychological studies to introduce the field, including studies by Lewin, Asch, and Milgram. These studies illustrate the central concept of social psychology: Situational factors can exert a powerful influence over human behavior. This selection is part of the *Discovering Psychology* series (Updated edition). (2001, 30 min.) Available from Annenberg/CPB Collection (800-532-7637).

Prejudice: The Eye of the Storm. If you did not (or will not) show this memorable video in the context of Chapter 4, you should consider showing it here. The video documents an exercise conducted by a third-grade teacher in which she divided her class into two groups as a function of their eye color, fed them some information about the superiority of one or the other group, and observed the groups' dramatic responses. In addition to the points about prejudice, this video illustrates the social influence the teacher had, as well as the conformity evident in the students as the divisions between the groups grew wider and wider. (1970, 25 min.) Available from Insight Media (800-233-9910).

Quiet Rage: The Stanford Prison Experiment. This video documents the controversial Stanford Prison Simulation conducted by Philip Zimbardo and his colleagues. Zimbardo narrates the film, which includes chilling footage of the study as well as fascinating follow-up interviews with some of the subjects. (1992, 50 min.) Available from Philip Zimbardo, P.O. Box 2996, Stanford, CA 94309 (415-725-2417).

Remember My Lai. This *Frontline* video would be excellent to use in conjunction with Lecture and Discussion Idea 3. It describes the cold-blooded massacre of an entire village of Vietnamese perpetrated by American soldiers, and it features interviews with some of these soldiers years later. This video can be used to explore issues concerning conformity, obedience, aggression, lack of self-awareness, prejudice, etc. (1989, 55 min.) Available from PBS Video (800-334-3337).

Socialization. The focus of this video is on how individuals' personalities are influenced profoundly by the sociocultural context in which they develop. It explores gender socialization, the social and cultural aspects of emotion and emotional expression, and the nature-nurture debate. It includes footage from the United States and the former Soviet Union to show the contrast in social settings. This video could be used as a way to illustrate how social norms can have profound influence on individuals' identities and behaviors. (1991, 30 min.) Available from Insight Media (800-233-9910).

The Wave. Based on a true story, this television movie dramatizes the "experiment" conducted by a high school teacher who uses his authority to create a fascistic group of students, demonstrating how vulnerable we all are to some of the underlying forces that helped make possible the obedience found in Nazi Germany. Particularly relevant and powerful is the scene toward the end of the film in which the teacher stuns the students when he reveals the identity of the person responsible for this movement to be Hitler. Unfortunately, the acting in this dramatic recreation is a bit "over-the-top," but it did win an Emmy Award. Available from Pennsylvania State University, Audio-Visual Services, University Park, PA 16802 (800-826-0132).

Internet

The National Social Norms Resource Center. This is an independent organization set up to support the application of the social norms approach to health promotion. Students can read about current research involving finding ways to reduce alcohol consumption and drunk driving, increase seat-belt use, reduce teen smoking, prevent sexual assaults, and increase compliance with tax laws. Visit this site at: http://www.socialnorms.org/casestudies.php.

The Stanford Prison Experiment Web Site. This site offers a comprehensive look at Philip Zimbardo's prison experiment. Visit this site at: http://www.prisonexp.org/

The Philip Zimbardo Web Site. In addition to the above site, students can visit http://www.zimbardo.com to watch the video of the Stanford University Prison Simulation, and to learn about Philip Zimbardo's research in general.

The Stanley Milgram Web Site. This site focusing on the work of Stanley Milgram is hosted by Thomas Blass. Visit this site at: http://www.stanleymilgram.com/

Milgram's Study of Obedience. This site, which is run by M. Partridge at the King Edward VII technology college in England, has audio clips of actual Milgram obedience studies that allow you to hear the screams of the "learners," the protests of the "teachers," and the admonitions of the experimenters. Visit this site at: http://learningat.ke7.org.uk/SocialSciences/Psychology/PsyRes13/Milgram.htm.

Computer Program

Compliance. This demonstration is modeled after the work of Asch concerning pressure to conform to a group norm. The computer generates pressure for subjects to appear self-consistent. By requiring estimates of the number of dots shown briefly under different conditions of feedback, the program illustrates independence and compliance. Instruction booklet included. (Macintosh & DOS.) Available from Life Science Associates, 1 Fenimore Road, Bayport, NY 11705-2115.

HANDOUT 7.1a CASE HISTORY: BOBBY JAMES

Bobby James was born in Bellevue Hospital in New York City. He was the sixth of eight children born before Mr. James abandoned the family once and for all when Bobby was five years old. During the next five years, Mrs. James and her eight children lived in a number of different apartments in the Bronx. Sometimes they moved because they could no longer pay the rent, and sometimes they moved because the older children got in trouble with the school officials or the police. Sometimes they moved simply because Mrs. James feared her children would be hurt or become involved with drugs or serious crime if they stayed where they were any longer.

After these five years, Mrs. James's health declined and Tommy, the oldest, assumed the authority in the family. Mrs. James relied heavily on Tommy to discipline the other children and to hold the family together. When the younger children got out of hand at home or in trouble at school or with the police, Tommy would slap them around, often brutally. Bobby and the younger children were terrified of their oldest brother and were relieved when he left two years later to join the army. Two other older brothers, Ray and Aaron, twins a year younger than Tommy, left the James family six months later when they were convicted of selling narcotics to other high school students.

After Tommy left for the army, Bobby began to get in more and more trouble at school. Whereas his elementary school teachers had described him as "scared," "anxious," "sullen," "uncommunicative," and "quiet," his eighth grade American History teacher called him "openly hostile, aggressive, and disruptive." His English teacher called him an "unruly animal." Bobby never studied out of class and was not promoted at the end of eighth grade.

Following each incident at school, Bobby was compelled to commit some new misbehavior. With each new punishment and failure, his conviction grew that his teachers, like everyone else, were out to get him.

At the same time, Bobby fell into more and more trouble with the police. The summer after he turned thirteen, Bobby and a friend were arrested for stealing a case of beer off a delivery truck. They were taken to the neighborhood police station. As Bobby described the incident, "Larry and me was sitting there waiting and these two cops come along and ask me if Aaron and Ray were my brothers so I said yes. One grabs me by the arm, twists it real hard, and says, 'Are you junkies too, you little bastard?'.... I hate them ****ing cops." The police stated that Bobby was quite unruly and verbally abusive to them and that he had not been provoked.

After several more run-ins with the police during the rest of the summer, Bobby was assigned to a juvenile court parole officer, Mr. Simmons. Mr. Simmons was friendly and at first spent a good deal of time with Bobby. Bobby's teachers found that he was making a tremendous effort to behave himself and complete his schoolwork. Despite his progress, however, one teacher described him as "a lit time bomb about to explode."

As the year passed, Mr. Simmons spent less time with Bobby. Bobby managed to get through the school year without much trouble and was promoted, but a possible summer job Mr. Simmons had mentioned didn't materialize. The summer had scarcely begun before Bobby was arrested for selling marijuana to some other teenagers from the Junior High School. Before he appeared in court, Mr. Simmons visited him. "Bobby," Mr. Simmons reported, "seemed unhappy but cool and detached, though once or twice, as we talked, he looked like he might cry. Perhaps if I had been able to spend more time with him, this wouldn't have happened."

HANDOUT 7.1b KINDNESS-PUNISHMENT SCALE

1. Love, kindness, and friendship are all that are necessary to make Bobby a better kid. If he can be placed in a less hostile environment—with a warm, friendly atmosphere—his troubles will clear up.

2. Bobby should be sent into new surroundings where the <u>most</u> emphasis will be placed on providing him with warmth and affection, but where he will be punished if he really gets out of hand.

3. Bobby should be sent into an environment where providing him with warmth and affection will be emphasized slightly more than punishing him, but where he'll have to shoulder some responsibility, and discipline and punishment will be frequent if his behavior warrants it.

4. Bobby needs an equal measure of both love and discipline. Thus, he should be placed in an atmosphere where he will be disciplined and punished if he does wrong, but rewarded and given affection if he behaves himself.

5. Though not too strong or frequent, punishment and discipline should be emphasized more than kindness and affection. Thus Bobby should be placed in an atmosphere of serious discipline but one which allows opportunities for warmth and kindness to be shown him.

6. Bobby should be sent into new surroundings where the <u>most</u> emphasis will be placed on discipline and punishment, but where praise and kindness will be presented when he behaves himself.

7. There's very little you can do with a kid like this other than to put him in a very severe disciplinary environment. Only by punishing Bobby strongly can you change his behavior.

HANDOUT 7.1c GUIDELINES FOR THE CONFEDERATE

You are to support the harshest treatment of Bobby James ("7" on the kindness-punishment scale). You must maintain this position regardless of the strength of the opposition.

As the session begins, each participant will be asked to choose a treatment for Bobby. The moderator will then let the discussion begin. No other instructions are given. Often, much of the communication is directed toward the confederate, particularly in the beginning. Be ready for this. You **should not** initiate the conversation but rather should wait to be spoken to. Sometimes, communication with the confederate falls off, with the other participants haggling over the differences between their positions. If this happens in your case, after several minutes of being ignored you should break back into the conversation to see if you will continue to be rejected. However, in some groups the confederate is never off the hook: The others in the group may continue to try to get you to change your mind. You should be polite but rigid, never switching from "7."

Come to class prepared with a set of arguments about why you believe in this position. Don't reveal all your arguments right away; save some for later points in the discussion.

The moderator will again poll the participants after the discussion has ended. You should not switch from your support of treatment "7."

HANDOUT 7.1d POST-DISCUSSION RATINGS

Be assured that your answers will be kept confidential. Please answer each item.

How well do you think your discussion went?

1	2	3	4	5	6	7

very poorly   very well

How much did you enjoy the discussion?

1	2	3	4	5	6	7

very poorly   very well

Try to guess which of the following types of movies each of the people in your discussion group would rate the most positively (in terms of enjoyment, not necessarily critical analysis): (a) light comedy, (b) heavy drama, (c) romantic comedy, (d) very violent, cold movie, (e) very sexual movie, (f) nonviolent suspense thriller, (g) science fiction, and (h) film biography or documentary. Write down the name of each group member (excluding yourself) and the type of movie he or she would pick. Feel free to cite the same type of movie more than once.

1. _____
2. _____
3. _____
4. _____
5. _____

Imagine that your group was asked to run a newspaper for a day. Below are five tasks that need to be done. You have to determine the best matches of person to task so that your paper will be run in the way that you think is best. Excluding yourself, assign one person from your group to each task by writing his or her name next to the task.

Writer. _____
Public relations. _____
Proofreader. _____
Political analyst. _____
Sales manager. _____

Please rank the other people in your group in terms of how <u>likable</u> you think they are (that is, in terms of how much you think you would like them if you got to know them). Again, keep in mind that your answers will be confidential. Because your responses are all relative, the "worst"-rated person may still be seen as quite likable in an absolute sense.

MOST LIKABLE

1. _____
2. _____
3. _____
4. _____
5. _____

LEAST LIKABLE

HANDOUT 7.2a COMPLIANCE STUDY
A

<u>Instructions for the Experimenter</u>

Approach one <u>same-sex</u> student you do not know, carry with you a stack of papers in an envelope, and say, "Hi, I'm trying to finish up a psychology experiment for my class. I have an attitude questionnaire I need people to fill out. It takes about 30 minutes. Would you be willing to do it?" (If the student asks "when," say that you will contact him or her with a list of available times for next week.) Record the answer below.

If the student says "YES," ask for his or her mailing address and say, "Unless it turns out that we already have enough subjects, I'll send you a note with a choice of times. Thanks." Later, throw out the mailing address.

Be sure to bring this completed form back to class.

A

Your name: _____

Your sex: M   F

In response to the request to complete a 30-minute questionnaire, the student said:

YES   NO

HANDOUT 7.2b COMPLIANCE STUDY

B

<u>Instructions for the Experimenter</u>

Approach one <u>same-sex</u> student you do not know, carry with you a stack of papers in an envelope, and say, "Hi, I'm trying to finish up a psychology experiment for my class. Would you be willing to help me out by answering a couple of questions right now?" If the student agrees, ask the following questions, and record the answers:

- Do you think alcohol should be banned at sporting events to control violence?

  YES, NO, UNDECIDED

- Do you think that restaurants should be required to have large no-smoking sections?

  YES, NO, UNDECIDED

Then say: "I have a questionnaire for you to fill out. It takes about 30 minutes. Would you be willing to do it?" (If the student asks "when," say that you will contact him or her with a list of available times for next week.) Record the answer below.

If the student says "YES," ask for his or her mailing address and say, "Unless it turns out that we already have enough subjects, I'll send you a note with a choice of times. Thanks." Later, throw out the mailing address.

Be sure to bring this completed form back to class.

B

Your name: _____

Your sex: M   F

In response to the request to complete a 30-minute questionnaire, the student said:

YES   NO

HANDOUT 7.2c COMPLIANCE STUDY

C

<u>Instructions for the Experimenter</u>

Approach one <u>same-sex</u> student you do not know, carry with you a stack of papers in an envelope, and say, "Hi, I'm trying to finish a psychology experiment for my class. I need students to volunteer for two 2-hour evening sessions. Would you be willing to do it?"

Assuming the student turns you down, say: "Well, I also have a questionnaire to be filled out. It takes about 30 minutes. Would you be willing to do that?" (If the student asks "when," say that you will contact him or her with a list of available times for next week.) Record the answer below.

If the student says, "YES" to either question, ask for his or her mailing address and say, "Unless it turns out that we already have enough subjects, I'll send you a note with a choice of times. Thanks." Later, throw out their mailing address.

If the student says "YES" to the first question, go to a second student and start the experiment again. In this case, record only the response of the second student.

Be sure to bring this completed form back to class.

C

Your name: _____

Your sex: M   F

In response to the request to complete a 30-minute questionnaire, the student said:

YES   NO

HANDOUT 7.4a OBSERVING NORMS FOR A DAY

ANSWER THE FOLLOWING QUESTIONS IN THE MORNING, PREFERABLY JUST BEFORE YOU LEAVE YOUR DORM, APARTMENT, OR HOUSE.

Is there a particular code of etiquette about how much time one can use the bathroom, shower, etc. in the morning? Is this different at other times of the day?

Is there a norm about clothing worn in, or to and from, the bathroom (e.g., bathrobe, full set of clothes, towel only, slippers)? Is this different at other times of the day?

If you share a room with others, is there a norm about being quiet in the morning, not turning lights on, turning alarm clocks off, taking turns using particular appliances, taking turns using the bathroom, etc.? Or is the situation pretty random?

When you decided what clothes to wear for the day, to what extent did considerations about norms play a role? If you were back in high school, would you have selected different clothes? If your friends started to wear clothes or hairstyles that are quite different from what they've been wearing, would you dress differently or change your hairstyle?

Are there other morning-related norms you've observed that might be of interest?

HANDOUT 7.4b OBSERVING NORMS FOR A DAY

IF YOU EAT LUNCH IN A DINING HALL, COMMON ROOM, CAFETERIA, OR OTHER LOCATION WITH SEVERAL OTHER PEOPLE, ANSWER THESE QUESTIONS DURING LUNCH.

What norms can you observe concerning the behavior of those around you?

Are there particular seating arrangements that tend to be consistent? Do people who sit together tend to be of the same race, from the same dorm, on the same team, at the same level of status or attractiveness, etc.?

What are the norms about what and how much to eat during lunch? What are the norms about what and how much to drink during lunch?

What are the norms about the order in which different foods or courses should be eaten? Are there norms about going back for seconds or thirds?

Are there norms about how much time one takes during lunch, or about whether one can read during lunch?

Does everyone throw out their trash and, if applicable, return their trays to the appropriate location?

HANDOUT 7.4c OBSERVING NORMS FOR A DAY

ANSWER THESE QUESTIONS SOON AFTER THE LAST CLASS OF THE DAY.

What are the norms about where to sit in class? That is, do certain students tend to sit in the same location most of the time? Do students avoid the front or the back rows? Are certain types or categories of students (e.g., athletes, students who like to talk a lot, students from a particular dorm, popular students, etc.) likely to sit in particular parts of the room? Do any of these norms vary across different classes?

What norms are there about class participation in your classes? How do these norms vary from one class to the next?

Is there a norm about whether and when students ask questions during class? Do you ever want to ask a question but feel uncomfortable doing so? If so, why?

Do your instructors seem to follow a norm about their appearance (e.g., in terms of clothes or hair)?

What are the norms about when to show up for various classes (e.g., a few minutes early, right on time, a few minutes late)? Are there norms about when to start packing up one's books to get ready to leave?

What other norms of behavior did you observe in your classes?

HANDOUT 7.4d OBSERVING NORMS FOR A DAY

ANSWER THESE QUESTIONS IN THE EVENING.

During a typical day, do you feel any pressure to conform to a norm about physical activity or extracurricular interests? Did you feel this pressure today?

During a typical day, do you feel any pressure to conform to a norm about studying or doing academic work? Did you feel this pressure today?

During this past day, in what ways do you think you conformed to the attitudes, opinions, or behaviors of others? What instances of others' conformity did you observe?

During this past day, in what ways do you think you resisted the social influence pressures exerted by others? What instances of others' resistance did you observe?

HANDOUT 7.5 VIOLATING NORMS

At some point between the end of this class and the beginning of the next one, I'd like each of you to deviate from at least one widely accepted norm. For example, you might wear very non-normative clothes to class or dinner. You might eat your meal in front of people while standing, or while singing. You might greet people or return others' greetings in a very unusual way. You might argue a point with other people who all disagree with your point. Try to be creative, but <u>be sure to do this in a way that is safe and that won't get you into trouble</u> (for example, disrupting a class, breaking a law, or saying hateful or prejudiced things would definitely be a bad idea). Just before you violate the norm, record your thoughts about your expectations, emotions, etc. in a notebook. As soon as you can after you've violated the norm, record how you felt as you were doing it and soon after. What were other people's reactions? Did you feel a great pressure to stop doing what you were doing, or did it feel fun or liberating? Why do you think you felt this way?

HANDOUT 7.6 PRIVATE OR PUBLIC CONFORMITY?

Read each of the following descriptions and decide if the event constitutes private or public conformity or a combination of both:

1. Jodie begged her parents to allow her to get her navel pierced because some of the popular girls in 6th grade had had theirs pierced.

2. John sees every big box-office smash movie that comes out, figuring that that many people can't be wrong and seeing it will give him something to talk about.

3. In the supermarket, Linda picked up the box of detergent after observing two other shoppers opting for the same brand.

4. Ella never dressed up, preferring to wear jeans everywhere. But when a good friend sent her a wedding invitation that specified "Black Tie," she went shopping for a formal gown.

5. Because the accident caused traffic to crawl on the highway, Lloyd got off at the first exit. Not knowing where to go, he followed the majority of cars, figuring that they would lead him to the next highway entrance.

6. Andy was fishing for a while without catching anything. Then he noticed that some of the other boys were fishing further down the river and he decided to go down there too.

7. Dr. Brown began prescribing the new heartburn drug after attending a convention at which he heard some other doctors touting it.

8. Melanie read in the fashion magazine that green was the new color for the fall season. She immediately went out and purchased a new green suit.

9. Although he hated the taste of liquor, Sam downed the glass of vodka because his friends were drinking.

10. When he took part in his first race, Ryan was wearing the khaki cotton pants that he always wore bike riding. After coming in last place, he decided to get the same kind of spandex bike shorts that other racers were wearing.

HANDOUT 7.7 SEQUENTIAL REQUEST STRATEGIES

For each of the following scenarios, decide which sequential request strategy is being used. Is it foot in the door, low-balling, door in the face, or that's not all?

1. Only after Jenna agreed to babysit for Mr. and Mrs. Williams' two-year-old twins for $5.00 an hour, was she told that their cousin, another toddler, was staying with them that night and that she would be watching him too.

2. Kevin thought the laptop was priced too high, but when he found out that it came with a free printer, he decided it was worth the asking price and he bought it, even though he already owned a perfectly good printer.

3. Students who were asked to help create blood donation campaign posters were more likely to donate blood when the campaign started a week later.

4. Linda was shopping for a new sweater. She was ready to spend around $50. Then she saw one that had a sale tag saying it had been reduced from $150 to $75. Even though it appeared to be almost identical to the less expensive sweaters, she bought it thinking it was a good deal.

5. Sixteen-year-old Kate asked her parents if she could go away for a skiing weekend with some older friends. Predictably, they said "No." The next day, when she asked if she could just go for the day, which is really all she wanted, they said "Yes."

6. Michael asked Brian, his teammate, to give him a ride home after the soccer game. Once they were on their way, he said, "You don't mind if we stop a little bit away from here and pick up three more people who are coming to my house, do you?"

7. Mr. and Mrs. Brown were looking to buy an outdoor table and chair set that was advertised at $500. After they said they'll take it, the salesman explained that they had to pay an extra $100 for the store to assemble the pieces, another $125 for the umbrella, and an additional $50 for the umbrella stand.

8. At the "little league" game, some parents were asked to volunteer to man the concession stand. None of them volunteered. Later, when the same parents were asked to contribute to a travel fund for the team, they gave much more money than parents who were not asked to volunteer to man the concession stand.

HANDOUT 7.8a MILGRAM'S RESEARCH

As you saw in the film excerpt, the "teacher" in Milgram's study gave shocks to the "learner" whenever the learner made a mistake. The intensity of the first shock given was 15 volts, and with each mistake the learner was supposed to receive a shock that was 15 volts greater than the previous one.

Below is a list of the range of voltage levels on the shock generator, along with the verbal designations associated with various voltage levels. Imagine that you were a participant in Milgram's study (without knowing what you know now, of course, about the purpose of the study). What do you think is the maximum voltage you would have given the learner if you were a participant? That is, would you have obeyed all the way and administered 450 volts, or would you have refused to obey the experimenter's instructions after reaching a particular point? In the appropriate column, please indicate the maximum voltage of shock that you think you would have given the learner.

In the next column, indicate the maximum voltage of shock that you think the **<u>average</u>** student in your psychology class would have given the learner if your classmates had been participants in the study. Finally, in the last column, indicate the maximum voltage of shock that you think the **<u>average</u>** participant in the actual study gave to the learner.

Voltage	Verbal Designation	Maximum shock I would have given	Maximum shock average classmate would have given	Maximum shock average participant would have given
15 volts	Slight Shock			
30				
45				
60				
75	Moderate Shock			
90				
105				
120				
135	Strong Shock			
150				
165				
180				
195	Very Strong Shock			
210				
225				
240				
255	Intense Shock			
270				
285				
300				
315	Extreme Intensity Shock			
330				
345				
360				

375	Danger: Severe Shock			
390				
405				
420				
435	XXX			
450				

What percentage of students in your class do you think would have obeyed all the way and administered 450 volts to the learner? _____%

What percentage of participants in Milgram's study do you think obeyed all the way and administered 450 volts to the learner? _____%

HANDOUT 7.8b MILGRAM'S RESEARCH: POST-FILM QUESTIONNAIRE

1. Compared to the average individual in the United States at the time of Milgram's research, how **moral** do you think the participants who obeyed all the way to 450 volts were?

1	2	3	4	5	6	7
much less than average						much more than average

2. Compared to the average individual in the United States at the time of Milgram's research, how **conformist** do you think the participants who obeyed all the way to 450 volts were?

1	2	3	4	5	6	7
much less than average						much more than average

3. Compared to the average individual in the United States at the time of Milgram's research, how much **integrity** do you think the participants who obeyed all the way to 450 volts had?

1	2	3	4	5	6	7
much less than average						much more than average

4. Compared to the average individual in the United States at the time of Milgram's research, how **intelligent** do you think the participants who obeyed all the way to 450 volts were?

1	2	3	4	5	6	7
much less than average						much more than average

5. What percentage of the "teachers" do you think would have obeyed all the way to 450 volts if the teachers had been women (and the "learner" continued to be a man)? ____%.

6. If you could be sent back in time to serve on a panel that was supposed to judge the ethics of Milgram's research and decide whether or not it should be conducted, what would your decision be, and why?

1	2	3	4	5	6	7
definitely would not allow the study to be conducted						definitely would allow the study to be conducted

    My reason for the above answer is as follows. [Please complete on the back.]

HANDOUT 7.10 STRATEGIES TO ELICIT OR RESIST CONFORMITY AND COMPLIANCE: ROLE PLAYING

Scenario 1:   You want to go to a stereotypically masculine/feminine (choose one) movie; your date wants to go to the opposite.

Scenario 2:   Your roommates want you to go to a party, but you feel that you have to study.

Scenario 3:   Your roommate wants to study, but you and your other roommates want him or her to go to a party with you.

Scenario 4:   An ex-friend of yours has an extra ticket to a concert that you'd love to attend, but you and your ex-friend have hardly spoken in months because you've drifted apart from each other.

Scenario 5:   You and your classmates want to persuade your professor to make the final exam optional.

Scenario 6:   You and your younger brother and younger sister want to convince your parents to give you each a separate phone line.

CHAPTER 8

Group Processes

LEARNING OBJECTIVES: GUIDELINES FOR STUDY

You should be able to do each of the following by the conclusion of Chapter 8.

1. Describe the reasons that people join a group. Discuss the process of adjustment to a new group. Explain the processes of group development, as well as how roles, norms, and cohesiveness influence groups. (*pp. 294-299*)

2. Explain how the presence of others affects task performance, and how Zajonc's social facilitation model accounts for these effects. Describe three alternative accounts for these effects. (*pp. 300-304*)

3. Describe how working with others on a task affects productivity. Explain the concept of social loafing, identify factors that can reduce the likelihood of loafing, and distinguish between situations likely to lead to social facilitation versus social loafing. (*pp. 304-306*)

4. Define deindividuation. Describe how environmental cues and a sense of identity can affect this process. (*pp. 307-309*)

5. Describe the different types of tasks that groups perform. Explain process loss and the relationship between group performance and type of task. Discuss the advantages and disadvantages of brainstorming. (*pp. 310-311*)

2. Describe group polarization and distinguish between the informational and normative processes through which it occurs. (*pp. 312-314*)

3. Define groupthink and its antecedents, behavioral symptoms, and consequences. Address how groupthink can be prevented. (*pp. 314-317*)

8. Describe the roles of biased sampling, information-processing biases, and transactive memory in group communication and performance. (*pp. 318-319*)

9. Discuss strategies for improving group performance. Address the role of diversity in considering this issue. (*pp. 319-322*)

4. Define social dilemma. Describe the prisoner's dilemma and resource dilemmas. Discuss mixed motives in the context of these dilemmas, and delineate psychological and structural factors that influence behavior in social dilemmas. (*pp. 323-327*)

5. Discuss how threat capacity and perceptions of others can lead to the escalation of group conflict. Explain how GRIT, negotiation, and finding a common ground can reduce group conflict. (*pp. 327-333*)

DETAILED CHAPTER OUTLINE

I.   Fundamentals of Groups
  A.   What is a Group?
  B.   Why Join a Group?
      1.   increases evolutionary survival
      2.   to gain social status and identity
  C.   Socialization and Group Development
  D.   Roles, Norms, & Cohesiveness
      1.   Resisting Norms
      2.   Culture and Cohesiveness
III. Individuals in Groups: The Presence of Others
  A.   Social Facilitation: When Others Arouse Us: Dominant responses are enhanced and
       subordinate responses are impaired by the presence of others, so performance improves on
       easy tasks and is impaired on hard tasks
      1.   The Zajonc solution: social facilitation occurs due to the mere presence of others that
           causes the arousal that creates the performance effects
      2.   Evaluation apprehension: social facilitation occurs because people are evaluating the
           performer
      3.   Distraction: the distraction-conflict theory argues that other people are arousing
           because they are a distraction, and the distraction-based arousal accounts for social
           facilitation phenomena
  B.   Social Loafing: When Others Relax Us
      1.   On pooled tasks people tend to produce less in the presence of others; this is called
           social loafing (Latane & colleagues, 1979)
      2.   When one's input is made identifiable, social loafing does not occur
      3.   Collective effort model: when individuals strive hard on a collective task because they
           personally value the final outcome.
      4.   Culture and social loafing: Females and people from collectivist countries are less
           likely to engage in social loafing than are males and people from individualist
           countries.
  C.   Facilitation and Loafing: Unifying the Paradigms
      1.   When the presence of others increases the possibility of evaluation
          a)   performance on easy tasks should be enhanced
          b)   performance on difficult tasks should be impaired
      2.   When the presence of others decreases the possibility of evaluation
          a)   performance on easy tasks should be impaired
          b)   performance on difficult tasks should be enhanced
  D.   Deindividuation
      1.   Environmental cues
          a)   accountability cues
          b)   attentional cues
      2.   From personal to social identity: social identity model of deindividuation effects
IIII. Group Performance: Problems and Solutions
  A.   Types of Tasks
      1.   additive task: product is the sum of all the members' contributions
      2.   conjunctive task: product is determined by the "weakest link"
      3.   disjunctive task: product is determined by the individual-best performance
  B.   Process Loss: reduction in group performance due to obstacles created by group processes
  C.   Brainstorming: coming up with ideas

D.   Group Polarization: Strengthened attitudes through group discussion
  1.   Persuasive arguments theory: in a group people hear more arguments that make attitudes more extreme
  2.   Social comparison: in a group people compare themselves to others and create more extreme norms for the group
E.   Groupthink
  1.   Behavioral symptoms
    a)   overestimation of the group
    b)   closed-mindedness
    c)   increased pressures toward uniformity
  2.   Research on groupthink
    a)   only mixed support for the model
    b)   groupthink is most likely to occur when the following conditions occur simultaneously: high cohesiveness, a strong controlling leader, and heightened stress
  3.   Preventing groupthink
    a)   groups should consult widely with outsiders
    b)   leaders should explicitly encourage criticism
    c)   subgroups should separately discuss the same issue
    d)   groups should engage in counterfactual thinking
F.   Escalation effects
G.   Communicating Information and Utilizing Experience
  1.   Biased sampling
    a)   groups fail to consider important information
    b)   group norms can promote either consensus or critical thinking
    c)   communication networks can hinder the flow of information
  2.   Information processing and Transactive Memory
    a)   groups are susceptible to the same information-processing biases as are individuals
    b)   transactive memory: groups remember information more efficiently than individuals
H.   Strategies for Improvement
  1.   Norms and Goals
  2.   Training and Intervention
  3.   Computer Technology, Group Support Systems, Virtual Teams
  4.   Diversity and Group Productivity
IV.   Conflict: Cooperation and Competition Within and Between Groups
A.   Mixed Motives and Social Dilemmas
  1.   The prisoner's dilemma
    a)   tit-for-tat strategy – respond as your partner does
    b)   win-stay, lose-shift strategy – stay with strategy if payoff is high, shift if payoff is low
  2.   Resource dilemmas
    a)   commons dilemma – if people take as much as they want of a limited resource that does not replenish itself, nothing will be left for anyone
    b)   public goods dilemma – if people do not contribute to a common pool of resources there will be nothing for anyone
  3.   Solving social dilemmas: groups and individuals
    a)   groups tend to be more competitive in mixed-motive situations than individuals
    b)   the importance of trust
    c)   The negative effect of anonymity

4.   Solving social dilemmas: culture and individual difference
    a)   people with a prosocial, cooperative orientation are more likely to work for the common good
    b)   those with competitive or individualistic orientation are more concerned with personal benefits
B.   Conflict Escalation and Reduction
  1.   Threat capacity: the ability to punish others often leads to escalation of conflict
  2.   Perceptions of others: we often exaggerate the bad qualities of our enemies and they do likewise
    a)   mirror image: what we see in our enemies is what our enemies see in us
    b)   dehumanization: we often dehumanize outgroups, which justifies the escalation of conflict
C.   Reducing Conflict through GRIT
  1.   True GRIT: a strategy for unilateral reduction in conflict
    a)   issue a statement of intention to reduce conflict
    b)   carry out your tension-reducing initiative as announced
    c)   once the other party cooperates, quickly reciprocate
    d)   maintain a retaliatory capability
D.   Negotiation
  1.   Keys to successful negotiating
    a)   integrative agreements – negotiated resolution where all parties come out ahead
    b)   characteristics of experienced negotiators
    c)   communication and disclosure of information
    d)   getting outside assistance: arbitrators and mediators
  2.   Gender differences
  3.   Culture and negotiation: cultural differences in communication and emotion
  4.   Finding common ground
    a)   superordinate identity: a larger group of which all other groups are a part
    b)   superordinate goals: goals that all parties share

LECTURE AND DISCUSSION IDEAS

Idea 1.   Choking in Sports and Social Facilitation

At the end of sporting events, players often have to perform in the clutch in w away that will leave them the hero or the goat. Social facilitation can make a prediction about what types of activities players are likely to make at the end of a contest and what types of activities they are less likely to make. For example, in basketball if a player is a good free-throw shooter, then shooting free throws is a fairly easy task and his or her performance should be improved at the end of a game. On the other hand, if the player is a poor free-throw shooter, then his or her performance should deteriorate at the end of the game. Similarly, short shots should get easier and long shots should get harder. While it is clear social facilitation cannot explain every instance of last minute heroics and failure, it does make interesting testable hypotheses.

Idea 2.   Mob Scenes and Deindividuation

Large diffuse crowds often turn to violence and property damage. One explanation of this phenomenon offered in the book is that in a crowd people experience a sense of deindividuation—a sense that they are not accountable for their own actions—and it is this deindividuation that accounts for the violent turn of events. Yet many large diffuse crowds rarely if ever turn violent—like the crowds going to work in most large cities. What makes some crowds turn violent while others do not? Ask your students if they have any explanations for this discrepancy. We can offer one possible explanation: Perhaps a crowd has to be fairly aimless, with little purpose, for the deindividuation that people experience to turn to violent activity.

The text discusses how deindividuation is facilitated by disguises, such as Halloween costumes. You might wish to point to another example that demonstrated deindividuation in disguised individuals. Andrew Silke (2003) investigated 500 politically motivated acts of violence in Northern Ireland. Silke found that when the attackers were disguised (in 206 of the cases), they inflicted more serious injuries, attacked more people, engaged in more vandalism, and were more likely to threaten people after the attacks.

Silke, E. Deindividuation. (2003). Anonymity, and violence: Findings from Northern Ireland. Journal of Social Psychology, 143, 493.

Idea 3.   Group Polarization and Cliques

Cliques are a permanent feature of many school situations. Those inside the clique usually see the group as reasonable and holding normal views, whereas those outside the clique often see the clique as holding extreme and unusual positions. Group polarization may be able to explain this phenomenon. In particular, this condition can provide a powerful example of the social comparison explanation of group polarization for those inside the clique and of the social categorization explanation for those outside the clique.

Idea 4.   The Blood Supply: A Public Goods Dilemma

In most parts of the country the nation's blood supply has a serious shortage. Most people freely admit that an adequate blood supply is an important community resource, yet few people give blood. This is an excellent example of a public goods dilemma. Everyone wants blood to be there if they or their family need it, but many (if not most people) are free-riders and do not contribute to the blood supply to make sure that there are adequate resources.

Idea 5.   Voter Turnout and Social Loafing

Voter turnout, or the percentage of eligible voters who actually exercise their vote, hovers around 50 percent in the US presidential elections. And the turnout is much lower among those who are between the ages of 18 and 25. Ask your students to discuss the reasons for why so many people do not bother to exercise their vote. Could it be that our political system with its Electoral College and two major parties makes an individual's vote appear insignificant? And is it the belief that one vote doesn't really matter that leads to mass social loafing?

In chapter 8 of the text, there is a list of factors that have been shown to reduce social loafing. Ask yours students which ones could be applied to encourage more people to participate in elections? What in their opinion will be the impact of Internet voting on turnout among the young in future presidential elections?

Idea 6.   Cooperation Through Competition

Benchmarking refers to knowing where you stand in comparison to others, especially those who are considered to be at the top. In an article in Forbes Magazine (2005), authors Ayres and Nalebuff tout the use of benchmarking to spur competition and thereby encourage countries to cooperate on various global issues, such as improving water quality, reversing overfishing, and controlling greenhouse gas emissions.

Such a technique, of using performance comparisons to motivate competition, has already been implemented by the Center for Environmental Law & Policy at Yale University. The Center releases an Environmental Sustainability Index that ranks 146 countries on 76 environmental and social measures. On the latest index, the US ranks at the top for quality of drinking water but near the bottom for greenhouse gas emissions, an embarrassing position that calls for corrective steps.

After the 2002 rankings came out, some countries immediately acted to improve their rankings. South Korea, for example, made substantial improvements in air and water pollution, which resulted in its moving up 22 places on the index for 2004. Likewise, Mexico instituted a set of specific environmental standards for each of its 32 states to strive for in the near future.

Ayres, I. & Nalebuff, B. (2005). Peer pressure. Forbes, 175, 7, 118.

Idea 7.   Groupthink and Famous Disasters

Much of the research on groupthink has focused on well-known disasters and blunders. Janis (1982) in his seminal analysis on groupthink evaluated several famous disasters: the Bay of Pigs fiasco, the decisions of the U.S. Navy that exacerbated the attack on Pearl Harbor, and the Watergate scandal. Many recent disasters could also be analyzed using the groupthink framework. For example, you might find news clippings describing the Space Shuttle *Challenger* explosion and the loss of the space shuttle Columbia, the Iran-Contra scandal, the Waco, Texas disaster, the Ruby Ridge shootings, or the Los Alamos fire. All of these recent disasters could be analyzed by using concepts related to groupthink.

Writing in the British Journal of Political Science, Steve Yetiv analyzes the Persian Gulf conflict of 1990–1991 in terms of groupthink. You might ask your students to consider whether the latest conflict in Iraq and the initial search for weapons of mass destruction reflects elements of groupthink as well.

Alternatively, you might also examine good decision making by looking for mechanisms that prevent groupthink. Janis did this in his book by contrasting the poor decision making in the above examples with the decisions made by the Kennedy administration during the Cuban missile crisis. He argued that the President and his cabinet operated in ways that reduced groupthink during this crisis. You might try to find accounts of successful decision making in the media and see if these decisions were made in ways that prevented groupthink.

Janis, I. L. (1982). Groupthink. (2nd ed.). Boston: Houghton.
Yetiv, S. (2003). Groupthink and the Gulf crisis. British Journal of Political Science, 33, 419.

Idea 8.   Group Processes in Television Reality Shows

In recent years, there have been several popular reality shows on television that are group-based. Some examples are *Big Brother*, *Survivor*, *Real World,* and *The Apprentice.*

After students have read the chapter, ask them to discuss a specific episode of a current or past reality show that pertains to one of the group processes mentioned in the text (social facilitation, social loafing, deindividuation, group polarization, or groupthink).

An article that explores the history and trends of reality-based television, by Edward D. Miller (2000), might be of interest to students. In it, Miller traces the roots of reality shows such as *Survivor* and *Big Brother* to the old television series *Gilligan's Island* and the book Lord of the Flies. In both cases, a group of strangers is thrown together in an unfamiliar and somewhat fantasy-like setting. Another precursor of present day reality shows is *The American Family*, which featured the Louds, a real family that was videotaped around the clock. According to Miller, that show set the precedent for MTV's *The Real World* and PBS's *The Old 1900 House*.

Miller, E.D. (2000). Fantasies of reality: Surviving reality-based programming. Social Policy, 31, 6.

CLASSROOM ACTIVITIES

Activity 1. Is this a Group?

The book defines collectives as, "people engaged in common activities but with minimal direct interaction." But, are collectives groups? The activity in **Handout 8.1** presents students with a number of different situations, and students are asked to decide whether they think the situation describes a group or not. This handout can be a good discussion starter. It should allow students to think about how their own view of groups is similar to or different from the book's definition.

> ●*What if this bombs?* This one should be bombproof. Any pattern of answers (whether students show consensus or lack of consensus in their answers) should lead to interesting discussion, and students will gain a clearer understanding of the definition of a group.

Activity 2. Deindividuation: What Would You Do?

David Dodd describes this highly effective and entertaining exercise in individuation that demonstrates how even normal, law-abiding college students are capable of deviant, antisocial acts under some conditions.

Have your students respond anonymously to the following question:

If you could be totally invisible for 24 hours and were completely assured that you would not be detected or held responsible for your actions, what would you do?

Ask students to write down their answers on a blank sheet of paper and to fold the papers before turning them in. Collect the papers, shuffle them, and randomly begin to read them aloud. Usually reading just a few of the responses will be enough. Students will likely be amused as typically the most popular response is "rob a bank." You can also classify the responses into rough categories such as prosocial, antisocial, and neutral. The antisocial responses will probably tend to predominate.

Dodd reports that the average number of antisocial responses given by his college students (36%) is the same as that given by inmates at a maximum security prison where he once taught.

> ●*What if this bombs?* This one should be bombproof. Students are most surely to come up with original ideas and, depending on the class size, you should be able to find at least one example from each category. The only aspect of this activity that could go astray is your disclosure that responses will be read aloud. Knowing this, students might be more likely to temper their responses. To maintain confidentiality, however, you should be careful to only read examples that will not disclose the author, thus maintaining students' confidentiality. Students are likely to be amused by the actions that their peers report.

Dodd, D. K. (1985). Robbers in the classroom: A deindividuation exercise, <u>Teaching of psychology</u>, <u>12</u>, 89-91.

Activity 3. Missiles vs. Factories: A Social Dilemma

This activity is meant to mimic, on a very small scale, the dilemma faced by countries in the age of nuclear weapons. Whereas many nations might agree that it be great if everyone got rid of nuclear weapons, no one wants to be caught without such weapons as long as anyone else has access to them.

Divide the class into an even number of small groups (3–5 students). These groups represent countries with nuclear weapons. Each group of students will play against one other group of students. Each team begins the game with five missiles. Over the course of five trials each team has the opportunity to convert <u>one</u> of their missiles into a factory (to disarm) or they may elect to do nothing that round (maintain their arsenal). This decision is made in secret and at the end of the five trials the payoff matrix (**Handout 8.3**) is used to compute each team's outcome. Note that the payoff matrix is actually very simple. Each team gets 1 point for each factory they have, 2 points for each missile more than the other team they possess, and –2 points for each missile less than the other team they possess.

If both countries disarm all of their missiles then the highest collective outcome is achieved but this is an unlikely outcome as each team is best served by having more missiles than their opponents at the end of the five trials.

♠*What if this bombs?* This one should be bombproof. Virtually any outcome will lead to stimulating classroom discussion. In the best case, some of the countries will cooperate with one another (mutually disarm) and others will not so the students can discuss different alternative outcomes from their own experiences with the exercise.

Pilisuk, M. (1984). Experimenting with the arms race. <u>Journal of Conflict Resolution</u>, <u>28</u>, 296-315.

Activity 4. Competitive versus Cooperative Behavior

Have students stand in a circle and toss a ball back and forth to each other. In the first game, tell students to cooperate by calling the name of the person they are throwing the ball to. Have at least one student record the number of misses in five minutes. In the second game tell students that the object of the game is to keep the ball in play for five minutes with as few errors as possible, and that when someone misses the ball they will be removed from the circle. If only one person is remaining in the end, that person will receive a prize for their excellent play. Again count the number of errors in this game within five minutes (if the game lasts that long). There are likely to be fewer errors in the first game as the implicit competition in the second game is likely to override the group goal.

♠ *What if this bombs?* This one should be bombproof. Even if the anticipated outcome does not result, students should find the exercise engaging and you will be able to discuss co-operation and competition within groups.

Adapted from Hollingsworth, F. (1990). Competitive versus cooperative behavior. In V. P., Makosky, L. G. Whittemore, C. P. Landry, & M. L. Skutley (Eds.), <u>Activities handbook for the teaching of psychology</u> (Vol. 3, pp. 145-146). Washington, DC: American Psychological Association.

Activity 5. Replication of Triplett's Social Facilitation Study

Triplett's (1897–1898) study of children's speed at winding a fishing reel alone or while competing against someone else is an easy and fun study to replicate. All you need is two old fishing reels with a lot of string on each reel. Unwind both of the reels. Then let one person wind up the reel, and time him or her. Then let another person wind up the second reel. Time him or her as well. Next unwind the reels and time two people as they compete in trying to wind the reels. You should find that people wind the reels faster when they are competing with someone else than when they are alone. You can repeat the alone phase and the competition phase a couple of times if you want to be sure that you get this social facilitation effect. Ask students why they thought they winded the reels faster when they competed.

♠ *What if this bombs?* This activity has a slight chance of bombing, but students should enjoy it anyway. The risk of not obtaining the social facilitation effect can be reduced if you have more students complete the task alone and competing. This activity should serve as a good introduction to social facilitation and will teach students a bit about the history of the field.

Tripplet, N. (1897-1898). The dynamogenic factors in pacemaking and competition. <u>American Journal of Psychology</u>, <u>9</u>, 507-533.

Activity 6. Social Loafing and Group Size

This activity is a replication of a study by North, Linley, & Hargreaves (2000) which found that social loafing was more likely to occur in larger (8-member) than in smaller (3-member) groups of students working on a cooperative task.

Tell the class that they'll be working on a task that will illustrate an important point that will be covered in the ensuing lecture. Assign them into groups of 3 (or 4) members and 8 members (see chart below for possible divisions). Inform them that they have 15 minutes to generate as many words as possible that contain the sequence of letters T-O-N. The letters must remain in that order but other letters can be inserted between them. No proper nouns can be used. One participant in each group should be designated to write down the words and maintain a word-count. That person is also allowed to generate words.

Allow students to leave the classroom and find a location where they can work, away from other groups, without being disturbed. Ask them to stop the task at exactly 15 minutes and return to the room.

When everyone has returned, have the scorekeepers figure out the mean number of words generated by each participant in each group (the total number of words produced by the group divided by the number of participants in each group). Write the numbers on the board under the headings of "small groups" and "large groups."

After briefly discussing the topic of social loafing, examine the means of the groups to see if there was any evidence of social loafing in the larger groups (i.e., smaller means). If there was, ask students to explain why social loafing was more likely to occur in large than in small groups.

Suggested groupings:

Total # of students	Small groups	Large groups
22	3 + 3	8 + 8
23	3 + 4	8 + 8
24	4 + 4	8 + 8
25	3 + 3 + 3	8 + 8
26	3 + 3 + 4	8 + 8
27	3 + 4 + 4	8 + 8
28	3 + 3 + 3 + 3	8 + 8
29	3 + 3 + 3 + 4	8 + 8
30	3 + 3 + 4 + 4	8 + 8
31	3 + 3 + 3 + 3 + 3	8 + 8
32	3 + 3 + 3 + 3 + 4	8 + 8
33	3 + 3 + 3	8 + 8 + 8
34	3 + 3 + 4	8 + 8 + 8
35	3 + 4 + 4	8 + 8 + 8
36	3 + 3 + 3 + 3	8 + 8 + 8

37	3 + 3 + 3 + 4	8 + 8 + 8
38	3 + 3 + 4 + 4	8 + 8 + 8
39	3 + 3 + 3 + 3 + 3	8 + 8 + 8
40	3 + 3 + 3 + 3 + 4	8 + 8 + 8
41	3 + 3 + 3	8 + 8 + 8 + 8

What if this bombs? This activity might bomb, but social loafing is a fairly robust and reliable phenomenon. Therefore, it seems likely that you will be able to replicate the effect in your classroom, at least to some extent. If there is no evidence of social loafing in any of the large groups, introduce the findings of the study and ask students to give possible explanations for the failure to replicate the results.

North, A.C., Linley, P.A., & Hargreaves, D.J. (2000). Social loafing in a co-operative classroom task. Educational Psychology, 20, 4, 389-392.

Activity 7. Group Polarization Exercise

Peter Gray (1993) suggests this simple exercise to demonstrate group polarization. Before students have read and discussed the chapter, have them declare how strongly they agree or disagree, on a scale of 1 to 6 (1 = very strongly agree, 2 = strongly agree, 3 = agree, 4 = disagree, 5 = strongly disagree, 6 = very strongly disagree) with some statement or idea (Gray suggests the idea that the next exam should be essay rather than multiple choice). Collect the responses and divide students into like-minded groups (of about 5–7 members) for a short, 5-minute discussion. Afterwards, have students rate their agreement with the proposition again. Ask them to raise their hands if their position became less extreme, remained the same, or became more extreme. The results should be consistent with group polarization: those who initially agreed should agree more strongly after group discussion, and those who initially disagreed should disagree even more strongly after group discussion. There should be more students who became more than less extreme.

According to Gray, asking your students to speculate about the causes of the effect should generate the same explanations generated by psychologists over the years (i.e., that members are exposed to new, persuasive arguments, and that members gradually take a more extreme position in order to be viewed positively by others).

What if this bombs? This activity might bomb. If it does, ask students to generate explanations for the failure. This would present a good opportunity to discuss the processes that contribute to group polarization.

Gray, P. (1993). Engaging student intellects: The immersion approach to critical thinking in psychological instruction. Teaching of Psychology, 20, 68-74.

Activity 8. Prisoner's Dilemma Exercise

Ask your students to imagine themselves in the following dilemma:

You and a friend committed some crime. The prosecution has enough evidence to convict both of you of a lesser offense, but they would like to convict at least one of you of the more serious charge. The prosecutor puts you and your friend into different rooms. The prosecutor offers to make you a deal. If you confess that you and your friend committed the more serious offense, and if your friend does not confess, you will get a much lighter sentence and your friend will get the more severe sentence. If your friend confesses and you don't, you get the severe sentence and your friend gets the reduced sentence.

If you both confess, each of you will receive a moderate sentence. If neither confesses, you both will receive a light sentence.

To illustrate these choices, show the students the matrix in **Handout 8.8a**. (See also Multimedia Resource for some computer software that can be used to help illustrate this classic dilemma.) Ask the students how they think they would respond in such a situation. What factors would make them more or less likely to confess?

After presenting the basic paradigm of the prisoner's dilemma, we suggest that you divide the students into pairs and make repeated decisions about whether they are going to cooperate or compete with their partner. To enact this multiple trial prisoner's dilemma, you can use **Handout 8.8b** or, if you have the facilities, one of the computer programs that allow students to play a multiple trials prisoner's dilemma game. To use Handout 8.8b have students make ten scraps of paper. Ask them to write on their first scrap of paper "cooperate" or "compete." Then have partners submit their actions (pieces of paper) simultaneously. Once the actions have been submitted, both players can compare their actions to Handout 8.8b and see how many points they won. Students should repeat this nine times and obtain a total of the number of points that they obtained. After completing the exercise, have students discuss the strategies they used and how effective they were. This activity should serve as a good way to introduce research reported in the text on strategies in multiple trial prisoner's dilemma situations.

> ● **What if this bombs?** This activity is fairly bombproof. Students will have a good time enacting the prisoner's dilemma situation and they should learn a lot by participating in the activity. Whatever patterns emerge should be interesting to discuss.

Activity 9. Tragedy of the Commons

The tragedy of the commons occurs when a natural resource is depleted due to selfish, competitive behavior. For example, when people have equal access to a lake and each member of a group wants to get the most fish out of the lake, which ultimately results in the lake being depleted.

To demonstrate an analog of the tragedy in class, you will need the following materials: A paper bag with 20–30 pistachio nuts, paper clips, large buttons, pennies, (or any other same number of a single item), an equal number of the same item for replenishment, and a watch.

The procedure is as follows:

Pick one row (4–6 seats would be ideal) of students to play the game. Explain that the game you are about to play has two rules.

Rule # 1: The number of objects (whatever they may be) left in the bag at the end of every

10 seconds will double.

Rule # 2: The object of the game is to acquire as many of the objects in the bag as

possible.

Ask the students in the designated row if they understand the rules. Tell them that when you say "go," they should start passing the bag down the row, from one end to the other and back again. Now say "Go!" and monitor your watch. After 10 seconds, stop the game and double the number of objects that are in the bag. Keep playing a few more rounds if objects remain in the bag. However, chances are that there will be no objects left in the bag. That as soon as you say "Go," the first, second, or third student will grab as many objects as he or she can before the others do, causing the game to end prematurely. Usually students focus on rule # 2, and quick to forget rule # 1.

> ●*What if this bombs?* This one should be nearly bombproof. However, students may figure out the game and try to hold off from taking any items. If they do, point out that they averted the tragedy of the commons.

Edney, J.J. (1979) The nuts game: A concise commons dilemma analog. Environmental Psychology and Nonverbal Behavior, 3, 252-254.

Hardin, G. (1968) The tragedy of the commons. Science, 162, 1243-1248.

Activity 11.   Brainstorming

People often assume that groups are better at solving problems than individuals in situations where that isn't necessarily the case. One popular example is brainstorming. Brainstorming is a method for generating ideas. A group of people gets together and everybody in the group says whatever ideas come into their heads on the topic of interest while a note-taker keeps track of all the ideas. Brainstorming has a great deal of intuitive appeal but little empirical support. One reason that has been offered to explain why brainstorming is generally ineffective is blocking, that is, that when one person is expressing their ideas they are simultaneously suppressing the other members of the group from expressing theirs. This blocking effect can easily be demonstrated in class.

Activity:

Assign half of the class to the "interactive groups" condition and half to the "non-interactive (nominal) groups" condition. Further divide those in the "interactive groups" condition into clusters of 5 or more students (the bigger the groups, the more pronounced the blocking effect should be).

Provide the following instructions:

Your task is to make a list of items that you would need to survive alone on a desert island for the span of ten years. You should try to come up with as many items as you can. Those of you in the interactive groups will use a standard brainstorming technique. Choose one person in the group to record your ideas (this person may also contribute ideas) and just say your ideas as they come to you for five minutes. Those of you in the non-interactive groups will work individually for the five minutes writing down your ideas on your own papers and will combine your ideas at the end of the time.

In coming up with your "total ideas" tally at the end of the activity, make sure that you only count each idea once. For example, even if four people in your group say that you need a cheese grater you only get to count the item one time.

What should happen: Even though the non-interactive groups have redundancy working against them (that is, they are likely to have a lot of overlap in their lists that don't benefit their final idea count) they are still highly likely to do better than the interactive groups due to the blocking effect. Again, the larger the groups are, the more pronounced the difference between the two should be.

> ● *What if this bombs?* It is highly likely that the results of the demonstration should turn out as planned (particularly when large groups are used). If it doesn't turn out as planned, however, all is not lost. If the interactive groups do better, this activity can be used as a springboard into discussing some of the benefits of group interaction including the motivating properties of working in a group (the interactive group students probably had more fun at the task and were more engaged than were the non-interactive group students).

Diehl, M. & Stroebe, W. (1991). Productivity loss in idea-generating groups: Tracking down the blocking effect. Journal of Personality & Social Psychology. 61, 392-403.

MULTIMEDIA RESOURCES

Video

Abilene Paradox, 2nd Edition. Vignettes from a variety of situations illustrate how well-intentioned but misguided consensus agreements can steer an organization into activity that directly contradicts individual desires and defeats group purpose. Shows how three key psychological principles—action anxiety, negative fantasies, and fear of ostracization—contribute to faulty group collusion, and demonstrates how to overcome these obstacles to reach successful and productive group decisions. (2002, 26 min.) CRM Learning, 2218 Faraday Ave., Ste. 110, Carlsbad, CA 92008. (800-421-0833).

The Anatomy of a Group. This film discusses the characteristics of a group and identifies a group as a collection of individuals with a common purpose, a participation pattern, a communication system, a well-developed social climate, mutually adopted standards, an organizational structure, and prescribed procedures to be followed in their relations. (1963, 30 min.) Audio-Visual Center, Indiana University, Bloomington, IN 47495-5901.

An Essay on War. The film presents, pictorially and verbally, an in-depth portrayal of the psychology of war. Explores the puzzle of war: why we wage it, how we justify it, and how we are affected as nations and individuals. (1971, 23 min.) Bureau of Audio Visual Instruction, University of Wisconsin - Extension, PO Box 2093, Madison, WI 53701-2093.

Gangs: The Consequences of Conformity. Explains elements that combine to form a group of any kind. Shows how a group often demands conformity and allegiance of members. Encourages observation and individual decisions about group participation. (1977, 16 min.) Bureau of Audio Visual Instruction, University of Wisconsin-Extension, PO Box 2093, Madison, WI 53701-2093.

Groups and Group Dynamics. This program describes different categories of groups and explains how they function, how they differ from other social entities, and how group membership is determined. It then looks at intra-group relationships, examining conformity and individualism. Finally, the interaction between groups is investigated. (1991, 30 min.) Available from Insight Media (800-233-9910).

Groupthink, 2nd Edition. This film illustrates eight symptoms of "groupthink": the illusion of invulnerability, shared stereotypes of the enemy, rationalization, the illusion of morality, self-censorship, the illusion of unanimity, direct pressure on the deviant member, and mindguarding—a device that protects the group from dissenting opinions. Uses the story of the space shuttle Challenger and other historical examples to explore and demonstrate the phenomenon of groupthink. Commentary by Drs. Irving Janis and David Kanouse. (1992, 22 min.) CRM Learning, 2218 Faraday Ave., Ste. 110, Carlsbad, CA 92008. (800-421-0833).

Group Dynamics in the Electronic Environment. This video examines group dynamics in cyber-communication. (1996, 30 min.) Available from Insight Media (800-233-9910).

Interviews with My Lai Veterans. Chilling documentary on the dehumanizing effects of the Vietnam War on American soldiers. Five My Lai veterans who participated in the massacre of Vietnamese civilians tell in detail what they did, how they felt while doing it, and how they feel about it now. Academy Award. (1970, 22 min.) http: //www.Video.BarnesandNoble.com.

Postwar Hopes, Cold War Fears. This feature explores the issue of conformity and the Cold War fears that dominated America during the late 1940s and well into the 1950s. Looks at how an economically strong and optimistic America came to distrust anyone who was "different"—artists were blacklisted, professors and certain intellectuals ostracized. Discusses how the McCarthy era was one of the first instances where mass merchandising brought the American public to near hysteria. (1984, 55 min.) Audio-Visual Center, Indiana University, Bloomington, IN 47495-5901.

Resolving Conflicts. Realistic vignettes illustrate two basic approaches to conflict resolution, showing how and when to use each method to achieve effective and positive results. Applicable to a wide variety of organizations. (1982, 22 min.) Video Learning Library, L.L.C. 15838 North 62nd Street, Scottsdale, Arizona 85254-1988. (800-383-8811).

Internet

Game Theory. This site will allow students to play the prisoner's dilemma against five different virtual personalities. Visit this site at: http://www.gametheory.net/web/pdilemma/

Peace Agreements. The United States Institute of Peace was established by the federal government to promote peaceful resolutions of international conflicts. The site includes an archive that contains every international peace agreement signed since 1989. You can visit the sight at: http://www.usip.org/library/pa.html

Prisoner's Dilemma. This site allows students to play the prisoner's dilemma online against a "wizard" opponent. You can visit the site at: http://serendip.brynmawr.edu/playground/pd.html

Computer Programs

Conflict & Cooperation (Version 2.0). Expanding on the classic prisoner's dilemma framework, this software allows students to author and then play out a wide variety of interactive decision-making scenarios constructed to represent political, business, or social situations in which participants vie for resources. Instruction booklet included. On-line help available. Although the kit may be more appropriate for use in the context of Ch. 11, it can be used here as an extension of a discussion of the prisoner's dilemma. (Windows) Available from Wisc Ware, Academic Computing Center, University of Wisconsin, 1210 W. Dayton St., Madison, WI 53706.

A Cooperative-Competitive Game. Students of social psychology, gaming, bargaining, and conflict resolution have observed a general tendency for people to compete even when they could do much better by cooperating. This program, based on work by Deutch and Krauss, puts each player in charge of a trucking company that transports goods to certain destinations via various routes, one of which is a one-way road. Players earn points depending on their time to reach a destination which is, in turn, determined by an optimal combination of private versus cooperative strategies. Instruction booklet included. (Macintosh & DOS) Educational Psychology Department, University of Calgary, Calgary, AL T2N 1N4.

HANDOUT 8.1

Is each of the following a group?

1. Y N   Stockbrokers trading on a stock exchange

2. Y N   Parents at a PTA meeting

3. Y N   Diners in a fancy restaurant

4. Y N   Members of the US Olympic ski team

5. Y N   Patients sitting in a doctor's waiting room

6. Y N   Relatives at a family reunion

7. Y N   Residents in the same apartment complex

8. Y N   Members of one of the teams on the television reality show *The Apprentice*

9. Y N   Students at the same school

10. Y N   The cast of a Broadway musical

11. Y N   Prisoners on the same cell block

12. Y N   Passengers on a commercial jet

HANDOUT 8.3

Missiles Vs. Factories Payoff Matrix

Number of Missiles Other Person Has Left

Number of Missiles You Have Left

	0	1	2	3	4	5
0	5 / 5	3 / 6	1 / 7	5 / 5	-1 / 8	-5 / 10
1	6 / 3	4 / 4	2 / 5	0 / 6	-2 / 7	-4 / 8
2	7 / 1	5 / 2	3 / 3	1 / 5	-1 / 5	-3 / 6
3	8 / -1	6 / 0	4 / 1	2 / 2	0 / 3	-2 / 4
4	9 / -3	7 / -2	5 / -1	3 / 0	1 / 1	-1 / 2
5	10 / -5	8 / -4	6 / -3	4 / -2	2 / -1	0 / 0

Left of diagonal is your payoff, right of diagonal is the other player's payoff

HANDOUT 8.8a THE PRISONER'S DILEMMA

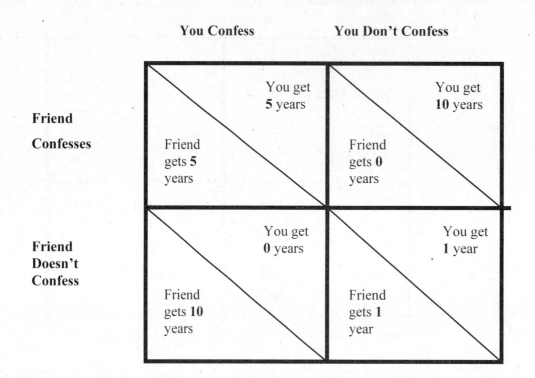

You Confess   **You Don't Confess**

Friend Confesses

You get **5** years

Friend gets **5** years

You get **10** years

Friend gets **0** years

Friend Doesn't Confess

You get **0** years

Friend gets **10** years

You get **1** year

Friend gets **1** year

HANDOUT 8.8b THE PRISONER'S DILEMMA

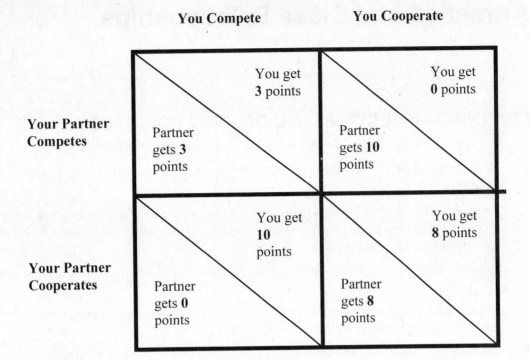

You Compete   **You Cooperate**

Your Partner Competes

Partner gets **3** points   You get **3** points

Partner gets **10** points   You get **0** points

Your Partner Cooperates

Partner gets **0** points   You get **10** points

Partner gets **8** points   You get **8** points

CHAPTER 9

Attraction and Close Relationships

LEARNING OBJECTIVES: GUIDELINES FOR STUDY

You should be able to do each of the following by the conclusion of Chapter 9.

1. Describe social anxiety and the need for affiliation. Address the relationship between affiliation and stress. (*pp. 339-342*)

2. Summarize the social difficulties associated with shyness and loneliness. Discuss factors that predict loneliness (e.g., age, transitions) and coping strategies that can be employed to deal with loneliness. (*pp. 342-343*)

3. Describe the role of familiarity in attraction, including issues of proximity and mere exposure effects. (*pp. 343-345*)

4. Distinguish between objective and subjective perspectives on physical attractiveness, drawing on data and observations that support both ideas. (*pp. 345-349*)

5. Describe the what-is-beautiful-is-good stereotype and why it endures. Explain the benefits and costs of being someone who is perceived to be beautiful. (*pp. 350-352*)

6. Explain the influence of similarity on attractiveness, including the matching and complementarity hypotheses. Discuss the role of reciprocity in liking. (*pp. 352-357*)

7. Explain the differences between evolutionary and sociocultural perspectives on mate preference. (*pp. 357-362*)

8. Explain social exchange theory. Define the concepts of comparison level, comparison level for alternatives, and investment. Explain how equity theory differs from social exchange theory. (*pp. 364-367*)

9. Distinguish between exchange and communal relationships and consider the role of attachment style in studying intimate relationships. (*pp. 367-369*)

10. Summarize different approaches to classifying love, such as Lee's love styles, Sternberg's triangular theory of love, and Hatfield's distinction between passionate and companionate love. (*pp. 369-370*)

11. Explain the relationship between arousal and attraction, as well as the role that both play in passionate love. (*pp. 370-372*)

12. Define self-disclosure, and describe typical patterns of disclosure in relationships. (*pp. 372-373*)

13. Discuss cultural and gender differences with regard to issues of attraction, intimate relationships, and sexuality. Consider how social psychologists study sexual orientation. (*pp. 374-380*)

14. Discuss communication and attribution patterns that can lead to conflict in relationships. Describe patterns of marital satisfaction and issues regarding the end of intimate relationships. (*pp. 380-384*)

DETAILED CHAPTER OUTLINE

I. Being with Others: A Fundamental Human Motive
    A.   The Thrill of Affiliation
        1.   Need for affiliation: a desire to establish contact with others
        2.   Stress leads to desire to affiliate
    B.   The Agony of Loneliness – To feel deprived about the nature of one's existing social relations
II. The Initial Attraction
    A.   Familiarity: Being There
        1.   The proximity effect
        2.   The mere exposure effect
    B.   Physical Attractiveness: Getting Drawn In
        1.   What is beauty?
            a)   some faces are seen as more attractive than others
            b)   composite averages of faces are seen as more attractive
            c)   even babies show preference for certain faces
            d)   beauty is also influenced by culture, time, and circumstance
            e)   viewing attractive models lowers people's evaluations of themselves and others
        2.   Why are we blinded by beauty?
            a)   it is inherently rewarding to be with beautiful people
            b)   what-is-beautiful-is-good stereotype
            c)   physical attractiveness stereotype is only accurate to a limited extent
            d)   the self-fulfilling prophecy probably maintains the physical attractiveness stereotype
        3.   The benefits and costs of beauty
            a)   attractive people gain benefits from the physical attractiveness stereotype
            b)   attractive people also have difficulty interpreting feedback: is it due to my looks or my performance?
            c)   attractive people might face more pressure to maintain their appearance
    C.   First Encounters: Getting Acquainted
        1.   Liking others who are similar
            a)   we associate with those who are similar
            b)   the matching hypothesis seems true; people tend to date and marry people with a similar level of attractiveness
        2.   Liking others who like us
            a)   balance theory predicts that we will like someone if they share our views of others
            b)   we like others when there is reciprocity: mutual give and take
        3.   Pursuing those who are hard to get
    D.   Mate Selection: The Evolution of Desire?
        1.   The evolutionary perspective
            a)   women are attracted to older men who are financially secure
            b)   men are attracted to women who are young, and physically attractive
            c)   women are jealous of emotional infidelity – intimacy with another partner
            d)   men are jealous of sexual infidelity
        2.   Sociocultural perspectives
            a)   women trade youth and beauty to gain economic power
            b)   men fear sexual infidelity because of what it implies about intimacy
            c)   sex differences are small compared to similarities

III. Close Relationships
    A. The Intimate Marketplace: Tracking the Gains and Losses
        1. Social exchange theory – relationships that provide more rewards and fewer costs will be more satisfying and endure longer
            a) comparison level – average expected outcome of a relationship
            b) comparison level for alternatives – expected outcome of other possible relationships
            c) investment – something a person puts into a relationship that he or she cannot recover
        2. Equity theory – people are most content when the ratio between what they get out of the relationship and what they put into it is similar for both partners
            a) overbenefited partner – receives more benefits that his or her contributions warrant
            b) underbenefited partner – receives fewer benefits than his or her contributions warrant
            c) both types of partners are likely to be unhappy and want to leave the relationship
    B. Types of Relationships
        1. Exchange and communal relationships
            a) exchange relationships are characterized by immediate tit-for-tat repayment of benefits
            b) communal relationships are characterized by partners responding to each other's needs without regard to benefits they have received
        2. Secure and insecure attachment styles
            a) based on models of infant attachment – three types: secure, avoidant, anxious
            b) people's rating of their attachment style predicts to some extent their adult relationships – securely attached people seem to have happier relationships
    C. How Do I Love Thee? Counting the Ways
        1. Triangular theory of love – love combines intimacy, passion, and commitment
        2. Passionate love: The thrill of it – two key ingredients
            a) heightened physiological arousal
            b) belief that the arousal was triggered by the beloved person
        3. Companionate love: The self-disclosure in it
            a) deep bond of trust and friendship
            b) characterized by self-disclosure – a willingness to open up and share intimate facts and feelings
            c) social penetration theory – proposes that as relationships develop self-disclosure becomes broader and deeper
    D. Culture, Attraction, andRelationships
    E. Relationship Issues: The Male-Female "Connection"
        1. Sexuality
        2. Sexual orientation
        3. The marital trajectory
        4. Communication and conflict
            a) negative affect reciprocity – a tit-for-tat exchange of expressions of negative affect – signals a troubled relationship
            b) demand/withdrawal interaction pattern – where one partner demands to discuss things only to be met by withdrawal from the situation by the other partner – signals trouble
            c) in healthy relationships partners deal with conflict in similar ways
            d) increasing rewards of the relationship and seeing the other's point of view can reduce conflict
            e) attributions that partners make for each other's behavior matter

5. Breaking up
   a) almost all relationships exhibit a decline in satisfaction over time – the steeper this decline, the more likely they are to break up
   b) people who are most committed to a relationship and who define themselves in terms of the other are most affected by a break up

LECTURE AND DISCUSSION IDEAS

Idea 1.   Introduction to Attraction and Intimate Relationships: Artists' Conceptions

One way to introduce the students to the issues of attraction and close relationships is to begin your first class on these topics with quotes, excerpts, lyrics, video excerpts, and pictures from popular sources to illustrate varied conceptions of what is considered attractive, how people conceptualize love, etc. Our students have found this to be both entertaining and thought provoking. The implicit and explicit theories of interpersonal attraction, or of the relationship between liking and loving, that can be illustrated in movie clips, for example, can be very illuminating and fun—particularly if you choose examples that are diverse and may even contradict each other.

For example, you could quote the famous line from Erich Segal's *Love Story*, or show the clip from the 1970 movie (which was a big hit at the box office) in which the line is stated: "Love means never having to say you're sorry" (which, in our opinion, is one of the most inaccurate statements ever written), and then show clips from any of dozens of romantic comedies in which one character (usually the male lead) grovels for forgiveness from the person with whom he or she is in love. Another film clip that can generate some good discussion is from the 1989 hit movie *When Harry Met Sally...*, in which the character played by Billy Crystal explains to the character played by Meg Ryan why men and women cannot be friends without physical attraction between them getting in the way. (Indeed, this character revises his theory at a few points during the movie; thus, by showing successive clips in which he alters his opinion, you can elicit some extra laughs and provide good material for discussion.) Ask the students to comment on this and to discuss the role that physical attraction can play in friendships.

Another film clip that may represent a perspective on attraction and relationships in a particularly memorable way is from Woody Allen's award-winning 1977 movie, *Annie Hall*. Show the last scene of the movie in which the Woody Allen character speaks directly to the camera and sums up his feelings about relationships.

Find contrasting quotes such as the following lines from Shakespeare, "...love is blind/and lovers cannot see the petty follies they themselves commit," and James Thurber's "Love may be blind, but lust doesn't give a good goddamn."

Song lyrics can be a particularly rich vein of material. Rock and rap music can offer dozens and dozens of provocative and very diverse conceptions of attraction, friendship, love, and relationships. Perhaps no form of contemporary music provides as many colorful, quotable statements about these issues as country-and-western music, with song titles such as "I Fell in a Pile of You and Got Love All Over Me," "If Love Were Oil, I'd Be a Quart Low," "Her Teeth Were Stained, But Her Heart Was Pure," "If You Don't Leave Me Alone, I'll Go and Find Someone Else Who Will," etc. On a more serious note, a particularly mature, unflinching examination of both the joys and challenges inherent in friendship, love, and relationships is Bruce Springsteen's 1988 album, *Tunnel of Love*.

In addition to your own examples, have your students bring to class examples that they can find from various sources, and have them explain how these examples relate to the theoretical accounts and empirical findings discussed in the textbook and in class. Consider dividing the class into smaller groups, each of which is assigned the task of finding interesting examples from different sources; for example, one group could bring in quotes from literature, another group could bring in lyrics from rap music, another group could bring in copies of works of art that depict attraction or love, etc. Encourage those students who are expert in searching the Internet to look there for sources and lists that can provide additional examples. Discuss how these popular conceptions of attraction and relationships are and are not consistent with social psychological theories and research findings. For example, the commonsensical notion of "opposites attract" is very popular in television and film, and yet the research indicates clearly that it is, in general, not accurate.

Idea 2.   Meeting People Online

An interesting topic that is new to the field of social psychology is how social interaction and forming relationships online differ from how the same processes take place in the non-Internet world. In a review of the research literature to date, McKenna and Bargh (2000) discuss these four major differences:

First, it is possible to maintain anonymity on the Internet. The result is deindividuation, whereby people who communicate by e-mail or other electronic venues, such as newsgroups, tend to be blunter, more hostile, more aggressive, and more nonconforming than those who communicate face-to-face. However, there's also the positive side of deindividuation. This was evident in a study (Gergen, Gergen, and Barton, 1973) in which individuals who met in a dark room disclosed more intimate information and felt more positive about each other than did those who met in a well-lit room. Likewise, the Internet encourages individuals to disclose more and sooner than they would in non-anonymous settings. Consequently, Internet relationships become more intimate, more quickly.

Second, because physical distance is unimportant on the Internet, an individual has the opportunity to interact with a much wider range and variety of others, with people from all over the world, provided they speak the same language.

Third, in online interactions, physical appearance is not as influential a factor in first meetings. Instead, liking, attraction, and friendships are often formed on a basis other than physical attributes. Shared interests and values become much more important. And because relationships are formed on a deeper level, they are more likely to endure. Moreover, newsgroups on the Internet allow individuals to easily find others who share their interests. So, with common ground to begin with, individuals can cut to the chase and find out what else they have in common much more quickly than they would in an offline setting.

Finally, the fourth major difference has to do with time. In Internet interactions, two people do not have to converse at the same time. Instead, they can respond at their leisure, and edit and change messages before sending them. This gives individuals much more control over their interactions, which coupled with anonymity, again encourages greater self-disclosure.

Gergen, K. J., Gergen, M. M., & Barton, W. H. (1973). Deviance in the dark. Psychology Today, 7, 129-130.

McKenna, K. Y. A., & Bargh, J. A. (2000). Plan 9 from cyberspace: The implications of the Internet for personality and social psychology. Personality and Social Psychology Review, 4, Issue 1.

Idea 3.   Beauty in Society

Discuss the role of beauty in our society. What is considered physically attractive in our society today? Does this differ from standards or ideals in other societies? Have these changed over time? Discuss some of the harmful side effects of our society's emphasis on the value of physical appearance, such as bulimia, anorexia nervosa, low self-esteem, etc. Look at examples in the media (television, movies, magazines, advertising, music videos, etc.) and discuss what role the media have played in emphasizing beauty and glamour. Are the popular media depictions of beauty more representative of some groups than others (e.g., in terms of racial, socioeconomic, sexual-orientation, religious, and other distinctions)? Who are today's role models for people of various generations? What impact has their physical appearance, relative to their personality or accomplishment, had on their rise to role-model status?

Bring magazines (particularly fashion or beauty magazines aimed at women) or clipped-out ads for discussion in class. Discuss the age, weight, race, gender, apparent socioeconomic status, clothing, body language, and implied skills and personality of the models depicted. Compare the effects of female and male models on women's and men's self-perceptions, attitudes, and behaviors. In addition to your own examples, have students bring in clips of ads and discuss their reactions to them.

Consider showing the video *Still Killing Us Softly*, concerning the depiction of women in print advertising, to help foster good discussion of these issues. We have shown this video in our classes for several years, and it never fails to elicit a powerful reaction in many of the students.

Ask students to comment on the recent initiative, which began in Madrid, to ban ultra-thin models from the fashion runways. In Madrid, officials banned models with a BMI (body mass index) lower than 18 in the fall of 2006. Milan followed suit by banning anyone with a BMI less than 18.5 (The World Health Organization considers anyone with a BMI less than 18.5 to be underweight).

The American fashion industry has so far resisted adopting similar regulations. Designers here argue that standards of beauty change often and that the current emphasis on extremely thin models will eventually shift back to more curvaceous ones. They also dispute doctors' claims that overly thin models contribute to eating disorders among teenaged girls, claiming that Hollywood celebrities are the real role models for the public, not the 14-year-old Eastern European models seen in magazine ads. What do your students think about these arguments?

On a more positive note, see if students are familiar with one advertiser's product message of "Campaign for Real Beauty." This is an attempt to acknowledge that attractive women come in a variety of shades, shapes, and sizes. The series of ads uses nice looking, average-sized women as opposed to the "anorexic, breast-implanted, tricked-up Barbie dolls" that are usually encountered in ads. Especially notable is their web spot titled "Evolution." The video shows a young, pretty-but-unexceptional looking woman who is being made up for a billboard ad. It takes a team of hairdressers, makeup artists, lighting specialists, and photo retouchers hours to produce the final product that looks nothing like the woman in the beginning of the film. Then a line appears on the screen reading: "No wonder our perception of beauty is distorted."

Garfield, B. (2006). Tackling ugly truth, Dove effort evolves beautifully. Advertising Age, 77, 44, 45.

Wilson, E. (Jan. 9, 2007). Doctors fault designers' stance over thin models. The New York Times, Section C, Column 1, Business/Financial Desk, 2.

Idea 4. The Warm-Glow Heuristic

Ask your students if they've ever heard or used that old pick-up line, "Don't I know you...?" Tell them that in some cases, it may not be as phony as it sounds.

According to a study done by Benoît Monin (2003), attractive people are more likely to seem familiar than are unattractive people. This phenomenon, which Monin termed the warm-glow heuristic, makes people, places, or things that we experience as pleasant seem familiar.

There are two explanations offered for this finding. First, attractive faces might seem familiar because they are prototypical and prototypes are likely to seem familiar. Second, in a confusing social world we are always asking ourselves, "Have I met this person before?" If a face is pleasant and leaves us with a positive "warm glow" reaction, we are more likely to interpret that feeling as familiarity. The fact that liking something is associated with prior experience can also be explained by the self-serving bias. We tell ourselves that our experiences are mostly superior, and a pleasant stimulus might very well be representative of them. So, we regard a beautiful face as one that we are more likely to have encountered than a plain face.

Have your students discuss the implications of the study. Does the warm-glow heuristic confer advantages to attractive people in the dating scene? Are there any disadvantages that might be associated with it?

Monin, B. (2003). The warm-glow heuristic: When liking leads to familiarity. Journal of Personality and Social Psychology, 85, 1035-1048.

Idea 5. Similarity vs. Complementarity

Discuss the differences between relationships based on similarity and those based on complementarity. Have your students cite examples of these kinds of relationships among celebrities, politicians, parents, friends, and others. Discuss the discrepancy between the media's fascination with "opposites attract" and the findings of the social psychological research concerning similarity. Ask the students to discuss why so many television shows and films depict attraction between dissimilar or complementary others—concerning both romantic attraction and friendships (e.g., in numerous "buddy" movies, the buddies often start out hating each other, and/or being complementary, as when one is disciplined and "by-the-book" and the other is undisciplined and impulsive). Ask the students to discuss why similarity seems to be the better predictor of attraction than complementarity. Discuss why dissimilarity is likely to repulse people, as discussed in terms of the theories and models described in Chapter 9. Ask students to compare and discuss the roles of similarity and complementarity in their own current or previous friendships and romantic relationships. Have they found one more important than the other in initial attraction? In predicting the quality and endurance of these relationships?

Or is it more a matter of having a combination of both similar and complementary traits? While most online dating sites, such as eHarmony and Chemistry.com, match people up only according to their similarities, the site PerfectMatch deems it important for some traits, like energy level and optimism, to match, but not others. As they see it, flexibility, perfectionism, and emotion are traits that need to be complemented in order for a marriage to work (2006).

Leonhardt, D. (March 29, 2006). Computing the mysteries of attraction. The New York Times, Section C, Column 1, Business/Financial Desk, 1.

Idea 6. Arranged Marriages

Arranged marriages have been around for quite a while. Your students might be surprised to learn that even today 60 percent of the world's weddings are arranged marriages. They are especially common in large parts of Africa, Asia, and the Middle East. The people who do the arranging are family members, professional matchmakers, religious leaders, or friends. Arranged marriages are based on the assumption that the decision about who to marry is complex and requires more information than is readily available. It is a decision that should not be entrusted to chance or to the young people who are involved.

But in some arranged marriages, the prospective bride and groom are given final say. In modern Indian families, for example, a common practice is the placement of personal ads in the newspapers by the arrangers, describing the person they represent and the candidate they are seeking. The young people are typically given the choice of vetoing any prospect before negotiations begin. In essence, the decision becomes who to choose from among many proposals.

In other, more tradition-bound settings, young people are not given the choice of rejecting their future mates. If they do reject the chosen mate, they risk alienating their families and possibly endangering their physical well-being, as well. After all, the honor of the two families is at stake. In her book, *Understanding Arabs*, Margaret Nydell (1987) equates the feelings of an Arab father whose son refuses to accept the family's choice of a bride with the feelings of a Western father who discovers that his son uses drugs.

Ask your students to discuss how people typically meet their mates in Western cultures. What are the advantages and disadvantage of "love American style" as opposed to the courtship patterns of arranged marriages? Do they agree that choosing a mate requires more information than is readily available (such as family standing)? Some proponents of arranged marriage point to lower divorce rates, but that doesn't necessarily mean that the marriages are more successful. Discuss other factors that might be at work (such as the importance of the family unit in collectivist societies and the powerlessness of women in some cultures).

Batabyal, A. (2001). On the likelihood of finding the right partner in an arranged marriage. Journal of Socio-Economics, 30, 273-281.

Carlin, F. (2004). Close quarters. Psychology Today, 37, 15-17.

Nydell, M. (1987). Understanding Arabs, Yarmouth, ME: Intercultural Press.

Idea 7.   Social Motives: The Needs for Affiliation and Intimacy

Discuss and contrast the need for affiliation and the need for intimacy. The textbook defines the former as "the desire to establish and maintain many rewarding relationships" and the latter as "the preference for warm, close, communicative relationships." The text goes on to characterize high need for affiliation as "inspiring active, controlling social behavior with an emphasis on the breadth and quantity of social contacts" and high need for intimacy as "inspiring more passive, less controlling social behavior with an emphasis on the depth and quality of social relations."

Ask the students to imagine where they stand on each of these dimensions, and why. Ask them for examples of specific behaviors that they think would be predicted by each of these dimensions. Consider summarizing or assigning some articles by Dan McAdams and colleagues concerning these different motives, such as "Intimacy and Affiliation Motives in Daily Living: An Experience Sampling Analysis," by McAdams and Constantian (1983), and/or, "Social Motives and Patterns of Friendship," by McAdams, Healy, and Krause (1984). These articles explain the distinction between these two social motives in greater detail than the textbook can, and they illustrate how these motives correlate with various patterns of behavior. See Activity 6 of this chapter for an exercise involving an individual-difference measure of four dimensions thought to underlie the need for affiliation.

Researchers typically assess social motives on the basis of participants' responses on the Thematic Apperception Test (TAT). To facilitate discussion about these issues, consider using Activity 6 of this chapter, which involves the use of the TAT and the coding system developed to assess need for affiliation and need for intimacy.

McAdams, D. P., & Constantian, C. A. (1983). Intimacy and affiliation motives in daily living: An experience sampling analysis. Journal of Personality and Social Psychology, 45, 851-861.

McAdams, D. P., Healy, S., & Krause, S. (1984). Social motives and patterns of friendship. Journal of Personality and Social Psychology, 47, 828-838.

Idea 8.   The Role of Self-Monitoring in Attraction and Dating Relationships

Does physical attractiveness play a more important role in determining attraction for some people than for others? Are some people more likely than others to end current relationships in order to pursue alternative partners? Research by Mark Snyder, Jeffrey Simpson, and their colleagues suggests that individual differences concerning self-monitoring should be correlated with such differences in attraction, dating, and related issues.

As is discussed in Chapter 3, self-monitoring refers to the tendency to change behavior in response to the self-presentation concerns of the situation. Snyder and his colleagues (1985) presented men who were either high self-monitors or low self-monitors with dating choices that pitted physical attractiveness against a good personality. When given the choice of dating a physically attractive woman who was difficult to get along with versus a woman who was relatively unattractive physically but who had an engaging and outgoing personality, a majority of the high self-monitoring individuals said that they would prefer to date the former woman, whereas a majority of the low self-monitoring individuals indicated a preference for the latter woman. Snyder and Simpson (1984) found that high self-monitoring individuals indicated a greater willingness than low self-monitoring individuals to end current relationships in favor of alternative partners; moreover, high self-monitoring individuals reported having dated a greater number of partners in a given period of time than did low self-monitoring individuals, and low self-monitoring individuals reported dating their current partners longer than did high self-monitoring individuals.

Discuss these findings with the class. Ask students to try to explain why self-monitoring should be correlated with these behaviors and attitudes. The scale that is used to assess individuals' self-monitoring is included in the materials for Chapter 3 in this *Instructor's Resource Manual*. Distribute copies of the scale to the class, and have each student complete and then score it to see where he or she stands on this dimension. (You may have already done this for an activity associated with Chapter 3—in which case you should simply remind the students about the contents of the scale and, if possible, have them look up their self-monitoring scores from the original copy of the scale.)

Snyder, M., Berscheid, E., & Glick, P. (1985). Focusing on the exterior and the interior: Two investigations of the initiation of personal relationships. Journal of Personality and Social Psychology, 48, 1427-1439.

Snyder, M., & Simpson, J. A. (1984). Self-monitoring and dating relationships. Journal of Personality and Social Psychology, 47, 1281-1291.

Idea 9.   Misattribution

Discuss the role of attribution in general, and misattribution in particular, in attraction. As Chapter 9 explains, the pattern of causal attributions that people make can exacerbate (or attenuate) social difficulties such as anxiety, loneliness, and depression. Give examples of the kinds of attributions that are likely to prolong one's social difficulties (i.e., attributions that are internal and stable), and discuss why these attributions are likely to have this effect.

Misattribution can also play an important role in determining how attracted a perceiver is to another person. One of our favorite studies in this regard illustrates how ambiguous our own feelings can be and how this ambiguity makes us vulnerable to perceptions of the self and others that are based on inaccurate attributions. Assign or summarize Dutton and Aron's (1974) article, which found that men seemed to be more attracted to a woman if they met her after having just taken a rather frightening stroll across a bridge than if they had just taken a less anxious walk. Their results suggest that the men in the former condition may have mistakenly attributed at least some of the arousal that had been elicited by the anxiety concerning the bridge to arousal due to physical attraction to the woman. Students tend to find this study interesting and amusing. Discuss how misattribution can occur, and explain its implications for self-perception and interpersonal attraction. Also discuss alternative explanations for the Dutton and Aron findings—for example, talking with the woman may have reduced the stress of the men who had just crossed the bridge, and thus her presence was rewarding to them. Ask students to discuss any conceptually similar experiences that they have had, such as meeting their boyfriend or girlfriend at an exciting game or very fun party.

Dutton, D. G., & Aron, A. P. (1974). Some evidence for heightened sexual attraction under conditions of high anxiety. Journal of Personality and Social Psychology, 30, 510-517.

Idea 10.   Does a Pretty Face Signify a Healthy Woman?

As discussed in Chapter 9 of the text, according to evolutionary theory, men prefer pretty women because their beauty signifies good health (and therefore good reproductive potential).

Perceptions of facial attractiveness have been shown to correlate with three characteristics: averageness, symmetry, and dimorphism (i.e., feminine traits in female faces and masculine traits in male faces).

In a review of all studies linking physical attractiveness and health (Weeden & Sabini, 2005), the authors found the following:

   a.   Average faces were judged to be more attractive and healthier than distinctive faces. However, there was only a very small relationship between actual health and averageness of faces.

   b.   Symmetrical faces (enhanced through computer manipulation) were judged to be more attractive and healthier than nonsymmetrical faces. However, there was no relationship between actual measured symmetry and perceived health, or between perceived symmetry (of actual faces) and actual health. There was also no meaningful relationship between actual measured facial symmetry and actual health.

   c.   The one study that involved the relationship between dimorphism in facial characteristics and health showed a positive correlation in males but no relationship between how feminine women's features were rated and their actual health.

   d.   In summarizing and averaging the results of four studies that asked participants to rate the overall attractiveness of faces, it was found that although rated face attractiveness and impressions of health are highly positively correlated (at around .60), women's facial attractiveness was only a weak predictor of their actual health.

In another, more recent study, researchers (Hutson, 2006) reported finding a negative correlation when it comes to pretty women and health. They explain their findings by suggesting that attractive women are more social, which means that they have more opportunities to come in contact with pathogens.

Hutson, M. (2006). When beauty misleads: pretty does not mean problem-free. Psychology Today, 39, 5, 26.

Weeden, J. & Sabini, J. (2005). Physical attractiveness and health in Western societies. Psychological Bulletin, 131, 5, 635-653.

Idea 11.   Can Passionate Love Last?

When most people think of passion they envision a passing whim or fancy, yet passionate love seems to be fairly robust. Although some studies show that passionate love decreases over time in a relationship (Acker & Davis, 1992), this decrease is relatively small (Tucker & Aron, 1993). For the most part, couples are able to keep a lot of thrills in their relationships and passion seems to be an important part of their connection to one another.

Acker, M., & Davis, M. H. (1992). Intimacy, passion and commitment in adult romantic relationships: A test of the triangular theory of love. Journal of Social and Personal Relationships, 9, 21-50.

Tucker, P., & Aron, A. (1993). Passionate love and marital satisfaction at key transition points in the family life cycle. Journal of Social and Clinical Psychology, 12, 135-147.

Idea 12.   The Dynamics of Same-Sex Friendships

What transforms an acquaintanceship into a friendship, what maintains a friendship, and what elevates a friend to a best friend status? An article in Psychology Today (2006) reviews the relevant findings of sociologists and social psychologists.

Acquaintances become friends when one party makes a self-disclosure and the other reciprocates. The phrase "Can I talk to you for a minute?" has been used to initiate many friendships. Once a friendship is established, it is maintained by reciprocal emotional understanding. Those who respond to their friends' self-disclosures with emotional expressiveness, unconditional support, acceptance, loyalty, and trust will develop satisfying same-sex relationships. As for the ability of friends to offer material support, that was judged by study participants to have only marginal relevance. In fact, the "Ben Franklin" effect appears to be true, in that people tend to appreciate others even more after they have done favors for them.

"Best" friendships are characterized by intimacy as well as social-identity support, which is the degree to which a friend supports one's place in society. We become best friends with those who boost our self-esteem by acknowledging our contribution to a group (You're a great dancer) or by affirming the status of the group with which we identify (You belong to the best dance troupe).

The intimate bond of best friendships will persist only if both parties will strive to nurture these four necessary factors:

1.   Self-disclosure: the ability to share the things that are happening in one's life.
2.   Supportiveness: the ability to empathize with and listen to each other.
3.   Interaction: in person, by phone, by e-mail, or by letters.
4.   Positivism: the give-and-take of intimate self-disclosure must leave both parties feeling good.

Karbo, K. (2006). Friendship: The laws of attraction. Psychology Today, 39, 6, 90-95.

Idea 13.   Communication in Relationships

The textbook outlines two negative communication patterns: negative affect reciprocity and the demand/withdraw interaction pattern. Ask your students whether they recognize these interaction patterns in their friends and relatives or even in their own relationships. Can your students think of other negative interaction patterns? Are there positive interaction patterns that make relationships more successful? Can your students describe the type of interaction patterns that they find enjoyable and rewarding? Ask your students to list both an interaction they have had that went badly and an interaction that went well. Have them try to characterize the interaction and note its most important aspects.

Idea 14.   Breakups in Relationships

As the textbook mentions, interdependence and a shared identity are associated with both longer-lasting relationships (Berscheid et al., 1989) and more post-breakup distress (Simpson, 1987). It seems that those people who are most closely identified with their partner receive the most benefits when a relationship goes well and the most pain when a relationship ends. Identification with a partner seems to operate in much the same way as passionate love: intense satisfaction when all is well, but intense dissatisfaction when things fall apart. How might passionate love and identification with a partner be related? Have your students discuss the possible relationship between these two interesting variables.

Berscheid, E., Snyder, M., & Omoto, A. M. (1989). The relationship closeness inventory: Assessing the closeness of interpersonal relationships. Journal of Personality and Social Psychology, 57, 792-807.

Simpson, J. A. (1987). The dissolution of romantic relationships: Factors involved in relationship stability and emotional distress. Journal of Personality and Social Psychology, 53, 683-692.

Idea 15   Love Stories

Are there prototypical types of love relationships? What happens when the partners in a relationship have different ideas about what a relationship is "supposed" to be like? An interesting topic for class discussion is Robert Sternberg's new theory about love relationships. This theory centers on the assumption that we have narratives involving romantic relationships (love stories) that tell us what relationships should be. Examples include the "soulmate" where the story is that once you find the right person everything will be perfect, "gardening" where the story is that the relationship is something that needs constant attention to develop, and the "police" story in which your love partner needs to be constantly monitored and "kept in line." You can ask the students to suggest other relationship stereotypes that they might have seen over and over again in movies, on TV, in plays, etc.

Sternberg, R. J. (1999). Love Is a Story: A New Theory of Relationships. Oxford University Press.

CLASSROOM ACTIVITIES

Activity 1.   Collecting and Analyzing Personals Ads

What qualities are men and women looking for when they seek potential mates? What do men and women think they need to offer to potential mates in order to attract them? Although self-report measures are often used to address these questions, one alternative approach that may be particularly informative is to analyze the personals ads that are published in many newspapers and magazines. As Lynn and Bolig (1985) noted, personal ads are particularly useful in addressing these questions because (1) their authors are not aware that their ads are being studied for research purposes, (2) compared to most laboratory or survey settings, the mundane realism is much higher and the consequences for the participants are greater, and (3) the people who submit these ads better represent the population at large on a variety of dimensions than do the college participants in the typical laboratory experiment.

This activity, therefore, involves students analyzing the content of personals ads. Divide the students into small groups, and either give each group, or have them find and bring to class, about a dozen "personals" from newspapers or magazines. Each group should have a different set of personals ads. There should be an equal number of ads by men and by women for each group. You might consider having some groups analyze homosexual or bisexual ads, or having each group analyze homosexual or bisexual ads along with the heterosexual ones. Only ads in which the advertiser lists his or her own sex and the sex (or sexes) of the people he or she is seeking should be used.

You should explain to the students what the various definitions used in these ads mean (indeed, some of the students may have to explain some of them to you), such as "SWDPF," meaning single, white, divorced, professional, female (at least that's what we think it means). You may need to call the editor of a local newspaper's personals section to help with some of the more obscure abbreviations or terms.

Findings in the literature. Several studies have analyzed the content of these ads to examine gender differences (e.g., Cameron, Oskamp, & Sparks, 1977; Deaux & Hanna, 1984; Gonzales & Meyers,

1993; Koestner & Wheeler, 1988). These studies have consistently found that women are more likely to offer physical attractiveness and to seek professional status, whereas men are more likely to offer professional status and to seek attractiveness. This finding is clearly consistent with the sociobiological account of mate selection, as well as with accounts based on sex-role stereotyping, power differences, and implicit theories of attraction.

Koestner and Wheeler (1988) also found that women were "relatively more likely to offer instrumental or 'male-valued' traits in their ads and to seek expressive or 'female-valued' ones, while men showed the reverse pattern. This paradoxical finding was interpreted to reflect the influence of implicit notions of attraction and role expectations" (p. 149). Another interesting finding in their study was that women were relatively more likely to offer weight and seek height, whereas men showed the opposite pattern.

Contrary to prior studies and their own predictions, Strassberg and Holty (2003) found that after placing four different "female seeking male" ads on an Internet bulletin board, the ad that was most popular used the key phrase "financially independent…successful and ambitious." It was 50% more popular than an ad that used the key phrase "lovely…very attractive and slim."

Moreover, a study mentioned in the text (Gangestad, 1993), as well as a more recent one cited in Psychology Today (2006), found that with increasing financial independence, women become more interested in good looks and less in wealth when it comes to choosing a prospective mate. That this trend has been noticed by males is evident in the recent proliferation of men's fashion and fitness magazines and the greater amount of time that men now devote to grooming tasks, such as taking care of their hair.

Characteristics to code. Each group of students should analyze the ads by taking note of particular characteristics that the advertiser either seeks in a mate or is "offering" or advertising about himself or herself to attract a mate. The students can code each ad in a variety of ways, in terms of whether the advertiser seeks or offers physical attractiveness, professional achievement, particular personality traits, etc. What characteristics you have your students examine depends on the kinds of ads that are included in your sample, what points about attraction you would like to address, etc. We suggest that you examine gender differences regarding what Koestner and Wheeler (1988) call the "status/attractiveness exchange hypothesis"—i.e., women offering attractiveness in exchange for status and men offering status in exchange for attractiveness. Also examine whether women offer characteristics assumed to be valued most by men and whether men show the opposite pattern, and whether advertisers seem to be seeking similar others or complementary others.

Handout 9.1 is a long list of specific and general factors to be coded. Either distribute copies of the handout to the students, or construct a smaller list from the characteristics included on the handout that would best suit your goals or situation. Either have each group of students code the ads collaboratively as a group, with students working together to decide how to code the ads and resolve any differences of opinion, or have each student within each group code the ads individually, and then have them get together to assess their inter-rater reliability and resolve differences of opinion by majority rule. The latter, individual approach is likely to be more methodologically sound, but the former, collaborative approach is likely to be more fun for the students.

At the top of Handout 9.1 appears: "_____ seeking _____." In those blanks should be written "Men" or "Women," as appropriate. That is, separate coding sheets should be kept for men seeking women, women seeking men, and, if you include these conditions, men seeking men, and women seeking women.

For each of the characteristics on Handout 9.1 or on an alternative coding sheet, the students should record the number of ads in which an advertiser was <u>offering</u> a characteristic (i.e., the advertiser mentions this characteristic or behavior about himself or herself), <u>seeking</u> a characteristic (i.e., the advertiser mentions this characteristic or behavior as being what he or she is looking for), or simply mentioning a characteristic (i.e., it is not clear if the person is seeking or offering it, but it is mentioned—e.g., the person describes the type of relationship he or she expects they will build together).

Note that some characteristics mentioned in a personals ad may apply to multiple characteristics on the coding sheet. For example, if a student examines an ad in which the advertiser seeks someone with a very attractive, athletic body, the student should check both "attractive" and "body."

When the ads have been coded, divide up the sample by gender (and, if you included ads for homosexual and/or bisexual relationships, divide up the sample further by sexual orientation). Calculate the proportions of women and men who offer, seek, or mention each of the characteristics that were coded.

Discussion. Discuss the results of the analysis with the students. Did the results replicate previous findings, such as the status/attractiveness exchange hypothesis? Why or why not? Did people tend to seek similar or dissimilar others? Were people more likely to emphasize personality, activities, status, or physical attractiveness? Discuss the results from a variety of theoretical perspectives, such as sociobiology, cultural influences, etc. Ask the students if they were able to learn what attributes or characteristics seem most attractive to the people who write the ads, whether some types of people seem especially likely to write ads, etc.

What if this bombs? This activity is bombproof. Although it certainly is possible that there will be no interesting differences as a function of gender, sexual orientation, or whatever other categories you compare, simply examining what kinds of characteristics are sought and offered in these ads should be very illuminating and lead to interesting discussion about many of the issues raised in Chapter 9. If previous findings are not replicated, ask students for their own ideas about why that might be. Is it likely that the people who submit ads to the newspapers selected for this activity are not representative of the population at large? Was the coding scheme not specific enough, leaving too many ambiguities about how to code particular ads? Was the sample analyzed too small to be very reliable? In any case, replicating previous findings is not at all necessary for this activity to be very successful in raising important issues and points for discussion.

Cameron, C., Oskamp, S., & Sparks, M. (1977). Courtship American style: Newspaper ads. The Family Coordinator, 26, 27-30.

Deaux, K., & Hanna, R. (1984). Courtship in the personal column: The influence of gender and sexual orientation. Sex Roles, 1, 363-375.

Gangestad, S. W. (1993). Sexual selection and physical attractiveness: Implications for mating dynamics. Human Nature, 4, 205-235.

Gonzales, M. H., & Meyers, S. A. (1993). "Your mother would like me": Self-presentation in the personals ads of heterosexual and homosexual men and women. Personality and Social Psychology Bulletin, 19, 131-142.

Koestner, R., & Wheeler, L. (1988). Self-presentation in personal advertisements: The influence of implicit notions of attraction and role expectations. Journal of Social and Personal Relationships, 5, 149-160.

Lynn, W. M., & Bolig, R. (1985). Personal advertisements: Sources of data about relationships. Journal of Social and Personal Relationships, 2, 377-383.

Strassberg, D.S. & Holty, S. (2003). An experimental study of women's Internet personal ads. Archives of Sexual Behavior, 32, 253-261.

Wolfer, S. (2006). Can't buy me love. Psychology Today, 39, 4, 25.

Activity 2.   Writing Personals Ads

As an alternative to the previous activity, or as an activity that could be done <u>before</u> Activity 1 (moreover, this activity should be done before students have read Chapter 9), have the students actually write their own personals ads. This activity can be used to make points similar to those made in Activity 1. Ideally, these two activities should be used together—conduct the present activity first, and then see how the students' own ads compare to the ads found in newspapers and magazines by conducting Activity 1. If, however, you are going to do only one or the other activity, consider the following: An important advantage of Activity 1 is that it concerns *real* personals ads rather than fictitious ones, and is therefore the more methodologically sound activity (for which reason we have listed it first); the advantage of Activity 2 is that students often find this activity to be particularly fun and memorable because they are forced to think about how they would write an ad, and they get to learn about what their classmates find attractive and valuable in relationships.

<u>Procedure.</u> Students should be told to imagine that they were going to write a personals ad to be published in a local newspaper, seeking someone for an intimate relationship. Emphasize as strongly as you can that the students should take this task seriously—that they should write the ads as if they really were going to submit them to the newspaper (which, of course, they will *not* do as part of the activity). Without this emphasis, many students would be likely to make a joke out of the activity and simply try to be outrageous or comical.

Tell them to indicate their sex and the sex of the persons they're hoping will answer the ad. Also tell them, "You can include anything else that you want, such as age, race, interests, physical characteristics, occupation, etc." We recommend that you do mention this list of characteristics so that they will be available in the students' memory.

Instruct the students to write their ads by themselves, with no assistance from anyone else, and that they should not look at anyone else's ads. Tell the students that the ads should be anonymous; they should not put their names in the ads or anywhere on the sheet of paper they will submit to you. Tell the students that they should write "OK" on the top-right corner of the page on which their ad is written to indicate that you have permission to read their ad to the rest of the class (without any names mentioned, of course), and to write "NO" on the top-right corner to indicate that they do not want you to read the ad to the class.

<u>Results and discussion.</u> Analyze the content of the ads your students submit based on the suggestions made in the previous activity (Activity 1). Discuss the results with the class. What kinds of characteristics seem most important to the students in determining their ideal mate? What characteristics were rarely mentioned that one might have expected would be important? Are there gender differences concerning whether they are seeking or offering physical appearance, status, personality characteristics, weight, height, etc.? Among the ads on which "OK" is indicated, choose a few representative ones to read to the class. If there seem to be some good "matches" apparent, read them to the class, volunteering your services as a matchmaker if both parties are interested; you might even get invited to their wedding in a few years.

> ● *What if this bombs?* Like the previous activity, this activity is bombproof, and for the same reasons. In both cases, replicating previous findings is not at all necessary for the activity to be very successful in raising important issues and points for discussion.

Activity 3. Images of Beauty in Advertisements

Activities 1 and 2 concern ways of getting insight about, among other things, what people find attractive, without asking simply for self-reports about attitudes or preferences. Another approach would be to examine what implicit messages about attractiveness are presented in the media through images in advertisements (i.e., ads for commercial products, not personals ads as in Activities 1 and 2).

This activity can be done in any of several ways. For example, you could have students bring in clippings of print ads or videotapes of TV commercials featuring women and men whom the students find attractive. Show the clips and video segments to the class and discuss whether there is a consensus among the students about who is and isn't attractive, what characteristics seem to be most important in determining attractiveness for women and for men, etc. What body types (e.g., thin, athletic, voluptuous, very muscular), shapes or colors of eyes, apparent attitudes, etc., are most preferred? What body types, attitudes, etc., are most used to sell what kinds of products? Discuss whether the women in the ads seem to be more dehumanized or objectified than the men, whether the women and men tend to be in stereotypical gender roles, to what degree flirtatiousness and sexuality are used in various kinds of ads, etc.

An interesting addition to this task would be to bring to class, or have students find and bring to class, examples of ads from various previous decades, such as the '50s, '60s, and '70s. (These may be found in newspapers and magazines in the library; in many libraries they are stored on microfilm and can be copied, although the quality of these copies is likely to be disappointing. Alternatively, it may be easier to try to find images of older ads on the Internet.) Compare the standards for physical beauty across these decades. How have things changed and, perhaps more interesting, how have they stayed the same?

A more methodologically rigorous approach would be to have students collect ads in a more objective manner. For example, you could assign groups of students to different newspapers and magazines and have them select ads based on criteria such as "Select every tenth ad that (prominently) features a woman, until you have collected five such ads. Then, start on a different page, and select every tenth ad that (prominently) features a man, and until you have collected five such ads." By using a procedure such as this, you can discuss all of the points raised above, but the discussion of such issues as whether the women in the ads seem to be more dehumanized or objectified than the men, whether the women and men tend to be in stereotypical gender roles, to what degree flirtatiousness and sexuality are used in various kinds of ads, etc. would be based on a less biased, more representative sample of ads.

Indeed, this more systematic approach to sampling ads would be an excellent way to lead up to or follow the showing of Jean Kilbourne's *Still Killing Us Softly*, a filmed lecture concerning the depiction of women in print advertising that is listed in the Multimedia Resources section of this chapter. We have found that the film itself almost always elicits very interesting and educational discussions in class, and the combination of the film and this activity can be especially memorable and educational.

🔥 ***What if this bombs?*** This activity is bombproof. Students find the analysis and discussion of images of beauty in advertisements to be a fascinating activity. The activity works well whether or not there is consensus among the students about who or what is attractive, whether or not consistent gender differences emerge, etc.

Activity 4. Images of Beauty in Children's Literature, Cartoons, and Films

What implicit messages about physical appearance and attractiveness are present in the literature, cartoons, and films to which young children are exposed? This is an especially important topic because these children's self-concepts and attitudes are just beginning to develop and be influenced by the world beyond their immediate families. How frequently is physical attractiveness correlated with goodness, warmth, and other qualities? For example, in many classic children's stories, the good are beautiful (and the beautiful girls or women are often helpless and waiting for a charming and handsome boy or man to come to the rescue), and the bad are often ugly and sometimes deformed. Consider the Wicked Witch or Captain Hook, for example; or Pinocchio, who clearly represents a correlation between morality and physical appearance. Ask the students to discuss the stories that they remember reading or watching as children. Was this correlation evident? What physical characteristics were most associated with good? For example, in old Westerns, the men with the white hats more often than not were good, and the men with the black hats bad. In children's stories, are the sweet damsels blonde and blue-eyed, and the sadistic villains considerably darker?

Have the students collect examples of the literature, cartoons, and films to which children are exposed today. If possible, have them collect examples from ten or twenty years ago as well. Assign small groups of students to research this together. Some groups could be assigned to go to a local community library and check out some of the more popular contemporary children's books, others could check out some popular books from an older generation, and still others could check out old and newer movies available on video. Some groups could also be assigned to analyze Saturday morning or weekday afternoon TV cartoons.

Compare and discuss the trends, or lack of trends, the students find. How have things changed, and how have they stayed the same? What characteristics are associated with physical attractiveness? What personality traits are associated with what physical characteristics?

What if this bombs? This activity is fairly bombproof. Students find the analysis and discussion of images of beauty in the stories told and shown to children to be very interesting, no matter what specific "results" are found in their analysis. The only potential for a negative outcome is if the students wind up spending a great deal of time researching their assignment; thus, we recommend that the students should work in groups and that the assignments given to each group should be relatively brief.

Activity 5. A Lexical Application of the Warm Glow Heuristic

Lecture and Discussion Idea 4 discusses the warm-glow heuristic, which is the phenomenon whereby liking leads to familiarity. In one study (Monin, 2003), attractive people appeared to be more familiar than did average looking people. In a related study, pleasant words, those with positive connotations appeared more familiar than did neutral or negative words. **Handouts 9.5a and 9.5b** will enable you to replicate the latter study.

Distribute Handout 9.5a upside down to all students. Tell them that this is an exercise in memory. That when you say "Go," they'll have 10 seconds to scan the list. Say "Go." After 10 seconds, instruct the students to turn their lists upside down. At this point, collect handouts 9.5a.

Now distribute Handout 9.5b. Instruct the students to read the list quickly and circle any words that they think might have appeared on the previous list. Ask them to read off the words that they circled. Put those words on the board in three columns "positive," "neutral," and "negative." Tell the students that there were no words that appeared on both lists. If more words are "remembered" under the heading of "positive," then the warm glow heuristic has been demonstrated.

What if this bombs? It's entirely possible that the exercise will bomb because it differs from the original study. In that study, there was no prior list at all. Instead, participants watched a screen with "X's" and "&'s" flashing at random locations as if to mask words, and were made to believe that words were presented subliminally. Because this exercise does contain a prior list of words, it's entirely possible that students will "remember" seeing words on Handout 9.5b because of their association to words on Handout 9.5a. For example, having seen "crime" might lead to a memory of "victim" (both negative words) and having seen "apparatus" might lead to a memory of "mechanism" (both neutral words). A little deception would encourage the students to "remember" a large number of words. Just tell them that a specific number of words were repetitions. In the original study, participants were told that about half the words on the target list were seen subliminally.

Kitayama, S. (1991). Impairment of perception by positive and negative affect. Cognition and Emotion, 5, 255-274.

Monin, B. (2003). The warm-glow heuristic: When liking leads to familiarity. Journal of Personality and Social Psychology, 85, 1035-1048.

Activity 6. Social Motives: The Thematic Apperception Test and Need for Intimacy

As noted, Lecture and Discussion Idea 7 suggests issues to raise in class about the two social motives discussed in Chapter 9: the need for affiliation and the need for intimacy. Parallel to Activity 6, which concerns a scale that can be used to assess students' affiliation motivation, is the present activity, designed to give students the chance to try to assess their intimacy motivation.

The need for intimacy is defined in Chapter 9 as "the preference for warm, close, communicative relationships." Discussion of this motive can be enhanced greatly by having the students try to assess each other on this dimension according to their responses to Thematic Apperception Test (TAT) pictures. Although the students' assessments will tend to be very inaccurate because they have had no training in coding TAT protocols, they should find the task of *trying* to code these protocols educational and fun. This activity will also teach them more about the social motive being examined.

TAT pictures. The TAT is a projective test originally designed by Morgan and Murray. The TAT is composed primarily of a series of pictures of people with ambiguous expressions in ambiguous situations. The people being tested are asked to look at each picture and make up a story about what is going on in the picture. They are told that the stories should have a clear beginning, middle, and end. The test is designed to obtain insight into the motives, concerns, fantasies, fears, etc., of individuals through the stories they create in response to these pictures. The TAT is available from Harvard University Press, Cambridge, MA.

Procedure. Multiple TAT protocols are analyzed for each person in the process of assessing that person's need for affiliation or need for intimacy. For the purposes of this activity, we suggest that you use only one TAT picture. Students should be given five minutes to write an imaginative story about the picture. We suggest that you use either the picture of two people sitting on a bench next to a river, or the picture of an older man and a younger woman walking through a field with horses and a dog. These two pictures can be found in McClelland and Steele (1972) and McClelland (1975), respectively.

Show the TAT picture to the students, and have them write their story on a piece of paper on which they should *not* write their name. Hand out paper clips to the students. They should use the paper clips to attach to their TAT story a piece of paper that contains only their name. Collect these stories and names. Assign a code number to each student (don't tell the students what their code numbers are, but you must keep track of this), discard the pieces of paper with their names on them, and write the appropriate code number above each student's TAT story (or stories).

Mix up the TAT stories and distribute them to the class, informing the students that if they receive their own story back, they should return it to you and get another one. Consult the McAdams (1984) scoring manual and explain to the students how you want them to score for intimacy motivation. Explain to the students that they would need a great deal of training if they were to score these stories for purposes of real research or evaluation, but that you want to give them a sense of how need for intimacy is assessed by having them analyze these TAT protocols. Return the paper clips to the students and have them report their "evaluation" of the TAT stories for need for intimacy on another piece of paper, to which they should attach the TAT story that they evaluated. Collect these materials and, using the code numbers on top of the TAT stories, return the stories to their original authors, along with the evaluations made from these stories. The students should get a big kick out of seeing how one of their classmates evaluated their need for intimacy based on their story.

Discussion. Discuss the social motive for intimacy. What needs or thoughts underlie this motive? What kinds of behaviors might be predicted by how strongly an individual is motivated to achieve intimacy? Contrast this motivation with the motivation for affiliation. How are they similar and how are they different? Chapter 9 reports the results of a longitudinal study by McAdams and Vaillant (1982) that suggests that one's need for intimacy may be a better predictor of an individual's overall psychosocial adjustment than is one's need for affiliation. Why might this be? Consider assigning or summarizing some of the articles published by McAdams and his colleagues on these issues, such as "Intimacy and Affiliation Motives in Daily Living: An Experience Sampling Analysis," by McAdams and Constantian (1983), or "Social Motives and Patterns of Friendship," by McAdams, Healy, and Krause (1984).

Discuss the process of scoring TAT protocols to assess need for intimacy. What were some of the challenges and problems? What were some of the advantages of using the TAT rather than self-report measures or questionnaires? Ask the students to discuss how accurate they thought the evaluation of their TAT story was in relation to their own need for intimacy. Were some evaluations very accurate? Why were these evaluations so accurate? Were others very inaccurate? Why were they inaccurate? How well can individuals assess their own need for intimacy? Consider reading to the students portions of the scoring manual used to assess need for affiliation from TAT protocols (Heyns, Veroff, & Atkinson, 1958) and comparing the two methods of evaluating TAT stories to assess social motives.

What if this bombs? As with the previous activity concerning the Interpersonal Orientation Scale, there is nothing to bomb in this activity. The students should be told at the beginning of the activity that they would need extensive training in order to be able to assess the TAT protocols accurately or reliably, so the success of the activity does not depend on how well the students do in determining each other's need for intimacy. The key point here is that the students will learn more about the motive for intimacy, about some of the factors that underlie this motive, and about what it is like to use responses on projective tests to try to discern information about individuals' motivations and personalities.

Heyns, R. W., Veroff, J., & Atkinson, J. W. (1958). A scoring manual for the affiliation motive. In J. W. Atkinson (Ed.), Motives in fantasy, action, and society (pp. 205-218). Princeton, NJ: Van Nostrand.

McAdams, D. P. (1984). Scoring manual for the intimacy motive. Psychological Documents, 14, No. 2613.

McAdams, D. P., & Constantian, C. A. (1983). Intimacy and affiliation motives in daily living: An experience sampling analysis. Journal of Personality and Social Psychology, 45, 851-861.

McAdams, D. P., Healy, S., & Krause, S. (1984). Social motives and patterns of friendship. Journal of Personality and Social Psychology, 47, 828-838.

McAdams, D. P., & Vaillant, G.E. (1982). Intimacy motivation and psychosocial adjustment: A longitudinal study. Journal of Personality Assessment, 46, 586-593.

McClelland, D. C. (1975). Power: The inner experience. New York: Irvington.

McClelland, D. C., & Steele, R. S. (1972). Motivation workshops. Morristown, NJ: General Learning Press.

Activity 7. Self-Esteem: Confidence and Desire

Chapter 9 discusses the interesting relationship between self-esteem and attraction. The research reported suggests that relative to people with high self-esteem, people with low self-esteem are more likely to have a strong desire to obtain social rewards from being with others and should therefore be more interested in seeking out and being attracted to others; but they also should be more likely to lack the confidence needed to pursue others. Thus, self-esteem has contradictory effects on the likelihood of individuals pursuing others for social rewards: high self-esteem may be associated with increased confidence and decreased desire, and low self-esteem may be associated with decreased confidence and increased desire.

To help facilitate discussion about this issue, consider giving students a self-esteem scale to complete, along with a set of questions concerning their confidence and desire to seek out social relationships. **Handout 9.7** contains a set of questions concerning confidence and motivation to seek out others for social rewards and intimate relationships. The set of questions on Handout 9.7 has not been tested or validated; we constructed the set of questions exclusively for this activity for purposes of facilitating discussion about the role of self-esteem in attraction.

Procedure. Distribute copies Handout 9.7 to the students. Ideally, this should be done <u>before</u> the students have read Chapter 9. Tell the students not to indicate their name anywhere on the handouts.

We recommend that you do not take the time during class to analyze the results. Rather, bring the results to a subsequent class. The ideal procedure would be to distribute the activity before the students read Chapter 9, and bring the results back to class for discussion on the first class in which you discuss attraction. Discuss the results with the students.

Results and discussion. Regarding the confidence and desire subscales of Handout 9.7, score items 1, 6, 8, and 14 in a positive direction (i.e., *strongly agree* = 4, *agree* = 3, etc.), and items 4, 11, and 13 in a reversed direction (i.e., *strongly agree* = 1, *agree* = 2, etc.). Add these scores to get a total score for confidence; higher scores indicate greater confidence about pursuing relationships. Next, score items 5, 7, and 10 in a positive direction, and items 2, 3, 9, and 12 in a negative direction, and add these scores to get a total score for the desire to obtain positive social rewards from others; higher scores indicate a greater desire.

🔹*What if this bombs?* There is a very real risk that the data from this activity will bomb. That is, because of the complexity of the relationships among self-esteem, confidence in pursuing social relationships, and desire for social rewards, and because the items in Handout 9.7 have not been constructed and tested for reliability and validity, there is a good chance that the correlations will all be very weak or confusing. Even if the correlations are not worth discussing, you can discuss the means and variability. Students should be interested to know the class averages for the items, as well as the range and degree of variability. Compare the averages and variability as a function of gender as well.

Activity 8. Proximity and Similarity Between Friends and Acquaintances

Perhaps the most under-appreciated factor in attraction is the role of proximity. Compared to its "sexier" counterparts such as physical appearance, similarity and complementarity, and psychological reactance, proximity seems rather, well, pedestrian. Students are therefore surprised to learn how important proximity is in determining friendships and intimate relationships.

Handout 9.8a and **Handout 9.8b** can be used to facilitate discussion of proximity, as well as of similarity concerning some demographic and attitudinal variables. Have each student think of one very good friend from school. Distribute copies of Handout 9.8a to the students and have them answer the questions on the handout about this friend. Next, distribute Handout 9.8b. Have each student find one student in the class whom he or she does not know very well, and have them interview each other in order to complete Handout 9.8b. The students should not complete the handout while they are in the presence of this other person—they should return to their own seats and complete Handout 9.8b privately. Handout 9.8b is identical to Handout 9.8a in all respects but two: Handout 9.8b refers to the student's classmate whom he or she interviewed rather than to a close friend, and Handout 9.8a contains one additional question (concerning why the student and the student's close friend became and remain friends).

Handout 9.8c and **Handout 9.8d** ask questions similar to those on Handout 9.8a and Handout 9.8b, respectively, but the open-ended questions used in Handouts 9.8a and 9.8b have been changed on Handouts 9.8c and 9.8d to questions that require students to respond using specific numbers or points on numerical scales. Consider using these latter handouts if you want to analyze the students' responses and compare means as a function of whether the responses concern friends or non-friend classmates. In contrast, Handouts 9.8a and 9.8b do not yield much data that can be analyzed easily; they are designed simply to get the students thinking about the issues of proximity and similarity. You can, however, have students code their responses on Handouts 9.8a and 9.8b in terms of whether they were closer in proximity to their friends when they first met than to their classmates, more similar to their friends than to their classmates, etc., and you can tally this information to see whether there is consensus concerning these comparisons.

> **What if this bombs?** The results from the handouts may indeed fail to produce good evidence for the roles of proximity or similarity. If this is the case, explain that the procedure used may have been too simple to test these factors well, and ask the students for some reasons why this might have been the case. For example, the way they selected a friend and a classmate for the activity was not determined by a random procedure and thus may have been subject to bias—e.g., perhaps they felt most comfortable approaching classmates whom they had seen frequently on campus because they lived near them. Also, the roles of proximity and similarity in a campus setting may not be as evident as elsewhere because on many campuses everyone lives fairly close to one another, and because the students are likely to be more similar to one another than is typically observed in the more general population. After explaining these caveats, shift the focus away from the data and toward the concepts themselves. Having inspired students' thoughts about the roles of proximity and similarity, this activity can be successful by generating a better discussion of these issues than would have been likely without it.

Activity 9. Similarity and Complementarity

Do "birds of a feather flock together" or do "opposites attract"? Chapter 9 indicates that the consensus from the research on this issue is clear: people tend to be attracted to similar rather than dissimilar others. This activity is designed to examine this phenomenon, and to compare the role of similarity in friendships, acquaintances, intimate relationships, and ideal romantic partners.

Distribute copies of **Handout 9.9** to students. When the students have completed the handouts, collect them and compare the roles of similarity and complementarity in determining friendships, intimate relationships, etc. Were outgoing people more likely to be in relationships with introverted people or with similar outgoing people? Were assertive, dominant people more likely to be friends with similar people or with passive, submissive others? Complementary pairs of characteristics included in the handout are: *outgoing* and *loner*; *optimistic* and *pessimistic*; *assertive/dominant* and *passive/submissive*; *physically active* and *physically lazy*; *independent* and *dependent*; *organized plans ahead* and *spontaneous*; *talkative* and *good listener*.

Compare the patterns of data as a function of the sex of the student. Take special note of the characteristics of students' ideal or fantasy romantic partners—do they seem very different from the students' actual friends and lovers? For example, a student may fantasize about a complementary, or better, other (e.g., more physically attractive than they) but in reality tend to form friendships or romantic relationships with similar others.

> **What if this bombs?** This activity is fairly bombproof. There is a lot to talk about based on these handouts, and the discussion of similarity and complementarity in attraction should be facilitated by this activity. If the data do not replicate the findings from the literature, the same caveats that are mentioned in the corresponding section of Activity 9 can be applied here. Shift the focus away from the data collected and toward the conceptual issues and empirical findings reported in the textbook.

Activity 10. What Characteristics Do You Find Desirable in the Opposite Sex?

In a survey, Robin Gilmour (1988) found that men and women look for totally different qualities when asked which characteristics they find desirable in the opposite sex. Men listed physical attractiveness first. That was followed by ability in bed, warmth and affection, social skills, and homemaking ability. Women listed a record of achievement first. That was followed by leadership qualities, job skills, earning potential, and a sense of humor.

To see if your students duplicate the survey results, ask them, on a blank sheet of paper, to list the five qualities that they find desirable in the opposite sex. Tell them not to put their names on the sheet, but to designate their gender with an "F" or an "M" at the top. Sort the papers into gender-separate piles and tabulate the results on the board. Discuss any gender differences that exist. Compare your students' results with those of Gilmour. Discuss how gender roles and stereotypes have changed if they had, or why they did not.

What if this bombs? There is no bomb potential. Either way, the results can lead to a lively discussion. If there are no gender differences, then students might be asked to explain how societal conditions have changed since the late 1980s. If results conform to Gilmour's findings, then you might ask your students to explain why the changing cultural conditions have not affected these gender differences.

Gilmour, R. (1988). Desirable and negative qualities. In P. March (Ed.), <u>Eye to Eye</u>, (p.197). Md.: Salem House Publishers.

Activity 11. Defining Intimate Relationships

The text defines intimate relationships as "close relationships between two adults involving at least one of the following: emotional attachment, fulfillment of psychological needs, and interdependence." The activity in **Handout 9.11** presents students with a number of descriptions of different relationships. Ask them to decide whether they think each relationship is an intimate relationship or not. This handout can be a good discussion starter. It should allow students to think about how their own views of intimate relationships are similar to or different from the textbook's definition.

What if this bombs? This one should be bombproof. Any pattern of answers (e.g., whether students show consensus or lack of consensus in their answers) should lead to interesting discussion, as students are always interested in exploring what makes up an intimate relationship.

Activity 12. Attachment-Style Questionnaire

Attachment style is thought to arise from early interactions between an infant and his or her primary caregiver. The original work in this area (Ainsworth et al., 1978) described three kinds of interaction patterns between children and their mothers: secure attachment, avoidant attachment, and anxious/ambivalent attachment. Hazan and Shaver (1987) have proposed that just as parent-child interactions can be characterized by attachment styles, so too can adults' romantic relationships. They have found that people with a secure attachment style tend to have relationships characterized by happiness, friendship, and trust; people with an avoidant attachment style tend to have relationships characterized by fear of closeness; and people with an anxious/ambivalent attachment style tend to experience extreme emotional reactions—joy and agony—in their romantic relationships. The scale reproduced in **Handout 9.12** has been used by Shaver et al. (1988) to classify people into one of the three attachment styles described above. Have students read the handout, and determine whether selection A, B, or C best describes their relationships. A indicates a secure attachment style, B indicates an avoidant attachment style, and C indicates an anxious/ambivalent attachment style.

💣 *What if this bombs?* This one should be bombproof. Even in small classes, it is likely that some students will select each of the three attachment styles to describe their relationships. In the unlikely event that all of your students fall into only one or two categories, the activity will still serve to get the discussion of attachment styles started.

Ainsworth, M., Blehar, M. C., Waters, E., & Wall, S. (1978). Patterns of attachment: A psychological study of the strange situation. Hillsdale, NJ: Erlbaum.

Hazan, C., & Shaver, P. (1987). Romantic love conceptualized as an attachment process. Journal of Personality and Social Psychology, 52, 511-524.

Shaver, P., Hazan, C., & Bradshaw, D. (1988). Love as attachment: The integration of three behavioral systems. In R. J. Sternberg & M. L. Barnes (Eds.), The psychology of love (pp. 68-99). New Haven, CT: Yale University Press.

Activity 13. Gender Differences in Jealousy

This activity is a partial replication of the classic study by David Buss (1992) on differences in what drives men and women's jealousy. Since it is discussed in the text, it should be carried out before students have read the chapter.

Handout 9.13 presents students with the following question:

> Please think of a serious or committed romantic relationship that you have had in the past, that you currently have, or that you would like to have. Imagine that you discover that the person with whom you've been seriously involved became interested in someone else. What would distress or upset you more (please circle only one):
>
> A) Imagining your partner falling in love and forming a deep emotional attachment to that person.
>
> B) Imagining your partner having sexual intercourse with that other person.

Students are asked to answer anonymously but to indicate their sex. After collecting the responses separately from males and females, tally the results on the board. In the original study, the finding was that females were much more likely to be upset about their man's emotional infidelity, whereas males were much more likely to be upset about their woman's sexual infidelity.

💣 *What if this bombs?* This one as well should be bombproof. It should lead to interesting discussion whether or not the results echo those of the original study.

Buss, D.M., Larsen, R.J., Westen, D., & Semmelroth, J. (1992). Sex differences in jealousy: Evolution, physiology, and psychology. Psychological Science, 3, 251-255.

Activity 14. Sexual orientation

The textbook stresses the point that sexual orientation cannot be divided into neat, discrete categories; that it should be viewed as varying along a continuum. This exercise reinforces the difficulty inherent in defining sexual behavior in rigid, categorical terms. It demonstrates to students that sexual orientation means more than just whom one has sex with, that it also involves such factors as psychological-emotional attachment, identification, erotic attractions, and relationship history.

Handout 9.14 describes 10 fictional individuals and asks students to categorize each one as heterosexual, bisexual, lesbian, or gay. Each description refers to some combination of the person's sexual attractions, current relationship status, relationship history, past and present sexual behavior, self-identification, psychological attachments, and community preferences. The first few examples are straightforward but the later ones are more involved. Students may work independently or in small groups (in which case they should be told that consensus is not required).

Afterwards, in full class discussion, ask for a show of hands to see how many students placed each individual into each of the four categories. There will likely be agreement in the first few examples. At this level, most students will base their answers on an individual's sexual behavior, relationships, or self-identification. (Most will agree that individual # 1 is lesbian, # 2 is gay, # 3 is bisexual, and # 4 is heterosexual.) Agreement will tend to be lower for the next few individuals because of inconsistencies between their sexual behavior, relationship history, self-identification, and attractions. Individual #8 will emphasize the point that sexual orientation does not mean sexual behavior.

🔴 *What if this bombs?* This activity is bombproof. Because there are no definitive right answers, many of the items are sure to generate a lively discussion relative to sexual orientation.

MULTIMEDIA RESOURCES

Video

Being Obese. Confronts America's prejudices about overweight people. Through interviews with children and adults, feelings and prejudices are examined. Experts discuss eating disorders, genetic predispositions, and dieting trends. (1985, 24 min.) Available from the Bureau of Audio Visual Instruction, University of Wisconsin at Madison, Madison, WI 53701.

Communication: The Nonverbal Agenda, 2nd Edition. An insightful and well-made exploration of the whole spectrum of nonverbal behavior: tone of voice, posture, facial expressions, gestures, use of space, eye contact, and body movement. This film employs excellent and sometimes humorous vignettes—mostly in organizational settings—to show how an understanding of nonverbal communication can enhance managerial effectiveness. For example, in separate meetings, a distasteful message is given to three individuals; the same words are spoken, but the effect varies from a severe reprimand to a friendly discussion, depending on the nonverbal cues given and received. (1988, 20 min.) CRM Learning, 2218 Faraday Ave., Ste. 110, Carlsbad, CA 92008. (800-421-0833).

Couples Arguing. Arguments between couples are an important aspect of interpersonal relationships. They allow the airing of divergent views so that a compromise becomes possible and violence is avoided. Here is the first documentary to investigate real couples in actual arguments. To capture this phenomenon with absolute spontaneity, the filmmakers had the couples call them whenever they were about to become embroiled in an argument. They would then go into separate rooms, wait for the documentary crew to arrive, and then resume their argument. Five couples are shown. They argue about issues such as money, sex, alcohol, and children. Differences of opinions are vented humorously, passionately, and sometimes venomously. One sees that despite seemingly irresolvable conflicts, many couples have positive feelings toward one another. In short, they argue as a way to be understood. (1987, 60 min.) Filmmakers Library, 124 East 40th Street, New York, NY 10016.

Dreamworlds. Using clips from more than 165 music videos, this explicit program explores the impact of seeing objectified images of women and sexual violence on viewers' thoughts and behaviors. This could be a provocative introduction to the course by challenging students to think about how these images, which most of them will have taken for granted, can have very serious social psychological implications and consequences. For mature audiences—some of the footage is explicit. (1995, 56 min.) Available from Media Education Foundation (800-897-0089).

Face Value: Perceptions of Beauty. Examines the theory that people's perceptions of attractiveness may be universal and biologically based, contrasting this idea with the perspective that perceptions of beauty change with time and place. The program considers computer analyses, shows contestants in a beauty contest, and examines the faces of today's "beautiful people." (1993, 26 min.) Available from Films for the Humanities and Sciences, P.O. Box 2053, Princeton, NJ 08543-2053 (800-257-5126).

The Familiar Face of Love. This film examines love and loving, and how we choose our mates and for what reasons. Dr. John Money of Johns Hopkins Hospital, author of numerous books on gender and sexuality, talks of a "love map"—a mental blueprint of the ideal relationship we carry with us. This is formed by attitudes and experiences from early childhood. Children at a kibbutz in Israel are observed as they engage in "sex rehearsal play," which Dr. Money feels is an essential stage in the development of a healthy love map. (1986, 47 min.) Available from Filmmakers Library, 124 East 40th Street, New York, NY 10016.

Friendship. This film examines the roles of factors such as proximity and similarity in influencing attraction and the strength of friendships. (1989, 30 min.) Available from Pennsylvania State University, Audio-Visual Services, University Park, PA 16802 (800-826-0132).

Human Sexuality (It's Personal). Sexuality is an integral part of human identity and a primary factor in human behavior. This video explores the development of sexual behavior and considers the range of sexual experience and preference that exists within contemporary human society. (2000, 28 min) Available from Insight Media (800-233-9910).

Impression Formation and Interpersonal Attraction. This film presents research on central traits, first impressions, implicit personality theory, and need complementarity. It also includes an enactment of a "warm/cold" experiment and demonstrates the effects of familiarity on attraction. If you did not use this film for Chapter 3, it can be used here instead. (1975, 27 min.) Available from University Films of Canada, 7 Hayden St., Suite 305, Toronto, Ontario, Canada M4Y 2P2.

Let's Get Married. This PBS *Frontline* video examines the public consequences of marriage and the social, political, and economic forces that converged to advance the modern-day marriage movement. (2002, 1 hour) Available from PBS Video (888-255-9231).

Looks! How They Affect Your Life. What are the psychological pressures that urge Americans to spend billions of dollars on cosmetics each year, or that lead so many people into plastic surgery? This video examines data that illustrate the social and psychological impact of fulfilling and not fulfilling the American "standards" of beauty. It features interviews with Elaine Hatfield, Judith Langolis, and others, including personal accounts given by children, teenagers, and adults. (1984, 51 min.) Available from the Bureau of Audio Visual Instruction, University of Wisconsin at Madison, Madison, WI 53701-2093.

Pain of Shyness. While two out of five Americans feel they are shy, few realize the extent to which a severe case of shyness can be handicapping. Dr. Philip Zimbardo of Stanford University explains some of the techniques that have been developed to overcome this handicap. The film illustrates some of these successful techniques, such as role playing, behavioral retraining, and desensitizing exercises. (1985, 17 min.) Available from Filmmakers Library, 124 East 40th Street, New York, NY 10016.

The Sexiest Animal. Examining human sexuality from social, political, and historical perspectives, this program reveals what is common, uncommon, acceptable, and unacceptable in modern Western culture. (1990, 38 min.) Bureau of Audio Visual Instruction, University of Wisconsin Extension, PO Box 2093, Madison, WI 53701-2093.

Stale Roles and Tight Buns. Sexism is a form of stereotyping that limits the roles of both men and women. The strength of sex-role stereotypes is subtly and continuously reinforced by common images. This video presents a selection of images of men found in consumer advertising. Through these, the viewer gains insight into the myths used to define and limit the American man. (1989, 29 min.) Available from the Bureau of Audio Visual Instruction, University of Wisconsin at Madison, Madison, WI 53701-2093.

Still Killing Us Softly: Advertising's Image of Women. Dr. Jean Kilbourne uses dozens of examples of ads from magazines and billboards to examine the images of women in advertising, and to examine the consequences of these images on women and men. Dr. Kilbourne explores the relationship of media images to various problems in society, such as violence and discrimination against women, eating disorders, etc. She illustrates how people's perceptions of what is considered attractive and valued in society is influenced in profound ways by the countless images to which women and men, and girls and boys, are exposed every day. This video of Dr. Kilbourne's lectures is an excellent way to get students thinking about these issues and to produce a thoughtful discussion. Available from Cambridge Documentary Films, P.O. Box 385, Cambridge, MA 02139 (617-354-3677).

The Ugly Truth. This ABC News *20/20* story focuses on "lookism," demonstrating how widespread is the discrimination faced by people as a function of their looks. From the opening images of two women—one average looking, one very attractive—seeking roadside assistance for their car, we see how differently people are treated based on their physical appearance. This story illustrates how lookism affects people's ability to get jobs, the pay they receive for their jobs, how much your students may like you, etc. (1991, 19 min.) Available from corVision Media (800-537-3130).

Internet

Beauty Check. This is the site of a research project on human facial attractiveness which was carried out by Regensburg and Rostock Universities in Germany. It contains many demonstrations on such topics as morphing of faces, averaged faces, symmetry, and babyfaceness. Visit this site at: http://www.uni-regensburg.de/Fakultaeten/phil_Fak_II/Psychologie/Psy_II/beautycheck/english/index.htm.

Go Ask Alice. At this site, which is run by Columbia University's Health Services, students can post any questions on health, relationships, and sexuality. Visit this site at: http://www.goaskalice.columbia.edu/

Ideal Beauty in Art. At this site, visitors can view the ideal human body as it has been expressed in art from the prehistoric Venus of Villendorf to Modigliani's Reclining Female Nude. Visit this site at: http://www.cichon.de/ideal-beauty/

Perception Laboratory. At this site, run by the school of psychology at the University of St. Andrews in Scotland, there are articles on research and online experiments on the topic of facial perception. There are also some links to other facial perception sites. Visit this site at: http://monty.st-and.ac.uk.

Symmetry Measurement & Analysis. This site allows you see what your face would look like if it was perfectly symmetrical. Visit this site at: http: www.symmeter.com/symfacer.htm.

Computer Program

Social Power Game. This computer program features an instructional game designed to teach undergraduate students the nature and process of power relationships. Instructional booklet included. On-line help available. (Dos.) McGraw-Hill College Division, 1221 Avenue of the Americas, New York, NY 10020.

HANDOUT 9.1 CODING THE PERSONALS

_____ seeking _____

Characteristic	Offers	Seeks	Mentions
attractiveness			
height			
weight			
body description (other than height or weight)			
blond hair color			
other hair color			
eye color			
personality (general)			
ambitious, goal-oriented			
Independent			
physically active			
kind/warm/sensitive			
extroverted/outgoing			
introverted/introspective			
good listener			

Characteristic	Offers	Seeks	Mentions
talker, communicator			
younger partner			
older partner			
range of age given (range includes more than 2 years older)			
education			
specific occupation			
"professional" status			
financial status			
"commitment" or "serious" relationship			

HANDOUT 9.5a WORD LIST

bone	pertinent	integrity	cash	worse
weakness	honeymoon	slaughter	eager	trend
formation	magnitude	execution	prize	fence
inhabitant	desirable	crime	enjoy	panel
emergency	manufacture	wonderful	pale	award
storm	destroyed	prominent	trace	translation
measurement	delightful	charm	trend	guilt
prisoners	custom	enthusiasm	ugly	humor
criticism	blame	extra	mature	corruption
apparatus	satisfying	conspiracy	route	objectives
angry	conspiracy	magnificent	wisdom	label
objectives	disturbing	outstanding	panic	impression
hatred	detect	margin	injury	terror
threatening				

HANDOUT 9.5b WORD LIST

comedy	border	destruction	fascinating	cancer
conception	talent	alienation	comfortable	locate
intentions	lucky	inadequate	stamp	attractive
mechanism	smile	dimension	dedication	track
resentment	victim	devil	isolation	funny
alternative	error	spare	excellence	trust
probability	waste	condemned	switch	glory
arrangement	fantastic	habit	proud	brilliant
happiness	joke	applicable	suffering	arrangement
stone	chair	dangerous	marvelous	sheet
pause	false	fool	favorable	residents
trembling	hung	snake	revolution	variables
violence	shame	wire		

HANDOUT 9.7

Based on the scale below, please write a number from 1 to 4 before each of the following statements so as to rate the extent to which you agree or disagree that the statement is true or descriptive for you.

1	2	3	4
strongly disagree	disagree	agree	strongly agree

___ 1. When I am attracted to someone, I usually make my feelings known to that person fairly quickly.

___ 2. I am not attracted to other people very easily.

___ 3. If someone I am attracted to is playing hard-to-get, I lose interest in this person pretty quickly and am no longer attracted to him or her.

___ 4. I frequently feel nervous and intimidated in the company of someone to whom I am attracted.

___ 5. It's a great feeling to know that someone whom I don't know very well likes me.

___ 6. If I try hard, I can usually make other people like me.

___ 7. There always seems to be at least a few people in my surroundings whom I would really love to get to know better.

___ 8. I have a lot of confidence when it comes to "making small talk" or first getting to know someone to whom I am attracted.

___ 9. I don't really care that much about what people other than my very close friends and my family think of me.

___ 10. I would be much happier if I had more close friends and/or romantic relationships.

___ 11. I get very nervous about risking rejection when I consider approaching people to whom I'm attracted.

___ 12. I do not spend much time thinking about who may be attracted to me or to whom I may be attracted.

___ 13. If I could change anything about myself it would be to develop more confidence and social skills.

___ 14. If I'm attracted to someone, I don't worry very much about the possibility of rejection but instead focus on the potential for a successful relationship.

HANDOUT 9.8a FRIENDSHIPS AND ACQUAINTANCES

Friend

1. How far away from each other did you and your friend live when you first met? How far away do you live now?

2. How old are you and your friend?

3. How similar do you think you and your friend are in terms of physical attractiveness?

4. How similar do you think you and your friend are in terms of your personalities and interests?

5. How similar do you think you and your friend are in terms of specific attitudes?

6. Are you and your friend opposite each other on any personality dimensions? For example, is one of you assertive and the other passive?

7. Why did you become friends with this person? Why do you remain friends?

HANDOUT 9.8b FRIENDSHIPS AND ACQUAINTANCES

Classmate

1.   How far away from each other did you and your classmate live when you first met? How far away do you live now?

2.   How old are you and your classmate?

3.   How similar do you think you and your classmate are in terms of physical attractiveness?

4.   How similar do you think you and your classmate are in terms of your personalities and interests?

5.   How similar do you think you and your classmate are in terms of specific attitudes?

6.   Are you and your classmate opposite each other on any personality dimensions? For example, is one of you assertive and the other passive?

HANDOUT 9.8c FRIENDSHIPS AND ACQUAINTANCES (FRIEND)

1. a. How far away from each other did you and your friend live when you first met?

    Circle the number of the most accurate answer:

    (1). shared same room or suite

    (2). rooms were close to each other

    (3). same building

    (4). nearby buildings

    (5). neither nearby nor very far away

    (6). relatively far away from each other

   b. How far away from each other do you and your friend live now?

    Circle the number of the most accurate answer:

    (1). share same room or suite

    (2). rooms are close to each other

    (3). same building

    (4). nearby buildings

    (5). neither nearby nor very far away

    (6). relatively far away from each other

2. How old are you and your friend?

    Your age: _____   Your friend's age: _____

3. How similar do you think you and your friend are in terms of physical attractiveness?

    1   2   3   4   5   6   7
    very dissimilar   very similar

4. How similar do you think you and your friend are in terms of your personalities and interests?

    1   2   3   4   5   6   7
    very dissimilar   very similar

5. How similar do you think you and your friend are in terms of specific attitudes?

    1   2   3   4   5   6   7
    very dissimilar   very similar

6. Are you and your friend opposite each other on any personality dimensions? For example, is one of you assertive and the other passive?

    Please circle one:

    no   yes, on 1 or 2 dimensions   yes, on many dimensions

7. On the reverse side, discuss why you became friends with this person, and why you remain friends.

HANDOUT 9.8d FRIENDSHIPS AND ACQUAINTANCES (CLASSMATE)

1. a. How far away from each other did you and your classmate live when you first met?

    Circle the number of the most accurate answer:

    (1). shared same room or suite

    (2). rooms were close to each other

    (3). same building

    (4). nearby buildings

    (5). neither nearby nor very far away

    (6). relatively far away from each other

   b. How far away from each other do you and your classmate live now?

    Circle the number of the most accurate answer:

    (1). share same room or suite

    (2). rooms are close to each other

    (3). same building

    (4). nearby buildings

    (5). neither nearby nor very far away

    (6). relatively far away from each other

2. How old are you and your classmate?

   Your age: _____   Your classmate's age: _____

3. How similar do you think you and your classmate are in terms of physical attractiveness?

1	2	3	4	5	6	7
very dissimilar						very similar

4. How similar do you think you and your classmate are in terms of your personalities and interests?

1	2	3	4	5	6	7
very dissimilar						very similar

5. How similar do you think you and your classmate are in terms of specific attitudes?

1	2	3	4	5	6	7
very dissimilar						very similar

6. Are you and your classmate opposite each other on any personality dimensions? For example, is one of you assertive and the other passive?

   Please circle one:

   no   yes, on 1 or 2 dimensions   yes, on many dimensions

HANDOUT 9.9 CHARACTERISTICS IN COMMON

For each characteristic listed below, place a checkmark in the appropriate column or columns to indicate that the characteristic is true of yourself, your close friend, an acquaintance who is not a close friend, your current or most recent romantic partner, and your ideal or fantasy romantic partner.

	Self	Friend	Acquaintance	Romantic partner	Romantic ideal
Ambitious	___	___	___	___	___
Assertive/Dominant	___	___	___	___	___
Dependent	___	___	___	___	___
Good listener	___	___	___	___	___
Good sense of humor	___	___	___	___	___
Independent	___	___	___	___	___
Intelligent	___	___	___	___	___
Introspective	___	___	___	___	___
Likes to take charge	___	___	___	___	___
Loner	___	___	___	___	___
Optimistic	___	___	___	___	___
Organized, plans ahead	___	___	___	___	___
Outgoing	___	___	___	___	___
Passive/Submissive	___	___	___	___	___
Pessimistic	___	___	___	___	___
Physically active	___	___	___	___	___
Physically attractive	___	___	___	___	___
Physically lazy	___	___	___	___	___
Politically active, aware	___	___	___	___	___
Responsible	___	___	___	___	___
Spontaneous	___	___	___	___	___
Talkative	___	___	___	___	___
Warm	___	___	___	___	___

HANDOUT 9.11 INTIMATE RELATIONSHIPS

Is this an intimate relationship?

1. Y N   Martha adores her dog Pepper, and spends a lot of time with her.

2. Y N   Harry has been infatuated with Ruth for years, but he never talks to her.

3. Y N   Bob and Ida have been married for thirty years, but now they hardly talk.

4. Y N   Maria and Al have just started dating and are preoccupied with thoughts about one another.

5. Y N   Oscar's mother has always been his best friend. He calls her almost about one another.

6. Y N   Nellie and Paula have been good friends since second grade, but they rarely see each other now.

7. Y N   Linda and Bill have been dating for two years, but they will be unable to see each other for another year because Linda's work takes her out of the country.

8. Y N   Hilda and Agnes talk to each other every day and are pleasant to each other, but secretly they both despise each other.

9. Y N   Mark and Ken regularly play golf and go bowling together, but they never share the details of their lives with one another.

10. Y N   Nancy and James are sixteen. They have been dating for two years and have decided to get married.

HANDOUT 9.12 ATTACHMENT STYLES

Which of the following best describes your feelings?

1. I find it relatively easy to get close to others and am comfortable depending on them and having them depend on me. I don't often worry about being abandoned or about someone getting close to me.

2. I am somewhat uncomfortable being close to others; I find it difficult to trust them completely, difficult to allow myself to depend on them. I am nervous when anyone gets too close, and often love partners want me to be more intimate than I feel comfortable being.

3. I find that others are reluctant to get as close as I would like. I often worry that my partner doesn't really love me or won't want to stay with me. I want to merge completely with another person, and this desire sometimes scares people away.

HANDOUT 9.13

Do not write your name on this handout. Instead, just circle the correct letter for your gender:

    M   F

Please think of a serious or committed romantic relationship that you have had in the past, that you currently have, or that you would like to have. Imagine that you discover that the person with whom you've been seriously involved became interested in someone else. What would distress or upset you more (please circle only one):

A) Imagining your partner falling in love and forming a deep emotional attachment to that person.

B) Imagining your partner having sexual intercourse with that other person.

HANDOUT 9.14

For each of the following people, identify whether the person is heterosexual (H), gay (G), lesbian (L), or bisexual (B), based on the information provided. For each person, briefly make note of your reasons for the decision.

Having had no sexual experiences in high school at all, this man started to have sexual encounters with men while he was a freshman in college. He has since graduated and joined the work force and has never attempted to date women.

As a teenager, this woman began to think of herself as a lesbian. In high school, however, she had two brief sexual relationships with men, since then, for the past two years, she has been involved with the same female partner.

This woman has had several intimate sexual relationships with both men and women, though her last three relationships were with men.

This woman who used to identify herself as a lesbian in her junior year in high school, has since then decided that she is attracted only to men

Although she has been happily married for the past fifteen years, this woman now admits to herself that she is strongly attracted to both men and women

For the first thirty-five years of his life, this man has always considered himself straight. Now, however, he finds himself attracted to a man that he has business dealings with.

This man who was in a homosexual relationship for six years is now in a monogamous relationship with a woman.

This man has never had relationships with either women or men.

This young man spent a year flirting with the idea that he was homosexual. After a year of experimentation, he decided that he was really heterosexual and is now dating women exclusively.

This woman who has recently been widowed, after a marriage of twenty-five years and four kids, has now moved in with a female partner.

CHAPTER 10

Helping Others

LEARNING OBJECTIVES: GUIDELINES FOR STUDY

You should be able to do each of the following by the conclusion of Chapter 10.

1. Discuss how evolutionary theory accounts for helping behavior. Explain kin selection and reciprocal altruism. (*pp. 391-394*)

2. Compare and contrast egoistic and altruistic motives for helping. Explain the empathy-altruism hypothesis and identify why a distinction between these two types of motives is important. (*pp. 399-402*)

3. Explain the bystander effect. Identify and explain the five steps in the helping process, discussing obstacles to each step. Consider how each of these obstacles contributes to the bystander effect. (*pp. 405-409*)

4. Describe the influence of other situational factors on helping behavior, such as time pressure, location, culture, mood, role models, and social norms. (*pp. 412-420*)

5. Explain how individual differences such as personality, moral reasoning, and family background may affect a person's likelihood of helping others. (*pp. 421-423*)

6. Describe how characteristics of people in need (e.g., attractiveness, perceived responsibility, gender) influence the likelihood that others will help them. Consider the role of fit between the characteristics of the help giver and receiver (i.e., similarity and closeness). (*pp. 423-426*)

7. Identify the factors that influence people's different reactions to receiving help. (*pp. 427-428*)

DETAILED CHAPTER OUTLINE

I. Evolutionary and Motivational Factors: Why Do People Help?
   A. Evolutionary Factors in Helping
      1. The selfish gene: kinship selection, we help our relatives
      2. Reciprocal altruism: reciprocity, we help those who help us
      3. Group-Level Altruism
      4. The Evolution of Morality, Parental Caregiving, and Empathy

   B. Rewards of Helping: Helping Others to Help Oneself
      1. The arousal: cost-reward model of helping
      2. Feeling good
      3. Being, or appearing to be, good
      4. Cost of helping, or of not helping
   C. Altruism or Egoism: The Great Debate
      1. Two motives for helping
         a) egoistic: desire to increase one's own welfare
         b) altruistic: desire to increase another's welfare
         c) perspective taking is the cognitive component of empathy
         d) there are two emotional components of empathy—empathic concern and personal distress

2. The empathy-altruism hypothesis
    a) perspective taking is the first step toward altruism
    b) in true altruism, the focus remains on the other person
    c) egoistic alternatives
3. Convergence of Motivations: Volunteering
D. Distinguishing among the Motivations to Help: Why Does it Matter?

II. Situational Influences: When Do People Help?
A. The Unhelpful Crowd
   1. The bystander effect: people are less likely to help when others are present
   2. Five steps where bystanders may impede helping
    a) noticing: sometimes it is hard to notice that others need help, especially when one is busy
    b) interpreting: when someone is in a helping situation it is easy to believe that he or she is the only one who thinks help is necessary; when everyone feels this way it is called pluralistic ignorance
    c) taking responsibility: when bystanders are around, people tend to believe that other people will or should take responsibility; this is called diffusion of responsibility
    d) deciding how to help: direct help is more likely when bystanders feel competent
    e) providing help: the arousal cost reward model of helping stipulates that both emotional and cognitive factors affect when there are bystanders; audience inhibition or the fear of making a bad impression is one cost in this model
   3. The bystander effect on-line
   4. The legacy of the bystander effect research: What to do to get help in a crowd
B. Time Pressure: People Help Less When They Are Late
C. Location and Helping
D. Culture and Helping
E. Moods and Helping
   1. Good moods and doing good
    a) the mood maintenance hypothesis suggests we may help to stay in a good mood
    b) we may help more because a good mood elicits positive thoughts
   2. Bad moods and doing good
    a) guilt can lead to helping
    b) the negative state-relief model suggests that we may help to avoid feeling bad
    c) negative moods only increase helping if we take responsibility for them
    d) self-awareness leads to helping if focus is on value of helping; can decrease helping if focus is on self-concerns
F. Role Models and Social Norms: A Helpful Standard
   1. How role models influence helping
   2. How social norms influence helping
    a) norms based on fairness: reciprocity and equity
    b) norms based on what is right: social responsibility and justice
G. Culture and Social Norms for Helping

III. Personal Influences: Who is Likely to Help?
A. Are Some People More Helpful than Others?
B. What is the altruistic personality?
   1. Helping appears to be situation-specific
   2. Empathy and moral Reasoning

IV. Interpersonal Influences: Whom Do People Help?
A. Perceived Characteristics of the Person in Need
   1. Attractiveness: attractive people are helped more
   2. Attributions of responsibility: people are helped more if they aren't blamed for their plight

    B.   The Fit between Giver and Receiver
        1.   Similarity and Ingroups: Helping those just like us
        2.   Closeness: A little help for our friends
            a)   self-evaluation maintenance theory predicts we help our friends more than strangers on low ego-relevant tasks
            b)   self-evaluation maintenance theory predicts we help our friends less than strangers on high ego-relevant tasks
        3.   Gender and helping
            a)   men help more when helping may be dangerous
            b)   women help more when help involves social support
V.   Reactions to Receiving Help
    A.   Help That Supports vs. Help That Threatens
        1.   Threat to self-esteem model
        2.   Two types of help
            a)   self-supportive help: help that makes the recipient feel cared for and appreciated
            b)   self-threatening help: help that makes the recipient feel inferior and overly dependent
    B.   Seeking Help from Others
        1.   Help may be seen as a threat
            a)   when the person in need has high self-esteem
            b)   when the person in need is helped by a similar other
            c)   when the person in need receives help from a significant other on an ego-relevant task
            d)   when the person in need is a member of a stigmatized group and the help is unsolicited
        2.   Help from another is usually seen as helpful
            a)   when it involves close relationships
            b)   when there is mutuality
            c)   when children receive help from adults
VI.   Culture and Who Receives Help
VII. The Helping Connection: Feeling Connected to Others Leads to More Helping

LECTURE AND DISCUSSION IDEAS

Idea 1.   Helping Jews During the Holocaust

In the debate over whether helping is ever truly altruistic, some have pointed to those who hid Jews from the Nazis in World War II and argued that this helping is an example of genuine altruism rather than self-interest. Ask your students what they believe. Without a doubt, helping in this instance clearly came at great risk to the helper, but is it an example of genuine altruism?

Many of your students will be familiar with the movie *Schindler's List*. Ask them to discuss why people like Oskar Schindler were willing to help Jews escape persecution despite the severe costs that the helpers may have incurred. Were Schindler's actions truly altruistic? Discussing this topic is a good way to introduce altruistic and egoistic models of helping.

While definitive answers may not be possible, the examples of Germans helping to protect Jews from the Nazis show the extent to which helping can occur and can provide a nice contrast to the somewhat pessimistic tone set by the research on bystander intervention.

Idea 2.   Why People Help after Disasters

As reported in the text, in the aftermath of the terrorist acts of September 11, 2001, there was a dramatic spike in helping behavior. The same thing happened in the wake of the Asian tsunami in 2004, and Hurricane Katrina in 2005. In each case, people donated huge sums of money and volunteered their time and effort to selflessly help others.

Ask students to discuss why disasters like these motivate people to engage in prosocial behavior.

In a study that documented helping behavior, in the form of volunteering following the attacks of 9/11, Louis Penner and colleagues (2005) offered the following theories to explain such actions:

1.   Modeling. In the days following these disasters, the media focused on stories of heroic and selfless acts. Watching such role models inspired others to follow their example because the media attention showed that such actions are valued by society.

2.   Threat to one's community. The terrorist attacks of 9/11 appeared to target the American people, rather than one specific ethnicity, which led to an increased sense of community and heightened patriotic feelings. These in turn spurred individuals to work for the common good of the country.

3.   Lerner's just-world theory. The belief that the world is a fair and just place is shattered when so many innocent people die. People help others after something bad happens in order to restore the balance of a just world.

4.   Terror management theory. Disasters remind people of their mortality. That in turn causes anxiety. One way to manage the anxiety is to raise one's self-esteem and feel that one is valued by society. Doing good for others can accomplish both.

5.   Negative state relief model. Watching others suffer makes people sad because they empathize with them. The observers are then more likely to help others because that allows them to change their mood from negative to positive.

Challenge your students to apply some of the other concepts mentioned in the text to the phenomenon of post-disaster helping behavior. For example, how might the arousal: cost-reward model fit these situations? What were the potential rewards that outweighed the potential costs? Is there evidence of perspective taking in people's response to these tragedies? Do they think that most people acted altruistically or egotistically when they offered help following these disasters? Do they think that diffusion of responsibility occurred as well?

Penner, L, Brannick, M.T, Webb, S. & Connell, P., (2005). Effects on volunteering of the September 11, 2001, attacks: An archival analysis. Journal of Applied Social Psychology, 35, 7, 1333-1360.

Idea 3.   The Kitty Genovese Tragedy

The Kitty Genovese case was an impetus to the research on bystander intervention. Recount the story of her death to your students. She was brutally attacked outside her New York City apartment at two in the morning. All her neighbors in her apartment building were awakened by her screams. Her attacker was scared away at one point, but came back a half hour later and killed her. None of her neighbors so much as called the police until she was dead. If any one of her thirty-eight neighbors would have helped she probably would have lived. After recounting the crime, ask your students whether they think any of the neighbors helped. When they find out that no one helped, ask them why they think that no one helped. Unless they have read the textbook, it is unlikely that they will note the number of bystanders as an important determinant in the lack of help Kitty Genovese received.

Idea 4.   Helping the Homeless

Despite being a very wealthy nation our country has many poor people and many with no place to live. Despite several programs, homelessness currently does not seem to be a problem that is high on the national agenda. Ask your students what beliefs about the homeless might contribute to people's unwillingness to address this problem. You might further ask what type of information about the homeless might make people more willing to donate money to this cause.

Idea 5.   Who Benefits from Help?

An article in Psychology Today (2003) reports on a study that followed 400 older married couples for a period of five years. The researchers found that those who provided emotional or practical support (such as driving or cooking) to others were 40–60 percent less likely to die within the next five years than did those who did not provide such help. The authors concluded that giving help produces positive emotions and those emotions tend to buttress cardiovascular health.

Several earlier research studies have documented the benefits for those who help others. Giving of one's self increases happiness and decreases depression; reduces distress and improves general mental and physical health; gives one a sense of belonging and mattering; and boosts the immune system.

So, clearly, giving or helping others improves the mental and physical health of givers, but why didn't all that help and giving do much for those on the receiving end? Ask your students to think of explanations for this finding. Why didn't those who received social support live as long as did those who gave it? One possible explanation (discussed in Ch. 14 of the text) is that the people receiving help lacked a perception of control, an ingredient that serves as a buffer against stress and has been shown to have a positive effect on health and longevity (Rodin & Langer, 1977; Schulz & Hanusa, 1978).

Ask students to discuss what the implications are for those who care for another person. How can you increase perception of control in those who need help?

Carlin, F. (2003) A boon for caregivers. Psychology Today, 36, 16.

Langer, E. J., & Rodin, J. (1976). The effects of choice and enhanced personal responsibility for the aged: A field experiment in an institutional setting. Journal of Personality and Social Psychology, 34, 191-198.

Schulz, R., & Hanusa, B. H., (1978). Long-term effects of control and predictability-enhancing interventions: Findings and ethical issues. Journal of Personality and Social Psychology, 36, 1194-1201.

Idea 6.   Altruism or Egoism

The textbook reviews research by Batson and his colleagues (1981) that suggests that helping can, under certain circumstances (particularly when it is motivated by empathy), result from altruistic motives. Cialdini and his colleagues (1987) have argued that people may be helping in these situations not out of altruism but egoistically. The basic finding by both teams is that when people experience empathy they are willing to help someone even when they have other ways to avoid the situation. Batson argues that this shows that they are motivated to really help the person. Cialdini, however, argues that people help in this situation simply to relieve the sadness they feel by empathizing with the person, and avoiding the situation does not relieve this sadness. The final resolution to this debate is unlikely in the near future even though both sides have continued to present evidence for their point of view.

One interesting way to begin to discuss this topic is to divide your students into small groups and have them discuss the basic issue for a short period of time. After they have discussed the issue you might ask them to try to develop a study that would disentangle altruistic and egoistic interpretations of helping. Having students discuss these issues before hearing about Batson's and Cialdini's research should allow them to appreciate both the elegant designs of these two programs of research and why it is so difficult to come to a resolution in this debate.

Batson, C. D., Duncan, B. D., Ackerman, P., Buckley, T., & Birch, K. (1981). Is empathic emotion a source of altruistic motivation? Journal of Personality and Social Psychology, 40, 290-302.

Cialdini, R. B., Schaller, M., Houlihan, D., Arps, K., Fultz, J., & Beaman, A. L. (1987). Empathy-based helping: Is it selflessly or selfishly motivated? Journal of Personality and Social Psychology, 52, 749-758.

Idea 7. What is a Heroic Act?

In order to see altruism in a more concrete light, consider acquainting students with the stories of real heroes. Five times a year, the Carnegie Hero Fund Commission awards a bronze medal and $3500.00 to persons, in the United States and Canada, who risk their lives to an extraordinary degree while saving or attempting to save the lives of others. The following individuals were included in the 2006 awards:

Cody James Griffin, 17, a high school student, saved Diane Brunner, 52, from drowning. Brunner had been trying to save a dog that broke through the ice on the White River in Vermont. She also broke through the ice. Cody, clad only in a basketball uniform, knelt at the edge of the hole and grasped her by the arms. Although she outweighed him, he managed to pull her from the water onto the ice. Then he took her to the bank of the river. Brunner and the dog recovered after three days. Cody, whose foot had broken through the ice, was not injured.

James W. Davies II, 22, a heavy machine operator from New Jersey, attempted to rescue Shannon Williams, 19, from assault. One night, Williams was being stabbed repeatedly by an estranged boyfriend in the hallway of her apartment building. Davies, who lived across the hall, ran out and shouted at the assailant to stop. The assailant stabbed him in the neck, sending him to the floor. He then stabbed Williams again and left. Davies called 911. The police captured the assailant. Davies and Williams were hospitalized for stab wounds. Davies had to undergo surgery for a lacerated jugular vein, a collapsed right lung, and nerve damage to his right arm.

Donald C. Wilkinson Jr., 67, a retired power plant employee, died after saving a five-year-old from drowning. The boy fell off the edge of a pier that extends 60 feet into the Gulf of Mexico. The water was eight feet deep. Wilkinson climbed the pier railing and lowered himself into the 60-degree water. He grasped the boy while holding on to one of the pier supports. A man came by in a boat and picked up the boy, but was unable to get Wilkinson into the boat. Wilkinson hung on while the boat drifted toward the shore. The boy was uninjured. Wilkinson lost consciousness in the shallow water. Paramedics took him to the hospital. He died the next day of complications of near drowning.

Jencie Regina Fagan, 43, a middle-school teacher, helped rescue an indeterminate number of people from assault. A 14-year-old student in Reno, Nevada, entered the school armed with a 38-caliber gun and three bullets. He went into the main corridor and fired three times, striking one student and hitting another with bullet fragments. Fagan, who was in the school gym at the time, ran into the corridor as the third shot was being fired. She yelled at other students to seek safety and told the assailant to drop the gun. He did and she held him until the police came. The two injured students recovered.

David S. Parks 38, and Warren Bennett, 55, rescued Andrew Sleigh, 75, and his wife Mary, 83 from burning in their home in West Virginia. The couple had been upstairs when fire broke out on the second floor. Parks was walking by when he saw the smoke. He went into the house and crawled upstairs through thick smoke. He grabbed Mr. Sleigh by the ankles and took him to the top of the stairs. Then he went downstairs to get a wet towel. Meanwhile, Bennett also saw the smoke and came in as well. He dragged Mr. Sleigh down the steps. Parks returned upstairs with the wet towel and led Mrs. Sleigh downstairs and out of the house. Sleigh was hospitalized for a long time for severe burns. His wife Mary, Parks, and Bennett were all treated for smoke inhalation.

Students who are interested in reading about other awardees can be directed to the Web site for the Carnegie Hero Fund Commission at: http://www.carnegiehero.org.

Idea 8.   Pluralistic Ignorance and Learning

In the Latané and Darley (1970) research on helping, they note that one way that a crowd can undermine helping is by making it more difficult to interpret a situation as an emergency. In explaining why this is the case, they argue that in a crowd people experience pluralistic ignorance, a state where they believe they are the only one who thinks and feels as they do when actually their thoughts and feelings are common. In an emergency, this state leads everyone to play it cool and prevents people from interpreting the situation as an emergency.

Understanding this concept will likely be difficult for your students at first. One way to bring this concept to life is to talk about another context where they are more likely to have noticed the feeling of pluralistic ignorance: in an academic setting or at a party. Miller and McFarland (1987) demonstrated that people can experience pluralistic ignorance in trying to understand a difficult article. In this study people read a very difficult article but displayed pluralistic ignorance in that they felt they were the only ones who couldn't understand it when in fact the article was incomprehensible to most other students. Prentice and Miller (1993) showed that students show pluralistic ignorance with respect to norms about drinking alcohol. In particular they found that students think they are the only ones who want to restrict their drinking. This pluralistic ignorance could lead people to drink more than they want and more than their friends want.

Your students are likely to be able to relate to these forms of pluralistic ignorance, particularly if they discuss them in groups with other students. In fact this sort of group discussion could serve to break down the pluralistic ignorance that students have on these topics. Further identifying pluralistic ignorance in these every-day situations should also help students understand how it could make helping more difficult in an emergency.

Latané, B., & Darley, J. M. (1970). The unresponsive bystander: Why doesn't he help? New York: Appleton-Century-Crofts.

Miller, D. T., & McFarland, C. (1987). Pluralistic ignorance: When similarity is interpreted as dissimilarity. Journal of Personality and Social Psychology, 53, 298-305.

Prentice, D. A., & Miller, D. T. (1993). Pluralistic ignorance and alcohol use on campus: Some consequences of misperceiving the social norm. Journal of Personality and Social Psychology, 64, 243-256.

CLASSROOM ACTIVITIES

Activity 1. What Is Altruism?

The text defines altruism as helping that is "motivated by the desire to increase another's welfare." The activity in **Handout 10.1** presents students with a number of different situations. They decide whether they think the situation exemplifies altruism or not. This handout can be a good discussion starter. It should allow students to think about how their own view of altruism is similar to or different from the book's definition.

> ●*What if this bombs?* This one should be bombproof. Any pattern of answers (whether students show consensus or lack of consensus in their answers) should lead to interesting discussion and should serve to clarify the definition for them.

Activity 2. Generating Empathy for the Disabled

In describing helping behavior, the text emphasizes that empathy is one important factor in increasing helping. This exercise provides students with an opportunity to step into the shoes of someone who has a physical disability. For this task you will need a small paper bag for each student. (Alternatively you can do the exercise with one or two students as a demonstration.) Each student places the paper bag over his or her hand, holds a pencil with the bag, and then writes a short paragraph or copies a simple design from one drawn on the blackboard. This exercise impairs people's ability to control their small muscles. It should allow them some sense of what it is like to have a disability in which these muscles are impaired all the time.

    ●*What if this bombs?* This one should be bombproof. As long as students actively engage in the exercise, they should have some impairment of the ability to write, and this should give them some sense of what it is like to have a disability.

Adapted from Fernald, C. D., & Fernald, S. S. (1990). Experiential activities for generating interpersonal empathy for people with developmental disabilities. In V. P. Makosky, L. G. Whittemore, C. P. Landry, & M. L. Skutley (Eds.), <u>Activities handbook for the teaching of psychology</u> (Vol. 3, pp. 206-208). Washington, D.C.: American Psychological Association.

Activity 3. An Experiment to Assess the Effectiveness of Different Appeals to Donations

This activity replicates an experiment (Perrine & Heather, 2000) that found that people were more likely to put money in a Humane Society donation box when the box had an appealing picture than when the box had nothing on it or the phrase "even a penny will help." In the original study, the effect was explained in terms of the pictures evoking a positive mood, which made people feel more generous.

Divide the students into groups of about six students. Let each group identify a worthy cause (on campus or otherwise) for which they would like to raise money. They can then contact the targeted beneficiary for official collection boxes or they can use makeshift boxes that they create themselves. (One suggestion being to take an appropriate-sized box from a supermarket product, and cover it with construction paper). Each group should have three boxes. One box should have a pleasant picture indicative of the type of charity that the box represents. A second box should have the phrase "even a penny will help" on it. And a third box should just have the name of the charity. The boxes should be placed in settings that are equally trafficked on campus. After a week, let students collect the boxes and report on the results.

    ●*What if this bombs?* It is possible that your students will not get the same results. In that case, it would be profitable to discuss why their findings differed. What conditions did they introduce, in terms of the pictures, boxes, or placements that deviated from the original study? Why did those changes impact the results as they did?

Perrine, R. & Heather, S. (2000, April). The effects of picture and even-a-penny. <u>Psychological Reports</u>, <u>86</u>, 551-559.

Activity 4. Committing Random Acts of Kindness

An article in Psychology Today (2006) touts the benefits of altruism in terms of long-term psychological fulfillment. It cites the work of Sonja Lyubomirsky of Stanford University whose students reported higher levels of happiness than a control group after carrying out good deeds for a week.

Alternatively, the same article also cites the work of Jonathan Haidt of the University of Virginia, who contends that doing acts of kindness for strangers is not likely to benefit the doer, whereas helping family members or friends will because it will result in a strengthening of a social relationship.

Challenge your students to commit random acts of kindness, daily, for a period of two weeks and to keep a journal of their actions, the response they received from those who were helped, and their own subsequent reactions.

Suggest that they focus their good deeds on strangers in the first week (for example, give up a seat on a bus or buy a meal for a homeless person) and on family members in the second week (for example, visit an elderly relation or help a sibling with homework).

After the two-week period, have students share their impressions of their experiences with other classmates. Did they find themselves feeling fulfilled as a result of helping others? Did they experience any change of attitude? Do they feel happier now than they did at the start of the activity? Was their subjective experience the first week (helping strangers) different from their subjective experience in the second week (helping family members)?

What if this bombs? This could bomb if students do the assignment and report feeling no change at all. In that case, ask them to discuss why they think their results differed from those obtained by the students mentioned in the article. Any other results should lead to an interesting discussion.

Svoboda, E. (Jul/Aug 2006). Pay it forward. Psychology Today, 39, 4, 51-52.

Activity 5. Investigating Negative Mood and Helping

This activity is a simple test of the negative state relief model of helping. It is not a replication of a previous study so it should be undertaken with caution. The negative state relief model of helping predicts that when people are in a sad mood they will help others in order to put themselves in a better mood (Cialdini et al., 1987).

To test this idea, have half your students read **Handout 10.5a** and have the other half read **Handout 10.5b**. These two stories should work as a mood manipulation. Students reading Handout 10.5a should be sadder than students reading Handout 10.5b. After reading the stories, have students complete **Handout 10.5c**. This handout is a very simple measure of behavioral intention to volunteer for several activities that are likely to be viewed as helpful by most people. If the negative state relief model of helping is correct, students should report a stronger behavioral intention to help after reading Handout 10.5a than after reading Handout 10.5b.

You should note that the negative state relief model of helping has only received mixed support. Some (Miller & Carlson, 1990) have argued that the model is not supported by the research while others (Cialdini & Fultz, 1990) have argued that the research does support the model. Discussing these different points of view would also provide a good opportunity to discuss how research problems are worked out in the field and how conflicting evidence is often the pattern.

What if this bombs? This activity has a pretty short fuse and may well blow up. The literature on the negative state relief model has often failed to find increased helping after negative mood. In addition, the materials for this activity are untested. Therefore, you should only undertake this activity if it does not bother you that the results may not turn out. One way to look at this activity is as more of a teaching exercise than as a replication of a known effect.

Cialdini, R. B., & Fultz, J. (1990). Interpreting the negative mood-helping literature via "mega" analysis: A contrary view. Psychological Bulletin, 107, 210-214.

Cialdini, R. B., Schaller, M., Houlihan, D., Arps, K., Fultz, J., & Beaman, A. L. (1987). Empathy-based helping: Is it selflessly or selfishly motivated? Journal of Personality and Social Psychology, 52, 749-758.

Miller, N., & Carlson, M. (1990). Valid theory-testing meta-analyses further question the negative state relief model of helping. Psychological Bulletin, 107, 215-225.

Activity 6. A Scale of Altruistic Behaviors

Handout 10.6 reproduces a scale of altruistic behaviors that was used in a survey of 2,623 participants by the National Opinion Center at the University of Chicago.

Students are asked to note how many times in the past year they performed each of the altruistic behaviors. After they have completed the handout, collect their papers, tabulate the results into a frequency distribution, and compare them to those of the original survey population.

The majority of participants said they performed a total of 10–15 altruistic acts in the past year. In order, the altruistic behaviors from most frequent (the number in parenthesis denotes how many times a year on average each was performed) to least frequent were:

1.   Spent time talking with someone who was a bit down or depressed (24)

2.   Helped someone outside your household with housework or shopping (16)

3.   Allowed a stranger to go ahead of you in line (12)

4.   Given directions to a stranger (11)

5.   Given money to a charity (10)

6.   Done volunteer work for a charity (7)

7.   Given food or money to a homeless person (6.5)

8.   Helped somebody to find a job (5)

9.   Looked after a person's plants, mail, or pets while they were away (4)

10. Carried stranger's belongings, like groceries, a suitcase, or shopping bag (4)

11. Offered your seat on a bus or in a public place to a stranger who was standing (4)

12. Let someone you didn't know well borrow an item of some value like dishes or tools (3.5)

13. Lent quite a bit of money to another person (3)

14. Returned money to a cashier after getting too much change (2)

15. Donated blood (0.6)

You might also go through the list of altruistic behaviors and ask students to consider circumstances under which each of these behaviors would actually be egoistic and not altruistic.

● *What if this bombs?* This activity should be fairly bombproof. Students should find it interesting to compare the frequency of their altruistic acts with those who were surveyed.

Smith, T.W. (2/9/2006). Altruism and Empathy in America: Trends and Correlates. An analysis of survey results of the National Opinion Research Center at the University of Chicago.

MULTIMEDIA RESOURCES

Video

Aspects of Behavior. This film relates psychology to the student's life experience and considers ethical issues such as obedience and authority, along with prejudice and attitude change. Includes treatment of childhood autism, physiological bases of behavior, abnormal psychology, and influence of environment on individual personality and behavior. Shows the Smoked-Filled Room experiment and interviews several noted psychologists. (1971, 31 min.) Bureau of Audio Visual Instruction, University of Wisconsin Extension, PO Box 2093, Madison, WI 53701-2093.

Helping and Prosocial Behavior. This video explores different norms including the norm of equity and the norm of social responsibility. Altruistic behavior of typical citizens is shown. (1989, 30 min.) Audio-Visual Services, Pennsylvania State University, Special Services Building, 1127 Fox Hill Road, University Park, PA 16803.

Human Instinct: Natural Born Heroes. This program examines the instinct to protect that prompts people to risk everything for the sake of others. It spotlights three stories: a mother who wrestled a cougar to save her son, a soldier who braves the enemy to save a fellow soldier, and two men who helped a woman in a wheelchair escape the collapse of the World Trade Center. It considers the impulse of self-sacrifice and the role of mirroring neurons in promoting empathy. (2002, 50 min.) Available from Insight Media (800-233-9910).

Invitation to Social Psychology. This program introduces the field of social psychology by examining subject matter studies, methods of investigation, and finding/discoveries. Includes dramatizations of classic experiments in affiliation, attribution theory, cognitive dissonance, conformity, aggression, and bystander intervention. (1975, 33 min.) Audio-Visual Center, Indiana University, Bloomington, IN 47495-5901.

Silent Witness: The Kitty Genovese Murder. This video focuses on the murder of Kitty Genovese and deals with the question of human apathy in the face of atrocity. (1999, 50 min.) Available from Insight Media (800-233-9910).

When Will People Help. What makes a bystander decide to help or to ignore a potential crisis? Daryl Bem, the film's consultant and narrator, discusses the problem and presents experiments by social psychologists. Tests indicate that physical danger, fear of legal harassment, need for a quick decision, and embarrassment result in nonintervention. The bystander, who must define the situation as an emergency and must feel the weight of responsibility, often is deterred by the presence of others. (1976, 25 min.) Pennsylvania State University Film Library, College Station, PA, 16801.

Internet

Carnegie Hero Fund Commission. At this site, which is discussed in Idea 7 of this manual, students can read about the heroic deeds of the people chosen by the Carnegie Fund to receive awards for their altruism. Visit this site at: http: www.carnegiehero.org/

Charity Navigator. Subtitled: Your Guide to Intelligent Giving, this site evaluates over 5,000 charities and posts related articles. Visit this site at: http://www.charitynavigator.org/

VolunteerMatch. This site is run by a national nonprofit organization that uses the Internet to connect volunteers and service organizations. Visitors to the site select a service category from a list of twenty-seven that includes health and medicine, animals, children and youth, disabled, seniors, immigrants and refugees, and crisis support. Individuals are then matched within their category of interest, via zip code, with local charitable or service organizations that are in need of volunteers. Visit this site at: http://www.volunteermatch.org/

HANDOUT 10.1

Is this an example of altruism?

1. Y N A man puts money in a blind beggar's tin cup.

2. Y N A woman gives money to United Way during the yearly campaign drive.

3. Y N A child helps her classmate with her homework.

4. Y N A mother gives her child a bath.

5. Y N A paramedic administers CPR at an accident.

6. Y N A family hides a political prisoner.

7. Y N A woman loans a friend five dollars.

8. Y N A professor helps a student during office hours.

9. Y N A man does the laundry for his family.

10. Y N A bank lends a family money to buy a house.

HANDOUT 10.5a

Try to imagine yourself as the main character as you read this story.

It is nearing the end of fall semester and John is really looking forward to winter vacation. The semester has been a little hectic and he is happy that he will have some time relaxing with his family.

The Sunday two weeks before finals John gets up early to catch up on some of his courses. He is in the shower thinking about what he will study when his roommate pulls him out of the shower telling him he has a phone call from his sister. By her strained voice, John knows something is wrong. She manages to say that his mother is sick in the hospital and they don't know what it is. Without finding out more, John decides to fly home immediately.

John finds the flight home confusing. He is dizzy trying to make sense of what is happening. He rehearses to himself, "My mom's o.k. I'm sure nothing is wrong." John finds it odd but he feels that the other people on the plane sense his distress and act sympathetically toward him.

When he arrives John takes the first cab he can find to the hospital. Once there he hurries to his mom's room. He sees the rest of his family with pale, drained faces and teary eyes huddled around his mother. She looks weakened and frail with yellowish skin. John is overwhelmed by the sight of his mother and the pain that he feels.

Somehow John goes to his mother's bed, kneels beside her and holds her legs. She is rocking side to side clenching her teeth. At times she whimpers from the pain deep within her body. Gradually, she looks up at John and her family. She seems to cry and smile at the same time. She raises her arms a little as if to reach out to them and says, "You're all here." "Of course we are," John replies through his tears. Then his mother says somewhat hesitantly, "It's sort of strange being in this place isn't it." Everyone reassures her that she will be alright but everyone knows this is simply a masquerade.

John's mother then speaks softly, "I feel like I'm spinning. All of you are spinning too." She then closes her eyes and dies. John can't believe what is happening. He reaches over and hugs his mom but he feels that everything is gone and empty and will never be the same.

HANDOUT 10.5b

Try to imagine yourself as the main character as you read this story.

Mary wakes up at 6:53 a.m. seven minutes before her alarm. She twists and turns looking for a comfortable position. She gets out of bed and sees her bedroom just the way she left it the night before, books scattered all over the place and an empty Coke can on the nightstand.

Mary gets into the shower and turns the water on full blast, ridding herself of yesterday's heat and humidity. After she dries off, she gets herself a bowl of cereal and turns on the TV. She becomes engrossed in a story about a very successful team of rescuers who have saved many earthquake victims.

Mary's roommate comes back and reminds her that she is about to be late for class. So, she throws her books in her backpack and flies out the door. By running Mary makes it to class only three minutes late. Class is just starting, but it turns out the professor has decided to spring a pop quiz. One of the questions seems impossible to Mary and she struggles with it, systematically attempting every approach she can think of. Her strategy pays off and she figures out the answer just in time. Mary turns in her quiz and collects her things, deciding to leave the lecture early.

A friend catches her as she leaves the lecture hall and suggests that she hang out with him on the lawn to enjoy the weather. They find some people they know and everyone enjoys themselves sitting around talking for a couple of hours. Finally, Mary decides that she has had enough so she picks up her things and goes home.

At home Mary dumps her stuff on the floor and heads straight for the kitchen, where she makes a sandwich for herself and her roommate who has just come in. Mary looks in the refrigerator but decides that there is nothing worthwhile inside so she runs to the store next door to buy a couple of apples and some Coke to finish off lunch. Mary's roommate bought a paper on the way home and offers it to Mary to read. She looks for interesting news but there is none so she turns to the comics.

After lunch Mary decides that she really has to find her lost sunglasses. She realizes that she has to bite the bullet and clean her room. She locates the sunglasses in the middle of a pile of clean laundry while she was putting the clothes away. After an hour she has transformed her room into a place that a human being could live in.

At 1:30 p.m. Mary decides to do some schoolwork. She decides to begin by reading an article for her anthropology course. The article is not required but she wants to read it anyway. She finds the topic, the status of women in polygamous societies, very interesting. But Mary realizes that she has to turn to the calculus assignment that she has been dreading all week. She gets the calculator out of her backpack and puts it on the desk. She notices that the numbers are blinking, indicating that the batteries are low. She replaces the batteries. She sharpens her pencil. She straightens her books. Finally, she realizes that she has to begin. Fortunately, she realizes that the first problem is just like the one her professor worked through in class. She is able to do the problem easily. The second problem requires the solving of simultaneous equations to determine the speed that a ping pong ball would travel in liquids of different densities. Mary is lost but her roommate helps her finish the problems in only an hour and a half.

HANDOUT 10.5c

Please rate your agreement to each of the following statements.

1.   I would like to volunteer at a peer counseling center.

1	2	3	4	5	6	7
Strongly Disagree						Strongly Agree

2.   I would like to volunteer at a soup kitchen.

1	2	3	4	5	6	7
Strongly Disagree						Strongly Agree

3.   I would like to volunteer at an AIDS clinic.

1	2	3	4	5	6	7
Strongly Disagree						Strongly Agree

4.   I would like to volunteer at a hospice.

1	2	3	4	5	6	7
Strongly Disagree						Strongly Agree

HANDOUT 10.6

During the past 12 months, about how many times have you done each of the following things:

a.   Donated blood _____

b.   Given food or money to a homeless person_____

c.   Returned money to a cashier after getting too much change _____

d.   Allowed a stranger to go ahead of you in line _____

e.   Done volunteer work for a charity _____

f.   Given money to a charity _____

g.   Offered your seat on a bus or in a public place to a stranger who was standing _____

h.   Looked after a person's plants, mail, or pets while he or she was away _____

i.   Carried a stranger's belongings, like groceries, a suitcase, or shopping bag _____

j.   Given directions to a stranger _____

k.   Let someone you didn't know well borrow an item of some value like dishes or tools _____

l.   Helped someone outside your household with housework or shopping _____

m.   Lent quite a bit of money to another person _____

n.   Spent time talking with someone who was a bit down or depressed _____

o.   Helped somebody find a job _____

CHAPTER 11

Aggression

LEARNING OBJECTIVES: GUIDELINES FOR STUDY

You should be able to do each of the following by the conclusion of Chapter 11.

1. Define aggression as well as related concepts, such as anger, hostility, and violence. Distinguish between instrumental aggression and emotional aggression. (*pp. 436-437*)

2. Discuss the role of culture in aggression and attitudes towards aggression. Consider various explanations for differences in aggression across cultures and across groups within cultures. (*pp. 437-442*)

3. Identify individual differences that have been found to predict aggression, paying particular attention to gender. In doing so, explain the different types of aggression (overt and relational) for which gender differences have been observed. (*pp. 442-443*)

4. Consider whether aggression is innate by reviewing the evolutionary perspective, and the role of biological and brain factors. Discuss how these different explanations account for gender differences in aggression. (*pp. 444-448*)

5. Consider whether aggression is learned by reviewing the concepts of reinforcement, punishment, and the social learning theory of aggression. Discuss how socialization accounts for gender and cultural variations in aggression. (*pp. 448-454*)

6. Explain the original version of the frustration-aggression hypothesis, including discussion of the concepts of displacement and catharsis. Identify problems with this hypothesis and summarize its subsequent reformulation. (*pp. 455-457*)

7. Discuss the role of affect, arousal, and cognition when it comes to aggression. Consider situational factors that influence these processes. (*pp. 457-461*)

8. Summarize the immediate as well as long-term effects on aggression of exposure to violent forms of media. Explain the concepts of habituation and cultivation. (*pp. 462-470*)

9. Discuss the influence of nonviolent and violent forms of pornography on nonsexual and sexual aggression, and consider the factors and psychological processes responsible for these effects. Consider types of interventions or education that might reduce these effects. (*pp. 470-472*)

10. Discuss the antecedents, prevalence, and consequences of different forms of violence among intimates. Discuss the role played by alcohol and rape myth attitudes in sexual aggression among college students and other populations. Discuss effective ways of reducing these forms of violence. (*pp. 473-478*)

DETAILED CHAPTER OUTLINE

I. What Is Aggression?
   A. Aggression and Violence
   B. Anger and Hostility
   C. Instrumental Aggression and Emotional Aggression

II. Culture, Gender, and Individual Differences
    A. Culture and Aggression
        1. Comparisons across societies
        2. Subcultures within a country
    B. Gender and Aggression
        1. Overt, physical aggression
        2. Indirect, relational aggression
    C. Individual Differences
III. Origins of Aggression
    A. Is Aggression Innate?
        1. Evolutionary psychology
            a) genetic survival
            b) gender differences
            c) inhibition of aggression against those who are genetically related
            d) criticisms and rebuttals
        2. Behavior genetics
        3. The role of testosterone
        4. The role of serotonin
        5. Brain and executive functioning
    B. Is Aggression Learned?
        1. The effects of rewards and punishments
        2. Social learning theory: The role of models
        3. Socialization
            a) as a factor in gender differences in aggression
            b) as a factor in cultural differences in aggression
    C. Gender Differences and Socialization
    D. Culture and Socialization; Cultures of Honor
    E. Nature versus Nurture: A False Debate?
IV. Situational Influences on Aggression
    A. Frustration: Aggression as a Drive
        1. The frustration-aggression hypothesis
            a) frustration is produced when a person's progress toward a goal is interrupted
            b) all aggression is caused by frustration
            c) displacement occurs when one cannot aggress against the source of the frustration
            d) catharsis as the reduction of the motive to aggress
        2. The frustration-aggression hypothesis: Does the evidence support it?
        3. Frustration-aggression theory revised
    B. Negative Affect
        1. Heat and aggression: Losing your cool
        2. Positive affect: Reducing retaliation
    C. Arousal: "Wired" for Action
        1. Arousal-affect model
        2. Reducing arousal can reduce aggression
    D. Thought: Automatic and Deliberate
        1. Situational cues: the weapons effect
        2. Higher-order cognitive controls
        3. Alcohol
    E. Situational Influences: Putting It All Together

V.   Media Effects
   A.   Violence in TV, Movies, Music Lyrics, and Video Games
      1.   Extent of media violence
      2.   Linking media violence to real-world violence
      3.   Immediate and long-term effects
      4.   Positive, pro-social effects?
   B.   Pornographic Materials
      1.   Nonviolent pornography
         a)   the type and intensity of the emotion elicited
         b)   reducing restraints against male-to-female aggression
         c)   habituation
      2.   Violent pornography
         a)   gender specificity of the effects
         b)   effects on men's attitudes
         c)   the "rapist's profile"
         d)   correlation between consumption of violent pornography and endorsing anti-women attitudes
VI. Intimate Violence: Trust Betrayed
   A.   Sexual Aggression among College Students
      1.   Acquaintance rape
      2.   Gender
      3.   Alcohol
      4.   Attitudes toward rape and toward women
   B   Domestic Violence: Partner and Child Abuse
      1.   The cycle of family violence
VII. Reducing Violence
   A.   Multiple Causes, Multiple Cures
      1.   Situational and sociocultural factors
      2.   Media effects
      3.   Intimate violence
   B. Conclusions

LECTURE AND DISCUSSION IDEAS

Idea 1.   War

War is the ultimate demonstration of the scope and horror of human aggression. A discussion of the social psychological factors that contribute to war, and to peace, can highlight the profound significance of the topic of aggression. For example, you could discuss factors relevant to the frustration-aggression hypothesis, such as frustration, displacement, and scapegoating, in the context of the buildup of World War II. Ask students to discuss accounts consistent with evolutionary psychology to explain wars and conflicts concerning "ethnic cleansing" and nationalism, or to discuss the roles of factors associated with social learning theory, such as reinforcement and modeling, to explain particular acts of aggression or altruism in the context of war.

Discussions of war and peace can help students tie together theory and research from Chapter 11 with those of several other chapters, such as expectations, self-fulfilling prophecies, and attributions (Ch. 4); stereotypes and prejudice (Ch. 5); conformity and obedience (e.g., see Lecture and Discussion Idea 2); groupthink, group polarization, and ingroup-outgroup distinctions (Ch. 8); and helping (e.g., see the opening to Ch. 10). A frank, serious discussion of war and its brutality can be a powerful topic in which you can integrate a great many issues in social psychology, beyond the issues addressed in the present chapter.

Idea 2.   The My Lai Massacre

Even in the context of war, some events prove so shocking and seemingly irrational that people begin to question their understanding of human nature. One such event was what came to be known as the My Lai massacre during the Vietnam War. A platoon of U.S. soldiers brutally killed an entire village of innocent men, women, and children in the village known to Americans as My Lai. By assigning and discussing Hammer's (1970) book *One Morning in the War*, or excerpts of the book (e.g., pp. 3-10, 115-155), along with reports from the popular press at the time, such as the *Newsweek* article "The Killings at Song My" (December 8, 1969), you can provide students with extremely powerful and memorable material to which they can apply the principles and findings discussed in the textbook. The My Lai incident is rich with social psychological factors discussed in Chapter 11, such as frustration, displacement of aggression and scapegoating, aggression cues, heat, arousal, excitation transfer (perhaps demonstrated most horrifically in the apparent rape and murder of a young girl), reinforcement, and modeling, as well as social psychological factors discussed in other chapters, such as self-awareness (Ch. 3), expectations (Ch. 4), stereotypes and prejudice (Ch. 5), cognitive dissonance (Ch. 6), conformity and obedience (Ch. 7), group processes (Ch. 8), altruism (Ch. 10), and stress (Ch. 14). This discussion is a highlight of the course for many of our students every year. The popular film, *Platoon*, directed by Oliver Stone includes a powerful scene of a (fictitious) massacre similar to My Lai. Consider showing this scene as part of this discussion.

In conjunction with the discussion of the My Lai massacre, you might also discuss the prisoner mistreatment in the Iraqi prison Abu Ghraib by American MPs. As in My Lai, the soldiers involved justified their actions by claiming to have been following orders; they claimed that superiors told them to "soften up" the prisoners for interrogation. And, as in My Lai, there were men who were moved to take action against the abuses they were witnessing.

After the Abu Ghraib incidents came to light, President George W. Bush characterized the seven accused soldiers as "a few bad apples." Commenting on the President's speech, Philip Zimbardo said that the abuse at Abu Ghraib was due not to some character flaws of the soldiers' personalities but rather to group dynamics and the situation into which they were placed. He also drew parallels between what took place at Abu Ghraib and the results of his Stanford prison experiment. In both cases, he said, abuse of prisoners could be blamed on lack of clear rules, lack of a well-trained staff that was aware of the rules, and lack of a system in place to punish violations of the rules (Wallis, et. als., 2004).

Hammer, R. (1970). <u>One Morning in the War</u>. New York: Coward-McCann.

Wallis, C., August, M., Bacon, Jr., P., Phillips, M., Crittle, S., Rawe, J., Ripley, A., Johnson, K., Morrissey, S., & Thornburgh, N. (5/17/2004). Why Did They Do It? <u>Time</u>, <u>163</u>, 20, 38-42.

Idea 3.   Violence in the Media

The television and movie industries have been under criticism for years for the amount and degree of violence they display. There is a great deal of public debate about this issue, which touches on related issues such as censorship and the First Amendment, family values, profitability versus social responsibility, and definitions of art, violence, and obscenity. Many of the people whose voices are loudest in these debates are quite ignorant of the empirical research concerning the effects of media violence on attitudes and behavior. Discuss what the research does, and does not, suggest about the correlational and causal relationships between exposure to violence depicted in the media and real-life aggressive attitudes or behaviors. What implications does this research have for policy decisions? How should parents who are concerned about the antisocial effects of exposure to violent images in television raise their children without barring television from the house? Can watching violent films or sports have a cathartic effect? To encourage discussion and student participation, ask the students to discuss their own reactions to such stimuli. Ask the students how they typically feel after watching various violent films, ranging from slasher films to more realistic, but graphic, depictions of violence. Do they feel aroused, satiated, repulsed, nothing? Do these reactions differ as a function of the type of film or show, and, if so, why? Does prolonged exposure to violence depicted in the media cause desensitization and thus require more intense exposure in order for viewers to be excited and satisfied? Another interesting, and important, question to ask students is how research in this field can be improved so as to better address the questions of causality; researchers in this area are challenged with pragmatic and ethical limitations—how would the students try to face these challenges?

The Multimedia Resources section of this chapter lists several videos that could be used in conjunction with this discussion.

Idea 4.   Violence and Sports

One topic that many students like to discuss is the issue of violence and sports. Ask students whether they think that sports that feature rough physical contact reduces, increases, or has no effect on subsequent aggression, among not only the participants but also the observers. One paper that could be assigned or summarized to the students is by Bennett (1991), in which he asserts that "the notion that hostile feelings can be catharted from the psyche by playing football or other aggressive sports was virtually destroyed by behavioral scientists....Educators realize that the sport actually increases aggression but hide behind the outdated hypothesis about catharsis to perpetuate the sport" (p. 415). Students will no doubt have their own opinions about this, and many students should be willing to share them with the class. Another topic that should generate good discussion is whether particular acts within the context of a sporting event should be considered aggression. Is a hard body check in hockey an act of aggression? A hit by a pitcher in baseball or softball? "Trash talking" or taunting on the field or court? This latter issue of taunting, boasting, etc., can be especially interesting for students today. Ask the students to explain the causes and potential consequences of such behavior from a number of social psychological perspectives, such as the frustration-aggression hypothesis, social learning theory, and the arousal-affect model.

A related issue to be discussed is what causes aggression among the fans who attend sporting events, most dramatically illustrated by the riots and "hooliganism" involving European, African, or South American soccer fans, motorcycle racing fans in Australia, and hockey fans in North America.

In a review of some possible factors that have been implicated in soccer riots, Gordon W. Russell (2004) included the following:

Need for excitement — to relieve boredom caused by rising unemployment, greater amounts of "down" time, and fewer opportunities for interesting risky adventures.

Frustration — caused by having to wait for hours for tickets to an event only to be told that it's sold out or by having a star player on one's team appear to be disciplined unfairly.

Outlaw behavior — sometimes an event is used as the staging ground by hooligans who arrive at the game ready to do battle, with the sporting event merely being a guarantee of media attention.

Emotional arousal — after a particularly triumphant win or an agonizing defeat, fans are highly aroused which leads to intense emotions.

Modeling — witnessing athletes engage in violent or aggressive behavior leaves fans more hostile and likely to aggress as well.

Situational and environmental factors — crowdedness, excessive heat, loud noise, second-hand smoke, darkness and foul odors have all been shown to increase the tendency to aggress. When any of them occurs during a sporting event, the likelihood of aggressive incidents rises. (For example, 69 percent of all fights among fans in American professional baseball occurred at night.)

Personality traits — troublemakers are likely to be single, young males, poorly educated, and employed in semiskilled jobs. They are also likely to have a recent history of fighting.

Group dynamics — it is rare for a single spectator to initiate trouble. Rioters tend to attend in groups. Groups of fans are angrier, more aggressive, more impulsive, and more sensation seeking than are individual fans.

Cognitive factors — some fans are "sore losers" who attribute their loss to "dirty" play, unfair officials, and bad luck. All are external factors, contributing to their feeling that it's not fair that they didn't win (because it was not due to inferior play), which leads them to riot.

False consensus effect — rioters tend to see their own behavior as appropriate under the circumstances, and think that anyone who does not participate is a deviant. (Hockey fans who admitted that they would join in a fight believed that most other hockey fans would do so as well.)

Additionally, an article in Forbes magazine (Seligman, 2005) suggests an evolutionary explanation for irrational fan behavior in sports venues. According to psychologist David C. Geary, for generations, the Darwinian impulse to survive has galvanized organized bands of males to engage other male groups in battles for physical resources and women. This resulted in men experiencing fierce loyalty toward their ingroup members and deep hatred and fear for males in outgroups. Eventually, those feelings transferred to sports teams.

Other articles that can be assigned or referred to are cited below; they concern hooliganism in Italy, England, and Africa. Also, a series of articles in a special issue of the journal *Current Psychology Research and Reviews* (1988-1989, Winter, Vol. 7) examines violence in and around sports such as boxing, hockey, and soccer.

Bennett, J. C. (1991). The irrationality of the catharsis theory of aggression as justification for educators' support of interscholastic football. Perceptual and Motor Skills, 72, 415-418.

Igbinovia, P. E. (1985). Soccer hooliganism in Black Africa. International Journal of Offender Therapy and Comparative Criminology, 29, 135-146.

Russell, G.W. (July, 2004). Sports riots: A social-psychological review. Aggression and Violent Behavior, 9, 4, 353-378.

Seligman, D. (3/28/2005). Root root for the home team. Forbes, 175, 6, 118.

Williams, J. (1991). When violence overshadows the spirit of sporting competition: Italian football fans and their sports clubs. Journal of Community and Applied Social Psychology, 1, 23-28.

Zani, B., & Kirchler, E. (1991). When violence overshadows the spirit of sporting competition: Italian football fans and their clubs. Journal of Community and Applied Social Psychology, 1, 5-21.

Idea 5.   Alcohol and Other Drugs

Just as students like to discuss the roles of media violence and sports in aggression, they also like to discuss the role of alcohol. What are the students' own experiences concerning the effects of alcohol on aggression? What about other drugs? What social psychological explanations are there for the effects of alcohol on aggression? This discussion can tie together the research and theory reported in Chapter 11 with the research on self-awareness reported in other chapters (such as Chs. 2 & 5). The issues of stereotypes and prejudice can also be brought into the discussion if you focus on prejudice-related violence and the role of alcohol in reducing the inhibitions against acting out these prejudices. A number of interesting and readable articles can be assigned or discussed on these topics. For example, assign the article by Claude Steele and Robert Josephs (1990) on "alcohol myopia" that is included in the book of readings, *Readings in Social Psychology: The Art and Science of Research*, which is available with the textbook. Some of this work is summarized in Steele's (1986) *Psychology Today* article, which discusses the effects of alcohol not only on aggression but also on helping, gambling, risk taking, self-disclosure, and a number of other topics relevant to social psychology. In addition, Cook and Moore (1993), and Taylor and Chermack (1993) offer readable reviews of this important topic. A recent review (Ito et al., 1996) meta-analyzes the results of forty-nine studies on the effects of alcohol on aggression; although your students might have some difficulty reading this entire article, you could summarize it or assign only the Introduction and Discussion sections.

Cook, P. J., & Moore, M. J. (1993). Violence reduction through restrictions on alcohol availability. Special Issue: Alcohol, aggression, and injury. Alcohol Health and Research World, 17, 151-156.

Ito, T. A., Miller, N., & Pollock, V. E. (1996). Alcohol and aggression: A meta-analysis on the moderating effects of inhibitory cues, triggering events, and self-focused attention. Psychological Bulletin, 120, 60-82.

Steele, C. M. (1986). What happens when you drink too much? Psychology Today, 20, 48-52.

Taylor, S. P., & Chermack, S. T. (1993). Alcohol, drugs, and human physical aggression. Journal of Studies on Alcohol, 11, 78-88.

Idea 6. Sports, Alcohol, and Sexual Aggression

Combined discussions of sports, alcohol, and aggression can be very compelling for students. A number of campuses throughout the country have experienced highly publicized incidents of members of sports teams abusing alcohol and drugs and behaving very violently, committing acts of aggression ranging from vandalism to rape. Such a discussion could be facilitated by assigning or describing any or all of the following articles:

Frinter, M. P., & Rubinson, L. (1993). Acquaintance rape: The influence of alcohol, fraternity membership, and sports team membership. Journal of Sex Education and Therapy, 19, 272-284.

Koss, M. P., & Gaines, J. A. (1993). The prediction of sexual aggression by alcohol use, athletic participation, and fraternity affiliation. Journal of Interpersonal Violence, 8, 94-108.

Parrot, A., Cummings, N., Marchell, T. C., & Hofher, J. (1994). A rape awareness and prevention model for male athletes. Journal of American College Health, 42, 179-184.

Idea 7. Pornography

Organize a discussion, or perhaps a debate, about the effects of pornography on aggression, and/or about the policy implications of these effects. This is an extremely interesting, controversial, and challenging topic, and it should therefore generate a great deal of debate and discussion, although students may be frustrated that they cannot easily resolve or come to consensus about the complex issues raised. Should erotica of all kinds be censored? Does it depend on the context or setting? What is the difference between art and pornography? What should be the definition of obscenity? Who should make these decisions?

One way to get students thinking about these issues is to assign readings from the popular press concerning high-profile murder cases in which exposure to pornography was cited as a possible contributing factor, such as the cases of Ted Bundy and Jeffrey Dahmer. Another way to get students thinking about these issues is to assign the transcript published in *Harper's* (November, 1984, pp. 31-45) from a roundtable debate featuring individuals such as Al Goldstein (publisher of the "adult" magazine called *Screw*), Erica Jong (author of *Fear of Flying*), Susan Brownmiller (founder of Women Against Pornography), and Aryeh Neier (former national executive director of the American Civil Liberties Union). This debate concerned psychological, legal, and moral issues involving pornography, such as whether or not pornography should be protected. Although this debate occurred many years ago and the level of discourse is somewhat disappointing, the issues remain very relevant today and the diversity of the panel of discussants is noteworthy.

In addition to policy implications, discuss the social psychological theories and research findings concerning the effects of pornography and aggression. Discuss the roles of thought, arousal, individual differences, and gender in the effects of exposure to pornography. Compare and contrast the predictions about the effects of pornography that could be offered from the various theoretical perspectives concerning aggression discussed in the chapter, such as: the frustration-aggression hypothesis (e.g., vicarious catharsis versus sexual frustration and displaced aggression), the arousal-affect model (positive versus negative emotions, levels of arousal, desensitization), social learning theory (observations of positive reinforcement, imitation), and concepts such as aggression cues and cultivation.

Malamuth, Donnerstein, and others have written numerous articles reviewing the effects of pornography on violence, and by assigning any of these you could help students understand both the research findings and the challenge of conducting empirical research on such a sensitive topic. As a way of connecting research with policy implications in your discussions, you might find it helpful and interesting to assign the brief article by Neil Malamuth in *American Psychologist* (1989), "Distinguishing between the Surgeon General's personal views and the consensus reached at his workshop on pornography," to illustrate some of the challenges that researchers often face when trying to bridge the gap between the research lab and government policy.

Finally, you might also assign students to read an article by Robert Bauserman (1996), who, after reviewing all existing studies investigating the relationship between pornography and sexual aggression, concluded that there is no relationship between exposure to nonviolent pornography and anti-female attitudes or acceptance of sexual aggression.

Bauserman, R. (1996). Sexual aggression and pornography: A review of correlational research. Basic and Applied Research, 18, 4, 405-427.

Malamuth, N. M. (1989). Distinguishing between the Surgeon General's personal views and the consensus reached at his workshop on pornography. American Psychologist, 44, 580.

Idea 8.   Gender Differences

Discuss the theoretical and empirical research concerning gender differences and aggression. Ask the students to summarize what the empirical findings are, and ask them to explain these findings from a variety of perspectives, including sociocultural perspectives, evolutionary psychology, biological accounts, sex-role stereotypes, and power differences. You can facilitate this discussion by assigning or summarizing some representative articles from these different perspectives. For example, summarize or ask students to skim a set of articles published in 1995 in *Psychological Inquiry*. The opening article, Buss's (1995) article, "Evolutionary psychology: A new paradigm for psychological science," provides a good introduction to the evolutionary perspective, and the article is followed by a variety of commentaries about this perspective, some supportive and some critical. Also consider using the book, *Sex, Power, Conflict: Evolutionary and Feminist Perspectives* (Buss & Malamuth, 1996), to get material for this discussion. Also, refer to the research cited in the textbook for more material to foster a strong debate.

Have the students debate the evolutionary and social-roles accounts. Challenge them to suggest ways that research could test these and other explanations. Is the evolutionary account falsifiable? Can a social-roles account be maintained in light of sex differences in aggression that are found across cultures and species?

In addition, ask the students to describe their own observations about this issue. Do they see gender differences in aggression on campus? Are these differences equally great or small for both physical and nonphysical (e.g., verbal, indirect, relational) aggression? Do they think that these differences are changing over time? How do the media portray aggression differently as a function of the gender of the aggressor? Susan Faludi's (1991) book, *Backlash*, offers an interesting discussion of the portrayals of aggressive women in the movie industry, and your class can discuss the portrayal of women in movies such as *Fatal Attraction*, *The Hand That Rocks the Cradle*, *The Temp*, *The Crush*, *Single White Female*, and *Disclosure*, comparing these portrayals to those of men in movies. What effects do such movie images have on boys and girls? Similarly, the students can be asked to discuss the media's portrayals of gays and lesbians in terms of aggression. In addition to the role of the media, discuss the role of parents and teachers. Do the students remember being taught, either explicitly or implicitly, very different messages about the appropriateness of various aggressive behaviors, such as aggressive play in sports or aggressive verbal play? Do they continue to observe, or not observe, such differences today?

Buss, D. M.(1995). Evolutionary psychology: A new paradigm for psychological science. Psychological Inquiry, 6, 1-30.

Buss, D. M., & Malamuth, N. M. (Eds.) (1996). Sex, power, conflict: Evolutionary and feminist perspectives. New York: Oxford University.

Faludi, S. (1991). Backlash: The undeclared war against American women. New York: Doubleday.

Idea 9.   Marital Violence

Discuss the phenomenon of spousal abuse from social psychological perspectives. What factors contribute to spousal abuse? Why do women remain in these relationships? An article in Psychology Today (Marano, 1993) presents the findings of various studies of violent couples. One researcher, who looked at the interaction patterns of fifty-seven severely violent couples, found that the vast majority of battered women in his study returned to their abusing husbands. The explanation usually offered for the phenomenon is the battered-wife syndrome, whereby a battered woman becomes so demoralized and degraded by the fact that she cannot predict or control the violence that she becomes psychologically paralyzed and unable to take any action to improve her situation. The researcher, however, concluded that there was another reason in most of the cases he observed; that these relationships, which are characterized by severe violence, often happen to be (aside from the violence) "highly romantic and deeply loving." As proof, he cites the finding that much of the interaction in these marriages is not of a violent nature.

The violence that takes place in these relationships is attributed mainly to the fact that the men are deficient in processing social information. They negatively misinterpret their wives' (often innocuous) behavior when it involves someone of the opposite sex. Oddly, he states that the reason for the violent reaction is that most batterers are extremely dependent on their wives. The dependency being a factor of the type of childhood these men experienced. Almost all the violent husbands that were studied came from homes where there was physical violence. The women didn't necessarily come from violent homes, but they lacked good mothering. So the abused boy and the unmothered girl ended up together, feeling safe in each other's company, but not trusting the outside world. Violence in such marriages is often related to jealousy and the security the men feel in being attached to another person. The thought of being abandoned by the women they totally rely on makes them violent. Some researchers have pointed out that the females in these relationships are often themselves violent and are more likely to initiate violent acts, but, according to the studies described in the article, women's violence usually appears only as a response to the husbands' violence.

There are also certain cultural norms that play a role in reinforcing the view that men can sometimes use violence and that women should tolerate it. This is particularly so in cultures of honor. In these cultures, there is great concern for a man's reputation, which is based on his toughness and ability to protect his family and possessions. Examples of cultures of honor are the Mediterranean societies, such as Greece, Italy, and Spain, Middle Eastern and Arab countries, Latin and South American cultures with Iberian roots, and the American South. Researchers Vandello and Cohen (2003) conducted an experimental study that tested this hypothesis. In the first part of the study (which is discussed in detail in Chapter 2 of the textbook), the Brazilian and US students responded to written scenarios involving fidelity and violence in married relationships. The Brazilians were more likely to say that the wife's infidelity reduced the masculinity and good character of her husband. Moreover, the Brazilians characterized the man who responded to infidelity by hitting his wife as more manly and loving of his wife than the one who merely yelled at her. In the second part of the study, participants (Latinos, Southern Anglos, and Northern Anglos) witnessed a staged jealousy-related argument between a couple (that included violent behaviors on the man's part) and later interacted with the female confederate. Latinos and Southern Anglos formed a more positive impression of the woman when she was contrite and expressed loyalty to her "fiancé" than did the Northern Anglos, who liked her more when she expressed assertiveness and said she was going to end the relationship.

Marano, H. E. (1993). Inside the heart of marital violence. Psychology Today, 26, 48-58.

Vandello, J. A., & Cohen, D. (2003). Male honor and female fidelity: Implicit cultural scripts that perpetuate domestic violence. Journal of Personality and Social Psychology, 84, 997-1010.

Idea 10.   Driving while Hostile

In a survey cited in the journal New Scientist (Byrne, 2000), one-sixth of drivers who described themselves as generally being mild-mannered in temperament admitted to often feeling angry when behind the wheel of their vehicles.

Ask students in what ways driving in traffic differs from walking on a crowded sidewalk. What social-psychological factors might account for automobiles provoking negative emotions?

Byrne cites the following causal factors:

   a.   Arousal and excitation transfer — when someone is cut off while walking, he or she might get all excited, but the very act of walking requires the exertion of energy so that any excitation soon dissolves. In a car, however, every time a person perceives that someone is doing something wrong, stress and tension build up with no physical release. Moreover, when one is driving, other drivers present a constant potential threat, something to watch out for, so the individual who is driving remains in a state of heightened arousal.

   b.   Deindividuation — cars confer a sense of anonymity on drivers. It's not possible to see clearly into one and identify a driver, especially if the vehicle is moving fast.

   c.   Lack of communication — when a person accidentally bumps into another on the sidewalk, a contrite expression or an expressed "excuse me" is all it takes to defuse the situation. However, on the road, there is less of an opportunity to communicate that one has made a regretful mistake.

   d.   Cars as valued possessions — a car is often a person's second most valuable possession. The type of car one drives also makes a statement to others as to the owner's social status, wealth, attitude, and personality. Because one's self-identity is tied up with the car, any threat to it is seen as a personal offense.

   e.   Traffic — crowding causes stress, as does being obstructed on the way to a goal. A person is more likely to encounter congestion and limitations when driving (e.g., speed limits, traffic, or slow drivers) than when walking.

Byrne, G. (2000). Road rage. New Scientist, 3838.

Idea 11.   The Social Psychology of the 9/11 Terrorists

Why would someone decide to become a terrorist? Are any of the factors mentioned in the text's discussion on the origins of aggression or in some of the other chapters relevant in explaining what motivates terrorists to kill themselves and others?

For example, might their aggressive instincts be innate characteristics? Are terrorists mentally unstable individuals with death wishes? When President Bush characterized the 9/11 hijackers as "evil cowards" and others in the government called them "craven homicidal maniacs" might they have been, as one researcher (Atron, 2003) claims, committing the fundamental attribution error (see Ch. 6)?

A recent study (Perina, 2002) of 32 suicide bombers discounted the idea that terrorists are mentally unstable individuals with death wishes. These particular thwarted terrorists appeared to have no particular psychopathology, social dysfunction (not more likely to be fatherless, friendless, or jobless), or suicidal symptoms. How might Milgram's obedience studies (see Ch. 7) be used to explain these findings?

What role do religion and culture play in the development of terrorists? Historically, martyrdom has been an integral part of the belief system of Shiite Islam as far back as the first Caliphates and the death of Husayn who martyred himself. The first major suicide terrorist attack in the Middle East in contemporary times was the December 1981 bombing at the Iraqi embassy in Beirut (killing 30 and injuring more than 100 people) believed to have been sponsored by the Ayatollah Khomeini. A year later came the assassination of the allegedly pro-Israel Lebanese President Bashir Gemayel by a suicide-bomber. Then, in October of 1983, a truck-bomb killed nearly 300 American and French servicemen in their barracks in Beirut. Dependent on how the Koran is interpreted, martyrdom also resonates with Sunni Moslems when religious or national leaders actively advocate it and is regarded as the highest honor in Islamic society when committed in defense of Muslim faith and lands (Burdman, 2003).

The 9/11 terrorists came from Middle East countries, which are cultures of honor. How might that have impacted their terrorist leanings? Arab families are typically authoritarian in nature. How might such an upbringing have influenced the terrorists (Ch. 7)? In what ways might the outgroup homogeneity effect (Ch. 5) have influenced the worldview of the terrorists? What draws potential terrorists to join organizations such as Al Qaeda? How might the "foot-in-the-door" compliance technique be used in training terrorists? What benefits does group affiliation confer on an unattached individual from a stressful background (Ch. 9)?

Could the frustration-aggression hypothesis be raised to explain what motivates terrorists? Or at least what makes them susceptible to indoctrination? The text discusses how aggressive behavior is strongly affected by learning. What role might learning (in the form of indoctrination) play in the development of suicide terrorists? One trait that all terrorists appear to share is a propensity for anger and rage (Plous & Zimbardo, 2004). How might such anger be channeled by a "teacher" into a desire for revenge against the West?

Atran, S. (2003). Genesis of suicide terrorism. Science, 299, 1534-1540.

Burdman, D. (2003). Education indoctrination and incitement: Palestinian children on their way to martyrdom. Terrorism and political violence, 15, 96-123.

Perina, K. (2002). Suicide terrorism: Seeking motives beyond mental illness. Psychology Today, 35, 15.

Plous, S. & Zimbardo, P. (2004). How social science can reduce terrorism. Chronicle of Higher Education, 51, 3, B9-B10.

Idea 12. Applying Social Psychology to Murder Trials in South Africa

By summarizing or assigning Colman's (1991) article, "Expert psychological testimony in two murder trials in South Africa," you can provide students with insight into how the social psychological theory and research reported in the textbook can be applied to the field of law. In these trials—each a retrial in which the defendants had been sentenced to receive the death penalty—the author and another social psychologist discussed a number of relevant social psychological concepts, such as frustration-aggression, self-awareness, and conformity, to help explain the defendants' behaviors. In both trials, the death penalty was withdrawn. Colman notes that until these cases came to trial, psychological evidence had never been taken into account as extenuating evidence in South Africa.

Colman, A. M. (1991). Expert psychological testimony in two murder trials in South Africa. Issues in Criminological and Legal Psychology, 1, 43-49.

Idea 13. War, Capital Punishment, and Criminal Violence

In the *Psychology Today* article "Murder in mind," John Wilkes (1987) discusses research that has led to this hypothesis: "When a nation does violence to human beings by conducting wars or executing criminals, it incites its citizens to more criminal violence than they would otherwise commit." Consider assigning this article as a way to initiate a discussion of the effects of the death penalty and war on subsequent aggression. Theoretical perspectives such as the cognitive-neoassociation analysis and social learning theory can be examined in this context.

Wilkes, J. (1987). Murder in mind. Psychology Today, 21, 26-32.

Idea 14. Televising Executions

Deborah Potter (2001), an expert on journalistic concerns, thinks that televised executions for public viewing are inevitable in the near future.

When Timothy McVeigh, the Oklahoma City bomber was executed in June of 2001, survivors and relatives of the victims were given the option to watch the execution on a close-circuit feed from the death chamber. This set a precedent. It was the first time that an execution was televised. A month earlier, sounds (but not pictures) were broadcast over national radio from the death chamber in Georgia. Soon after, an independent radio producer managed to pick up official tapes of past executions and he developed an hour-long audio program that was played on ABC's *Nightline*.

When the decision was made to execute McVeigh, legitimate news organizations expressed no interest in the taping the event. However, an entertainment Web site, best known for soft-core porn, petitioned the court for the right to tape the execution, claiming First Amendment rights. The Web site was prepared to charge online users $1.95 to view the tape. It was turned down.

Ask your students how they feel about televised executions. Do they think that such broadcasts would act as a deterrent to crime, resulting in decreased aggression? Or would they arouse more violent instincts and thereby increase societal aggression? What does the research on violence in the media lead them to expect? Would such broadcasts lead to habituation and cultivation? Or, would such airings be, as a producer of *60 Minutes* said, "No big deal. Just another guy on a gurney getting a needle in his arm, something viewers see every week on ER." (Potter, 2001).

Potter, D. Witnessing the final act. American Journalism Review, 23, 76.

Idea 15.   Cyberbullying

Bullying occurs when children try to cause harm to other children physically, verbally, or through social ostracism. It happens in elementary grades through high school, although it is most common in middle school (grades 6 through 8). In the past, bullying was bad enough when it occurred in the school yard. These days, however, some bullies have taken their act to cyberspace. Using e-mail, chat rooms, cell phones, instant messaging, web page "slams," text messaging, and online voting booths, they spread hurtful information about their chosen victims.

Ask students to discuss how this new form of bullying differs from the old-fashioned kind. What effect do they think anonymity (provided by the use of fake screen names on the Internet) has had on the expressed levels of aggression? How might a typical online bully differ from a typical offline bully? Do they expect there to be any different gender patterns? In what ways is a digital form of taunting more hurtful than a face-to-face one?

In one article about teen cyberbullies (Education Digest, 2005), the authors contend that online bullying is more damaging to the victims because the humiliation is so much more public. Moreover, the lack of face-to-face contact means that bullies are less likely to empathize, feel compassion for, or regret their actions. The anonymity factor also emboldens bullies because it makes it difficult to trace the source of hurtful messages and punish the perpetrators.

As for the bullies themselves, in real life, they are most often male and larger than their victims. On the Internet, however, size is less relevant and a bully might be an undersized weakling. In addition, female bullies actually predominate on the Internet because girls are more likely than boys to be e-mailing, text messaging, or chatting online.

Strom, P.S. & Strom, R.D. (Dec., 2005). When teens turn cyberbullies. Education Digest, 71, 4, 35-41.

CLASSROOM ACTIVITIES

Activity 1. What Is Aggression?

The question of what is and what is not aggression can be more difficult to answer than students initially think. Challenging students to define and identify aggression is a good way to begin a lecture or discussion of aggression because it gets them to think carefully about the prevalence and diversity of aggression, about the assumptions that underlie the definition of aggression that is offered in the textbook, and about how different types or manifestations of aggression may signal very different social psychological causes and processes.

Handout 11.1 contains a long list of a variety of actions, many of which are likely to be difficult to classify as either aggression or not aggression. Before each action are two blank lines. Distribute copies of this handout to the class (consider using only the first page if time is short, or distributing the first 25 questions to half the class and the other 25 to the rest of the class), and ask the students to place a check on the first blank line in front of every action that they feel would satisfy their own personal criteria of what constitutes aggression. Once they have done this, ask them to place a check on the second blank line in front of every action that they feel would satisfy the criteria of the textbook's definition of aggression—i.e., "behavior intended to injure another person who does not want to be injured." It might be interesting to distribute this handout before the students have read Chapter 11 and have them do only the first task, and then have them do the second task (applying the textbook definition) after they have read the chapter.

When students have completed these tasks, have them discuss the difficulties they faced in deciding what was and was not aggression. On what items was there much consensus? Why? On what items was there little consensus? Why? (You can determine consensus either by asking for a show of hands for various actions or by collecting the handouts and calculating the percentages. You might consider asking students to write an "M" or an "F" on the handouts to indicate their gender and then calculating the consensus separately as a function of gender to see if there are interesting gender differences.) On what items did the students' own judgments differ from those suggested by the textbook's definition? In larger classes, you might consider breaking the students into smaller groups to discuss these issues.

This discussion can provide a good transition to a discussion of the different theories and causes of aggression. To what extent, for example, does aggression seem instinctual? Are there gender differences? What is the role of conscious thought? Of intention? Of mitigating circumstances? Of frustration or arousal?

> *What if this bombs?* This exercise is bombproof. Any pattern of results can inspire interesting discussion. Either extreme, from a great deal of consensus among the students on most of the items to very little consensus, as well as a mix of some items leading to consensus and others not, should lead to interesting discussions.

Activity 2. Social Learning Theory and the Bobo Doll

For over two decades, we have seen instructors turn this demonstration into what many of their students consider to be one of the most memorable and fun experiences of the entire course (we thank social psychologists Joel Cooper and James Hilton for being particularly inspirational examples). Although your results may vary, it is hard to imagine that this demonstration could ever fail to work (i.e., in the absence of defective props or injury). After watching their instructor jump around in front of the class and pummel a plastic doll, students rarely forget the research conducted in the 1960s by Bandura, Ross, and Ross concerning social learning theory. Students appreciate both the creativity of the research itself and the important social psychological points suggested by the results.

Overview of the research. In this research, Bandura and colleagues investigated the effects of exposure to aggressive models on children's subsequent verbal and physical aggressiveness. In the study (Bandura et al., 1961) illustrated in this classroom activity, a child was placed in a room with a same-sex or opposite-sex adult, along with a variety of toys. One of the toys was a large, inflatable plastic doll (typically 3–5 feet tall) that returns to a standing position after being knocked over. This toy used to be known as a Bobo doll (named after the clown who was depicted on early versions of this toy; today, a variety of cartoon characters may be featured). The adult and the child each played with some toys quietly. After a while, in the aggressive-model conditions, the adult stood up and made a dramatic approach to the Bobo doll. The adult yelled at the doll and aggressed toward it in strange verbal and physical ways. The researchers were interested in determining the extent to which the children would later imitate these acts of aggression when they subsequently were left alone in a room with toys that included the Bobo doll. Bandura and his colleagues found that children did indeed tend to imitate these novel acts of aggression, particularly when the aggressive model was of the same sex as the child. In subsequent studies (e.g., Bandura et al., 1963) these researchers found that children exposed to aggressive models on television, whether human or cartoon, also seemed to learn aggressive behaviors from the models and would act them out under the right conditions (e.g., when they believed they would not get punished for it).

Procedure. The classroom exercise described below can ensure that this research has an impact on the students. It consists of acting out the behavior of the aggressive adult model. This is particularly effective when students are not very familiar with the details of the study, so if you assign a reading concerning this study, the students should read it after the demonstration. There is a great deal of room for variation in the details of the procedure, but here is one way of simulating this study:

1.   Without fanfare or warning, tell the class that you're going to demonstrate a classic study.

2.   Retrieve a bag that you had been hiding, and slowly and quietly take out about a half-dozen toys, one at a time. (The variety and quality of the toys can be used as a source of humor; students find it very amusing when they see their instructors play with particularly goofy toys.)

3.   After bringing out all of the other toys, get the Bobo doll from a hidden location and set it down some distance away from the other toys.

4.   Play with the other toys for a minute or so.

5.   Suddenly, and dramatically, stop playing with the other toys and slap your hands down hard on the table or podium. Stare angrily at the Bobo doll. Do not smile.

6.   Keep your arms and legs very stiff, and goose-step slowly and dramatically toward the doll. A few feet away from it, yell loudly, "Clear the way!"

7.   Begin punching it lightly, then harder. With every couple of punches, yell things such as "Sock him in the nose...," "Pow...," "Boom. Boom. Boom...," "Hit him down....," "He keeps coming back for more. He sure is tough." Throw the doll up in the air a few times and hit it as it comes down.

8.   Take out a mallet (at which point you can briefly "break character" and twirl the mallet toward the class, as if to say, "I'm going to have some fun with this"), and hit the doll lightly, and then a bit harder. Be careful not to break the doll (and make sure that the head of the mallet does not come flying off and hit a student). Continue to yell things such as "Pow! Boom!" at the doll as you hit it.

9.   Begin to walk away, as if the demonstration is over. Suddenly, run back toward the doll and pounce on it, hitting its nose with the mallet as you kneel on top of it.

10. Depending on your athletic skill and the layout of the room, you might finish the demonstration with a huge kick, sending the doll flying.

Some variations of this demonstration include throwing various things at the doll (such as tennis balls or plastic darts); putting on a leather "biker" jacket or revealing a cut-off T-shirt or a shirt with an aggressive (or very pacifist) saying on it just before attacking the Bobo doll; etc. The key is to have fun with this. The more surprising your behavior is to the students, the better. Indeed, if your teaching style is rather "distinguished" and "formal" or if you usually come across as rather quiet and reserved, this kind of demonstration can be very entertaining for the students. We know of junior and senior faculty, men and women, and athletic and nonathletic types, all of whom have performed this in front of their classes with great success.

Discussion. After you catch your breath, explain to the students that you have demonstrated, with some minor modifications, what a child in the Bandura et al. (1961) study might have seen. Ask the students to guess why your specific behaviors (the use of the mallet, the things you yelled) were so unusual and even bizarre. The answer is that the researchers wanted to see if the children actually learned novel ways to aggress (both verbally and physically), and thus they exposed the children to acts of aggression that the children would not otherwise be expected to perform. Then, summarize the results of the study (i.e., on measures of physical aggression and of verbal aggression, the children tended to imitate the adult model's acts of aggression; the children were much more aggressive after having seen an aggressive than a nonaggressive adult model—particularly when the aggressive model was of the same sex as the child). Discuss how Bandura and his colleagues (1963) also found this kind of effect when the model was seen on film rather than live. This can lead to a discussion of the effects on children of aggressive models such as parents and teachers, as well as aggressive characters (both human and cartoon) on television.

What if this bombs? Unless you injure yourself, hit a student, or too quickly maim the Bobo doll beyond repair, this demonstration is virtually bombproof. At the very least it helps to illustrate an important study, and at the most it can inspire good discussions of the methods and implications of the research concerning social learning theory. It also is a lot of fun, especially for your audience.

Bandura, A., Ross, D., & Ross, S. (1961). Transmission of aggression through imitation of aggressive models. Journal of Abnormal and Social Psychology, 63, 575-582.

Bandura, A., Ross, D., & Ross, S. (1963). Imitation of film-mediated aggressive models. Journal of Abnormal and Social Psychology, 66, 3-11.

Activity 3. Television Violence

The third Lecture and Discussion Idea for this chapter concerns the issue of violence in the media. After discussing this issue, assign the following exercise to heighten students' awareness of the current patterns of violence on television. Politicians, journalists, various community groups, and many, many others have been criticizing television producers and the television networks with increasing intensity in recent years concerning the amount and degree of violence depicted. Some counter that there is much more violence on the network news than on fictionalized television programs, suggesting that these television programs simply reflect a very violent society. These discussions and assertions rarely include actual data to support anyone's claims. This exercise, therefore, emphasizes the role of research in this dialogue, and may provide a "reality check" against some of the claims and accusations that have garnered a lot of attention.

Depending on the size of the class, each student should watch either one or each of the following three types of programs on a major network: a children's Saturday morning or after-school cartoon, a prime-time program, and the network news. While watching the program, the students should use **Handout 11.3** to code the content for various scenes of physical or verbal aggression or related issues.

Sampling. There are two ways of determining which students should watch which programs: either with or without random sampling of the programs within each category. Random sampling is the more methodologically sound way of doing this exercise, and it can thus serve to illustrate to the students how best to examine issues of this kind. However, it also takes more work to set up. If you choose to use a method approximating random sampling, get a listing of the television program schedule for the major networks. Assign a number to every cartoon show targeted toward children on these networks on Saturday morning or Monday afternoon, to every prime-time program (from 8:00 PM to 11:00 PM) on these networks from Monday through Thursday night, and to these networks' weekday evening news programs (usually scheduled at 6:30 or 7:00 PM). Using these numbers, either (1) randomly select for each student one program of each type (i.e., cartoon show for children, prime-time show, network news), or (2) randomly select for one student a cartoon show, for the next student a prime-time show, for the next student a network news program, and so on. (If a student's schedule conflicts with one or more of these times, select other programs at random.) If random sampling seems too cumbersome, then have the students select one program of each type themselves, but discuss why random sampling is a much better way to conduct the research than is a more haphazard method of sampling.

Distribute Handout 11.3 and tell the students to watch their assigned programs carefully and to use the handout to code the various acts of aggression and related incidents. For consistency's sake, each program selected should be coded for 30 minutes (minus commercials). For programs that last an hour or more, the students should flip a coin and select either the first or last 30 minutes.

In large classes, to help students get to know each other and to increase the fun, you might have students work in pairs or small groups to watch and code these programs together.

Collect the completed handouts and calculate the average number of the various incidents for each category of program. Ask the students to predict the averages before you report them. Are the actual numbers higher or lower? Discuss the implications of these results, in the context of the issues raised in the chapter and suggested by the Lecture and Discussion Ideas in this manual.

What if this bombs? This exercise is bombproof. Virtually any pattern of results could inspire interesting discussion. For example, if the results suggest that there is a great deal of violence on television, this would support the research discussed in the text. If the results suggest the opposite, this could lead to a discussion of why this finding is discrepant from those often reported (i.e., Is TV in the process of changing? Was the sample used in this exercise too small or unrepresentative? Are the reports from groups opposed to TV violence not objective?) There are many interesting questions to pursue, such as whether there is more violence in the news than on other programs, whether children's cartoons are particularly violent, what kinds of aggression are depicted most and least frequently, and so on.

Activity 4. Violent Lyrics and Aggression

Research appears to support the hypothesis that exposure to violent media, such as television, movies, and video games produces an increase in aggression-related variables, such as thoughts, feelings, and behavioral impulses (Anderson & Bushman, 2002). Music videos also appear to increase such aggressive tendencies (Anderson & Bushman, 2001).

Most students would probably argue that violent music without the video would produce no such effects. For one thing, the lyrics are rarely discernible unless one is paying very close attention. For another, people often listen to the music (not the lyrics) or use the music as a background for other activity. Therefore, students may be surprised to learn that a recent study by Anderson, Carnagey, and Eubanks (2003) found that songs with violent lyrics do produce aggressive tendencies in their listeners.

One of the dependent variables used by the researchers to measure aggressive cognition was a task created by Bushman (1996) that asks participants to rate the similarity between aggressive and ambiguous words. The logic being that violent lyrics increase the accessibility of aggressive thoughts in semantic memory, which will cause ambiguous words to be interpreted in a more aggressive vein. An activity based on a portion of this study can be executed as follows:

Ask students to bring in a pair of contemporary rock songs that have the following characteristics: One song has to have clearly violent content, whereas the other has to have minimal or no violent content. They should both be of the same type of music and by the same group. Randomly assign half the class to Group A and the other half to Group B. If you have use of another room, let both groups listen to the tapes at the same time. Immediately afterwards ask them to complete **Handout 11.4**. (If there's only one classroom available, send one group out of the classroom while the other is listening to the tape and completing Handout 11.4).

After they have completed Handout 11.4, ask them to total the ratings. Write the total ratings on the board and compute the means for the two groups. If the violent lyrics do cause aggressive thoughts to increase, then the group that listened to violent lyrics should have a significantly higher mean of similarity ratings.

What if this bombs? The exercise might bomb and fail to replicate the results of the original study for several reasons. First, it might be difficult to obtain two audio tapes, by the same group, that are distinctly violent and nonviolent. Second, the similarity ratings scale is one-fourth the size of the original scale. Third, the sample size will be smaller than the one used in the original study. And fourth, if they're involved in choosing the music, the students might anticipate the purpose of the study. Nevertheless, the experiment is likely to engage the students and even if it bombs, the students can profit from discussing the reasons that it did.

Anderson, C.A., & Bushman, B.J. (2002). The effects of media violence on society. Science, 295, 2377-2378.

Anderson, C.A., Carnagey, N.L., & Eubanks, J. (2003). Exposure to violent media: The effects of songs with violent lyrics on aggressive thoughts and feelings. Journal of Personality and Social Psychology, 84, 960-971.

Bushman, B.J.(1996). Individual differences in the extent and development of aggressive cognitive-associative networks. Personality and Social Psychology Bulletin, 22, 811-819.

Johnson, J.D., Adams, M.S., Ashburn, L., & Reed, W. (1995). Differential gender effects on African American adolescents' acceptance of teen dating violence. Sex Roles, 33, 597-605.

Activity 5. Context and Gender Differences in Aggression

This activity is based on an experiment by Mary Harris (1994), which investigated the role of context in gender differences in aggression. In that study, undergraduates were asked to respond to four anger-eliciting scenarios. In the three scenarios that did not involve dating, males tended to be more aggressive. But in the fourth scenario, which did involve dating, the females tended to be more aggressive.

Handout 11.5 presents students with four different scenarios, in which aggressive tendencies might be aroused. The first three, which involve strangers, are: having someone steal a parking spot, having someone ruin a term paper, and having someone push ahead in a line for concert tickets. The fourth scenario, which involves dating, asks students to imagine being slapped and falsely accused of cheating by a boyfriend/girlfriend at a party. For each scenario, students are asked to choose their most likely response on an escalating scale of aggression, from of 1 to 5, with 1 being a nonaggressive response and 5 being a physically aggressive response.

After students have completed responding to the four scenarios, tally the results for each of the first three scenarios, separately by gender. If the findings mimic those of the Harris (1994) study, then males should have higher totals for scenarios A, B, and C. This is because males tend to be more verbally and physically aggressive in nondating or relationship situations than females.

Now tally the results of scenario D, separately by gender. This scenario is different than the others in that it involves a dating situation, it requires a response to physical aggression (in the form of a slap), and the gender is understood (so males are being asked if they would respond aggressively against a female, and vice versa). Because this is a dating situation and because males are less likely to physically aggress against a female (than females are to aggress against a male in a dating relationship), females should show a higher level of aggression than males for this scenario.

What if this bombs? This activity should be relatively bombproof. Even if the results are not as expected, students would likely be eager to discuss why they deviated from the results of Harris' study.

Harris, M. B. (1994). Gender of subject and target as mediators of aggression. Journal of Applied Social Psychology, 24, 453-471.

Activity 6. Designing a Better Laboratory Aggression Paradigm

Writing in the Journal of Experimental Psychology: Applied (2005), Dominik Ritter and Mike Eslea critiqued five classic and three new research designs that are being used to measure aggression in the laboratory. This activity challenges students to design a research study using a new paradigm.

Begin by presenting the eight existing paradigms to your students and citing the criticisms associated with each one. The designs are as follows;

1. Teacher/learner — In this classic paradigm, the "teacher" is the participant and the "learner" is a confederate. The participant is asked to teach the learner (who is typically in another room) a memory task and to punish each mistake with an electric shock.

2. Essay evaluation — This paradigm is similar to the preceding one except that here participants are asked to evaluate essays supposedly written by confederates. Both designs are problematic in that the participant might be moved to give shocks for prosocial reasons (to help teach the learner), the aggression is sanctioned by an authority figure, the victim is separated from the aggressor, and the only possible responses are aggressive ones. All those factors are not likely to be present pin real life circumstances that involve aggression.

3. Competitive reaction time game — This procedure is presented as a game in which the participant and the confederate are playing against each other. The participant is told to press a button as quickly as possible after a signal, so as to beat out the confederate. For each trial that the participant "wins," he or she gets to decide how severe an electric shock will be administered to the "losing" confederate. One problem with this paradigm is that its iterative nature may encourage an aggressive response for self-defense, to weaken one's opponent, or just to be fair, and not necessarily to cause harm. As in the previous two paradigms, this one also separates the aggressor from the target, does not allow for any response other than an aggressive one, and features an authority figure that encourages the aggression.

4. Bobo doll modeling paradigm — This is the well-known procedure wherein small children watch an adult play aggressively with an inflatable Bobo doll. After the children are frustrated, they are observed to see whether they copy the adult's aggressive behavior when presented with the same doll. It remains unclear whether the children are being aggressive or if they're simply enjoying rough-and-tumble play.

5. Point subtraction aggression paradigm — This classic paradigm has the participant seated at a computer screen. He or she is told that pressing one button will earn him or her money, whereas pressing another will deduct money from another person. Supposedly, that other person is playing the game in another room. Participants are shown a running total of their earnings (from pressing the first button) and losses (from their non-existent opponent who is said to be pressing a second button). Although in this instance the participant can choose to respond non-aggressively by simply not pressing the second button, the only available way to interact with the one's opponent is to use aggressive action. And, again, there are the problematic matters of separation of aggressor from victim and the authority figure's approval of the aggression.

6. Hot sauce paradigm — This is the first of three newer laboratory methods used to test for aggression. In this procedure, the participant sets the amount of hot sauce that another individual must down. The "victim" is someone who is said to dislike spicy food and who has taken some provocative action against the participant (such as insulting him or her). The authors question whether the administration of hot sauce can be construed as a hostile act, since study results have found the participants to be in a better mood than the controls. If this really was an aggressive action, they say, it would render the participants in a negative mood.

7. Bungled procedure paradigm — Participants are given an opportunity to use a pellet or paintball gun to shoot at a female target who is wearing protective gear. The shooting never takes place as

participants are informed that there was an error and they are actually in the control condition. The aggressive measure has to do with the power of the gun and the number of pellets participants select for the shooting. This procedure only allows for potentially aggressive intentions as no aggressive actions are allowed to take place. Another problem is that those who score highest appear to have antisocial or psychotic tendencies, and may enjoy the idea of shooting at the target but are not especially intent on doing harm. In fact, the protective gear may stress the point that this is all in fun and no one will get hurt.

8.   Experimental graffiti and tearing procedure — This paradigm asks participants to perform two tasks. First, they are presented with an illustration titled "Adam and Eve in the Garden of Paradise" on which they are told to draw. Aggression is measured by how much graffiti is added, how damaging it is, and whether it has sexual or aggressive content. In the second task they are given an illustration titled "Samson and the Lion." In this case, they are instructed to tear the illustration in pieces and place all in a small envelope. The aggressive measure is the number of pieces produced. The authors question whether the illustrations are viewed as valuable objects by the participants, or simply as worthless items that are meant for destruction. Like the Bobo doll paradigm, this one might simply be measuring enjoyment in rough-and-tumble play.

According to Ritter and Eslea, all the existing paradigms are weak in that they disregard motivating variables such as anger, fear, or hostile thoughts. Without taking such variables into consideration, they say, it is not possible to determine if an aggressor intended to do harm. Another area of criticism has to do with the limited number of response options available to the participants (For example, in the hot sauce paradigm, participants cannot choose the degree of spiciness that will be administered and in the Bungled procedure they cannot choose to hit an inanimate rather than a live target). All the paradigms, except for the "Bungled procedure," are criticized for separating the aggressor from the target. Also, the fact that aggression is produced in response to the demands of the authority figure makes it unclear if the responses are aggressive or merely compliant.

As for what would characterize a good paradigm, the authors set the following conditions: Give participants an opportunity to aggress without requiring or permitting it. Make sure there is direct contact between the aggressor and the target. Use behavior that is unambiguously harmful (cannot be interpreted as rough-and-tumble play). Provide a range of response items that includes prosocial and non-aggressive acts. And make the measured behavior resemble aggression in the real world without being unethical.

Divide your students into groups of 4 to 6 and challenge them to come up with a research design that uses a new aggression paradigm that avoids the pitfalls of the existing paradigms and follows the authors' guidelines with regard to what defines a good paradigm. Have each group appoint a spokesperson to present their idea to the class and have the class debate the strengths and weaknesses of each proposed paradigm.

   What if this bombs? There is very little chance that this activity will bomb. Even if students are unable to come up with good proposals, they are likely to find the topic engaging and to benefit from the discussion about what they did right or wrong.

Ritter, D. & Eslea, M. (2005). Hot sauce, toy guns, and graffiti: A critical account of current laboratory aggression paradigms. Journal of Experimental Psychology: Applied, 31, 407-419.

Activity 7. Debates

Using a debate format, assign students to one of two sides: "Men are inherently more aggressive than women, regardless of society's norms and practices," versus "Men are not inherently more aggressive than women." Discussions of sex differences are often provocative and memorable for the students. Another provocative debate topic concerns violence in the media and censorship. Among the possible topics are "Violence on television should [should not] be censored," "It is appropriate [inappropriate] for the government to exert a great deal of pressure on television networks to reduce the depictions of violence," "Record stores that sell to children music that contains graphic lyrics should [should not] be punished," and "Only very violent films should receive ratings of 'NC-17' (no children under 17 admitted); the sexual content should not matter."

> 💣 *What if this bombs?* There is very little chance that this activity will bomb completely. Debates can be excellent ways to engage students in the material, in that they provide an opportunity for students who might be reluctant to reveal their own attitudes or questions to be able to contribute to class discussion and make important points by speaking from behind an assigned position, and to help the students see the complexities of the issues at hand. If the quality of the debate is poor, or if one side is far superior to the other, you can shift the focus away from the debate itself and toward the issues raised in the debate, asking students to drop their roles and analyze the particular issues raised (and, perhaps, to consider issues that were not raised). Thus, the debate would be seen as the *beginning* of a discussion rather than as a substitute for one.

Activity 8. Guest Speakers

Colleges and universities often have a number of resources concerning prevention of aggression and coping in the aftermath of violence. Inviting a guest speaker to discuss some of these issues with the class can be a powerful way of getting students to see the reality of aggression and its real-world consequences, and to become familiar with some of the resources that are available. The speaker can shed light on some of the demographic issues, current statistics about the prevalence and financial costs of some of these problems, the effectiveness of various kinds of treatments, the community's support or lack of support for their efforts, etc. Among the experts to pursue for such an invitation are individuals from a local women's shelter, who could discuss issues of spousal abuse or family violence; rape-prevention or sexual-abuse clinic or group; or law enforcement, judicial, or social service agency.

> 💣 *What if this bombs?* The best way to avoid a bomb here is through good preparation. Be sure your speaker knows the level at which he or she should talk to your students about the issue at hand. Be sure the speaker knows what the students have read and heard in class, how much time you expect for lecture, questions, and discussion, and what your goals are for the talk. If possible, ask the speaker to make an outline of what he or she will be saying and discuss this outline with the speaker in advance of the class, so that you can provide feedback for the speaker and get the students ready for the talk. Even in cases where the talk is not very engaging, students typically learn a lot from guest speakers who have had experiences with these issues first-hand. Of course, if the speaker really does bomb, you can rely on the contrast effect to make your own lectures seem better by comparison.

Activity 9. Instigators of Aggression

In his *Teaching of Psychology* article entitled "The dirty dozen: Classroom demonstration of twelve instigators of aggression," William Davidson (1990) suggests a classroom activity in which students view scenes from movies that depict aggression and judge "the scenes for the presence or absence of 12 instigators of aggression" (p. 252). In this article Davidson describes the procedure involved in this activity and discusses its pedagogical benefits.

This is a good activity to conduct <u>after</u> the students have read Chapter 11. Discuss how prevalent the students think these instigators are in the media and in other aspects of life. How do the instigators relate to the theoretical concepts and empirical findings discussed in the textbook? What can be done to minimize the prevalence or effects of each of these instigators?

🔥 ***What if this bombs?*** There is nothing to bomb here. The activity is designed to initiate discussion of the nature and causes of aggression, and the material is interesting, accessible, and important enough that the potential for a good discussion is very strong.

Davidson, W. B. (1990). The dirty dozen: Classroom demonstration of twelve instigators of aggression. Teaching of Psychology, 17, 252-253.

MULTIMEDIA RESOURCES

Video

Aggression: The Explosive Emotion. This film probes the roots of aggression in human behavior, determines the difference between constructive and destructive aggression, and examines various outlets for aggression. Mental health experts discuss the dangerous results of not dispelling anger with constructive forms of aggression, such as sports and physical exercise; they also question whether drugs should be used to control aggression. From the Thin Edge series. Produced by NET. (1975, 58 min.) Available from Pennsylvania State University, Audio-Visual Services, University Park, PA 16802 (800-826-0132).

The Aggressive Impulse. Explores the idea that the urge to be violent is inborn and provides suggestions of ways to control aggression. Given the "nature vs. nurture" debate discussed in Chapter 11, this film can lead to some very compelling discussions. (1977, 18 min.) Available from Encyclopedia Britannica, Educational Corp., 425 N. Michigan Avenue, Chicago, IL 60611.

Battered Women: Violence Behind Closed Doors. This film features group discussions and individual interviews in which female victims reveal how getting beaten up can become an almost accepted part of married life, and male perpetrators show how a number of prevalent attitudes toward women in our society contribute to cases of wife beating. It also examines cultural aspects of their aberrant behavior and suggests remedies such as community shelters, counseling, and education. (1977, 23 min.) Available from Pennsylvania State University, Audio-Visual Services, University Park, PA 16802 (800-826-0132).

Bowling for Columbine. The United States is notorious for its astronomical number of people killed by firearms for a developed nation without a civil war. With angry humor, film activist Michael Moore explores the roots of this bloodshed in an award-winning documentary. Produced by United Artists and Alliance Atlantis. (2003, 119 min.) Available from MGM Home Entertainment.

Child Abuse: Cradle of Violence. Using intimate interviews with abusive parents in the areas of child behavior and discipline, this film provides an insight into child abuse and explains the need to break the cycle. It also presents alternatives to moral punishment and potential stress situations. (1976, 20 min.) Available from Pennsylvania State University, Audio-Visual Services, University Park, PA 16802 (800-826-0132).

Cyberbullying – Cruel Intentions: 9/14/06. This ABC Primetime program shows how cell phones, digital cameras, and personal Web sites encourage and amplify teenage meanness. Teens use the new technology to invade privacy, spread gossip, and publicly humiliate one another. In one example, girls bring a camera phone into a locker room in order to get back at a girl they dislike. (September 14, 2006). Available at http://www.transcripts.tv (818-848-6500 x 101).

Does TV Kill? This episode of *Frontline* investigates television's role in our increasingly violent society and examines how violent images change children—and adults. We strongly recommend using this program. (1995, 90 min.) Available from PBS Video (800-344-3337).

Human Aggression. This video depicts spontaneous occurrences of aggression, such as the activities of a youth gang, and relates these examples to scientific principles and laboratory findings. The video covers the psychological training of police, the Bobo doll experiment of Bandura and colleagues discussed in Activity 2 above, Milgram's work with group influence on aggression, and the legitimization of aggression in delinquent groups; it also includes a statement by former Attorney General Ramsey Clark on aggression among the disadvantaged. From the Social Psychology series. (1976, 24 min.) Available from Pennsylvania State University, Audio-Visual Services, University Park, PA 16802 (800-826-0132).

The Impact of Violence on Children. This program looks at the sources of violence that affect children, and reports staggering statistics about the amount of violence that children today are exposed to. Among the experts featured in the video are Dr. James Garbarino, Director of Cornell University's Family Life Development Center; James Stayer, President of Children Now; and Dr. Kathleen Kostelny, Erikson Institute. (1995, 28 min.) Available from Films for the Humanities and Sciences (800-257-5126).

The In Crowd and Social Cruelty. This is a videotape of an ABC News program that dealt with cliques and bullying. (2002, 41 min.) It is available from Films for the Humanities and Sciences (800-257-5126).

Konrad Lorenz: An Intimate Portrait of the Founder of the Science of Animal Behavior. Presents the seminal ideas of Nobel Prize-winner Konrad Lorenz, known as the father of ethology, a science dealing with all the forces at work in animal behavior. Lorenz himself tells how he developed his central concepts of imprinting, domestication, and aggression. (1978, 25 min.) Available from Pennsylvania State University, Audio-Visual Services, University Park, PA 16802 (800-826-0132).

The Lessons of Littleton. This video examines the shootings in Columbine High School in Littleton, Colorado and examines the roots of violent behavior. (1999, 90 min.) Available from Insight Media (800-233-9910).

Machismo. Originally shown on *60 Minutes*, this video examines the issues of sex-role stereotyping and the ways in which aggression against women can be an accepted part of one's culture. It demonstrates how in Brazil a man can, with impunity, kill his wife because he imagines she may have glanced at another man or simply because she did not serve dinner on time. The most severe "punishment" received by the man who has murdered his wife is that he is to disappear for a few days, after which he cannot be punished for defending his honor. (1988, 16 min.) Available from Films for the Humanities and Sciences (800-257-5126).

Rage: A Social Analysis. This program examines the emotional causes and social dangers of road rage, workplace aggression, and sports spectators' violence. Nonviolent ways to assert needs and grievances are highlighted. (2004, 48 min.) Available from Films for the Humanities and Sciences (800-257-5126).

Rape: An Act of Hate. This program, hosted by actress Veronica Hamel, seeks to determine why people rape. It examines the history and mythology of rape, explains who its most likely victims are, and contains interviews with experts in the fields of media, law enforcement, and sociology. (1986, 30 min.) Available from Films for the Humanities and Sciences (800-257-5126).

The Rape Drug: A New Menace. Examines the growing use of the drug Rohypnol, an odorless and flavorless drug that can be mixed with alcohol. This video explains how some men use this drug to sedate women in order to take advantage of them on dates. The video follows two such cases through interviews with victims and their attorneys. This program presents "a thorough examination of a growing social problem." (1997, 26 min.) Available from Films for the Humanities and Sciences (800-257-5126).

Skinheads USA: The Pathology of Hate. This award-winning program provides an unprecedented inside look at an actual neo-Nazi skinhead organization, its operations, and its personalities. "The program powerfully captures firsthand the distorted idealism and openly racist objectives of the neo-Nazi youth movement." Caution: This video contains profanity and footage of violence and brutality.

Instructors should preview this video before showing it to their students. (1993, 54 min.) Available from Films for the Humanities and Sciences (800-257-5126).

Spanking. This *Dateline* NBC program focuses on the debate about whether and how to use physical punishment when disciplining children. Does spanking cause children to become more aggressive, rather than less? Does "sparing the rod" lead to "spoiling the child"? The program includes interviews with social scientists and physicians. (June 29, 1997). Available from NBC (800-420-2626).

Talked to Death: Have TV Talk Shows Gone Too Far? This HBO program focuses on the growing phenomenon of depictions of violence, hatred, and other extreme, sensational behaviors and emotions on talk shows, demonstrating how far producers and hosts are willing to go to win high ratings. The video includes interviews with Geraldo Rivera, Phil Donahue, Maury Povich, and Morton Downey, Jr., as well as producers, lawyers, and guests. The video shows producers trying to elicit rage from a timid guest, a woman posing as an unhappy wife, and footage of the never-broadcast *Jenny Jones Show* episode in which a gay man revealed his attraction for a heterosexual man, who later killed him, allegedly because of the revelation made on the show. (1996, 60 min.) Available from Films for the Humanities and Sciences (800-257-5126).

Teen Violence: Wot U Lookin' At? Is violent behavior a product of nature or nurture? This documentary explores the causes of antisocial behavior in young urban males. The video includes candid interviews with young criminals, and it encourages viewers to question various theories about the origins of aggression. A BBC production. (1998, 60 min.) Available from Films for the Humanities and Sciences (800-257-5126).

TV Violence and You. George Gerbner (his research on cultivation is discussed in the textbook) analyzes one week of television shows to determine their level of violence. Violence in the news, on cartoons, at sports events, and on prime-time programs are discussed. The put-down, frequently seen in sitcoms, is also analyzed. The effects of these depictions of violence on viewers are discussed. Violent relationships portrayed between men and women are analyzed within the context of the growing incidence of rape. (1995, 30 min.) Available from Films for the Humanities and Sciences (800-257-5126).

Violence Against Women. Hosted by a policewoman and a television news anchor, this award-winning video examines domestic violence, the secrecy that often surrounds it, and some of the practical and legal issues that abused women face. (1995, 46 min.) Available from Films for the Humanities and Sciences (800-257-5126).

Violence: An American Tradition. Using archival photos and footage, as well as discussions by experts in a variety of fields, this video explores the recurring patterns of violence in our society. "Hosted by civil rights activist Julian Bond, the program examines many of the most notorious acts of violence that have scarred the American psyche over the past 200 years." An HBO production. (1995, 55 min.) Available from Films for the Humanities and Sciences (800-257-5126).

Note: Films for the Humanities and Sciences (800-257-5126) offers a great many videos relevant to the topic of domestic violence. This list summarizes only a small sample of what is available.

INTERNET

International Society for Research on Aggression. This organization is devoted to the scientific study of aggression and violence. It provides links to several other sites involved with studying or reducing aggression. Visit this site at: http://www.israsociety.com/

Lion and Lamb Project. This organization aims at stopping the marketing of violent toys to children. The site's creators conduct "violent toy trade-ins" all over the country, where children exchange violent toys for nonviolent ones and then cooperatively produce a peace sculpture from the discarded violent toys. Visit this site at: http://www.lionlamb.org/

HANDOUT 11.1 WHAT IS AGGRESSION?

Yes   No

1. A child punches a large plastic doll.
2. A group of children refuse to let a new classmate play with them.
3. A murderer is executed in the electric chair after being sentenced to death.
4. A hunter kills an animal and has it mounted on his living room wall.
5. A person kills an animal in order to eat it.
6. A starving person steals some food from a supermarket.
7. A child chases a frightened cat around the house.
8. A cat kills a mouse.
9. A person commits suicide.
10. A parent spanks his child who has broken some house rule.
11. A wrestler intentionally grabs his opponent's injured left knee as often as he can during a meet.
12. A doctor gives a shot to a child.
13. A baseball pitcher intentionally throws a pitch near a batter's head.
14. A man almost always arrives late to meet his girlfriend.
15. A woman kicks a vending machine that "ate" her money.
16. An undercover police officer punches a uniformed police officer in front of others in order to try to maintain his cover.
17. A participant in a psychology experiment administers an electric shock to another participant to signify a wrong response.
18. A student who gets a bad grade gives the teacher very low ratings on a course evaluation that will be seen by the teacher's superiors.
19. A teacher lowers a student's grade on a paper because it was submitted late.
20. A soldier shoots and kills a soldier from an opposing army.
21. A man kisses a woman without warning on their first date.
22. A teenager drives his parents' car recklessly.
23. A married person commits adultery.
24. A person withholds sex from his/her lover when angry at him/her.
25. A woman shoots and kills someone who has broken into her home.
26. A group of men stare and whistle at a woman as she walks past them.
27. A group of women stare and whistle at a man dancing at a dance club.
28. A boy plays too rough with his younger sister until she starts to cry.
29. A woman who feels that her ex-boyfriend is still in love with her says hurtful things to him to try to get him to move on with his life.
30. A baseball player curses loudly and smashes his bat after striking out.
31. Two brothers light a firecracker near their younger brother to scare him.
32. After encountering a mouse in their house, a couple sets up mouse traps in several rooms.
33. A teacher embarrasses a student who has not done her homework by making her sit in the corner of the room away from everyone else.
34. A person sells drugs to another person.
35. A prostitute whips and beats a man who has hired her to do this.

____	____	36.	A pregnant woman abuses alcohol.
____	____	37.	A driver flashes her high-beam lights because the car in front of her is going below the speed limit and won't let her pass.
____	____	38.	An artist creates a work that is designed to repulse most people.
____	____	39.	A man shoots a drug dealer because he sells drugs to children.
____	____	40.	An individual tells a joke that some might perceive to be racist or sexist.
____	____	41.	An auto mechanic hangs pictures of nude women in his garage.
____	____	42.	A drunk driver crashes into another car, killing two people.
____	____	43.	A motorist chooses not to pull over and help someone with car trouble.
____	____	44.	A man chooses not to call the police when he hears a woman scream near his apartment building.
____	____	45.	A person shoots in the back two men who attempted to mug him.
____	____	46.	A driver honks his horn at someone who has cut him off.
____	____	47.	A woman kills her husband who has been abusing and threatening her for years.
____	____	48.	A prison guard hits a prisoner who is slow to go back to his cell.
____	____	49.	A journalist reports a potentially scandalous story about unsubstantiated charges that a person made about an important political candidate.
____	____	50.	A governor cuts the budget for schools by 30% in order to lower taxes.

HANDOUT 11.3 VIOLENCE ON TELEVISION

In the columns below, keep track of the number of violent incidents and aggressive acts, both physical and verbal, shown in each program.

	Children's Cartoon	Prime-Time Program	Network News Program
Physical assaults that involve using a weapon or object			
Physical assaults that do not involve a weapon or object			
Verbal threats of harm			
Insults or derogatory remarks			
Violent deaths			
Accidents in which someone is hurt			

HANDOUT 11.4 RATINGS OF SIMILARITY OF PAIRED WORDS

Rate each of the following pairs of words based on how similar, related, or associated the pair seems to be:

1.   butcher :: alley

1	3	5
not similar at all	somewhat similar	extremely similar

2.   fight :: bottle

1	3	5
not similar at all	somewhat similar	extremely similar

3.   hatchet :: movie

1	3	5
not similar at all	somewhat similar	extremely similar

4.   kill :: police

1	3	5
not similar at all	somewhat similar	extremely similar

5.   wound :: rock

1	3	5
not similar at all	somewhat similar	extremely similar

6.   butcher :: bottle

1	3	5
not similar at all	somewhat similar	extremely similar

7.   fight :: movie

1	3	5
not similar at all	somewhat similar	extremely similar

8.   hatchet :: police

1	3	5
not similar at all	somewhat similar	extremely similar

9.   kill :: rock

1	3	5
not similar at all	somewhat similar	extremely similar

10.   wound :: alley

1	3	5
not similar at all	somewhat similar	extremely similar

11.   butcher :: movie

1	3	5
not similar at all	somewhat similar	extremely similar

12.   fight :: police

1	3	5
not similar at all	somewhat similar	extremely similar

13. hatchet :: rock

                    1   3   5
            not similar at all   somewhat similar   extremely similar
14. kill :: alley

                    1   3   5
            not similar at all   somewhat similar   extremely similar
15. wound :: bottle

                    1   3   5
            not similar at all   somewhat similar   extremely similar
16. butcher :: police

                    1   3   5
            not similar at all   somewhat similar   extremely similar
17. fight :: rock

                    1   3   5
            not similar at all   somewhat similar   extremely similar
18. hatchet :: alley

                    1   3   5
            not similar at all   somewhat similar   extremely similar
19. kill :: bottle

                    1   3   5
            not similar at all   somewhat similar   extremely similar
20. wound :: movie

                    1   3   5
            not similar at all   somewhat similar   extremely similar
21. butcher :: rock

                    1   3   5
            not similar at all   somewhat similar   extremely similar
22. fight :: alley

                    1   3   5
            not similar at all   somewhat similar   extremely similar
23. hatchet :: bottle

                    1   3   5
            not similar at all   somewhat similar   extremely similar
24. kill :: movie

                    1   3   5
            not similar at all   somewhat similar   extremely similar
25. wound :: police

                    1   3   5
            not similar at all   somewhat similar   extremely similar

HANDOUT 11.5

For each of the following scenarios, pick the response that comes closest to what you would do in a similar situation:

You're late for an appointment because you've been circling the block for the past twenty minutes looking for a parking spot. Then you spot one. You put your signal light on and position yourself two cars ahead to allow the person who is maneuvering out enough room. Then, as soon as she pulls out, and you get ready to back in, another car comes from down the street and pulls right into the spot. You tell the driver that you were there first, but he laughs at you and proceeds to walk out of his car. What do you do?

Nothing; look for another spot.

Mutter some choice words under your breath and proceed to look for another spot.

Curse the driver out loud.

Wait till the driver leaves and do some damage to the car.

Punch the driver.

You're standing in a long line for two hours waiting for the box office to open so you could get concert tickets for your favorite rock group. The group's tour was supposed to have been sold out, but yesterday they announced that one additional performance was scheduled. You hope you'll be able to get two tickets. Out of nowhere, comes an individual who pushes his way into the line right in front of you and says, "I was here earlier. I had to go and now I'm back." You tell the person to get on the end of the line but the person refuses. What do you do?

You do nothing.

Soundlessly mutter a few choice words about the person.

Call the person a liar and other things out loud.

'Accidentally' shove into the person a few times.

Hit the person until the person leaves the spot.

You're sitting in the cafeteria, having lunch. Your stuff is on the table in front of you. You have a couple of books and a social psychology paper that you've worked on diligently for the past two weeks. Today's the due date, but that's okay, because you're prepared to hand it in right after lunch. Two people whom you don't know begin to argue. In the midst of verbal accusations, one picks up a full paper cup and hurls it in the direction of the other person. That person ducks and orange soda spills all over your social psychology paper and ruins it. What do you do?

You leave the cafeteria to locate your professor and explain what happened.

You silently curse the two persons who were fighting while you dry your books.

You scream obscenities at the person who threw the cup.

You pick up your drink and hurl it at the person who threw the cup.

You hit the person who threw the cup.

You and your date (someone you're in a serious relationship with) are at a party. Your date mingles with others for a while, then comes over, accuses you of cheating, and slaps your face. What do you do?

Calmly deny it.

Say, "We're through. I never want to see you again."

Use curse words.

Do nothing now but plan to ruin your date's reputation later.

Return the slap.

CHAPTER 12

Law

LEARNING OBJECTIVES: GUIDELINES FOR STUDY

You should be able to do each of the following by the conclusion of Chapter 12.

1. Identify the three stages of jury selection. Consider the role of intuition and scientific data in the process of jury selection. (*pp. 487-491*)

2. Consider the role of race in legal decision making. Discuss how and under what circumstances the race of a defendant and the racial composition of a jury can affect verdicts. (*pp. 491-492*)

3. Describe the purpose of death qualification and the controversy surrounding the effects of this process on trial verdicts. (*pp. 492-493*)

4. Describe the approaches used by police to extract confessions from suspects. Differentiate false confessions that result from compliance from those that result from internalization, and identify the conditions under which people are most likely to internalize false confessions. Discuss the difficulties that juries face when they try to evaluate a confession introduced into evidence at trial. (*pp. 494-498*)

5. Describe a polygraph, and identify the assumptions and potential problems underlying its use. (*pp. 498-499*)

6. Summarize the acquisition, storage, and retrieval stages of eyewitness testimony. Describe how these stages are susceptible to errors caused by factors such as arousal, the weapon-focus effect, the cross-race identification bias, misinformation, the suggestibility of young children, and lineup procedures. (*pp. 499-506*)

7. Explain the difficulties facing jurors as they try to distinguish credible from noncredible eyewitnesses. Summarize how experts may help jurors become more competent judges of eyewitnesses. (*pp. 506-509*)

8. Summarize the general effects of pretrial publicity and inadmissible evidence on jurors' perceptions of defendants. Identify the factors that contribute to the finding that judges' instructions often have little impact on jurors. (*pp. 509-512*)

9. Describe the jury deliberation process. Discuss the importance of a jury's first vote and explain the concept of the leniency bias. Describe factors that affect jury deliberation, including informational and normative influences, jury size, and the unanimous decision rule. (*pp. 513-517*)

10. Discuss how defendants are treated after being found guilty in a court of law. Define the sentencing disparity, and why it occurs. Summarize factors that may affect a convict's experience in prison. (*pp. 517-521*)

11. Differentiate between decision and process control and their effects on perceptions of justice. Contrast the adversarial and inquisitorial models of justice, and consider the role of culture in studying issues related to law and justice. (*pp. 521-524*)

DETAILED CHAPTER OUTLINE

I.   Jury Selection—Voir Dire and Peremptory Challenges
    A.   Trial Lawyers as Intuitive Psychologists
    B.   Scientific Jury Selection
    C.   Juries in Black and White: Does Race Matter?
    D.   Death Qualification

II.   The Courtroom Drama
    A.   Confession Evidence
        1.   Police interrogations: Social influence under pressure
        2.   The risk of false confessions
            a)   compliance
            b)   internalization
        3.   Confessions and the jury: An attributional dilemma
    B.   The Lie-Detector Test
    C.   Eyewitness Testimony
        1.   Acquisition
            a)   weapon-focus effect
            b)   cross-race identification bias
        2.   Storage
            a)   misinformation effect
            b)   children's memory
        3.   Retrieval
            a)   lineup construction
            b)   lineup instructions
            c)   lineup format
            d)   familiarity-induced biases
        4.   Courtroom testimony
        5.   The eyewitness expert
    D.   Nonevidentiary Influences
        1.   Pretrial publicity
        2.   Inadmissible testimony
    E.   The Judge's Instructions
        1.   Comprehension
        2.   Jury nullification

III.   Jury Deliberation
    A.   Leadership in the Jury Room
    B.   The Dynamics of Deliberation
        1.   Three stages
            a)   orientation
            b)   open conflict
            c)   reconciliation
        2.   Majority rules
        3.   Leniency bias
    C.   Jury Size: How Small Is Too Small?
    D.   Less-Than-Unanimous Verdicts

IV.   Posttrial: To Prison and Beyond
    A.   The Sentencing Process
        1.   Goals of sentencing
        2.   Sentencing disparity

            3.   The anchoring effect
            4.   The race bias
      B.   The Prison Experience
V.   Justice: A Matter of Procedure?
      A.   Decision Control and Process Control
      B.   Adversarial Model and Inquisitorial Model
      C.   Culture, Law, and Justice
VI.   Closing Statement

LECTURE AND DISCUSSION IDEAS

Idea 1.   Setting the Context: High-Profile Cases

Several very high-profile trials in recent years have raised issues relevant throughout Chapter 12. The two trials (criminal and civil) of O. J. Simpson; the Oklahoma City bombing trials of Timothy McVeigh and Terry Nichols; The DC sniper cases;; the trial of Scott Peterson, accused of murdering his pregnant wife and unborn son; the government cases against Martha Stewart—these are some of the high-profile cases that have focused much attention on the legal system in the United States in recent years. During the media hype surrounding these cases, hundreds of "talking heads" appeared before the television cameras to share their wisdom about the psychological issues concerning the defendants, the lawyers, the judges, the juries, the media, etc. Although some of these observations were valid and intelligent analyses consistent with the findings of empirical research, many more were misleading, wildly speculative, or just plain wrong. As you introduce the material in Chapter 12, begin by discussing some of these cases with your students and explain that by reading the material in Chapter 12 they may have more and better knowledge of the psychology of law than many of the so-called experts they've seen in the media coverage of these trials.

Each of these trials is rich with material relevant to the chapter. Jury selection, for example, was thought to play a critical role in all of these cases, perhaps most memorably in the O. J. Simpson case. Inadmissible evidence and testimony, the use of expert witnesses, and the use of video, audio, and computer technology—these were controversial issues in these various trials. Prejudice was an issue in the first Simpson trial; discuss the case in light of the research reported in Chapter 5 on stereotypes and prejudice. The content of the judges' instructions was scrutinized and debated in each of these trials; discuss the research concerning judges' instructions that is summarized in Chapter 12. Jurors sold their stories to tabloid magazines and news shows, cashing in on the intense curiosity of the public who wanted to know what went on during deliberations; discuss the practical, legal, and ethical concerns that this phenomenon raises.

To help with discussion, consider having the students read popular accounts of some of these cases; there is no shortage of magazine and newspaper articles summarizing these cases from a number of different angles and points in time.

Idea 2.   Ethical Considerations of Scientific Jury Selection

Discuss the ethical considerations of scientific jury selection, some of which are raised in Chapter 12. For example, should psychologists involved in jury selection be required to provide their findings to both sides? Why are psychologists employed primarily by the defense, and does this affect their impartiality? Should all juries, not just juries in cases in which a lot of money can be spent by one or the other side, be selected through scientific means? Should peremptory challenges be abolished so that lawyers cannot have too much control over what kind of jury is selected (e.g., the racial or gender composition of the jury)?

Students should have a wide range of opinions on these issues. Discuss the controversies concerning jury selection in the high-profile cases mentioned above. For example, the original Rodney King case involved an all-White jury—selected from a politically conservative, pro-police community—and four defendants who were White police officers. In the O. J. Simpson murder trial, in which the defendant was African-American and the defense team argued that racist police officers framed the defendant, the jury was selected from a community that was largely suspicious of the police, and the jury that decided the case consisted predominantly of African-Americans.

William Kennedy Smith (accused of rape in 1991) and O. J. Simpson had a number of very high-priced, famous lawyers on their sides (indeed, Simpson had such a powerful group of lawyers that they were called "The Dream Team"), and both were acquitted of the crimes of which they had been charged. Many argue that cases such as these illustrate how biased the legal system can be in favor of wealthy clients who can afford the kind of counsel that gives them a much better chance of winning their case. The ability to afford scientific jury selection is one of the ways in which wealthy clients may get an edge. Discuss this issue with the students, and ask them for their opinions about the ethical implications of this, and how they think the system should be run.

In addition to discussing the ethical considerations, also discuss when and how scientific jury selection is effective for the client who uses it. Contrast scientific jury selection with some of the less valid techniques used by many very high-priced jury consultants, such as looking at the body language, hair style, and jewelry of prospective jurors.

Idea 3.   Rape Myths and Rape Shield Laws

Several of the most high-profile cases in recent years have involved charges of rape or sexual assault. These cases raise some particularly sensitive issues that could be the focus of a serious class discussion.

Discuss the issue of rape myths and how and why jurors' attitudes about rape myths are likely to predict their verdicts in cases involving rape. Refer to the rape myth acceptance scale discussed in Activity 4 of Chapter 11 in this *Instructor's Resource Manual* (the scale can be found in Handout 11.4a in that chapter). Discuss whether individual differences in acceptance of these myths seemed to play a role in the Kennedy Smith and the Tyson trials. (In those trials, a great deal of discussion centered around whether the women were implicitly giving consent to sex by being with these men in the settings involved; for example, many defended Tyson by saying that the woman was "asking for it" by going to his hotel room so very late at night.)

Discuss where these myths come from, and how the prosecution and defense may try to use these in one way or the other. For example, how might the prosecution in a rape trial attempt to convince jurors that many of their attitudes about rape are untrue and dangerous? Does the defense ever try to implicitly encourage jurors to rely on their rape myths when examining the evidence?

In addition to the issue of rape myths, discuss rape shield laws. These are statutes used in many states that restrict the kinds of personal questions lawyers can ask rape victims who take the witness stand. This kind of restriction played a crucial role in the sexual assault trial of sportscaster Marv Albert. In the Kobe Bryant case, however, the accuser was required to give three hours of closed-door testimony about her sexual history, despite Colorado's tough rape-shield laws. What kinds of questions should be permitted and what kinds should be prohibited in cases involving rape or sexual assault? Are these laws fair? One related issue concerns protecting the anonymity of the person who alleges to have been raped. Some members of the media protect the anonymity of this person (e.g., you could refer to, or show videotape of, the infamous "blue dot" that obscured the face of the woman who accused Kennedy Smith of rape), whereas a few chose to reveal the person's name. Should the media be encouraged, or required, to protect this person's anonymity? If so, should the accused have this same right? For example, people accused falsely of rape may have their reputations ruined, even if they are eventually acquitted. Should they, therefore, be left anonymous until the conclusion of the trial?

Although rape shield laws may protect the accuser in the court, the person who accuses another of rape is often put on "trial" in a more public way through the media. For example, Kobe Bryant's accuser received hundreds of death threats and thousands of obscene messages. Similarly, the life of the accused is no longer private, and information that would not be admissible in court becomes known by the general public outside the court. What effects does this information have on the trials? What responsibilities should the media have concerning these issues? This issue is raised again concerning pretrial publicity in Lecture and Discussion Idea 13 of this chapter.

Idea 4.   Death Qualification

Discuss the issue of death qualification in capital cases. Summarize the issues raised by social psychological research about how death-qualified juries differ from other juries. Discuss the implications of these differences. Assign Ellsworth's (1985) *Psychology Today* article, "Juries on trial," to help produce discussion about these issues. Ellsworth summarizes the relevant research, including findings that death-qualified juries not only tend to be more punitive but also are more likely to reject due-process considerations and less likely to include African-Americans and women.

Discuss why the U.S. Supreme Court rejected the American Psychological Association's argument that death-qualified juries are biased. Summarize the contrasting points made by Ellsworth (1991) and Elliott (1991) about whether the Supreme Court should have been persuaded by the empirical evidence presented by the American Psychological Association. This is a controversial and psychologically interesting topic that should generate some good debate and discussion among students.

Elliott, R. (1991). Social science data and the APA: The Lockhart brief as a case in point. Law and Human Behavior, 15, 59-76.

Ellsworth, P. C. (1985, July). Juries on trial. Psychology Today, 44-46.

Ellsworth, P. C. (1991). To tell what we know or wait for Godot? Law and Human Behavior, 15, 77-90.

Idea 5.   Capital Punishment

In addition to the issue of death qualification, the issue of the death penalty itself is an important and controversial issue about which many people feel quite strongly. Many argue that capital punishment is barbaric and is used in a discriminatory manner (e.g., people who kill Whites are more likely to get the death penalty than are people who kill others); moreover, many argue that the death penalty is not an effective deterrent against murder and is more expensive than is keeping murderers in prison for life (primarily due to the costs of appeals in capital punishment cases). On the other hand, others argue that capital punishment sends the important message that the community takes violent crime very seriously and will punish it severely, that it is the only sure way to keep convicted violent criminals off the streets, that it is impossible to determine its value as a deterrent because there have been too few executions to be able to judge their effects reliably, and that it can help the victims and/or their families recover from their ordeal. Have the students discuss and debate these issues. After some discussion, ask the students to consider what role social psychologists can and should play in this debate. What kinds of studies should be conducted to examine some of these issues? How do processes and models discussed in other chapters of the textbook relate to this issue (e.g., social learning theory of aggression in Chapter 11).

Ellsworth and Ross (1983) and Lord and his colleagues (1994) have published articles that raise some important issues about opinion polls concerning attitudes toward capital punishment and how these attitudes correspond to jurors' actual decisions. These articles report results of surveys that indicate that a majority of Americans say that they are in favor of the death penalty for particular kinds of crimes (and many of these individuals advocate that the death penalty be mandatory for these crimes). However, these studies suggest that if these proponents of capital punishment are put in a situation in which they learn some irrelevant but humanizing and non-stereotypic information about a particular convicted murderer, they become less likely to recommend the death penalty for this person. That is, even if people say in the abstract that the death penalty should be automatic for particular kinds of crimes, when faced with a real individual who may deviate from their images of what a murderer should be like, they may recommend a lesser sentence. The authors suggest, therefore, that the results reported from opinion polls may be misleading somewhat in that they reflect, in part, symbolic attitudes rather than real attitudes. Consider assigning or summarizing either or both of these articles.

Ellsworth, P. C., & Ross, L. (1983). Public opinion and capital punishment: A close examination of the views of abolitionists and retentionists. Crime and Delinquency, 29, 116-169.

Lord, C. G., Desforges, D. M., Fein, S., Pugh, M. A., & Lepper, M. (1994). Typicality effects in attitudes toward social policies: A concept-mapping approach. Journal of Personality and Social Psychology, 66, 658-673.

Idea 6.   Court Appearance

Whether the defendant appears to be innocent or guilty in the eyes of a jury depends on more than just the evidence of the case. Many studies have shown that appearance also matters. In one study (Stewart, 1980), for example, attractive looking people who were found guilty received more lenient sentences than less attractive people.

The physical attractiveness of a defendant affects trial outcomes in civil matters as well. In one classic study (Stephan & Tully, 1977), when college students were given case summaries with either a photo of an attractive plaintiff or an unattractive plaintiff attached, they were more likely to find in favor of and to award larger monetary sums to the attractive plaintiff.

Ask your students to explain why it is that good looking people are judged more favorably in court. One explanation offered by social psychologists involves the "halo effect," the phenomenon whereby what is beautiful is also considered to be good. Conversely, the opposite, or "horns effect," whereby the unattractive is seen as bad, also affects trial outcomes. And since first impressions are important and are largely based on appearances, looks significantly impact jurors' initial judgments as to defendants' culpability.

But attractiveness is not the only quality that is equated with innocence. Jurors are also swayed by how contrite and sincere defendants appear to be. One study (Antonio, 2006) found that when defendants who were facing the death penalty appeared to be emotionally involved during their trials, they were judged to be sincere and regretful and were more likely to get a life sentence. On the other hand, those who appeared to be emotionally uninvolved or bored during their trials were more likely to receive the death penalty.

Clothing also makes a difference. In a Psychology Today article (Paul, 1997), titled *Judging by Appearances*, the author says that the old advice that lawyers gave clients was to wear to court what they would wear to church. These days, however, in a more secular society, clients are advised to wear what they would to a business meeting. Such executive attire connotes a person who works for a living, someone who's not too rich but who is gainfully employed. It's also a disguise for a complicated individuality. The business suit says: "I'm just like every other working person."

Because what the defendant wears in court sends a message to the jury that can be interpreted favorably or unfavorably with regard to culpability, clothing decisions carry a lot of weight. Increasingly, jury consultants in high-profile cases are called on to counsel clients on what to wear to court. Before the O. J. Simpson trial began, there was a press release to the effect that a jury consultant prescribed the suit, shirt, and tie that Simpson would wear to court each day. Simpson was instructed to wear solid-white or light blue shirts, which are intended to convey an understated, humble look. His shirts sported a preacher collar, which gently curves inward around the tie and supposedly makes the wearer appear to be more virtuous. The consultant was apparently not specific enough about the suits, however. Alan Dershowitz (Zinczenko, 1996), one of Simpson's lawyers, recounts that on the first day of the trial, he looked at his client and was appalled to see that he was wearing a $1,000 suit (in front of a jury that makes a thousand dollars a month at most). He recommended that henceforth Simpson wear less expensive suits. Pricey suits, he said, put the jury in a situation where they don't relate to the defendant as an equal. Dershowitz also taboos the wearing of accessories, such as necklaces, bracelets, lapel stickers, handkerchiefs, and expensive watches to court for all his clients. He believes that all scream for attention and make the defendant appear to be different from the jurors who are judging him. The idea is to wear something with neutral associations, to be homogenized to look like everyone else. Dershowitz, himself, says that he wears a $30 calculator watch in court.

Some defendants in recent high-profile cases have been criticized in the media for what they chose to wear to court (Puente, 2004). Martha Stewart, for example, who attended her trial in the prescribed business suits, was carrying, contrary to advice, an extremely expensive bag. One *Washington Post* columnist wrote that "…it (the bag) may lead people on the jury to assume the worst: that Stewart is an arrogant woman who thinks she's above the law." Kobe Bryant appeared in a pretrial hearing without a necktie. His continued failure to wear one, warned one paper, could be interpreted by a jury as arrogant disrespect for the legal system.

Antonio, M.E. (2006). Arbitrariness and the death penalty: How the defendant's appearance during trial influences capital jurors' punishment decision. Behavioral Sciences and the Law, 24, 215-234.

Paul, A. M. (Nov./Dec., 1997). Judging by appearances. Psychology Today, 30, 20.

Puente, M. (Jan. 30, 2004). Fashions make their opening statements. USA Today.

Stephan, C. & Tully, J.C. (1977). The influence of physical attractiveness of a plaintiff on the decisions of simulated jurors. The Journal of Social Psychology, 101, 149-150.

Stewart, J. E. (1980). Defendant's attractiveness as a factor in the outcome of criminal trials: An observational study. The attraction-leniency effect in the courtroom. Journal of Applied Social Psychology, 10, 348-361.

Zinczenko, D. (Sep, 1996). How to dress for any occasion. Men's Health, 11, 136-144.

Idea 7.   Confessions

The issue of police confessions is a particularly fascinating one from a social psychological perspective. What techniques of conformity, compliance, obedience, and persuasion do the police use to produce confessions?

How often are the extracted confessions false? In December of 2002, the five teens that confessed in the rape and assault of the Central Park jogger had their convictions reversed when another prisoner confessed to the crime. A month after the charges were vacated, the police admitted that even that confession might have been false.

In January 2003, Governor George Ryan of Illinois commuted the sentences of 150 inmates on death row to life in prison due to concerns about false confessions. In a review of murder cases of the last ten years, the state found 247 confessions that were judged as suspect.

Why would anyone confess to a crime that he or she did not commit? In an article in *Psychology Today* (Perina, 2003), Saul Kassin, a co-author of the textbook, lists some possible explanations. Suspects with low IQ's are particularly likely to be vulnerable to police interrogations and to misunderstand the consequences of confessing. They might believe that by doing so, the police will be lenient and allow them to go home. Others who might falsely confess are suspects with suggestible, compliant, or anxious personalities and drug addicts or alcoholics. All can be made to believe in their own guilt.

How do individuals come to internalize false confessions that they gave? Discuss the tactics that police use to produce confessions (see Table 12.2). Why do they work? How ethical are they? Should these tactics be illegal? If so, why?

If students are very quick to attack these strategies, ask them to imagine that they or a loved one was a victim of a terrible crime, and that there is good but not good enough evidence pointing to a particular suspect—would they be upset if the police tried to trick the suspect into confessing?

Consider assigning textbook co-author Saul Kassin's (1997) article, which reviews the literature concerning confession evidence. Also, *Dateline NBC* did a special program on police interrogations and false confessions (see Multimedia Resources below).

Kassin, S. M. (1997). The psychology of confession evidence. American Psychologist, 52, 221-233.

Perina, A. (2003). I confess. Psychology Today, 36, 11-12.

Idea 8.   The Latest in Lie Detetction

You might wish to elaborate on the text's brief discussion of the latest advances in lie detection. An article in Scientific American Mind (Metzinger, 2006) features some of the new inventions that are currently being tested.

The idea behind this new generation of lie detector technology is that when a person tells a lie, he is consciously doing so and therefore leaving a neurological record in the brain. One technique, the development of which is being funded by the FBI and CIA, is called brain fingerprinting. It records brain waves on an electroencephalogram (EEC). The suspect who wears a helmet with electrodes is shown something which is familiar (like the photo of a crime scene). There is a specific brain wave known as P300 that forms whenever we recognize something that we have seen before. If the person lies and says he was not at the crime scene, the presence of a P300 wave will indicate that the crime scene is familiar which indicates that he is not telling the truth.

Critics of this technique assert that anxiety, alcohol, and drug use can affect the formation of P300 waves as well. They also note that if one aspect of the crime scene is familiar, like the brand of sneakers worn by the victim, it could give rise to a false positive. In spite of that, tests of the device are currently under way and it has already been used (in Iowa, in 2003) to exonerate a man who had been convicted of murder and who served 25 years in prison.

A second novel technique called the "guilty knowledge test" uses magnetic resonance imaging (MRI). According to its inventor, deliberate lying shows up in the anterior cingulated gyrus and the prefrontal cortex, areas of the brain that are associated with conflict. One drawback to this method is that it requires a cooperative subject who would remain absolutely still inside the scanner. Another is that simply knowing that the person is conflicted does not necessarily mean that he is lying; he may just be conflicted about whether or not to lie.

A third device, currently under development, consists of a headband that sends near-infrared light into the skull and captures its reflection. Sensors are able to detect changes in the prefrontal cortex, which signify that decision making is taking place, as when a person decides to tell a lie.

The fourth apparatus is a heat-sensing camera that detects a rush of blood to the face, especially around the eyes, that occurs when a person tells a lie. This technique has the advantage of being non-invasive, quick, and simple enough for use with a large number of people, as in airline screening. The accuracy of the procedure is still unclear.

Finally, the fifth new form of lie detector is a device that is able to read microexpressions, tiny facial movements that cannot be deliberately controlled. It is being developed by the psychologist Paul Ekman who says he has no interest in the device being used for judicial purposes because it is not 100 percent accurate.

One problem inherent in all of these new devices is that the contents of memory change over time, so that a person might have a false memory without deliberately trying to lie. Another problem is that some people, (e.g., mentally retarded individuals or drug addicts) are not able to store memories accurately.

Ask students how they feel about having someone read their own brainwaves. Do they think that the contents of one's brain should remain private and off limits to law enforcement? If the devices are approved and become highly reliable, can they be put to other uses? For example, what if they were available for sale to the public, would your students consider using them? If yes, under what circumstances? Should employers be allowed to implement them in job interviews? Would it be beneficial to read the minds of candidates for political office?

Metzinger, T. (2006). Exposing Lies. <u>Scientific American Mind,</u> <u>17</u>, 5, 32-37.

Idea 9.   Eyewitness Testimony

Eyewitness testimony often plays the most critical role in a trial, and yet people have strong misconceptions about it. Discuss the issues raised in Chapter 12 about the nature of memory and the biases to which eyewitnesses' memories are vulnerable. Contrast the acquisition stage, storage stage, and retrieval stage. Explain how the presence of weapons can interfere with accurate acquisition, and how this weapon-focus effect runs counter to many jurors' intuitions about the accuracy of an eyewitness who saw a weapon. Ask the students to provide reasons for why there is a cross-race identification bias.

Discuss the controversial issue of reconstructive memory, and of the misinformation effect (see Lecture and Discussion Idea 10 to follow). Discuss also the difficult issues concerning children's testimony. How can social psychologists contribute to this debate and help design fair and reliable ways of asking questions of eyewitnesses—particularly of children?

If the students have not yet read Chapter 12, ask them to describe what they imagine a typical lineup would be like, and what factors should increase or decrease the validity of these lineups. Then review the results of research concerning lineups. Discuss issues of lineup construction, the instructions used, the format employed, and familiarity-induced biases. See Activity 3 below for an exercise concerning lineups.

A particularly interesting point to discuss concerns how people's intuitions about eyewitness testimony can lead them to make inaccurate inferences about the validity of such testimony. People assume that the more confident a witness appears to be, the more accurate the witness's testimony is likely to be. Research has shown, however, that witnesses' confidence does not reliably predict their accuracy. Ask your students to discuss the factors that may explain this surprising finding.

Idea 10.   Reconstructive Memory

This is a very controversial issue that touches on a number of important social psychological issues, as well as on issues of cognitive, clinical, and perhaps developmental psychology. Assign and/or summarize some of Loftus's work (e.g., Loftus, 1979, 1993). Explain the debate concerning whether postevent information actually changes a witness's memory for an event or whether the memory remains intact but is not retrieved due to the interference of biasing information. That is, has the *storage* been altered, or is there simply an obstacle temporarily interfering with an individual's ability to *retrieve* what is in storage?

A very provocative and controversial issue that you might choose to discuss is how therapists, counselors, police detectives, and others may—intentionally or not—use their power and social influence to change the beliefs or behaviors of vulnerable individuals in subtle but very powerful ways, possibly to the point where they believe that they have particular psychopathologies or to the point where they develop false memories. This is a very controversial and sensitive issue that you should handle with great care, but it raises some fascinating questions about eyewitness memory, the misinformation effect, and confessions (as well as about issues in other chapters of the textbook, such as conformity). Consider assigning or summarizing Loftus's (1993) article, "The reality of repressed memories," which argues that most (and perhaps all) "recovered" memories (i.e., memories of events that allegedly were repressed from consciousness and are then recalled many years after the events in question, either through therapy or by exposure to some triggering cue or event) are not real memories but are rather constructed at the time of "recall" and often stem from the suggestions made by a therapist or other people. This article also raises the issue about the statute of limitations for crimes that allegedly had been committed many years ago but that had just recently been remembered or recovered. Along with the article, assign the commentaries that follow the article. All of these issues can be included in an interesting and informative discussion.

There are some Internet sites that speak to these issues from both sides of the debate. See Multimedia Resources below.

Loftus, E. F. (1979). Eyewitness testimony. Cambridge, MA: Harvard University Press.

Loftus, E. (1993). The reality of repressed memories. American Psychologist, 48(5), 518-537.

Idea 11.   U.S. Supreme Court Guidelines for Eyewitness-Identification Evidence

Present the U.S. Supreme Court's legal standards, which define five conditions to be considered in the evaluation of eyewitness-identification evidence. These guidelines, specified in *Neil v. Biggers* (1972, 409 U.S. 188, 93 S. Ct. 375, 34 L. Ed. 2d 401), are: (1) the opportunity for the witness to view the criminal at the time of the crime, (2) the length of time between the crime and the identification, (3) the level of certainty demonstrated by the witness at the identification, (4) the witness's degree of attention during the crime, and (5) the accuracy of the witness's prior description of the criminal. As an exercise for the students to apply their knowledge of the three stages of memory, have the students explain how these guidelines relate to the three stages of memory. (Acquisition involves the opportunity to view [guideline 1] and the witness's degree of attention [guideline 4]; storage involves the length of time between crime and identification [guideline 2]; and retrieval involves the level of certainty [guideline 3] and accuracy of prior description [guideline 5].) Ask the students to assess the validity of each guideline.

Idea 12.   Cameras in the Court

Court TV was launched in 1991 and became wildly popular during the O. J. Simpson trial in 1995. After Judge Ito's rulings and the antics of O. J. Simpson's defense lawyers were widely criticized, some judges and lawyers began thinking that maybe cameras in the courtroom may not be to their advantage. Many judges have since limited camera access in their trials, for example, permitting them only during opening and closing statements, when their own participation is minimal.

Ask students to discuss what they think the founding fathers might have said about cameras in the courtroom. Did they intend trials to be public or private affairs? Does the public have a right to know that criminals are being punished and that defendants' rights are being respected? Is there a difference between allowing a newspaper reporter to follow the proceedings of a trial versus allowing a camera to film them for television? If a person is accused of a crime, is having her name in a newspaper comparable to having her face appearing on millions of television screens? Do cameras in court constitute a violation of privacy?

Could cameras affect the behavior of witnesses? Is it possible that cameras might intimidate some people who would then refuse to testify?

What might be the repercussions of having cameras in the jury room? An article in Time Magazine (2002) reported on PBS's Frontline's filming of the jury deliberations in the trial of a 17-year-old who was facing the death penalty. The article lists the pros and cons of such filming as follows:

Pros:

1.   Accountability: if jurors know they are being watched, they might act more responsibly.

2.   Transparency: a public record of what goes on in the jury room would document misconduct.

3.   Civic education: juries are empowered to sentence people to death but Americans know very little about the institution.

Cons:

1.   Privacy: having an audience might distract the jurors from doing their job.

2.   Fairness: some jurors will refuse to serve because of cameras, which will skew the selection. Others will be wary of taking an unpopular stand if they know they're being watched. Inarticulate individuals or those who lack confidence may be reluctant to speak.

3.   Tradition: the jury has always deliberated in private. The system works most of the time and there is no need to tamper with it.

Labi, N. & Fowler, D. (12/9/2002). Cameras? Jury's still out. Time, 160, 24, 66.

Idea 13.   Pretrial Publicity

Ask the class why pretrial publicity typically is biased in favor of the prosecution, and why in many particularly high-profile cases it may be biased in favor of the defense. (The answer is that the former is due to the access to the media that the police and the district attorney's office have, and the latter is due to the amount of fame, money, power, and resources that some high-profile clients have relative to the prosecution.) Discuss how pretrial publicity can affect a trial. What steps can be taken to reduce these effects?

Assign the article by Dexter and colleagues (1992) that is included in *Readings in Social Psychology: The Art and Science of Research*, the book of readings that is available with the textbook. This article, along with other research discussed in Chapter 12 of the textbook, illustrates that despite the fact that attorneys and judges are confident that through the jury selection process they can choose a jury that has not been biased by pretrial publicity, the voir dire often is not successful in eliminating these biases.

Discuss the potential role of pretrial publicity in the high-profile cases mentioned in Lecture and Discussion Idea 1 above, such as the O. J. Simpson trial. See an article by Fein et al. (1997) that discusses pretrial publicity in the Simpson trial.

Dexter, H. R., Cutler, B. L., Moran, G. (1992). A test of voir dire as a remedy for the prejudicial effects of pretrial publicity. Journal of Applied Social Psychology, 22, 819-832.

Fein, S., Morgan, S. J., Norton, M. I., & Sommers, S. R. (1997). Hype and suspicion: Effects of pretrial publicity, race, and suspicion on jurors' verdicts. Journal of Social Issues, 53, 487-502.

Idea 14.   Inadmissible Testimony

Why are jurors influenced by inadmissible testimony that leaks into the trial? Discuss the various reasons with your students. Demonstrate the difficulty of thought suppression by asking them not to think about something, such as a white bear. Discuss the potential contrast between what is considered *legally* relevant and what is *psychologically* relevant to jurors. That is, whereas a piece of evidence may be considered legally irrelevant because of some technicality, that piece of evidence may be extremely relevant to a juror's sense of whether or not the defendant truly is guilty. Discuss how once such information is learned, processes such as those described in Chapter 4 of the textbook concerning the primacy effect, information integration, and confirmatory hypothesis testing may influence jurors' subsequent processing of information, making them even more affected by the original piece of inadmissible evidence. Discuss also the role of reactance in making jurors likely to use information that the judge commands them to disregard.

One kind of evidence that is likely to be inadmissible but that has the potential to influence the jury greatly concerns coerced confessions. Discuss the role of the fundamental attribution error in making jurors more likely to be influenced by confessions that have been coerced. Discuss the different reactions that jurors have to confessions that were produced by threat of punishment and to confessions that were produced by promises of leniency. Why are jurors less likely to discount the confessions in the latter case than in the former?

Idea 15.   Deliberation

Jury deliberation is a hotbed of social psychological processes. Discuss the roles of conformity (including normative and informational influence, majority vs. minority influence), persuasion, group processes (such as group polarization, groupthink) social comparison processes, stress, leadership, expectancy effects, and attribution. Consider dividing the class into groups and have each group apply one of these processes to the issue of jury deliberation.

One interesting point of discussion that you could raise is the issue of using non-unanimous verdicts. What are the pros and cons? Have the students comment on Table 12.7 from the textbook; it presents conflicting opinions on this issue written by two U.S. Supreme Court justices. Which side do the students endorse? Discuss also the issue of using juries with fewer than twelve people—what are the pros and cons?

The O. J. Simpson murder trial illustrated, among many other things, what an ordeal jurors can go through while being sequestered during a long trial. In the Simpson murder trial, despite the tremendous amount of evidence that was introduced into trial, the jurors deliberated for less than four hours before reaching their verdict. Some believe that this short deliberation was a result of the jurors being exhausted and disgusted with being sequestered for so long. During those many months, the jurors only spent a fraction of the time in court. Countless delays, hearings outside the presence of the jury, and frequent sidebars contributed to the inefficiency of the process. Can your students recommend any ways around such problems?

One potential, and rather radical, solution for some trials might be to videotape them, but in the absence of jurors (or media). Once the trial is completed, a jury can be selected. The jury would watch an edited videotape, with all "dead" time edited out. Moreover, any inadmissible evidence can be edited out— thereby successfully doing what the judges' instructions to the jury are supposed to do but rarely achieve. The editing of the tape would be supervised by the prosecution and the defense. Suggest this idea to the students and ask them to discuss the pros and cons of it. What suggestions can they propose for how leaks to the media can be avoided? How would watching a videotape of a trial affect jurors' processing of information relative to watching it live and in person?

Idea 16.   *Twelve Angry Men*: A Fictional Case Study of Jury Deliberation

Show the film *Twelve Angry Men* (see Multimedia Resources). This film can be used to help spark discussion of issues such as majority and minority influence in deliberations, the role of the foreperson, eyewitness testimony, defendant characteristics, less-than-unanimous verdicts, group polarization, etc. This film is described briefly in Chapter 12 in the textbook.

Idea 17.   Functions of Sentencing and Prison Reform

Ask the students what functions are served by sentencing a criminal to prison. Four functions that have been identified are incapacitation, deterrence, rehabilitation, and retribution. Ask the class which of these is most important. How do considerations of these different functions affect the severity of sentencing? What factors make one or more of these functions particularly likely to be relevant when a judge is about to sentence an individual? Discuss the success or failure of the current prison system in facilitating these functions.

Those who are calling for prison reform fall into two groups. The first group wants to strengthen the deterrence function of sentencing. Accordingly, its members call for changes to make prisons tougher. In answer to their demands, some states have reverted to chain gangs and gravel smashing. Others have established militaristic style "boot camp" prisons (mainly for young, nonviolent offenders) that stress discipline. And some have begun to build "Supermax" prisons, facilities where inmates spend all but three hours a week confined to solitary cells without reading material, opportunities for education, or social contact. Ask students if they believe that any of these efforts will be successful in deterring future crime. If not, do they at least serve the function of retribution? And how does retribution compensate the victim of a crime?

Conversely, the second group of prison reformers wants to strengthen the rehabilitation function of sentencing. Accordingly, its members call for liberalizing changes that will make prisons more humane. Taking that view to an extreme, an article in the New York Times Magazine (Holt, 2004) describes a movement called abolitionism that is attempting to totally eliminate the prison system in the future. For now, they're calling for the release of all non-violent prisoners. As for the violent criminals, they recognize the need to protect society from these individuals but want them kept in conditions that are humane and not degrading or punishing (incapacitation without retribution). The author cites research showing that the most violent criminals are unable to control their aggressive impulses because of damage to their prefrontal lobes, supporting the contention that punishing them is unjust.

You might ask students to envision a prison system where inmates live in dormitory-style rooms, address guards by first names, and get generous home leaves. Such a system exists in Finland, which used to have a severe penal system modeled after the Russians'. That was 30 years ago. Thanks to this liberal form of prison, they now have the smallest imprisonment rate in Europe. Do your students believe that the Finnish system would work in this country?

Finally, consider bringing to class some recent examples of trials concerning crimes ranging from driving while intoxicated to murder, and ask the students what sentences they would recommend, and why. Compare these sentences to the ones that were actually given in these trials (in which the defendant was found guilty).

Holt, J. (8/15/2004). Decarcerate? New York Times Magazine, 20.

Idea 18.   The Stanford University Prison Simulation

One of the most controversial studies ever conducted in social psychology was conducted by Philip Zimbardo and his colleagues (Haney et al., 1973; Zimbardo et al., 1973) as a simulation of a prison experience. A mock prison was established in the basement of the psychology department building at Stanford University, and a group of young men volunteered to participate in a two-week study of prison life. Each participant was randomly assigned to play the role of either a prisoner or guard. During the few days that this study ran (before the researchers terminated it due to ethical concerns), the young men assigned to the role of prison guards quickly became more and more hostile and sadistic, whereas the young men assigned to the role of prisoners became increasingly weak, compliant to the guards, and distrustful of each other.

Although this study can be used for discussions of conformity and obedience (Ch. 7) and of group dynamics (Ch. 8), consider using it in the context of discussing the prison experience. The film of this study (see Multimedia Resources below) is very powerful, and it should help generate a good discussion.

There are many points to discuss. In addition to discussing points about conformity, obedience, group polarization, and the power of roles, use this study as a context in which to discuss the functions of sentencing described in the Lecture and Discussion Idea presented above. What suggestions can the students make for prison reforms to avoid the kinds of outcomes observed in this study?

Any discussion of the Stanford Prison study should include a discussion of the ethics of the research. The study should have been terminated much sooner than it was in light of the behaviors and emotions displayed by the participants. Zimbardo makes the important point about how the researchers themselves got caught up in their own roles and failed to appreciate that their "prison" was not a prison but was part of a research study, thereby letting the study go on longer than it should have.

Haney, C., Banks, W. C., & Zimbardo, P. G. (1973). Interpersonal dynamics in a simulated prison. International Journal of Criminology and Penology, 1, 69-97.

Zimbardo, P. G., Banks, W. C., Haney, C., & Jaffe, D. (1973, April 8). The mind is a formidable jailer: A Pirandellian prison. New York Times Magazine, pp. 38-60.

Idea 19.   Do jails have to be violent settings?

Following the discussion of the Stanford prison experiment, ask your students whether they think that jails are inevitably violent because of the inmates' aggressive tendencies.

Writing in *Psychology Today (*1987), Richard Wener, William Frazier, and Jay Farbstein detail a recent trend in jail design called direct-supervision that appears to reduce violence. In jails that utilize the design and philosophy of direct-supervision, violent incidents are reduced by 30 to 90 percent and homosexual rape virtually disappears. The rates of vandalism and graffiti similarly drop dramatically.

One of the reasons for the drop in violence and destruction, according to the authors, is that the physical and social environment of an institution sets the behavioral norm. In a traditional jail, animalistic behavior is expected, as inmates are placed behind bars and the staff keeps a safe distance. Direct-supervision jails, on the other hand, send a message that good behavior is expected.

A second reason is that correction officers can head off violence before it goes too far because they're right on the scene. In direct-supervision jails, the correction officers are in direct contact with the inmates at all times. There is no enclosed booth. Officers spend their time in the living area of the inmates. Instead of just observing the inmates, they supervise and interact.

Complementing the direct-supervision arrangement is a design philosophy that sees inmates in a more humane light. It typically features a more open setting with multiple activity spaces, noninstitutional, softer colors and materials, and fixtures that can be moved and controlled by inmates. There is also more privacy afforded inmates, which allows them to cool off rather than respond violently to every provocation. The more normal feel of the place also encourages normal behavior.

Correction officers in these facilities require different training. Instead of brute strength, they need to acquire skills in interpersonal communication, counseling, and negotiation.

Wener, R., Frazier, W., and Farbstein, J. (June, 1987). Building better jails. Psychology Today, 40-49.

CLASSROOM ACTIVITIES

Activity 1. Age Bias in Sentencing

This activity is loosely based on a study by Bergeron and McKelvie (2004), which found that younger (20-year-old) and older (60-year-old) defendants were treated more leniently by mock juries than were middle-aged (40-year-old) defendants. The study confirmed previous archival and mock-jury studies, which have generally shown that people over the age of 53 and those under 23 are treated more leniently in criminal court than are middle-aged people, especially when it comes to some lesser crimes, such as shoplifting or burglary.

Handouts 12.1a–12.1c each describes three crime scenarios that involve shoplifting, burglary, and second degree murder, respectively. The only difference between the handouts is that the ages of the perpetrators vary. In Handout 12.1a, the shoplifter is 20 years old, the burglar is 60 years old, and the murderer is 40 years old. In Handout 12.1b, the shoplifter is 40 years old, the burglar is 20 years old, and the murderer is 60 years old. In Handout 12.1c, the shoplifter is 60 years old, the burglar is 40 years old, and the murderer is 20 years old.

Randomly distribute one of the three handouts to each member of the class. Ask students to read the scenarios, consider the facts in each case and make a sentencing decision (from 0–99 years). Collect the handouts. Solicit the help of three students to tabulate the mean sentencing period for each age group within each handout. Place the resulting means in a table as follows (the letter in the parenthesis signifies the corresponding handout):

	Shoplifting	Burglary	Murder
20-year-old	(a)	(b)	(c)
40-year-old	(b)	(c)	(a)
60-year-old	(c)	(a)	(b)

If your results conform to the results of the original study, then the mean number of years the younger and older persons will be sentenced to will be significantly lower than the mean number of years that the 40-year-olds will be sentenced to for both shoplifting and burglary. Age should not make a difference in the sentencing for murder.

According to the study's authors, even though age is not supposed to be a mitigating factor in sentencing, judges may see a younger person as more likely to be rehabilitated than a middle-aged one, therefore justifying greater leniency. There is also the perception that younger people are more likely to be harmed by prison. As for older people, they are generally viewed as being less blameworthy and less of a threat to society than are middle-aged individuals. When it comes to serious crimes that involve death, age effects are less likely because all sympathy is focused on the victim.

● *What if this bombs?* The only way that this might bomb is if there are no age effects at all. Any other pattern, even one that does not agree with the original study's findings, could lead to an interesting discussion. If age effects are absent, you might ask students to analyze why their results differed from those of the original study.

Bergeron, C. E. & McKelvie, S. J. (2004). Effects of defendant age on severity of punishment for different crimes. Journal of Social Psychology, 144, 1, 75-90.

Activity 2. Witnessing a Staged Event During Class

One activity that many instructors use concerns staging a sudden, dramatic event during the middle of class, and then asking the students to "testify" about what they witnessed.

Procedure. Arrange for a confederate (unknown to the students) to burst into your classroom in the middle of a lecture, mumble a few words, pull out a brightly colored water pistol (the water pistol is important because it draws attention away from the culprit's face, but be sure that its appearance is such that it is clear that it is a toy and not a weapon—you don't want to cause panic or trauma), steal something from you (such as your briefcase), and run out—all within just a few seconds.

You may consider having multiple confederates burst into class at the same time and do different things, to add to the confusion. When the shock and laughter have died down, inform the students that they are all witnesses to a crime and should not communicate with one another. Then distribute **Handout 12.2**—or create and distribute your own version of the handout modified to fit the event you will stage—to obtain students' recollections of the event. (Students should get multiple forms if multiple confederates were used.) Collect the forms, read the responses, and discuss how accurate and consistent the students' reports are. For this demonstration to be most effective, you should know in advance the confederate's (or each confederate's) height, weight, hand in which the water pistol will appear, clothing worn, what will be said, the order in which particular things will be done, and so on.

Consider <u>not</u> reporting the answers to the students for a few days. After this delay, have the students complete Handout 12.2 again (distribute new copies), and have them compare their current recollections with their initial recollections. How much change was there? Then report the true answers, and have the students examine how accurate they were at both times.

Finally, you may want to have students fill out the appropriate sections of another copy of Handout 12.2—this time describing someone whom they saw for a significantly longer period of time, such as a guest speaker from a previous week, or have them describe you (while you're not in the room) or a teaching assistant. Many students' observations are likely to be somewhat inaccurate even when describing a familiar person (see Activity 5).

Discussion. The disparities in students' descriptions are often amusing and quite surprising to them. Discuss the reasons for such disparity. Ask the students to indicate how confident they were in their recollections. Ask a few students who reported observations that were quite different from one another to discuss their conflicting observations, and ask them to see if they can infer who, if any, is most accurate.

Report the correct answers. Ask students who were very accurate and students who were not very accurate to explain how they made their observations. Ask the students whether or not their confidence predicted their accuracy very well. Discuss the results in the context of the issues raised in Chapter 12 about eyewitness memory (particularly relevant in this activity is the acquisition stage; if you introduce a delay between the event and recall, the storage and retrieval stages become relevant as well) and eyewitness testimony.

You might want to show a very engaging *Dateline NBC* program about eyewitness testimony (see Multimedia Resources) in the context of this activity—<u>after</u> the demonstration, but either during or after the discussion.

> ● *What if this bombs?* This activity is virtually bombproof. It should be a good way to introduce issues concerning eyewitness memory and testimony—whether or not the students' observations are very accurate. The only real potential for problems is if the students are upset by the incident. To reduce the chances of this happening, make sure that it is clear that the event is staged and safe; consider having one of the confederates come in wearing a clown suit and throwing candy (indeed, this should be quite distracting and make the students less accurate in their observations of other details). Also to minimize the chances of students being upset, you should not look frightened or concerned but rather should smile or laugh as the "crime" is taking place.

Activity 3. Lineups

You can use a version of Activity 2 to examine the issues relevant to lineups. Have a confederate who was seen doing something unusual in Activity 2 appear for one or a series of lineups, along with several "foils"—people who were <u>not</u> seen by the students.

<u>General Procedure</u>. Show the students one or more lineups. The lineup(s) should consist of a number of foils and, depending on the version(s) of the activity you choose to conduct, you may or may not include the true culprit in the lineup. Have the students take out a piece of paper and either write down "Don't Know" or write down the number of the confederate (from left to right) who was the culprit. Next to their response the students should indicate the degree to which they are confident that they are correct.

<u>Version 1</u>. The simplest way to do this activity is to have the confederate and several foils come into class, stand in the front of the room and face the students, have them turn to either side, and so on, as if they were in a real lineup. Explain to the students that they would not want to send an innocent person to jail so they should not identify any of the people in the lineup unless they are quite sure that he or she is the right one.

<u>Version 2</u>. If you have enough confederates, consider having two or three lineups, only one of which contains the true culprit. Before the first lineup is brought out, explain to the students that in any one lineup the true culprit may not be present.

<u>Version 3</u>. Another way to conduct this activity is to compare the accuracy of witness' identifications while varying factors that, according to the research reported in the textbook, can have important effects on lineup identifications. Divide your students into a number of groups. Call one group at a time into another room in which they will receive instructions and see the lineup.

One variable to manipulate is the <u>construction</u> of the lineups. Have some groups view a lineup containing the culprit along with foils who do not resemble the culprit at all, and have other groups view a lineup containing the culprit along with foils who do resemble the culprit to some extent (e.g., in height, weight, clothing).

Another variable concerns the <u>instructions</u> given to the students. Instruct some groups that the culprit is in the lineup, and instruct other groups that the culprit may or may not be present. Then present both groups with the same lineups consisting of nothing but foils—that is, the culprit should not be in the lineup. Do witnesses identify someone anyway?

Consider also trying to demonstrate a <u>familiarity-induced bias</u>. Have some groups examine pictures (which you should call "mugshots") of "suspects" before viewing a lineup. There should be at least a dozen pictures, and the students should not know any of the individuals in these pictures. The pictures you show should not include a picture of the culprit. After a delay, have these groups view a lineup consisting of nothing but foils—that is, the culprit should not be in the lineup. However, one (and only one) of the people whose pictures students had seen should be in the lineup. Have other groups of students view the same lineup, but these students should not be exposed previously to this person's picture. Are the students in the former condition more likely than those in the latter condition to misidentify this individual as the culprit?

Consider combining variables to find even stronger effects. For example, the familiarity-induced bias should be more likely to emerge if these students are given the instructions that the culprit is in the lineup.

<u>Discussion</u>. Show the class the true culprit (either live or via a picture). How accurate were the students? Determine whether students had correctly identified the culprit (a "hit"), incorrectly identified a foil (a "false alarm"), identified no one while in a condition in which the true culprit was in the lineup (a "miss"), or identified no one while in a condition in which the true culprit was not in the lineup

(a "correct rejection"). If you used Version 3 of this activity, compare the accuracy as a function of the various conditions used. Do the results illustrate how factors such as construction, instructions, and use of mugshots can influence witnesses' lineup identifications?

Compare and contrast the three stages of memory, and ask the class to explain what stages are implicated in this activity. Discuss the ethical and practical issues concerning how the police use lineup instructions, construction, format, and mugshots in ways that might increase the likelihood that a witness will identify a particular suspect as the culprit.

Consider assigning or summarizing the article by Wells and Lüüs (1990) that discusses the issue of the validity and fairness of lineups in terms of social psychological and methodological considerations. This framework clarifies why and how particular factors influence the validity of lineups. Discussing this reasoning also helps students practice and apply their critical thinking skills concerning methodological issues.

> ● *What if this bombs?* This activity should be successful in introducing issues concerning eyewitness memory and testimony—whether or not the students' observations are very accurate. If you used Version 3 of this activity and found no differences as a function of the manipulations, ask students to speculate about why this might be. What should come out of this discussion is that factors such as stress and the desire to cooperate with a real investigation probably make individuals in real lineup situations more vulnerable to these manipulations. Also, your ability to find confederates who could play foils was probably limited, and you therefore did not have the flexibility to construct lineups as you wanted (e.g., if the students tended to be quite accurate, this may reflect the fact that you didn't have enough foils or that they looked too different from the culprit).

Wells, G., & Lüüs, E. (1990). Police lineups as experiments: Social methodology as a framework for properly conducted lineups. Personality and Social Psychology Bulletin, 16, 106-117.

Activity 4. The Misinformation Effect

After viewing a crime, eyewitnesses may be exposed to post-event information that can alter their memory of the crime. This is the misinformation effect. Two potential sources of misleading information are biased questioning about the event and the testimony of a second eyewitness. This activity should demonstrate how each of those two factors can distort the memory of an event and thus result in the misinformation effect.

In **Handout 12.4a**, students are asked to imagine that they are working at an airport car-rental agency. They are then presented with descriptions of ten customers that they supposedly waited on that morning.

After students have read the handout, it is collected. You then distribute Handouts **12.4b**, **12.4c**, and **12.4d**, so that each third of the class receives a different handout. In all three handouts, the students learn that someone driving one of the agency's cars has robbed a bank, killing a security guard, and that the police need help in identifying the criminal. The three handouts differ as follows: Handout 12.4b asks the students to answer some open-ended questions about one of the customers. Handout 12.4c asks the students to answer questions about the same customer, but this time the questions are misleading. Handout 12.4d presents the students with the purported (erroneous) testimony of a co-worker, describing the same customer, and asks them to collaborate it.

After students have completed their handouts, describe the alleged perpetrator and compare the accuracy of the memory of those who received Handout 12.4b (no post-event information), Handout 12.4c (misleading questions), and Handout 12.4d (erroneous testimony of another witness).

🖤*What if this bombs?* The experiment might bomb in two ways. First, those in condition *c* (misleading information) and those in condition *d* (error-filled testimony of another) might do better than those in condition *a* (a memory task with no post-event information). Second, the accuracy rates across all three conditions might turn out to be similar, either all low or all high.

In either case, you might wish to elicit student explanations for the bombing. If the results show that the post-event information actually improved memory, the students in conditions *c* and *d* might volunteer that they suspected deception and automatically eliminated the given choices, which made their task easier. If overall accuracy was high (everyone did well in all three conditions) or too low (everyone did poorly), the students might attribute the results to the length of time allotted to visualize the suspects (too long or too short) or to the number of suspects involved (too few or too many).

Activity 5. Interrogating a Suspect

This activity is designed to illustrate some ways in which police might interrogate and try to extract confessions from suspects. Examples of this kind of interrogation can be found in many popular movies such as *L.A. Confidential* (1997) or in television shows (such as *NYPD Blue*, *Homicide*, and *The Wire*). In this activity, the students are placed into the roles of security officers, and a confederate is placed into the role of a suspect who is pressured to confess to a crime. The primary purpose of the activity is to see what kinds of strategies the students choose to use to try to elicit confessions, and to what extent these strategies are consistent with those used by the police. This activity can be conducted before or after the students have read Chapter 12, but it would be preferable to run it <u>before</u> they have read the chapter. Also, the activity may be too difficult to conduct in very large classes.

<u>Procedure</u>. Distribute copies of **Handout 12.5a** to the students. The handout gives the students some background information about their role. On this handout is space for a telephone number and times to call that number. Fill in this information before making copies of the handout. The phone number should be that of a male confederate who will play the role of a maintenance supervisor named MacKenzie whom the students suspect may have stolen car batteries. The times listed should be when he can be reached at that number for purposes of this activity. Be sure to tell the students how much time they have for the activity and where they should turn in their completed forms.

Depending on the size of your class, you can have the students work individually or in groups. The students are to call this number (and do not tell them whose number it is), identify themselves, and try to extract a confession from MacKenzie using whatever strategies they choose.

The confederate playing MacKenzie should be told to take note of the strategies used by the various students. **Handout 12.5b** includes some of the categories of strategies that may be used. The confederate should confess if he thinks that it clearly would be in his best interests. Our best advice about how the confederate should make this judgment is that he should imagine that for some reason he really can't remember if he stole the batteries, but that it wouldn't be beyond the realm of possibility. The confederate should not confess very quickly or easily, but he <u>should</u> confess to some of the first students or groups who call him so that word might get around among the students that it is possible to produce a confession.

Consider running a more ambitious version of this activity by manipulating the gender of the suspect (and, of course, the confederate). See if the strategies that students use differ as a function of the gender of the student and of the suspect.

<u>Discussion</u>. Compare the students' reports with the confederate's reports. To the extent that there are discrepancies, use the confederate's reports if he (or she) is confident in them.

Calculate the proportion of students using each of the various strategies (many students or groups will use more than one strategy). Calculate the proportions overall, and separately for men and women. If your students do this activity in groups, consider using same-sex groups if possible. Report which strategies were most likely to elicit confessions.

Explain that the primary purpose of the activity was to see what kinds of strategies the students chose to use to try to elicit confessions, and to what extent these strategies are consistent with those used by the police. Ask the students to discuss how they chose the strategies to use. Ask them to discuss these strategies from a social influence perspective and from an ethical perspective. Ask the confederate to report about his (or their) feelings and observations during the activity and relate them to the class. Discuss the issues raised about confessions in the textbook, including the types of strategies used by police. Discuss the issue of false confessions—both in terms of compliance and internalization. See the *Dateline NBC* video described in the Multimedia Resources.

> ●*What if this bombs?* This activity is virtually bombproof. Any pattern of data should be quite interesting and has the potential to lead to a good discussion. Students typically find this to be a fun, memorable, and informative activity. Although some students do concentrate too much on whether or not they were able to produce a confession, you should emphasize during the post-activity discussion that the point of the activity was to examine and discuss the strategies they used and to discuss what effects these strategies have in real-life situations, not whether they were able to produce a confession from your confederate.

Activity 6. Jury Selection: Voir Dire

According to the text, the first goal of lawyers in the voir dire portion of jury selection is to eliminate biased prospective jurors. A second goal is to eliminate those who are intuitively believed to be most likely to vote against them. To do that, the lawyers use their peremptory challenges. This activity presents students with the opportunity to play the roles of the lawyers in a voir dire.

There are three separate cases described in **Handouts 12.6a–f**. Students will be asked to represent both sides of each case. So, you will need to divide the students into six groups (a, b, c, d, e, and f). Groups a, c, and e (the recipients of **Handouts 12.6a, 12.6c**, and **12.6.e**) will represent the defense in jury selection. Groups b, d, and f will represent the other side. (They will receive **Handouts 12.6b, 12.6d,** and **12.6f**)

After completing the questions on their respective handouts, the groups representing both sides in each of the three cases can read their case and discuss their answers with the rest of the class.

> ●What if this bombs? This is very unlikely to bomb. Students will likely enjoy the activity because it allows them to exercise creative critical thinking. You might also consider extending the role playing potential of the activity by allowing the "lawyers" to use students who are not involved with their particular case as prospective jury members who actually have to answer the lawyers' questions.

Activity 7. Jury Deliberation

Have students read or watch a brief summary of a trial. This can be a trial transcript that you select from the literature, or an excerpt from a videotape from *Court TV* or some other source. Try to choose a trial in which there is some ambiguity about whether the defendant is guilty or innocent. Divide the class into six-person or twelve-person juries to deliberate for about fifteen minutes in an effort to reach a unanimous verdict. Have each jury choose a foreperson.

Students enjoy the experience of playing the role of jurors. This exercise generates lively discussion of how majorities try to persuade minorities. One way is that the majority may call for open, rather than secret, ballots, so that the pressure is placed on those whose votes do not concur with the majority opinion. You may also want to discuss the ways in which deliberation tends to produce a leniency bias; ask students why this occurs.

Discuss whether the deliberations seemed to follow the pattern of orientation, open conflict, and reconciliation. What happened in the deliberations that did not follow this pattern? How did the jurors choose forepersons? How often was the first juror who spoke chosen to be foreperson? Were the forepersons disproportionately likely to be male? What roles did the foreperson tend to play? Relative to the other jurors, did the foreperson have greater influence over the verdict?

Depending on the case you've chosen, discuss various aspects of the case. What evidence seemed to be particularly influential?

Alternative procedures. You might consider giving one-third of the juries a transcript that contains some testimony that is very powerful for the prosecution but that is ruled inadmissible (and the judge instructs the jury to disregard the information), another third the same transcript except that the inadmissible testimony is very powerful for the defense, and another third the same transcript except that the inadmissible testimony is not included. Determine the extent to which the inadmissible evidence influenced the students' deliberations or verdicts.

Also consider distributing the juror bias scale to the students (see previous activity) at some time before you conduct this activity, and then calculate the average juror bias score for the students in each jury. Then correlate these scores with the juries' verdicts. Were juries that were comprised of prosecution-leaning students more likely to convict than juries comprised of defense-leaning students?

♦*What if this bombs?* Students should be very interested in this activity, and it always has the potential to elicit a good discussion of the issues raised in Chapter 12, no matter what patterns of verdicts are found in the activity. If you included a manipulation of inadmissible evidence and it did not have any effect, discuss this with the students and ask the juries in the different conditions how they dealt with the information. Did it come up during deliberation? Did jurors want to bring it up but feel that they could not? Ask the students to explain why the effects of inadmissible evidence may be much greater in a real trial (e.g., the jurors care much more about whether or not the defendant committed the crime, the judge may elicit reactance, there is so much more evidence to sift through in a real trial that jurors may not realize the causes of their judgments, etc.). If you correlated the juror bias scores with the juries' verdicts and the correlation was very weak, examine the data to see if there was not enough variability either in the juror bias scores or the verdict. You may have chosen a trial, for example, about which the large majority of the students are in agreement, so this would not be a sensitive enough measure to detect differences as a function of juror bias. If so, explain that this illustrates that the evidence in a trial can overwhelm individual differences among jurors. In more ambiguous cases, however, these individual differences may be more likely to play a critical role.

Activity 8. Jury Size and Size of Awards in Civil Cases

This activity is partly based on a study by Davis, et al., (1997) that examined how the size of a jury affects the size of damage awards allocated by mock civil juries.

Divide the class into "jury" groups of 6 and 12. Ideally, there should be equal numbers of large and small jury groups. Any remaining individuals not assigned to groups should be instructed to work alone without discussing the cases with anyone else.

Distribute **Handout 12.8** to everyone in the class. The handout outlines four negligence case scenarios. Students are told that all four cases were decided in favor of the plaintiffs and it is up to them to award damages. Tell those who are working in groups that they need to discuss each case to reach a consensus of opinion on the amount to be awarded by their group. (You might set a specific time limit for each case, of say 3–5 minutes.)

When all the monetary amounts have been designated, review the data to see if the results conformed to those of the original study. In that study, the 12-person juries awarded the plaintiff less money than did the 6-person juries. Moreover, groups awarded less money than did individuals working alone.

> ●*What if this bombs?* It is possible that this activity will bomb, meaning that there will be no clear differences between amounts awarded by the large groups versus small groups or by groups versus individuals. In that case, introduce the findings of the original study and ask students to explain its results. It is also possible that the class results will be totally opposite to those of the original study, meaning that the larger juries will award more money than the smaller juries, who in turn will award more money than individuals working alone. In that case, tell the class that in the recent past larger juries did mete out bigger awards. This was explained in terms of larger groups experiencing more interaction relative to small groups, and group interaction increasing the salience of shared social norms. The social norm in this context is the "deep-pockets bias," which is the tendency of juries to award inordinately generous sums of money to ordinary citizens suing large corporations.
>
> That is no longer the case, however, as there was negative public reaction against some large, highly publicized awards in the past few years. Consequently, social trends have changed and juries have begun to scale back on the amounts awarded. Since larger jury groups are more attuned to current social trends, they are also presently expected to award less money relative to smaller jury groups. In class, however, because students are aware that they're not actually giving out monies, they might be less influenced by current social norms and instead revert back to the "deep-pockets bias."
>
> Another point to make if there are no clear differences, or if the results are contradictory, is that it is necessary to use a very large number of participants in order to properly study the effect of group size on group-level actions.

Davis, J. H., Au, W. T., Hulbert, L., Chen, X., & Zarnoth, P. (1997). Effects of group size and procedural influence on consensual judgments of quantity: The example of damage awards and mock civil juries. Journal of Personality and Social Psychology, 73, 4, 703-718.

Activity 9. Expert Testimony: Using Guest Speakers or Field Trips

The topic of social psychology and law is a great one to explore through field trips or guest speakers. Possible places to take field trips include the courthouse, the police department, a probation and parole center, and a local jail or correctional facility. For example, you can meet with a police sketch artist and have the students try to describe someone to the artist to make a composite sketch. Have someone administer a lie-detector test to some volunteer students. Ask the police officers or detectives to discuss the uses and challenges of these procedures. Guest speakers could discuss their experiences in the legal field. Invite a police officer, judge, private attorney, prosecutor, public defender, correctional officer, jury or trial consultant, or psychologist who often gives expert testimony in court.

What if this bombs? There is very little chance of this bombing. Students should find such speakers or trips to be very informative, and it can provide vivid, concrete examples of the issues raised in Chapter 12. To avoid disappointment, discuss in advance with your hosts or guests what the students will have read and what you hope the students will learn from the visit, and go over as much of the details as you can about what your guests or hosts will be saying and demonstrating so that you can help ensure that this will be a productive activity. If a speaker does not do a very good job anyway, enjoy the chance to take advantage of the contrast effect when you do your next lecture.

MULTIMEDIA RESOURCES

Video

Burden of Innocence. This PBS program explores what happened to five wrongfully convicted prisoners who were exonerated because of DNA evidence and were released from prison without psychological, social, or economic support. (2003, 60 min.) Available from Insight Media (800-233-9910).

Capital Punishment: An Evolving Standard. This DVD examines several issues surrounding capital punishment in the US. Among them are the Supreme Court's decision to abolish capital punishment for juvenile offenders, applications of international standards to US law, and the 8th constitutional amendment which protects against cruel and unusual punishment. (2005, 30 min.) Available from Insight Media (800-233-9910).

Criminally Insane. This video explores the world of a maximum-security institution for the criminally insane. (1999, 60 min) Available from Insight Media (800-233-9910).

Eyewitness Testimony. *Dateline NBC* ran a fascinating story on eyewitness testimony, and how easy it is to identify the wrong suspect. This program featured Professor Roy Malpass and included a staged "crime" during a lecture at Brooklyn Law School. (Aired on August 8, 1995.) Available from NBC (800-420-2626).

False Confessions. This *Dateline NBC* program examines the tactics that police sometimes use to extract confessions from suspects, and how these tactics can elicit false confessions from innocent people. (First aired on December 23, 1997.) Available from NBC (800-420-2626).

Fidelity of Report. This old black-and-white film begins with a 60-second vignette of a woman being robbed. The projector is stopped and a series of questions is asked of the students. (1946, 6 min.) Available from Pennsylvania State University, Audio-Visual Services, University Park, PA 16802 (800-826-0132).

Justice on Trial. Top authorities in criminal justice are interviewed about sentencing disparities. (1977, 49 min.) Available from CRM-McGraw-Hill Films, 110 Fifteenth Street, Del Mar, CA 92014 (619-453-5000).

Order in the Court. This DVD explains courtroom terminology and procedure, differentiates between adult and juvenile proceedings, discusses the pretrial process, indictment, pretrial release, bail, and arraignment, explores plea bargaining, direct examination, cross-examination, and rebuttal, and defines alibi, burden of proof, and reasonable doubt. (2001, 30 min.) Available from Insight Media (800-233-9910).

Prisons: Questioning the System. This set of videos features legal professionals, academics, and community service professionals debating the merits of a penal system that is seen by some as practical and essential, and by others as a misguided failure of humanity. (1999, 2 VHS cassettes- 30 min. each) Available from Insight Media (800-233-9910).

Quiet Rage: The Stanford Prison Experiment. This video documents the controversial Stanford Prison Simulation conducted by Philip Zimbardo and his colleagues. Zimbardo narrates this film, which includes chilling footage of the study, as well as fascinating follow-up interviews with some of the subjects. If you didn't use this video for Ch. 9 or Ch. 11, it would work very well with Ch. 12. (1992, 50 min.) Available from Philip Zimbardo, P.O. Box 2996, Stanford, CA 94309 (415-725-2417).

Rethinking the Death Penalty. This video traces the history of the death penalty in the US since 1935. (2000, 22 min.) Available from Insight Media (800-233-9910).

The Psychology of Criminal Behavior. This video examines criminal behavior and traces societal views on crime. It addresses biological theories, environmental and sociological factors, and other considerations. (2001, 25 min) Available from Insight Media (800-233-9910).

The Story of a Trial. This video follows two men from the time they are arrested through their arraignments and trials. It shows how the rules of criminal procedure work in practice and emphasizes the importance of due process. (1982, 22 min.) Available from Insight Media (800-233-9910).

The Trial of Bernhard Goetz. An American Playhouse presentation, this is a true-to-life drama about the trial of Bernhard Goetz, who was called New York City's "subway vigilante" in the 1980s. The trial raised issues of confession, self-defense, insanity, racism, pretrial publicity, sentencing disparity, etc. Goetz's confession and trial were restaged from 4,600 pages of court transcripts. The script is a verbatim representation of the trial. (1988, 135 min.) Available from Today Home Entertainment, Inc., 9200 West Sunset Boulevard, Penthouse 1, Los Angeles, CA 90069 (213-278-6490).

Twelve Angry Men. Jury deliberation is depicted in this classic film. Illustrates majority and, particularly, minority influence. Henry Fonda leads an impressive cast. (1957, 95 min.) Available from United Artists, 727 Seventh Avenue, New York, NY 10019.

Internet

And Justice for All? At this *Dateline NBC* site, students can listen in from the perspective of a lawyer who receives letters from young men who were sentenced to life in prison. The cases are real and students get to decide whether they believe the prisoners' stories or not. In addition, students get to find out if their decision was correct. The site can be visited at: http://www.thejusticeproject.org/press/popculture/television/dateline.html.

Eyewitness Identification Laboratory. At this site, which is run by the University of Northern Iowa, students can view a series of actual lineups that present problems of fairness. They can also access research on eyewitness memory and identification and face recognition. Visit this site at: http://www.uni.edu/psych/eyewitness.html.

Innocence Project. Innocence Project is a non-profit legal clinic affiliated with the Benjamin N. Cardozo Law School at Yeshiva University. It is dedicated to exonerating wrongfully convicted people through DNA testing. As of March 5, 2007, 195 people have been released through its efforts. Students can read their case profiles at: http://www.innocenceproject.org/

Ontario Centre for Religious Tolerance. This Web site contains an extensive summary of information and links to other sites concerning, among other things, issues relevant to discussions of reconstructive memory. Links to numerous sites concerning ritual abuse cases, including information about the Paul Ingram case and the McMartin preschool case (both of which are discussed briefly in Chapter 12) that may be relevant for discussions of the social psychology of confessions and of the controversy concerning the theory of reconstructive memory. Links are provided to a variety of sites with a range of opinions on these issues, such as the *False Memory Syndrome Foundation* (whose site contains numerous quotes and references from social and cognitive psychologists who often testify in court as expert witnesses) and the *Cult Awareness and Information Centre.* http://limestone.kosone.com/people/ocrt/ocrt_hp.htm

Computer Programs

Mac-a-Mug Pro (Macintosh); **Identi-Kit** (PC). These programs are used to produce high-quality facial composites. A seemingly infinite combination of features can be selected by eyewitnesses to develop composite sketches for use in eyewitness identification. No artistic ability is required to quickly and easily construct these composites. Warning: These are expensive packages (particularly the Identi-Kit). Mac-a-Mug Pro available from Shaherazam, P.O. Box 26731, Milwaukee, WI 53226 (414-442-7503). Identi-Kit available from Identi-Kit Co., Inc., 2100 Roosevelt Avenue, Springfield, MA 01101 (413-781-8300).

Conflict & Cooperation. (Version 2.0). A social game construction kit. Expanding on the classic prisoner's dilemma framework, this software allows students to author and then play out a wide variety of interactive decision-making scenarios constructed to represent political, business, or social situations in which participants vie for resource allocations. Instruction booklet included. Online help available. Although the kit may be more appropriate for use in the context of Chapter 11, it can be used here as an extension of a discussion of the Prisoner's Dilemma. (Windows) Available from Wisc Ware, Academic Computing Center, University of Wisconsin, 1210 W. Dayton Street, Madison, WI 53706.

HANDOUT 12.1a

Each of the following scenarios describes a crime for which the defendant has been found guilty. It is your job to read each case, consider the circumstances, and decide on the appropriate sentence.

1. Twenty-year-old Mark was apprehended in an electronics store by a guard who had seen him slip a small $400 camera into a coat pocket. When the suspect was searched, police also found that he had stolen a portable music player and a mobile phone.

Since Mark was found guilty of shoplifting, I recommend sentencing him to serve _____ years in prison. (from 0–99)

2. Sixty-year-old Simon was caught burglarizing the apartment of an opera star. After questioning, Simon admitted to burglarizing the homes of several show-biz performers, in each case planning the burglary by reading the paper, noting the star's schedule, and paying a visit to the house when its owner was absent.

Since Simon was found guilty of burglary, I recommend sentencing him to serve _____ years in prison. (from 0–99)

3. Forty-year-old Lenny went to the apartment building of an acquaintance who owed him a substantial amount of money. He saw the fellow in the hallway taking out the garbage. Lenny confronted him and demanded that he pay him back that day. The victim laughed and told Lenny that he had no intention of ever paying him back. Lenny became enraged. He grabbed him and they scuffled for a while until Simon managed to push him so that he tumbled down a flight of steps. The victim died of a broken neck.

Since Lenny was found guilty of second degree murder, I recommend sentencing him to serve _____ years in prison. (from 0–99)

HANDOUT 12.1b

Each of the following scenarios describes a crime for which the defendant has been found guilty. It is your job to read each case, consider the circumstances, and decide on the appropriate sentence.

1. Forty-year-old Lenny was apprehended in an electronics store by a guard who had seen him slip a small $400 camera into a coat pocket. When the suspect was searched, police also found that he had stolen a portable music player and a mobile phone.

Since Lenny was found guilty of shoplifting, I recommend sentencing him to serve _____ years in prison. (from 0–99)

2. Twenty-year-old Mark was caught burglarizing the apartment of an opera star. After questioning, Mark admitted to burglarizing the homes of several show-biz performers, in each case planning the burglary by reading the paper, noting the star's schedule, and paying a visit to the house when its owner was absent.

Since Mark was found guilty of burglary, I recommend sentencing him to serve _____ years in prison. (from 0–99)

3. Sixty-year-old Simon went to the apartment building of an acquaintance who owed him a substantial amount of money. He saw the fellow in the hallway taking out the garbage. Simon confronted him and demanded that he pay him back that day. The victim laughed and told Simon that he had no intention of ever paying him back. Simon became enraged. He grabbed him and they scuffled for a while until Simon managed to push him so that he tumbled down a flight of steps. The victim died of a broken neck.

Since Simon was found guilty of second degree murder, I recommend sentencing him to serve _____ years in prison. (from 0–99)

HANDOUT 12.1c

Each of the following scenarios describes a crime for which the defendant has been found guilty. It is your job to read each case, consider the circumstances, and decide on the appropriate sentence.

1. Sixty-year-old Simon was apprehended in an electronics store by a guard who had seen him slip a small $400 camera into a coat pocket. When the suspect was searched, police also found that he had stolen a portable music player and a mobile phone.

Since Simon was found guilty of shoplifting, I recommend sentencing him to serve _____ years in prison. (from 0–99)

2. Forty-year-old Lenny was caught burglarizing the apartment of an opera star. After questioning, Lenny admitted to burglarizing the homes of several show-biz performers, in each case planning the burglary by reading the paper, noting the star's schedule, and paying a visit to the house when its owner was absent.

Since Lenny was found guilty of burglary, I recommend sentencing him to serve _____ years in prison. (from 0–99)

3. Twenty-year-old Mark went to the apartment building of an acquaintance who owed him a substantial amount of money. He saw the fellow in the hallway taking out the garbage. Mark confronted him and demanded that he pay him back that day. The victim laughed and told Mark that he had no intention of ever paying him back. Mark became enraged. He grabbed him and they scuffled for a while until Mark pushed him so that he tumbled down a flight of steps. The victim died of a broken neck.

Since Mark was found guilty of second degree murder, I recommend sentencing him to serve _____ years in prison. (from 0–99)

HANDOUT 12.2 WITNESS'S DESCRIPTION

Describe the person who committed the crime(s):

Sex: _____ Race: _____ Age: _____ years old

Height: _____ Weight: _____ lbs. Build (thin, muscular, etc.): _____

Hair color: _____ Hair length: _____

Hair style (wavy, straight, how combed, etc.):_____

Eyes (color, size, etc.): _____ Ears (small, prominent, etc.): _____

Nose (small, large, broad, pug, etc.): _____ Glasses (describe frame): _____

Mustache or beard (color, shape, etc.): _____

Mask or false face (type, color, etc.): _____

Scars or marks (tattoos, birthmarks, blemishes, etc.): _____

Distinguishing characteristics (How would you pick him/her out of a crowd?):

Clothing - Describe what was worn (e.g., hat, coat, jacket, suit, dress, pants, skirt, shorts, shirt, blouse, tie, shoes, jewelry, other) *and their color, type of material, style, etc.* (Use reverse side if necessary.)

Describe each of the following:

Weapon (what kind, in what hand was it held, etc.):

Speech (accent, pitch, peculiarity):

Any names used:

Mannerisms (unusual walk, nervous habit, etc.):

Crime(s) committed by this person:

How long did you observe this person?

HANDOUT 12.4a ME

Imagine that you are employed as the sales agent behind the counter at a car-rental agency at a busy airport. This morning, you rented cars to six people. Below are the descriptions that represent your impressions of them at the time. As you read each description, try to visualize each individual.

Stewart Allen, 30 years old, has an Ohio driver's license. He has longish hair that is tied in a ponytail. He is wearing blue jeans with a large silver buckle, a blue denim shirt, and brown cowboy boots. He is talking excitedly into a cell phone.

Peter Lynn, 36 years old, has a New Jersey driver's license. He is an African-American businessman. He is slightly balding and wears glasses. He's carrying a briefcase. He has on a three-piece pinstripe gray suit, with an orange shirt, and an expensive looking tie.

Bob Mars, 39 years old, has a Tennessee driver's license. His brown hair is short and curly. His eyes are brown. He is trim and muscular. He's wearing blue jeans, white cotton sweater, and black hiking boots. In his hand, he has a paperback book.

Jim Smith, 27 years old, has a California driver's license. Jim is tall and wears his reddish hair in a crew cut. He is wearing a baseball cap, a hockey jersey, and black chinos. He is carrying a guitar case. He is accompanied by his teenaged brother.

Scott Jones, 25 years old, has a New Hampshire driver's license. He is short and stocky. He is wearing a black tee shirt and black shorts. He wears one gold hoop earring on his left ear and has a tattoo of a butterfly on his left arm. His girlfriend Mary is with him.

Ernest Bates, 65 years old, has a Pennsylvania driver's license. Ernest has blue eyes and sparse gray hair. He is wearing a plaid shirt, gray pants, and a wrinkled beige raincoat. He is holding a digital camera. He is accompanied by his overweight wife.

HANDOUT 12.4b ME

The police suspect that one of the people that you rented a car to this morning, a Mr. Bob Mars, used the vehicle in a bank robbery that involved the killing of a security guard. To help them capture the suspect, please answer each of the following questions as best you can. If you're not sure of an answer, take your best guess.

Bob Mars' driver's license is from which state? _____

How old is Bob Mars? _____

What was Bob Mars wearing? _____

Was Bob Mars by himself or with someone? _____

Do you remember anything about Bob Mars' looks? _____

Was Bob Mars carrying anything? _____

HANDOUT 12.4c ME

The police suspect that one of the people that you rented a car to this morning, a Mr. Bob Mars, used the vehicle in a bank robbery that involved the killing of a security guard. To help them capture the suspect, please answer each of the following questions as best you can. If you're not sure of an answer, take your best guess. If you disagree with the given choices, write a different answer on the blank.

Was Bob Mars' driver's license issued in California or New Hampshire?

_____

Is Bob Mars 25, 27, or 29 years old?

_____

What color cowboy boots was Bob Mars wearing?

_____

Who accompanied Bob Mars, a male or a female?

_____

Do you remember anything about what Bob Mars was wearing? For example, what color were his shorts?

_____

What musical instrument was Bob Mars carrying?

_____

HANDOUT 12.4d ME

The police suspect that one of the people you rented a car to this morning, a Mr. Bob Mars, used the vehicle in a bank robbery that involved the killing of a security guard. Your co-worker at the rental-car agency has just given the police the following testimony concerning the suspect. Please review her testimony to see if you agree with everything that she says. If you disagree about anything, please add it on the lines below her testimony.

"I remember Bob Mars. He was the short, stocky guy who came with a girlfriend. He wore black jeans, a plaid shirt, and cowboy boots. According to his New Hampshire driver's license, his age was 29. He had reddish hair, with a scar on the side of his face. I believe he was carrying a cell phone."

_____

_____

HANDOUT 12.5a INTERROGATING A SUSPECT

Introduction to Your Assignment:

Imagine that you were hired as a part-time security officer for the local office of your State Department of Transportation (SDT). One of your duties is to investigate complaints against SDT employees who may be subject to disciplinary proceedings. The procedure in such cases is that your supervisor sends you a memo describing the case and telling you what to do, and you follow his or her instructions as closely and as quickly as you can.

The enclosed form concerns the first disciplinary case you have been asked to work on. You know very little about SDT procedures beyond what is described in the memo, and you are not aware of the processes by which investigations are initiated and final decisions made.

Since this is your first case, and you are still a probationary employee, this assignment is very important to you. Do your best to follow the directions carefully and promptly, and return the completed form to me as soon as possible.

State Department of Transportation

Disciplinary Investigation, Form SDT-D331

To:

From: William V. Hippel

Re: John MacKenzie, SDT ID No. 68-479

Charges: Since the three-day weekend last month, several car batteries have been missing from the SDT Garage. MacKenzie works there as a maintenance supervisor. We've identified him as the thief, and are conducting an investigation to fire him.

Action Requested: We are not sure if MacKenzie did it, but we need a statement from him. It would save us a lot of time and money if you could get him to confess. Call him as soon as possible to get his story. He can be reached at the following phone number:

_____, and he can be reached at that number during the following times only:

MacKenzie knows about the missing batteries—they're his responsibility—but he hasn't been told we're on to him. If he asks why you're calling or what information you have, you may tell him. Do what you can to get a confession.

Be sure to write down carefully what you and he say, and return this form to me as soon as possible.

Report on Investigation:

(Use back of form if necessary)

HANDOUT 12.5b INTERROGATING A SUSPECT

Instructions to confederate playing the role of MacKenzie

For each interrogator who calls, have a clean copy of this form ready, and note the following things:

1. Sex of the interrogator: _____

2. Which tactic or tactics were used to try to get you to confess (circle all appropriate ones):

    - **Sympathy** / Trying to be your **friend**

    - **Promises** (e.g., promises of leniency)

    - **Claims of evidence**

        - no specifics mentioned

        - eyewitness

        - physical

        - videotape

        - other (specify)

    - **Threats**

        - will make your life tough

        - will physically hurt you

        - will call police

        - will make you take a lie detector test

    - **Other** (Please specify below):

3. Did the interrogator (circle one):

    a.   accuse you of the crime

    b.   state that he or she suspects you may have done it

    c.   do neither (a) nor (b), but simply asked questions of you.

4.

    a.   Did you confess: YES   NO

    b.   If you did confess, indicate why:

5. On the other side of the page, indicate any other observations that might be of interest.

HANDOUT 12.6a JURY SELECTION: VOIR DIRE (Case # 1-defendant)

You are representing the defendant (the State) in Case # 1.

First decide on the profile of the ideal defense juror.

Then decide on the profile of the juror that you would most like to excuse from the jury.

Then list five questions that you would ask prospective jurors in order to maximize a favorable finding for the defense.

For each question, outline the answer that would be most ideal for the defense.

For each question, outline the answer that would be least favorable for the defense.

Case # 1

James is serving a five-year sentence in the state penitentiary for assault with a deadly weapon. He is suing the State, claiming that a correction officer used excessive force when returning him to his cell after a visit from his sister. He says the officer crushed his back against the cell wall, which caused him to have a severely painful back injury.

HANDOUT 12.6b JURY SELECTION: VOIR DIRE (CASE # 1-PLAINTIFF)

You are representing the plaintiff (James) in Case # 1.

First decide on the profile of the ideal plaintiff's juror.

Then decide on the profile of the juror that you would most like to excuse from the jury.

Then list five questions that you would ask prospective jurors in order to maximize a favorable finding for the plaintiff.

For each question, outline the answer that would be most ideal for the plaintiff.

For each question, outline the answer that would be least favorable for the plaintiff.

Case # 1

James is serving a five-year sentence in the state penitentiary for assault with a deadly weapon. He is suing the State, claiming that a correction officer used excessive force when returning him to his cell after a visit from his sister. He says the officer crushed his back against the cell wall, which caused him to have a severely painful back injury.

HANDOUT 12.6c JURY SELECTION: VOIR DIRE (CASE # 2-DEFENDANT)

You are representing the defendant (the automobile company) in Case # 2.

First decide on the profile of the ideal plaintiff's juror.

Then decide on the profile of the juror that you would most like to excuse from the jury.

Then list five questions that you would ask prospective jurors in order to maximize a favorable finding for the plaintiff.

For each question, outline the answer that would be most ideal for the plaintiff.

For each question, outline the answer that would be least favorable for the plaintiff.

Case # 2

Paula is suing a car company because her 65-year-old husband, a retired air force pilot, was killed while driving an SUV that skidded and turned over. The automobile company claims that their car is safe but that the victim was driving recklessly and at excessive speed under dangerous conditions (the road was icy).

HANDOUT 12.6d JURY SELECTION: VOIR DIRE (CASE # 2-PLAINTIFF)

You are representing the plaintiff (Paula) in Case # 2.

First decide on the profile of the ideal plaintiff's juror.

Then decide on the profile of the juror that you would most like to excuse from the jury.

Then list five questions that you would ask prospective jurors in order to maximize a favorable finding for the plaintiff.

For each question, outline the answer that would be most ideal for the plaintiff.

For each question, outline the answer that would be least favorable for the plaintiff.

Case # 2

Paula is suing a car company because her husband was killed while driving an SUV that skidded and turned over. The automobile company claims that their car is safe but that the victim was driving recklessly and at excessive speed under dangerous conditions (the road was icy).

HANDOUT 12.6e JURY SELECTION: VOIR DIRE (CASE # 3-DEFENDANT)

You are representing the defendant (Paul) in Case # 3.

First decide on the profile of the ideal defense juror.

Then decide on the profile of the juror that you would most like to excuse from the jury.

Then list five questions that you would ask prospective jurors in order to maximize a favorable finding for the defense.

For each question, outline the answer that would be most ideal for the defense.

For each question, outline the answer that would be least favorable for the defense.

Case # 3

After receiving a tip from a disgruntled student, the police raid a fraternity and arrest Paul on charges of possession of illegal drugs. Paul, a new member, recently moved into the fraternity house. The drugs, Ecstasy and marijuana, were found concealed in a small cardboard box on top of a bookshelf that was not visible from the floor below.

HANDOUT 12.6f JURY SELECTION: VOIR DIRE (CASE # 3-PROSECUTION)

You are representing the prosecution (the government) in Case # 3.

First decide on the profile of the ideal defense juror.

Then decide on the profile of the juror that you would most like to excuse from the jury.

Then list five questions that you would ask prospective jurors in order to maximize a favorable finding for the defense.

For each question, outline the answer that would be most ideal for the defense.

For each question, outline the answer that would be least favorable for the defense.

Case # 3

After receiving a tip from a disgruntled student, the police raid a fraternity and arrest Paul on charges of possession of illegal drugs. Paul, a new member, recently moved into the fraternity house. The drugs, Ecstasy and marijuana, were found concealed in a small cardboard box on top of a bookshelf that was not visible from the floor below.

HANDOUT 12.8 JURY DELIBERATION IN CIVIL CASES

Imagine that you are part of a jury that has just heard the following cases. Negligence was already found and now, for each case, you must decide on the appropriate amount to award the injured party or the estate:

1. A 65-year-old woman was driving a 2005 sedan at highway speed when one of the tires exploded. In court, it was proven that the tire company knew that they had a defective tire but they continued producing it for the market because they faced considerable costs if production was halted. The plaintiff suffered a broken hip bone and has had limited mobility since, which is not expected to improve.

    Your award is: _____

2. A 34-year-old man died when an elevator door opened and the man stepped forward and fell six stories down an open shaft because the elevator wasn't there. In court, it was determined that the elevator was not properly maintained or inspected.

    Your award is: _____

3. A 28-year-old woman was shopping in an office supply store when one of the employees in the next aisle shoved a large box so that it went over the edge to the opposite side and crashed on her head, knocking her unconscious. She sustained a permanent head injury and has been having severe migraine headaches ever since.

    Your award is: _____

4. A 19-year-old construction worker was standing on the top rung of a ladder when the step gave way and broke. In court, it was shown that the ladder was defective because it was manufactured using aluminum that was too thin to comply with standard regulations. The plaintiff injured his back, resulting in a permanently compressed disk. He suffers from frequent attacks of pain and will need to undergo physical therapy for many years.

    Your award is: _____

CHAPTER 13

Business

LEARNING OBJECTIVES: GUIDELINES FOR STUDY

You should be able to do each of the following by the conclusion of Chapter 13.

1. Define industrial/organizational psychology. Explain the Hawthorne effect and its role in triggering interest in industrial/organizational psychology. (*pp. 529-531*)

2. Describe the effectiveness of the traditional employment interview when it comes to personnel selection. Consider the role of expectations in job interviews. Discuss the effectiveness of the various alternatives to the traditional job interview. (*pp. 531-537*)

3. Discuss social psychological perspectives on the debate concerning affirmative action in hiring and promotion. Discuss the effects of diversity on organizational morale and performance. (*pp. 537-542*)

4. Differentiate objective from subjective criteria for performance appraisals. Identify the potential problems associated with supervisors' evaluations of their subordinates as well as self-evaluations. Identify factors that improve the accuracy of performance appraisals and explain the due process model of performance appraisal. (*pp. 542-545*)

5. Compare and contrast views of leadership that emphasize a trait approach with those that emphasize interactions between the person and situation. Explain the concepts of transactional and transformational leaderships. Discuss some of the problems faced by women and ethnic minorities when it comes to advancement in the workplace, and consider gender differences in leadership styles and preferences. (*pp. 545-553*)

6. Summarize the economic factors that affect employee satisfaction. Discuss expectancy theory, equity theory, and the differences between intrinsic and extrinsic motivation. (*pp. 553-558*)

7. Consider psychological perspectives on economic decision making. In particular, identify the influence of money on social judgment, social influences on investor behavior, and the significance of concepts such as commitment, entrapment, and escalation. (*pp. 558-563*)

DETAILED CHAPTER OUTLINE

I. Introduction
    A. Industrial/Organizational Psychology: The study of human behavior in business and other organizational settings
    B. Hawthorne Effect: The finding that workers who were observed increased their productivity regardless of what actual changes were made in the work setting
II Personnel Selection
    A. The Typical Job Interview
    B. "Scientific" Alternatives to the Traditional Interview
        1. Polygraph
        2. Standardized tests
            a) cognitive abilities
            b) integrity tests

        3.   Structured interviews
           a)   compared to conventional interviews
           b)   assessment centers
           c)   personnel selection as a two-way street
    C.   Affirmative Action
    D.   Culture Organizational Diversity
III. Performance Appraisals
    A.   Supervisor Ratings
        1.   Halo effect
        2.   Contrast effect
        3.   Restriction of range problem
    B.   Self-Evaluations
    C.   New and Improved Methods of Appraisal
    D.   Due Process Considerations
IV. Leadership
    A.   The Classic Trait Approach
    B.   Contingency Models of Leadership
        1.   Fiedler's contingency model
           a)   task-oriented leaders
           b)   relations-oriented leaders
           c)   situational control
        2.   Normative model of leadership
    C.   Transactional Leadership
    D.   Transformational Leadership
    E.   Leadership among Women and Minorities
V.   Motivation at Work
    A.   Economic Reward Models
        1.   Types of rewards
        2.   Expectancy theory
    B.   Bonuses, Bribes, and Intrinsic Motivation
        1.   Undermining intrinsic motivation with rewards
        2.   Controlling versus informational value of rewards
    C.   Equity Considerations
        1.   Equity in the workplace
        2.   Gender differences in perceived equity
VI. Economic Decision Making
    A.   The Symbolic Power of Money
    B.   Social Influences in the Stock Market
    C.   Commitment, Entrapment, and Escalation
        1.   Entrapped by initial commitments
        2.   Escalation effect
        3.   Sunk-cost principle

LECTURE AND DISCUSSION IDEAS

Idea 1.   Personnel Selection Interviews

Many assessment techniques are used to select individuals for organizational roles. These include application forms, references, intelligence tests, special ability tests (e.g., math or language), personality tests, work simulation exercises, and various kinds of interviews. Ask students to discuss some of the reasons an organization would choose to use a particular assessment test rather than others, and to identify some of the limitations of each of these assessment devices. To aid in the discussion, generate a list of jobs (e.g., accountant, carpenter, cashier, college president, college professor, doctor, elementary school principal, social worker), and discuss what assessment devices students think would be most useful for each job and why.

The textbook indicates that interviewers' expectations about candidates can bias how they interview them, potentially leading to poor selection decisions. Ask the class to think of other limitations of the conventional interview for personnel selection. These include: The disproportionate power of early impressions, candidates may lack interviewing skills but be perfectly suited for the job, contrast effects, halo effects, the disproportionate weight given to negative over positive information, prejudice, and the disproportionate weight given to subjective impressions (as influenced by perceived attractiveness and skill at self-promotion) rather than objective information (e.g., work history, academic qualifications, or extracurricular activities) (e.g., see Graves & Powell, 1988; Kinicki, Lockwood, Hom, & Griffeth, 1990).

Unstructured interviews are notoriously bad predictors of subsequent job performance. In a classic 1929 study, twelve independent interviewers in a company each interviewed 57 applicants (Hollingworth, 1929). There was wild variation in interviewer preferences. Some candidates who were ranked first by one interviewer were ranked last by another. Given results such as these, why do interviews continue to be so widely used? Reasons include: Although they may acknowledge that other employers may not conduct valid interviews, employers think that they personally are not biased and that they are good judges of character; employers want a chance to meet an applicant in person before making the offer of a job; interviews can be useful for identifying how well job candidates will "fit" into organizational culture; etc. Also, few other assessment devices allow the interviewers to have such a good "feel" for the person whom they are hiring. This subjective, intangible evaluation is very important to the organizational members doing the hiring.

Interviews are often used in conjunction with personal references or letters of recommendation from previous employers. Research has found that letters have poor predictive validity (Paunonen, Jackson, & Oberman, 1987; Reilly & Chao, 1982). They often present a false picture of the applicant, and they may deliberately mislead potential employers. Moreover, many organizations no longer supply evaluative information to other organizations or individuals for fear of lawsuits. For example, a busy insurance executive in Houston got a call from a private investigator hired by a former employee who had been fired. The PI posed as a potential employer. When asked what kind of person the employee was, the former employer described him as "Jekyll and Hyde, a classic sociopath." The former employee sued the company, and it had to pay him almost $2 million. Because of stories like this, some organizations will only give out performance data that are objectively verifiable. Tell this story to your class, and have the students discuss this complex issue. Ask them how they would write letters of recommendation for someone they felt lukewarm about, and how they go about asking professors and others to write letters for them.

Ask students to discuss their experiences with job interviews. What factors seemed to play the most important roles in how well the interviews went? Did the interviews seem fair? Were they structured or unstructured interviews? Ask students to suggest ways that traditional interviews can be improved so as to increase their predictive validity and fairness. What other methods of personnel selection would the students advocate instead of, or in addition to, traditional interviews (see Lecture and Discussion Idea 2 below for more discussion of this issue).

Discuss the relevance of principles and findings from previous chapters in the textbook for the issue of personnel selection. This could serve as a good way to review various concepts from the course, including: methodological issues such as validity and expectancy biases (Ch. 2); self-perception, self-presentation, and social comparison (Ch. 3); attributions, heuristics, self-fulfilling prophecies, impression formation, primacy effect, central traits, and information integration

(Ch. 4); stereotypes, prejudice, and discrimination (Ch. 5); cognitive dissonance and persuasion (Ch. 6); compliance tactics (Ch. 7); social facilitation (Ch. 8); physical attractiveness, similarity, and self-disclosure (Ch. 9); mood (Ch. 10).

Graves, L., & Powell, G. (1988). An investigation of sex discrimination in recruiters' evaluations of actual applicants. Journal of Applied Psychology, 73, 20-29.

Hollingworth, H. L. (1929). Vocational psychology and character analysis. New York: Appleton.

Kinicki, A.J., Lockwood, C. A., Hom, P. W., & Griffeth, R. W. (1990). Interviewer predictions of applicant qualifications and interviewer validity: Aggregate and individual analyses. Journal of Applied Psychology, 75, 477-486.

Paunonen, S. V., Jackson, D. N., & Oberman, S. M. (1987). Personnel selection decisions: Effects of applicant personality and letter of reference. Organizational Behavior and Human Decision Processes, 40, 96-114.

Reilly, R. R., & Chao, G. T. (1982). Validity and fairness of some alternative employee selection procedures. Personnel Psychology, 35, 1-62.

Idea 2. "Scientific" Alternatives to the Selection Interview

Are "scientific" alternatives to the selection interview an improvement over the traditional interview? Discuss each of the alternatives described in Chapter 13, and ask the students to consider whether they would consider them to be valid alternatives to more traditional means of personnel selection, and why.

Discuss the validity and the ethics involved in using polygraphs. Is the use of polygraphs an invasion of individuals' privacy? Should it be acceptable to use them to screen candidates for jobs in which security is an extremely important issue? The Employee Polygraph Protection Act, passed in the United States in 1988, limits the use of lie-detector tests to jobs in law enforcement, national security, and public safety. Should any employer be allowed to use the polygraph or similar devices when they interview candidates or to check on their employees? A related issue for debate concerns the use of drug testing. What are the ethical considerations of drug testing candidates for jobs such as for school bus drivers or air traffic controllers or for other kinds of jobs? How would the students react if they had to be tested for drugs at random times during the year if they receive any money from the school for jobs, scholarships, or financial aid? Ask them to imagine that they were taxpayers who helped fund these jobs, scholarships, or financial aid—would they feel differently about the drug testing?

Graphology (handwriting analysis) is used by an estimated 2,000–3,000 U.S. companies, and by many more in Europe, despite the results of research suggesting that it lacks predictive validity. Discuss why graphology is not likely to be valid, and why so many companies continue to use it. Ask the students what they would do if they were on a job interview and were asked to submit material for a handwriting analysis.

Ask the students to apply their social psychological knowledge to the question of why structured interviews help reduce some of the biases associated with traditional interviews. Among the issues that should be raised are the biasing effects of expectancies, confirmatory hypothesis testing, and self-fulfilling prophecies (Ch. 4) that are more likely to be a factor in unstructured interviews. Discuss why employers may be resistant to the use of structured interviews. Discuss also the potential for bias in the questions used for structured interviews (e.g., use as an analogy the criticisms of standardized achievement tests, such as the SAT, concerning cultural biases).

Discuss the use of situational interviews, which present specific dilemmas faced on the job and ask candidates to choose how they would behave in these situations. Some research suggests that they are more valid than structured interviews (Latham, 1988; Maurer & Fay, 1988).

Draw an analogy between the use of assessment centers for personnel selection and the use of multiple methods in researching a set of hypotheses (Ch. 2). A discussion of this can illustrate to the students the importance of applying issues of methodology in general, and validity and reliability in particular, to real-world situations such as personnel selection.

Latham, G. P. (1988). Human resource training and development. Annual Review of Psychology, 39, 545-582.

Maurer, S. D., & Fay, C. (1988). Effect of situational interviews, conventional structured interviews, and training on interview rating agreement: An experimental analysis. Personnel Psychology, 41, 329-344.

Idea 3. Affirmative Action

The textbook examines some of the difficult issues involved in implementing affirmative action in organizations. Of course, this is a very hot topic in politics, education, and business, and it is good material for a serious discussion. Try to emphasize the social psychological points that often are missed in debates about affirmative action. You can draw on important points about stereotypes, prejudice, and discrimination from Chapter 5 and about group dynamics and diversity in work groups in Chapter 8, as well as the research reviewed in Chapter 13. For example, you should point out how research concerning "modern racism," implicit bias, and other forms of covert discrimination suggest that the problem of discrimination is much deeper and more pervasive than many people think, and that employers who truly believe that they are fair and non-prejudiced in their judgments could in fact be biased in their assessments of job candidates or employees.

If affirmative action can lead women and minorities to devalue their own performance, as suggested by research cited in the text, what actions can managers in organizations take to prevent this from happening? The use of "diversity training" to help organizational members be sensitive to issues of diversity is one method used by many corporations. Relevant readings on the topic can be used in class lecture or discussion. Consider assigning Murray's (1993) New York Times article that examines some of the difficulties of effectively using diversity training; this can lead to an interesting and informative discussion of the practical obstacles to obtaining the benefits of affirmative action. An article by Milliken and Martins (1996) reviews some of the effects of diversity in organizational groups. Finally, a more recent systematic analysis by Kalev, Dobbin, and Kelly (2006) tracks the effectiveness of three broad approaches to increasing diversity: establishing organizational responsibility to implement diversity goals, diversity training and evaluation of managers, and networking and mentoring initiatives meant to reduce the isolation of women and minority workers.

Kalev, A., Dobbin, F., & Kelly, E. (2006). Best practices or best guesses? Assessing the efficacy of corporate affirmative action and diversity policies. American Sociological Review, 71, 4, 589-617.

Milliken, F. J., & Martins, L. L. (1996). Searching for common threads: Understanding the multiple effects of diversity in organizational groups. Academy of Management Review, 21, 402-433.

Murray, K. (1993, August 1). The unfortunate side effects of 'diversity training.' The New York Times, Sec. 3, p. 5.

Idea 4. Leadership

Ask students to name individuals who are/were great leaders, and write the names on the board. Discuss why these individuals were great leaders. What individual traits were important in making them great leaders? What situational factors were important?

Discuss these leaders and whether their success as leaders seems to support the trait approach or interactional models of leadership. This exercise may be more likely to support the former because the first people that come to mind as successful leaders are likely to be unusually dynamic, powerful individuals. Thus, be ready to give examples that are more consistent with interactional models, such as coaches in team sports who achieve terrific success as a leader of one team but great failure when in a different situation, or team players who were respected leaders on and off the field while still players but who could not lead effectively when they became coaches or managers (e.g., basketball's Magic Johnson was a fantastic leader as a player who felt he could not communicate with his players when he became a coach), or, outside the realm of sports, politicians who are effective leaders in one context (e.g., Congress) but not in another (president).

Ask the students to discuss their experiences as leaders of organizations or groups, or their observations of people who led them. What were typical challenges? Does Fiedler's contingency model seem to apply well to these experiences? Have they ever known any leaders whom they would consider to be transformational leaders? Is it sufficient for a team captain to quietly lead by example, or does he or she have to play a vocal, prominent role in rallying the rest of the team? How important is good leadership, relative to other skills or characteristics such as intelligence, good decision-making ability, and integrity, for a variety of different kinds of jobs, such as president or prime minister, or captain of a team or club?

Idea 5.   Elaborating on the Role of Gender Stereotypes in Upholding the Glass Ceiling

According to the text, one of the reasons that more women do not reach the top echelon in the corporate world is that gender stereotypes portray them as unsuited for leadership positions. In an article in the *Journal of Social Issues* (2001), Madeline Heilman asserts that there are actually two types of gender biases involved in producing the "glass ceiling." The first is the descriptive norm, which describes characteristics that are typically masculine or feminine. According to this bias, men are "agentic" and characterized by such achievement-oriented traits as aggressiveness, forcefulness, independence, and decisiveness. Women, on the other hand, are labeled as "communal." Accordingly, they are characterized as helpful, sympathetic, kind, and concerned about others.

Managerial and executive-level positions are almost always described in terms of "male" traits. They are thought to require achievement-oriented aggressiveness and emotional toughness. The stereotyped view of what women are like and the male trait characterization of what top business positions are combine to produce a perceived 'lack of fit.' In the case of women, the fit between the job requirements and their characteristic traits is poor. Accordingly, the expectations for women in top managerial and executive positions are low; they are expected to fail at these jobs. Women are thought to not have the required personalities to be effective leaders. They are deemed too "nice" to occupy top positions in the corporate world.

The second gender bias is the prescriptive norm, which dictates how men and women *should* and *should not* behave. Typically, the *should nots* include behaviors that are typical of the opposite sex, but are seen as incompatible with the behavior desirable for one's own gender. In the case of women, the agentic behaviors of men are considered off limits; women cannot remain feminine if they are being competitive, aggressive, independent, forceful or decisive. When women go against the norm and express agentic traits and succeed at "man's work," they are shunned and disliked. This dislike is then likely to translate into a negative evaluation by their superiors.

In one study (Glick & Rudder, 1999), undergraduate volunteers were asked to rate men and women who were vying for a managerial position in a computer lab. They were given essays purportedly written by the job applicants and they watched tapes of the job applicants' interviews. They were asked to rate the applicants on competence, social skills, and hirability. Females who rated high on competence tended to rate consistently lower on social skills than men who rated comparably high in competence. Consequently, the women received lower ratings on hirability than did the men. Moreover, men who were competent were described as hirable, even if they rated low on social skills.

This study reflects a double standard that is ironically the result of the "feminization" of companies. In an effort to reduce gender discrimination, many companies have redefined the characteristics that make for a good leader. Instead of looking for leaders with stereotypically male traits like aggressiveness and assertiveness, they are seeking leaders with qualities that are more stereotypically feminine, like interpersonal sensitivity and people skills. It's no longer enough for a woman to be as competent as a man, she also needs to be seen as feminine. But it's sort of a Catch 22 because a competent woman will be characterized as masculine. Competence is seen as incompatible with femininity. So women, who need to be seen as possessing both traits, often can't succeed in getting to the top. A discussion of Hillary Clinton's campaign for President in 2008 might also allow you to touch on many of these issues.

Glick, L. & Rudder, P. (1999). Feminized management and backlash toward agentic women: The hidden costs to women of kinder, gentler images of middle managers. Journal of Personality and Social Psychology, 77, 1004-1011.

Heilman, M. E. (2001). Description and prescription: How gender stereotypes prevent women's ascent up the organizational ladder. Journal of Social Issues, 57, 657-674.

Idea 6.   Learning from The Apprentice

The reality television show *The Apprentice* features 18 young men and women vying for a position with the Donald Trump organization by performing various team tasks. The show has been referred to by Mr. Trump as a 14-week job interview. Accordingly, episodes of the show (or segments) can be used to illustrate and spur discussion on many topics relevant to this chapter, such as alternative interview techniques, performance appraisals, self-evaluation and self-promotion, teamwork, models of leadership, gender differences in leadership styles, leadership decision making, and motivation.

You might also ask students to discuss how the show diverges from the reality of the business world. An article posted at CNN.com (Gyenes, 2007) quotes some business school professors who are enthusiastic about using the show and others who have reservations about its useful as an educational tool. Those in the latter category state that the show is too artificial, that it only allows for an evaluation of people's skills in terms of how quickly they can solve short-term tasks, and that it presents a distorted balance of power where the employees are totally dependent on the boss and he has little need for them.

Gyenes, K. (April 15, 2004). 'Apprentice' sparks classroom discussions. Article posted at: http://www.cnn.com/2004/SHOWBIZ/TV/04/15/apprentice.biz.schools/index.html.

Idea 7.   Escalation of Commitment in Organizations

Have students read a presentation of the escalation of commitment that took place in Expo '86 held in Vancouver, British Columbia (Ross & Staw, 1986), or briefly summarize the case for them. This is a fascinating case study of commitment breeding subsequent commitment (Ch. 7 of the textbook) and of the sunk-cost trap (Ch. 13) (in addition, you can tie in the issues of group polarization, groupthink, and entrapment from Ch. 8). Ross and Staw examine how a proposed $78 million project continued to escalate and eventually became a $1.5 billion project that lost millions of dollars.

Discuss what led to escalation in Expo '86. Specifically, what were the project determinants, psychological determinants, social determinants, and structural determinants? Each of these categories is discussed in the Ross and Staw analysis. After analyzing the causes of escalation, ask students to consider steps that could be taken in a project to reduce or eliminate a tendency toward escalation. (These are examined in detail in the article). These include explicitly rewarding bad news, building in "backing-off" times, and recognizing signs of overcommitment.

Consider showing the video *Abilene Paradox* (see Multimedia Resources below) to provide more good material for this discussion.

Ross, J., & Staw, B. M. (1986). Expo '86: An escalation prototype. Administrative Science Quarterly, 31, 274-297.

CLASSROOM ACTIVITIES

Activity 1. Replicating the Hawthorne Effect

The Hawthorne effect is the phenomenon whereby people behave differently (usually better) when they are being observed. To mimic the effect, students are asked to undertake an activity, with you, the instructor, monitoring only half of the class. Afterwards, you compare the work produced by the "watched" students with the work produced by the "unwatched."

Decide in advance which half of the class you will be monitoring. This might be dictated by the placement of their chairs. Optimally, you should be able to look over the shoulders of the students who are being monitored.

Tell the class that they will be participating in an experiment on word fluency. Put the word WORKPLACE on the board, and say, "When I tell you to start, you'll have five minutes to make as many words as possible out of the letters in the word "workplace." Do not use any letter more than once in any one word and do not share your list with anyone else. The lists will not be collected, so there's no need to put your name on them."

Say "Start." After one minute, begin your monitoring. Walk back and forth behind the "watched" students, reading a word or two and moving on. Be careful not to let your eyes stray in the direction of the "unwatched" students.

After five minutes, tell them to stop writing and count the number of words that they produced. Draw a vertical line on the board. On one side, write "Group A," and on the other side, write "Group B." Ask the students in the "unwatched" group to read off their totals first. Then ask the "watched" group to do the same. If there is a marked difference (with an advantage for the "watched group" – Group B), then you have mimicked the Hawthorne effect. To launch the discussion, ask the students if anyone figured out the experimental treatment.

> *What if this bombs?* There are two possibilities for bombing. First, the experiment could bomb if the "watched" group performs worse than the "unwatched" group. In that case, remind the students what they learned about social facilitation (in Ch. 8), namely, that the presence of others impedes performance on difficult tasks because it puts pressure on the individual to perform while being evaluated. Second, the experiment might bomb if there is no (or only minimal) difference between the two groups. If that happens, ask the students to explain why the effect was not attained. Perhaps, the "unwatched" group was expecting to be evaluated as well.

Activity 2. Personnel Selection: The Typical Interview

This role-playing exercise is designed to give students an opportunity to identify and understand some of the limitations of job interviews and to consider how to improve personnel selection techniques. The exercise requires at least one hour of class time. The suggested times below are guidelines to help structure class time. The activity can be conducted before or after students read Chapter 13.

Choosing a job. First, take five minutes with the class to identify an interesting job to use in the exercise. Explain to the students that they will be doing an exercise that involves designing and conducting an interview and evaluating the validity of the job interview as a technique to select personnel. Ask the students to discuss what kinds of jobs they would like to have after graduation. After a list of several jobs has been generated, have students vote on which job will be used for the exercise. Ask the class to describe what kinds of skills, experience, and personality the ideal candidates for this job should have. Ask them to consider what a classified advertisement for this job should say.

If time is a problem, you can skip this step by choosing a job ahead of time, and even bringing in a real classified advertisement to use in the activity. Selecting a job that some students might be applying for upon graduation will help make this activity more interesting and relevant for the class.

Interview preparation. Second, students should spend ten minutes on interview preparation. After dividing the class into groups of four to five, assign half of the groups to play the role of interviewers who are making personnel selection decisions within an organization, and the other half to the role of candidates for the job openings.

The interviewers should meet in their small groups and discuss exactly what qualifications they think the ideal job candidate should have. They should then decide how they want to design and conduct interviews in order to choose the best job candidate. Each group is free to do this as it sees fit, with one exception: each job candidate must be interviewed or otherwise evaluated by *at least* two interviewers (and preferably more). This can be accomplished via group interviews, multiple one-on-one interviews, or other combinations.

The job candidates should use this time to construct and write their own résumés. Depending on the job selected for this activity, you may want to encourage the job candidates to feel free to exercise some creativity in inventing appropriate qualifications, or you may encourage them to be fairly honest about their qualifications and experiences.

The interviews. Each group of candidates should be matched with a group of interviewers. The interviewers and candidates should introduce themselves to each other by name. At the beginning of each interview, the interviewers and candidates should write down each other's names for future reference. The students should then be given about twenty minutes to conduct the interviews.

Post-interview. Each interviewer should receive a copy of **Handout 13.2a**. They should complete the handout individually. When each has completed the handout, the group should discuss their selections of the best candidate and compare notes for about five to ten minutes. They should not change their written responses on the handout, but by the end of the discussion they should all try to agree on one candidate to hire for the job.

In the meantime, the job candidates should complete individual copies of **Handout 13.2b**. Next, the candidates should meet in small groups for about five to ten minutes and discuss their interview experiences. Were they surprised by the questions asked? Did they think that other questions *should* have been asked? For those candidates who were interviewed by the same interviewer, how similar were their experiences? Did they have similar impressions of the fairness of the interviewer and his or her questions? The candidates should share with each other their responses from the handout—how much consensus was there?

General discussion. The rest of the class time should consist of a discussion of the activity. How did interviewers select the best candidate? How much consensus was there among the interviewers who interviewed the same job candidates? How did the various groups of interviewers decide to conduct the interviews? Which groups conducted group interviews, and which conducted one-on-one interviews? What seemed to be the pros and cons of each approach? Did the candidates tend to prefer group interviews or one-on-one interviews? Did the job candidates think that the interviews were valid and fair? How much consensus was there among the job candidates about the various interviews, about what questions should have been asked, etc.?

Ask students to discuss what some of the advantages and limitations are of the interview as a selection tool. Discuss how some of the limitations of the interview can be overcome with the use of other selection devices, such as those discussed in Chapter 13.

> ●*What if this bombs?* This exercise cannot bomb because it will stimulate students to think about the interview situation, its advantages and limitations. Students may criticize the role-playing situation as being too artificial and not reasonably approximating a "real-life" interview. This issue can be used to introduce a discussion of what it is "really like" to conduct an interview or to be interviewed, and the limitations and advantages of interviews can be discussed in the context of these real-world situations. Emphasize that the point of this exercise was not to simulate actual personnel selection experiences but instead to put the students in a position that makes them think about these issues in a compelling way.

Activity 3. Motivation

This activity is designed to give students the opportunity to apply different theoretical approaches to motivation to an organizational setting, and then to compare these approaches in class discussion.

Background. There are many different theories of motivation that are employed by I/O psychologists. The three theoretical approaches to motivation suggested for this exercise are: expectancy theory (Nadler & Lawler, 1991), equity theory (Greenberg, 1988—available in *Readings in Social Psychology: The Art and Science of Research*, which is available with the textbook), and job enrichment theory (Hackman, Oldham, Janson, & Purdy, 1994). While job enrichment theory is not introduced in the chapter, it is a very popular and accessible theory that specifies a model for how to design jobs in order to be motivating. It is an interesting theory that students should enjoy using in an applied exercise like this one. (If you can't get access to the Hackman et al. chapter, consider using instead an article by Oldham, Hackman, and Pearce, 1976.)

Procedure. Students should be introduced to each of the three theoretical approaches in some depth either in a lecture or through assigning them the readings cited above (particularly the Hackman et al. or Oldham et al. readings because this approach is not discussed in the textbook). Students should understand each approach and have an opportunity to have any questions answered before the exercise. If this will take up too much time, the exercise can be done effectively with only one or two of the theoretical approaches to motivation.

Break the class into groups of four to five. Assign a theoretical approach (expectancy, equity, or job enrichment) to each group. Each group will use that theory to analyze and improve the motivational potential of a specific job. Some examples of jobs that could be used in this exercise include cashier, fast-food employee, waitress, lawyer, or college professor. Then, give the groups some time (15 to 20 minutes) to discuss how to apply their assigned theory to make the job as motivating as possible. Specifically, tell them to play the role of organizational consultant, and ask them what they would tell the manager of these employees about how to maximize employee motivation. All of the groups should be assigned to improve the motivational potential of the same job or jobs. Tell the groups that they will have five minutes to present their analysis to the class.

Discussion. After all of the groups have presented to the class, discuss which ideas the students thought would work best to make a job motivating. Discuss which theories students find most compelling and why. Ask how their assessments of the utility of theories might be different if they applied the theory to enhancing the motivation of a very different type of job.

A variant of this exercise is to assign one group to the role of "managers" who will choose which "consultants" to hire after hearing all of them present. While the "consultants" groups are conducting their analysis, the "managers" group can be deciding what criteria they will use in their hiring decision.

Students usually enjoy having this fun-spirited element of competition introduced into the class exercise and discussion.

> ●*What if this bombs?* Because this exercise gives students an opportunity to apply different theories of motivation, this activity has little chance of failing completely. It is possible that students may be skeptical about the utility of the theories for addressing applied issues. The motivating role of positive inequity posited by equity theory in particular is often greeted with skepticism. Expectancy theory also is often criticized because many students do not believe that people actually calculate expected utilities while in a work setting (you should explain that people are not necessarily aware of the extent to which they are influenced by issues of equity—i.e., this does not have to be a conscious process). This skepticism should generate healthy discussion of the strengths and limitations of the different theoretical perspectives for both theoretical understanding and management practices.

Adams, J. S. (1965). Inequity in social exchange. In L. Berkowitz (Ed.), <u>Advances in experimental social psychology</u> (Vol. 2, pp. 267-299). New York: Academic Press.

Hackman, J. R., Oldham, G., Janson, R., & Purdy, K. (1994). A new strategy for job enrichment. In B. A. Gold (Ed.), <u>Exploring organizational behavior: Cases, readings, and experiences</u> (pp. 75-93). Ft Worth, TX: Dryden.

Nadler, D. A., & Lawler, E. E. (1991). Motivation: A diagnostic approach. In B. M. Staw (Ed.), <u>Psychological dimensions of organizational behavior</u> (pp. 43-64). New York: Macmillan.

Oldham, G. R., Hackman, J. R., & Pearce, J. L. (1976). Conditions under which employees respond positively to enriched work. <u>Journal of Applied Psychology</u>, <u>61</u>, 395-403.

Activity 4. Dollar Auction

This exercise illustrates the escalation effect that can emerge in economic decision-making situations. Decision makers frequently commit more and more resources into a failing project in order to try to justify their initial investment. Because this exercise is discussed in the textbook, you should use it <u>before</u> students read Chapter 13.

Begin by explaining to the class that there is going to be an auction in which you will be auctioning off (real) dollar bills to the highest bidder. The rules of the auction require that the top <u>two</u> bidders pay their last bid, although only the top bidder is awarded the money. Thus, the second highest bidder will pay the amount of his or her bid, but receive nothing. The use of real money by both students and instructors will enhance the effectiveness and the fun of this demonstration. You may want to suggest that bids must be multiples of five cents.

After explaining these rules to the students, answer their questions, but do not let them talk among themselves. Then, auction off each dollar. You may only need to auction off one. If, however, the first dollar goes cheap, the later ones probably will not. Instruct the students not to talk to each other during the activity—you don't want there to be any alliances or side deals among groups of students that could ruin your auction.

After the auction, discuss what happened. In this exercise, multiple student bids of greater than fifty cents guarantee a profit to the auctioneer. It is not unusual for students to bid even more than fifty cents. In many classes in which this demonstration has been used, individual students' bids have even exceeded one dollar—which is a perfect demonstration of the escalation effect! Ask students to explain their own and their fellow students' behavior during the course of the auction. Why did people become involved in the bidding? Why did they stop when they did? For the highest bidders, why didn't they stop earlier? Relate this discussion to the issues suggested in the Lecture and Discussion Idea 7 above.

What if this bombs? One way to help ensure that student bids add up to more than a dollar is to plant a confederate in the classroom who will help escalate the bidding if the class members were very timid early on in the bidding. The identity of the confederate would be disclosed after the auction, and discussion of the confederate's role in the class dynamics would ensue. If you use a confederate, you should return your winnings back to the students (indeed, you might consider doing this even if you didn't use a confederate).

Activity 5. Economic Risk Taking: Following the Stock Market

In this activity, students read the business pages in the *Wall Street Journal* or another major financial publication and predict the performance of a particular stock. Students can do this individually or in small groups of four or five. Each group/individual should choose a stock from the over-the-counter stocks listed in the newspaper and decide, over a two- or three-week period, whether to keep the stock or sell the stock and use the money to invest in another stock. A relatively long time-frame is necessary to allow students to watch the trends of the market. During this time, students should log and chart the progress of their selected stock. When the monitoring period is over, have the students explain why they chose their particular stock, how their stock performed, and how this fit with their expectations. Did students tend to buy low and sell high, or did they buy stocks that were on the rise and sell those that were already on the decline. Research cited in the textbook found that people tend to adopt the latter, less effective strategy. Discuss why students did or did not engage in effective economic decision making about their chosen stock. Specifically, use the exercise as a way to discuss the non-economic criteria that influence economic decision making, such as contagion, social comparison, and conformity.

A great way to test how effective the students' management of their stocks were would be to compare their performance to that of a more random strategy, such as asking a small child to make the same decisions based on their whims, or rolling some dice. How do the performances compare?

What if this bombs? Most students will enjoy this opportunity to think critically about economic decision making in a real-world context. Those who had success with their decisions will want to share their "effective strategies" and those who were not so successful will appreciate an opportunity to talk about the role of different biases in their poor performance. Relevant research on economic decision making will be very interesting for students to discuss in light of their own experiences.

Activity 6. Gambler's Fallacy

The gambler's fallacy can be very costly for people when making economic decisions. This fallacy is the false belief that random processes are self-correcting, such that if one flips a coin and gets "heads" three times in a row that this increases the likelihood that the next flip will be "tails," because the coin is "overdue" for it. A gambler who is on a cold streak might decide to risk more money because he or she now feels due to win. The same kind of flawed logic could impair people's business decisions about investing money or resources in some project, stock, or other investment.

Demonstrate the gambler's fallacy for your class by flipping a coin 15 times. Ask a confederate to announce the outcomes of each coin toss. Have him or her announce the following sequence to the class: HTHTTHTTTTTTTTT. Before each flip of the coin, ask your students to predict the outcome. Record the predictions and the phony outcomes that are dictated by the confederate. According to the gambler's fallacy, the number of students who predict H should increase above the 50-50 rate as they observe the long succession of T's.

Discuss the reason for the gambler's fallacy and why it is a fallacy (i.e., people have an image of what a random pattern of numbers should look like, even though, by definition, there is no prototypical pattern of randomness). Discuss how people often attribute causality to random events, and how this can affect economic decision making.

●*What if this bombs?* If students are already familiar with the gambler's fallacy (e.g., from an introductory or cognitive psychology class), they may not succumb to it in this demonstration. All is not lost, however. Ask students why they think the gambler's fallacy is so common in the real world. Is there something about the situation (a classroom simulation) that may have influenced their predictions? Ask students what factors might influence someone in a real gambling situation to fall prey to the gambler's fallacy.

Activity 7. Guest Speakers

Most students are very interested in how social psychology applies in the business world, and the discussions and activities suggested in this chapter should make them even more interested in these topics. This would be the perfect opportunity, therefore, to bring to class one or more guests who can share with the class their expertise and experience in these matters. Among the ideas for speakers:

Someone who has experience in personnel selection. Professionals who have experience interviewing job candidates could talk about how they construct their interviews, how they try to minimize biases, and how valid they think their procedures are. You could also bring in some people from the Admissions office to talk about how they select students. Have the students ask questions about alternative procedures and why these professionals or admissions personnel don't use them.

People in positions of leadership. There are many types of leaders that you could draw on here, including business executives, supervisors, coaches, local politicians, theater directors, musical conductors, military officers, the president of the college or university, and so on. Try to bring in more than one such person to talk about their approaches to leadership, what challenges they face and how they deal with them, what *they* think makes a good leader, and whether they think that they'd be more or less effective as a leader if they were in a different setting. Have the students discuss with these individuals the different theories of leadership presented in the textbook. This could make for fascinating discussions.

●*What if this bombs?* The best way to avoid a bomb here is through good preparation. Be sure your speaker knows the level at which he or she should talk to your students. Be clear about how much time you expect for lecture, questions, and discussion (some guests like to go on and on, so give the speaker a specific amount of time to talk), and what your goals are for the talk. Even in cases where the talk is not very engaging, the students should be interested in asking a lot of questions about issues relevant to Chapter 13, and so you could try to steer the speaker away from lecturing and toward more give-and-take with the class. Prepare a list of good discussion questions in advance that you could use if the students are reticent about asking a lot of questions.

MULTIMEDIA RESOURCES

Video

Abilene Paradox 2nd Edition. This amusing yet very compelling video features vignettes from a variety of situations that illustrate how well-intentioned but misguided consensus agreements can steer an organization into activity that directly contradicts individual desires and defeats group purpose. Shows how three key psychological principles—action anxiety, negative fantasies, and fear of ostracization—contribute to faulty group collusion, and demonstrates how to overcome these obstacles to successful and productive group decisions. (2002, 26 min.) Available from CRM Learning, 2218 Faraday Ave., Suite 110, Carlsbad, CA 92008. (800-421-0833).

All Together: Organizational Behavior. Explaining that each organization has its own culture, this program looks at organizational behavior. It discusses the ideas of Frederick Taylor, scientific management, corporate culture, and the pitfalls of bureaucracy. (2005, 30 min.) Available from Insight Media (800-233-9910).

Beyond Wall Street: The Art of Investing. If you discuss and conduct an activity concerning economic decision making or the stock market, consider showing some or all of this video, which features advice from eight well-respected investment experts. (1997, 30 min.) Available from PBS Video (800-344-3337).

Groupthink, 2nd Edition. This film illustrates eight symptoms of "groupthink": the illusion of invulnerability, shared stereotypes of the enemy, rationalization, the illusion of morality, self-censorship, the illusion of unanimity, direct pressure on the deviant member, and mindguarding — a device that protects the group from dissenting opinions. Uses the story of the space shuttle Challenger and other historical examples to explore and demonstrate the phenomenon of groupthink. Commentary by Drs. Irving Janis and David Kanouse. (1992, 22 min.) CRM Learning, 2218 Faraday Ave., Ste. 110, Carlsbad, CA 92008. (800-421-0833).

Motivating People in Today's Workplace. This video seminar teaches how to inspire involvement, enthusiasm, and productivity in the workplace, through the use of internal motivators and external rewards. (1995, 3 volumes, 180 min. total) Available from PBS Video (800-344-3337).

Motivation: Organizational Behavior. This program outlines the theories of Abraham Maslow and Douglas McGregor. Using interviews with behavioral scientists, workers, and managers, it explores what makes a person satisfied and productive at work. (1978, 26 min.) Available from Insight Media (212-721-6316); and from PBS Video (800-344-3337).

Personality: Assessment Methods. This video shows a psychologist administering a battery of tests to one participant. It discusses the value of interviews, outside description, and self-description in assessment, as well as a number of clinical and cognitive tests (which you might want to skip for this class). This video is old, but it does touch on important issues in personnel selection. (1971, 30 min.) Available from PBS Video (800-344-3337).

Personnel Selection. Uses the selection of fighter pilots to illustrate how I/O psychologists devise tests that predict which candidates are more likely to succeed. Discusses issues of validity, reliability, and predictability. The video follows the progress of one hypothetical candidate through interviews and psychometric tests. (1991, 24 min.) Available from Insight Media (800-233-9910).

Pygmalion Effect: The Power of Expectations. According to the Pygmalion effect, people fulfill the expectations that others have for them. This video shows managers four ways that expectations can be transmitted to subordinates in order to raise their performance. (2001, 22 min.) Available from CRM Learning, 2218 Faraday Ave., Suite 110, Carlsbad, CA 92008 (800-421-0833).

Team Building. Everyone is involved at some time or another in group making or decision making. This video examines factors that can make people work together better and more productively as a team. It also examines pitfalls that are common to group situations. (1983, 18 min.) Available from the Bureau of Audio Visual Instruction, University of Wisconsin at Madison, Madison, WI 53701-2093.

What to Do When Conflict Happens. Shows through vignettes how conflict between coworkers or between employees and supervisor can be resolved in four easy steps. (2007, 21 min.) Available from CRM Learning, 2218 Faraday Ave., Suite 110, Carlsbad, CA 92008 (800-421-0833).

Working Solutions: Empowering Workers. Examines how successful companies are adapting to the challenge of decentralization and worker empowerment. (1993, 30 min.) Available from PBS Video (800-344-3337).

Working Solutions: Workforce Diversity. Examines how successful companies are adapting to the challenge of managing an increasingly diverse workforce. (1993, 30 min.) Available from PBS Video (800-344-3337).

Internet

The following Internet sites and e-mail discussion groups and list servers contain information and discussions relevant to many of the issues raised in Chapter 13, as well as related issues concerning the application of social psychological principles to businesses and organizations.

Harvard Business School Publishing. Contains a large number of case studies, simulations, videos, and other teaching material relevant to business. You can order case studies about how particular businesses try to motivate employees, how they develop work teams, etc. http://www.hbsp.harvard.edu

Homepage of the Society for Industrial & Organizational Psychology. Contains many resources and links relevant to industrial/organizational psychology. http://www.siop.org/

Social Psychology Network. This extensive homepage maintained by Scott Plous contains many links relevant to Chapter 13, including sites about group performance, teams, affirmative action, leadership, and many aspects of industrial/organizational psychology. http://socialpsychology.org/

Organizational Management (ORGMGT-1). E-mail group concerning organizational and management studies and related topics. Send e-mail to list owner at hees@siswo.uva.nl

Organizations and Culture List. E-mail group concerning the issues of organizational culture and organizational change. mail to: orgcult@commerce.uq.edu.au

CD-ROM

Who Do You Think You Are? The Berkeley Personality Profile. One issue concerning personnel selection concerns using standardized tests to assess candidates' personalities and skills. You can use this CD-ROM as an example of a way to assess people's personalities. Based on the book by Keith Harary and Eileen Donahue, this CD-ROM asks users to respond to thirty-five questions and then graphs a score. It also features video clips that allow students to test their first impressions of people and compare them to personality profiles of these people. (1996, Mac/Windows CD-ROM). Available from PBS Video (800-344-3337).

HANDOUT 13.2a INTERVIEWER'S EVALUATION OF JOB CANDIDATES

1. Which of the job candidates whom you interviewed would you select for the job?

2. Which of the job candidates whom you interviewed would you pick as the second best candidate for the job?

3. Explain your selections of the best candidate. What were the two most important reasons for your selection of this person? What other reasons were there?

Use the form below to rate each of the candidates you interviewed on each of several dimensions. Use the following scale:

1	2	3	4	5	6	7
very below average			average			very above average

JOB CANDIDATE NUMBER:

(you should write in the name of the candidate above his or her number)

	#1	#2	#3	#4	#5
Ambitious	____	____	____	____	____
Creative	____	____	____	____	____
Easy to get along with	____	____	____	____	____
Good fit for job	____	____	____	____	____
Hard worker	____	____	____	____	____
Honest	____	____	____	____	____
Independent	____	____	____	____	____
Intelligent	____	____	____	____	____
Likes to take charge	____	____	____	____	____
Organized	____	____	____	____	____
Passive/Submissive	____	____	____	____	____
Responsible	____	____	____	____	____
Warm	____	____	____	____	____

HANDOUT 13.2b CANDIDATE'S EVALUATION OF INTERVIEWERS

1.   How well designed and conducted were the interviews?

1	2	3	4	5	6	7
very poor						very good

2.   How valid do you think these interviews will be in determining who is the best candidate for the job?

1	2	3	4	5	6	7
not valid at all						very valid

3.   How biased or fair do you think the questions were?

1	2	3	4	5	6	7
very biased						very fair

4.   To what extent do you think you were able to present yourself to the interviewers in an accurate, representative way?

1	2	3	4	5	6	7
not at all						very much

5.   Which interviewer did you feel did the best job interviewing you? What were the two most important reasons for your selection of this person?

6.   What were the strangest, or most irrelevant, questions asked of you? Why do you consider them to be strange or irrelevant?

Use the form below to rate each of your interviewers on each of several dimensions. Use the following scale:

1	2	3	4	5	6	7
very poor						very good

INTERVIEWER NUMBER:

(you should write in the name of the interviewer above his or her number)

	#1	#2	#3	#4	#5
Quality of questions	____	____	____	____	____
Open-mindedness	____	____	____	____	____
Fairness	____	____	____	____	____
Easy to talk to	____	____	____	____	____

CHAPTER 14

Health

LEARNING OBJECTIVES: GUIDELINES FOR STUDY

You should be able to do each of the following by the conclusion of Chapter 14.

1. Define health psychology. Define stress and identify its causes, including major crises, positive and negative life events, and microstressors of everyday life. (*pp. 569-575*)

2. Consider how the body responds to stress. Describe the three stages of the general adaptation syndrome. Explain how the experience of stressful events affects the heart, the immune system, and the likelihood of experiencing other short-term and chronic disease. (*pp. 575-582*)

3. Discuss the physical and mental health implications of attributional and explanatory tendencies. Discuss the negative effects engendered by learned helplessness and a depressive explanatory style. (*pp. 583-584*)

4. Consider the psychological tendencies that contribute to the human capacity for resilience, including self-efficacy and optimism. (*pp. 584-588*)

5. Define the two principal types of coping with stress, problem- and emotion-focused coping. Identify the strengths and limitations of each coping style, as well as the types of stress towards which each is best suited. (*pp. 588-596*)

6. Explain what is meant by "proactive coping." Discuss the role of social support, religion, and culture on the manner in which people cope with stress. (*pp. 596-601*)

7. Identify the social psychological components of a successful approach to treatment, and explain why they are effective. Outline factors that promote prevention of risky behaviors. (*pp. 601-605*)

8. Consider the wide range factors that affect the pursuit of happiness and subjective well-being. Describe when people are most likely to be happy and when they are least likely to be happy. (*pp. 605-609*)

DETAILED CHAPTER OUTLINE

I. Stress and Health
   A. Stress: An unpleasant state of arousal in which people perceive the demands of an event as taxing or exceeding their ability to satisfy or alter those demands
   B. Appraisal: The process by which people make judgments about the demands of potential stressful events and their ability to meet those demands
   C. Coping: Efforts to reduce stress
II. What Causes Stress?
   A. Crises and Catastrophes
      1. Environmental disaster can have profound psychological effects
      2. War and other highly stressful experiences
      3. These major events can lead to posttraumatic stress disorder, a condition in which a person experiences enduring physical and psychological symptoms after an extremely stressful event

    B.   Major Life Events
        1.   Change itself is probably not inherently stressful
        2.   Negative life events are associated with physical illness and psychological distress
    C.   Microstressors: The Hassles of Everyday Life
        1.   Crowded prisons and dorms can lead to stress
        2.   Work stress which can cause burnout is another important microstressor
        3.   The stress of commuting
        4.   Economic pressure

III.   How Does Stress Affect the Body?
    A.   The General Adaptation Syndrome: Three phases in response to stress
        1.   Alarm: mobilization of the fight or flight response
        2.   Resistance: body remains aroused and on the alert
        3.   Exhaustion: overuse causes our body to break down
    B.   What Stress Does to the Heart
        1.   Type A behavior pattern: competitive drive, a sense of time urgency, anger, cynicism, and hostility
           a)   is associated with heart disease
           b)   is measured more accurately by the interview method
           c)   the main toxic ingredient is hostility
        2.   Type B behavior pattern: a more laid-back style in contrast to Type A pattern
        3.   Psychocardiology: the study of the heart and mind
    C.   What Stress Does to the Immune System
        1.   Psychoneuroimmunology: the study of the effects of stress on the immune system
        2.   Stress weakens the immune system
           a)   behaviors people engage in under stress decrease immune cell activity
           b)   stress triggers release of adrenaline which decreases immune cell activity
    D.   The Links Between Stress and Illness

IV.   Processes of Appraisal
    A.   Attributions and Explanatory Styles
        1.   Learned helplessness
           a)   original model: uncontrollable events create passive behavior
           b)   reformulated model: stable, global, internal attributions for uncontrollable negative events lead to learned helplessness
        2.   Depressive explanatory style: attribution consistent with the reformulated model of learned helplessness
    B.   The Human Capacity for Resilience
        1.   Hardiness
           a)   control: the belief that one's outcomes are controlled by one's actions
           b)   challenge: the perception that change is a normal part of life
           c)   commitment: having a sense of meaning and mastery in one's life
        2.   Self-efficacy: the belief that one can perform a specific behavior, usually associated with positive coping with a stressor
        3.   Dispositional optimism
           a)   Optimism is associated with better health outcomes
           b)   Biological and behavioral explanations for the optimism-health connection
    C.   Pollyanna's Health: Positive thinking is associated with positive health outcomes
        1.   Positive thinking is associated with good health
        2.   Still unclear whether positive thinking *causes* good health

V.   Ways of Coping with Stress
    A.   Problem-Focused Coping: Cognitive and Behavioral Efforts to Alter a Stressful Situation
        1.   Control: the need for flexibility

            a)   actual control of a situation can be stressful

            b)   the trick is to know when one can exercise control and when one can't

      2.   Blame: where to place it?

            a)   blaming others is associated with poor adjustment

            b)   behavioral self-blame, which is unstable, is associated with positive adjustment but may not help one cope with extremely traumatic events

            c)   characteriological self-blame, which is stable, is associated with negative adjustment

  B.   Emotion-Focused Coping: Cognitive and Behavioral Efforts to Reduce Distress Brought on by a Stressful Situation

      1.   Positive emotions: the building blocks of emotion-focused coping

            a)   Fredrickson's two-step theory

      2.   Shutting down: suppressing unwanted thoughts

            a)   distraction can be an effective coping strategy

            b)   suppressing unwanted thoughts can lead to increased awareness of these thoughts

      3.   Opening up: confronting one's demons

            a)   opening up and discussing one's problems seems to promote health

            b)   increased health probably occurs because of the insight that one obtains in opening up

      4.   Self-focus: getting trapped versus getting out

            a)   the self-focus model of depression suggests that self-focus can lead to a vicious circle of negative thoughts that can intensify depression

            b)   passive ruminative thinking about one's problems maintains depression

            c)   active thinking aimed at understanding is associated with reduced depression

  C.   Proactive Coping: Up Front Efforts to Ward Off or Modify the Onset of a Stressful Event

      1.   Social support: support from others increases one's ability to cope with stress

            a)   number of social contacts model: it may be the number of social contacts that is important in social support

            b)   intimacy model: it may be that having a close relationship is important in social support

            c)   perceived availability model: it may be that perceiving that others will help is important in social support

      2.   The religious connection

  D.   Culture and Coping: Differences Between Individualistic and Collectivist Cultures

VI.   Treatment and Prevention

  A.   Treatment: The "Social" Ingredients

      1.   Social support

      2.   Hope

      3.   Choice

  B.   Prevention: Getting the Message Across

      1.   To be willing to engage in a healthy behavior, people must be convinced that there is a health risk if they do not engage in the healthy behavior

      2.   Healthy behaviors are promoted by positive models

      3.   Healthy behaviors are promoted by positive subjective norms

      4.   A sense of self-efficacy may be necessary for the adoption of positive life changes

      5.   AIDS prevention

VII. The Pursuit of Happiness

  A.   Measuring Subjective Well-being

  B.   Predictors of Happiness

      1.   Social relationships

      2.   Employment status

      3.   Physical health

C.   Why Money Can't Buy Happiness?
1.   Social comparison theory
2.   Adaptation-level theory
3.   The baseline level of happiness

LECTURE AND DISCUSSION IDEAS

Idea 1.   Stress Produced by Crowding in Prisons and Dorms

One of the microstressors discussed in the text is a crowded living situation. Baum and Valins (1979) have found that the more people sharing a common space in dorms, the higher their level of stress. Similar findings have been obtained in prisons. Paulus (1988) has found that the number of prisoners sharing a common space is a better predictor of stress than the total amount of common space. Ask your students if they feel stress as a result of their living situations. You might even have them break up into groups and discuss the positive and negative aspects of their living situations.

Baum, A., & Valins, S. (1979). Architectural mediation of residential density and control: Crowding and the regulation of social contact. In L. Berkowitz (Ed.), <u>Advances in experimental social psychology</u> (Vol. 12, pp. 131-175). New York: Academic Press.

Paulus, P. B. (1988). <u>Prison crowding: A psychological perspective</u>. New York: Springer-Verlag.

Idea 2.   Posttraumatic Stress Disorder and Rape

The textbook discusses posttraumatic stress disorder (PTSD) in connection with environmental catastrophes and war. Another major crisis that can bring on posttraumatic stress disorder, characterized by physical and psychological problems following an extremely stressful event, is rape. Unfortunately, rape is all too common, at least twelve million women were raped in 1990 alone (Kilpatrick et al., 1992). This significant social problem is likely to be a significant source of posttraumatic stress disorder. The video, *Post-Traumatic Stress Disorder: The Woman's Perspective*, listed in the Multimedia Resources is one compelling way to present this topic.

You might also allude to a recent article in the New York Times Magazine (Corbett, 2007) which reported that in the first Gulf War, female soldiers experienced post traumatic stress disorder at double the rate of male soldiers. Ask students to discuss this gender difference.

One possible factor for the disparity in rates of PTSD for men and women is that women have stronger reactions to the horrors of combat. Another is that they are more likely to be diagnosed. That could be because women do a better job of describing their symptoms or because they present with more typical symptoms. Researchers believe that men with PTSD are more likely to abuse alcohol or become aggressive, whereas women with the disorder are more likely to cry frequently and feel depressed.

Students could argue that the hyper-macho military culture might stigmatize men who report emotional symptoms. However, women are not more likely than men to ask for help. In fact, those who return from the front with symptoms are actually likely to take longer than men to request treatment.

According to the article, much of the gender difference is due to the fact that many women in military service experience the "double whammy" of sexual assault and combat trauma.

Studies have found that both sexual harassment and assault rise during wartime. Consequently, women in the military tend to have a higher risk for being sexually assaulted than do civilian women. That is reflected in a 2003 Department of Defense report stating that one-third of female veterans seeking health care through the V.A. said they experienced rape or attempted rape during their service. Ask students to discuss what aspects of the military environment make sexual assault so prevalent.

Research has also shown that sexual assault is more likely to precipitate posttraumatic stress disorder in women than exposure to combat. In fact, for women, being raped is considered to be the more "toxic" experience. Moreover, being assaulted by a fellow soldier may be extra-traumatic because enlistees are taught to expect that others in the military will do their utmost to protect them.

Corbett, S. (March 18, 2007). The women's war. The New York Times Magazine, 41-72.

Kilpatrick, D. G., Edmunds, C. N., & Seymour, A. (1992). Rape in America. Arlington, VA: National Victim Center.

Idea 3.   Problems with the Type A Construct

The story of the development, propagation, and subsequent questioning of the Type A construct can provide an excellent example of the way that psychological theories and research develop and relate to the general population. As detailed in the textbook, this construct originally arose from heart doctors' observations of their patients. It quickly gained acceptance and was included as a risk factor in heart disease by the National Heart, Lung, and Blood Institute. Further research, however, found that the Type A behavior pattern had varying relations to heart disease and that its measurement was suspect. Today it seems that hostility may be the critical component, although further evidence is needed. This example poses some interesting questions. When should scientific findings be accepted? When should they be disseminated to the general public? What are the implications if researchers present findings to the general public that are later questioned?

You might also introduce students to the Type D construct. This is a newly coined personality type with the D standing for distressed. Type D people tend to manifest negative emotions, such as anxiety, irritability, and depression, and, at the same time, they tend to inhibit those emotions in social interactions because they fear that expressing them will drive others away. Research findings (Harvard Heart Letter, 2005) indicate that Type D personality is associated with increased risk for early death, for developing cardiovascular problems after a heart attack, for poor response to treatment for heart disease, and for increased risk for sudden cardiac arrest. These results are from small, preliminary studies, however, and will need to be replicated with larger samples and different populations. The authors of the article in the Harvard Heart Letter caution that there was a Type C construct kicked around for a while, as well, with C standing for cancer-prone, and that that personality type was totally discredited.

You might want to use Activity 14.3 in conjunction with this idea. This activity lets students see how difficult it can be to develop a measure of a psychological construct.

Lee, T. H. (Ed.). (Aug. 2005). Type "D" for distressed. Harvard Heart Letter, 15, 12, 5-6.

Idea 4.   Is Negative Social Support Possible?

The textbook describes several models of social support: the number of social contacts model, the intimacy model, and the perceived availability model. These models seem to share the assumption that contact with other people is likely to be beneficial. But we can all probably think of instances in which some of our social contact, or some of our helpers, or even people we are intimate with, end up causing us more stress when they try to help us. Can social support in some instances be a detriment to health? When might social support have this paradoxical effect?

Chris Crandall (1988) provides an example where this appears to have occurred. In this set of studies he showed that social pressure in two sororities at the University of Michigan promoted binge eating. That is the social group that most of these women probably saw as a source of social support encouraged them to engage in a behavior that could undermine their health. Ask your students if any of their sources of social support encourage them to engage in unhealthy behaviors.

Crandall, C. S. (1988). The social contagion of binge eating. Journal of Personality and Social Psychology, 55, 588-598.

Idea 5. Should You Shut Down or Open Up after Trauma?

In discussing emotion-focused coping, the text describes two effective ways of coping with a traumatic event: shutting down and opening up. When people are able to distract themselves after traumatic events or when they are able to express how they feel about these events, they seem to have some relief and report feeling better. Is this pattern of results contradictory?

You might ask your students to discuss this question. In addition, you could break this question down further by asking them, "When is distraction likely to be ineffective in dealing with a traumatic event?" and similarly, "When is expressing your feelings likely to be ineffective in dealing with traumatic events?" You might want to further explore what the long-term consequences of each strategy are. Currently, there is little research that addresses these questions; therefore, you might ask your students to try to develop a way to test their answers to these questions.

Idea 6. Should Everyone Count Their Blessings?

Is it better to focus on what is wrong with one's life or on what is right? Research (Emmons & McCullough, 2003) has shown that having a grateful outlook has a positive effect on one's well-being. In one study, participants kept daily records of up to five things for which they were grateful or thankful for in their lives. Compared to a control group or another group of participants who focused on daily hassles, the grateful participants experienced fewer symptoms of physical illness, felt better about their lives as a whole, were more optimistic about the future, and spent significantly more time exercising.

Ask your students to explain the finding. Is gratitude generally a pleasant emotion? What about its negative side? Gratitude also means that one is a recipient of someone's favor, that one is indebted, or even dependent on another person. Feeling that you need to reciprocate could be an unpleasant emotion. So why does being reminded that you should be grateful have a positive effect on emotional and even physical health?

Emmons, R.A. & McCullough, M.E. (2003). Counting blessings versus burdens: An experimental investigation of gratitude and subjective well-being in daily life. Journal of Personality and Social Psychology, 84, 377-389.

Idea 7. Positive Psychology

In conjunction with the text's discussion of optimism as a factor in health, you might want to discuss the movement of positive psychology. Martin Seligman founded the movement, which focuses on self-awareness and optimistic thinking. Self-awareness comes from knowing what your strengths are. Seligman encourages people to log on to his Web site (http: //authentic happiness.sas.upenn.edu/) and take the Values in Action strengths test. This test measures people's five "signature" traits, the ones that define their personality. According to Seligman, most people are familiar with three or four of the strengths, but one or two may surprise them. Knowing what your strengths are, he says, will allow you to make better decisions in your life and make it easier for you to achieve a meaningful kind of happiness. This is a happiness that comes from knowing that you are maximizing your potential to the good of a cause or institution outside of yourself. It is this meaningful kind of happiness that gives rise to optimistic thinking.

Besides the VIA (Values in Action) strengths test, Seligman lists other exercises on his Web site that are meant to promote an optimistic outlook. Among them are:

"Make a Beautiful Day" – This is an exercise that encourages the individual to schedule a day or half day that will take advantage of his or her talents and attributes. For example, if the person's top traits are love of learning and curiosity, the day might include a morning in a museum and the afternoon spent reading. Or, if a person's top strength is capacity to love, the day might revolve around hosting friends or family members.

"Good Things in Life" – This is a gratitude exercise that mimics the Emmons and McCullough (2003) study (see Idea 6). The individual writes down three good things that happen each day, and for each one, he asks himself or herself, "What did I have to do with it?" Eventually, says Seligman, it becomes easier to think of good things and harder to dismiss one's role in making them happen.

"Start a Fight" – Also called the ABCDE method for disputing negative thoughts. This is an exercise that is helpful for when things go badly. It's a way to see things in a good light even if at first they seem bleak. The (A) stands for adversity. The (B) stands for automatic pessimistic beliefs. The (C) stands for the consequences of these pessimistic thoughts. The (D) stands for disputing or arguing with yourself about these beliefs. And the (E) stands for the energizing feeling you get from not succumbing to the inevitable pessimism that an unfortunate event usually brings on.

Lawson, W. (Jan/Feb 2004). The glee club. Psychology Today, 37, 34-39.

Idea 8.   Stress and Burnout

Many of your students may be interested in entering a human service profession. Research (Cordes & Dougherty, 1993; Lee & Ashforth, 1996; Maslach, 1982) shows that these professions show a high incidence of burnout. People who experience burnout describe themselves as used up, drained, frustrated, callous, hardened, apathetic, lacking in energy, and without motivation.

You might ask your students to discuss why it is that they think that human service professionals experience such a high level of these feelings. You might also ask whether they think they will experience burnout in the occupation that they enter.

Posing these questions should provide a good opportunity to discuss themes covered throughout the class. You are likely to find that most students will display the self-serving bias in answering these questions and think that other people will burn out but they will not. They are also likely to ignore the power of the situation—lack of resources, such as social support and too many job demands—that research suggests is the critical factor in burnout. On the bright side, perhaps your students will have learned these lessons well and be able to apply these concepts to their situation. In any event, you can point out that when deciding on an occupation and a particular job in the future, they are likely to be better served by looking at the features of the situation than in trying to decide if they are the type of person who will suffer burnout.

Cordes, C. L., & Dougherty, T. W. (1993). A review and integration of research on job burnout. Academy of Management Review, 18, 621-656.

Lee, R. T., & Ashforth, B. E. (1996). A meta-analytic examination of the correlates of the three dimensions of job burnout. Journal of Applied Psychology, 81, 123-133.

Maslach, C. (1982). Burnout: The cost of caring. Englewood Cliffs, NJ: Prentice Hall.

CLASSROOM ACTIVITIES

Activity 1. Explanatory Styles

The reformulated model of learned helplessness (Abramson & colleagues, 1989) suggests that people experience depression when they interpret negative stressful events as originating from internal, stable, and global causes. **Handout 14.1** provides students with the opportunity to see which types of attributions they would choose in one particular set of circumstances.

What if this bombs? This one should be bombproof. Any pattern of results (e.g., whether students show consensus or lack of consensus on their scores) should lead to interesting discussion, as students are always interested in how, and why, they each score as they do.

Abramson, L. Y., Metalsky, G. I., & Alloy, L. B. (1989). Hopelessness depression: A theory-based subtype of depression. Psychological Review, 96, 358-372.

Activity 2. The Illusion of Control and Picking a Card

Bring a standard deck of cards to class and announce that you are going to play a simple card game whereby the person who gets the highest card will win a prize (of course you can offer whatever you want as a prize). Then give cards to some students and allow other students to pick their own cards. Make sure you stress that they are not to look at their cards. After distributing cards to six to ten people, ask them what they think their chance of winning is. Typically the people who have chosen their own cards will estimate a higher probability of winning than will those who were given cards, demonstrating the illusion of control. All students will be likely to over-estimate their chances of winning.

What if this bombs? The easiest way to handle this activity if it bombs is just to repeat the process with another group of students before telling the class the purpose of the demonstration. If the demonstration still doesn't work, point out that using a small number of people often leads to inconsistent results.

Adapted from Dollinger, S. J. (1990). The illusion of control. In V. P. Makosky, L. G. Whittemore, C. P. Landry, & M. L. Skutley (Eds.), Activities handbook for the teaching of psychology (Vol. 3, pp. 170-171). Washington, D.C.: American Psychological Association.

Activity 3. Understanding the Type A Behavior Pattern

This activity requires students to generate specific observable behaviors that are characteristic of the three dimensions of the Type A behavior pattern: excessive competitiveness and achievement motivation, time urgency and impatience, and easily aroused anger and hostility. **Handout 14.3a** should facilitate their completion of this task. Divide the class into relatively small groups of four to six students each and allow them to work on this task. Once they have generated a list of behaviors, found in their own lives, compare these behaviors with the indicators generated by Friedman and Ulmer (1984).

To score Handout 14.3b reverse code items 3, 7, 11, 15, 29, 33, and 37 then add up all the responses. Higher numbers indicate more of a Type A behavior pattern. Lower numbers indicate more of a Type B behavior pattern.

What if this bombs? This one should be bombproof—again, because any pattern of results will likely lead to interesting discussion.

Adapted from Eagleston, J. R. (1985). Understanding the Type A behavior pattern. In V. P. Makosky, L. G. Whittemore, & A. M. Rogers (Eds.), Activities handbook for the teaching of psychology (Vol. 2, pp. 153-155). Washington, D.C.: American Psychological Association.

Friedman, M.,& Ulmer, D. (1984). Treating Type A behavior – and your heart. New York: Knopf.

Activity 4. A Journal Exercise Utilizing the Theory of Inhibition and Confrontation

Much of the research that Pennebaker (1990) has done concerning the theory of inhibition and confrontation has journal entries about upsetting events in people's lives. When Pennebaker and his colleagues (1990) asked students to write their "very deepest thoughts and feelings about coming to college," they found that the students who did so were actually healthier. Consider asking your students to keep such a journal and to process some upsetting event. Not only will this experience teach them the methodology of Pennebaker's work, but it might be good for them as well.

What if this bombs? This one should be bombproof as well, assuming your students follow through with the assignment. You will no doubt have some students who take the assignment more seriously than others, and you will see varying depths of thoughts and feelings. In any case, through this type of exercise students can connect their classes with their everyday lives.

Pennebaker, J. W. (1990). Opening up. New York: Morrow.

Pennebaker, J. W., Colder, M., & Sharp, L. K. (1990). Accelerating the coping process. Journal of Personality and Social Psychology, 58, 528-537.

Activity 5. College-Related Stressors and Preferred Coping Styles

This activity is meant to help students analyze what they found stressful in the school environment during the semester and to determine if they have a predominant coping style.

First, elicit a general list of potential college-related stressors from the class. The list might include assignments, tests, other students, teachers, school organizations, financial expenses tied to the school, etc. Write the items on the board if the majority of the class agrees that they are potential stressors that are related to being in college.

Next, ask students to think about the period from the beginning of the semester until now and write down a list of 15 specific incidents that they found to be personally stressful in the school environment during that time. When everyone is done, ask them to note next to each stressor how they reacted to the stress at the time.

    a.   At this point, review the four methods of coping with stress that are discussed in the text:

    b.   Approach problem-focused coping — taking control and confronting the problem head on

    c.   Avoidance problem-focused coping — taking action to avoid having to deal with the problem by procrastinating or through prioritizing

    d.   Approach emotion-focused coping — opening up and acknowledging and expressing feelings

    e.   Avoidance emotion-focused coping — shutting down and suppressing unwanted thoughts and feelings

Now ask students to classify their way of coping with each stressor as P+ (approach-problem), P- (avoidance-problem), E+ (approach-emotion), or E- (avoidance-emotion). For example, if, during a test, someone found it stressful that another student was copying off his or her answer sheet, that individual might classify the response as follows:

Shifting position so that the copier couldn't see the paper – P+ (approach-problem)

Continuing to do the test as if nothing was going on – P- (avoidance-problem)

Feeling upset the whole time – E+ (approach-emotion)

Not caring that the other person was copying – E- (avoidance-emotion)

Have your students tally the number of each type of coping to see if they have a dominant way of responding to stress.

> ●*What if this bombs?* This activity should be bombproof. Students should find it interesting to see if they have one habitual method of coping, or if they react differently in various situations.

Activity 6. Television and Health-Related Messages

As discussed in the text, the modeling of healthy or unhealthy behavior by celebrities is likely to have great influence on people's behavior. In 1997 and 1998, researchers (Will, Porter, Geller, and DePasquale, 2005) examined the depiction of automobile driving, violence, sexual activity, and use of alcohol, tobacco, and illicit drugs in primetime network shows to gauge the frequency of risky health-related behavior. This activity, which is based on that study, asks students to monitor current shows to determine if negative health-related messages are evident in current programming.

Begin the activity by asking students to list some risky health-related behaviors that they may have seen modeled on television in the past. Alternatively, you could present students with the Will, Porter, Geller, and DePasquale (2005) target behaviors—not using a seatbelt in a moving vehicle, disobeying traffic laws, use of alcohol, tobacco, or illegal drugs, using physical violence, and having unprotected sex, or sex with a stranger—and ask them to add other health-related risky behaviors to that list.

Divide the class into four groups and assign each group to one of the four major networks used in the study (ABC, CBS, FOX, and NBC). Explain that each person in the group will be responsible for reporting on a different popular weekly television program. (There should preferably be an even mix of half-hour situation comedies and one-hour dramas.) After all group members have selected the shows they will be monitoring, distribute **Handout 14.6a** to each student. This handout will be used to record incidents of risky health-related behaviors and their consequences. Each group should also select a coordinator who will present the findings of the group as a whole. Give each of the four coordinators a copy of **Handout 14.6b** to aid them in summarizing their group's results. Allow students at least one week to view the shows and complete the handouts.

Discussing the results:

Ask each of the four coordinators to report the total number of scenes depicting risky behaviors that his or her group recorded. Add the four totals and divide by the total number of hours of television viewing reported on by the class. How does that number compare with the 4 instances per hour reported in the 1997-1998 study? Ask students to explain any discrepancy. Note that the original study results were based on 242 episodes of 24 programs, viewed over a period of one television "season," whereas the class results are based on single episodes of shows viewed over a period of one week.

Discuss how often risky behavior was followed by negative consequences. In the original 1997-1998 study, risky behavior was seldom followed by negative consequences, except for violence, which had negative consequences only 60 percent of the time. Ask students what impact a lack of consequences for risky behavior might have on viewers.

Find out if students encountered any risky behaviors that were not listed initially. Determine which particular shows had the most scenes of risky behaviors. Ask students which age group those shows were aimed at.

Other questions that could be brought up for discussion are: Which substance appears most frequently in scenes of substance abuse? Was alcohol, tobacco, or illegal drugs used by main characters? How often was a main character shown using violence? What difference does it make if a behavior is modeled by a main character or an incidental one? Was violence ever rewarded? Was it glamorized?

What kind of messages are the networks sending about casual sex? How do they think network shows compare with cable shows when it comes to the modeling of health-related behavior?

Finally, ask students what they can conclude on the basis of their findings concerning popular network television programs and the messages they send concerning health-related issues.

> 🍍 *What if this bombs?* There is no bombing potential unless students fail to carry out the assignment, which is not likely, as it is sure to engage their interest. Not only will any results lead to a lively discussion, the activity also has the added bonus of making students more aware of the negative messages that they are exposed to when watching their favorite television shows.

Will, K. E., Porter, B. E., Geller, E. S., & DePasquale, J. P. (2005). Is television a health and safety hazard? A cross-sectional analysis of at-risk behavior on primetime television. Journal of Applied Social Psychology, 35, 1, 198-222.

MULTIMEDIA RESOURCES

Video

Acute and Posttraumatic Stress Disorder. This film identifies the criteria for stress disorders and the disabling symptoms suffered by those affected by trauma. It uses interviews with educators to discuss the need for early intervention and examine how acute stress disorder can evolve into a chronic condition. (DVD, 2003, 22 min.) Available from Insight Media (800-233-9910).

Emotion and Illness. New work in immunology research has shown that emotions do play a role in physical health. Women with incurable breast cancer who have been through psychotherapy have actually lived twice as long as women without such therapy. People have been able to lower their blood pressure and decrease medication by dealing with the causes of anger and depression. This program visits classes for people under stress, hospital cancer wards, and a support group for breast cancer patients to show how emotions are being treated in order to improve health. (1995, 30 min.) Films for the Humanities and Sciences, PO Box 2053, Princeton, NJ 08543-2053.

Health, Mind, and Behavior (*Discovering Psychology* Series). In psychological theory, the bio-psychosocial model is replacing the traditional biomedical model. Accordingly, this film explains how recent research is reexamining the relationship between mind and body. (1989, 28 min.) Audio-Visual Center, Indiana University, Bloomington, IN 47495-5901.

Health, Stress, and Coping. Provides a number of good examples that illustrate the relationship between psychological states and physical reactions. Also discusses Selye's General Adaptation Syndrome. (1990, 30 min.) Insight Media, 121 West 85th Street, New York, NY 10024.

Managing Stress. Examines ways to cope with common stressors in our environment. (1989, 33 min.) CRM/McGraw-Hill Films, 2233 Faraday Avenue, Carlsbad, CA 92008.

Pain and Healing (*The Mind* Series). While examining the mind's role in healing the body and controlling pain, this film explores the ways in which attitudes affect patterns of disease and pain. It tours a pain clinic at the University of Washington in Seattle where patients with chronic pain participate in a three-week course designed to ease their suffering. It reveals that patients under hypnosis dissociate with painful sensory input, demonstrating that the brain is actually an interpreter of pain. Also describes how the body's pain-killing mechanisms respond to expectation and placebos, allowing the mind to make associations that have a powerful effect on the healing process. (1989, 20 min.) Audio-Visual Center, Indiana University, Bloomington, IN 47495.

Post-Traumatic Stress Disorder: The Woman's Perspective. The puzzling nervous disorder, originally associated with former Vietnam combat veterans, has since become a recognized health problem for millions of American women. In truth, more women than men suffer from PTSD. This program examines the symptoms and suspected causes of the disorder, including feelings of helplessness suffered by victims of child abuse, sexual assault, or domestic violence. Doctors and sufferers discuss the ongoing problem of PTSD misdiagnosis, along with the treatments and therapies that have proven effective in controlling its disabling symptoms. (1998, 20 min.) Films for the Humanities and Sciences, PO Box 2053, Princeton, NJ 08543-2053.

Social Side of Health (*Triangle of Health* Film Series). This film emphasizes the equal importance of all three sides of health: social, physical, and mental. It also points out that, however important it is for each person to nurture his or her own individuality, humans must accept the fact that they are, by nature, social beings with a basic need to relate to others and to find acceptance and recognition in group membership. (1969, 10 min.) Bureau of Audio Visual Instruction, University of Wisconsin Extension, PO Box 2093, Madison, WI 53701-2093.

Stressed to the Limit. Exploring the connection between stress and health, this film examines the fight-or-flight response, lymphocytes, cytokines, heart disease, and the psychological lure of smoking. It offers insights into such issues as control, social support, resilience, and the search for meaning. (DVD, 2006, 30 min.) Available from Insight Media (800-233-9910).

Stress: You Can Live With It. Three dramatized case histories depict the risk-taking patterns typical of Type A workaholics, illustrating how stress control, proper nutrition, exercise, and abstaining from smoking can enrich and extend lives – and increase productivity. (1983, 26 min.) J. Gary Mitchell Film Company (800-301-4050).

Internet

American Institute of Stress. This site is maintained by the American Institute of Stress (AIS), a non-profit organization, which was established in 1978 at the request of Dr. Hans Selye to serve as a clearinghouse of information on stress-related topics. Visit this site at: http://www.stress.org.

Authentic Happiness. This site, mentioned in Idea 7 of this manual, is run by the University of Pennsylvania and features Dr. Martin Seligman, the founder of Positive Psychology. Visitors can fill out questionnaires and receive feedback concerning emotions, meaning, engagement, and life satisfaction. Visit this site at: http://www.authentichappiness.sas.upenn.edu/

Health Psychology. This site, which is run by the APA, provides many links to online resources on the subject of health psychology. Visit this site at: http://www.health-psych.org.

Medline Plus. This site is run jointly by the US National Library of Science and the National Institutes of Health. Here, visitors can view a slideshow on stress management, take a stress assessment test, and read many articles on stress-related topics. Visit this site at: http://www.nlm.nih.gov/medlineplus/stress.html.

Computer Program

Typecat (Type A-B Behavior). In this module, students take a brief personality test and then discuss the implications of the results. The module gives careful qualifications for making generalizations based on these simple test results. The students' main objective is to learn how test scores on the Type A-B test are used to link behavioral patterns and illness. (DOS) Houghton Mifflin Company; see your sales representative.

HANDOUT 14.1 EXPLANATORY STYLES

Imagine that the situation described below happened to you. What would you feel caused it? Events may have many causes, but we want you to pick only one—the major cause if this event happened to you. Please write this cause in the blank provided. Next we ask you some questions about this cause. Circle one number for each answer.

Situation: Your car ran out of gas in the middle of a highway.

1.   Write down the one major cause _____

2.   Is this cause due to something about you or to something about other people or circumstances?

Totally due to other people or circumstances							Totally due to me
1	2	3	4	5	6	7	

3.   In the future, will this cause again be present?

Will never again be present							Will always be present
1	2	3	4	5	6	7	

4.   Is the cause something that influences just this situation, or does it also influence other areas of your life?

Influences just this particular situation							Influences all situations in my life
1	2	3	4	5	6	7	

HANDOUT 14.3a TYPE A BEHAVIOR PATTERN

Create a list of specific observable behaviors that exemplify each of the three categories below that make up the Type A behavior pattern.

Excessive Competitiveness and Achievement Motivation	Time Urgency and Impatience	Easily Aroused Anger and Hostility

HANDOUT 14.6a RISKY HEALTH-RELATED BEHAVIOR CHECKLIST

While watching your assigned show, record each scene depicting a risky health-related behavior. Also list any consequences that result from the behavior.

Network: _____

Name of show: _____

Check this box if the show you watched had no scenes involving risky health-related behavior: ☐

Scene	Type of risky behavior	Consequences, if any
1		
2		
3		
4		
5		
6		
7		
8		
10		
11		
12		
13		
14		
15		

a.   The total number of scenes of risky health-related behavior in the show: _____

b.   The number of scenes of risky health-related behavior that were NOT followed by negative consequences: _____

c.   The percentage of risky health-related behaviors that were not followed by negative consequences — (answer to line (b) ÷ answer to line (a)) x 100%: _____

HANDOUT 14.6b RISKY BEHAVIOR GROUP TOTALS

Network: _____

Name of show	Length of show ½ hour or 1 hour	Number of risky health-related behaviors
1.		
2.		
3.		
4.		
5.		
6.		
7.		
8.		
9.		
10.		

a. The total number of scenes involving risky behavior viewed by my group is — (total of all answers to line (a) on Handout 14.6a): _____

b. The total number of hours of programming viewed by my group is: _____

c. The mean percentage of scenes of risky health-related behaviors viewed by my group that were not followed by negative consequences — (average of all answers to line (c) on Handout 14.6a): _____

Test
Bank

CHAPTER 1

What is Social Psychology?

MULTIPLE CHOICE

1. Social psychologists do *not* generally
    a)   work in settings outside of an academic context.
    b)   consider the effects of external, nonsocial factors on behavior.
    c)   study phenomena about which commonsense beliefs are held.
    d)   pay more attention to group behavior than the behavior of individuals within groups.
    Ans: d   LO: 1   Page: 5   Type: F

2. Which of the following questions would a social psychologist be *most* likely to study?
    a)   Are crime rates different among people of higher versus lower socioeconomic status?
    b)   What risk factors contribute to the onset of schizophrenia?
    c)   Is there a link between playing violent video games and engaging in aggressive behavior?
    d)   Do citizens in countries with democratic governments report greater life satisfaction than citizens in countries with autocratic governments?
    Ans: c   LO: 1   Page: 5   Type: C

3. Which of the following questions would a social psychologist be *least* likely to study?
    a)   What kinds of persuasion techniques are the most effective in product advertising?
    b)   What are the most important qualities people look for in a romantic partner or friendship?
    c)   Why do people sometimes behave differently in a group setting than they do on their own?
    d)   Have attitudes toward gay marriage in the U.S. changed in the last five years?
    Ans: d   LO: 1   Page: 5-6   Type: C

4. Social psychology is all of the following *except*
    a)   a science addressing a diverse array of topics.
    b)   the study of how people think, feel, and behave.
    c)   a compilation of anecdotal observations and case studies.
    d)   an approach applying the scientific method of systematic observation, description, and measurement.
    Ans: c   LO: 1   Page: 5-6   Type: F

5. Social psychology is primarily concerned with the ways in which
    a)   group factors contribute to the functioning of social institutions.
    b)   unconscious forces influence conscious motivations and desires.
    c)   specific personality characteristics predict behavior across situations.
    d)   individuals think, feel, and behave with regard to others.
    Ans: d   LO: 1   Page: 5-6   Type: F

6. Social psychology differs from history and philosophy in its
    a)   attention to the scientific method.
    b)   concern with human behavior.
    c)   greater focus on cultural influences.
    d)   more narrow and refined bandwidth of interest.
    Ans: a   LO: 1   Page: 5-6   Type: F

7. Which of the following is *not* considered an important part of the scientific method?
    a)   Systematic observation
    b)   Variable Definition
    c)   Intuition
    d)   Measurement
    Ans: c   LO: 1   Page: 5-6   Type: F

8.   Anita wants to spend her career studying the factors that predict whether the members of a couple are satisfied with their marriage. If she chooses to do so as a social psychologist, it is likely that her pursuit will
     a)   focus more on people's thoughts than on their actual behavior.
     b)   emphasize the importance of different personality types, such as "fun-loving" and "open to new experiences."
     c)   examine couples rather than individuals as the unit of analysis.
     d)   include systematic observation and measurement of couples.
     Ans: d   LO: 1   Page: 6-7   Type: A

9.   Mariano is interested in how the diversity of a group affects its performance. If Mariano is a social psychologist, it is *unlikely* that he will
     a)   conduct experiments that compare diverse and non-diverse groups.
     b)   focus more on the details of recent Supreme Court rulings regarding affirmative action than examining the actual behavior of groups.
     c)   be interested in the thoughts as well as behaviors of people within those groups.
     d)   expect the perceived influence of diversity among the members of the groups to be as influential as the actual changes in performance caused by diverse demographics.
     Ans: b   LO: 1   Page: 6-7   Type: A

10. Which of the following is a central part of the definition of social psychology?
     a)   It uses historical events as its primary source of data.
     b)   It assumes that thoughts and behaviors are influenced by other people.
     c)   It focuses more on the behavior of groups than on that of individuals.
     d)   It emphasizes the solitary nature of human behavior.
     Ans: b   LO: 1   Page: 6-7   Type: F

11. Which of the following statements about social psychology is *false*?
     a)   A goal of social psychology is to develop general principles that describe human behavior.
     b)   An assumption of social psychology is that only social factors influence human behavior.
     c)   Social psychology relies on the scientific method to learn about human behavior.
     d)   Social psychology is concerned with the way in which the imagined presence of others influences individuals.
     Ans: b   LO: 1   Page: 6-7   Type: C

12. A social psychologist would be *least* likely to conduct a study examining the effect of
     a)   sleep on concentration ability.
     b)   temperature on highway shootings.
     c)   political attitudes on friendship formation.
     d)   academic performance on self-esteem.
     Ans: a   LO: 1   Page: 6-7   Type: C

13. Sarunas is a social psychologist. Of the following studies, he is probably *most* interested in reading about one demonstrating the effects of
     a)   attitude similarity on interpersonal attraction.
     b)   immigration patterns on stock market activity.
     c)   distraction on attention to a visual display.
     d)   narcotic substances on neurotransmitter activity in the brain.
     Ans: a   LO: 1   Page: 6-7   Type: A

14. Which of the following is *not* an important theme in social psychological research?
     a)   The power of the situation
     b)   The role of the individual's cultural background
     c)   The motivation to be liked
     d)   The role of unconscious drives
     Ans: d   LO: 1   Page: 6-7   Type: F

15. Courses in social psychology are often required for students majoring in which of the following fields?
    a) Education
    b) Journalism
    c) Business
    d) All of these.
    Ans: d   LO: 1   Page: 6-7   Type: F

16. The study conducted by Fein et al. (2007) on perceptions of a political debate focuses on
    a) how a candidate's nonverbal behaviors influences viewers' evaluations of his performance.
    b) differences in viewers' perceptions of male versus female candidates.
    c) cross-cultural differences in political preferences.
    d) the influence of other people's reactions on viewers' perceptions of candidate performance.
    Ans: d   LO: 2   Page: 7-8   Type: F

17. The results of the political debate study conducted by Fein et al. (2007) indicate that
    a) participants rated a candidate more positively when they heard him make jokes during the debate.
    b) a candidate's efforts to make jokes during the debate did not influence participants' ratings of his performance.
    c) a candidate making jokes during the debate led participants to like him more when people in the audience laughed at those jokes.
    d) a candidate making jokes during the debate led participants to like him less when no one in the audience laughed at those jokes.
    Ans: d   LO: 2   Page: 7-8   Type: C

18. Extrapolating from the Fein et al. (2007) study of political debates, when a cable TV channel shows viewers at home real-time data regarding the debate perceptions of a focus group
    a) the attitudes of the viewers at home are not likely to be influenced.
    b) the attitudes of the viewers at home are likely to change in the same direction as the attitudes of the focus group.
    c) the attitudes of the viewers at home are likely to change in the opposite direction of the attitudes of the focus group.
    d) viewers at home are likely to get distracted and confused.
    Ans: b   LO: 2   Page: 7-8   Type: A

19. Which of the following conclusions regarding the Fein et al. (2007) study of political debates is *false*?
    a) Participants were more influenced by other people's reactions to the candidate than by what the candidate actually said.
    b) The reactions of other people to the candidate were only influential when those people were in the same room as the participant.
    c) The factors in our social context that influence our perceptions and behaviors are often subtle.
    d) Telling jokes during a political debate is risky because the payoff in terms of audience perception is small and the potential costs are great.
    Ans: b   LO: 2   Page: 7-8   Type: C

20. Sociologists tend to study behavior at the _____ level, whereas social psychologists study behavior at the _____ level.
    a) group; individual
    b) interpersonal; cultural
    c) specific; general
    d) social; cognitive
    Ans: a   LO: 2   Page: 8-9   Type: F

21. Sociologists studying the effects of media violence would be more likely than social psychologists to
    a) conduct experiments manipulating the amount of media violence viewed by participants.
    b) assess changes in television availability and in murder rates over the last thirty years.
    c) concern themselves with situational variables that moderate the effects of media violence on its viewers.
    d) focus on the types of individuals who choose to view media violence.
    Ans: b   LO: 2   Page: 8-9   Type: C

22. To examine the relationship between economic conditions and violence, Gunther compares the murder rates for counties with different median incomes. Gunther's research *best* characterizes what field of study?
     a)   Social psychology
     b)   Clinical psychology
     c)   Personality psychology
     d)   Sociology
     Ans: d   LO: 2   Page: 8-9   Type: A

23. To examine the relationship between temperature and violence, Priti manipulates the thermostat in her laboratory while participants are engaged in a military simulation game. She then looks at the effect of this manipulation on their aggressive behavior during the game, comparing participants in the "warm" condition to those in the "comfortable" condition. Priti's research *best* characterizes what field of study?
     a)   Sociology
     b)   Social psychology
     c)   Clinical psychology
     d)   Personality psychology
     Ans: b   LO: 2   Page: 8-9   Type: A

24. Brad is a social psychologist. Marion is a sociologist. Which of the following research questions is *most* likely of interest to both of them?
     a)   How do societal and immediate factors influence racial differences in academic achievement?
     b)   How does positive and negative feedback impact conceptions of the self?
     c)   Do different socioeconomic groups express different political attitudes?
     d)   Can an authority figure influence people to act in ways that they normally would not?
     Ans: a   LO: 2   Page: 8-9   Type: A

25. Which of the following statements concerning social psychology and sociology is *false*?
     a)   Sociologists tend to study societal level variables, whereas social psychologists focus on more specific and immediate variables.
     b)   Social psychology studies human behavior at the level of the individual, whereas sociology studies human behavior at the group level.
     c)   Social psychologists and sociologists often study the same issues and publish in the same journals.
     d)   Sociologists are more likely than social psychologists to rely on experimentation to study human behavior.
     Ans: d   LO: 2   Page: 8-9   Type: C

26. When comparing social psychology to sociology, a major difference is the
     a)   target populations studied.
     b)   number of variables explored.
     c)   focus on the individual or the group.
     d)   emphasis on how social context affects behavior.
     Ans: c   LO: 2   Page: 8-9   Type: C

27. Marilyn is interested in whether schizophrenic individuals tend to interpret verbal feedback from others as negative even if it is positive. It might be said that Marilyn is doing research at the intersection of social psychology and
     a)   evolutionary psychology.
     b)   sociology.
     c)   personality psychology.
     d)   clinical psychology.
     Ans: d   LO: 2   Page: 8-9   Type: A

28. Although related to other fields, social psychology is distinct in that its emphasis is on
     a)   understanding the immediate situational factors that influence human behavior.
     b)   classifying and treating psychological disorders.
     c)   identifying individual characteristics that are relatively stable across time.
     d)   describing the relationship between human behavior and societal variables.
     Ans: a   LO: 2   Page: 8-9   Type: C

29.   Which of the following is *true* regarding social psychology and clinical psychology?
      a)   Researchers in both fields might conduct studies investigating outcomes such as anxiety or
            depression.
      b)   Research in social psychology utilized the scientific method, whereas research in clinical psychology
            does not.
      c)   Both fields are primarily concerned with the underlying causes of atypical behavior.
      d)   Psychologists in both fields must become certified in therapy aimed towards helping individuals with
            mental illness.
      Ans: a   LO: 2   Page: 9   Type: C

30.   Research concerning how depressed and non-depressed individuals process social information is at the
      intersection of what two fields of study?
      a)   Personality psychology and cognitive psychology
      b)   Social psychology and clinical psychology
      c)   Social psychology and sociology
      d)   Clinical psychology and sociology
      Ans: b   LO: 2   Page: 9   Type: A

31.   Which of the following branches of psychology is *most* interested in "the power of the situation"?
      a)   Clinical psychology
      b)   Cognitive psychology
      c)   Personality psychology
      d)   Social psychology
      Ans: d   LO: 2   Page: 9   Type: F

32.   What distinguishes social psychology from other specialties in psychology is its
      a)   use of the scientific method in research design.
      b)   emphasis on correlational research design.
      c)   attention to the influence of situational context on behavior.
      d)   willingness to consider cross-cultural differences in human behavior and cognition.
      Ans: c   LO: 2   Page: 8-9   Type: C

33.   Astrid has developed a 12-item questionnaire to help her identify individuals who tend to be skeptical of
      authority figures across different situations. Astrid is most likely a _____ psychologist.
      a)   cognitive
      b)   social
      c)   clinical
      d)   personality
      Ans: d   LO: 2   Page: 10   Type: A

34.   The interaction between individual characteristics and situational constraints on the way people behave *best*
      reflects the intersection of
      a)   cognitive and personality psychology.
      b)   personality and social psychology.
      c)   social and clinical psychology.
      d)   clinical and developmental psychology.
      Ans: b   LO: 2   Page: 10-11   Type: C

35.   Hyunwoo believes that image-oriented ads will be more persuasive for individuals concerned with the way
      they appear to others, whereas ads that stress product quality will be more effective for individuals who are
      less concerned with their public image. This belief represents the intersection of what two fields of study?
      a)   Social psychology and clinical psychology
      b)   Social psychology and cognitive psychology
      c)   Social psychology and personality psychology
      d)   Social psychology and sociology
      Ans: c   LO: 2   Page: 10-11   Type: A

36. Diane is interested in whether women with nurturing personalities are more reliable friends both inside and outside the workplace. Rebecca is interested in the hypothesis that women tend to be more nurturing outside the workplace because others expect them to be nurturing. It is likely that Diane is a _____ psychologist and Rebecca is a _____ psychologist.
    a)   social; personality
    b)   clinical; personality
    c)   personality; clinical
    d)   personality; social
    Ans: d   LO: 2   Page: 10-11   Type: A

37. Which of the following research questions does *not* involve the interaction of social and cognitive psychology?
    a)   What situational factors influence whether someone interprets an event as an emergency and then makes a decision to offer help to a stranger?
    b)   How does injury to a particular part of the brain influence the ability to form new memories?
    c)   How does a threat to self-esteem influence people's ability to pay attention to complex stimuli?
    d)   How do stereotypes influence our memory of social interactions?
    Ans: b   LO: 2   Page: 11   Type: C

38. Antoine investigates the extent to which depressed individuals have difficulty forming accurate memories of social interactions, particularly when those interactions are stressful. His research is *best* described as being at the intersection of
    a)   personality, cognitive, and clinical psychology.
    b)   cognitive, social, and personality psychology.
    c)   social, clinical, and cognitive psychology.
    d)   clinical, personality, and social psychology.
    Ans: c   LO: 2   Page: 9-11   Type: A

39. Which of the following "common sense" findings is indeed *true*?
    a)   Most of us expect beautiful people to be unintelligent.
    b)   Playing violent video games is a safe way to release aggressive tendencies.
    c)   People come to like an activity more when they are given a large reward for engaging in it.
    d)   People tend to overestimate the extent to which others agree with their points of view.
    Ans: d   LO: 2   Page: 11-12   Type: F

40. It could be argued that social psychology supplements common sense about human behavior in all of the following ways *except* that
    a)   social psychology tests commonsense assumptions using scientific methods.
    b)   social psychology addresses many of the same issues about which people have intuitions.
    c)   social psychological theories are as broad in scope as common sense.
    d)   social psychological findings tend to support most intuitive beliefs about human behavior.
    Ans: d   LO: 2   Page: 11-12   Type: C

41. Social psychological research is a necessary endeavor because our commonsense intuitions
    a)   tend to be very unstable.
    b)   often contradict each other.
    c)   are not as shared by other people as we think.
    d)   are generally accurate but are held with little confidence.
    Ans: b   LO: 2   Page: 11-12   Type: F

42. Social psychology differs from common sense in that
    a)   common sense tends to produce more accurate knowledge about human behavior than social psychology.
    b)   common sense captures the full complexity of human behavior.
    c)   social psychology is far more intuitive than common sense.
    d)   social psychology relies on the scientific method to test its theories.
    Ans: d   LO: 2   Page: 11-12   Type: C

43. The field of social psychology emerged as a distinct discipline around the turn of the
     a)   17th century.
     b)   18th century.
     c)   19th century.
     d)   20th century.
     Ans: d   LO: 3   Page: 12   Type: F

44. Ringelmann and Triplett are *best* labeled as
     a)   the first researchers to explore conformity.
     b)   sociologists who established social psychology as a distinct discipline.
     c)   pioneers in the field of social cognition.
     d)   the founders of social psychology.
     Ans: d   LO: 3   Page: 13   Type: F

45. Among the following social psychologists, who was one of the original founders of social psychology?
     a)   Norman Triplett
     b)   Stanley Milgram
     c)   Michael Norton
     d)   Philip Zimbardo
     Ans: a   LO: 3   Page: 13   Type: F

46. Which of the following people is credited with publishing the first research article in social psychology?
     a)   Max Ringelmann
     b)   Norman Triplett
     c)   Floyd Allport
     d)   John Haharwood
     Ans: b   LO: 3   Page: 13-14   Type: F

47. Blaine works in a factory producing car stereos. He notices that workers produce more stereos by the end of the day when they work together in the same room than when they work in separate rooms. His observation is consistent with a classic study conducted by which of the following classic researchers?
     a)   Lewin
     b)   Asch
     c)   Triplett
     d)   Sherif
     Ans: c   LO: 3   Page: 13-14   Type: A

48. "Founders of social psychology" Norman Triplett and Max Ringelmann both did research examining
     a)   the influence groups exert on their members.
     b)   the impact of the presence of others on performance.
     c)   how behaviors are shaped by perceptions.
     d)   the impact of different leadership strategies on group performance.
     Ans: b   LO: 3   Page: 13   Type: C

49. Which of the following events is regarded as having established social psychology as a distinct field of study?
     a)   The publication of the first three textbooks in social psychology
     b)   The publication of the first research article in social psychology
     c)   The formation of the Society for the Psychological Study of Social Issues
     d)   The introduction of the interactionist perspective to the field of psychology
     Ans: a   LO: 3   Page: 13   Type: F

50. Floyd Allport's social psychology textbook, published in 1924, is credited with
     a)   establishing the field's emphasis on the scientific method.
     b)   imbuing the field with a cross-cultural orientation.
     c)   introducing the major theories of social psychology.
     d)   bridging the "hot" and "cold" perspectives on behavior and cognition.
     Ans: a   LO: 3   Page: 13-14   Type: F

51.   Which of the following people did *not* author one of social psychology's first textbooks?
      a)   William McDougall
      b)   Muzafer Sherif
      c)   Edward Ross
      d)   Floyd Allport
      Ans: b   LO: 3   Page: 13-14   Type: F

52.   If a student wants to find the first source that established social psychology as a separate field with an emphasis on experimentation, he or she should probably read
      a)   Allport's (1924) text.
      b)   Ringelmann's (1913) article.
      c)   McDougall's (1908) text.
      d)   Triplett's (1897–1898) article.
      Ans: a   LO: 3   Page: 13-14   Type: C

53.   According to your textbook, one of the people who had the greatest impact on the developing field of social psychology was *not* a psychologist. Who was this person?
      a)   Plato
      b)   Charles Lindbergh
      c)   Adolf Hitler
      d)   Jackie Robinson
      Ans: c   LO: 3   Page: 13   Type: F

54.   Which historical event sparked great interest in and gave shape to the field of social psychology?
      a)   The Great Depression
      b)   The use of two atomic bombs by the United States during World War II
      c)   The Nazi Holocaust during World War II
      d)   The American Civil Rights Movement
      Ans: c   LO: 3   Page: 13   Type: F

55.   Of the following important figures in the history of social psychology, who most explicitly emphasized application of the field to social problems in society?
      a)   Gordon Allport
      b)   Fritz Heider
      c)   Max Ringelmann
      d)   Muzafer Sherif
      Ans: a   LO: 3   Page: 13-14   Type: F

56.   Which of the following classic investigations is *not* thought to have arisen from the researcher's attempt to understand events in Nazi Germany?
      a)   Adorno's research on prejudice
      b)   Triplett's research on performance in groups
      c)   Milgram's study of destructive obedience
      d)   Lewin's research on conservation
      Ans: b   LO: 3   Page: 13-14   Type: C

57.   Which of the following is *least* characteristic of research in social psychology between the 1930s and 1950s?
      a)   An emphasis on the application of social psychology to practical concerns
      b)   An integration of social and cognitive processes that determine behavior
      c)   Attention to the topics of conformity and prejudice
      d)   The use of experimentation in research
      Ans: b   LO: 3   Page: 13-14   Type: C

58. Which social psychologist is credited with demonstrating that complex social processes could be studied scientifically?
    a) Sherif
    b) F. Allport
    c) Heider
    d) Lewin
    Ans: a   LO: 3   Page: 13-14   Type: F

59. The work of Muzafer Sherif was important for the development of social psychology because he
    a) demonstrated the interaction between personality characteristics and situational factors.
    b) developed professional associations for social psychologists.
    c) showed that complex social behavior could be examined scientifically.
    d) helped to find solutions to the crisis in the field during the 1960s and 1970s.
    Ans: c   LO: 3   Page: 13   Type: F

60. Muzafer Sherif's research was crucial for the development of social psychology because it
    a) introduced the idea of cognitive dissonance.
    b) marked the beginning of the pluralistic approach that continues to characterize the field.
    c) firmly established the importance of an interactionist perspective.
    d) demonstrated the feasibility of studying complex social issues in a rigorous, scientific manner.
    Ans: d   LO: 3   Page: 13-14   Type: C

61. Which of the following is *not* one of the fundamental principles of social psychology established by Lewin?
    a) Behavior depends on how we perceive and interpret the world around us.
    b) Behavior is a function of the interaction between the person and the environment.
    c) Social psychology should be applied to important, practical issues.
    d) Behavior should be conceptualized as an interaction of cognition and motivation.
    Ans: d   LO: 3   Page: 14   Type: F

62. Jack and his girlfriend Diane dine out about three times a week. Jack believes that they hardly ever dine out, whereas Diane thinks they dine out all the time. This illustrates what important theme in social psychology?
    a) Behavior is a function of the interaction between a person and his or her environment.
    b) Different people can see the same situation very differently.
    c) Complex social behaviors can be studied using the scientific method.
    d) Social psychological theories can be applied to the solution of real-world problems.
    Ans: b   LO: 3   Page: 13-14   Type: A

63. According to the interactionist perspective, behavior is a result of the interaction between
    a) motivation and cognition.
    b) introverts and extraverts.
    c) personality and situations.
    d) theoretical and practical concerns.
    Ans: c   LO: 3   Page: 13-14   Type: F

64. By stressing both internal differences among individuals and differences among external situations, the interactionist perspective is an approach combining
    a) personality psychology with social psychology.
    b) social psychology with clinical psychology.
    c) cognitive psychology with social psychology.
    d) social psychology with sociology.
    Ans: a   LO: 3   Page: 13-14   Type: C

65. An emphasis on experiments addressing the interaction of individuals and their social context is particularly clear in the writings of
    a) Rich Petty and John Cacioppo.
    b) Max Ringelmann and Norman Triplett.
    c) Norman Triplett and Kurt Lewin.
    d) Kurt Lewin and Floyd Allport.
    Ans: d   LO: 3   Page: 13-14   Type: C

66. Phoebe is a graduate student in social psychology who will only agree to conducting research that will help address an ongoing social problem. Phoebe's desire is *most* consistent with the philosophies of which of the following pairs of individuals?
   a)   Gordon Allport and Floyd Allport
   b)   Floyd Allport and Kurt Lewin
   c)   Kurt Lewin and Fritz Heider
   d)   Fritz Heider and Gordon Allport
   Ans: b   LO: 3   Page: 13-14   Type: A

67. Which of the following is *true* regarding Kurt Lewin?
   a)   His interactionist perspective argues that human behavior is mostly a function of situational pressures.
   b)   His push for practical research was met with great resistance in the early days of social psychology.
   c)   He was the first to test social psychological hypotheses in a scientific manner.
   d)   He was instrumental in generating research on how groups function.
   Ans: d   LO: 3   Page: 13-14   Type: C

68. Lewin's research concerning both how to promote economical and nutritious eating habits, and what kinds of leaders elicit the best work from group members, was important in establishing which of the following?
   a)   Different topics require different research strategies.
   b)   Social psychology could be used to understand and help solve practical problems.
   c)   Early theories in social psychology were often historically and culturally limited.
   d)   Social psychologists may unwittingly influence the behavior of research participants.
   Ans: b   LO: 3   Page: 13-14   Type: C

69. Because of his research on practical issues, such as the research he conducted in the 1940s concerning promotion of more economical and nutritious eating habits, Kurt Lewin could be considered one of the founders of
   a)   evolutionary social psychology.
   b)   psychoneuroimmunology.
   c)   "hot" theories of social psychology.
   d)   applied social psychology.
   Ans: d   LO: 3   Page: 14   Type: F

70. Mona would like to understand the interactionist perspective. She has enough time to skim two textbooks. She should probably read one textbook in social psychology and one in
   a)   evolutionary psychology.
   b)   cognitive psychology.
   c)   clinical psychology.
   d)   personality psychology.
   Ans: d   LO: 3   Page: 13-14   Type: A

71. Which of the following *best* illustrates Lewin's interactionist perspective?
   a)   Sally is a very creative kind of person who likes to build things.
   b)   Jerry only works because he receives a very large income.
   c)   Rikki is usually shy, but at work she appears to be quite outgoing.
   d)   Maury gives money to charities because he wants other people to think he is very generous.
   Ans: c   LO: 3   Page: 14   Type: C

72. Abe subscribes to a psychoanalytic view of human behavior. Abe's view probably differs from that of Kurt Lewin in that Abe is more likely to emphasize the power of
   a)   external rewards.
   b)   internal motives.
   c)   situational factors.
   d)   interpersonal relationships.
   Ans: b   LO: 3   Page: 14   Type: A

73.   Galen studies stereotypes and prejudice; Dan studies how people make attributions about others' behavior.
       Galen and Dan probably feel particular gratitude to _____ and _____, respectively, for helping to establish
       these areas in social psychology.
       a)   Asch; G. Allport
       b)   G. Allport; Heider
       c)   Heider; Sherif
       d)   Sherif; Asch
       Ans: b   LO: 3   Page: 14   Type: A

74.   Suppose that research on how people make attributions about others' behavior was linked to the way in
       which people compare themselves with others. This would *best* represent an intersection of the work done
       by which of the following pairs of social psychologists?
       a)   Festinger and Hovland
       b)   Hovland and Asch
       c)   Asch and Heider
       d)   Heider and Festinger
       Ans: d   LO: 3   Page: 14   Type: C

75.   Thibaut and Kelley share Heider's interest in
       a)   the roots of prejudice.
       b)   people's desire to sustain consistency.
       c)   the perceptions people have in relationships.
       d)   applying their research to understanding propaganda.
       Ans: c   LO: 3   Page: 13-14   Type: C

76.   Elliot is interested in how people cope with holding two thoughts that are not consistent with each other. He
       would do best to read the writings of which of the following pairs of social psychologists?
       a)   Allport and Asch
       b)   Asch and Heider
       c)   Heider and Festinger
       d)   Festinger and Milgram
       Ans: c   LO: 3   Page: 13-14   Type: A

77.   Which of the following is correctly matched with its founder?
       a)   Attribution theory; Heider
       b)   Social comparison theory; Triplett
       c)   Social cognition; Festinger
       d)   Cognitive dissonance theory; Asch
       Ans: a   LO: 3   Page: 13-14   Type: C

78.   Hovland and his colleagues are *best* known for their research concerning
       a)   attribution theory.
       b)   stereotypes and prejudice.
       c)   interpersonal relationships.
       d)   attitudes and persuasion.
       Ans: d   LO: 3   Page: 13-14   Type: F

79.   Dimitri would like to read about social psychological research on conformity. He should look at the
       research of
       a)   Asch.
       b)   Thibaut and Kelley.
       c)   Adorno.
       d)   Heider.
       Ans: a   LO: 3   Page: 13-14   Type: A

80. Research on the social psychological underpinnings of prejudice might be said to have its roots in research by
    a)   Adorno and Allport.
    b)   Allport and Asch.
    c)   Asch and Festinger.
    d)   Festinger and Adorno.
    Ans: a   LO: 3   Page: 13-14   Type: F

81. One thing that Heider and Festinger have in common is that they were both concerned with
    a)   why prejudice develops.
    b)   how individuals behave in groups.
    c)   how people resolve inconsistencies.
    d)   why people conform to social norms.
    Ans: c   LO: 3   Page: 13-14   Type: C

82. Much of the debate in social psychology during the period of "Confidence and Crisis" occurred in reaction to
    a)   the usefulness of applied research.
    b)   the use of laboratory experiments.
    c)   new technological developments in the research lab.
    d)   Lewin's interactionist perspective.
    Ans: b   LO: 4   Page: 15   Type: F

83. The reference to social psychology in the 1960s and 1970s as being in the midst of "Confidence and Crisis" reflects an expansion in the types of issues studied by researchers, as well as increased criticism that largely came from
    a)   sociologists.
    b)   fellow social psychologists.
    c)   the general public.
    d)   the popular media.
    Ans: b   LO: 4   Page: 15   Type: F

84. Which of the following was *not* a criticism of laboratory experimentation in the 1960s and 1970s?
    a)   Experiments were sometimes unethical.
    b)   Experimenters' expectations might influence the results.
    c)   The theories being tested in the laboratory were often historically and culturally limited.
    d)   Experiments did not allow researchers to draw conclusions about the causal relationship between variables.
    Ans: d   LO: 4   Page: 15   Type: F

85. Which of the following represented a critique of social psychology in the 1960s and 1970s?
    a)   The discipline failed to address topics of social relevance.
    b)   It failed to distinguish itself from other fields of psychology.
    c)   Researchers had not yet agreed upon a conventional methodology.
    d)   The findings were limited to current historical circumstances.
    Ans: d   LO: 4   Page: 15   Type: C

86. Mel criticized the field of social psychology during the 1960s and 1970s. It is likely that Mel despaired about the inability of social psychological researchers to do all of the following *except*
    a)   suggest possible solutions to everyday social concerns.
    b)   acknowledge their role in artificially producing the results of their studies.
    c)   consider the cultural context in which their findings were obtained.
    d)   design ethical experimental contexts.
    Ans: a   LO: 4   Page: 15   Type: A

87. Arguably, the most famous research in social psychology focused on the situational factors influencing obedience to authority and was conducted by
    a) F. Allport.
    b) G. Allport.
    c) Festinger.
    d) None of these.
    Ans: d   LO: 4   Page: 15   Type: F

88. During the 1960s and 1970s, social psychologists who favored laboratory experiments rebuffed critics by arguing that
    a) critics' concerns regarding experimenter bias were exaggerated and misplaced.
    b) it did not matter that some studies were unethical because the benefits of running these experiments outweighed the costs.
    c) experimental studies were easier to conduct than non-experimental studies.
    d) the theoretical principles being tested in the lab were widely applicable across eras and cultures.
    Ans: d   LO: 4   Page: 15   Type: C

89. Social psychologists reacted to critiques of the field in the 1960s and 1970s by doing all of the following *except*
    a) adopting more rigorous and formalized ethical standards.
    b) paying more attention to cross-cultural differences in cognition and behavior.
    c) denouncing experiments as unacceptably artificial.
    d) developing more stringent procedures to avoid the effects of experimenter bias.
    Ans: c   LO: 4   Page: 15   Type: F

90. Social psychology in the period from the middle 1970s through the 1990s can *best* be described as a time of
    a) confidence and crisis.
    b) social activism.
    c) pluralism.
    d) interactionism.
    Ans: c   LO: 4   Page: 15-16   Type: F

91. When Taka is teaching his social psychology class, he emphasizes that the field must encompass a range of research techniques and cultural perspectives if it is to flourish. Taka's emphasis reflects a(n)
    a) contextualist orientation.
    b) empirical approach.
    c) "hot" approach to studying social behavior.
    d) pluralistic orientation.
    Ans: d   LO: 4   Page: 15-16   Type: A

92. A pluralistic approach to social psychology
    a) encourages research outside of controlled settings.
    b) emphasizes the motivational more than the cognitive underpinnings of behavior.
    c) has been supplanted by other approaches in the past thirty years.
    d) limits the kinds of topics that social psychologists can study.
    Ans: a   LO: 4   Page: 15-16   Type: C

93. Pluralism in social psychology can be seen in all of the following areas *except* the
    a) procedures used to secure government funding.
    b) integration of "hot" and "cold" perspectives.
    c) methods social psychologists use to study behavior.
    d) inclusion of various cultural perspectives.
    Ans: a   LO: 4   Page: 15-16   Type: C

94. Social psychologists use a multi-method approach to study behavior because
     a)   shifting sentiments in the field lead different methodologies to fall out of and back into favor.
     b)   different topics require different types of research strategies.
     c)   some methods are more expensive than others.
     d)   None of these.
     Ans: b   LO: 5   Page: 15-16   Type: C

95. A multi-method approach to the study of social psychological phenomena is advantageous because it
     a)   allows researchers to study many more variables within a single experiment.
     b)   increases confidence in the research findings.
     c)   requires fewer research participants.
     d)   permits multiple interpretations of the same result.
     Ans: b   LO: 5   Page: 15-16   Type: C

96. Marta is interested in how behavior is influenced by the way people think about their social world. Marta
     subscribes to the _____ perspective in social psychology.
     a)   "cold"
     b)   interactionist
     c)   multi-cultural
     d)   cross-cultural
     Ans: a   LO: 5   Page: 17   Type: A

97. The "hot" perspective in social psychology emphasizes _____, whereas the "cold" perspective emphasizes
     _____.
     a)   positive information; negative information
     b)   feelings; behavior
     c)   facts; motives
     d)   emotion; cognition
     Ans: d   LO: 5   Page: 17   Type: F

98. Fernando studies the relationship between emotions and behavior in social settings. Fernando's research
     epitomizes the _____ perspective in social psychology.
     a)   pluralistic
     b)   interactionist
     c)   "cold"
     d)   "hot"
     Ans: d   LO: 5   Page: 17   Type: A

99. A contemporary social psychologist studies both "hot" and "cold" explanations for social behavior. This
     approach is an example of
     a)   the cognitive revolution.
     b)   applied social psychology.
     c)   pluralistic orientation.
     d)   a cross-cultural perspective.
     Ans: c   LO: 5   Page: 17   Type: C

100. Benny wants to adopt both a "hot" and "cold" perspective in his research on why married couples get
     divorced. Which of the following *best* exemplifies his approach?
     a)   He wants to understand what motivates people to stay in marriages that they know from past
          experience will only get worse.
     b)   He wants to study the difference between passive and active aggression in marriages.
     c)   He wants to investigate how spur-of-the-moment marriage problems are solved relative to ongoing
          problems.
     d)   He wants to determine whether simple factors, such as mismatches in attitudes, can predict breakups
          better than communication patterns.
     Ans: a   LO: 5   Page: 17   Type: A

101. Jeff is a social psychologist who favors the "cold" approach to understanding human behavior. He is conducting research on why people fail to use condoms even when they know that they can reduce their risk of obtaining HIV by doing so. Jeff is *least* likely to devote his attention to people's
    a) drive to avoid this inconsistency.
    b) ability to detect the inconsistency.
    c) awareness of the actual risk of unprotected sex.
    d) memory for past cases in which they have behaved in a manner inconsistent with their attitudes.
    Ans: a   LO: 5   Page: 17   Type: A

102. Which of the following would *best* represent the "hot" perspective in social psychology?
    a) A good mood can foster attitude change.
    b) Distraction can lead to overdependence on first impressions.
    c) Failure to recognize that a situation is an emergency can interfere with helping.
    d) People can be genetically programmed to aggress against others.
    Ans: a   LO: 5   Page: 17   Type: A

103. Which of the following is *not* identified by your textbook as an influential factor in today's social psychology?
    a) New technological advances
    b) Behavioral genetics
    c) The split between "red" and "blue" states in the U.S.
    d) The Internet
    Ans: c   LO: 5   Page: 17-19   Type: F

104. All of the following are characteristic of the field of social psychology today *except*
    a) an interest in the way cognition and motivation interact.
    b) an emphasis on the role of culture in shaping behavior.
    c) an integration of biological and social perspectives.
    d) a concern for the lack of ethical standards in research.
    Ans: d   LO: 5   Page: 17-19   Type: C

105. Social cognition can be *best* described as the study of
    a) how we perceive, remember, and interpret information about the self and others.
    b) how cultural differences are manifested in social behavior.
    c) the extent to which social behavior is rooted in the chemistry of the brain.
    d) the interaction of people and new "thinking" computers.
    Ans: a   LO: 5   Page: 17   Type: F

106. Social psychologists interested in how we learn, store, and recall information about other people are interested in the subfield of
    a) evolutionary psychology.
    b) behavioral genetics.
    c) social cognition.
    d) multicultural psychology.
    Ans: c   LO: 5   Page: 17   Type: F

107. A contemporary social psychologist who studies stereotyping is likely to focus on
    a) controlled, but not automatic processes.
    b) automatic, but not controlled processes.
    c) both controlled and automatic processes.
    d) None of these.
    Ans: c   LO: 5   Page: 17   Type: F

108. Social neuroscience is *best* described as the study of
    a) the evolution of the brain.
    b) the interplay between genes and the environment.
    c) the social functioning of neurons.
    d) the interaction of social and neural processes.
    Ans: d   LO: 6   Page: 18   Type: F

109. Which of the following is concerned with how the brain influences social behavior?
    a)   Evolutionary psychology
    b)   Social cognition
    c)   Social neuroscience
    d)   Behavioral genetics
    Ans: c   LO: 6   Page: 18   Type: F

110. Which of the following questions would be of *most* interest to a social psychologist who studies behavioral genetics?
    a)   To what extent are attitudes inherited?
    b)   What brain structures are involved in describing the self?
    c)   Does high self-esteem help people to resist disease?
    d)   What role does testosterone play in aggression?
    Ans: a   LO: 6   Page: 18   Type: A

111. Which of the following statements regarding recent advances in behavioral genetics is *false*?
    a)   These developments have led to increased attention to the role of genes in processes of interpersonal attraction and mate selection.
    b)   These developments are of interest to clinical but not social psychologists.
    c)   These developments raise questions regarding the extent to which some social behaviors, such as aggression, reflect inherited traits.
    d)   These developments demonstrate the extent to which social psychology has become an increasingly interdisciplinary field drawing on many different perspectives.
    Ans: b   LO: 6   Page: 18   Type: C

112. Which of the following is *true* of behavioral genetics?
    a)   It is a subfield of sociology.
    b)   It examines the extent to which behavioral tendencies may be inherited.
    c)   It is synonymous with evolutionary psychology.
    d)   It considers social experiences to have a negligible effect on behavior.
    Ans: b   LO: 6   Page: 18   Type: F

113. The role of natural selection processes in the development of social behavior is a concern in
    a)   behavioral genetics.
    b)   social cognition.
    c)   personality psychology.
    d)   evolutionary psychology.
    Ans: d   LO: 6   Page: 18   Type: F

114. Izzy finds that when people vacate a parking spot, they do so more slowly when there is someone waiting to take their spot than if there is no one waiting. He attributes this behavior to an innate predisposition towards territoriality. It might be said that Izzy's findings represent a combination of work in social psychology and
    a)   clinical psychology.
    b)   behavior genetics.
    c)   anthropology.
    d)   evolutionary psychology.
    Ans: d   LO: 6   Page: 18   Type: A

115. Kareem is trying to explain to his class the difference between behavioral genetics and evolutionary psychology by using altruistic behavior as an example. In order to make the distinction clear, he should probably emphasize
    a)   sex differences in altruistic behavior.
    b)   the adaptiveness of altruistic behavior.
    c)   the role of social factors in producing altruistic behavior.
    d)   the cognitive versus motivational influences on altruistic behavior.
    Ans: b   LO: 6   Page: 18   Type: A

116. Fatma investigates whether the tendency for people to return favors is the result of natural selection. Fatma's research is in the area of
    a)   evolutionary psychology.
    b)   cross-cultural psychology.
    c)   personality psychology.
    d)   multicultural psychology.
    Ans: a   LO: 6   Page: 18   Type: A

117. Jessica and Nick are behavioral researchers. Jessica believes that her sons have been aggressive from birth because she and her husband Nick have inborn aggressive tendencies. Nick, however, believes that their sons are aggressive because throughout history it has been adaptive for men to be aggressive so that they can protect their territory and possessions. Nick's beliefs reflect the influence of _____, whereas Jessica's beliefs reflect _____.
    a)   behavioral genetics; multicultural psychology
    b)   multicultural psychology; cross-cultural psychology
    c)   cross-cultural research; evolutionary psychology research
    d)   evolutionary psychology; behavioral genetics
    Ans: d   LO: 6   Page: 18   Type: A

118. Cross-cultural research regarding attitudes about the self indicate that
    a)   people from individualistic cultures are more likely than people from collectivist cultures to seek out information that makes them feel good about themselves.
    b)   people from individualistic cultures are more likely than people from collectivist cultures to seek out information that points to a need for self-improvement.
    c)   people from individualistic cultures write more balanced and accurate self-descriptions than do people from collectivist cultures.
    d)   None of these.
    Ans: a   LO: 6   Page: 18-19   Type: C

119. Cross-cultural research by Carl Falk and colleagues (2009), in which self-ratings by Canadian and Japanese participants were compared, indicated that
    a)   Canadian participants endorsed more positive traits about the self than did Japanese participants.
    b)   Canadian participants endorsed a more balanced and accurate self-description than did Japanese participants.
    c)   Canadian participants endorsed more negative traits about the self than did Japanese participants.
    d)   there were no significant differences in the self-descriptions endorsed by Canadian and Japanese participants.
    Ans: a   LO: 6   Page: 18-19   Type: F

120. Christine conducts cross-cultural research and Betty conducts multicultural research. Which of the following is probably *true*?
    a)   Christine is more interested in discovering differences between her samples than Betty is.
    b)   Betty is more likely to use social psychological research methods.
    c)   Christine is more likely to sample individuals from many different countries.
    d)   Betty is more likely to find differences between her samples than Christine is.
    Ans: c   LO: 6   Page: 18-19   Type: A

121. Of the following, which *best* illustrates an interest in multicultural psychology?
    a)   Identifying what behaviors are caused more by culture than by genetics
    b)   Evaluating the behavior of two different racial groups within the same country
    c)   Understanding the historical forces that have led to hatred between groups
    d)   Endorsing a "hot" perspective more than a "cold" perspective of human behavior
    Ans: b   LO: 6   Page: 18-19   Type: C

122. Virtual reality allows social psychologists to
    a)   more effectively deceive research participants.
    b)   test questions that might otherwise be impractical or unethical.
    c)   scan the brain as it processes stimuli.
    d)   explore "hot" processes more so than "cold" processes.
    Ans: b   LO: 6   Page: 20-21   Type: F

123. Positron emission tomography (PET) and functional magnetic resonance imaging (MRI) are technologies that enable social psychologists to
    a)   record research participants' true attitudes without their awareness.
    b)   present visual stimuli to research participants at one-hundredth of a second.
    c)   see images of the brain as people think, feel, and behave.
    d)   induce a particular mood state in people.
    Ans: c   LO: 6   Page: 20-21   Type: F

124. Which of the following is a new technology used in contemporary social psychological research?
    a)   Positron emission tomography
    b)   Functional magnetic resonance imaging
    c)   Virtual reality
    d)   All of these.
    Ans: d   LO: 6   Page: 20-21   Type: F

125. Which of the following is an accurate statement regarding the relationship between the Internet and contemporary social psychology research?
    a)   The Internet facilitates collaboration among researchers, but is also, in and of itself, a provocative topic for empirical inquiry.
    b)   The Internet has increased the number of different variables that can be studied at one time, but at the same time has led to an unfortunate increase in the cost of running psychological studies.
    c)   The Internet allows researchers to combat the artificiality of laboratory experiments, and increases the demographic diversity of the participant sample used in most studies.
    d)   The Internet is still years away from having a significant impact on the nature and topics of research in social psychology.
    Ans: a   LO: 6   Page: 20-21   Type: C

ESSAY

126. How does social psychology differ from each of the following: (a) sociology, (b) the other subdisciplines of psychology, and (c) the approach taken by a journalist who examines the social behaviors of various individuals?
    Ans: Although social psychologists and sociologists often study related issues, an important difference between social psychology and sociology is the level of analysis used in each discipline. Sociologists tend to classify people in terms of groups, such as socioeconomic class, nationality, or race, whereas social psychologists tend to focus on the individual, even in the context of groups. In addition, social psychologists use experiments to study human behavior to a greater extent than do sociologists. Compared to the other subdisciplines of psychology, social psychology is more concerned with human behavior in social situations—that is, with thoughts, feelings, beliefs, and desires that are relevant to social behavior. A critical difference between social psychology and the approach taken by a journalist who examines the social behaviors of various individuals is that social psychologists use the scientific method of systematic observation, description, and measurement, whereas the journalist would tend to use much less scientific methods and might rely more on personal observation and specific anecdotal observations.   Page: 9-12

127. Max Ringelmann, Floyd Allport, and Kurt Lewin all made singularly important contributions to the development of social psychology as a field. Summarize these contributions.
Ans: *Max Ringelmann was an engineer who, around the beginning of the twentieth century, found that individuals who carry out simple tasks in the presence of other people tend to perform worse than they would if they carried out the task by themselves. Because this finding represents an effect of social factors on performance, it is social psychological in nature. Thus, Ringelmann is often considered one of the founders of the field. Floyd Allport wrote one of the first social psychology textbooks, and helped establish the use of the scientific method and the focus on individuals in a social context as part of the field's doctrine. Kurt Lewin emphasized the importance of seeing behavior as an interaction between an individual's personality and the situational factors influencing that individual, and also argued that social psychology must be applicable to important, practical issues. Social psychology today is applied to many domains, including law, business, health, politics, education, medicine, and many others. Page: 12-14*

128. The middle of the 20th century was an important period in the establishment of social psychology as a field. Name two general themes in the topics studied by researchers of that era, and give examples.
Ans: *Because of the events of World War II (and in particular, Nazi Germany), one general theme in research of that era was an investigation of social influence. For example, Asch and Sherif conducted studies with the aim of understanding the conditions under which people conform with majority behavior, Milgram studied destructive obedience to authority figures, and Hovland and others studied persuasion and attitude change. Another theme concerned social perception, or the ways in which we judge ourselves and others. For example, Heider was interested in how we make attributions for others' behaviors, Adorno and G. Allport were interested in the development of stereotypes and prejudice toward others based on group membership, and Festinger was interested in the extent to which we observe others in order to draw conclusions about ourselves. Page: 15-16*

129. The field of social psychology endured significant critique in the 1960s and 1970s. What were the most important elements of this critique, and how has the field addressed them?
Ans: *During that time, social psychology was criticized because some thought that its findings did not take historical and cultural context into consideration, and that its use of an experimental methodology suffered from ethical problems, artificiality, and potential experimenter bias. Social psychology has responded to the latter problems by adopting a multi-method approach while at the same time tightening ethical standards for conducting experiments and taking measures to reduce experimenter bias. Moreover, many social psychologists are now considering cross-cultural and multicultural similarities and differences in human behavior. All of these changes represent a more "pluralistic" approach to research in the field. Page: 15-16*

130. Define social cognition, and explain how this subfield of social psychology developed from its early days to current times.
Ans: *Social cognition is the study of how we perceive, remember, and interpret information about ourselves and others, and represented social psychology's contribution to the "cognitive revolution" of the 1980s. At first, social cognition research adopted a largely "cold" perspective, meaning that it attributed feelings and behaviors to people's thoughts. However, recent research in this subfield has merged motivation and emotion (or "hot" influences) with cognitive processes, such as in attempts to determine how people's motivations might affect how they think or interpret behavior in social situations. Page: 17*

CHAPTER 2

Doing Social Psychology Research

MULTIPLE CHOICE

1. One major difference between research in social psychology versus research in other fields such as chemistry is that
    a) social psychology is less of a science than many other fields.
    b) many people have common sense intuitions about the questions that social psychologists study empirically.
    c) social psychologists are less likely to rely on empirical observation to draw conclusions.
    d) in social psychology, researchers are less concerned with theories and more concerned with data.
    Ans: b   LO: 1   Page: 26   Type: C

2. Social Psychologists use the scientific method when they study human behavior in order to
    a) allow other social psychologists to attempt to replicate the findings.
    b) ensure that the right people get credit for the research.
    c) provide a solid theoretical foundation for social psychological research.
    d) encourage social psychologists to conduct more basic, rather than applied, research.
    Ans: a   LO: 1   Page: 26-27   Type: C

3. Sebastian is learning about research methods in his social psychology course. All of the following are benefits he is likely to experience *except*
    a) the findings he learns about in class will be easier to understand and remember.
    b) it will improve his reasoning about everyday events.
    c) he will become a more critical consumer of information in general.
    d) he will develop a better appreciation for the advantages of uncontrolled anecdotal observations.
    Ans: d   LO: 1   Page: 26-27   Type: A

4. All social psychological research must begin with a(n)
    a) question.
    b) independent variable.
    c) subject variable.
    d) control group.
    Ans: a   LO: 1   Page: 27   Type: F

5. Which of the following concerning research questions in social psychology is *false*?
    a) Research questions can be inspired by real-world events.
    b) Social psychologists sometimes develop research questions based on their own personal experiences and observations.
    c) Social psychologists can only develop testable research questions by reading about prior research in the field.
    d) Music, poetry, and literature can all inspire research questions.
    Ans: c   LO: 1   Page: 27   Type: C

6. Which of the following is *not* listed by your textbook as a primary means by which social psychologists discover what past research has been conducted on a given topic?
    a) Electronic databases such as PsycINFO
    b) The reference sections of other published articles
    c) Calling other researchers personally
    d) Textbooks
    Ans: c   LO: 1   Page: 28   Type: F

7. Which of the following *best* describes the process of "treeing" when searching the psychology literature?
    a) Searching for all articles on a given topic using an electronic database such as PsycINFO
    b) Breaking down the size of an electronic search by using several limiting terms
    c) Limiting searches to articles that have been cited by many other articles
    d) Using the reference sections of relevant articles to find other relevant articles
    Ans: d   LO: 1   Page: 28   Type: F

8. Social psychologists use electronic databases, such as PsycINFO to
    a) find published research on a particular topic.
    b) determine the scientific and moral value of their research question.
    c) help them select a random sample of participants from the population of interest.
    d) increase the external validity of their research.
    Ans: a   LO: 1·   Page: 28   Type: F

9. A hypothesis provides a means of _____ a theory.
    a) testing
    b) proving
    c) generalizing
    d) creating
    Ans: a   LO: 2   Page: 28-29   Type: C

10. Which of the following is *not* a testable hypothesis?
    a) Women tend to have more opposite-sex friends than men.
    b) Stereotypes are more likely to impact judgments when people are tired.
    c) People smile more when they are lying than when they are telling the truth.
    d) Refusing to help someone in need is morally wrong.
    Ans: d   LO: 2   Page: 28-29   Type: C

11. Hypotheses must be all of the following *except*
    a) explicit.
    b) testable.
    c) predictive.
    d) comprehensive.
    Ans: d   LO: 2   Page: 28-29   Type: F

12. A hypothesis is a(n)
    a) organized set of principles used to explain and predict observed phenomena.
    b) specific procedure for manipulating or measuring variables in an experiment.
    c) explicit testable prediction about the conditions under which an event will occur.
    d) measure of the strength and association between two or more variables.
    Ans: c   LO: 2   Page: 28-29   Type: F

13. All else being equal, social psychologists prefer a(n) _____ theory to a(n) _____ theory.
    a) complex; simple
    b) simple; complex
    c) intuitive; counterintuitive
    d) popular; unpopular
    Ans: b   LO: 1   Page: 28-29   Type: F

14. Britney believes that exposure to violent television increases aggressive behavior by making people's own aggressive thoughts more accessible. Christina believes that violent television increases aggressive behavior by impairing people's cognitive abilities, which in turn makes them worry less about the consequences of their behavior as well as more likely to have aggressive thoughts. If we knew that violent television indeed increases aggressive behavior but knew nothing else on this topic, which of the two theories should we prefer?
    a) Britney's because it is more testable than Christina's.
    b) Britney's because it is simpler than Christina's.
    c) Christina's because it is more empirical than Britney's.
    d) Christina's because it is more testable than Britney's.
    Ans: b   LO: 1   Page: 28-29   Type: A

15.   Which of the following is *most* consistent with Bem's theory of self-perception?
      a)   People prefer to perceive themselves in positive rather than negative terms.
      b)   Becoming aware of one's own actions is threatening to the self-concept.
      c)   The way that people see themselves is determined only by their private thoughts and feelings.
      d)   Individuals sometimes rely on their own behavior to infer their attitudes and feelings.
      Ans: d   LO: 2   Page: 28-29   Type: F

16.   Which of the following statements concerning theories in social psychology is *true*?
      a)   Theories can develop from hypotheses, but hypotheses do not develop from theories.
      b)   Theories are valued to the extent that they are generative.
      c)   Complex theories tend to be valued more than simple theories.
      d)   Theories must be accurate to be useful.
      Ans: b   LO: 2   Page: 28-29   Type: C

17.   Which of the following is *not* a common attribute of theories in social psychology?
      a)   They are high in simplicity.
      b)   They encompass a wide range of relevant information.
      c)   They preclude the need for testing further hypotheses.
      d)   They address limited and specific aspects of the way people behave.
      Ans: c   LO: 2   Page: 28-29   Type: C

18.   All of the following are goals of basic research *except*
      a)   solving practical or real-world problems.
      b)   testing psychological theories.
      c)   building a foundation of knowledge for the field.
      d)   discovering general principles of behavior.
      Ans: a   LO: 1   Page: 29-30   Type: C

19.   Melissa's research examines the cognitive processes involved in persuasion and how those processes can be used to persuade women to have yearly mammograms. This work represents an integration of
      a)   hypothetical and theoretical research.
      b)   specific and general research.
      c)   basic and applied research.
      d)   independent and dependent research.
      Ans: c   LO: 1   Page: 29-30   Type: A

20.   Which of the following *best* describes the primary goal of basic research?
      a)   To examine human behavior in real-world settings
      b)   To test specific hypotheses derived from a specific theory
      c)   To integrate the different research methodologies within one subfield of social psychology
      d)   To solve practical problems
      Ans: b   LO: 1   Page: 29-30   Type: F

21.   In encouraging social psychologists to generate useful, practical theories, Kurt Lewin
      a)   set apart reliability issues from validity issues.
      b)   urged the synthesis of basic and applied research.
      c)   reduced the distinction between hypotheses and theories.
      d)   emphasized the importance of experimental methodologies.
      Ans: b   LO: 1   Page: 29-30   Type: C

22.   Which of the following is *not* true of applied research in social psychology?
      a)   It was pioneered by Kurt Lewin.
      b)   It is more experimental than basic research.
      c)   It contributes to solutions of social problems.
      d)   It is often conducted by researchers who also conduct basic research.
      Ans: b   LO: 1   Page: 29-30   Type: F

23. Sapna is interested in the influence of nutrition on reaction time. She assigns participants to eat a salad and fruit for dinner every day for a week or to eat fast food each day. She then brings participants into the lab and asks them to push a button on a keyboard as fast as they can every time they hear a particular sound. What are the operational definitions of the variables in Sapna's study?
   a) Nutrition; whether participants eat a salad or fast food
   b) Nutrition; reaction time
   c) Whether participants eat salad or fast food; reaction time
   d) Whether participants eat salad or fast food; how quickly they push the button when they hear the sound
   Ans: d   LO: 2   Page: 30-31   Type: A

24. A researcher wanted to see if alcohol consumption raises or lowers a person's self-esteem. In one condition, he gives participants three glasses of punch spiked with alcohol and in the other he gives participants three glasses of plain punch. After participants finish their punch, they complete the Rosenberg (1965) self-esteem scale. In this study, self-esteem is the _____ and the Rosenberg questionnaire is the _____.
   a) conceptual independent variable; operational independent variable
   b) conceptual dependent variable; operational dependent variable
   c) operational dependent variable; conceptual dependent variable
   d) conceptual independent variable; operational dependent variable
   Ans: b   LO: 2   Page: 30-31   Type: A

25. Which of the following statements about conceptual variables is *false*?
   a) They are more general and less abstract than operational definitions.
   b) There is usually only one way to operationally define them.
   c) In social psychology, they are often intangible and assessed indirectly.
   d) Any social psychological study includes at least one of them.
   Ans: b   LO: 2   Page: 30-31   Type: C

26. Construct validity is *best* defined as the extent to which
   a) the independent variable caused the observed change in the dependent variable.
   b) the operational definitions reflect the conceptual variables of interest.
   c) the experimental procedures are involving and meaningful to the participants.
   d) different constructs within the study are correlated with one another.
   Ans: b   LO: 2   Page: 31   Type: F

27. Which of the following is *false* about construct validity?
   a) It is relevant to both the dependent and independent variables in a study.
   b) It can be identical for two researchers who have different operational definitions of the same conceptual variable.
   c) It ensures that the study is high in internal validity.
   d) It facilitates the testing of both hypotheses and theories.
   Ans: c   LO: 2   Page: 31   Type: C

28. In a study concerning the cues that signal deception, Winston uses the number of times a person shifts in his or her seat as a measure of lying. Virginia points out that people may shift their position because they are nervous about being perceived as a liar, even though they are actually telling the truth. Virginia is questioning the _____ of Winston's measure of lying.
   a) construct validity
   b) inter-rater reliability
   c) mundane realism
   d) internal validity
   Ans: a   LO: 2   Page: 31   Type: A

29. Which of the following statements concerning self-report measures is *false*?
   a) They allow researchers access to individuals' private thoughts and feelings.
   b) They are not influenced by the phrasing of a question or the response options provided.
   c) They are sometimes inaccurate because people intentionally present themselves in a socially desirable way.
   d) One problem they have is that individuals may not explicitly remember the thoughts or behaviors they are asked about.
   Ans: b   LO: 3   Page: 31-32   Type: F

30. Your book describes a study in which participants were provided with information about either the success
     rate or failure rate of condoms. The findings of this study indicate that
     a)   college students tend to be naively ignorant of the risks associated with some of their behaviors.
     b)   the simple wording and/or positioning of a question can have a drastic effect on self-report responses.
     c)   participants often lie when they are asked about sensitive personal issues.
     d)   All of these.
     Ans: b   LO: 3   Page: 32   Type: C

31. Which of the following has been shown to increase the accuracy of self-reports?
     a)   Experimental research
     b)   Construct validity
     c)   Bogus pipeline
     d)   Random sampling
     Ans: c   LO: 3   Page: 31-32   Type: F

32. Dr. Gillig is worried that when he asks participants to indicate on a questionnaire how they feel about
     members of other racial groups, they will respond in a socially desirable manner instead of indicating how
     they really feel. If Dr. Gillig uses a bogus pipeline in his research, he is hoping to convince participants
     a)   that it is not important whether they look good or look bad.
     b)   he can tell when they are lying as opposed to telling the truth.
     c)   that their responses are completely anonymous and confidential.
     d)   he, too, is biased, so they should feel free to admit their own racial biases.
     Ans: b   LO: 3   Page: 31-32   Type: A

33. Unlike questionnaire studies, narrative studies require
     a)   that participants answer specific questions.
     b)   that participants forsake anonymity.
     c)   coding of participant responses.
     d)   strict time limits.
     Ans: c   LO: 3   Page: 33   Type: A

34. Researchers have developed interval-contingent, signal-contingent, and event-contingent report methods in
     order to
     a)   reduce the time that elapses between an actual experience and the person's report of it.
     b)   observe participants' behavior unobtrusively.
     c)   strengthen the ethical standards used in experiments.
     d)   incorporate a more diverse sample of participants and cultures in their research.
     Ans: a   LO: 3   Page: 32-33   Type: C

35. In her research on mood, Selena asks research participants to keep a journal for a period of one month. In
     this journal, participants write as much as they can about the various emotions they experience each day.
     Selena's research would *best* be described as
     a)   relying on signal-contingent self-reports.
     b)   high in inter-rater reliability.
     c)   a narrative study.
     d)   archival research.
     Ans: b   LO: 3   Page: 33   Type: A

36. In comparison to self-report measures, observational measures are *not* affected by
     a)   experimenter expectancy effects.
     b)   participants' social desirability concerns.
     c)   sampling biases.
     d)   participants' memory biases.
     Ans: d   LO: 3   Page: 33   Type: F

37. Self-report measures and observational measures are similar in that both
    a) can be influenced by social desirability concerns.
    b) require high inter-rater reliability to be considered accurate.
    c) are subject to biases and distortions in memory.
    d) provide direct access to people's thoughts and feelings.
    Ans: a   LO: 3   Page: 31-33   Type: C

38. To assess the extent to which students are reading their textbooks, a professor notes how creased the spine of each book is. This professor is relying on
    a) a descriptive study.
    b) signal-contingent self-reports.
    c) event-contingent self-reports.
    d) observational measures.
    Ans: d   LO: 3   Page: 33   Type: A

39. The use of machines to measure dependent variables in observational studies can reduce the need for
    a) internal validity.
    b) random sampling.
    c) construct validity.
    d) inter-rater reliability.
    Ans: d   LO: 3   Page: 33   Type: C

40. Which of the following examples *best* reflects the use of inter-rater reliability?
    a) In a study examining the creativity of children's paintings, several judges are asked to rate the creativity of each painting. The degree to which the judges agree in their ratings is assessed.
    b) In a study examining the favorite foods of college students, a large sample of students rate several foods according to their preferences. The degree to which students' responses are correlated is assessed.
    c) In a study examining toy preferences of toddlers, the children are left alone to play with several toys for an hour. During the first half hour, one researcher observes their play. During the second half hour, a second researcher observes their play. The researchers' observations are then compared.
    d) In a study examining well-being in the elderly, respondents living in different nursing homes are asked to rate the quality of their nursing home. Researchers then obtain a copy of participants' medical records. The relationship between the quality ratings and actual health is assessed.
    Ans: a   LO: 3   Page: 33   Type: A

41. Which of the following is *not* mentioned in your book as a new technology used by social psychologists in obtaining observational data?
    a) Polygraphs (lie detector machines)
    b) Eye tracking
    c) fMRI
    d) Computer-based reaction time measurement
    Ans: a   LO: 4   Page: 33-34   Type: F

42. The different research methods used by social psychologists tend to emphasize all of the following *except*
    a) an objective approach.
    b) a variable approach.
    c) a systematic approach.
    d) a quantifiable approach.
    Ans: b   LO: 4   Page: 34-35   Type: F

43. Social psychologists tend to prefer which of the following research methods above all others?
    a) Meta-analysis
    b) Correlational research
    c) Experimentation
    d) Descriptive research
    Ans: c   LO: 4   Page: 34   Type: F

44. Social psychologists use descriptive research in order to describe
    a) general patterns and trends in the variables of interest.
    b) cause-and-effect relationships between independent and dependent variables.
    c) associations between two or more variables of interest.
    d) the strength of an observed effect.
    Ans: a   LO: 4   Page: 34   Type: C

45. A study that examines existing records or databases is referred to as a
    a) case study.
    b) archival study.
    c) anecdotal study.
    d) survey.
    Ans: b   LO: 4   Page: 35   Type: F

46. For which of the following questions would a researcher be *most* likely to use an observational study?
    a) Is memory for television commercials influenced by the content of the programs in which the commercials appear?
    b) Is there any relationship between taking social psychology courses and happiness later in life?
    c) Does the consumption of alcohol lead to increased aggressiveness?
    d) Do banks tend to offer heterosexual couples lower interest rates on home mortgages than homosexual couples?
    Ans: d   LO: 4   Page: 35   Type: C

47. To examine potential gender differences in the qualities individuals seek in their romantic partners, HaeJin compares the personal ads placed by men and women. HaeJin is conducting a(n)
    a) survey study.
    b) observational study.
    c) archival study.
    d) experiment.
    Ans: c   LO: 4   Page: 35   Type: A

48. Latrell, the editor of a popular sports magazine, would like to know more about the demographics of the magazine's readers. He designs a questionnaire to assess this information and sends it to a random sample of the magazine's readers. Latrell is conducting a(n)
    a) survey.
    b) observational study.
    c) archival study.
    d) experiment.
    Ans: a   LO: 4   Page: 35-36   Type: A

49. The *most* important aspect of sampling in a survey study is
    a) its inclusion of equal numbers of individuals from different groups in the population.
    b) the number of people in the sample.
    c) the ratio of the sample size to the population size.
    d) the extent to which the sample in this study matches the population proportionally in terms of demographic variables.
    Ans: d   LO: 4   Page: 35-36   Type: F

50. A television producer is interested in whether women like soap operas more than sitcoms. The producer uses a random number table to select a sample of one hundred households, and then makes phone calls to these households every afternoon for three weeks. Of those who were home when the producer called, 75% reported they liked soap operas more than sitcoms. Which of the following might raise questions about the results?
    a) The use of archival data
    b) The representativeness of the sample
    c) The construct validity of the measure
    d) The operational definition advanced by the magazine
    Ans: b   LO: 4   Page: 35-36   Type: A

51. Which of the following does *not* make use of random sampling?
    a) Public opinion polling
    b) Election Day exit polling
    c) Market research telemarketing surveys
    d) A Population Census
    Ans: d   LO: 4   Page: 36   Type: A

52. In principle, the purpose of random sampling is to make sure that research participants
    a) have the right to withdraw from a study without incurring any penalty.
    b) are fully informed as to the procedures and hypotheses of the study.
    c) do not differ from one another in systematic ways.
    d) constitute a representative sample from the population of interest.
    Ans: d   LO: 4   Page: 36   Type: C

53. What is one general difference between descriptive and correlational research methods?
    a) Descriptive research does not look at relationships between variables.
    b) Descriptive research is more useful when one wants to infer causation.
    c) Correlational research cannot make use of archival data.
    d) Correlational research imbues the researcher with more control over the research participants.
    Ans: a   LO: 5   Page: 36   Type: C

54. Luke would like to know if there is a relationship between the number of psychology courses people take and their level of empathy. He surveys a randomly selected group of college students. Each student indicates the number of psychology courses he or she has taken and then completes an empathy scale. Luke's research is *best* described as a(n)
    a) correlational study.
    b) experiment.
    c) prospective study.
    d) archival study.
    Ans: a   LO: 5   Page: 36-38   Type: A

55. The primary goal of using correlational research is to
    a) determine the causal relationship between an independent and dependent variable.
    b) describe the population's average score on a particular measure.
    c) manipulate one variable but hold the other constant.
    d) determine the nature and strength of the association between two measured variables.
    Ans: d   LO: 5   Page: 36-38   Type: C

56. Which of the following statements concerning correlational research is *true*?
    a) In correlational research, variables are measured, but not manipulated.
    b) In correlational research, one variable is manipulated and one is measured.
    c) Correlational research can be conducted using observational, but not archival, measures.
    d) Correlational research can be conducted using archival, but not observational, measures.
    Ans: a   LO: 5   Page: 36-38   Type: C

57. The stronger the relationship between two variables
    a) the further from zero the correlation coefficient will be.
    b) the less appropriate is a correlational research design.
    c) the greater the probability that the observed association was due to chance.
    d) the more likely the correlation coefficient is to be a positive number.
    Ans: a   LO: 5   Page: 37   Type: F

58. Which of the following correlation coefficients reflects the *strongest* meaningful relationship?
    a) −0.67
    b) 0
    c) +0.86
    d) +1.25
    Ans: c   LO: 5   Page: 37   Type: F

59. When decreases in one variable are accompanied by decreases in another variable, the variables are described as
     a)   negatively correlated.
     b)   positively correlated.
     c)   causally related.
     d)   prospectively related.
     Ans: b   LO: 5   Page: 38   Type: C

60. Which of the following is *not* a causal explanation that would be consistent with a positive correlation between the number of hours a person sleeps per night and her level of positive mood?
     a)   The more sleep a person gets, the better her mood.
     b)   People who are happy are less likely to suffer from insomnia.
     c)   Stress causes people to sleep less and be in a bad mood.
     d)   People who are depressed tend to need more sleep than other people.
     Ans: d   LO: 5   Page: 38   Type: A

61. Vito finds a correlation of –0.35 between procrastination behaviors and academic achievement. Which of the following is an appropriate conclusion for Vito to draw?
     a)   Procrastination leads students to perform more poorly.
     b)   Poor academic performance causes more procrastination.
     c)   Elimination of procrastination behaviors will lead students to perform better.
     d)   None of these.
     Ans: d   LO: 5   Page: 37-38   Type: A

62. Carmella finds a correlation of +0.47 between self-esteem and academic achievement. Which of the following is the *most* appropriate interpretation of this correlation?
     a)   High self-esteem motivates students to achieve more academically.
     b)   Doing well academically increases students' self-esteem.
     c)   The higher students' self-esteem, the greater their academic achievement.
     d)   As self-esteem increases, academic achievement decreases.
     Ans: c   LO: 5   Page: 37-38   Type: A

63. Which of the following is an example of a negative correlation?
     a)   The more pets you own, the greater your physical health tends to be.
     b)   The more money people make the bigger their house tends to be.
     c)   The more alcohol you consume, the lower your GPA tends to be.
     d)   The more points the higher the score.
     Ans: c   LO: 5   Page: 38   Type: C

64. Suppose the correlation between the number of times couples go to the movies and the number of times they go out to dinner is +0.79. Among the following conclusions, which one is *not* consistent with this computation?
     a)   The more often that couples go to the movies, the more often they go out to dinner.
     b)   The less often that couples go to the movies, the less often they go out to dinner.
     c)   There is a strong positive correlation between the number of times couples go to the movies and the number of times they go out to dinner.
     d)   Because the correlation coefficient is less than 1.0, the association between these two variables is very weak and probably unreliable.
     Ans: d   LO: 5   Page: 37-38   Type: A

65. Dr. Vandelay found the correlation between shoe size and sexual deviancy to be +0.83. Which of the following can you conclude from this correlation?
     a)   As shoe size increases, sexual deviancy increases.
     b)   As shoe size increases, sexual deviancy decreases.
     c)   There is virtually no relationship between shoe size and sexual deviancy.
     d)   Engaging in sexually deviant acts causes your feet to grow.
     Ans: a   LO: 5   Page: 37-38   Type: A

66. Camryn uses a survey to measure the association between students' grade point average and weekly consumption of alcohol. She finds that higher GPAs tend to predict lower levels of alcohol consumption (and vice versa). This study is best described as a(n)
    a) experiment.
    b) observational study.
    c) concurrent study.
    d) correlational study.
    Ans: d   LO: 5   Page: 37-38   Type: A

67. To examine the relationship between media violence and aggressive behavior, Lomez first measures the number of hours of violent television watched per week for a sample of boys. Ten years later, the same boys are contacted and asked to complete a questionnaire to measure their aggressiveness. Lomez's work is *best* described as a(n)
    a) experiment.
    b) observational study.
    c) concurrent study.
    d) prospective study.
    Ans: d   LO: 5   Page: 37-38   Type: A

68. In a correlational study, the researcher _____; in an experiment the researcher _____.
    a) is limited in what she can study by practical and ethical constraints; examines the full range of two variables
    b) considers both independent and dependent variables; can draw causal conclusions
    c) may be worried about random selection; compares the responses of two or more groups of participants
    d) must use random assignment to condition; manipulates a variable and measures another variable
    Ans: c   LO: 5   Page: 37-39   Type: C

69. One of the many advantages of correlational research is that
    a) it allows researchers to study variables that cannot be manipulated in the lab.
    b) it allows the researcher to test for and determine the nature of causal relationships.
    c) it exhibits high internal validity.
    d) it tends to be statistically significant.
    Ans: a   LO: 5   Page: 38-39   Type: C

70. Which of the following statements concerning correlational research is *false*?
    a) Correlational research aids researchers in the development of new hypotheses.
    b) Correlational research permits researchers to determine whether one variable can predict another.
    c) Correlational research is often useful for studying phenomena for which experimentation is impractical or unethical.
    d) Correlational research allows researchers to measure relationships between independent and dependent variables.
    Ans: d   LO: 5   Page: 37-38   Type: C

71. Which of the following statements about correlational studies is *false*?
    a) They are useful for studying questions that can't be examined by experiments for practical reasons.
    b) They are often more sophisticated than descriptive studies.
    c) Their major limitation involves their inability to speak directly to issues of causality.
    d) They free a researcher from any type of ethical concerns in collecting the data.
    Ans: d   LO: 5   Page: 37-38   Type: C

72. Which of the following is *true* of correlational research?
    a) It is a powerful way to establish causal relationships between variables.
    b) It allows an experimenter to control extraneous variables.
    c) It permits researchers to determine whether one variable is predictive of another.
    d) It is limited to the study of variables that can be measured in the laboratory.
    Ans: c   LO: 5   Page: 37-38   Type: C

73.   Relative to experimental studies, the primary *disadvantage* of correlation studies is that
      a)   they are more labor-intensive.
      b)   cause and effect cannot be determined with them.
      c)   the results are more difficult to understand.
      d)   the choice of variables that can be studied is limited.
      Ans: b   LO: 5   Page: 38   Type: F

74.   Causation cannot be inferred from correlational studies because
      a)   they are so low in external validity.
      b)   they do not involve the manipulation of variables.
      c)   they are always conducted outside of the research lab.
      d)   researchers have too much control over the variables in correlational research.
      Ans: b   LO: 5   Page: 38   Type: C

75.   Experiments require all of the following *except*
      a)   equal treatment of participants in different groups except for the manipulation of the independent
            variable.
      b)   control over experimental procedures.
      c)   manipulation of an independent variable.
      d)   a laboratory environment.
      Ans: d   LO: 6   Page: 39-40   Type: F

76.   In a well-designed experiment, all participants must
      a)   be treated in exactly the same manner except for the specific differences the experimenter wants to
            create.
      b)   not realize that they are involved in an experiment.
      c)   be influenced by experimenter expectancy effects.
      d)   be allowed to choose their own experimental conditions without interference or bias from the
            experimenter.
      Ans: a   LO: 6   Page: 39   Type: F

77.   Buster runs an experiment in which she finds that participants placed in a good mood by a happy film clip
      are more likely to offer help to a fellow participant than participants who see a sad film clip. Gob suggests
      that perhaps this difference simply results from the fact that the participants in the happy film clip condition
      were more helpful people to begin with. What methodological aspect of a successful experiment can Buster
      point to in order to refute this criticism?
      a)   External validity
      b)   Random selection
      c)   Random assignment
      d)   Manipulation
      Ans: c   LO: 6   Page: 39-40   Type: A

78.   Among the following, which is *most* relevant to ensuring that any differences one obtains after the
      experimental manipulation of a study have been produced only by that manipulation?
      a)   Statistical interactions
      b)   External validity
      c)   Construct validity
      d)   Experimenter control
      Ans: d   LO: 6   Page: 39-40   Type: C

79.   Random assignment is a defining feature of an experiment. It means that
      a)   participants are able to select the particular experimental manipulations they wish to experience.
      b)   participants were randomly selected from the population of interest.
      c)   whether participants are in one condition or another is determined at random.
      d)   participants are assigned to the experimental conditions on the basis of their pre-existing differences.
      Ans: c   LO: 6   Page: 39-40   Type: F

80. A researcher was interested in the effects of mood on aggression. She decided to see how receiving an insult or a compliment affects aggression, and she measured aggression by having participants administer small shocks to another participant. The researcher found that participants in the insult condition were more aggressive than those in the compliment condition. One of her colleagues reads about this research and voices concern that people in the insult condition may have been more naturally aggressive than people in the compliment condition, causing the differences observed by the researcher. This concern about pre-existing differences between participants in the two conditions would only be valid if
    a) participants were not a representative sample of the population.
    b) participants were not randomly assigned to the condition.
    c) participants were not randomly selected from the population.
    d) All of these.
    Ans: b   LO: 6   Page: 39-40   Type: C

81. Random assignment is essential to establishing causality because it
    a) permits researchers to verify that they have a diverse and representative sample of participants.
    b) reduces the possibility that individual characteristics of the participants produced the observed results.
    c) increases the external validity of the experiment.
    d) allows researchers to determine whether or not their operational definitions reflect the variables of interest.
    Ans: b   LO: 6   Page: 39-40   Type: C

82. The procedure used to ensure that research participants have an equal chance of being placed in either the experimental or control group in an experiment is called
    a) random assignment.
    b) random sampling.
    c) debriefing.
    d) experimental realism.
    Ans: a   LO: 6   Page: 39-40   Type: F

83. In comparison to field experiments, laboratory experiments
    a) permit researchers greater control.
    b) allow more naturalistic observation of behavior.
    c) are less susceptible to experimenter expectancy effects.
    d) have fewer problems caused by the limitations of self-report data.
    Ans: a   LO: 6   Page: 40-41   Type: C

84. One advantage of field research is that
    a) random assignment is more likely to be used in field experiments.
    b) they pose fewer threats to external validity than lab studies.
    c) participants are more likely to behave naturally in the field than in the lab.
    d) they face fewer potential ethical problems than do lab experiments.
    Ans: c   LO: 6   Page: 41   Type: F

85. In an experiment, the independent variable is _____ while the dependent variable is _____.
    a) held constant; varied
    b) correlational; descriptive
    c) manipulated; measured
    d) general; specific
    Ans: c   LO: 6   Page: 42   Type: C

86. Subject variables are characterized by all of the following *except*
    a) They are neither dependent nor truly independent variables.
    b) They cannot be manipulated or randomly assigned.
    c) They may include gender and ethnicity of participants.
    d) They are essential for field experiments.
    Ans: d   LO: 6   Page: 42   Type: C

87. To examine the impact of group size on conformity behavior, Stanley has groups of two, five, or ten people
     stand on a city street and stare up at a window. Stanley then records the number of passersby who stop and
     stare at the window. This study is an example of a(n)
     a)   meta-analysis.
     b)   archival study.
     c)   experiment with one independent variable.
     d)   experiment with two independent variables.
     Ans: c   LO: 6   Page: 42   Type: A

88. Dr. Van Nostrand studies the impact of pornography on attitudes toward women. Attitudes toward women
     are the _____ in this research. '
     a)   independent variable
     b)   control factor
     c)   interaction
     d)   dependent variable
     Ans: d   LO: 6   Page: 42   Type: A

89. Vera thinks that having pets increases psychological functioning and well-being. To test this, one group of
     randomly selected nursing home residents is each given a pet while a second group is not. Over two months,
     the overall level of psychological functioning is evaluated on a daily basis. What is the independent variable
     in this study?
     a)   Having pets increases psychological functioning
     b)   Whether or not the residents received a pet
     c)   The level of psychological functioning demonstrated by the residents
     d)   This is a correlation study, so there is no independent variable.
     Ans: b   LO: 6   Page: 42   Type: A

90. Barb examines the impact that sitting in front of a mirror has on the academic performance of female
     adolescents. In her study, the number of math questions answered correctly appears to be the
     a)   conceptual independent variable.
     b)   conceptual dependent variable.
     c)   operational definition of the independent variable.
     d)   operational definition of the dependent variable.
     Ans: d   LO: 6   Page: 42   Type: A

91. Castilla wonders whether environmental factors influence how long juries take to select a foreperson. Mock
     jurors are brought into a room with either a rectangular table or a round table. The jurors are asked to select
     a foreperson before starting deliberation. Castilla records how long it takes each jury to select a foreperson.
     The shape of the table is the
     a)   independent variable.
     b)   dependent variable.
     c)   subject variable.
     d)   control variable.
     Ans: a   LO: 6   Page: 42   Type: A

92. Robinson manipulates two variables in his experimental investigation of test-taking performance: the
     number of participants seated in the room and the room temperature. He finds that regardless of the
     temperature in the room, participants do better on the test when the room is less crowded. Which of the
     following statements about this study is *true*?
     a)   There are two independent variables in this study.
     b)   There is one independent variable in this study.
     c)   There are two dependent variables in this study.
     d)   None of these
     Ans: a   LO: 7   Page: 42   Type: A

93.   Natasha finds that men speak more often in the classroom than do women, and that this is true both when they are assigned to sit in the front of the room versus the back of the room. Natasha's study has found a statistically significant effect for
      a)   the independent variable she manipulated.
      b)   a subject variable.
      c)   the conceptual, but not the operational variable.
      d)   the experimental, but not the correlational variable.
      Ans: b   LO: 7   Page: 42   Type: A

94.   What does it mean to say that an experiment has two independent variables?
      a)   The researcher has created a study with two different conditions.
      b)   The researcher has come up with two different measures to take in order to test the hypothesis.
      c)   The researcher is manipulating two different variables in the course of the study.
      d)   The effects of one variable in the study have nothing to do with the effects of the other variable.
      Ans: c   LO: 7   Page: 42   Type: C

95.   To examine the impact of mood on prosocial behavior, Leila had participants watch a video intended to put them in either a positive or neutral mood before asking them to make a donation to a fictitious charity. Which of the following is the operational dependent variable in this study?
      a)   mood
      b)   happy or sad video
      c)   prosocial behavior
      d)   donation to charity
      Ans: d   LO: 7   Page: 42   Type: A

96.   Theo administered an intelligence test to freshmen and seniors at Faber College and at Hillman College and compared performance across these four groups. Which of the following statements about the study is *true*?
      a)   It has one independent variable.
      b)   It has two subject variables.
      c)   It has two dependent variables
      d)   None of these.
      Ans: b   LO: 7   Page: 42   Type: A

97.   Achieving _____ is typically more of a challenge in a field study than in a laboratory study.
      a)   high external validity
      b)   high internal validity
      c)   high mundane realism
      d)   cross-cultural reliability
      Ans: b   LO: 7   Page: 43-44   Type: C

98.   The study conducted by Tobias Greitemeyer (2009) in which participants were exposed to different types of music illustrates

      a)   the ethical difficulties inherent to field research.
      b)   the limitations posed by reliance on self-report measures.
      c)   the usefulness of correlational research for devising new hypotheses to be tested.
      d)   None of these
      Ans: d   LO: 7   Page: 41   Type: A

99.   Tobias Greitemeyer (2009) conducted a set of studies in which he examined the effect of media exposure on mood and helping behavior. He found that
      a)   the type of music listened to had no effect on participants' likelihood of donating their money.
      b)   participants were more likely to donate their money if they had listened to socially positive than neutral song lyrics.
      c)   participants that listened to neutral song lyrics were more likely to donate their money.
      d)   participants that listed to socially positive song lyrics were less likely to donate their money.
      Ans: b   LO: 7   Page: 41   Type: F

100. The study by Claire Ashton-James et al. (2009) (in which mood and cultural differences were explored) examined whether
      a)   mood could cause individuals to act in novel ways.
      b)   Western participants were more likely to act in ways that are inconsistent with cultural norms.
      c)   East Asian participants were less likely to choose the uncommon color pen.
      d)   positive mood would make all participants more likely to choose the common color pen.
      Ans: a   LO: 7   Page: 41   Type: F

101. The color pen that participants chose in the Ashton-James (2009) study is best described as a(n)
      a)   dependent variable.
      b)   subject variable.
      c)   manipulated variable.
      d)   independent variable.
      Ans: a   LO: 7   Page: 41   Type: A

102. A subject variable in the Ashton-James (2009) study was
      a)   the color pen that the participant selected.
      b)   the type of music that the participant listened to.
      c)   whether the participant was from a Western or East Asian background.
      d)   the mood of the participant at the end of the study.
      Ans: c   LO: 7   Page: 41   Type: A

103. When researchers find that the results of their studies could have occurred by chance only 5 or fewer times in 100 possible outcomes, they conclude that the results
      a)   are statistically significant.
      b)   reflect an interaction between the dependent variables.
      c)   are theoretically meaningful.
      d)   are null because of their low level of reliability.
      Ans: a   LO: 7   Page: 43   Type: C

104. Zachary observes a significant negative correlation between binge drinking and grades among college students. Which of the following is *true*?
      a)   There is a 5 percent probability or less that this correlation occurred by chance.
      b)   Zachary cannot be sure what causes what, but he can be sure that either binge drinking causes lower grades or vice versa.
      c)   Zachary will probably try to replicate his findings by conducting an experiment.
      d)   Zachary would not have been able to conduct the study if students received written evaluations from instructors rather than grades.
      Ans: a   LO: 7   Page: 43   Type: A

105. According to standard convention, a researcher must be ___ % sure that the difference she observed between experimental conditions were not simply the result of chance in order to conclude that the difference is statistically significant.
      a)   90
      b)   95
      c)   99
      d)   99.9
      Ans: b   LO: 7   Page: 43   Type: F

106. One reason that social psychologists attempt to replicate the results of their research is that doing so
      a)   reduces the probability that the results are due to chance.
      b)   increases the construct validity of the experiment.
      c)   allows them to examine multiple relationships among variables.
      d)   increases the likelihood that participants have been treated ethically.
      Ans: a   LO: 7   Page: 43   Type: C

107. Participants who are subjected to all of the experimental procedures *except* the experimental manipulation are called
    a) raters.
    b) confederates.
    c) samples.
    d) controls.
    Ans: d   LO: 7   Page: 44   Type: F

108. The purpose of using control groups is to
    a) address ethical concerns about experiments.
    b) determine if there are any interactions among the independent variables.
    c) ensure a high level of experimental realism.
    d) provide a baseline against which to compare the effects of the independent variables.
    Ans: d   LO: 7   Page: 44   Type: C

109. Which of the following *best* represents a challenge to internal validity?
    a) Failure to use a randomization procedure when selecting a sample
    b) Use of a dependent measure high in inter-rater reliability but low in construct validity
    c) Differential compensation given to two groups in an experiment
    d) Designing laboratory conditions to be very different from everyday conditions
    Ans: c   LO: 7   Page: 43-44   Type: C

110. The *best* solution to the problem of experimenter expectancy effects is
    a) the use of different experimenters in different conditions.
    b) letting participants choose their own condition.
    c) keeping experimenters uninformed about group assignment.
    d) strict attention to random assignment.
    Ans: c   LO: 7   Page: 44   Type: F

111. You are a new researcher in a social psychology lab. The study you are working on is examining the effects of alcohol on aggressiveness. You are aware of the hypotheses of the study and eager to find evidence that supports them, and you find yourself acting in a less polite manner with participants who are assigned to the alcohol condition. This differential treatment of participants across conditions will threaten
    a) the statistical significance of the results.
    b) the internal validity of the study.
    c) the external validity of the study.
    d) None of these.
    Ans: b   LO: 7   Page: 43-44   Type: A

112. Rosenthal and Fode (1968) asked students to teach a rat to learn a maze. Some students were told they had been given a genetically engineered "intelligent" rat, whereas others were told that they had a "dull" rat. Although there were no actual differences among the rats, the "intelligent" rats learned the maze more quickly than the "dull" rats. Which of the following topics discussed in your book can best explain the results of this experiment?
    a) experimenter expectancy effects.
    b) mundane realism.
    c) experimental realism.
    d) high construct validity.
    Ans: a   LO: 7   Page: 44   Type: A

113. External validity refers to the degree to which
    a) there can be reasonable certainty that the independent variables in an experiment caused the observed effects on the dependent variables.
    b) there can be reasonable confidence that the same results would be obtained for other people and in other situations.
    c) participants were assigned to the various conditions on the basis of representative criteria.
    d) the experimental situation engages participants and leads them to behave naturally and spontaneously.
    Ans: b   LO: 7   Page: 44-45   Type: F

114. If a study is high in external validity,
    a)   the theoretical constructs are accurately represented by the study's manipulations and measures.
    b)   the results can be generalized to different types of people and situations.
    c)   changes in the dependent variable are caused by changes in the independent variable.
    d)   the theory that the study is testing is correct.
    Ans: b   LO: 7   Page: 44-45   Type: F

115. A social psychologist wants to study the impact of listening to classical music on people's level of comfort in social interactions. She runs a study using a convenience sample of college undergraduates. The use of this particular sample is a threat to
    a)   mundane realism.
    b)   experimental realism.
    c)   internal validity.
    d)   external validity.
    Ans: d   LO: 7   Page: 44-45   Type: A

116. Joel argues that the use of confederates provides for real interactions that emulate the types of reactions that occur in real life. Dale argues that the use of confederates simply makes an experiment more involving for the participant. Which of the following is *true*?
    a)   Joel and Dale both believe that confederates increase mundane realism.
    b)   Joel and Dale both believe that confederates increase experimental realism.
    c)   Joel believes that confederates increase mundane realism; Dale believes that confederates increase experimental realism.
    d)   Joel believes that confederates increase experimental realism; Dale believes that confederates increase mundane realism.
    Ans: c   LO: 7   Page: 45   Type: A

117. The reliance of many social psychology studies on college student participants poses a threat to
    a)   internal validity.
    b)   external validity.
    c)   mundane realism.
    d)   experimental realism.
    Ans: b   LO: 7   Page: 44-45   Type: C

118. Which of the following is *not* a benefit of using deception in social psychological research?
    a)   Experimental realism is increased.
    b)   Future meta-analyses become unnecessary.
    c)   Participants' reactions tend to be more natural and less affected by social desirability.
    d)   It allows researchers to study potentially harmful or controversial behaviors in a relatively safe environment.
    Ans: b   LO: 7   Page: 46   Type: C

119. Research using meta-analysis procedures
    a)   computes correlations among more than two variables.
    b)   approaches a research question using both correlational and experimental studies.
    c)   statistically assesses the consistency of several tests of the same hypothesis.
    d)   is used when self-report data regarding a particular topic are not available.
    Ans: c   LO: 7   Page: 46   Type: F

120. Which of the following is *true* regarding ethical standards of social psychological research?
    a)   All participants in any study must provide informed consent.
    b)   All participants in any study must be debriefed at the end of the study.
    c)   Even archival analyses of data obtained from participants many years ago must be approved by an Institutional Review Board beforehand.
    d)   Participants must be told the hypotheses being tested when providing informed consent.
    Ans: c   LO: 8   Page: 48-49   Type: F

121. Which of the following types of studies must be approved by an Institutional Review Board
   a)   Experiments using deception
   b)   Correlational studies
   c)   Descriptive studies
   d)   All of these.
   Ans: d   LO: 8   Page: 48-49   Type: C

122. Providing research participants with information concerning the potential risks and benefits of their participation
   a)   is part of obtaining informed consent.
   b)   is usually done only after a study is over.
   c)   tends to increase the internal validity of a study.
   d)   tends to increase the external validity of a study.
   Ans: a   LO: 8   Page: 48-49   Type: F

123. The disclosure made to participants after research procedures are completed, in which the researcher explains the purpose of the research, is called
   a)   informed consent.
   b)   a post-hoc test.
   c)   experimenter expectancy effects.
   d)   debriefing.
   Ans: d   LO: 8   Page: 48-49   Type: F

124. Which of the following statements concerning personal values and morals in social psychology is *false*?
   a)   Values can influence the questions social psychologists choose to ask.
   b)   The impact of values can be reduced through the use of the scientific method.
   c)   Values impact the hypotheses researchers advance.
   d)   Values do not affect the research methods selected to address a particular issue.
   Ans: d   LO: 8   Page: 48-49   Type: C

125. It is probably fair to say that
   a)   institutional review boards have had little effect on the types of research conducted by social psychologists.
   b)   most social psychologists believe they have a moral imperative to study important topics even if doing so poses high risk for the study participants.
   c)   social psychology research is devoid of human biases.
   d)   strict adherence to scientific methods reduce but do not eliminate human biases in social psychology.
   Ans: d   LO: 8   Page: 48-49   Type: C

ESSAY

126. Explain the difference between random sampling and random assignment, and indicate how these procedures affect a study's internal and external validity.
   Ans: A random sample indicates that all members of the target population have an equal chance of being selected for the study. Random samples are particularly attractive because they are more representative than other samples (such as convenience samples) of the populations from which they are taken. Moreover, because representative samples allow one to generalize the findings of a study to the larger population, random sampling increases external validity. Random assignment is a procedure that is only relevant when conducting an experiment; in this case, members of the sample (who have already been chosen, randomly or not) have an equal chance of being assigned to any of the experimental conditions. This procedure assures that, on average, members of experimental groups are equivalent in all ways before a study begins. This allows the researcher to infer that any differences between groups at the end of the study must be the result of the manipulation. In other words, it is random assignment that allows the researcher to conclude with confidence that the independent variable caused the changes in the dependent variable, which means that random assignment to condition increases internal validity.   Page: 40, 42

127. What are the advantages and the primary disadvantage of doing correlational research rather than experiments? Give an example of two variables that you think probably are negatively correlated with each other. Explain why you think so.

Ans: An important advantage of doing correlational research rather than experiments is that correlational research can study associations of naturally occurring variables that cannot be manipulated or induced due to practical constraints, such as participants' gender, age, race, height, etc. Correlational research can also examine phenomena that would be difficult or unethical to create for research purposes, such as certain kinds of violence, love, abuse of alcohol, etc. Correlational research also offers more flexibility than experiments because a wide range of variables can be measured, including those obtained in the field, using archives, through national surveys, etc. The primary disadvantage of doing correlational research rather than experiments is that a correlational study cannot demonstrate causation. That is, correlations cannot demonstrate cause-and-effect relationships between variables. A well-designed experiment, in contrast, can demonstrate that changes in one variable can cause a change in another variable. Two variables are negatively correlated if as one variable increases the other decreases (and vice versa). One pair of variables that should be negatively correlated with each other is the amount of time spent studying and the number of courses failed. As the amount of time one spends studying increases, the number of courses one fails should decrease.   Page: 36-38

128. What are the two essential characteristics of an experiment? Why, and how, is each of these important for the internal validity of the experiment?

Ans: One essential characteristic of an experiment is that the researcher has control over the experimental procedures. The researcher manipulates the variables of interest and keeps all else uniform. That is, all participants should be treated exactly the same way--except for the manipulations that the experimenter is investigating. The other essential characteristic of an experiment is that all participants are assigned randomly to the different conditions. Because of random assignment to condition, at the beginning of the study there should be no systematic differences between the groups of participants. Internal validity is the degree to which there can be reasonable certainty that the independent variables in an experiment caused the effects obtained on the dependent variable. By having a great deal of control over the experimental procedures, researchers can help ensure that the only differences between conditions are the manipulations themselves and not some other factors. If other factors vary along with the independent variables, then it is less clear that the independent variables are the cause of any differences found in the dependent variable, thereby reducing the internal validity of the experiment. Even if the researcher has a great deal of control and ensures that the only differences in the treatment received by the participants across conditions are the manipulations of the independent variables, it is possible that the participants in one condition are different from the participants in other conditions in important ways just by random chance. If this is the case, the differences found in the dependent variable may be a function of these other differences rather than the result of the manipulations. If the participants are randomly assigned to the conditions, however, the chances that the participants differed in ways other than those created by the manipulations become very improbable, especially with larger samples. Differences found in the dependent variable can thus be attributed to the manipulations of the independent variables rather than to pre-existing differences among the participants, thereby creating internal validity.   Page: 39-41, 43-44

129. Imagine that some researchers are interested in college students' self-reports about their reactions to various stressful situations. Rather than simply asking the students to recall various stressful situations and their reactions to them, the researchers want to reduce the time between the students' self-reports about the situations and the actual situations themselves. Describe two methods that have been developed by social psychologists that could serve this purpose.

Ans: The textbook describes three such methods: interval-contingent, signal-contingent, and event-contingent. Using the interval-contingent method, the researchers would have the students report their experiences at regular intervals, such as once a day. Using the signal-contingent method, the researchers would ask the students to report their experiences as soon as possible after being signaled to do so, as with a beeper. Using the event-contingent method, the researchers would ask the students to report on a designated set of events as soon as possible after such events occurred; for example, the students might be asked to report their experiences as soon as possible after being confronted with a stressful situation. Page: 29-31

130.   What is informed consent? What is debriefing? Why are they important in conducting research in social
       psychology? What is the responsibility of institutional review boards?
       *Ans: Informed consent is the individual's deliberate, voluntary decision to participate in research, based on
       the researcher's description of what will be required during such participation. Individuals must be given
       enough information about the research in order to make an informed decision about whether or not they
       wish to participate. Debriefing is a disclosure, made to participants after research procedures are
       completed, in which the researcher explains the purpose of the research, attempts to resolve any negative
       feelings, and emphasizes the scientific contribution made by individuals' participation. Both informed
       consent and debriefing are very important in protecting the welfare of the individuals who participate in the
       research. Informed consent, for example, is critically important from an ethical perspective. Human
       participants should know what the possible risks and dangers are of participating in some research before
       they agree to do so. The debriefing is also important from an ethical perspective. During the debriefing the
       researcher should attempt to make the participants feel good about having participated in the research, and
       any possible negative effects of having been in the study should be eliminated. Institutional review boards
       exist at all institutions that seek federal funding for research involving human participants. Their
       responsibility is to review research proposals to ensure that the physical and psychological welfare of the
       individuals who participate in the proposed research will be protected, both in the short-term and long-
       term.   Page: 48-50*

CHAPTER 3

The Social Self

MULTIPLE CHOICE

1. The "ABCs of the self" refer to affect, behavior, and cognition. Which of these three concepts is most relevant to the idea of self-esteem?
    a) Affect
    b) Behavior
    c) Cognition
    d) All of these.
    Ans: a   LO: 1   Page: 55-56   Type: F

2. Which of the "ABCs of the self" is most relevant to the idea of the self-concept?
    a) Affect
    b) Behavior
    c) Biology
    d) Cognition
    Ans: d   LO: 1   Page: 55-56   Type: F

3. The cocktail party effect refers to the tendency for people to
    a) become more self-conscious in large groups.
    b) get nervous in social settings and forget the names of those to whom they have been introduced.
    c) hear the mention of their own name even from across a loud and crowded room.
    d) become more focused on self-presentational concerns in group settings.
    Ans: c   LO: 1   Page: 56   Type: F

4. From a social psychological perspective, the cocktail party effect illustrates
    a) the importance of the self when it comes to attentional processes.
    b) the origination of the fundamental attribution error.
    c) that alcohol can alter interaction patterns.
    d) the power of situational factors to influence behavioral tendencies.
    Ans: a   LO: 1   Page: 56   Type: C

5. While talking to a friend at a noisy party, Julianna stops in the middle of a sentence and turns her head. According to the cocktail party effect, what did she probably hear?
    a) Her name
    b) Laughter
    c) Uninhibited behavior
    d) A funny joke
    Ans: a   LO: 1   Page: 56   Type: A

6. The term self-concept refers to the
    a) sum total of a person's beliefs concerning his or her own personal characteristics.
    b) evaluation of one's own abilities and attitudes through comparison to similar others.
    c) whether a person's self-evaluation is positive or negative.
    d) general disposition to focus on either the inner feelings or outer image of the self.
    Ans: a   LO: 1   Page: 56   Type: F

7. Beliefs about the self that guide the processing of self-relevant information are called
    a) self-awareness cues.
    b) autobiographical memories.
    c) flashbulb memories.
    d) self-schemas.
    Ans: d   LO: 1   Page: 56   Type: F

8.   Bernie considers intelligence to be an important part of his self-concept, and he feels that he is more intelligent than most other people. Bernie would be described as
     a)   low in emotional intelligence.
     b)   schematic with respect to intelligence.
     c)   high in public self-consciousness.
     d)   low in public self-regard.
     Ans: b   LO: 1   Page: 56   Type: A

9.   Helene is schematic concerning honesty. She is likely to do all of the following *except*
     a)   see herself as more honest than most other people.
     b)   consider honesty a central part of her self-concept.
     c)   notice the honest and dishonest behaviors of others.
     d)   engage in more strategic self-presentation than most other people.
     Ans: d   LO: 1   Page: 56   Type: A

10. Research using new technologies has determined that
     a)   different areas of the brain are activated when people are shown photos of themselves as opposed to photos of others.
     b)   different areas of the brain are activated when American participants are shown photos of themselves as opposed to photos of others, but such differentiation does not occur among Korean participants.
     c)   brain activity does not vary depending on whether or not a stimulus is self-relevant.
     d)   PET scans are not particularly informative for investigations of the self-concept, but fMRI is.
     Ans: a   LO: 1   Page: 57   Type: C

11. When Gallup (1977) placed different species of animals in front of a mirror, it was only the great apes who
     a)   exhibited social responses to their reflection in the mirror.
     b)   greeted their reflection with vocalizations.
     c)   used their reflection in the mirror to groom themselves.
     d)   attempted to attack their reflection.
     Ans: c   LO: 2   Page: 57-58   Type: F

12. Developmental psychologists have shown that children begin to recognize their own image in a mirror between
     a)   0 and 6 months of age.
     b)   6 and 12 months of age.
     c)   12 and 18 months of age.
     d)   18 and 24 months of age.
     Ans: d   LO: 2   Page: 57-58   Type: F

13. Yulia stands in front of a mirror. She notices a red spot on the forehead of the image she sees in the mirror. She then brings her hand up to her own forehead and touches the red spot, trying to brush it off. Yulia is demonstrating
     a)   self-recognition.
     b)   self-verification.
     c)   self-regulation.
     d)   the looking-glass self.
     Ans: a   LO: 2   Page: 57-58   Type: A

14. According to the looking-glass model of self-concept development, the self-concept develops
     a)   from one's physical appearance.
     b)   from the way one is viewed by others.
     c)   slowly, reaching its complete form only in old age.
     d)   quickly, but is quite fragile and subject to change.
     Ans: b   LO: 2   Page: 58   Type: F

15. Gallup's research revealed that when apes were raised in isolation they were unable to recognize themselves in the mirror. This research provides support for
    a)   the non-social origins of the self-concept.
    b)   self-perception theory.
    c)   the idea that humans are the only animals capable of self-recognition.
    d)   the concept of the looking-glass self.
    Ans: d   LO: 2   Page: 58   Type: C

16. Our self-concept appears to be influenced by all of the following sources *except*
    a)   introspection.
    b)   our perceptions of our own behavior.
    c)   the culture in which we live.
    d)   the way other people actually see us.
    Ans: d   LO: 2   Page: 58-64   Type: C

17. The process of reflecting on your own inner thoughts and feelings in order to gain self-knowledge is called
    a)   introspection.
    b)   self-verification.
    c)   self-monitoring.
    d)   autobiographical memory.
    Ans: a   LO: 3   Page: 58-60   Type: F

18. According to research by Nisbett and Wilson (1977),
    a)   introspection is a valid and accurate source of information about the self.
    b)   the development of the self-concept begins at birth.
    c)   people are often unable to give accurate explanations for the causes of their own behavior.
    d)   people compare themselves with similar others for self-verification.
    Ans: c   LO: 3   Page: 58-59   Type: F

19. A high school class goes to the Metropolitan Museum of Art and enjoys one of the exhibitions very much. If the teacher wanted the students to gain accurate self-insight regarding why they liked the exhibition, the teacher should ask the students to
    a)   compare the different exhibitions they had seen.
    b)   focus upon their feelings about the paintings in the exhibition.
    c)   give a list of reasons for why they liked particular paintings in the exhibition.
    d)   discuss the historical context in which the paintings were done.
    Ans: b   LO: 3   Page: 58-59   Type: A

20. Wilson (1985) found that the more people consider the reasons why they like something,
    a)   the more negative their reasons become over time.
    b)   the lower the correlation between their attitudes and behavior.
    c)   the more accurate they are in making self-judgments.
    d)   the greater their extrinsic motivation.
    Ans: b   LO: 3   Page: 59   Type: F

21. Research by David Dunning suggests that one problem concerning self-assessment is that people tend to
    a)   overestimate their own skills, prospects for success, and opinion accuracy.
    b)   underestimate their own skills, prospects for success, and opinion accuracy.
    c)   pay too little attention to past successes in evaluating future prospects.
    d)   dwell too much on past failures in assessing present competencies.
    Ans: a   LO: 3   Page: 59   Type: C

22. Which of the following statements concerning introspection is *true*?
    a)   Contrary to popular perceptions, introspection can sometimes impair self-knowledge.
    b)   Analyzing the reasons why we like something typically leads to accurate self-insight.
    c)   People tend to underestimate the duration of their emotional reactions.
    d)   One way to improve affective forecasting is to focus on a single event without considering the impact of other life experiences.
    Ans: a   LO: 3   Page: 58-60   Type: C

23. During a discussion with some friends just prior to a school election, Sandra states that she is certain she will be devastated for months if she isn't elected class president. This is an example of
    a)   the overjustification effect.
    b)   the impact bias.
    c)   basking in reflected glory.
    d)   implicit egoism.
    Ans: b   LO: 3   Page: 59-60   Type: A

24. Research regarding affective forecasting indicates that
    a)   people are remarkably good at estimating how future events will impact their own happiness.
    b)   people are remarkably good at estimating how future events will impact the happiness of others.
    c)   people tend to underestimate the impact of future events on their own happiness.
    d)   None of these.
    Ans: d   LO: 3   Page: 59-60   Type: C

25. The impact bias in affective forecasting refers to the phenomenon in which
    a)   voters predicted that they would be much happier one month after an election if the candidate for whom they voted won as opposed to lost.
    b)   people tend to overestimate the strength and duration of their emotional reactions to events.
    c)   people are generally accurate predictors of how they will feel about future events.
    d)   people tend to underestimate how happy they will be several months after winning the lottery.
    Ans: b   LO: 3   Page: 59-60   Type: C

26. According to self-perception theory, when people are uncertain about their thoughts or feelings regarding an activity, they will
    a)   infer their thoughts and feelings regarding that activity from their behavior.
    b)   infer their thoughts and feelings from what others tell them about their engagement in the activity.
    c)   focus on past behavior that relates to the current activity to make inferences about their thoughts and feelings regarding the activity.
    d)   think about their self-schemas and decide whether the behavior is congruent or incongruent with the self-schema before engaging in the activity.
    Ans: a   LO: 4   Page: 60-61   Type: F

27. Marcia is unsure about whether Jan is her best friend. She thinks about how many times she has listened to Jan complain about her boyfriend, helped Jan study for difficult exams, and brought soup to Jan when she was sick. Marcia realizes that she speaks to Jan almost every night. After thinking about all this, Marcia concludes that Jan must be her best friend. This conclusion is based on a process described by
    a)   self-perception theory.
    b)   social comparison theory.
    c)   self-awareness theory.
    d)   self-discrepancy theory.
    Ans: a   LO: 4   Page: 60-61   Type: A

28. Justin falls asleep during a movie that he had been waiting all week to see. If he relies on self-perception to determine his feelings about the movie, he will *most* likely decide that
    a)   he would stay awake if he saw the movie a second time.
    b)   his perceptions of the movie match his perceptions of himself.
    c)   the movie was one of the best he's ever seen.
    d)   he found the movie to be quite boring.
    Ans: d   LO: 4   Page: 60-61   Type: A

29. Goldstein and Cialdini's 2007 study on vicarious self-perception demonstrated that
    a)   people sometimes infer something about themselves by observing the behavior of those who they believe to be biologically similar to them.
    b)   people's self-perceptions are not affected by others' actions.
    c)   people only pay attention to their self-perception when in the presence of those that who they perceive as similar to them.
    d)   People lose their sense of self when observing the behavior of someone with whom they identify.
    Ans: a   LO: 4   Page: 61   Type: C

30. Newman is having a very bad day—he overslept for his final exam, spilled coffee on himself at work, and got a speeding ticket on the way home. According to the facial feedback hypothesis, what will happen if he increases tension in the facial muscles normally active during frowning?
    a) It will reduce the intensity of his negative emotional experience.
    b) It will intensify his negative emotional experience.
    c) It will create a competing positive emotion.
    d) Because he is already in a bad mood, it will have no impact on his emotional experience.
    Ans: b   LO: 4   Page: 61-62   Type: A

31. Kira hates her calculus class. As a social psychologist, which of these tactics would you recommend to Kira to help improve her mood during class?
    a) Kira should try to empathize more with her instructor.
    b) Kira should force herself to smile throughout class.
    c) Kira should try to suppress or block out her negative feelings during class.
    d) All of these.
    Ans: b   LO: 4   Page: 61-62   Type: A

32. Which of the following is *most* consistent with the facial feedback hypothesis?
    a) Facial expressions are necessary for the experience of emotion.
    b) Facial expressions can trigger and magnify emotional states.
    c) Although facial expressions can influence emotions, they do not produce any real physiological changes.
    d) In order for facial expressions to evoke a corresponding emotion, people must be aware of their outward expression.
    Ans: b   LO: 4   Page: 61-62   Type: C

33. According to theories regarding self-perception of emotions, what would be the likely effect of sitting at your desk slumped over in the chair with a bowed head?
    a) You would feel proud.
    b) You would feel dejected.
    c) You would make other people frown in response.
    d) You would buffer your self-esteem against potential future threats.
    Ans: b   LO: 4   Page: 61-62   Type: A

34. When asked to clean his room, Miguel does so, but only after being assured by his parents that he will receive an allowance in exchange for cleaning up. Miguel's behavior is *most* likely motivated by
    a) social comparison.
    b) egocentric biases.
    c) self-monitoring.
    d) extrinsic motivation.
    Ans: d   LO: 4   Page: 62-64   Type: A

35. Dara loves to paint in her spare time. Painting is an enjoyable activity for her. Her desire to paint may *best* be explained by
    a) need-driven motivation.
    b) intrinsic motivation.
    c) extrinsic motivation.
    d) self-verification motivation.
    Ans: b   LO: 4   Page: 62-64   Type: A

36. Motivation that is driven by rewards and punishments is called
    a) instrumental motivation.
    b) intrinsic motivation.
    c) extrinsic motivation.
    d) egoistic motivation.
    Ans: c   LO: 4   Page: 62-64   Type: F

37. The tendency for extrinsic rewards to undermine intrinsic motivation is called
     a)   self-discrepancy theory.
     b)   implicit egoism.
     c)   the durability bias.
     d)   the overjustification effect.
     Ans: d   LO: 4   Page: 62-64   Type: F

38. Kerri is a teaching assistant for a large lecture class. She enjoys grading student tests, alphabetizing them,
     and entering the scores in the grade book, but the professor thinks she takes too long to complete this
     process. Hoping to speed things up, the professor offers Kerri a small cash reward for grading each
     assignment quickly and accurately. This solution works until the professor runs out of money. Now Kerri
     complains about her grading responsibilities all the time, and she takes even longer than before to complete
     her work. She asks if the professor can force the 150 students to sit in alphabetical order during the test to
     save her time alphabetizing them later, and when the professor declines, she tells him how much she hates
     grading. Which of the following *best* explains what happened to Kerri?
     a)   The extrinsic motivation of the monetary reward has come to undermine Kerri's intrinsic motivation
            to grade.
     b)   Kerri's extrinsic desire to grade was replaced by an intrinsic motivation to make money.
     c)   Kerri lost her intrinsic motivation to grade at the same time that the professor ran out of money.
     d)   Kerri sabotaged her own performance by engaging in self-handicapping.
     Ans: a   LO: 4   Page: 62-64   Type: A

39. Josephine bought her 6-year-old nephew, Joseph, a new set of paints for his birthday. Hoping to encourage
     the little artist, Josephine promised Joseph $1 for every painting. Joseph thinks that is quite a lot of money.
     According to research by Lepper, Greene, and Nisbett (1973) on overjustification effects, which of the
     following is *most* likely to occur?
     a)   Joseph will come to see painting pictures as a way to make money, not as something enjoyable in
            itself.
     b)   Joseph will develop a love for painting and will want to be an artist when he grows up.
     c)   Joseph will continue to paint even if his aunt eventually stops rewarding him with money.
     d)   The paintings for which Joseph receives money will be judged as better quality than the paintings for
            which he does not receive any money.
     Ans: a   LO: 4   Page: 62-64   Type: A

40. Which of the following strategies would be the *most* effective way to use rewards to motivate behavior, but
     avoid overjustification effects?
     a)   Only use monetary rewards.
     b)   Make sure the rewards are contingent upon the desired behavior and are clearly expected.
     c)   Present the rewards as a special bonus for the desired behavior and be sure that the reward is
            unexpected.
     d)   Create an expectation that rewards will be given for the desired behavior, but then do not actually
            provide the reward.
     Ans: c   LO: 4   Page: 62-64   Type: C

41. According to Warneken and Tomasello (2008), how can moms best encourage their young toddlers to help
     them out?
     a)   Give a reward before asking for help.
     b)   Give no reward at all..
     c)   Give a reward after they have successfully completed a helping task.
     d)   Never give verbal praise for helpfulness, but give more tangible rewards instead.
     Ans: b   LO: 4   Page: 62-64   Type: A

42. A person's spontaneous self-description can often be changed by an alteration of that person's
     a)   self reference.
     b)   social surroundings.
     c)   social desirability.
     d)   feelings of uncertainty.
     Ans: b   LO: 5   Page: 65   Type: C

43. People's spontaneous self-descriptions are *most* likely to include
     a)   their age, regardless of their social surroundings.
     b)   their gender, regardless of their social surroundings.
     c)   characteristics that set them apart from others in the immediate vicinity.
     d)   characteristics that make them seem similar to others in the immediate vicinity.
     Ans: c   LO: 5   Page: 65   Type: F

44. D'Brickashaw is the only man and the only African-American enrolled in a Women's Studies seminar.
     McGuire's work on spontaneous self-descriptions suggests that compared to other contexts, in this specific
     situation D'Brickashaw will be *more* likely to mention his _____ in his self-description.
     a)   race, but not gender
     b)   gender, but not race
     c)   race as well as gender
     d)   distinctive name
     Ans: c   LO: 5   Page: 65   Type: A

45. Klein (1997) asked participants to make a series of judgments regarding various pieces of art. He found that
     participants' self-assessments
     a)   did not reflect the influence of social comparison processes on such a subjective task.
     b)   were more accurate when they chose to compare themselves to others who performed better on the
           task.
     c)   were more influenced by information regarding their performance relative to others than by
           information regarding their absolute score.
     d)   were more influenced by information regarding their absolute score than by information regarding
           their performance relative to others.
     Ans: c   LO: 5   Page: 65   Type: F

46. Marion is a sprinter on her high school track team. According to social comparison theory, Marion is most
     likely to look to which of the following groups to assess how fast a sprinter she is?
     a)   Other female high school track athletes
     b)   Other female students at her school who are not on the track team
     c)   Male members of her track team
     d)   U.S. Olympic track team members
     Ans: a   LO: 5   Page: 65   Type: A

47. According to social comparison theory, people are *most* likely to compare themselves to others who are
     a)   friendly.
     b)   lonely.
     c)   popular.
     d)   similar.
     Ans: d   LO: 5   Page: 65   Type: F

48. According to Festinger, social comparison is *less* likely to occur
     a)   under conditions of uncertainty.
     b)   when a person's self-esteem is threatened.
     c)   when objective criteria are available.
     d)   with similar others.
     Ans: c   LO: 5   Page: 65   Type: F

49. Schachter (1959) found that participants expecting to receive painful electric shocks preferred the company
     of others who were in the same situation. These results suggest that
     a)   social comparison processes are used to evaluate emotions.
     b)   emotions have a strong physiological component.
     c)   self-handicapping is more about self-presentation than self-enhancement.
     d)   people are relatively inaccurate at affective forecasting.
     Ans: a   LO: 5   Page: 66-67   Type: C

50.   Schachter (1959) examined the preferences of participants who were expecting to receive a series of painful electric shocks. He found that these participants preferred to wait in a room
      a)   by themselves.
      b)   with participants who were not expecting shocks.
      c)   with participants who were also expecting shocks.
      d)   with participants who had already received shocks.
      Ans: c   LO: 5   Page: 66-67   Type: F

51.   The two-factor theory of emotion proposes that emotional experience
      a)   is independent of social comparison processes.
      b)   requires a combination of positive and negative physiological arousal.
      c)   is independent of physiological arousal.
      d)   is based on physiological arousal and a cognitive label for that arousal.
      Ans: d   LO: 5   Page: 66-67   Type: F

52.   The important conclusion that can be drawn from Schachter and Singer's (1962) study on emotions is that
      a)   every emotion experienced by humans has a specific and distinct set of physiological symptoms.
      b)   physiological arousal is one of the few human experiences not susceptible to variations in subjective interpretation.
      c)   social context can determine the way in which physiological arousal is interpreted.
      d)   the two major factors of emotion are arousal and happiness.
      Ans: c   LO: 5   Page: 66-67   Type: C

53.   According to the two-factor theory of emotion, social context *most* directly affects
      a)   facial expressions of emotion.
      b)   the physiological component of emotion.
      c)   the cognitive interpretation of emotion.
      d)   the self-perception of emotion.
      Ans: c   LO: 5   Page: 66-67   Type: C

54.   On his first day of class, Professor Saccamano thinks he is nervous because his blood pressure is up and his hands are shaking. He continues to feel this way, however, before every class meeting of the semester, and eventually realizes that his arousal is due to the five flights of stairs he must climb up to the classroom. Which theory *best* explains his misattribution?
      a)   Downward comparison theory
      b)   Self-handicapping theory
      c)   Self-perception theory
      d)   Two-factor theory of emotion
      Ans: d   LO: 5   Page: 66-67   Type: A

55.   People's recollection of a sequence of events that directly touched their lives is called
      a)   private self-consciousness.
      b)   the hindsight bias.
      c)   the distinctiveness effect.
      d)   autobiographical memory.
      Ans: d   LO: 6   Page: 67-68   Type: F

56.   In terms of autobiographical memory, to what does the phrase "reminiscence peak" refer?
      a)   The more negative the memory, the more likely it is to be remembered.
      b)   Older adults tend to retrieve a larger number of memories from adolescence and early adulthood than other periods of life.
      c)   Once people turn a certain age, they start to forget many of the events that happened to them in earlier stages of life.
      d)   People tend to remember a wide range of "firsts" in recounting their personal experiences.
      Ans: b   LO: 6   Page: 67-68   Type: C

57. Which of the following statements concerning autobiographical memories is *false*?
    a) Older adults tend to recall a large number of memories from adolescence and early adulthood.
    b) People tend to have greater recall of transitional life periods.
    c) In general, people tend to recall more events from the recent past than the distant past.
    d) People tend to have the most accurate recall for emotional versus unemotional events.
    Ans: d   LO: 6   Page: 67-68   Type: C

58. Herman remembers exactly what he was doing and where he was when he first heard about the September 11th terrorist attacks. Brown and Kulik (1977) would refer to this vivid image as
    a) the hindsight bias.
    b) a memory heuristic.
    c) memory inflation.
    d) a flashbulb memory.
    Ans: d   LO: 6   Page: 68   Type: A

59. Which of the following is *most* consistent with the notion that memory is biased rather than objective?
    a) When asked about her college experiences, most of Jennifer's memories are about her first day of college and her graduation.
    b) John spent most of his 65th birthday party reminiscing about his high school years and his time in the military before he turned 20.
    c) Jordan will never forget the day when he heard about Princess Diana's death on the news.
    d) Jessica recalls that she has always hated meat, even though she only recently became a vegetarian.
    Ans: d   LO: 6   Page: 68   Type: C

60. Jason fills out an application for college with the grades he remembered getting throughout high school. While reviewing the application with a guidance counselor, the counselor points out that Jason seems to have inflated a few of his lower grades. Which of the following is the *most* likely explanation for Jason's behavior?
    a) Jason is displaying the reminiscence peak characteristic of autobiographical memories.
    b) Jason fell prey to the tendency to revise personal histories to reflect favorably on the self.
    c) Jason relied on introspection and consequently impaired his self-knowledge of his grades.
    d) Jason was affected by the impact bias, which skewed his memory of his grades.
    Ans: b   LO: 6   Page: 68   Type: A

61. A husband and wife are asked to estimate how much each of them contributes to the household chores. Based on the research concerning autobiographical memory, which of the following patterns of results is *most* probable?
    a) Husband 50%, wife 50%
    b) Husband 50%, wife 70%
    c) Husband 70%, wife 50%
    d) Husband 70%, wife 70%
    Ans: d   LO: 6   Page: 68   Type: C

62. Rebecca fills out a survey in which she asserts complete agreement with the statement, "I enjoy being unique and different from others." With which cultural orientation does she *most* likely identify?
    a) Individualism
    b) Collectivism
    c) Multiculturalism
    d) Cooperativism
    Ans: a   LO: 7   Page: 69   Type: A

63. April was born and raised in an Eastern culture. She is more likely than people raised in Western cultures to
    a) compare herself to others.
    b) make friends easily.
    c) view relationships as an important part of her self-concept.
    d) experience anxiety in group settings.
    Ans: c   LO: 7   Page: 69-71   Type: A

64. Jomei feels that he cannot be happy if his family is not happy. Jomei has an _____ view of self.
     a)   individualistic
     b)   independent
     c)   interdependent
     d)   international
     Ans: c   LO: 7   Page: 69-70   Type: A

65. Cross-cultural research indicates that Americans are more likely than Asians to
     a)   perceive themselves as unique.
     b)   assume blame for failures.
     c)   strive for community belonging.
     d)   see themselves as others tend to see them.
     Ans: a   LO: 7   Page: 69-71   Type: C

66. According to Markus and Kitayama (1991), people from collectivist cultures are more likely than those from individualist cultures to
     a)   derive satisfaction from personal achievement.
     b)   see themselves as less similar to others.
     c)   take personal credit for their successes.
     d)   underestimate their contributions to a team effort.
     Ans: d   LO: 7   Page: 69-71   Type: F

67. Multilingual American and Japanese citizens are asked to describe themselves. Which of the following groups is *least* likely to focus on group affiliations?
     a)   U. S. citizens asked to respond in English
     b)   Japanese citizens asked to respond in English
     c)   U. S. citizens, regardless of language
     d)   Japanese citizens, regardless of language
     Ans: a   LO: 7   Page: 69-71   Type: C

68. Dialecticism, a concept grounded in Eastern traditions, can best be defined as
     a)   a system of thought characterized by the acceptance of contradictions.
     b)   the notion that if one option is right, the other must be wrong
     c)   the idea that one's "true self" is stable in all situations
     d)   a characteristic of individualist cultures
     Ans: a   LO: 7   Page: 71   Type: F

69. When Maria, a Latin American student, is asked to describe herself in one word during her college interview, she wants to truly express her Latina culture. Which of the following characteristics is she most likely to emphasize?
     a)   intelligence.
     b)   graciousness
     c)   drive
     d)   strength
     Ans: b   LO: 7   Page: 71-72   Type: A

70. English and Chen's (2007) study of college students of European and Asian descent found that
     a)   even within a particular context, Asian students see their identity as relatively fluid and variable..
     b)   European students tended to see the self in more stable terms across situations.
     c)   European students had smaller discrepancies between their ideal and actual selves.
     d)   All of these
     Ans: b   LO: 7   Page: 71-72   Type: C

71. Self-esteem is all of the following *except*
     a)   an affectively charged component of the self-concept.
     b)   responsive to success and failure.
     c)   a state of mind that can change depending on the situation.
     d)   a single, stable disposition.
     Ans: d   LO: 8   Page: 72   Type: F

72. People with unstable, fluctuating self-esteem react more strongly to _____ events than those with stable self-esteem.
     a)   positive
     b)   negative
     c)   both positive and negative
     d)   neither positive nor negative
     Ans: c   LO: 8   Page: 72-73   Type: F

73. Jade feels great about herself when she gets an A on her calculus test, but then hates herself when she forgets to meet a friend at the library. Jade seems to have
     a)   high self-esteem.
     b)   low self-esteem.
     c)   unstable self-esteem.
     d)   an independent view of self.
     Ans: c   LO: 8   Page: 72-73   Type: A

74. Consuela has a positive self-image. She is likely to do all of the following *except*
     a)   persist longer at difficult tasks.
     b)   expect to succeed.
     c)   blame herself if she fails.
     d)   sleep better at night.
     Ans: c   LO: 8   Page: 72-73   Type: A

75. Which of the following does *not* appear to be associated with low self-esteem?
     a)   The expectation of failure
     b)   The ability to effectively resist peer pressure
     c)   A sense of pessimism about the future
     d)   A reduced ability to ward off disease
     Ans: b   LO: 8   Page: 73-74   Type: F

76. Research by Crocker and Park (2004) suggests that the pursuit of self-esteem
     a)   is a necessary antecedent of positive mental health.
     b)   enables people to avoid anxiety and stress-related problems.
     c)   increases one's sensitivity to the needs of others.
     d)   None of these.
     Ans: d   LO: 8   Page: 74   Type: C

77. Which of the following is *not* a potential cost of the pursuit of self-esteem, as identified by Crocker and Park (2004)?
     a)   An increase in stress-related health problems
     b)   Anxiety
     c)   Unwanted social attention
     d)   Avoidance of worthwhile activities that carry a risk of failure
     Ans: c   LO: 8   Page: 74   Type: C

78. William Swann and others (2007) found that people with specific domains of self-esteem benefit in what ways?
     a)   they are likely to feel good about themselves
     b)   they are likely to do well in school
     c)   they are likely to outperform others in the specific situations for which they have high self-esteem
     d)   they are likely to try new things
     Ans: c   LO: 8   Page: 74   Type: C

79. According to Twenge and Crocker (2002),
     a)   White Americans have higher self-esteem on average than do African Americans.
     b)   White Americans tend to have much higher self-esteem than Latino Americans.
     c)   African Americans have higher self-esteem than all other racial groups except Asian Americans.
     d)   racial differences in self-esteem are far smaller than gender differences.
     Ans: d   LO: 8   Page: 75   Type: F

80. Higgins's (1979) self-discrepancy theory suggests that we each have an "actual self," an "ought self," and an "ideal self." According to Higgins, discrepancies between the _____ self and the actual self often lead to low self-esteem and feelings of _____.
    a)   ought; frustration
    b)   ought; shame
    c)   ideal; superiority
    d)   ideal; hostility
    Ans: b   LO: 9   Page: 75-76   Type: F

81. According to self-discrepancy theory, experiencing negative emotions, such as anxiety or depression, is often caused by
    a)   the content of the actual, ought, and ideal selves.
    b)   the stability of the actual, ought, and ideal selves.
    c)   the degree of incongruity among the actual, ought, and ideal selves.
    d)   the degree of incongruity between individuals' actual and ideal selves and their perception of important others' views of their actual and ideal selves.
    Ans: c   LO: 9   Page: 75-76   Type: C

82. Jenna is fairly high-strung. This attribute conflicts more with Jenna's ideal self than with her ought self. Jenna is more likely to experience _____ than she is to experience _____.
    a)   disappointment; fear
    b)   anxiety; sadness
    c)   fear; anxiety
    d)   sadness; disappointment
    Ans: a   LO: 9   Page: 75-76   Type: A

83. According to self-discrepancy theory, the disorder *most* likely to develop from a discrepancy between the real self and the ought self is
    a)   depression.
    b)   anxiety disorder.
    c)   antisocial personality disorder.
    d)   schizophrenia.
    Ans: b   LO: 9   Page: 75-76   Type: F

84. Jasper is feeling guilty and ashamed because he did not help his mother paint the house. Jasper is *most* likely suffering from a discrepancy between what two aspects of the self?
    a)   The ideal self and the ought self
    b)   The ideal self and the actual self
    c)   The ought self and the actual self
    d)   The actual self and the real self
    Ans: c   LO: 9   Page: 75-76   Type: A

85. According to self-awareness theory, which of the following behaviors is *least* likely to draw attention to self-discrepancies?
    a)   Sitting in a crowded, darkened theater
    b)   Seeing one's reflection in a mirror
    c)   Posing for a photograph
    d)   Standing on stage in front of an audience
    Ans: a   LO: 10   Page: 76   Type: C

86. Higher levels of self-awareness often
    a)   increase the use of stereotypes when describing others.
    b)   improve the natural flow of athletic performance.
    c)   help alcoholics avoid relapses into drinking.
    d)   result in a temporary reduction in self-esteem.
    Ans: d   LO: 10   Page: 76   Type: F

87.   When people are self-focused, they
      a)   exhibit temporary increases in self-esteem.
      b)   have a lower incidence of alcoholism, anxiety, and other clinical disorders.
      c)   are less likely to find themselves in a bad mood.
      d)   tend to behave in ways that are consistent with their personal standards.
      Ans: d   LO: 10   Page: 77   Type: F

88.   Baumeister (1991) suggests that drug abuse, sexual masochism, spiritual ecstasy, binge eating, and suicide
      may all be attempts to
      a)   increase self-awareness.
      b)   reduce self-awareness.
      c)   increase public self-consciousness.
      d)   increase private self-consciousness.
      Ans: b   LO: 10   Page: 77-78   Type: F

89.   Hideo tends to be very hard on himself, thinking he doesn't live up to his goals, but when drunk, he usually
      feels a lot better about himself. Hideo is probably experiencing
      a)   alcohol myopia.
      b)   intoxicated depression.
      c)   objective self-awareness.
      d)   drunken self-inflation.
      Ans: d   LO: 10   Page: 78   Type: A

90.   Missy always calls Delfina to discuss and coordinate her choice of clothes each morning before leaving for
      school. If Delfina disapproves or suggests an alternative outfit, Missy always changes her clothes
      accordingly. Missy is probably
      a)   high in private self-consciousness.
      b)   high in public self-consciousness.
      c)   low in self-monitoring.
      d)   low in self-handicapping.
      Ans: b   LO: 10   Page: 78-79   Type: A

91.   Research concerning private and public self-consciousness shows that people who are
      a)   privately self-conscious are very sensitive regarding the extent to which others share their opinions.
      b)   privately self-conscious are very aware of their internal body states.
      c)   publicly self-conscious are highly motivated to meet their own internal standards.
      d)   publicly self-conscious are quicker to make self-descriptive statements.
      Ans: b   LO: 10   Page: 78-79   Type: C

92.   The process by which we seek to control or alter our thoughts, feelings, behaviors, and urges is called
      a)   self-handicapping.
      b)   self-verification.
      c)   self-presentation.
      d)   self-regulation.
      Ans: d   LO: 11   Page: 79-80   Type: F

93.   Which of the following statements is *most* consistent with Muraven and Baumeister's (2000) theory of self-
      control?
      a)   Self-control is a limited inner resource that can be temporarily depleted.
      b)   Exerting self-control in one situation makes it easier to exert control on a subsequent occasion.
      c)   People have many inner sources of self-control from which they can draw.
      d)   Self-control is simply an illusion used to maintain a positive self-image.
      Ans: a   LO: 11   Page: 79   Type: C

94.   Anquan is frustrated by the incompetence of his professor during class today, and it takes a great deal of effort for him to refrain from standing up during the lecture to tell her she does not know what she is talking about. According to Muraven and Baumeister's (2000) theory of self-control, which of the following outcomes is most likely to occur?
      a)   When he gets back to his dorm after class, Anquan eats an entire pint of cookie dough ice cream.
      b)   Next week, he has an even tougher time sitting quietly though lecture.
      c)   When he goes to the gym after class, he is able to stay on the elliptical machine for 20 minutes longer than he ever has before.
      d)   He decides to work even harder in the course and winds up earning a final grade of A+.
      Ans: a   LO: 11   Page: 79   Type: A

95.   What physical symptom did Gailliot (2007) show to occur during acts of self-regulation?
      a)   heart palpitations.
      b)   high blood pressure.
      c)   reduced blood glucose levels
      d)   headaches.
      Ans: c   LO: 11   Page: 80   Type: F

96.   Which of the following statements about ironic processes of mental self-control is *false*?
      a)   They are more likely to occur when a person is cognitively busy.
      b)   They result from a concern about failing to maintain mental self-control.
      c)   They happen more among individuals who are low in stress.
      d)   They may affect athletic performance.
      Ans: c   LO: 11   Page: 80-81   Type: F

97.   Ruben is trying to lose weight, but his roommate keeps a stash of peanut butter cups in the refrigerator. Ruben has little willpower over his urge to eat peanut butter cups. Given the research regarding ironic processes, Ruben is *most* likely to think about the peanut butter cups if he tells himself
      a)   not to think about them and is distracted by something else.
      b)   to think about them, but then is distracted by something else.
      c)   not to think about them and is not distracted by something else.
      d)   not to think about them over and over.
      Ans: a   LO: 11   Page: 80-81   Type: A

98.   Research has consistently demonstrated that when it comes to perceptions of the self, people have a tendency to
      a)   underestimate their intellectual and social abilities.
      b)   rate negative traits as more self-descriptive than positive ones.
      c)   exaggerate their control over life events.
      d)   rate themselves less positively than others rate them.
      Ans: c   LO: 12   Page: 83-84   Type: F

99.   The fact that people rate the letters in their own names more favorably than other letters of the alphabet is best described as an example of
      a)   implicit egoism.
      b)   basking in reflected glory.
      c)   self-handicapping.
      d)   self-verification.
      Ans: a   LO: 12   Page: 83   Type: C

100. People enhance their self-esteem in all of the following ways *except*
      a)   basking in reflected glory.
      b)   self-serving cognitions.
      c)   upward social comparison.
      d)   self-handicapping.
      Ans: c   LO: 12   Page: 83-86   Type: F

101. Which of the following is *not* a self-serving tendency used to enhance self-esteem?
    a)   People tend to take credit for their successes, but not their failures.
    b)   People underestimate the probability of positive outcomes and overestimate the probability that they will experience negative outcomes.
    c)   People overestimate the extent to which they can control personal outcomes.
    d)   People bolster their optimism by linking their individual attributes to desirable outcomes.
    Ans: b   LO: 12   Page: 83-86   Type: F

102. Research by Pronin and colleagues (2006) indicates that imagining an event before it occurs can lead people to
    a)   take credit for influencing the event.
    b)   exhibit more accurate memory for the event.
    c)   overcome the illusion of mental causation.
    d)   suppress unwanted thoughts about the event.
    Ans: a   LO: 12   Page: 84   Type: F

103. Carlos is nervous about giving a class presentation because he doesn't think he can communicate very well with everyone watching him. If Carlos attempts to deal with his anxiety by self-handicapping, he will *most* likely
    a)   rehearse his presentation in front of a mirror.
    b)   rehearse his presentation in front of a group of friends.
    c)   stay out all night partying the night before the presentation.
    d)   compare himself to others who are eloquent speakers.
    Ans: c   LO: 12   Page: 84-85   Type: A

104. Which of the following *best* exemplifies self-handicapping?
    a)   Attributing poor performance on an exam to having just heard of a family member's cancer diagnosis prior to the exam
    b)   Telling someone you were lucky after winning a tournament
    c)   Procrastinating in writing a paper
    d)   Attributing one's failure to get a summer job to stable personality characteristics
    Ans: c   LO: 12   Page: 84-85   Type: C

105. Prior to the championship basketball game, Jocelyn reminds everyone that she really isn't as good a player as everyone thinks, that their opponent has had an undefeated season, and that it is unlikely she and her teammates will triumph. Jocelyn is engaging in
    a)   sandbagging.
    b)   implicit egoism.
    c)   downward social comparison.
    d)   cutting off reflected failure.
    Ans: a   LO: 12   Page: 85   Type: A

106. A young boy is an avid Mets fan. He reads the statistics for the team in the newspaper every day and goes to Shea Stadium a couple of times each summer to see the Mets play. After the Mets have a particularly bad losing streak, the boy decides that he also likes the Yankees and starts to root for them. This is an example of
    a)   self-handicapping.
    b)   cutting off reflected failure.
    c)   strategic self-presentation.
    d)   ironic processes.
    Ans: b   LO: 12   Page: 85-86   Type: A

107. Which of the following concerning the impact of others on self-esteem is *false*?
    a)   People are less likely to bask in reflected glory when their self-esteem is threatened.
    b)   A merely coincidental association is sufficient to serve as the basis for basking in reflected glory.
    c)   Reflected failure may have physiological effects on the body.
    d)   Both the success and failure of others with whom we identify can impact our self-esteem.
    Ans: a   LO: 12   Page: 85-86   Type: A

108. The tendency for people to think of those worse off than themselves when faced with difficulties of their own is called
    a)   social comparison jealousy.
    b)   self-handicapping.
    c)   downward social comparison.
    d)   public self-consciousness.
    Ans: c   LO: 12   Page: 86-88   Type: F

109. Someone victimized by a crime, disease, or other tragic life event is likely to
    a)   affiliate and compare themselves with others in the same situation.
    b)   affiliate and compare themselves with others who are worse off.
    c)   affiliate with others who are worse off, but compare themselves to others in the same situation.
    d)   affiliate with others who are in the same situation, but compare themselves to others who are worse off.
    Ans: d   LO: 12   Page: 86-88   Type: C

110. Research on social comparison shows that
    a)   people generally bask in reflected glory when they have accomplished siblings.
    b)   patients like to affiliate with other patients who are coping well.
    c)   breast cancer victims engage in more upward than downward comparison.
    d)   children have higher self-esteem when surrounded by others who are equally competent.
    Ans: b   LO: 12   Page: 86-88   Type: C

111. Research by Tesser suggests that when someone close to you performs more poorly than you on a dimension that is central to your self-concept, you are likely to engage in _____ social comparison with this person, resulting in _____ feelings about yourself and the other person.
    a)   upward; negative
    b)   upward; positive
    c)   downward; negative
    d)   downward; positive
    Ans: d   LO: 12   Page: 86-88   Type: C

112. Physical appearance is extremely important to Adriana. When she enters a beauty contest, she beats all but one of the other contestants and finishes in second place. However, the one contestant that beats her is her neighbor and arch-rival, Lisa. Research by Tesser (1988) suggests that Adriana
    a)   will be jealous of Lisa, but will receive a boost in self-esteem from beating the other candidates.
    b)   will avoid future contact with Lisa in order to avoid further threats to her self-esteem.
    c)   will bask in the reflected glory of Lisa's win.
    d)   will seek out situations that increase her level of self-awareness.
    Ans: b   LO: 12   Page: 87-88   Type: A

113. Taylor and Brown (1988) suggest that people are more likely to have realistic views of themselves when they are
    a)   depressed.
    b)   happy.
    c)   high in self-esteem.
    d)   low in self-awareness.
    Ans: a   LO: 12   Page: 88-89   Type: F

114. Erving Goffman (1959) argued that life was much like a theater and that people act out various roles. Goffman's ideas are clearly evident in the social psychological study of
    a)   self-awareness.
    b)   self-presentation.
    c)   public self-consciousness.
    d)   norm formation.
    Ans: b   LO: 13   Page: 91   Type: C

115. In the company of liberals, Mitt expresses favorable attitudes toward abortion and gay marriage; in the company of conservatives, he expresses negative attitudes toward these same issues. Mitt's behavior exemplifies
    a)   self-awareness.
    b)   self-complexity.
    c)   strategic self-presentation.
    d)   private self-consciousness.
    Ans: c   LO: 13   Page: 91-92   Type: A

116. The type of self-presentational strategy that describes acts motivated to establish one's competence is
    a)   self-promotion.
    b)   self-verification.
    c)   ingratiation.
    d)   self-handicapping.
    Ans: a   LO: 13   Page: 92   Type: F

117. Supriya considers it more important for her new boss to value her skills than to like her. The self-presentational strategy she is *most* likely to use is
    a)   self-verification.
    b)   self-handicapping.
    c)   ingratiation.
    d)   self-promotion.
    Ans: d   LO: 13   Page: 92   Type: A

118. A new research study indicates that people with high self-esteem tend to seek out partners who view them positively. Such a finding would be an example of
    a)   self-verification, but not self-enhancement.
    b)   self-enhancement, but not self-verification.
    c)   both self-verification and self-enhancement.
    d)   neither self-verification nor self-enhancement.
    Ans: c   LO: 13   Page: 92-93   Type: C

119. A new research study indicates that people with low self-esteem tend to seek out partners who view them negatively. Such a finding would be an example of
    a)   self-verification, but not self-enhancement.
    b)   self-enhancement, but not self-verification.
    c)   both self-verification and self-enhancement.
    d)   neither self-verification nor self-enhancement.
    Ans: a   LO: 13   Page: 92-93   Type: C

120. The desire for others to perceive us in the same way that we see ourselves is called
    a)   self-verification.
    b)   self-enhancement.
    c)   implicit egoism.
    d)   self-handicapping.
    Ans: a   LO: 13   Page: 92-93   Type: C

121. Alex changes his behavior in response to self-presentation concerns and various situations, exhibiting a high level of
    a)   self-monitoring.
    b)   self-complexity.
    c)   self-verification.
    d)   self-esteem.
    Ans: a   LO: 14   Page: 94-95   Type: A

122. An individual who tends to self-verify is more likely to be _____ than is an individual who does not.
    a)   high in public self-consciousness
    b)   more introspective
    c)   a low self-monitor
    d)   schematic with regard to many aspects of the self-concept
    Ans: c   LO: 14   Page: 94-95   Type: F

123. Compared to high self-monitors, low self-monitors are more likely to
    a)   gather information about others.
    b)   maintain consistency in behavior.
    c)   know the rules of appropriate action.
    d)   adjust their behavior to fit the situation.
    Ans: b   LO: 14   Page: 94-95   Type: C

124. Research on self-monitoring generally suggests that
    a)   it is a global trait.
    b)   high self-monitors conform even in situations that demand autonomy.
    c)   low self-monitoring is more socially adaptive.
    d)   one's scores on the self-monitoring scale decline with age.
    Ans: d   LO: 14   Page: 94-95   Type: F

125. Of the following, the person who would be *least* likely to fit Goffman's portrayal of people's social behavior is someone
    a)   low in self-monitoring.
    b)   high in public self-consciousness.
    c)   with an interdependent view of the self.
    d)   high in self-awareness.
    Ans: a   LO: 14   Page: 94-95   Type: C

ESSAY

126. Sometimes introspection leads to accurate self-knowledge; other times it does not. Explain the distinction.
    Ans: Research has produced the surprising finding that introspection often interferes with our self-knowledge, yet this negative effect does not always occur. As Millar and Tesser (1989) have noted, introspection can lead people astray in domains that are primarily affective, such as romantic relationships, but can actually sharpen self-knowledge in domains that are primarily cognitive, such as investment decision making.   Page: 58-60

127. Identify two biases in autobiographical memory, and give illustrative examples.
    Ans: First, people exhibit an egocentric bias, whereby they overestimate their contribution to a group goal. For example, athletes tend to overestimate the effect of their play on a team outcome. Second, people exhibit a hindsight bias, or a feeling that the outcome of an event could have been known all along. This bias is related to our tendency to revise knowledge of the past in a manner consistent with that which we want to believe in the present. For example, if we change our attitude, we may revise our memory such that we believe our attitude has always been what it is now.   Page: 67-68

128. Describe self-discrepancy theory, and explain how it accounts for certain emotional reactions. Also explain the role of self-awareness in these reactions.
    Ans: Self-discrepancy theory states that people's emotional reactions are the result of discrepancies between their ideal and actual self-conceptions. In general, self-discrepancies bring about negative emotional reactions, and the greater the discrepancies the stronger the negative reactions. This process is affected by self-awareness inasmuch as one must be aware of a self-discrepancy before it can bring about a negative emotional reaction. The emotional reactions that result depend on the nature of the self-discrepancies: Discrepancies between the actual and ought selves provoke feelings of guilt, shame, and resentment, whereas discrepancies between the actual and ideal selves provoke feelings of disappointment, frustration, and sadness.   Page: 75-79

129. Describe three biases that lead to self-enhancement. Explain how these biases bolster the self-concept.
     *Ans: The textbook describes four biases that lead to self-enhancement: self-serving cognitions, self-handicapping, basking in reflected glory, and downward social comparisons. Self-serving cognitions are unjustified positive beliefs that people hold about themselves. For example, people may exaggerate their actual performance on the SAT or be much more optimistic about their chances of avoiding a divorce or getting cancer than the rates corresponding to these events justify. Self-serving cognitions provide evidence of the robust nature of the self-concept and comprise the means by which positive self-conceptions are maintained even when they are not accurate. Self-handicapping is the purposeful engagement in actions that will undermine a later performance. These actions provide the self-handicapper with a reasonable excuse for poor performance on the later task, thereby bolstering his or her self-concept from the negative implications of failure (as well as making actual success all the more impressive). Basking in reflected glory refers to the desire to affiliate with individuals or groups that are successful. For example, people are much more likely to wear team colors after the team wins a game than after it loses. By associating with the winning group, people can claim some of its success, thus bolstering their self-concepts. Finally, downward social comparisons are comparisons with others who are doing worse than you are. These comparisons can bolster the self-concept by placing the self in a context where it appears to be doing relatively well.
     Page: 83-88*

130. Discuss the relationship between self-presentation and self-monitoring.
     Ans: Self-presentation is the portrayal of oneself to others in an effort to put forward a positive image. Self-monitoring refers to the ability to read the situation one is in and to adjust behavior accordingly. High self-monitors seem to have a repertoire of selves from which to draw and are especially sensitive to strategic self-presentation concerns that vary from one situation to the next, whereas low self-monitors express themselves more consistently across different situations. Therefore, self-monitoring can be an important ingredient of effective self-presentation.   Page: 90-95

CHAPTER 4

Perceiving Persons

MULTIPLE CHOICE

1. All of the following could be categorized as sources of "raw data" for social perception *except*
   a) a person's physical appearance.
   b) knowledge of what situation a person is in.
   c) a person's behavior.
   d) accounts given by others about a person.
   Ans: d   LO: 1   Page: 102   Type: C

2. The study of social perception addresses all of the following *except*
   a) how people explain the behavior of others.
   b) how people form impressions of others.
   c) the strategies people use to create a positive self-image.
   d) the way that expectations can distort reality.
   Ans: c   LO: 1   Page: 102   Type: F

3. The study of social perception involves consideration of how one individual (X) makes judgments about another individual (Y). The terminology typically used to describe the roles of X and Y are
   a) evaluator and actor.
   b) perceiver and target.
   c) judge and stimulus.
   d) rater and subject.
   Ans: b   LO: 1   Page: 102   Type: F

4. Fritz is a social psychologist who specializes in studying the processes of social perception. Given this interest, Fritz is *least* likely to specialize in which of the following research questions?
   a) How do employers infer traits and abilities about job candidates based on observing their behavior in a job interview?
   b) How do police officers and customs agents make judgments concerning how truthful or deceptive particular individuals are?
   c) How are consumers influenced in their choices by the packaging and positioning of different products?
   d) How does the performance of athletes vary as a function of their coach's expectations about their ability and potential?
   Ans: c   LO: 1   Page: 102   Type: A

5. As social perceivers, people's impressions of others are
   a) formed only after knowing the person for a considerable period of time.
   b) uninfluenced by superficial attributes of a person.
   c) formed at first encounter and completely unchangeable.
   d) influenced by the physical appearance of a person.
   Ans: d   LO: 1   Page: 102-104   Type: C

6. Willis and Todorov (2006) showed college students photos of strangers' faces and found which of the following?
   a) Participants were unable to rate the personality of the individuals in the photos when they only saw the faces for less than one second.
   b) Even when they saw the photos for less than one second, participants' ratings of the faces were highly correlated with the ratings made by others who were allowed to look at the faces for as long as they wanted to.
   c) Participants who only saw the faces for less than one second rated the faces as possessing more negative traits than others who were allowed to look at the faces for as long as they wanted to.
   d) The longer it took participants to rate each face, the more accurate their ratings were.
   Ans: b   LO: 1   Page: 102-103   Type: F

7.   Sam Gosling (2008) found that social perceivers often form impressions of people based on all of the following *except*
       a)   objects found in their offices.
       b)   the pitch of their voices.
       c)   their Facebook pages.
       d)   their height
       Ans: d   LO: 1   Page: 103-104   Type: F

8.   Hassin and Trope's (2000) study of physiognomy found that participants assigned traits to others based on their
       a)   hair style.
       b)   facial features.
       c)   perceived age.
       d)   perceived race.
       Ans: b   LO: 1   Page: 104   Type: F

9.   Research by Zebrowitz and her colleagues on facial appearance has shown that people who have baby-faced features tend to be perceived as
       a)   warm.
       b)   intelligent.
       c)   dishonest.
       d)   dominant.
       Ans: a   LO: 1   Page: 104   Type: F

10.   Different attributes are ascribed to people who have baby-faced features than to those who have mature facial features. Which of the following has *not* been offered as an explanation for this phenomenon?
       a)   Faces that appear happier are perceived as more trustworthy.
       b)   People overgeneralize attributes of babies to baby-faced adults.
       c)   People are genetically wired to have a nurturing response to baby-like features.
       d)   People are positively reinforced by others to perceive baby-faced adults the way they do.
       Ans: d   LO: 1   Page: 104   Type: C

11.   Todd, considered to have a baby-face, and Martin, viewed as having more mature features, are both being interviewed for the same position in a bank. Which of the following is the *most* probable outcome?
       a)   Because of his more mature features, Martin will be recommended for the position.
       b)   Todd will be recommended for the position because baby-faced individuals are perceived as more honest.
       c)   Todd will be recommended for the position because baby-faced individuals are judged as more qualified for employment than mature-faced individuals.
       d)   Their facial features will not impact the hiring decision and the more qualified candidate will get the job.
       Ans: a   LO: 1   Page: 104   Type: A

12.   Scripts are often culture-specific. This means that
       a)   there is a great deal of agreement about the order of events across cultures.
       b)   the more experience one has with a particular behavior, the more successfully one can execute the relevant script.
       c)   the more general the script is, the greater cross-cultural consistency it has.
       d)   the same behaviors may be perceived very differently in different cultures.
       Ans: d   LO: 2   Page: 105   Type: C

13.   In research by Pryor and Merluzzi (1985), the script for a first date
       a)   was more easily recalled and organized by participants with extensive dating experience.
       b)   varied widely by gender.
       c)   varied widely by sexual orientation.
       d)   was similar across cultures.
       Ans: a   LO: 2   Page: 105   Type: F

14. Which of the following is *not* a way in which scripts influence social perception?
    a) People use their scripts to help explain behavior.
    b) Scripts allow people to discount their expectations.
    c) People can use scripts to fill in missing information.
    d) Scripts can provide a context for understanding nonverbal behavior.
    Ans: b   LO: 2   Page: 105   Type: C

15. Research regarding perception of complex systems, such as sporting events, indicates that compared to people who break the event up into gross units, those who break the event up into fine units tend to
    a) remember more details about the event.
    b) lose sight of the big-picture outcome of the event.
    c) rely more on the expectations of others in evaluating the event.
    d) enjoy their observation of the event more.
    Ans: a   LO: 2   Page: 106   Type: C

16. Andrew tends to view the behavior of others in gross units, whereas Angela tends to break others' behavior down into fine units. Andrew is more likely than Angela to
    a) pay more attention to the behavior.
    b) detect more meaningful actions.
    c) remember fewer details about the behavior.
    d) form a more positive impression of an actor.
    Ans: c   LO: 2   Page: 106   Type: C

17. Research by Gray and colleagues (2007) has indicated two dimensions on which people "perceive minds." These dimensions are referred to as
    a) depth and breadth.
    b) morality and rationality.
    c) agency and experience.
    d) contextual and focal.
    Ans: c   LO: 2   Page: 107   Type: C

18. Behavior that communicates a person's feelings without words is called
    a) scripted behavior.
    b) fine-unit behavior.
    c) perceptually salient behavior.
    d) nonverbal behavior.
    Ans: d   LO: 3   Page: 107-109   Type: F

19. While traveling around the world, Teun shows various people pictures of men and women from his hometown who are smiling and frowning, and he asks these people to infer what emotions the individuals in the pictures are experiencing. According to the research on perceptions of primary emotions, Sven should find that
    a) perceptions of the emotions vary widely as a function of the people's culture.
    b) perceptions of the emotions are relatively consistent across most cultures.
    c) little can be inferred about the emotions unless the behaviors of the individuals in the pictures are also described.
    d) little is inferred about the emotions unless the situational contexts of the individuals in the pictures are also described.
    Ans: b   LO: 3   Page: 107-108   Type: A

20. All of the following are considered "primary" emotions *except*
    a) happiness.
    b) surprise.
    c) disgust.
    d) anxiety.
    Ans: d   LO: 3   Page: 107   Type: F

21. Cross-cultural research on perception of emotion, such as that conducted by Elfenbein and Ambady (2003), indicates that
    a) people are uniformly good at perceiving the emotional states of others based on nonverbal cues, regardless of whether perceivers and targets are from the same culture.
    b) people are fairly successful at perceiving the emotional states of individuals from other cultures, but we are better at judging emotions of individuals from our own culture.
    c) people are actually better at perceiving the emotional states of individuals from other cultures because they are not distracted by language use and other verbal cues.
    d) language comprehension plays a central role in the evaluation of emotion.
    Ans: b   LO: 3   Page: 108   Type: C

22. Which of the following research findings is *most* consistent with Darwin's hypothesis that the ability to interpret emotion from facial expressions has survival value?
    a) People are quicker to recognize angry faces than happy faces.
    b) People are better able to interpret emotions from video than still pictures.
    c) People are able to identify six primary emotions.
    d) People sometimes infer emotions from situations rather than facial expressions.
    Ans: a   LO: 3   Page: 108   Type: C

23. The "anger superiority effect" in social perception refers to the finding that
    a) people are quicker to look away from an angry face in a crowd than a neutral face.
    b) people are quicker to look away from an angry face in a crowd than a happy face.
    c) people are quicker to spot an angry face in a crowd than a neutral or happy face.
    d) cross-cultural differences in the perception of angry faces are greater than they are for faces with other emotions.
    Ans: c   LO: 3   Page: 108   Type: C

24. The importance of nonverbal behavior when it comes to social perception can be seen by the fact that email messages
    a) are often misinterpreted, especially when the writer is trying to be funny or sarcastic,
    b) have a stronger emotional impact on those who read them than do voice mail messages.
    c) are typically longer than text messages.
    d) are the preferred means of communication among younger but not older Americans.
    Ans: a   LO: 3   Page: 108   Type: A

25. Jerry makes frequent eye contact with the person to whom he is talking. This is *most* likely to elicit
    a) an impression that Jerry is domineering and likes power.
    b) an impression that Jerry is insecure and needy.
    c) a positive impression if the person to whom Jerry is talking is a friend, and a negative impression if this person is an enemy.
    d) a positive impression if the person to whom Jerry is talking is a woman, and a negative impression if this person is a man.
    Ans: c   LO: 3   Page: 109   Type: A

26. A target's "gaze disengagement" tends to lead perceivers to
    a) believe that a target is overly confident.
    b) rate a target as more physically attractive.
    c) have difficulty forming an accurate impression of a target.
    d) form a negative impression of a target.
    Ans: d   LO: 3   Page: 109   Type: C

27. Which of the following has been demonstrated by Henley's (1977) research on touching?
    a) Women initiate more touching than men.
    b) Men initiate more touching than women.
    c) Women initiate more touching than men early in a relationship, but this difference decreases later in the relationship.
    d) Lower-status individuals initiate more touching than do higher-status individuals.
    Ans: b   LO: 3   Page: 109-110   Type: F

28. Research conducted by Hall and colleagues suggests that we tend to believe that dominant people touch others more than do subordinate people, and behavioral data indicate that
    a)   this expectation is accurate.
    b)   this expectation leads us to be hesitant to make physical contact during interactions.
    c)   this expectation is not accurate.
    d)   this expectation is only accurate regarding male targets, and not for female targets.
    Ans: c   LO: 3   Page: 109-110   Type: C

29. Cross-cultural differences in the perception of nonverbal behavior are *least* prevalent in which of the following types of judgments?
    a)   Evaluations of emotions and facial features
    b)   Interpretations of head-nodding and hand signals
    c)   Preference for personal space
    d)   Inferences drawn regarding eye contact
    Ans: a   LO: 3   Page: 110   Type: C

30. One of the reasons that we are *not* very successful at detecting deception is because
    a)   we focus too much attention on nonverbal cues and not enough on verbal cues.
    b)   we fail to attend to the nonverbal cues that actually signal deception.
    c)   we are motivated to believe that others are telling the truth.
    d)   detecting deception is an evolutionary adaptive strategy.
    Ans: b   LO: 4   Page: 110-112   Type: F

31. Deception is *most* likely to be detected by attending to which channel of communication?
    a)   Spoken words
    b)   Body posture
    c)   Voice pitch
    d)   Facial expression
    Ans: c   LO: 4   Page: 110-112   Type: C

32. Which of the following is supported by research on deception?
    a)   People are more accurate at detecting deception if they focus on facial expressions rather than voice cues.
    b)   Police officers and FBI agents are better at detecting deception than most other people.
    c)   People tend to have an accurate sense of their lie-detecting abilities.
    d)   People are more accurate at detecting deception if they focus on body movements rather than facial expressions.
    Ans: d   LO: 4   Page: 110-112   Type: C

33. Research on detecting deception has consistently shown that
    a)   people are generally very good at distinguishing between truth and lies.
    b)   there are small individual differences in people's ability to detect lies.
    c)   people are only slightly better than chance when it comes to distinguishing between truth and lies.
    d)   experts, like police detectives and judges rarely make errors in lie detection.
    Ans: c   LO: 4   Page: 110-112   Type: F

34. Bella is a teacher who suspects that a student is trying to deceive her. Under which of the following conditions does Bella have the *best* chance of being accurate in her attempts to detect whether or not the student is lying?
    a)   Bella reads a written transcript of the student's story.
    b)   Bella sees a silent video of the student's face as the student tells the story.
    c)   Bella reads a written transcript of the student's story and sees a silent video of the student's face as the student tells the story.
    d)   Bella asks the student to recount her story in reverse chronological order.
    Ans: d   LO: 4   Page: 110-112   Type: A

35.   According to a survey about lying, people believe that liars tend to fidget and avert their eyes. The problem
       with relying on these kinds of cues to determine if someone is lying is that
       a).   People are not good at looking for these signs
       b)   Truth tellers may be just as likely to exhibit the same kinds of stress in real-life situations.
       c)   Some people might be "good liars" and not exhibit these behaviors.
       d)   This strategy does not take voice pitch into account.
       Ans: c   LO: 4   Page: 110-112   Type: C

36.   People are more likely to search for explanations for events that are
       a)   expected.
       b)   positive.
       c)   personally relevant.
       d)   ordinary.
       Ans: c   LO: 5   Page: 113-114   Type: C

37.   Veronica is talking to her parents about her French professor and claims that he gave her a failing grade on
       her last paper because he is arrogant, cold, and indifferent to the progress of his students. Veronica is
       making a(n)
       a)   personal attribution.
       b)   situational attribution.
       c)   external attribution.
       d)   counterfactual attribution.
       Ans: a   LO: 5   Page: 113-114   Type: A

38.   Colin and Erin are waiting to meet with their caterer so that they can discuss the menu for their wedding.
       The caterer is 30 minutes late and still hasn't arrived. Colin suggests that the caterer is probably delayed
       because of traffic. Erin suggests that the caterer is probably disorganized and unreliable. Colin is making
       a(n) _____attribution, whereas Erin is making a(n) _____ attribution.
       a)   dispositional; situational
       b)   situational; personal
       c)   expected; unexpected
       d)   correspondent; dispositional
       Ans: b   LO: 5   Page: 113-114   Type: A

39.   Jorge watches his friend Nina interacting with others and makes a situational attribution for her behavior.
       Jorge believes that
       a)   Nina's behavior is best explained by the circumstances surrounding the encounter.
       b)   Nina's way of relating to people stems from particular characteristics of her personality.
       c)   Nina is not acting the way other people would act in the same situation.
       d)   Nina's actions are not consistent with the social norms governing that particular situation.
       Ans: a   LO: 5   Page: 113-114   Type: A

40.   Lindy is trying to decide whether or not Marisa's behavior is dispositional. If Lindy relies on correspondent
       inference theory, she would consider all of the following factors *except*
       a)   whether Marisa freely chose the behavior.
       b)   whether Marisa knew she was being observed during the behavior.
       c)   if Marisa's behavior was expected given the situation.
       d)   the intended consequences of Marisa's behavior.
       Ans: b   LO: 5   Page: 114-115   Type: A

41.   According to correspondent inference theory, in which of the following situations would a personal
       attribution be *most* appropriate?
       a)   Serena, a professor, helps students during her office hours.
       b)   Sally, a naval officer, salutes when her commanding officer enters the room.
       c)   Sam, a wealthy athlete, is ordered by the court to attend a drug rehabilitation program.
       d)   Steve, a world renowned playboy, joins a monastery and takes a vow of celibacy.
       Ans: d   LO: 5   Page: 114-115   Type: C

42. In Jones and Davis's correspondent inference theory, observers trying to infer whether a particular behavior corresponds to an enduring personal characteristic of the actor would ask all of the following questions *except*
    a) Did the behavior violate any social norms?
    b) What were the consequences of the behavior?
    c) What is the actor's perception of the behavior?
    d) Did the actor freely choose to perform the behavior?
    Ans: c   LO: 5   Page: 114-115   Type: C

43. Which of the following reflects the primary question underlying Jones's correspondent inference theory?
    a) Do attributions correspond with pre-existing beliefs?
    b) Does an individual's beliefs correspond with that individual's behavior?
    c) Does an observer infer that an actor's behavior corresponds with the actor's personality?
    d) Does an observer infer that an actor's behavior is consistent with that of the observer?
    Ans: c   LO: 5   Page: 114-115   Type: C

44. According to correspondent inference theory, correspondent inferences are *most* likely to occur when a person's behavior is
    a) not freely chosen, expected, and results in many desirable outcomes.
    b) freely chosen, expected, and results in few desirable outcomes.
    c) freely chosen, unexpected, and results in many desirable outcomes.
    d) freely chosen, unexpected, and results in few desirable outcomes.
    Ans: d   LO: 5   Page: 114-115   Type: C

45. George is leaving his job at Vandalay Industries, a latex manufacturer. According to correspondent inference theory, in which of the following scenarios would you learn the *most* about George?
    a) The company is downsizing and many employees, including George, are being terminated.
    b) The company is expanding as a result of record-breaking profits, and compensation for employees in the sales department where George worked has increased 30% this year.
    c) By leaving, George will no longer have to work incredibly long hours, in unhealthy air quality, under a demanding and mean supervisor.
    d) The company is offering a great retirement deal to all of their senior management and, like the other senior managers, George has decided to retire early.
    Ans: b   LO: 5   Page: 114-115   Type: A

46. Kelley's theory of attribution suggests that, in trying to discern personal characteristics from behavioral evidence, people
    a) behave like scientists and engage in informal experiments.
    b) use cognitive heuristics improperly.
    c) usually attribute behavior to both personal and situational factors.
    d) fail to adequately consider consensus information.
    Ans: a   LO: 5   Page: 115-116   Type: F

47. According to Kelley's covariation principle
    a) actors attribute behavior to the situation, but observers attribute behavior to persons.
    b) people fail to use statistical information, instead relying on intuitive theories to make personality inferences.
    c) people infer that something is the cause of a behavior if it is present when the behavior occurs and absent when it does not occur.
    d) people infer the causes of a behavior as a function of the intended consequences of the behavior.
    Ans: c   LO: 5   Page: 115-116   Type: F

48. Everyone you know seems to love the TV show *The Apprentice*. You're a huge fan of reality TV as well, as you never miss an episode of *The Amazing Race*, *American Idol*, or *Project Runway*. But every time you watch *The Apprentice*, you have the same reaction: you hate it with a passion. According to Kelley's (1967) covariation theory of attribution, your dislike of this show would be
    a) high in consensus, low in distinctiveness, and high in consistency.
    b) low in consensus, high in distinctiveness, and high in consistency.
    c) high in consensus, high in distinctiveness, and low in consistency.
    d) low in consensus, low in distinctiveness, and low in consistency.
    Ans: b   LO: 5   Page: 115-116   Type: A

49. Among your group of friends, Chandler is the only one who is ever late for your weekly game of tiddlywinks. You've noticed that he is late every week and that he is also late for class, parties, movies, weddings, sporting events, and dental appointments. According to Kelley's covariation model of attribution, Chandler's behavior would be described as
     a)   low in consensus, high in consistency, and low in distinctiveness.
     b)   low in consensus, high in consistency, and high in distinctiveness.
     c)   low in consensus, low in consistency, and low in distinctiveness.
     d)   high in consensus, high in consistency, and high in distinctiveness.
     Ans: a   LO: 5   Page: 115-116   Type: A

50. Although he professes to hate sports, Andy never fails to watch the finals of the America's Cup yachting race. Andy's behavior is
     a)   high in distinctiveness.
     b)   low in consistency.
     c)   high in consensus.
     d)   low in consensus.
     Ans: a   LO: 5   Page: 115-116   Type: A

51. According to the covariation principle, a personal attribution is *most* likely to result when consistency is _____, consensus is _____, and distinctiveness is _____.
     a)   low; low; low
     b)   low; high; high
     c)   high; low; low
     d)   high; high; high
     Ans: c   LO: 5   Page: 115-116   Type: F

52. According to the covariation principle, a situational attribution is *most* likely to result when consistency is _____, consensus is _____, and distinctiveness is _____.
     a)   low; low; low
     b)   low; high; high
     c)   high; low; low
     d)   high; high; high
     Ans: d   LO: 5   Page: 115-116   Type: F

53. According to the covariation principle, consistent behaviors are attributed to the stimulus when
     a)   consensus and distinctiveness are low.
     b)   consensus and distinctiveness are high.
     c)   consensus is high, but distinctiveness is low.
     d)   consensus is low, but distinctiveness is high.
     Ans: b   LO: 5   Page: 115-116   Type: F

54. When _____ is low, it is difficult for the perceiver to attribute behavior to either the person or the stimulus; instead, the best that can be said is that the behavior was caused by transient circumstances.
     a)   consensus
     b)   distinctiveness
     c)   expectedness
     d)   consistency
     Ans: d   LO: 5   Page: 115-116   Type: F

55. Estimates of the probability that an event will happen based on the ease with which one can recall previous instances of this event reflect the
     a)   base-rate fallacy.
     b)   fundamental attribution error.
     c)   two-step attribution process.
     d)   availability heuristic.
     Ans: d   LO: 6   Page: 116-117   Type: F

56. Monica uses the availability heuristic much more frequently than does Ross. Therefore, Monica is more likely than Ross to
    a)   rely heavily on situational cues that are available in the stream of behavior she observes.
    b)   perceive and utilize the available consensus information.
    c)   make judgments that are more resistant to the false-consensus effect.
    d)   estimate the likelihood of an event in terms of the ease with which instances of it come to mind.
    Ans: d   LO: 6   Page: 116-117   Type: A

57. You are asked what percentage of psychology majors at your school are female. If you answer this question by thinking of how many female psychology majors come to mind quickly, you are relying on the
    a)   hindsight bias.
    b)   fundamental attribution error.
    c)   availability heuristic.
    d)   false consensus bias.
    Ans: c   LO: 6   Page: 116-117   Type: C

58. Carol is asked to rate her husband in terms of how helpful he is with the household chores. Because she cannot think of a single instance of helpful behavior, she gives him a very low rating. Carol relied on _____ to make her judgment.
    a)   counterfactual thinking
    b)   the base-rate fallacy
    c)   the availability heuristic
    d)   a confirmation bias
    Ans: c   LO: 6   Page: 116-117   Type: A

59. Sophia voted for Barack Obama in the 2008 U.S. Presidential election. She believes that approximately 90% of college students also voted for Obama, when in reality that number is much lower. Sophia's overestimation is consistent with
    a)   the false-consensus effect.
    b)   the confirmation bias.
    c)   the self-fulfilling prophecy.
    d)   the representativeness heuristic.
    Ans: a   LO: 6   Page: 117   Type: C

60. Abigail loves her social psychology class and thinks that most of the other students in the class love it as well. Lily is in the same class and absolutely hates it. Lily is thoroughly convinced that most of the other students also dislike it. These distorted perceptions are an example of
    a)   hindsight bias.
    b)   the confirmation bias.
    c)   counterfactual thinking.
    d)   the false-consensus effect.
    Ans: d   LO: 6   Page: 117   Type: A

61. The false-consensus effect is especially strong when
    a)   predicting the behavior of individuals in other cultures.
    b)   perceivers bring to mind the attitudes of people they like.
    c)   the actual percentage of others who agree is low.
    d)   considering behaviors rather than opinions.
    Ans: c   LO: 6   Page: 117   Type: C

62. The availability heuristic contributes to all of the following *except*
    a)   counterfactual thinking.
    b)   the base-rate fallacy.
    c)   the false-consensus effect.
    d)   belief in a just world.
    Ans: d   LO: 6   Page: 116-117   Type: C

63.   The base-rate fallacy reflects
       a)   a failure to use consensus information.
       b)   a failure to use consistency information.
       c)   the actor-observer effect.
       d)   an excessive reliance on situational attributions.
       Ans: a   LO: 6   Page: 117-118   Type: F

64.   Stephon knows someone whose brother received a very lucrative contract to play professional basketball for
       the National Basketball Association (NBA). With this success story in mind, he ignores the statistics that
       indicate a very low probability that anyone will make it to the NBA and overestimates his own chances of
       making it. This scenario *best* illustrates
       a)   the covariation principle.
       b)   the base-rate fallacy.
       c)   non-correspondent inferences.
       d)   the actor-observer effect.
       Ans: b   LO: 6   Page: 117-118   Type: A

65.   Whenever Elaine goes to the casino, the noise from all the winning slot machines convinces her that she
       will be able to win enough money to pay off all her debts. Elaine is a victim of
       a)   counterfactual thinking.
       b)   the base-rate fallacy.
       c)   the confirmation bias.
       d)   the false-consensus effect.
       Ans: b   LO: 6   Page: 117-118   Type: A

66.   Participants in one study rated fictional food additives that were more difficult to pronounce as more
       hazardous to health. These results demonstrate that
       a)   people tend to fear things that sound unfamiliar.
       b)   people prefer to eat things that they have heard of.
       c)   people underestimate their own fears and anxieties.
       d).   People are unlikely to eat something that they can't pronounce
       Ans: a   LO: 6   Page: 117   Type: C

67.   The tendency to mentally undo events or to ask "What if…?" is called
       a)   base-rate fallacy.
       b)   attribution.
       c)   counterfactual thinking.
       d)   fundamental attribution error.
       Ans: c   LO: 7   Page: 118   Type: F

68.   Based on research on counterfactual thinking, in which of the following scenarios is Jamal *most* likely to
       wonder what life might have been like had he been richer?
       a)   Financially, Jamal is in the upper-middle class. His parents were slightly wealthier.
       b)   Financially, Jamal is in the upper-middle class. His parents were lower-middle class.
       c)   Financially, Jamal is in the working class. His parents were also working class.
       d)   Financially, Jamal is in the middle class. His parents were extremely rich.
       Ans: a   LO: 7   Page: 118   Type: A

69.   Britney wonders if she would have been happier had she married Justin instead of Kevin. This illustrates
       a)   counterfactual thinking.
       b)   the fundamental attribution error.
       c)   the availability heuristic.
       d)   false-consensus bias.
       Ans: a   LO: 7   Page: 118   Type: A

70. Which of the following has *not* been demonstrated in research on counterfactual thinking?
    a)   Positive mood prompts counterfactuals about how much worse things could have been.
    b)   Negative mood prompts counterfactuals about how much better things could have been.
    c)   Counterfactual thoughts can influence how we feel about an event.
    d)   The things we fail to do are more likely to prompt counterfactuals than the things we do.
    Ans: d   LO: 7   Page: 118   Type: C

71. Vito finished first in the school spelling bee, Fabrizio finished second, and Luigi finished third. The first place winner gets a cash prize and the opportunity to compete at the regional spelling bee, but the others get nothing. Which of the following is *most* likely to occur?
    a)   Fabrizio will engage in more counterfactual thinking than Luigi.
    b)   Luigi will engage in more counterfactual thinking than Fabrizio.
    c)   Fabrizio and Luigi will engage in counterfactual thinking to about the same extent, but more so than Vito.
    d)   Fabrizio and Luigi will engage in counterfactual thinking to about the same extent, but less so than Vito.
    Ans: a   LO: 7   Page: 118   Type: A

72. According to Medvec's research on counterfactual thinking among Olympic medalists, which of the following is *true*?
    a)   Bronze and ilver medalists are equally likely to think "What if… I had won the Gold?"
    b)   Silver medalists are happier with their standing than Bronze medalists, because Silver medalists think about how they could have done worse and received the Bronze.
    c)   Silver medalists are less happy with their standing than Bronze medalists, because Silver medalists think about how they could have done better and won the Gold.
    d)   Bronze medalists are envious of Silver medalists.
    Ans: c   LO: 7   Page: 118-119   Type: F

73. The fundamental attribution error is the tendency to attribute
    a)   one's own behavior to personal factors rather than to the situation.
    b)   one's own behavior to the situation rather than to personal factors.
    c)   another person's behavior to personal factors rather than to the situation.
    d)   another person's behavior to situational factors rather than to personal factors.
    Ans: c   LO: 8   Page: 119-121   Type: F

74. In the Jones and Harris (1967) study, participants read essays that either supported or opposed Cuban leader Fidel Castro. Participants were either led to believe that the essay writers had chosen their own stance to write about (*choice* condition), or that the writers had been forced to adopt the position put forth in the essay (*forced* condition). Which of the following statements about the findings of this study is *false*?
    a)   Only in the *choice* condition did participants believe that the arguments in the essay were somewhat indicative of the writer's true Castro attitudes.
    b)   Participants in the *choice* condition were more likely to believe that the essay revealed information about the writer's true Castro attitudes than participants in the *forced* condition.
    c)   Even in the *forced* condition, participants believed that the arguments in the essay were somewhat indicative of the writer's true Castro beliefs.
    d)   The findings demonstrate support for the idea of the fundamental attribution error.
    Ans: a   LO: 8   Page: 119   Type: C

75. You hear Tiger Woods doing a radio commercial for Buick. Even though you know that Woods did not write the commercial himself, was paid to provide the voice-over for the commercial, and probably does not drive a Buick in real life, you still think that at some level, at least, Woods must think highly of Buicks. This is an example of
    a)   actor-observer effect.
    b)   false consensus bias.
    c)   availability heuristic.
    d)   fundamental attribution error.
    Ans: d   LO: 8   Page: 119-121   Type: A

76. LeBron is eating at a restaurant on a first date when his date spills spaghetti all over his lap. Which of the following conclusions would LeBron be most likely to draw if he commits the fundamental attribution error?
    a)   His date gets nervous on first dates.
    b)   His date is a slob.
    c)   His date is even more attractive than he originally thought.
    d)   His date is even less attractive than he originally thought.
    Ans: b   LO: 8   Page: 119-121   Type: A

77. A politician asked her speechwriter to write a speech that supports the death penalty. The fundamental attribution error would be *most* clearly seen in this case if the speechwriter
    a)   changes her attitude to support the death penalty.
    b)   is perceived by others to support the death penalty.
    c)   comes to believe that most other people support the death penalty.
    d)   is perceived by others to have written the speech because of a request from her boss.
    Ans: b   LO: 8   Page: 119-121   Type: A

78. Research suggests that people seem to commit the fundamental attribution error
    a)   only if they use the availability heuristic to make attributions.
    b)   only if they are unaware of the actor's feelings about the particular behavior.
    c)   even when they attempt to explain their own behavior.
    d)   even when they are aware of the situational constraints of the behavior.
    Ans: d   LO: 8   Page: 119-121   Type: F

79. According to the two-step model of the attribution process, people make an
    a)   automatic first step of weighing situational and personal attributions equally, and then an effortful second step of considering the initial inference.
    b)   automatic first step of making a personal attribution, and then an effortful second step of considering situational factors.
    c)   effortful first step of weighing situational and personal attributions equally, and then an automatic second step of making a dispositional inference.
    d)   automatic first step of making a situational attribution, and then an effortful second step of considering personal factors.
    Ans: b   LO: 8   Page: 120-121   Type: C

80. The "Quiz Show" study by Ross and colleagues found that in judging the general knowledge of the contestant and questioner,
    a)   observers fell victim to the fundamental attribution error, but the questioner and contestant did not.
    b)   participants did not fall victim to the fundamental attribution error because they knew that the quiz show roles were assigned at random.
    c)   observers and even contestants fell victim to the fundamental attribution error.
    d)   men were more likely to commit the fundamental attribution error than women.
    Ans: c   LO: 8   Page: 119-120   Type: F

81. According to Gilbert's two-step model of social perception, distraction should make the fundamental attribution error more likely to happen because it
    a)   discourages personal attributions, but has little effect on situational attributions.
    b)   inhibits perceivers from using distinctiveness information, but allows them to take consistency information into account.
    c)   does not interfere with the automatic process of making personal attributions, but does interfere with the more difficult process of making adjustments for situational factors.
    d)   changes the interrelationship between the figure and the background in social perception.
    Ans: c   LO: 8   Page: 120-121   Type: C

82. Al, Saul, Steve, and Ken are each observing Phoebe behave during a group meeting. Which of them should be the *most* likely to commit the fundamental attribution error when making inferences from Phoebe's behavior?
  a)   Al, who is not cognitively busy or distracted
  b)   Saul, who is very motivated to make accurate inferences about Phoebe
  c)   Steve, who is suspicious of Phoebe's motives
  d)   Ken, who is focused more on Phoebe's actual behavior than on the overall context
  Ans: d   LO: 8   Page: 120-121   Type: A

83. Suppose an experiment was conducted where people were asked to watch a political debate between two candidates that had been previously judged by political pundits to have been a tie. Half of the participants saw a videotape of the debate where the camera focused on candidate A. The other half of the participants saw a videotape of the debate where the camera focused on candidate B. It is likely that
  a)   the majority of the participants declared the debate a tie.
  b)   both groups saw candidate A as victorious.
  c)   the group that viewed candidate A thought she was victorious, whereas the group that viewed candidate B thought he was victorious.
  d)   the group that viewed candidate A thought candidate B was victorious, whereas the group that viewed candidate B thought candidate A was victorious.
  Ans: c   LO: 8   Page: 120-121   Type: A

84. When the saleswoman doesn't reply to his "hello," Mario concludes that she is simply a cold person. Yet the next day when Mario doesn't reply to the saleswoman who greets him, he realizes that he is just having a bad day. These differing attributional tendencies illustrate
  a)   the fundamental attribution error.
  b)   the actor-observer effect.
  c)   counterfactual thinking.
  d)   the false-consensus effect.
  Ans: a   LO: 8   Page: 119-121   Type: A

85. Which of the following has been demonstrated by research examining the role of culture in the attribution process?
  a)   Children reared in Western cultures are more likely to make the fundamental attribution error than those reared in Eastern cultures.
  b)   Children reared in Western cultures are less likely to make the fundamental attribution error than those reared in Eastern cultures.
  c)   Adults in Western cultures are more likely to make the fundamental attribution error than those in Eastern cultures.
  d)   Adults in Western cultures are less likely to make the fundamental attribution error than those in Eastern cultures.
  Ans: c   LO: 8   Page: 121-123   Type: C

86. Miller (1984) examined the attributions of American and Indian participants and found that
  a)   no cultural differences emerged with young children, but among adults, Americans were more likely to make personal attributions and Indians were more likely to make situational attributions.
  b)   no cultural differences emerged with young children, but among adults, Americans were more likely to make situational attributions and Indians were more likely to make personal attributions.
  c)   among young children, Americans were more likely to make personal attributions and Indians were more likely to make situational attributions; no cultural differences emerged with adult participants.
  d)   among young children, Americans were more likely to make situational attributions and Indians were more likely to make personal attributions; no cultural differences emerged with adult participants.
  Ans: a   LO: 8   Page: 122   Type: F

87. Research using bicultural participants, such as China-born students attending college in the U.S., indicates that
     a)   attributional style is dictated by the culture in which one is born and does not vary much due to cultural influences later in life.
     b)   at some point such individuals completely abandon the attributional tendencies of their nation of origin and replace them with the tendencies of their new country of residence.
     c)   people can simultaneously hold differing cultural worldviews, either of which can influence attributional tendencies depending on the situation.
     d)   All of these.
     Ans: c   LO: 8   Page: 122-123   Type: C

88. Which of the following is *not* an example of the positivity bias in attribution?
     a)   People tend to seek out more information about their own strengths than about their weaknesses.
     b)   People overestimate their contributions to group efforts.
     c)   People underestimate the amount of control they have over outcomes in life.
     d)   People are overly optimistic in predicting their own future.
     Ans: c   LO: 9   Page: 124   Type: C

89. The study by Balcetis and Dunning (2006) in which participants thought that they were taking part in a taste-testing experiment showed that?
     a)   People tend to see what they want to see.
     b)   People prefer orange juice to greenish drink.
     c)   People's perceptions are objective analyses of the facts
     d)   People are unlikely to make self-serving attributions.
     Ans: a   LO: 9   Page: 124   Type: C

90. Manuel observes Diana giving very good answers to a series of questions as she practices for a general knowledge contest. Under which of the following conditions is Manuel *most* likely to attribute Diana's success to external, unstable causes?
     a)   Manuel knows that Diana will be his teammate in the contest.
     b)   Manuel knows that Diana will be his opponent in the contest.
     c)   Manuel has had no previous experience with questions of the type that Diana answered.
     d)   Manuel has had considerable previous experience with questions of the type that Diana answered.
     Ans: b   LO: 9   Page: 124-125   Type: A

91. One way of defending our belief in a just world when we observe a victim suffering is to
     a)   identify strongly with the victim.
     b)   disparage the victim.
     c)   disparage the oppressor.
     d)   become very concerned with our own situation out of fear of suffering in the future.
     Ans: b   LO: 9   Page: 125   Type: F

92. The tendency to think that most victims of Hurricane Katrina were irresponsible and naive for not evacuating their homes before the storm hit is *most* likely to result from which of the following tendencies?
     a)   Belief in a just world
     b)   Implicit personality theory
     c)   False consensus effect
     d)   Priming
     Ans: a   LO: 9   Page: 125-126   Type: A

93. Perceivers judge accident victims as more responsible for their fate if
     a)   the victim's situation is very different from that of the perceiver.
     b)   the accident is mild rather than severe.
     c)   the perceiver is worried about threats to the self.
     d)   the perceiver can aid the victim in some way.
     Ans: c   LO: 9   Page: 125-126   Type: C

94.   Which of the following psychological processes best explains why it is that people sometimes react to news of a natural disaster or violent crime with something less than full sympathy on behalf of the victims?
       a)   Counterfactual thinking
       b)   False consensus effect
       c)   Availability heuristic
       d)   Belief in a just world
       Ans: d   LO: 9   Page: 125   Type: A

95.   _____ theory combines the personal dispositions of the perceiver with a weighted average of the target person's characteristics.
       a)   fundamental attribution error
       b)   information integration
       c)   motivational bias
       d)   covariation.
       Ans: b   LO: 10   Page: 126-127   Type: F

96.   The finding that moderately positive traits can dilute the impact of extremely positive traits on impressions is *most* consistent with the
       a)   role of central traits in impression formation.
       b)   influence of priming effects in impression formation.
       c)   averaging model of impression formation.
       d)   summation model of impression formation.
       Ans: c   LO: 10   Page: 126-127   Type: F

97.   The idea that impressions are based on a perceiver's disposition to form certain impressions and a weighted average of the target person's characteristics is *most* consistent with
       a)   correspondent inference theory.
       b)   cognitive heuristics.
       c)   the actor-observer effect.
       d)   information integration theory.
       Ans: d   LO: 10   Page: 126-127   Type: C

98.   When forming impressions of others,
       a)   people see their own skills and abilities as less desirable to have.
       b)   people use the significant others in their lives as a frame of reference.
       c)   people differ in the particular traits they are likely to notice.
       d)   there is less overlap between the descriptions provided by the same perceiver than between those provided for the same target.
       Ans: c   LO: 10   Page: 127   Type: C

99.   Research by Forgas and Bower (1987) demonstrated that good moods can lead to
       a)   more negative perceptions of others, particularly among individuals high in need for closure.
       b)   more negative perceptions of others, particularly when the mood is induced by an unexpected surprise.
       c)   more positive perceptions of others, particularly among individuals skilled at making correspondent inferences.
       d)   more positive perceptions of others, particularly when judging others who require more effort to be understood.
       Ans: d   LO: 10   Page: 127   Type: F

100.   Priming refers to the tendency
       a)   to infer unknown personality characteristics on the basis of known dispositions.
       b)   for recently used concepts to come to mind easily and influence the interpretation of new information.
       c)   for people to underutilize target characteristics and rely on their own traits when forming impressions of others.
       d)   to continue to believe pre-existing impressions even after they are discredited.
       Ans: b   LO: 10   Page: 127-128   Type: F

101. During her social psychology course this morning, Leticia learned about the situational obstacles that often prevent people from offering assistance to others in emergency situations. As she is eating lunch with her friends after class, one of them begins coughing and Leticia immediately starts to consider whether her friend is choking and how she will best be able to help her if she is in need of assistance. Leticia's behavior is *most* likely the result of
    a)   counterfactual thinking.
    b)   actor-observer effect.
    c)   priming.
    d)   false-consensus effect.
    Ans: c   LO: 10   Page: 127-128   Type: A

102. All of the following have been shown in research on priming *except* that priming
    a)   is more likely when people are aware of the exposure.
    b)   may have effects on our social perceptions of others.
    c)   may affect our social behavior.
    d)   demonstrates the effects of recent events on our perceptions.
    Ans: a   LO: 10   Page: 127-128   Type: C

103. While on an airplane, John completes a crossword puzzle in which *interrupt*, *rude*, and *blunt* are all answers. After landing, John gets in line to speak to someone at the ticket counter, but the ticket agent does not notice him because he is too busy talking with another employee. Research on priming suggests that John will be likely to
    a)   leave and get in line at another gate to ask his question.
    b)   interrupt the ticket agent to ask his question.
    c)   wait patiently until the agent finishes his conversation.
    d)   forget about asking his question and go look for something to eat.
    Ans: b   LO: 10   Page: 127-128   Type: A

104. Reena meets Rachael for the first time. Rachael is perceived as smart, funny, sociable, but rude. Although Reena perceived Rachael to have many positive qualities, her rudeness outweighed them, and Reena forms a negative impression of Rachael. This illustrates
    a)   an implicit personality theory.
    b)   the trait negativity bias.
    c)   the summation model of impression formation.
    d)   the primacy effect.
    Ans: b   LO: 10   Page: 129   Type: A

105. Social perceivers are most likely to agree in their judgments of which of the following traits?
    a)   Openness to experience
    b)   Extroversion
    c)   Agreeableness
    d)   Emotional Stability
    Ans: b   LO: 10   Page: 129   Type: F

106. The trait negativity bias refers to the tendency for
    a)   people to view others' traits more negatively than their own.
    b)   moderately favorable traits to negatively impact the favorability of overall impressions.
    c)   negative impressions to become more positive over time.
    d)   negative trait information to have a greater impact on impressions.
    Ans: d   LO: 10   Page: 129   Type: F

107. Negative information about a target
    a)   cannot be primed.
    b)   weighs less heavily on the brain than positive information.
    c)   is typically ignored by perceivers younger than 10 years old.
    d)   causes electrical activity in different areas of the brain than positive or neutral information.
    Ans: d   LO: 10   Page: 129   Type: F

108. Which of the following traits would produce the *most* extreme impression of a target?
    a)   Honesty
    b)   Cruelty
    c)   Maturity
    d)   Intelligence
    Ans: b   LO: 10   Page: 129   Type: C

109. Implicit personality theories suggest that if we know Yael is an extrovert, we would
    a)   be less likely to form an overall positive impression of her.
    b)   be more likely to form an overall positive impression of her.
    c)   look for situations in which one ought to be extroverted.
    d)   assume she also possesses other traits related to extroversion.
    Ans: d   LO: 11   Page: 130   Type: A

110. Traits that suggest the presence of other traits and that exert a powerful influence on final impressions are called
    a)   implicit traits.
    b)   central traits.
    c)   priming traits.
    d)   confirming traits.
    Ans: b   LO: 11   Page: 130   Type: F

111. People most often and easily differentiate each other based on which of the following two dimensions?
    a)   warm vs. cold.
    b)   introvert vs. extrovert.
    c)   kind vs. mean.
    d)   positive vs. negative
    Ans: a   LO: 11   Page: 130-131   Type: C

112. The primacy effect refers to the tendency for
    a)   people's impressions of others to be influenced by their memory of events that have just recently occurred.
    b)   perceivers to choose to make personal versus situational attributions as a function of which type is initially available.
    c)   people to first make situational attributions and then, only later, to insufficiently correct these attributions so as to take dispositions into account.
    d)   people's impressions of others to be more affected by information that is learned early rather than late in a sequence.
    Ans: d   LO: 11   Page: 131-132   Type: F

113. Imagine that you are grading the exams of two students, Michael and Fredo. They both get only half the questions correct. However, Michael gets most of his questions right on the first half of the test, whereas Fredo gets most of his questions right on the last half of the test. According to Asch's work on primacy effects in impression formation, you would be likely to conclude that
    a)   Michael is smarter than Fredo.
    b)   Fredo is smarter than Michael.
    c)   Michael and Fredo are equally unintelligent.
    d)   Michael became overconfident while taking the exam.
    Ans: a   LO: 11   Page: 131-132   Type: A

114. Research has shown that the strength of first impressions is even greater for individuals who
    a)   are high in need for closure.
    b)   have been primed.
    c)   are in a bad mood.
    d)   believe in a just world.
    Ans: a   LO: 11   Page: 132   Type: F

115. The finding that people's initial impressions of someone affect their interpretation of subsequent information about that person is *most* consistent with the
    a)   change-of-meaning hypothesis.
    b)   trait negativity bias.
    c)   summation model of information integration.
    d)   self-fulfilling prophecy.
    Ans: a   LO: 11   Page: 132   Type: C

116. One explanation for the primacy effect is that
    a)   information obtained early is usually more important than information obtained later.
    b)   people tend to pay closer attention to central trait information.
    c)   the meaning of information obtained later is often altered to fit with earlier impressions.
    d)   people tend to use initial impression information as a basis for comparing and contrasting subsequent impression information.
    Ans: c   LO: 11   Page: 131-132   Type: F

117. A confirmation bias refers to people's tendency to
    a)   agree with others whose attitudes differ from theirs.
    b)   behave according to others' expectations.
    c)   interpret, seek, and create information in ways that support existing beliefs.
    d)   reinterpret earlier information to make it more consistent with subsequent information.
    Ans: c   LO: 12   Page: 133   Type: F

118. A baseball manager who clings to old strategies that are ineffective, a lawyer who selects juries according to false stereotypes, and a political leader who does not withdraw support for a failing program are all exhibiting
    a)   belief perseverance.
    b)   confirmatory hypothesis testing.
    c)   the fundamental attribution error.
    d)   need for closure.
    Ans: a   LO: 12   Page: 133   Type: A

119. Esmeralda is a new reporter who has been asked to conduct an interview with an up-and-coming Hollywood celebrity. Esmeralda, who is concerned about the accuracy of her impressions, would be *most* likely to produce an unbiased interview if she _____ formed an impression of the celebrity and _____.
    a)   has not yet; is allowed to develop her own interview questions
    b)   has already; is allowed to develop her own interview questions
    c)   has not yet; is given the questions she is to ask during the interview
    d)   has already; is given the questions she is to ask during the interview
    Ans: a   LO: 12   Page: 133-134   Type: A

120. Darley and Gross (1983) conducted a study in which they asked participants to evaluate the intellectual ability of a 9-year-old named "Hannah." Some participants were led to believe that she came from a high socioeconomic (SES) background; others were led to believe she came from a low SES background. Kelley (1950) conducted a study in which students' expectations regarding a guest lecturer's personality were manipulated. Some students were told that the lecturer was a warm person; others were told he was a cold person. Which of the following statements about these studies is accurate?
    a)   In both studies, only for perceivers who actually met the target (i.e., Hannah or the lecturer) in person did expectation influence perceptions.
    b)   In both studies, perceivers' expectations determined the way they behaved towards the target, which in turn influenced the target's behavior.
    c)   In both studies, perceivers' expectations led them to fail to notice clear limitations of the target's actual performance.
    d)   In both studies, perceivers' expectations affected their perceptions of the target's performance, even when that performance was identical across conditions.
    Ans: d   LO: 12   Page: 133-134   Type: A

121. Cosmo is convinced that his accountant is a drug addict. To determine whether he is correct, Cosmo asks his friends if the accountant sniffs a lot, uses slang when he speaks, or frequently excuses himself to use the men's room—three behaviors Cosmo believes are characteristic of drug addicts. Cosmo's methods illustrate
    a)   the false-consensus effect.
    b)   a self-fulfilling prophecy.
    c)   confirmatory hypothesis testing.
    d)   the trait negativity bias.
    Ans: c   LO: 12   Page: 135   Type: A

122. Which of the following is the *best* example of a self-fulfilling prophecy?
    a)   When poor school children are expected to perform less well than wealthy school children
    b)   When an athlete visualizes a superior performance and then goes out and actually wins.
    c)   When minority candidates perform more poorly in interviews because interviewers act on their expectations that these candidates are unprepared
    d)   When people focus on the first information they have about another individual when making an impression
    Ans: c   LO: 12   Page: 135-138   Type: C

123. Vernell is being interviewed for a job. Though it isn't really true, the interviewer suspects that Vernell is incompetent. Because the interviewer doesn't expect much from Vernell, he sits far away from her during the interview, interrupts her frequently, and seems distracted when she speaks. As a result, Vernell becomes nervous, starts to stutter, and loses her train of thought several times. The interviewer's final impression is that Vernell is, as he suspected, incompetent. This impression is *most* likely the result of
    a)   the trait negativity bias.
    b)   a self-fulfilling prophecy.
    c)   primacy effects.
    d)   the fundamental attribution error.
    Ans: b   LO: 12   Page: 135-138   Type: A

124. Which of the following statements *best* describes our current state of knowledge regarding social perception?
    a)   People frequently make errors judging others and are rarely accurate in impression formation.
    b)   People frequently exhibit bias in their perceptions of others. However, their biases do not necessarily result in inaccurate impression formation.
    c)   People frequently exhibit bias in their perceptions of others. Such bias results in inaccurate impression formation.
    d)   People infrequently exhibit bias and, as a result, rarely make errors in impression formation.
    Ans: b   LO: 13   Page: 138-139   Type: C

125. Social perceivers are more likely to form accurate judgments of others if they
    a)   rely exclusively on cognitive heuristics.
    b)   make broad, global judgments.
    c)   are motivated to be accurate.
    d)   ignore the rules of probability and logic, and trust their instincts.
    Ans: c   LO: 13   Page: 138-139   Type: C

ESSAY

126. How are adults with baby-faced facial features perceived and treated differently than adults with mature facial features? What are two explanations for these effects?

Ans: Research has shown that adults with baby-faced features (i.e., large round eyes, high eyebrows, round cheeks, a large forehead, smooth skin, and a rounded chin) tend to be seen as relatively warm, kind, naive, weak, honest, and submissive, whereas adults with mature features (i.e., small eyes, low eyebrows, a small forehead, wrinkled skin, and an angular chin) tend to be seen as stronger, more dominant, and less naive. Furthermore, baby-faced individuals are considered more favorably by judges in cases of intentional wrongdoing, and by employers interviewing candidates for a day-care teaching position. There are three explanations for these effects. First, human beings may be genetically predisposed to respond gently to infantile features in order to ensure that real babies are treated carefully. Second, we may learn to associate infantile features with helplessness and expect this to be true of both infants and adults. Finally, there is the possibility of an actual link between baby-facedness and behavior, meaning that these differences in perception are driven by real differences in behavioral tendencies.   Page: 104

127. On what cues should social perceivers focus in order to try to detect if someone is trying to deceive others? Conversely, on what cues do social perceivers typically focus, and why are these cues less revealing?

Ans: Research has shown that of the four channels of communication (i.e., words, the face, the body, and the voice), the voice is the least controllable by the deceiver, and thus is the most revealing cue. The voices of people who are lying, particularly when they are highly motivated to deceive, tend to rise in pitch, and there is an increase in speech hesitations. The next most revealing cue is the body. Fidgety movements of the hands and feet and restless shifts in posture tend to be evident in someone who is lying. Perceivers, however, typically focus on the less revealing cues. Perceivers tend to focus on the words that people say, as well as on the face. This strategy is likely to fail because people can control these channels of communication fairly well, even when they are lying.   Page: 110-112

128. Describe the availability heuristic. Explain how it can lead to the false-consensus effect.

Ans: The availability heuristic is an information processing "rule-of-thumb" that people often use when making judgments. Specifically, it is the tendency for people to estimate the likelihood of an event by how easily instances of it come to mind. So, for example, people often think airplanes are more dangerous than cars because plane crashes get a lot of media attention—examples of plane crashes often come to mind more easily even though car accidents are much more frequent. It can give rise to the false-consensus effect, which is the tendency for people to overestimate the extent to which others share their opinions, attributes, and behaviors. Because people often associate with others who are similar to them in important ways, it is relatively easy to think of other people who share their opinions, attributes, and behaviors. And because these instances come to mind easily, people tend to overestimate the likelihood that others share their opinions, attributes, and behaviors.   Page: 116-117

129. Explain Gilbert and Malone's two-step process of making attributions, and identify when in this process the fundamental attribution error occurs.

Ans: According to Gilbert and Malone, we first identify a behavior and then make the initial assumption that it is caused by the actor's disposition. We then seek more information about the situational influences on the actor's behavior, and adjust our attribution accordingly. Naturally, the latter step is the more difficult and effortful one. The fundamental attribution error (the tendency to overattribute another person's behavior to disposition) occurs when we do not adjust adequately. This may occur because we do not have the adequate amount of cognitive resources to complete the second step properly. When people have the time and motivation to make accurate judgments, they are more likely to take account of situational constraints, and thus less likely to make the fundamental attribution error.   Page: 120-121

130. Describe the self-fulfilling prophecy. What factors can help prevent a self-fulfilling prophecy from occurring?

Ans: The self-fulfilling prophecy is the process by which a perceiver's expectations about a person can eventually lead that person to behave in ways that confirm those expectations. Self-fulfilling prophecies are less likely to occur if the perceiver is highly motivated to seek the truth and form an accurate assessment of the target, or if the perceiver is primarily motivated to make a good impression and be liked. If targets are aware of the perceiver's expectations about them, they may be able and motivated to disconfirm these expectations and thus avoid the self-fulfilling prophecy. Also, if the perceiver's expectations clash with the target's self-concept, the target's behavior may be less likely to be influenced by expectation.   Page: 135-138

CHAPTER 5
Stereotypes, Prejudice, and Discrimination

MULTIPLE CHOICE

1. Stereotypes, prejudice, and discrimination are
    a)   strictly an American phenomenon.
    b)   limited to collectivist cultures.
    c)   problematic world-wide.
    d)   all considered to be affective phenomena.
    Ans: c   LO: 1   Page: 147-148   Type: F

2. The ABC's of social psychology are affect, behavior, and cognition. Put the three major concepts of Chapter 5 in this ABC order by considering whether they correspond to affect, behavior, or cognition.
    a)   Stereotyping, prejudice, discrimination
    b)   Prejudice, discrimination, stereotyping
    c)   Discrimination, prejudice, stereotyping
    d)   Stereotyping, discrimination, prejudice
    Ans: b   LO: 1   Page: 147-148   Type: C

3. Which of the following is *not* discrimination?
    a)   Believing that baby-faced men are harmless
    b)   Giving a pink toy to a girl and a blue toy to a boy
    c)   Signing a petition to keep a minority group out of the neighborhood
    d)   Hiring a thin candidate rather than an obese one with the same credentials
    Ans: a   LO: 1   Page: 147-148   Type: C

4. Bridgette thinks short people are lazy and Barbara refuses to let short people join her book club. Bridgette is exhibiting _____, whereas Barbara is exhibiting _____.
    a)   discrimination; prejudice
    b)   stereotyping; discrimination
    c)   prejudice; stereotyping
    d)   prejudice; discrimination
    Ans: b   LO: 1   Page: 147-148   Type: A

5. Samantha thinks that all social psychology professors are intelligent, attractive, and fabulously good dancers. This is an example of
    a)   prejudice.
    b)   discrimination.
    c)   social categorization.
    d)   a stereotype.
    Ans: d   LO: 1   Page: 147-148   Type: A

6. Bonnie dislikes all lawyers. This is an example of
    a)   prejudice.
    b)   discrimination.
    c)   social categorization.
    d)   a stereotype.
    Ans: a   LO: 1   Page: 147-148   Type: A

7. Negative feelings directed at others strictly because of their membership in a particular social category is called
    a)   discrimination.
    b)   prejudice.
    c)   the outgroup homogeneity effect.
    d)   the ingroup homogeneity effect.
    Ans: b   LO: 1   Page: 147-148   Type: F

8.   Stereotypes differ from prejudice and discrimination in that stereotypes concern
     a)   positive feelings about a social group.
     b)   negative feelings about a social group.
     c)   positive or negative beliefs about a social group.
     d)   negative behavior directed at members of a social group.
     Ans: c   LO: 1   Page: 147-148   Type: C

9.   A set of beliefs about a group *cannot* be considered a stereotype if it is
     a)   positive.
     b)   negative.
     c)   true.
     d)   None of these.
     Ans: d   LO: 1   Page: 147-148   Type: C

10. Modern racism can be distinguished from what has been termed "old-fashioned" racism in that modern
     racism is
     a)   more prevalent than "old-fashioned" racism.
     b)   less obvious than "old-fashioned" racism.
     c)   less destructive than "old-fashioned" racism.
     d)   more likely to be revealed later in life than "old-fashioned" racism.
     Ans: b   LO: 1   Page: 149-150   Type: C

11. Jane is from race X and Jean is from race Y. Which of the following scenarios *best* demonstrates modern
     racism?
     a)   Jane yells racial slurs and spits on Jean who is a stranger.
     b)   Jane and Jean work together. Jane thinks Jean is not doing her share of the work. For this, Jane gives
          Jean a more negative evaluation than is deserved.
     c)   Jane and Jean are on the same athletic team. The social norm of the team is for everyone to be
          friendly and personable to one another. Jane never talks to Jean.
     d)   Jane is interviewing Jean as a pianist for her club. Jane is looking for a piano player who will play
          jazz. Jean plays classical music. Jane doesn't hire Jean for the job.
     Ans: b   LO: 1   Page: 149-150   Type: A

12. A form of prejudice that surfaces in subtle ways when it is safe, socially acceptable, and easy to rationalize
     is called
     a)   modern racism.
     b)   relative deprivation.
     c)   illusory correlation.
     d)   reverse discrimination.
     Ans: a   LO: 1   Page: 149-150   Type: F

13. Consider the Implicit Associations Test in which people are asked to categorize words as well as
     White/Black names. If you were to design a similar measure to assess implicit associations related to age,
     and more specifically, implicit negative beliefs about older people, which pattern of results might your IAT
     produce to indicate such ageism?
     a)   Participants report that they like younger-sounding names (e.g., Dylan, Carter) more than older-
          sounding names (e.g., Gladys, Sydney).
     b)   Participants take longer to pair positive words with older-sounding names and negative words with
          younger-sounding names than vice versa.
     c)   Participants primed with words related to old-age (e.g., "Florida," "Bingo," "wheelchair") internalize
          stereotypes regarding the elderly and demonstrate slower reaction times to the categorization tasks.
     d)   Participants are quicker to recognize and categorize photos of young faces than photos of older faces.
     Ans: b   LO: 1   Page: 150-152   Type: A

14. Which of the following has *not* been used by psychologists to measure implicit forms of racism?
    a) Functional magnetic resonance imaging (fMRI)
    b) Implicit Association Test (IAT)
    c) Common Ingroup Identity Model (CIIM)
    d) eye contact
    Ans: c   LO: 1   Page: 150-152   Type: F

15. Research by British researchers Hutchings and Haddock (2008) found that when White students were shown photos of racially ambiguous faces
    a) they tended to categorize the faces as Black when they believed the photos were of known criminals.
    b) they tended to categorize the faces as White when a happy videoclip had previously put them in a good mood.
    c) they tended to categorize the faces as Black when the images depicted angry, as opposed to happy faces.
    d) they were quicker to categorize these faces than they were to categorize racially unambiguous faces.
    Ans: c   LO: 2   Page: 153   Type: C

16. fMRI research has often found increased activation in the amygdala for White participants shown photos of Black faces. The amygdala is a region of the brain often implicated in the perception of
    a) hatred.
    b) threat.
    c) sympathy.
    d) callousness.
    Ans: b   LO: 2   Page: 153   Type: C

17. Research by Jennifer Richeson, Nicole Shelton and colleagues demonstrates that White individuals who score high on a measure of implicit racism
    a) must exert a great deal of cognitive effort in order to avoid prejudice when interacting with African-Americans.
    b) are usually good at hiding their biases and therefore tend to have comfortable interactions with African-Americans.
    c) have relatively low levels of amygdala activation when presented with photos of African-American faces.
    d) All of these
    Ans: a   LO: 2   Page: 154   Type: F

18. Research indicates that White individuals' concern about appearing prejudiced during interracial interactions can
    a) lead them to try to avoid such interactions altogether.
    b) lead them to sit closer to Black conversation partners in the effort to make a good impression.
    c) lead them to go out of their way to demonstrate how often they think about and notice race-related issues.
    d) All of these
    Ans: a   LO: 2   Page: 154   Type: C

19. Research by Apfelbaum and colleagues (2008) indicates that when it comes to norms regarding the acknowledgment of race
    a) the older White kids get, the more comfortable they are discussing race.
    b) 8- and 9-year-old kids are even more concerned about political correctness than 10- and 11-year-olds.
    c) it is not until early adulthood that people start to develop concerns about race-related norms.
    d) unlike younger children, older children are sometimes willing to sacrifice task performance for the goal of avoiding uncomfortable race-related conversation.
    Ans: d   LO: 2   Page: 155   Type: C

20.   Negative feelings directed at women's abilities, values, and ability to challenge the power of men are referred to as
      a)   ambivalent sexism.
      b)   modern sexism.
      c)   benevolent sexism.
      d)   hostile sexism.
      Ans: d   LO: 3   Page: 155-156   Type: F

21.   Affectionate feelings towards women based on the belief that women need protection are referred to as
      a)   ambivalent sexism.
      b)   patronizing sexism.
      c)   benevolent sexism.
      d)   hostile sexism.
      Ans: c   LO: 3   Page: 156   Type: F

22.   In their study of sexism in nineteen different countries, Glick et al. (2000) found that countries with the greatest degree of political and economic inequality exhibited
      a)   the highest levels of both hostile and benevolent sexism.
      b)   the lowest levels of both hostile and benevolent sexism.
      c)   high levels of hostile sexism but low levels of benevolent sexism.
      d)   low levels of hostile sexism but high levels of benevolent sexism.
      Ans: a   LO: 3   Page: 156   Type: F

23.   In a study by Phelan and colleagues (2008), participants read about male and female candidates for a managerial position. Compared to comparable male candidates, female candidates who emphasized their independence and leadership ability were rated as
      a)   lower in competence and in social skills.
      b)   lower in both competence but higher in social skills.
      c)   higher in competence but lower in social skills.
      d)   higher in both competence and social skills.
      Ans: c   LO: 3   Page: 158   Type: F

24.   In a study by Holloway and Johnston (2006), male job applicants who had just gone on an unsuccessful job interview were more likely to
      a)   disparage their interviewer when he was a man versus a woman.
      b)   disparage their interviewer when she was a woman versus a man.
      c)   envy their interviewer when he was a man versus a woman
      d)   envy their interviewer when she was a woman versus a man.
      Ans: b   LO: 3   Page: 158-159   Type: F

24.   Wes finds himself in a dark parking lot after having seen a scary horror movie. Research suggests that he is
      a)   likely to seek out affiliation with the first person he sees, regardless of their group status.
      b)   likely to mistakenly interpret another person's emotional state as angry when this individual is from an outgroup.
      c)   likely to experience increased activation in his amygdala upon encountering an individual from his ingroup.
      d)   likely to exhibit a desire for proximity to outgroup versus ingroup members.
      Ans: b   LO: 4   Page: 159-160   Type: A

25.   Michigan and Ohio State are rival universities. Students at the two schools only interact when the athletic teams they play for compete against each other. Sherif's Robbers Cave experiment suggests that the students will
      a)   limit their competition to the playing field and behave cooperatively off the field.
      b)   only change their negative stereotypes of one another once they have interacted on the playing field.
      c)   develop positive views of one another and behave in a friendly manner.
      d)   develop negative views of one another and behave in a hostile manner.
      Ans: d   LO: 4   Page: 160-161   Type: A

26. A junior high coach decides to separate his basketball players into an A team and a B team. These two teams regularly play each other and compete for rewards, such as time at the drinking fountain and use of the new basketballs. The Robbers Cave experiment would suggest that the coach's new arrangement is likely to
    a) promote team unity.
    b) lead to animosity between the A team and the B team.
    c) encourage the development of leadership skills.
    d) lead to less vigorous practices.
    Ans: b   LO: 4   Page: 160-161   Type: A

27. The Robbers Cave experiment demonstrated that
    a) ingroup favoritism is inevitable.
    b) group categorization is automatic.
    c) prejudice is a function of social class.
    d) prejudice can result from intergroup competition.
    Ans: d   LO: 4   Page: 160-161   Type: C

28. The Jets and the Sharks are two groups of local youths who regularly—and belligerently—compete against each other. The Robbers Cave experiment would suggest that one way of healing the rift between these groups is to
    a) allow the youths to date each other.
    b) encourage them to "air" their differences.
    c) have them work together on a goal that requires cooperative efforts.
    d) have each group note the good qualities of the other group.
    Ans: c   LO: 4   Page: 160-161   Type: A

29. One conclusion that can be drawn from the Robbers Cave study is that
    a) propaganda is not a particularly effective means of eliminating group conflict.
    b) imaginary competition does not lead to group conflict.
    c) the best way to reduce intergroup conflict is simply to bring group members together under noncompetitive circumstances, even if they do not get the chance to interact with each other.
    d) young boys exhibit greater aggressive tendencies than young girls.
    Ans: a   LO: 4   Page: 160-161   Type: C

30. The results of the Robbers Cave experiment can be extrapolated to suggest that prejudice between groups can be *increased* when the groups are placed in a situation where
    a) they compete against one another.
    b) appropriate ways of interacting are unclear.
    c) the groups communicate with one another.
    d) groups must jointly carry out multiple tasks.
    Ans: a   LO: 4   Page: 160-161   Type: F

31. Which of the following *best* exemplifies realistic conflict theory?
    a) The conflict over land ownership between Arabs and Israelis in the Middle East
    b) The conflict between Protestants and the Catholics in Ireland due to religious differences
    c) The conflict between Democrats and Republicans regarding U.S. political ideology
    d) The conflict between those who support "Pro-Choice" and those who support "Right to Life" on the issue of abortion
    Ans: a   LO: 4   Page: 161-162   Type: A

32. Realistic conflict theory proposes that
    a) conflict between groups is a function of interpersonal hostility.
    b) intergroup hostility arises from competition among groups for scarce but valued resources.
    c) intergroup conflict is largely a function of how realistically groups view one another.
    d) realistic groups do not have to worry about intergroup conflict.
    Ans: b   LO: 4   Page: 161-162   Type: F

33. Prejudice is not always limited to situations where an individual feels directly threatened by an outgroup. This fact is particularly difficult to explain from the perspective of which of the following theories?
    a)   Social role theory
    b)   Social identity theory
    c)   Minimal paradigm theory
    d)   Realistic conflict theory
    Ans: d   LO: 4   Page: 161-162   Type: C

34. Some border-town residents dislike illegal immigrants because they fear that the immigrants will take jobs away from them. These feelings can *best* be explained by
    a)   social role theory.
    b)   social identity theory.
    c)   social categorization theory.
    d)   realistic conflict theory.
    Ans: d   LO: 4   Page: 161-162   Type: A

35. Student groups at the school union must compete with each other for a limited supply of offices and money to support their projects. Over time, these groups are likely to
    a)   view each other in negative terms.
    b)   work together in an effort to acquire more resources.
    c)   ignore each other and work for their own causes.
    d)   become irritated with the university system.
    Ans: a   LO: 4   Page: 162   Type: A

36. The cooks at Burger Barn dislike the counter workers because the cooks think the counter workers get better health-care options. The cooks' perceptions would be described as
    a)   relative deprivation.
    b)   subtyping.
    c)   stereotype threat.
    d)   superordinate goals.
    Ans: a   LO: 4   Page: 162   Type: A

37. Latrell is not satisfied with his $5 million annual salary because he feels that other basketball All-Stars are paid far more money. Latrell's dissatisfaction is *most* likely the result of
    a)   realistic conflict theory.
    b)   ingroup favoritism.
    c)   outgroup homogeneity.
    d)   relative deprivation.
    Ans: d   LO: 4   Page: 162   Type: A

38. Which of the following statements concerning the relationship between competition and prejudice is *false*?
    a)   Imagined competition can lead to prejudice just as much as actual competition.
    b)   The perception that one is not doing as well as outgroup members is sufficient to produce prejudice.
    c)   Prejudice can result from competitive threat to the ingroup as well as the individual.
    d)   Superordinate goals help diffuse conflict between children, but not adults.
    Ans: d   LO: 4   Page: 162-163   Type: C

39. Minimal groups are groups
    a)   consisting of only two people.
    b)   that occupy low status positions in society.
    c)   based on trivial, often arbitrary, distinctions.
    d)   with a long history of competition and antagonism.
    Ans: c   LO: 5   Page: 162   Type: F

40. The main contribution of research using the minimal group paradigm is the finding that
   a) only people who strongly identify with a particular ingroup are likely to discriminate against the outgroup.
   b) random assignment of people to groups fails to lead to ingroup favoritism.
   c) a history of antagonism and competition makes people more likely to discriminate against an outgroup.
   d) None of these.
   Ans: d   LO: 5   Page: 162   Type: C

41. Which of the following has been demonstrated through the use of minimal groups?
   a) Competition for limited resources is necessary for ingroup favoritism.
   b) Ingroup favoritism will not occur in trivial laboratory groups.
   c) Ingroup cohesion is necessary to produce ingroup favoritism.
   d) Mere categorization is sufficient to produce ingroup favoritism.
   Ans: d   LO: 5   Page: 162   Type: C

42. Condoleezza is quick to defend U.S. foreign policy from criticism by foreign diplomats because she takes great pride in being an American. Condoleezza's feelings are *most* consistent with
   a) social role theory.
   b) gender-role orientation.
   c) illusory correlations.
   d) social identity theory.
   Ans: d   LO: 5   Page: 162   Type: A

43. According to social identity theory, people display ingroup favoritism
   a) as a way of displacing negative feelings toward the outgroup.
   b) as a means of increasing self-esteem.
   c) because they expect to be treated unfairly by outgroup members.
   d) because intergroup competition demands it.
   Ans: b   LO: 5   Page: 162   Type: C

44. Fein & Spencer (1997) conducted a study in which participants evaluated a job applicant whom they believed to be either Jewish or Italian. Which of the following statements about this study is *false*?
   a) Participants were more likely to discriminate against the Jewish applicant when they had previously been given negative feedback about their own abilities.
   b) Participants who were able to avoid discriminating against the Jewish applicant demonstrated the biggest boost to their own self-esteem.
   c) The study was conducted on a campus where negative stereotypes about Jewish women were pervasive.
   d) Their results provide supporting evidence for one of the basic predictions of social identity theory.
   Ans: b   LO: 5   Page: 163   Type: C

45. Which of the following is *not* predicted by social identity theory?
   a) Self-esteem is derived from positive ingroup associations.
   b) Threats to self-esteem tend to decrease ingroup favoritism.
   c) Expressions of ingroup favoritism tend to increase self-esteem.
   d) Self-esteem is increased to the extent that the ingroup is perceived as better than the outgroup.
   Ans: b   LO: 5   Page: 162-163   Type: C

46. Zena just learned that she did not get into the college of her choice. She comes upon Alec, a resident of a nearby neighborhood and one that most outsiders find distasteful. It is likely that the news Zena just received will cause her to judge Alec more _____, making her feel _____ about herself.
   a) positively; worse
   b) negatively; worse
   c) positively; better
   d) negatively; better
   Ans: d   LO: 5   Page: 162-163   Type: A

47. The individual *most* likely to exhibit ingroup favoritism and outgroup derogation is a member of a _____
     group who _____ with the group.
     a)   minority; strongly identifies
     b)   minority; does not strongly identify
     c)   majority; strongly identifies
     d)   majority; does not strongly identify
     Ans: a   LO: 5   Page: 162-163   Type: C

48. Hiral is pledging a sorority. She is *most* likely to display prejudice against members of other sororities if she
     a)   has not yet formed a strong identification with her sorority.
     b)   is generally low in prejudice.
     c)   is in the presence of the sorority president.
     d)   is from a collectivist culture.
     Ans: c   LO: 5   Page: 162-163   Type: A

49. Cross-cultural research indicates that people from collectivist cultures are _____ likely to boost their
     self-esteem through overt ingroup bias and _____ likely to draw sharp distinctions between ingroup and
     outgroup members than are people from individualist cultures.
     a)   more; more
     b)   more; less
     c)   less; more
     d)   less; less
     Ans: c   LO: 6   Page: 164-165   Type: F

50. Which of the following is *false*?
     a)   People from collectivist cultures draw sharper distinctions between ingroup and outgroup members.
     b)   Members of low status, stereotyped groups tend to have lower self-esteem.
     c)   People eager to join a group judge outgroups more negatively than do other members of the group in
          which membership is desired.
     d)   Social identity theory best predicts the reactions of individuals who derive a lot of their self-esteem
          from group memberships.
     Ans: b   LO: 6   Page: 162-165   Type: C

51. Individuals from collectivist cultures
     a)   never show ingroup favoritism.
     b)   exhibit more ingroup favoritism than people from individualistic cultures.
     c)   draw sharper distinctions between ingroups and outgroups than do people from individualistic
          cultures.
     d)   are less likely to engage in system justification than are people from individualistic cultures.
     Ans: c   LO: 6   Page: 164-165   Type: C

52. Eddie, an Oscar-nominated actor who is very proud of his profession, just learned that Hugh, a fellow actor,
     was arrested for possession of narcotics. Eddie is likely to
     a)   try to make excuses for Hugh's behavior because they are part of the same ingroup.
     b)   judge Hugh less harshly than an outgroup member in the same situation.
     c)   judge Hugh more harshly than an outgroup member in the same situation.
     d)   judge Hugh just as harshly as an outgroup member in the same situation.
     Ans: c   LO: 6   Page: 165   Type: A

53. Individuals with a strong social dominance orientation are *least* likely to
     a)   prefer to live in an egalitarian society.
     b)   strongly identify with their ingroup.
     c)   want their ingroup to be of higher status than other groups.
     d)   endorse government policies that oppress outgroups.
     Ans: a   LO: 6   Page: 165   Type: C

54.   System justifying beliefs are
      a)   more likely to be held by groups in power.
      b)   rarely if ever found in collectivist cultures.
      c)   associated with decreased levels of ingroup/outgroup bias
      d)   more common among women than men in most cultures.
      Ans: a   LO: 6   Page: 165   Type: C

55.   Which of the following best epitomizes the cultural perspective on explaining stereotypes?
      a)   Larry tends to sort objects into groups rather than thinking of each item as unique, and he does the same thing when perceiving other people.
      b)   Cheryl relies on stereotypes because it saves her cognitive effort and energy.
      c)   Jeff thinks that all Italians are loud and easily excited because he has heard his father describe them in this manner.
      d)   Susie responds to threats to her self-esteem by stereotyping other groups to make herself feel better.
      Ans: c   LO: 7   Page: 164-165   Type: A

56.   Social categorization is advantageous because it
      a)   leads to more accurate social perception.
      b)   encourages us to take longer to make judgments about others.
      c)   frees up cognitive resources.
      d)   is generally based on realistic assumptions.
      Ans: c   LO: 7   Page: 166-167   Type: F

57.   Social categorization leads people to
      a)   perceive group members more accurately.
      b)   perceive others as individuals rather than group members.
      c)   overestimate differences between groups.
      d)   overestimate differences within groups.
      Ans: c   LO: 7   Page: 166-167   Type: F

58.   All of the following result from social categorization *except*
      a)   overestimation of differences between groups.
      b)   underestimation of differences within groups.
      c)   increased confidence that differences between groups are biologically based.
      d)   increased tendency to notice behaviors inconsistent with group stereotype.
      Ans: d   LO: 7   Page: 166-167   Type: C

59.   Groups to which the self belongs are called _____, and groups to which the self does not belong are called _____.
      a)   ingroups; outgroups
      b)   social categories; self categories
      c)   implicit categories; explicit categories
      d)   self-groups; social-groups
      Ans: a   LO: 7   Page: 167-168   Type: F

60.   The tendency to perceive members of an outgroup as less variable, or more similar to one another, than members of the ingroup is called the
      a)   minimal group effect.
      b)   outgroup homogeneity effect.
      c)   ingroup homogeneity effect.
      d)   contrast effect.
      Ans: b   LO: 7   Page: 167-168   Type: F

61.   The belief "they're all the same" best epitomizes which of the following concepts?
      a)   Minimal group effect
      b)   Outgroup homogeneity effect
      c)   Ingroup heterogeneity effect
      d)   Contrast effect
      Ans: b   LO: 7   Page: 167-168   Type: A

62.   Buffy is a member of a sorority. She considers the stereotypes about her sorority to be gross
       overgeneralizations, but claims that the stereotypes about other sororities seem to have a kernel of truth.
       Buffy's thinking *best* illustrates
       a)   the outgroup homogeneity effect.
       b)   realistic conflict.
       c)   reverse discrimination.
       d)   social role theory.
       Ans: a   LO: 7   Page: 167-168   Type: A

63.   Ingroup members display the outgroup homogeneity effect because
       a)   ingroups and outgroups always compete for shared resources.
       b)   they lack familiarity with members of the outgroup.
       c)   they lack sufficient information to judge the variability of their own group.
       d)   they usually encounter the most typical members of the outgroup.
       Ans: b   LO: 7   Page: 167-168   Type: C

64.   Which of the following does *not* contribute to the outgroup homogeneity effect?
       a)   Ingroup members have little information concerning outgroup members.
       b)   Ingroup members are unlikely to have frequent contact with outgroup members.
       c)   Ingroup members accurately perceive the lack of diversity within the outgroup.
       d)   Ingroup members interact with a non-representative sample of outgroup members.
       Ans: c   LO: 7   Page: 167-168   Type: C

65.   Charles is a Red Sox fan who does not think highly of Yankees fans. Which of the following statements
       Charles made in the past week is most consistent with the concept of outgroup homogeneity?
       a)   "Obnoxious, rude, and prone to throwing batteries… if you've seen one Yankees fan, you've seem
             them all."
       b)   "I knew one Yankees fan who wasn't bad, but his wife was a Red Sox fan, so he doesn't count."
       c)   "The thing about Yankees fans is that some of them just jump on the bandwagon and root for their
             team through good times and bad times."
       d)   "My two favorite teams are the Red Sox and anyone who's playing against the Yankees."
       Ans: a   LO: 7   Page: 167-168   Type: A

66.   Arnold is not a cheerleader and doesn't know any cheerleaders personally, but when he sees them at the
       football games, they are always smiling. Arnold is likely to
       a)   think about specific cheerleaders rather than the group stereotype.
       b)   notice the ways in which each cheerleader is unique.
       c)   be able to distinguish cheerleaders from one another only if they are smiling.
       d)   think that all cheerleaders are happy.
       Ans: d   LO: 7   Page: 167-168   Type: A

67.   Sociocultural factors that influence stereotyping include all of the following *except*
       a)   the effects of priming.
       b)   popular images of groups in the media.
       c)   group norms.
       d)   parental examples.
       Ans: a   LO: 7   Page: 167-168   Type: F

68.   Hugenberg and Corneille (2009) exposed White participants to the faces of unfamiliar people. They found
       that compared to faces of outgroup members, faces of ingroup members were processed more
       a)   slowly.
       b)   holistically.
       c)   sequentially.
       d)   reluctantly.
       Ans: b   LO: 7   Page: 168   Type: F

69. Research findings regarding dehumanization indicate that
    a)   people tend to process outgroup faces in a manner similar their processing of nonhuman objects.
    b)   dehumanization of outgroups is typically associated with reactions of greater empathy.
    c)   only members of the racial majority tend to be aware of cultural associations between racial minority group members and particular animal characteristics.
    d)   All of these
    Ans: a   LO: 7   Page: 168-169   Type: C

70. All of the following are mechanisms that perpetuate stereotypes *except*
    a)   illusory correlations.
    b)   the jigsaw classroom.
    c)   subtyping.
    d)   self-fulfilling prophecies.
    Ans: b   LO: 8   Page: 169-172   Type: C

71. Gunner thinks that Jews are particularly funny. He overestimates the association between being a stand-up comedian and being Jewish because both characteristics are very distinctive from the normal population. This demonstrates
    a)   a contrast effect.
    b)   the outgroup homogeneity effect.
    c)   an illusory correlation.
    d)   social role theory.
    Ans: c   LO: 8   Page: 169-170   Type: A

72. Participants in an experiment learn about eight positive and four negative behaviors performed by members of group A. They also learn about four positive and two negative behaviors performed by members of group B. Which pattern of results is *most* likely?
    a)   Group B will be liked more because they performed the fewest number of negative behaviors.
    b)   Group A and B will be liked equally well because the ratio of positive to negative behaviors is the same.
    c)   Group A will be liked less because of a perceived link between the distinctive events of membership in the larger group and performing more negative behaviors.
    d)   Group B will be liked less because of a perceived link between the distinctive events of membership in the smaller group and performing fewer negative behaviors.
    Ans: d   LO: 8   Page: 169-170   Type: C

73. Liston believes that psychology professors are absentminded. Given the research on illusory correlations, he is likely to
    a)   notice when his psychology professor remembers students' names.
    b)   overestimate how often his psychology professor forgets to bring materials to class.
    c)   underestimate the ways in which his psychology professor is like other psychology professors.
    d)   make situational attributions for the stereotype-consistent behavior of his psychology professor.
    Ans: b   LO: 3   Page: 169-170   Type: A

74. The tendency to overestimate the extent to which members of stereotyped groups possess attributes and perform behaviors consistent with the group stereotype results from
    a)   subtyping.
    b)   illusory correlations.
    c)   stereotype threat.
    d)   ingroup favoritism.
    Ans: b   LO: 8   Page: 169-170   Type: C

75. Subtyping is *least* likely when confronted with a group member who
    a)   is dramatically different from the group.
    b)   causes observers to bring to mind others who confirm the stereotype.
    c)   is perceived to have violated a stereotype for situational reasons.
    d)   deviates from the stereotype on only a few dimensions.
    Ans: d   LO: 8   Page: 170   Type: C

76.   The fundamental attribution error may promote stereotypes because
      a)   observers see stereotype-consistent behavior as dispositional.
      b)   it is so prevalent that it is unaffected by personal motivations.
      c)   the more a stereotype is violated, the more observers cling to that stereotype.
      d)   we often perceive members of outgroups as having ulterior motives.
      Ans: a   LO: 8   Page: 170   Type: C

77.   Emily, an avid sports fan, notices that a disproportionate number of professional football players are African American. Because of the quick and violent nature of the game of football, Emily comes to assume that the average African American is relatively athletic as well as aggressive. This thought process is best explained as an example of
      a)   a minimal group paradigm.
      b)   a self-fulfilling prophecy.
      c)   the fundamental attribution error.
      d)   subtyping.
      Ans: c   LO: 8   Page: 170   Type: A

78.   In explaining the behavior of outgroup members, people tend to make
      a)   situational attributions for negative behaviors, but personal attributions for positive behaviors.
      b)   situational attributions for positive behaviors, but personal attributions for negative behaviors.
      c)   situational attributions for both positive and negative behaviors.
      d)   personal attributions for both positive and negative behaviors.
      Ans: b   LO: 8   Page: 170   Type: C

79.   Paloma thinks that all gay men have a superior fashion sense. She knows that her chemistry professor is gay, and notices that he is not a particularly snappy dresser. She rationalizes this by saying, "well, he's a gay *professor*—they don't know how to dress that well." This is an example of how
      a)   subtyping can lead to stereotype perpetuation.
      b)   social identity can influence stereotyping.
      c)   intergroup contact can alter stereotype exceptions.
      d)   social categorization can color stereotype formation.
      Ans: a   LO: 8   Page: 170   Type: A

80.   Forming subtypes for individuals who do *not* conform to a group stereotype
      a)   makes it easier to change the content of the stereotype.
      b)   serves to protect the stereotype from change.
      c)   prevents the stereotype from being applied to other group members.
      d)   has the greatest impact on atypical group members.
      Ans: b   LO: 8   Page: 170   Type: C

81.   You think all professors are uncoordinated, but then you see your social psychology professor make a diving catch down the left-field line an intramural softball game against the Arts Department team. You also notice that your professor hits lead-off for the team and is able to score from second base on a ground-out. You maintain your original stereotype of professors as uncoordinated by deciding that this one individual is an exception to the rule because he is a "young professor." This is an example of
      a)   social identity theory.
      b)   implicit personality theory.
      c)   subtyping.
      d)   None of these
      Ans: c   LO: 8   Page: 170   Type: A

82.   You think all professors are a bit nerdy and have esoteric interests. You find out that your social psychology professor can sing the theme song to any television show that aired in the 1970s or 1980s, and is also fluent in the *Star Trek* language of Klingon. You believe that your stereotype has been confirmed by this professor. This is an example of
      a)   confirmation bias.
      b)   implicit personality theory.
      c)   self-fulfilling prophecy.
      d)   None of these.
      Ans: a   LO: 8   Page: 171-172   Type: A

83. Lyons and Kashima (2001) had Australian participants transmit a story about a football player from one person to the next. Their results indicated that
    a) as the story went from person to person, the stereotype-inconsistent information was eventually weeded out.
    b) as the story went from person to person, the stereotype-inconsistent information was eventually exaggerated.
    c) as the story went from person to person, the stereotype-consistent information was often distorted.
    d) as the story went from person to person, its content remained relatively consistent.
    Ans: a   LO: 8   Page: 171-172   Type: F

84. Allport and Postman's (1947) study using a photograph of a subway car demonstrated how racial stereotypes
    a) evolve over generations.
    b) facilitate memory accuracy and conserve cognitive energy.
    c) can be controlled.
    d) distort social perception and memory.
    Ans: d   LO: 8   Page: 171   Type: F

85. Suppose a study of males was conducted in which half of the participants were subliminally exposed to pictures of females coupled with gender-stereotypical words such as "passive" and "submissive." Each of the males then worked with a female on a problem-solving task. Results revealed that the men who were subliminally primed asserted more agency and control in the problem-solving task than those who had not been primed. In turn, the females who worked with them responded in a more passive manner. The phenomenon that *best* explains these findings is
    a) illusory correlation.
    b) subtyping.
    c) self-fulfilling prophecy.
    d) the fundamental attribution error.
    Ans: c   LO: 8   Page: 171-172   Type: A

86. Self-fulfilling prophecies perpetuate stereotypes by
    a) increasing the likelihood that perceivers create subtypes.
    b) eliciting stereotype-confirming behavior from targets.
    c) threatening individual self-esteem.
    d) reducing ingroup favoritism.
    Ans: b   LO: 8   Page: 171-172   Type: C

87. Which of the following statements regarding the relationship between self-fulfilling prophecy and stereotyping is *inaccurate*?
    a) Stereotypes lead to a form of confirmation bias in that they provide expectations that color social perception.
    b) People often seek out less information when meeting members of a stereotype group, thus preventing them from disconfirming the stereotype.
    c) The fact that some stereotypes may have a kernel of truth to them reflects, in part, the influence of a perceiver's expectations on a target's behavior.
    d) Confirmation bias often colors perceptions of a target, but not the actual, objective behavior of that target.
    Ans: d   LO: 8   Page: 171-172   Type: C

88. Conclusions regarding the accuracy of stereotypes are best described as
    a) mixed because some stereotypes seem to be based on completely inaccurate information whereas others seem to have a kernel of truth.
    b) definitive indicators that stereotypes are distortions and not accurate in the least.
    c) definitive indicators that stereotypes are exaggerations, but almost always based on a kernel of truth.
    d) more accurate when held by entity theorists as opposed to incremental theorists.
    Ans: a   LO: 8   Page: 172   Type: C

89. Word and colleagues (1974) conducted a study examining the influence of racial stereotyping on job-interview performance. This study demonstrated that
     a)   a job interviewer's nonverbal behavior is not influenced by an applicant's race, though verbal behavior shows signs of self-fulfilling prophecy.
     b)   job interviewers who are trained with explicit instructions to treat job applicants the same way regardless of race are able to avoid the self-fulfilling prophecy.
     c)   a job interviewer's behavior can create a self-fulfilling prophecy that leads applicants of a particular race to objectively perform more poorly than other applicants.
     d)   job applicants who are negatively stereotyped are more sensitive to nonverbal cues during the course of an interview, and therefore more likely to fall victim to the self-fulfilling prophecy than are other applicants.
     Ans: c   LO: 8   Page: 172   Type: C

90. Which of the following does *not* demonstrate the influence of gender stereotypes?
     a)   Parents see their newborn sons as stronger and more alert than their newborn daughters.
     b)   Parents underestimate the crawling ability of their infant girls and overestimate that of their infant boys.
     c)   When a baby boy cries in response to a toy, he is thought to be angry. When a baby girl exhibits the same response, she is thought to be afraid.
     d)   Newborn boys tend to be taller and weigh more than newborn girls.
     Ans: d   LO: 9   Page: 173-174   Type: C

91. Two nine-month-old babies (one boy and one girl) are shown a jack-in-the-box. When the toy springs up, they both cry. In this situation, people are likely to perceive that the boy baby is _____ and the girl baby is _____.
     a)   startled; sad
     b)   angry; frightened
     c)   sad; startled
     d)   frightened; angry
     Ans: b   LO: 9   Page: 173-174   Type: A

92. Research regarding the relationship between parents' endorsement of gender stereotypes and their young children's gender-related thinking indicates
     a)   a strong correlation such that children's beliefs tend to reflect those of their parents.
     b)   a strong correlation such that children tend to rebel against their parents and display the opposite type of beliefs.
     c)   no reliable relationship, as children do not develop gender stereotypes of their own until much later in life.
     d)   a strong correlation in individualistic, but not collectivist cultures.
     Ans: a   LO: 9   Page: 173-174   Type: C

93. Gender stereotypes are prescriptive. This means that gender stereotypes
     a)   identify what men and women should be like.
     b)   can be used to predict when men and women are likely to behave in stereotype-consistent ways.
     c)   are more accurate than other kinds of stereotypes.
     d)   are less influenced by cultural standards than other stereotypes.
     Ans: a   LO: 9   Page: 173-174   Type: C

94. With regard to portrayal of the sexes in the media,
     a)   portrayal of men and women in counter-stereotypical ads and in stereotypical ads leads to similar self-perceptions in female viewers.
     b)   female viewers who are gender schematic are more attentive to gender stereotypes on television than male viewers who are gender schematic.
     c)   focus on the face is more evident in photographs of women than of men in the print media.
     d)   the behavior a male displays toward a woman can be influenced by whether he has just seen an ad where a woman is portrayed as a sex object.
     Ans: d   LO: 9   Page: 175-177   Type: F

95. According to social role theory, gender differences in social behavior are the result of
     a)   the unequal gender-based division of labor.
     b)   unrealistic expectations about how men and women should behave.
     c)   biologically based differences in social dominance.
     d)   the forces of natural selection.
     Ans: a   LO: 9   Page: 175   Type: C

96. According to social role theory, gender differences that arise from social roles provide a continuing basis for
     a)   minimal groups.
     b)   jigsaw classrooms.
     c)   old-fashioned racism.
     d)   gender stereotypes.
     Ans: d   LO: 9   Page: 175   Type: C

97. Both Jorge and Jocelyn are applying for two residencies after medical school: orthopedic surgery (a traditionally male-dominated residency) and pediatrics (a traditionally female-dominated residency). If Jorge and Jocelyn have similar academic records, it is likely that
     a)   Jorge will get more interviews for both types of residencies.
     b)   Jocelyn will get more interviews for both types of residencies.
     c)   Jorge will get more orthopedic surgery interviews and Jocelyn will get more pediatric interviews.
     d)   Jocelyn will get more orthopedic surgery interviews and Jorge will get more pediatric interviews.
     Ans: c   LO: 9   Page: 175   Type: A

98. Paluck's (2009) field experiment in Rwanda in which civilians listened to a radio soap opera demonstrates
     a)   the intractability of many intergroup conflicts.
     b)   the cross-cultural differences in how prejudice manifests itself.
     c)   the potential influence of media on shaping norms related to intergroup relations.
     d)   the automaticity of many stereotypical beliefs.
     Ans: c   LO: 9   Page: 177   Type: C

99. The stereotype content model of Cuddy, Fiske , and colleagues groups stereotypes along the two dimensions of
     a)   intelligence and morality.
     b)   competence and warmth.
     c)   directness and indirectness.
     d)   dehumanization and impulsivity.
     Ans: b   LO: 9   Page: 177-178   Type: F

100. According to the stereotype content model, migrant farm workers who move to an area with a shortage of farming jobs would likely be viewed as
     a)   high in warmth and low in competence.
     b)   low in warmth and high in competence.
     c)   low in warmth and low in competence.
     d)   none of the abve
     Ans: c   LO: 9   Page: 177-178   Type: A

101. Stereotypes appear to bias perceptions
     a)   even when we don't endorse them.
     b)   for outgroup members, but not for ingroup members.
     c)   only when we are aware that the stereotype was activated.
     d)   only when the stereotype was unconsciously activated.
     Ans: a   LO: 10   Page: 178-179   Type: F

102. Which of the following was *not* an argument of Devine's (1989) early work on the automatic activation of stereotypes?
    a) Exposure to a member of a stereotyped group is sufficient to activate the stereotype.
    b) Stereotype activation is automatic, but stereotypes cannot influence judgments without conscious intent.
    c) Exposure to some content of the stereotype will activate the general stereotype.
    d) Automatic stereotype activation biases subsequent judgments in the direction of the activated stereotype.
    Ans: b   LO: 10   Page: 178-179   Type: F

103. Which of the following has been demonstrated in research on the automatic nature of stereotypes?
    a) Exposure to stereotype content influences subsequent judgments for both high and low prejudiced individuals.
    b) Exposure to category labels influences subsequent judgments for both high and low prejudiced individuals.
    c) Automatic activation effects are less likely to occur if self-esteem is threatened.
    d) Stereotypes influence subsequent judgment only when people are aware that the stereotype has been activated.
    Ans: a   LO: 10   Page: 178-179   Type: C

104. Whose judgments are *least* likely to be influenced by automatic stereotype activation?
    a) A highly sexist person exposed to the label "woman."
    b) A non-sexist person exposed to the label "woman."
    c) A highly sexist person exposed to information consistent with negative stereotypes regarding women.
    d) A non-sexist person exposed to information consistent with negative stereotypes regarding women.
    Ans: b   LO: 10   Page: 178-179   Type: C

105. Sinclair and Kunda (1999) found that White participants who believed they were praised by an African-American doctor _____ racial stereotypes, whereas Whites who believed they were criticized by this doctor _____ stereotypes about African Americans.
    a) suppressed; activated
    b) activated; suppressed
    c) subtyped; contrasted
    d) perpetuated; subtyped
    Ans: a   LO: 10   Page: 179-180   Type: F

106. Research on age and stereotype suppression indicates that
    a) younger and older individuals are equally successful at suppressing stereotypes.
    b) younger individuals have less success with stereotype suppression than older individuals.
    c) older individuals have less success with stereotype suppression than younger individuals.
    d) None of these.
    Ans: c   LO: 10   Page: 181   Type: F

107. Which of the following factors makes automatic activation of stereotypes *more* likely?
    a) Exposure to neutral information about a group or target
    b) A personal motivation to avoid prejudice
    c) Being too cognitively busy to notice category membership of a target
    d) None of these.
    Ans: d   LO: 10   Page: 179-181   Type: A

108. People can counter the potentially negative effects of stereotype activation by
    a) taking the perspective of a member of the stereotyped group.
    b) trying very hard not to think about the stereotype.
    c) thinking about the stereotyped group as a whole.
    d) thinking about recent instances in which they made fair judgments.
    Ans: a   LO: 4   Page: 179-181   Type: F

109. Now that Betty knows she has to work with Barney on a project in their education class, she is
    a)   more likely to see him in a stereotypical manner.
    b)   less likely to enjoy her education class.
    c)   less likely to display contrast effects in evaluating him.
    d)   more likely to pay attention to his personal characteristics.
    Ans: d   LO: 10   Page: 179-181   Type: A

110. Research by Bodenhausen (1990) on the cognitive functioning of "morning people" vs. "night people"
    demonstrates that the influence of stereotypes depends on the
    a)   personal information a perceiver has about a target.
    b)   motivation of the perceiver.
    c)   age of the perceiver.
    d)   cognitive resources available to the perceiver.
    Ans: d   LO: 10   Page: 179-181   Type: F

111. In the aftermath of the Amadou Diallo shooting, several psychologists have investigated the influence that a
    suspect's race might play in police decisions to shoot or not shoot. The results of these studies suggest that
    a)   race does not influence police officers who have been trained to look past a suspect's skin color.
    b)   race can influence the thought processes of police officers, but very rarely their actual behavior.
    c)   police will react differently to an African-American suspect depending on their own level of racial
          prejudice.
    d)   mere awareness of racial stereotypes is enough to influence police behavior, even if the officers do
          not endorse these stereotypes.
    Ans: d   LO: 10   Page: 182-186   Type: C

112. Which of the following have been used by psychologists to investigate the influence of race on police
    behavior?
    a)   Studies using police participants
    b)   Video game simulations
    c)   Virtual reality
    d)   All of these
    Ans: d   LO: 10   Page: 183-185   Type: C

113. Recent studies examining police behavior in "shoot or don't shoot" simulations have found that
    a)   police and civilian participants show no differences in performance.
    b)   racial bias in performance on the task tends to increase over time, unlike college student participants,
          who show the opposite pattern of results.
    c)   even when they are able to avoid racial bias in their decisions, they sometimes take longer to make
          decisions that go against racial stereotypes.
    d)   None of these
    Ans: c   LO: 10   Page: 183-185   Type: C

114. Hightower is a new recruit in the police academy about to begin his very first day of training with a
    computer simulation task in which White and Black men are portrayed holding ambiguous, weapon-like
    objects. Research on race and the perceptions of police officers would predict that Hightower
    a)   would have little trouble distinguishing between White and Black targets in such a simulation.
    b)   would respond differently to the simulation depending on his personal endorsement of race-related
          stereotypes and prejudicial attitudes.
    c)   demonstrate more and more bias in his responses the longer his training went on.
    d)   None of these
    Ans: d   LO: 10   Page: 183-185   Type: A

115. Many targets of discrimination respond to these circumstances by
    a)   experiencing a drop in self-esteem.
    b)   disliking all members of the dominant group.
    c)   blaming themselves for the discrimination.
    d)   attributing both positive and negative outcomes to prejudice.
    Ans: d   LO: 11   Page: 186-187   Type: F

116. A stereotype exists in many cultures that men are better than women at math. Ramya is about to take a
      diagnostic achievement test in math. According to research on stereotype threat, under which of the
      following conditions is Ramya most likely to perform *poorly* on the test?
      a)   Ramya does not believe that the test is an accurate measure of math ability.
      b)   Ramya is asked to indicate her gender at the beginning of the test.
      c)   Ramya does not include math as an important part of her identity.
      d)   Ramya has been raised in a cave by a mathematical genius and is unaware of the cultural stereotype
              concerning gender and math.
      Ans: b   LO: 11   Page: 187-188   Type: A

117. Research on stereotype threat suggests that underperformance by Blacks in academic settings may be due to
      a)   a fear of confirming negative stereotypes of Blacks.
      b)   an overemphasis on superordinate goals in instruction.
      c)   receiving negative feedback based on racist motives.
      d)   the desegregation that tends to occur even in so-called integrated schools.
      Ans: a   LO: 11   Page: 187-188   Type: C

118. Which of the following experimental procedures would a researcher investigating stereotype threat be *least*
      likely to use?
      a)   Having women complete a math test
      b)   Having non-English speaking students complete a verbal skills test in English
      c)   Having African-Americans complete an athletic task
      d)   Having individuals with a history of mental illness complete a logical reasoning task
      Ans: c   LO: 11   Page: 187-188   Type: A

119. Which of the following is an essential requirement in order for stereotype threat to occur?
      a)   The individual in question must be a member of a minority group.
      b)   The individual in question must be aware of negative stereotypes about his or her group.
      c)   The individual in question must have below-average ability for the task in question.
      d)   All of these.
      Ans: b   LO: 11   Page: 187-188   Type: C

120. Research on stereotype threat indicates that
      a)   only a handful of minority groups experience such threats.
      b)   such threats can be attenuated by giving targets the opportunity to self-affirm.
      c)   stereotypes are just as likely to lift the math scores of women as they are to threaten them.
      d)   it is an exclusively American phenomenon.
      Ans: b   LO: 11   Page: 187-188   Type: C

121. The idea that, under certain conditions, direct contact between hostile groups can reduce prejudice is *most*
      consistent with
      a)   the theory of minimal groups.
      b)   contrast effects.
      c)   illusory correlation.
      d)   the contact hypothesis.
      Ans: d   LO: 12   Page: 192-194   Type: C

122. Two neighboring high schools have been feuding since the annual football game ended in a tie. The
      principals of the schools decide that the tension may subside if the two schools participate in joint activities,
      such as assemblies that would allow the students to hear a local band. The strategy is likely to be
      ineffective, however, because the
      a)   two groups have equal status.
      b)   students at the two schools know each other too well.
      c)   students at the two schools are unlikely to have personal contact.
      d)   principals have established the wrong social norm.
      Ans: c   LO: 12   Page: 192-194   Type: A

123. One possible explanation for the failure of school desegregation to promote better racial relations is that it was
    a)   a simplistic idea with no chance of working.
    b)   carried out on too large a scale.
    c)   often carried out without supportive social norms.
    d)   a strategy that provided too much racial contact.
    Ans: c   LO: 12   Page: 192-194   Type: A

124. Mr. Belding wants to reduce prejudice toward incoming minority students at his elementary school. Before the minority students arrive, Mr. Belding puts up posters showing children of all nationalities holding hands. Next, he plans a scavenger hunt in which incoming students are mixed with current students and divided into small groups. Each student receives a secret clue critical to his or her group's success in finding the treasure. Mr. Belding's actions reflect his understanding of
    a)   primacy effects.
    b)   social identity theory.
    c)   social role theory.
    d)   the contact hypothesis.
    Ans: d   LO: 12   Page: 192-194   Type: A

125. Aronson's jigsaw classroom work is similar to Sherif's Robbers Cave experiment because both illustrated how
    a)   social roles can influence the use of stereotypes.
    b)   superordinate goals can reduce prejudice.
    c)   social identification with a group can increase ingroup favoritism.
    d)   overcoming feelings of relative deprivation can decrease prejudice.
    Ans: b   LO: 12   Page: 194   Type: C

ESSAY

126. Describe the Robbers Cave experiment, and explain how it relates to realistic conflict theory.
    Ans: The Robbers Cave experiment, conducted at several summer camps, investigated the interactions among adolescent boys who were divided into two groups. Sherif found that competition between the two groups led to hostility and intense dislike that even propaganda could not eliminate. Peace was restored to some extent when the two groups worked together on tasks with superordinate goals that could be achieved only through cooperation from both groups. Simply bringing the two groups together under noncompetitive circumstances or exposing them to positive propaganda concerning the other group did not alleviate the conflict. The study suggests that group animosity can grow out of competition—the main tenet of realistic conflict theory.   Page: 160-162

127. Explain how social identity theory accounts for ingroup favoritism.
    Ans: Social identity theory proposes that people favor their own group over others in order to maintain a positive image of their group. The theory further argues that people seek to have a positive image of their group in order to promote positive self-esteem. When their self-esteem is challenged, people are more likely to be prejudiced toward others, a tendency that then restores positive self-regard.   Page: 162-165

128. Describe three mechanisms that help explain why stereotypes persist even when people are presented with stereotype-inconsistent information.
     Ans: Illusory correlation is one mechanism that can lead to the maintenance of stereotypes even in the presence of disconfirming information. It results from the tendency of people to see a relationship between infrequent events and negative events. People tend to think that groups that are in the minority are more likely to engage in infrequent acts. Because stereotypes are often about minority groups and because negative events are usually infrequent, illusory correlation can lead to the maintenance of negative evaluations of minority groups. A second mechanism is subtyping, the process whereby people refine a stereotype to include inconsistent individual members of a group while maintaining the overall negative evaluation of the group. Throughout this process, although evaluations of an individual member may not be consistent with the stereotype, evaluations of the group remain the same. A third mechanism is the confirmation bias, which causes people to seek out and pay more attention to stereotype-consistent information than to stereotype-inconsistent information. Confirmation biases lead people to discount information that is inconsistent with the stereotype, to interpret ambiguous information in an expectation-consistent manner, and even to elicit behavior that confirms their expectations.   Page: 169-172

129. Describe two ways in which gender stereotypes are strengthened and maintained.
     Ans: Gender stereotypes are strengthened and maintained through cultural institutions and social roles, among other mechanisms. Cultural institutions, particularly the media, portray women (as well as members of others groups) in a stereotypic fashion. These portrayals can have a cumulative effect on people's views of women. Although social roles may have begun as a division of labor based in part on biology and in part on social factors, over time many people act in ways that are consistent with their roles. In turn, the behaviors that result from these roles often come to justify the original division of labor.   Page: 171

130. How do group stereotypes affect the self-esteem and performance of individuals belonging to that group?
     Ans: Stereotyped individuals are greatly affected by the stereotypes attached to their groups. For example, such individuals often discount positive feedback and exhibit lower self-esteem after receipt of such feedback because they believe it is not genuine. By the same token, their self-esteem may not be decreased after negative feedback because they can attribute the feedback to the stereotype. Another way in which stereotypes can affect such individuals is when they approach performance situations with the anxiety that they might fail, thus confirming a negative view held of their group. Several experiments show that both women and Blacks may perform worse on academic tasks due to this "stereotype threat" particularly when the stereotype is made salient. More recent studies have found that such stereotype threat effects can occur for members of any group about which negative stereotypes exist, even White men.   Page: 186-188

CHAPTER 6
Attitudes

MULTIPLE CHOICE

1. Attitudes are *best* understood as
    a) being either entirely positive or entirely negative.
    b) being initially positive, but increasingly negative as new information arises.
    c) varying in strength along both positive and negative dimensions.
    d) ranging on a continuum from positive to negative.
    Ans: c   LO: 1   Page: 203-204   Type: C

2. Which of the following would *not* be considered an attitude?
    a) Darnell likes to play chess.
    b) Daphne hates liver.
    c) Daisy strongly favors universal health insurance.
    d) Dalton drives a silver minivan.
    Ans: d   LO: 1   Page: 203-204   Type: C

3. The feeling of ambivalence can be described as an attitude that is both _____ and _____.
    a) strong; mixed in terms of positive versus negative valence
    b) weak; extremely positive
    c) inconsistent over time; strong
    d) consistent over time; weak
    Ans: a   LO: 1   Page: 203-204   Type: F

4. Antonio describes himself as high in need for evaluation. It is likely that Antonio
    a) does not tend to make evaluative judgments about his daily experiences.
    b) prefers to be with people who are judgmental of him.
    c) has strong opinions about a variety of issues and people.
    d) avoids situations where he will be asked for his opinion.
    Ans: b   LO: 1   Page: 203-204   Type: A

5. Attitudes are useful because they
    a) allow us to judge whether something we encounter is good or bad.
    b) bias the way we interpret new information.
    c) make it more likely that we will change our minds later.
    d) allow us to take more time to evaluate others.
    Ans: a   LO: 1   Page: 203-204   Type: F

6. Sammy and Mark watched a ballgame together. Sammy favored the home team, while Mark was an avid fan of the road team. The star player for Sammy's team made a great play and started to celebrate in a rather demonstrative fashion. Sammy got caught up in the celebration, while Mark was angered because he felt this display was an insult to the players of his team. This demonstrates that
    a) two people's evaluations of the same event are more likely to be similar than to be different.
    b) we often interpret events and behavior based upon pre-existing attitudes.
    c) central route processing leads to stronger opinions than peripheral route processing.
    d) we can hold both positive and negative evaluations about the same object.
    Ans: b   LO: 1   Page: 203-204   Type: A

7. Public opinion pollsters, in trying to assess attitudes about particular subjects, have become aware that attitude responses seem to be affected by all of the factors below *except*
    a) the context in which the question appears.
    b) the wording of the question.
    c) the specific response options given.
    d) the length of the questionnaire.
    Ans: d   LO: 1   Page: 204-205   Type: C

8. The most direct and straightforward way to assess an attitude is through the use of
   a) covert measures.
   b) implicit measures.
   c) self-report measures.
   d) behavioral observation.
   Ans: c   LO: 1   Page: 204-205   Type: C

9. Shaniqua plans to use a self-report measure in which people indicate their agreement or disagreement with a list of statements. She is using
   a) a Likert scale.
   b) the luncheon technique.
   c) a categorical matrix.
   d) an agreement index.
   Ans: a   LO: 1   Page: 204-205   Type: A

10. One potential problem with self-report measures is that
    a) they do not provide information concerning the intensity of an attitude.
    b) they do not provide information concerning the direction of an attitude.
    c) respondents might not respond truthfully.
    d) it is not possible to assess the validity of self-report measures.
    Ans: c   LO: 1   Page: 204-205   Type: C

11. Jacqueline, an attitude researcher, is interested in how people feel about alcohol. She would be well-advised to use a
    a) Likert scale because it is not as susceptible to social desirability effects.
    b) bogus pipeline because it is not as susceptible to social desirability effects.
    c) Likert scale because it is more likely to be affected by social desirability.
    d) bogus pipeline because it is more likely to be affected by social desirability.
    Ans: b   LO: 1   Page: 205   Type: A

12. One way to increase the accuracy of self-report measures of attitudes is to
    a) offer many, rather than fewer, response options.
    b) use a single attitude scale, rather than multiple scales.
    c) focus on attitudes regarding sensitive and personal issues.
    d) convince respondents that any deception can be detected
    Ans: d   LO: 1   Page: 204-205   Type: C

13. Which of the following is *not* used in order to overcome the limitations of traditional self-report methodology?
    a) Bogus pipeline
    b) Likert scale
    c) Facial electromyograph
    d) Covert videotaping
    Ans: b   LO: 1   Page: 205-206   Type: C

14. Wells and Petty (1980) videotaped students as they listened to a speech. The results of this study indicated that
    a) students revealed the intensity, but not the direction, of their attitudes through their body language.
    b) students' self-reported attitudes did not agree with their observed attitudes.
    c) students signaled their attitudes by nodding or shaking their heads.
    d) horizontal head movements indicate agreement, whereas vertical head movements indicate disagreement.
    Ans: c   LO: 1   Page: 206   Type: F

15. When used to measure attitudes, physiological measures such as heart rate and perspiration
    a) are particularly susceptible to social desirability bias.
    b) reveal the intensity of an attitude.
    c) reveal whether an attitude is positive or negative.
    d) are easier to control than behaviors such as nodding.
    Ans: b   LO: 1   Page: 206   Type: F

16. Measuring attitudes by assessing physiological arousal tends to identify the _____ but not the _____ of the attitude.
    a) intensity; direction
    b) direction; accuracy
    c) accuracy; intensity
    d) direction; automaticity
    Ans: a   LO: 1   Page: 206   Type: A

17. Cacioppo and Petty (1981) recorded facial muscle activity of college students as they listened to a message with which they agreed or disagreed. The results of this study indicated that listening to a(n) _____ message increases activity in the _____.
    a) disagreeable; cheek muscles
    b) disagreeable; chin muscles
    c) agreeable; cheek muscles
    d) agreeable; muscles in the forehead and brow area
    Ans: c   LO: 1   Page: 206-207   Type: F

18. Which of the following concerning the use of facial electromyography (EMG) to assess attitudes is *true*?
    a) Facial EMG can detect muscular changes not observable to the naked eye.
    b) Facial EMG does not provide information about the direction of attitudes.
    c) One problem with using facial EMG is that the same pattern of activity could be interpreted as happiness or sadness.
    d) Facial EMG is only an accurate measure of attitudes if people know their attitudes are being assessed, so it is susceptible to the same social desirability biases as self-reports.
    Ans: a   LO: 1   Page: 206-207   Type: C

19. In a study about political attitudes and opinions during the 2004 presidential election, researchers used brain imaging to examine what happened in the brain when participants listened to positive or negative statements about the candidate of their choice. They found that most affected were those areas of the brain associated with which of the following?
    a) Emotion
    b) Cognitive reasoning
    c) Speech
    d) Mood
    Ans: a   LO: 1   Page: 207   Type: C

20. Tsuyoshi has positive implicit attitudes about himself. We know this because on an Implicit Association Test, he was quickest to associate _____ with photos of himself.
    a) positive words
    b) negative words
    c) male faces
    d) female faces
    Ans: d   LO: 1   Page: 207-209   Type: A

21. An attitude is implicit if you
    a) try to hide it.
    b) are not aware of it.
    c) cannot measure it.
    d) disagree with it.
    Ans: b   LO: 1   Page: 207-209   Type: C

22. Implicit Association Tests (IAT's) can detect implicit attitudes by measuring
    a) the participants' mood after responding to word pairings.
    b) the time it takes participants to complete the whole test.
    c) participants' facial muscles as they are exposed to positive or negative stimuli.
    d) the speed at which participants associate stimuli with a positive or negative word.
    Ans: d   LO: 1   Page: 207-209   Type: C

23.   Implicit attitudes can be difficult to measure because
      a)   people are not aware of having them.
      b)   physiological measures are not effective in assessing them.
      c)   they can only be measured by direct techniques.
      d)   they are prone to the effects of social desirability.
      Ans: a   LO: 1   Page: 207-209   Type: F

24.   Miss Roberto is concerned that Talia and Emily avoid playing with Michael because he is Black. Which of
      the following strategies would best enable her to assess any unconscious dislike these two students feel
      towards Michael?
      a)   Ask them why they don't want to play with him.
      b)   Measure the girls' brain activity when they are forced to play with Michael.
      c)   Administer an IAT to examine the girls' racial attitudes.
      d)   Administer a self-report questionnaire examining the girls' racial attitudes.
      Ans: c   LO: 1   Page: 207-209   Type: A

25.   Research on the attitudes of twins suggests
      a)   that genetics are not useful in predicting the attitudes different people will hold.
      b)   the attitudes of identical twins are more similar than the attitudes of fraternal twins.
      c)   the attitudes of twins who are reared apart from one another are more dissimilar than the attitudes of
            twins raised together in the same household.
      d)   that the first-born twin is likely to be more conservative than the second-born twin, even when their
            births are only separated by minutes.
      Ans: b   LO: 1   Page: 209-210   Type: F

26.   The hypothesis that there is a genetic component to some attitudes would be supported by the finding that
      a)   attitudes of identical twins are more similar than those of fraternal twins.
      b)   adults who shared certain physiological characteristics also had common political beliefs.
      c)   when asked about attitudes for which there seems to be a genetic predisposition, research participants
            were quicker to respond to questions and less likely to alter their views toward social norms.
      d)   All of these
      Ans: d   LO: 1   Page: 209-210   Type: C

27.   Which of the following statements regarding LaPiere's (1934) study of attitudes is *false*?
      a)   Even though respondents who were asked self-report questions claimed that they would not be
            racially prejudiced, their behavior showed clear discrimination.
      b)   The study examined racial attitudes at a time when prejudice was much more overt and blatant than it
            currently is.
      c)   LaPiere was not a psychologist.
      d)   Over 90% of the respondents claimed that they would not offer service to a Chinese patron.
      Ans: a   LO: 2   Page: 210-211   Type: C

28.   Ichiro is a member of a campus political group and is interested in finding out how many students plan to
      vote in the 2012 election. According to the theory of planned behavior, which of the following questions
      Ichiro could ask would be the best predictor of whether or not a particular student would actually vote in the
      2012 November election?
      a)   What are your attitudes about U.S. politics?
      b)   What are your attitudes about voting in U.S. Presidential elections?
      c)   What are your attitudes about the politicians in general?
      d)   What are your attitudes about the Bush vs. Gore Presidential election of 2000 and the fact that the
            winner of the election received fewer popular votes than the loser?
      Ans: b   LO: 2   Page: 211-212   Type: A

29.   Which of the following theories suggests that intentions to perform a behavior are *best* predicted by
      attitudes toward the behavior, subjective norms, and perceived behavioral control?
      a)   Theory of planned behavior
      b)   Cognitive dissonance theory
      c)   Self-perception theory
      d)   Self-affirmation theory
      Ans: a   LO: 2   Page: 211-212   Type: F

30. The theory of planned behavior posits that behavior is a function of attitudes, subjective norms, behavioral intentions, and
    a) the amount of time we have considered engaging in the behavior.
    b) the correspondence between the attitude and the behavior.
    c) the amount of control we perceive to have over our behavior.
    d) the costs of engaging in the behavior.
    Ans: c   LO: 2   Page: 211-212   Type: F

31. Jacob wants to learn how to water-ski. Which of the following would *not* be required by the theory of planned behavior?
    a) He feels confident that he can learn the skills associated with waterskiing.
    b) He fully intends to learn how to water-ski.
    c) Many of his friends are water-skiers and are encouraging him to join them.
    d) He recognizes the dangers associated with waterskiing.
    Ans: d   LO: 2   Page: 211-212   Type: A

32. According to the theory of planned behavior, one reason that a person's behavior might not be consistent with that person's attitudes is that the behavior
    a) is determined by norms that are consistent with the person's attitudes.
    b) is one that the person feels is within his or her control.
    c) is determined by norms that are counter to the person's attitudes.
    d) occurs only when the person is self-aware.
    Ans: c   LO: 2   Page: 211-212   Type: C

33. Gloria has a negative attitude toward smoking, but she continues to smoke two packs of cigarettes a day. According to the theory of planned behavior, one reason that her attitude and behavior are *inconsistent* could be that
    a) her attitude is based on feelings rather than beliefs.
    b) she doesn't believe that she can control her smoking behavior.
    c) her family and friends also have negative attitudes toward smoking.
    d) her attitudes are usually accessible when she reaches for a cigarette.
    Ans: b   LO: 2   Page: 211-212   Type: A

34. Which of the following is *not* supported by social psychological research?
    a) Situational factors can bring attitudes into awareness.
    b) Attitude similarity among twins raised apart is as high as attitude similarity among twins raised together.
    c) People feel more strongly about an object when the attitude is based on direct experience.
    d) Attitude-behavior consistency is unrelated to knowledge about the attitude object.
    Ans: d   LO: 2   Page: 212-213   Type: F

35. All of the following factors can distinguish strong from weak attitudes *except*
    a) the personal relevance of the issue.
    b) the importance of the issue to family and friends.
    c) the amount of perceived behavioral control.
    d) the extent to which the issue concerns important values.
    Ans: c   LO: 2   Page: 212-213   Type: F

36. According to research by Tormala and Petty (2002), an attitude can be ____ by a persuasive message or argument ____ it.
    a) weakened; for
    b) strengthened; against
    c) weakened; against.
    d) strengthened; for.
    Ans: b   LO: 2   Page: 213-214   Type: C

37. Professor Zavala would like to reduce cheating in her classes. She knows that students strongly oppose cheating but, in spite of these negative attitudes, cheating is quite common. Which of the following tactics would be *least* effective at reducing cheating?
  a) To strengthen attitudes toward cheating, ask students to write and sign a statement indicating that they will not cheat prior to each exam.
  b) To increase anxiety, make sure students are not well-informed about what behaviors constitute cheating or what consequences might result from cheating.
  c) To increase accessibility, ask students to spend a few moments before each exam thinking about their attitudes toward cheating.
  d) To increase self-awareness, publicly videotape the class during exams.
  Ans: b   LO: 2   Page: 213-214   Type: A

38. The mirrors in shopping malls may reduce shoplifting because
  a) shoppers are distracted by seeing their reflections, which makes them less likely to behave in accord with their positive attitudes toward shoplifting.
  b) people focus on the image they see and their negative attitudes toward shoplifting are weakened.
  c) mirrors create a sense of luxury invoking the "you get what you pay for" heuristic.
  d) mirrors increase self-awareness, which makes negative attitudes toward shoplifting accessible.
  Ans: d   LO: 2   Page: 213-214   Type: C

39. Mara pays close attention to the quality of the speaker's arguments in making up her mind on an issue. She is demonstrating
  a) the primacy effect.
  b) insufficient justification.
  c) the central route to persuasion.
  d) the peripheral route to persuasion.
  Ans: c   LO: 3   Page: 215-216   Type: A

40. The process by which a person is persuaded by cues in the persuasion context rather than thinking critically about the content of a persuasive message is called
  a) psychological reactance.
  b) theory of planned behavior.
  c) the peripheral route to persuasion.
  d) the central route to persuasion.
  Ans: c   LO: 3   Page: 216-217   Type: F

41. While watching the presidential debate on television, Matilda critically evaluated the arguments made by each candidate and was persuaded to support a particular candidate because of the quality of her arguments. Matilda exhibited
  a) psychological reactance.
  b) central route persuasion.
  c) peripheral route persuasion.
  d) insufficient justification.
  Ans: b   LO: 3   Page: 215-216   Type: A

42. Which of the following conditions is *not* specified in Hovland's model of persuasion as necessary for persuasion to occur?
  a) Message recipients must elaborate the message.
  b) Message recipients must attend to the message.
  c) Message recipients must comprehend the message.
  d) Message recipients must be motivated to accept the message.
  Ans: a   LO: 3   Page: 215-216   Type: F

43. Which of the following statements about the central route to persuasion is *false*?
  a) It is more commonly used by advertisers in collectivist cultures (e.g., Korea) than it is by advertisers in individualistic cultures (e.g., the United States).
  b) It leads audience members to be more influenced by a two-sided argument than a one-sided argument.
  c) It is a more thoughtful process than the peripheral route.
  d) It renders the quality of arguments more important than the quantity of arguments.
  Ans: a   LO: 3   Page: 215-216   Type: A

44. The primary difference between the models of persuasion proposed by Hovland and McGuire and that proposed by Greenwald is that Greenwald's model
    a)   does not allow for central route processing.
    b)   emphasizes the role of elaboration in producing persuasion.
    c)   does not include reception as one of the information-processing steps in persuasion.
    d)   proposes that memory of message content is the most important determinant of persuasion.
    Ans: b   LO: 3   Page: 215-216   Type: C

45. Eric does not really know how to answer the essay question about cognitive dissonance on his social psychology exam. He decides to write as many facts as he knows about the topic of attitudes in his bluebook, hoping that the professor will not read the exams too closely and will be impressed enough by the length of his essay to give him a good score. Eric is hoping to take advantage of
    a)   the sleeper effect.
    b)   the peripheral route to persuasion.
    c)   the central route to persuasion.
    d)   dissonance-related insufficient justification.
    Ans: b   LO: 3   Page: 216-217   Type: A

46. The dual-process model proposed by Petty and Cacciopo (1986) assumes that
    a)   people do not always process communications the same way.
    b)   people are never persuaded by the strength and quality of arguments.
    c)   people always think about both sides of an argument.
    d)   people are always strongly influenced by superficial cues.
    Ans: a   LO: 3   Page: 217   Type: C

47. When message recipients use central route processing, which of the following will be *true*?
    a)   Difficult messages will be more persuasive than easily learned messages.
    b)   Memorable messages will be more persuasive than forgettable ones.
    c)   Weak messages will engender more favorable responses than strong messages.
    d)   Elaboration of message content will be objective and unbiased.
    Ans: b   LO: 3   Page: 217   Type: C

48. Which of the following pairs of characteristics matter more for the central route to persuasion than the peripheral route?
    a)   Whether the message is well-conceived, and whether it addresses possible counterarguments from the other side of the issue
    b)   Whether the message is memorable, and whether it is given by a speaker with an honest reputation
    c)   Whether the message is given by a speaker with an honest reputation, and whether it is short
    d)   Whether the message stimulates favorable elaboration, and whether the message elicits cheers from an audience
    Ans: a   LO: 3   Page: 217   Type: C

49. Oscar, an advertiser, develops a commercial for Crispy Crunch Crackling Cereal. Suppose children, processing information via the central route, watch the commercial. The commercial will be more likely to persuade the kids to want the cereal if it has all of the following *except*
    a)   a spokesperson who asks viewers whether they want to try the cereal.
    b)   a simple straightforward message that the kids can learn easily.
    c)   a little jingle about the great qualities of the cereal that the children will remember.
    d)   an attractive spokesperson.
    Ans: d   LO: 3   Page: 215-217   Type: A

50. A two-sided argument is most likely to convince an audience that is
    a)   from a collectivist culture.
    b)   using the central route to persuasion.
    c)   using the peripheral route to persuasion.
    d)   distracted.
    Ans: b   LO: 3   Page: 215-216   Type: C

51. When an audience member does not feel personally involved or invested in the topic of a persuasive message, she is likely to
    a)   focus primarily on the strength of the message, ignoring the apparent expertise of the message source.
    b)   be influenced immediately by the sleeper effect.
    c)   engage in a central, but not peripheral route to persuasion.
    d)   None of these.
    Ans: d   LO: 3   Page: 215-217   Type: A

52. Which of the following concerning the impact of body movements on persuasion is *true*?
    a)   People who nod their heads up and down express greater agreement with a persuasive message than those who nod their heads side to side.
    b)   Stimuli associated with stretching the arms outward are rated more positively than those associated with flexing the arms inward.
    c)   Nodding the head side to side makes people more likely to engage in central route processing than does nodding the head up and down.
    d)   Stretching the arms outward makes people less likely to engage in central route processing than does flexing the arms inward.
    Ans: a   LO: 3   Page: 216-217   Type: C

53. The central route to persuasion requires
    a)   intelligence and strong arguments.
    b)   involvement and an expert source.
    c)   ability and motivation.
    d)   knowledge of the issue and a credible source.
    Ans: c   LO: 3   Page: 215-216   Type: F

54. An audience member is more likely to use the peripheral route to persuasion if
    a)   the argument is a familiar one.
    b)   the message is personally significant.
    c)   the audience is small.
    d)   the speaker is unattractive.
    Ans: a   LO: 3   Page: 216-217   Type: C

55. Gino, a salesperson, wants to use techniques that will lead his potential customers to rely on peripheral route persuasion. He should do all of the following *except*
    a)   speak quickly when presenting information about his product.
    b)   get the customer to nod in the affirmative while he is presenting his sales pitch.
    c)   present his sales pitch to customers who are clearly in a rush.
    d)   approach prospective buyers who obviously care deeply about his product.
    Ans: d   LO: 3   Page: 216-217   Type: A

56. Dan is listening to the dean of the college speak about banning fraternities on campus. Dan is *most* likely to evaluate the quality of the dean's arguments if
    a)   she speaks very quickly.
    b)   Dan is a member of a fraternity.
    c)   Dan is doing his calculus homework while listening to the speech.
    d)   the dean indicates that most students think fraternities should be banned.
    Ans: b   LO: 3   Page: 218-219   Type: A

57. The more products a celebrity endorses the
    a)   more competent she becomes in the eyes of consumers.
    b)   less trustworthy she becomes in the eyes of consumers.
    c)   more likeable she becomes in the eyes of consumers.
    d)   less likely an audience member is to use to peripheral route to persuasion.
    Ans: b   LO: 4   Page: 218-219   Type: F

58. Vicki is a lawyer who is trying to decide which of two forensic experts she should hire to provide testimony in a case. There is a large discrepancy in the fees each of the experts demands for their services. If Vicki wants the jurors to perceive her expert as trustworthy—and if she expects the witness' fees to become part of the trial record when he testifies—then she should select
    a)   the more expensive expert.
    b)   the less expensive expert.
    c)   either one because of their status in their field.
    d)   the expert who has the most experience testifying in court.
    Ans: b   LO: 4   Page: 218-219   Type: A

59. Because communicator trustworthiness is important, people tend to be readily impressed by speakers who
    a)   take popular stands.
    b)   argue against their own interests.
    c)   talk slowly and deliberately.
    d)   are well-dressed.
    Ans: b   LO: 4   Page: 218-219   Type: C

60. Brady and Quinn are trying to develop an ad campaign in which a key element is the trustworthiness of the message's communicator. Toward this end, they may wish to utilize
    a)   a public service message.
    b)   overheard communications.
    c)   novel advertising.
    d)   political campaigns.
    Ans: b   LO: 4   Page: 218-219   Type: A

61. Which of the following source characteristics best explains why a company might recruit a supermodel to endorse its products?
    a)   Similarity
    b)   Credibility
    c)   Likeability
    d)   Trustworthiness
    Ans: c   LO: 4   Page: 220-221   Type: A

62. Roger and Mike always seem to disagree on music. When Roger tells Mike that he has heard a new song on the radio that he likes a lot, this experience is likely to lead Mike to
    a)   like the song more than he would have had he not talked to Roger ahead of time.
    b)   like the song less than he would have had he not talked to Roger ahead of time.
    c)   be skeptical about Roger's motivation for telling him about the song.
    d)   view Roger as an unlikable message source.
    Ans: b   LO: 4   Page: 220-221   Type: A

63. The physical attractiveness of a spokesmodel will have the *greatest* effect if the product endorsed is
    a)   life insurance.
    b)   clothing-related.
    c)   birth control.
    d)   an insecticide.
    Ans: b   LO: 4   Page: 220-221   Type: A

64. Dr. Flinstone, president of Quarry College, needs to convince students that the college must double its tuition beginning in five years. He is hiring someone to promote this idea, as well as developing supportive arguments. Would he need to adopt a different strategy if he instead wanted to implement the change in the next academic year?
    a)   No. He should do the same thing either way.
    b)   Yes. If the change is to happen next year, the strength of the arguments will matter more than whom he hires to promote the idea.
    c)   Yes. If the change is to happen next year, the person he hires will matter more than the strength of the arguments.
    d)   Yes. If the change is to happen next year, obtaining a credible promoter and generating strong arguments will both be more crucial than if the change will happen in five years.
    Ans: b   LO: 4   Page: 221-222   Type: A

65. As personal involvement regarding an issue increases
    a) the quality of the arguments becomes a more important determinant of persuasion.
    b) the credibility of the speaker becomes a more important determinant of persuasion.
    c) the attractiveness of the speaker becomes a more important determinant of persuasion.
    d) the likelihood of central route persuasion decreases.
    Ans: a   LO: 4   Page: 221-222   Type: F

66. While shopping at the local mall, Ihno is approached by a man who asks her to sign a petition for stricter gun control laws. If Ihno uses the central route to decide whether to sign the petition, then she will be more likely to sign if the man who approaches her
    a) is physically attractive.
    b) is a member of the National Rifle Association.
    c) is a police officer.
    d) presents strong arguments.
    Ans: d   LO: 4   Page: 221-222   Type: A

67. A sleeper effect occurs when
    a) persuasion occurs in response to subliminal stimuli.
    b) a persuasive message from a noncredible source becomes more persuasive over time.
    c) distraction interferes with the ability to pay attention to a persuasive message.
    d) people fall asleep during exposure to a persuasive message.
    Ans: b   LO: 4   Page: 222-224   Type: F

68. Hope read a persuasive message written by a source who she considered to be incompetent and untrustworthy. The sleeper effect would suggest that her attitude toward the issue should
    a) change over time.
    b) show greater change over time in the direction advocated by the speaker.
    c) show greater change over time in the opposite direction than that advocated by the speaker.
    d) decrease over time.
    Ans: a   LO: 4   Page: 222-224   Type: A

69. Sleeper effects can be reduced by reminding people that the source of a persuasive message was not credible. This supports which explanation of sleeper effects?
    a) The inoculation hypothesis
    b) The discounting cue hypothesis
    c) Psychological reactance theory
    d) Cognitive dissonance theory
    Ans: b   LO: 4   Page: 222-224   Type: C

70. Josue listened to a speech on the radio advocating the increased use of automobiles that are not reliant on fossil fuels. One would expect the sleeper effect to be greatest if Josue found out about the background of the speaker _____ the speech and was asked about his views about the issue _____.
    a) before; that same day
    b) after; that same day
    c) before; a few weeks later
    d) after; a few weeks later
    Ans: d   LO: 4   Page: 222-224   Type: C

71. Cairan, a college student, wants to persuade her friends that residence halls should have curfews. Assuming her friends consider this issue to be personally involving, Cairan would be smart to
    a) present only strong arguments that support her position.
    b) present her weak arguments first followed by her strong arguments.
    c) present the strong arguments first and then follow with the weak arguments.
    d) point out how similar her friends are to her.
    Ans: a   LO: 5   Page: 224-225   Type: A

72. Jon and Kate give consecutive speeches on opposing sides in a debate on solar energy. Audience members are asked to register their view a few weeks later. How might the order of the speeches affect the audience's decision?
    a) It should yield a primacy effect.
    b) It should yield a subliminal effect.
    c) It should yield a recency effect.
    d) It should not have any effect.
    Ans: a   LO: 5   Page: 224-225   Type: A

73. At a computer trade show, a representative from Mad Dog Computers presents its product to the audience, and is immediately followed by a representative from Smelly Cat Computers, who demonstrates the benefits of her product. If surveyed immediately after the show, the audience is likely to report having been
    a) more persuaded by Mad Dog Computers.
    b) more persuaded by Smelly Cat Computers.
    c) equally persuaded by both companies if the presentations were comparable.
    d) persuaded by neither company.
    Ans: c   LO: 5   Page: 224-225   Type: A

74. Which of the following is *true* of issues that are personally important to us?
    a) We are more stubborn and resistant to change regarding those issues.
    b) We follow the peripheral route when others try to change our minds about these issues.
    c) The best way for others to change our minds about such issues is to take a position very discrepant from how we feel.
    d) Others will find it much easier to change our minds about these issues if we are first put in a bad mood.
    Ans: a   LO: 5   Page: 225-226   Type: F

75. Michael believes that one's family is more important than one's career. In order for him to successfully convince his achievement-oriented friend Ronald that he should also possess such a value system, Michael should
    a) take the very discrepant position that careers never provide satisfaction anywhere close to what a family provides.
    b) use peripheral cues.
    c) present as many arguments for his position as possible.
    d) suggest more of a balance between family and career concerns than is currently true for Ronald.
    Ans: d   LO: 5   Page: 225-226   Type: A

76. Which of the following concerning the use of fear appeals is *not* supported by research?
    a) Fear appeals may motivate change by increasing the incentive to think carefully about the arguments in the message.
    b) Fear appeals are generally less effective than messages that do not provoke fear.
    c) Fear appeals are most effective when they include specific information on how to avoid the threat.
    d) Fear arousal may reduce the ability of already fearful message recipients to carefully process a message.
    Ans: b   LO: 5   Page: 226-227   Type: F

77. Research by Landau and colleagues (2004) in which participants were exposed to subliminal images of the 9/11 terrorist attacks and then asked questions about then-President George W. Bush leads to the conclusion that
    a) the fear of death leads people to choose the central route to persuasion.
    b) reminders of mortality lead people to prefer one-sided messages to two-sided messages.
    c) fear arousal can influence even attitudes as important as political opinions.
    d) the higher the level of fear arousal in a persuasive communication, the stronger the agreement with it.
    Ans: c   LO: 5   Page: 226-227   Type: C

78.   Louie runs a clinic that helps individuals to quit smoking and he would like to use fear to motivate his clients. Which of the following strategies would be *most* effective?
   a)   First scare clients by showing them gory lung-cancer operations. Then outline the specific steps they could follow to stop smoking.
   b)   First scare clients by showing them gory lung-cancer operations. Then allow them to come up with their own ways of quitting smoking so that they are more committed.
   c)   Present statistics concerning the health hazards of smoking, but nothing too scary. Then allow the clients to come up with their own ways of quitting smoking so that they are more committed.
   d)   Present statistics concerning the health hazards of smoking, but nothing too scary. Then outline the specific steps they could follow to stop smoking.
   Ans: a   LO: 5   Page: 226-227   Type: A

79.   Professor Shackleford is elated because she has just learned that her paper has been accepted for publication. When a student passes her in the hallway and tells her that he missed the latest exam in order to stay home with his depressed cat, her good mood renders her likely to
   a)   be even more skeptical than usual about such an unlikely excuse.
   b)   be less skeptical than usual about the excuse.
   c)   overlook the student's cognitive dissonance.
   d)   fall victim to the sleeper effect.
   Ans: b   LO: 5   Page: 227-228   Type: A

80.   Wegener et al. (1995) found that happy participants used the central route to persuasion when presented with a pro-attitudinal message, but used the peripheral route to persuasion when presented with a counter-attitudinal message. This finding suggests that
   a)   positive mood disrupts the ability to process persuasive information.
   b)   people in a positive mood rely on superficial processing strategies.
   c)   positive mood affects different people in different ways.
   d)   happy people avoid processing only if it threatens to destroy their mood.
   Ans: d   LO: 5   Page: 227-228   Type: C

81.   Which of the following *best* summarizes the results of research regarding the effectiveness of subliminal self-help tapes?
   a)   Subliminal messages delivered verbally have a powerful and long-lasting impact on behavior.
   b)   The content of subliminal self-help tapes is the best predictor of their effectiveness.
   c)   Beliefs about the content of the tapes produce both perceived and actual behavioral changes.
   d)   Beliefs about the content of the tapes produce perceived but not actual behavioral changes.
   Ans: d   LO: 5   Page: 228-230   Type: C

82.   Research indicates that subliminal influence
   a)   never occurs.
   b)   usually occurs in the short-term for simple judgments.
   c)   is more likely among people high in the need for cognition.
   d)   can persuade people to take action even when they were previously unmotivated to do so.
   Ans: b   LO: 5   Page: 228-230   Type: F

83.   The study by Strahan and colleagues (2002) found that subliminal cues regarding thirst influenced how much Kool-Aid participants drank only
   a)   when the participants had previously been given water to drink.
   b)   when they were given something to eat as well.
   c)   when they were high in the need for cognition.
   d)   None of these.
   Ans: d   LO: 5   Page: 228-230   Type: F

84.   The "Lipton Ice" and dextrose pill research demonstrated that subliminal messages are most effective when participants
   a)   cared very much about the issue.
   b)   were low in self-monitoring.
   c)   were low in the need for evaluation.
   d)   really needed the item being advertised.
   Ans: d   LO: 6   Page: 228-230   Type: A

85. People high in need for cognition are
    a)   more likely to process a message along the central route.
    b)   most persuaded by image-oriented appeals.
    c)   more likely to agree with a message if they are in a good mood.
    d)   more persuaded by the reputation and appearance of the source.
    Ans: a   LO: 6   Page: 230-231   Type: C

87. The idea that people are more likely to be influenced by messages that match their frame of mind is known as
    a)   self-verification.
    b)   regulatory fit.
    c)   the matching hypothesis.
    d)   the affect congruency effect.
    Ans: b   LO: 6   Page: 231-232   Type: C

88. _____ oriented individuals are protective of what they have while _____ oriented individuals are drawn to the pursuit of success and achievement.
    a)   prevention; promotion.
    b)   motivational; persuasive.
    c)   promotion; prevention.
    d)   persuasive; motivational.
    Ans: a   LO: 6   Page: 231-232   Type: C

89. Research demonstrates that exposure to weak versions of a persuasive argument tends to increase later resistance to that argument. This is consistent with
    a)   the discounting cue hypothesis.
    b)   self-perception theory.
    c)   cognitive dissonance theory.
    d)   the inoculation hypothesis.
    Ans: d   LO: 6   Page: 232-233   Type: F

90. Tariq doesn't want his kids to give in to peer pressure to smoke. According to the inoculation hypothesis, one way he could build up their resistance to potential peer pressure is to
    a)   let them smoke so that their attitudes will be based on direct experience.
    b)   present them with weak arguments for smoking so that they can generate counterarguments.
    c)   present them with very strong arguments against smoking on which to base their attitudes.
    d)   have them listen to subliminal anti-smoking messages.
    Ans: b   LO: 6   Page: 232-233   Type: A

91. A negative reaction to the feeling that one's freedom is being threatened is called
    a)   cognitive dissonance.
    b)   psychological reactance.
    c)   forewarning.
    d)   the inoculation hypothesis.
    Ans: b   LO: 6   Page: 233   Type: F

92. Selma's friends can't stand her new girlfriend, Patty, and have been pressuring Selma to stop seeing her. Selma gets agitated and feels that her friends should mind their own business and not try to "run her life" for her. According to the concept of _____, Selma would be most likely to respond by _____.
    a)   psychological reactance; breaking up with Patty
    b)   psychological reactance; feeling even more dedicated to her relationship with Patty
    c)   attitude inoculation; eventually becoming persuaded by her friends' attitudes about Patty
    d)   attitude inoculation; taking out her frustrations on Patty
    Ans: b   LO: 6   Page: 233   Type: A

93. Which of the following advertising slogans for a new stereo system would be *most* appealing to someone in a collectivist culture?
     a) "Play all of your favorite CDs and hear every nuance."
     b) "Invite your friends over so they can dance to music of the highest clarity."
     c) "Don't you want to have the best stereo in your neighborhood?"
     d) "You work hard every day—why not treat yourself to something special?"
     Ans: b   LO: 6   Page: 234   Type: A

94. Elias believes that gun control is necessary. Which of the following would cause Elias to change his attitude the *most*?
     a) He hears a speech *against* gun control, then gives a speech that takes a similar position.
     b) He anticipates giving a speech *against* gun control, and then gives the speech.
     c) He anticipates giving a speech *for* gun control, and then must give a speech *against* it.
     d) He gives a speech *for* gun control, followed by a speech *against* gun control.
     Ans: b   LO: 7   Page: 234-235   Type: A

95. Which of the following has *not* been demonstrated in research on role-playing?
     a) People show greater attitude change after writing a persuasive speech than after reading one.
     b) Self-generated arguments are better remembered than arguments provided by others.
     c) Expecting to have to present a persuasive communication to another person increases the impact of the communication.
     d) Role-playing effects are stronger among those low in need for cognition than those high in need for cognition.
     Ans: d   LO: 7   Page: 234-235   Type: C

96. An unpleasant psychological state often aroused when people hold two conflicting cognitions is called
     a) cognitive dissonance.
     b) attitude ambivalence.
     c) functional inconsistency.
     d) self-persuasion.
     Ans: a   LO: 7   Page: 236   Type: F

97. The findings of the classic Festinger and Carlsmith (1959) experiment indicate that
     a) participants paid $20 to lie about how fun a boring task was come to believe they actually enjoyed the task more than participants paid $1 to lie.
     b) participants in the $20 condition experience insufficient justification for lying, and therefore are more likely to exhibit attitude change.
     c) participants in the $1 condition experience greater discomfort and agitation when lying about how fun the task was than do participants in the $20 condition.
     d) participants are only willing to lie to a fellow student when they are compensated generously for doing so.
     Ans: c   LO: 7   Page: 236-237   Type: F

98. How do Festinger and Carlsmith (1959) determine the level of cognitive dissonance experienced by participants in their classic peg-turning study?
     a) By observing their performance on the peg-turning task.
     b) By assessing their attitudes regarding how fun the experimental peg-turning task was.
     c) By measuring their level of physiological arousal.
     d) By asking them if they would return the money they were paid for lying.
     Ans: b   LO: 7   Page: 236-237   Type: C

99. In an experiment some participants are asked to write a counter-attitudinal essay, but others are forced to write the essay. Based on cognitive dissonance theory, which of the following results should be expected?
    a) Participants asked to write the essay should change their attitudes, but only if they are paid very little money.
    b) Participants asked to write the essay should change their attitudes, but only if they are paid a large sum of money.
    c) Participants forced to write the essay should change their attitudes, but only if they are paid very little money.
    d) Participants forced to write the essay should change their attitudes, but only if they are paid a large sum of money.
    Ans: a   LO: 7   Page: 236-237   Type: C

100. Participants in an extremely boring experiment are asked to lie and say that the experiment was fun and exciting. Which of the following participants will exhibit the *most* favorable attitudes toward the experiment?
    a) Elaine, who consumes an entire bottle of Hennigans scotch immediately after telling the lie
    b) George, who attributes his discomfort to the bulky Gortex coat he was wearing when he lied
    c) Kramer, who is convinced that nobody believes him whether he tells the truth or lies
    d) Jerry, who thinks that his lie will lead other participants to expect the experiment will be fun
    Ans: d   LO: 7   Page: 236-237   Type: A

101. A social psychology graduate student who works long hours for little pay becomes increasingly convinced that she loves social psychology. This student's attitude toward her chosen field of study is *most* likely the result of
    a) psychological reactance.
    b) self-affirmation.
    c) insufficient justification.
    d) insufficient deterrence.
    Ans: c   LO: 7   Page: 237-238   Type: C

102. The phenomenon of insufficient justification does *not* support
    a) the notion that people strive for cognitive consistency.
    b) the assumption that larger rewards produce greater change.
    c) the self-perception interpretation of cognitive dissonance.
    d) the hypothesis that cognitive dissonance requires negative consequences.
    Ans: b   LO: 7   Page: 237-238   Type: C

103. Imagine that Festinger and Carlsmith (1959) ran a follow-up to their classic peg-turning study. In this new version, participants are either paid $10 to lie to the next participant (actually a confederate), or are given no choice and forced to lie by being told that failure to do so will result in a loss of any course credit that was to be earned for having participated in the study. The most likely results of this new experiment would be that participants who are given no choice and forced to lie (through the threat of no course credit) would _____ than participants in the $10 condition.
    a) experience less cognitive dissonance
    b) rate the experimental peg-turning task as more enjoyable
    c) demonstrate more physiological arousal after lying to the confederate
    d) be less likely to agree to lie to the confederate
    Ans: d   LO: 7   Page: 237-238   Type: A

104. A condition in which people refrain from engaging in a desirable activity, even though only mild punishment is threatened, is called
    a) self-monitoring.
    b) negative attitude change.
    c) insufficient justification.
    d) insufficient deterrence.
    Ans: d   LO: 7   Page: 238   Type: F

105. Research by Aronson and Carlsmith (1963) shows that severe punishment
    a) is less likely than mild punishment to inspire cognitive dissonance.
    b) leads to attitude change only when a self-affirmation is possible.
    c) causes dissonance-induced physiological arousal to increase.
    d) changes behavior only when attitudes change as well.
    Ans: a   LO: 7   Page: 238   Type: F

106. When she first joined the Army, Stephanie was not entirely sure she would like it, but was excited about the thought of traveling around the world. By the end of the grueling basic training program, she absolutely loved Army life and was totally committed to it, despite the fact that she had been stationed in New Jersey and never got to leave the country. Stephanie's attitude toward the army is *most* likely the result of
    a) self-monitoring.
    b) effort justification.
    c) insufficient deterrence.
    d) psychological reactance.
    Ans: b   LO: 7   Page: 238-239   Type: A

107. Sam hates Celine Dion with a passion. One day he meets Celine at a party. She tries to win him over by giving him her new CD. In which of the following scenarios would Sam's attitudes towards Celine be most likely to change after hearing the CD?
    a) She holds a gun to his head, forcing him to listen to it.
    b) She offers him a coupon for 10% off his next dry cleaning order in exchange for listening to it.
    c) He decides to read suggestive passages aloud from a romantic novel while listening to it.
    d) She tells him to suppress his negative thoughts about her while he listens to it.
    Ans: b   LO: 7   Page: 238-239   Type: A

108. Shawna wants to join a sorority. This sorority has recently decided to put incoming members through various forms of initiation. Based on the findings of Aronson and Mills (1959), which of the following types of initiations is most likely to lead Shawna to come to identify strongly with the sorority and to value her membership in the group in the effort to avoid cognitive dissonance?
    a) A mildly pleasant initiation
    b) A neutral initiation
    c) A mildly unpleasant initiation
    d) A severely unpleasant initiation
    Ans: d   LO: 7   Page: 238-239   Type: A

109. In deciding where to go to college, Sophie was torn but finally picked Faber College over State University. Which of the following facts would be *least* likely to lead her to experience post-decision dissonance?
    a) State has a good football team and a cool mascot; Faber has not won a game in three seasons and its mascot is an 18th century French explorer.
    b) State is less expensive than Faber.
    c) All of the Faber professors she looks up on www.ratemyprofessor.com have lousy teaching ratings.
    d) She overhears her college counselor referring to State as a "safety school."
    Ans: d   LO: 7   Page: 239   Type: A

110. Which of the following situations should prompt the *least* decisional dissonance?
    a) Though he would rather be playing football with his friends, Wyatt decides to start his 20-page philosophy paper rather than his 25-page history paper.
    b) Elmer likes both duck and rabbit, but he decides to order the rabbit for dinner.
    c) Audrey doesn't like cats much, so she decides that her new pet will be a dog.
    d) Tevin would like to spend his vacation in both Italy and Greece, but can only afford to travel to one place, so he decides to go to Greece.
    Ans: c   LO: 7   Page: 239   Type: C

111. Marcia has two boyfriends, Davie and Mickey, both of whom she likes very much. She has decided that dating both of them is making her life too complicated and, after careful deliberation, has decided to stop seeing Davie and continue dating only Mickey. According to cognitive dissonance theory, which of the following should happen next?
    a)   Marcia will develop an intense dislike for Mickey.
    b)   Davie will seem more attractive than ever, making Marcia regret her decision.
    c)   Mickey will seem more attractive than ever, convincing Marcia that she made the right choice.
    d)   Marcia, Davie, and Mickey will appear on the Jerry Springer Show.
    Ans: c   LO: 7   Page: 239   Type: A

112. Trista had to choose between two potential mates, Charlie and Ryan, on the final episode of the original *The Bachelorette*. In the end, she chose Ryan. Several weeks later, a reporter interviewed Trista about her feelings towards the two men. Which of the following predictions regarding her feelings at the time of the interview would be most likely if she is trying to avoid post-decision dissonance?
    a)   Trista says that her attitudes about both men have become more negative with the benefit of hindsight.
    b)   Trista suggests that she was impressed by his career ambitions at first, but has come to realize that Charlie's busy work schedule would have been an obstacle to a successful relationship.
    c)   Trista has come to notice a variety of "little things" about Ryan that are starting to annoy her, including his penchant for writing really lousy poetry.
    d)   Trista reports that she believes Charlie to be one of the most attractive men she has ever met in person.
    Ans: b   LO: 7   Page: 239   Type: A

113. Abby compliments Sharon on her new outfit, despite thinking it is not flattering at all. According to the "new look" at dissonance theory,
    a)   Abby must feel physiological arousal after her lie in order to feel cognitive dissonance.
    b)   Abby will feel dissonance because she felt her only choice was to flatter Sharon when Sharon asked her "How do I look?"
    c)   Abby will not feel dissonance because Sharon's outfit is not personally important to Abby.
    d)   Abby will come to believe that Sharon's outfit is flattering in the same way that an observer might infer Abby's attitude from her behavior.
    Ans: a   LO: 8   Page: 239-241   Type: A

114. All of the following are necessary conditions for cognitive dissonance specified by Cooper and Fazio (1984) *except*
    a)   people must freely choose to engage in the attitude-discrepant behavior.
    b)   people must assign responsibility for the behavior to an outside source.
    c)   people must experience physiological arousal as a result of their behavior.
    d)   people must attribute their arousal to the attitude-discrepant behavior.
    Ans: b   LO: 8   Page: 239-241   Type: F

115. According to research by Balcetis and Dunning (2007) in which participants were asked to walk across a college campus wearing an embarrassing costume, which of the following is true?
    a)   students in the high-choice condition underestimated how far they had walked relative to those in the low-choice condition.
    b)   students in the low-choice condition underestimated how far they had walked relative to those in the high-choice condition.
    c)   students with insufficient justification for their embarrassing actions overestimated how far they had walked relative to those with sufficient justification.
    d)   the motivation to reduce dissonance had no .effect on participants' visual representations of the natural environment.
    Ans: a   LO: 8   Page: 240   Type: F

116. The idea that we infer our own attitudes by coolly observing ourselves and the circumstances of our behavior is *most* consistent with
    a)   planned behavior theory.
    b)   self-perception theory.
    c)   cognitive dissonance theory.
    d)   elaboration-likelihood theory.
    Ans: b   LO: 9   Page: 242-243   Type: C

117. Those who argue that self-perception theory better explains why people change their attitudes in research studies than does cognitive dissonance theory do *not* believe that
    a)   changes in attitudes are motivated by a desire to reduce unpleasant feelings.
    b)   private attitudes truly change in these experiments.
    c)   the changed attitude must be directly related to the attitude-discrepant behavior.
    d)   observers are fairly accurate in predicting others' attitudes.
    Ans: a   LO: 9   Page: 242-243   Type: C

118. Marge believes rather strongly that more money should be devoted to environmental concerns. However, she is agitated because she just signed a petition for a friend advocating the logging of a local forest in order to create new jobs. She then seems to soften her stance about the environment. This is *best* explained by
    a)   cognitive dissonance theory.
    b)   self-affirmation theory.
    c)   the inoculation hypothesis.
    d)   self-perception theory.
    Ans: a   LO: 9   Page: 242-243   Type: A

119. A major difference between cognitive dissonance theory and self-perception theory involves the extent to which _____ is necessary in order to lead to self-persuasion and attitude change.
    a)   normative social influence
    b)   physiological arousal
    c)   self-affirmation
    d)   an implicit attitude
    Ans: b   LO: 9   Page: 242-243   Type: C

120. The basic prediction of_____ theory is that attitude change occurs when people infer how they feel by observing their own behavior.
    a)   cognitive dissonance
    b)   the "new look" at cognitive dissonance
    c)   self-perception
    d)   elaboration likelihood
    Ans: c   LO: 9   Page: 242-243   Type: C

121. Impression management theory suggests that people change their attitudes to match their behaviors in an effort to
    a)   be consistent.
    b)   appear consistent.
    c)   reduce physiological arousal.
    d)   restore a positive self-image.
    Ans: b   LO: 9   Page: 243   Type: C

122. Elena changes her attitude about nuclear weapons after giving a speech supporting their development to a group of classmates. Brett gives the same speech, but to an empty classroom, and does not change his attitude. The difference between Elena and Brett supports
    a)   cognitive dissonance theory.
    b)   impression management theory.
    c)   self-perception theory.
    d)   self-affirmation theory.
    Ans: b   LO: 9   Page: 243   Type: A

123. After giving the matter a great deal of thought, Iris declared chemistry rather than physics as her major. Having made this decision, she went out and had a good time with her classmates, who reminded her what a great friend she was. At that point, Iris was able to look at her choice and see both its pros and cons without glamorizing it. Her behavior can *best* be explained by the concept of
   a) self-perception.
   b) cognitive dissonance.
   c) impression management.
   d) self-affirmation.
   Ans: d   LO: 9   Page: 243-245   Type: A

124. After narrowing their choices to a Toyota and a Honda, Tammy Faye and James have decided to buy a Toyota. It is likely that after making this decision, Tammy Faye and James will
   a) soon begin to question whether they should have bought the Honda instead of the Toyota.
   b) feel less dissonance about their decision if they are told by friends that they have decorated their house nicely.
   c) tell friends looking for a new car both the pros and cons of buying a Toyota.
   d) feel more dissonance than they felt before making the decision.
   Ans: b   LO: 9   Page: 243-245   Type: A

125. Cross-cultural research indicates that cognitive dissonance
   a) exists in similar situations and manifests itself the same way in collectivist and individualistic societies.
   b) does not exist in collectivist societies.
   c) can be seen across cultures, but emerges in different situations in different cultures.
   d) is more common among women in individualistic cultures, but among men in collectivist cultures.
   Ans: c   LO: 8   Page: 245   Type: C

ESSAY

126. According to the theory of reasoned action and the theory of planned behavior, how do attitudes influence behavior and what limits their impact?
   Ans: According to these theories, the influence of attitudes on behavior results from deliberate decision making. However, this influence is limited by (1) the specificity of the attitude (the more specific the attitude is regarding a specific behavior, the more influential it is), (2) subjective norms, (3) perceived control (individuals believe they have the capability to engage in the behavior), and (4) intentions (intentions do not always result in behavior).   Page: 210-212

127. Identify and explain the process whereby the source of a message gradually loses its impact over time.
   Ans: This process, known as the sleeper effect, occurs when the source of a message gradually loses its impact over time. Initially, people are more readily persuaded by credible sources than by noncredible sources, but over time they seem to lose the connection between the source and the message, becoming equally persuaded by both types of sources. The sleeper effect tends to occur only when the source of the message is introduced after the message itself and explains why a low-credibility source (e.g., the National Enquirer) *can be just as persuasive as a high-credibility source (e.g.,* the New York Times) *in the long-run. Page: 222-224*

128. Explain how both the cognitive content and emotional content of a message affect its persuasiveness. Be sure to discuss the relationship of both types of content to the central and peripheral routes to persuasion.
   Ans: The cognitive content of a message has its greatest impact when the message is processed through the central route to persuasion. Owing to the elaboration of the cognitive content through this route, the message is more persuasive if it is of high quality and two-sided, and less persuasive if it is of poor quality or one-sided. Conversely, the emotional content of a message has its greatest impact when the message is processed through the peripheral route to persuasion. In the latter case, heuristics and attributions affect the persuasiveness of the message. Both heuristics (rules of thumb) and attributions (quick analyses of the speaker's motives) avoid the content of the message, in favor of more superficial cues.   Page: 224-228

129. Describe the phenomenon of insufficient justification, and explain its relationship to cognitive dissonance.

    Ans: Insufficient justification occurs when people cannot find a good enough reason to explain their behavior. Often this results in attitude change in the effort to eliminate the unpleasant arousal caused by the behavior. The relationship between insufficient justification and cognitive dissonance is made clear by the 1959 study of Festinger and Carlsmith. In this study, subjects who had been paid only $1 for their participation in an unpleasant task (and thus received insufficient justification for doing so) were more inclined to exaggerate their enjoyment of the task (thereby reducing their cognitive dissonance) than were subjects who had been paid $20. The $1 was insufficient justification to account for why the participants had lied to someone else about how fun the task was, so participants adjusted their attitudes about the task accordingly in order to alleviate the cognitive dissonance. The $20 participants had sufficient justification for their behavior, and therefore no attitude change was necessary.   Page: 236-239

130. Discuss three alternatives to cognitive dissonance theory.

    Ans: Whereas cognitive dissonance theory posits a state of psychological tension that people are motivated to reduce by bringing their attitudes more in line with their behaviors, (1) self-perception theory suggests that people interpret their attitudes by observing their behaviors and that physiological arousal is not necessary for self-persuasion to occur, (2) impression-management theory maintains that what matters is not the consistency between attitudes and behaviors but the appearance of such consistency, and (3) self-affirmation theory proposes that attitude change is spurred by threats to the self-concept.   Page: 242-245

CHAPTER 7

Conformity

MULTIPLE CHOICE

1. Which of the following is *not* an example of social influence?
   a) A sports fan who decides to join the other members of the stadium crowd in doing the wave
   b) A student who hears that some of his fellow classmates may have been exposed to a noxious gas and immediately comes to feel a bit nauseated himself
   c) A model who catches a glimpse of herself wearing a swimsuit in a mirror and suddenly becomes self-conscious about the way she looks
   d) A guest at a dinner party who does not understand a joke told by the host, but laughs anyway because everyone else is laughing
   Ans: c   LO: 1   Page: 252-254   Type: A

2. The ways in which people are affected by the real or imagined presence of others is called
   a) social influence.
   b) psychological reactance.
   c) pluralistic ignorance.
   d) the autokinetic effect.
   Ans: a   LO: 1   Page: 252-254   Type: F

3. Which of the following *best* exemplifies automatic influence?
   a) People are more likely to purchase a product if they have been given a free sample.
   b) In trying to guess how much a point of light moves in a dark room, people use the estimates of others as an anchor.
   c) Beginning shortly after birth, infants often mimic simple gestures such as sticking out the tongue or moving the head .
   d) Adolescents often go along with the behavior of popular others to avoid social rejection.
   Ans: c   LO: 1   Page: 252-254   Type: C

4. The tendency to unconsciously mimic the nonverbal behavior of others is called
   a) reciprocation wariness.
   b) pluralistic ignorance.
   c) the ally effect.
   d) the chameleon effect.
   Ans: d   LO: 1   Page: 253-254   Type: F

5. Chartrand and Bargh (1999) had experimental accomplices mimic the mannerisms of some participants but not others. They found
   a) participants whose mannerisms were mimicked liked the accomplice more than participants who were not copied.
   b) participants whose mannerisms were copied by an accomplice reported being more uncomfortable during the interaction than those who were not mimicked.
   c) imitating the mannerisms of the participants tended to reduce the nonverbal behaviors exhibited during the interaction.
   d) participants who were not mimicked by their interaction partners indicated a greater willingness to interact with that person again in the future.
   Ans: a   LO: 1   Page: 253-254   Type: F

6.   As he spoke at the beginning of the faculty meeting, Klaus clasped his hands behind his head and reclined
      in his chair. Within minutes, three other faculty members were sitting in the same manner, demonstrating
      the psychological tendency referred to as
      a)   psychological reactance.
      b)   the chameleon effect.
      c)   low-balling.
      d)   idiosyncrasy credits.
      Ans: b   LO: 1   Page: 253-254   Type: A

7.   Frank gets a bit anxious in social situations and tends to scratch his nose when he speaks. Toward which of
      the following people is he *most* likely to feel positively?
      a)   Felicia, who mimics Frank's behavior and scratches her nose while they speak
      b)   Fletcher, who stares quizzically at Frank every time he scratches his nose
      c)   Florence, who averts her gaze and stares at the floor every time Frank scratches his nose
      d)   Faisal, who appears quite at ease with Frank's behavior and reaches out several times to scratch
            Frank's nose for him
      Ans: a   LO: 1   Page: 253-254   Type: A

8.   Which of the following has *not* been demonstrated by research on mimicry?
      a)   Within a few days of birth, infants mimic the facial expressions of adults.
      b)   Various species of non-human animals demonstrate rudimentary forms of mimicry.
      c)   People often mimic the facial expressions of others, but never mimic their overt behaviors.
      d)   People sometimes mimic facial expressions of which they are not even consciously aware.
      Ans: c   LO: 1   Page: 253-254   Type: C

9.   According to research by Emily Pronin and others (2007), which of the following explains why people
      perceive others to be more conforming than themselves?
      a)   People are poor judges of others' motivations.
      b)   People tend to judge others by their overt behavior while judging themselves by focusing inward.
      c)   People judge themselves in the same way that that they judge others.
      d)   People judge others by asking them about their inner thought processes.
      Ans: b   LO: 2   Page: 255   Type: F

10.   In comparison to obedience and compliance, conformity
      a)   involves less direct pressure from others.
      b)   occurs only in response to the behavior of a group of others.
      c)   requires the physical presence of at least one other person.
      d)   is more likely to produce destructive behaviors.
      Ans: a   LO: 2   Page: 254-255   Type: C

11.   A half dozen high school students are going to a concert. Chantal wants to wear a new colorful outfit that
      she just received as a gift, but she assumes that her five friends will all be wearing nothing but black leather.
      Chantal decides to do likewise, and leaves her colorful outfit in the closet. Chantal's behavior is an example
      of
      a)   reciprocation wariness.
      b)   idiosyncrasy credits.
      c)   resistance.
      d)   conformity.
      Ans: d   LO: 2   Page: 254-255   Type: A

12.   The tendency to alter thoughts, feelings, and behavior in ways that are consistent with group norms is called
      a)   psychological reactance.
      b)   compliance.
      c)   obedience.
      d)   conformity.
      Ans: d   LO: 2   Page: 254-255   Type: F

13. Everyone in the fast-food restaurant seemed to be leaving their leftovers on the table as opposed to throwing them away on their way out the door, so Jeff left his tray on the table as well. This is best described as an example of
    a) conformity.
    b) obedience.
    c) compliance.
    d) deindividuation.
    Ans: a   LO: 2   Page: 254-255   Type: A

14. Sherif (1936) asked groups of participants to estimate the distance moved by a point of light. He found that
    a) participants were more accurate when they were alone than when they were in groups.
    b) participants were more accurate in groups than when they were alone.
    c) as the study progressed, the participants' estimates began to converge with each other.
    d) as the study progressed, the participants' estimates began to diverge from each other.
    Ans: c   LO: 3   Page: 255-257   Type: C

15. You're out with friends when a talk show host walks up and asks if you'll answer a few trivia questions on camera. When he asks how many feet are in a mile, your first friend says 2,000 and your second friend says 3,000. You don't know the correct answer, so you say 2,500. Your response is similar to the judgments made by participants in which study?
    a) Langer et al. (1978)
    b) Sherif (1936)
    c) Asch (1951)
    d) Two of the above are correct
    Ans: b   LO: 3   Page: 255-257   Type: C

16. Sherif's (1936) research using the autokinetic effect demonstrated that
    a) people often look to others as a source of information.
    b) people are particularly concerned about social rejection.
    c) conformity is difficult to establish in the laboratory.
    d) only those with whom one has an existing relationship have the power to influence behavior.
    Ans: a   LO: 3   Page: 255-257   Type: C

17. Many participants in the social influence study conducted by _____ gave public responses that they privately knew to be inaccurate.
    a) Sherif
    b) Asch
    c) Milgram
    d) Zimbardo
    Ans: b   LO: 3   Page: 255-257   Type: C

18. The primary difference between the research of Sherif (1936) and Asch (1955) is that
    a) Sherif was able to demonstrate conformity whereas Asch was not.
    b) Asch was able to demonstrate conformity whereas Sherif was not.
    c) Sherif relied on an ambiguous task, whereas Asch used an unambiguous task.
    d) Asch relied on an ambiguous task, whereas Sherif used an unambiguous task.
    Ans: c   LO: 3   Page: 255-257   Type: C

19. Participants in Asch's line judgment study conformed approximately _____ of the time.
    a) 25%
    b) 37%
    c) 50%
    d) 100%
    Ans: b   LO: 3   Page: 255-257   Type: F

20. Which of the following statements regarding Asch's (1951) line similarity study is *false*?
     a) The results demonstrated that conformity is only likely in situations where the correct response is ambiguous.
     b) A follow-up study indicated that having an ally in the situation makes it easier for participants to resist conforming.
     c) Some participants failed to conform at any point during the study.
     d) A follow-up study suggested that conformity is less likely when participants can give their line judgments privately instead of out loud in front of the group.
     Ans: a   LO: 3   Page: 255-257   Type: F

21. Informational influence occurs primarily because people
     a) believe that others are correct in their judgments.
     b) fear the negative social consequences of appearing deviant.
     c) are motivated to appear consistent in their feelings and behaviors.
     d) respond to social norms automatically and without any thought.
     Ans: a   LO: 3   Page: 257-258   Type: F

22. Normative influence tends to occur primarily when people
     a) are uncertain regarding the correct answer to a question and therefore look to others for guidance.
     b) fear the negative social consequences of appearing deviant.
     c) are motivated to appear consistent in their feelings and behaviors.
     d) feel that their freedom to choose a particular course of action has been threatened.
     Ans: b   LO: 3   Page: 257-258   Type: F

23. The conformity seen in Sherif's (1936) study was *most* likely the result of
     a) normative influence.
     b) private conformity.
     c) public conformity.
     d) informational influence.
     Ans: d   LO: 3   Page: 257-258   Type: C

24. Imagine that some researchers conducted a study and interpreted the results of the study as indicative of normative influence. These researchers are *most* likely to reach this conclusion if participants in their study
     a) were truly convinced that the majority was correct in their opinions.
     b) behaved in the way that would be considered normal to people in Western cultures.
     c) did what they felt was morally right, even if it violated social norms in the process.
     d) conformed because they feared the social consequences of appearing deviant.
     Ans: d   LO: 3   Page: 257-258   Type: C

25. Because no one else seems concerned about the welfare of the man lying down on the sidewalk, Mo steps over him as well, figuring that he is simply drunk or asleep and not in need of emergency assistance. Mo's behavior is an example of
     a) informational social influence.
     b) normative social influence.
     c) compliance.
     d) obedience.
     Ans: a   LO: 3   Page: 257-258   Type: A

26. _____ is most likely to occur in an ambiguous situation where the correct response is unclear, as opposed to a straightforward situation with no ambiguity.
     a) Public conformity
     b) true acceptance
     c) Cognitive dissonance
     d) Superordinate identity
     Ans: b   LO: 3   Page: 259-260   Type: A

27.   Which of the following is the *best* example of normative influence?
       a)   When patients adhere rigidly to doctors' recommendations
       b)   When people estimate how far a stable dot has moved by referring to others' estimates
       c)   When people wear a particular type of shoe because it is considered fashionable even though it is
             uncomfortable
       d)   When military personnel follow a superior's orders that are morally questionable
       Ans: c   LO: 3   Page: 257-258   Type: A

28.   Joanie and Chachi have just started to attend church. Joanie pays attention to when the rest of the
       congregation sits and stands because she wants to be sure to stand and sit at the appropriate times. Chachi
       stands up and sits down when the rest of the congregation does because if he doesn't the elderly couple
       across the aisle scowl at him. Joanie has conformed because of _____, whereas Chachi has conformed
       because of _____.
       a)   normative influence; informational influence
       b)   informational influence; normative influence
       c)   compliance; obedience
       d)   obedience; compliance
       Ans: b   LO: 3   Page: 257-258   Type: A

29.   Arnold wears suits every day to his job at the bank, but when he is at home in the evening and on weekends,
       he spends most of his time naked because that is what he finds most comfortable. Arnold's daytime behavior
       illustrates
       a)   perceptual contrast.
       b)   private conformity.
       c)   conversion.
       d)   public conformity.
       Ans: d   LO: 3   Page: 259-260   Type: A

30.   Asch's line length judgment study demonstrates how vulnerable people are to
       a)   informational social influence.
       b)   normative social influence.
       c)   two-step compliance techniques.
       d)   obedience to authority.
       Ans: b   LO: 3   Page: 258-260   Type: C

31.   Though she initially attended the pro-choice rally because all her friends were going, Marion now firmly
       believes in a woman's right to choose when it comes to abortion. Marion's new beliefs illustrate
       a)   true acceptance.
       b)   public conformity.
       c)   reciprocation ideology.
       d)   reciprocation wariness.
       Ans: a   LO: 3   Page: 259-260   Type: A

32.   Participants in an experiment are asked to look at pictures of different infants and rate the attractiveness of
       each infant on a 10-point scale. The participants are tested in groups of three and indicate their ratings
       aloud. For almost all of the infants, the participants tend to give ratings similar to other group members. We
       can be *most* certain that their ratings represent private conformity rather than public conformity if
       a)   they exhibit much less conformity in the presence of the experimenter.
       b)   they give the same ratings alone as they do in the group.
       c)   their ratings result from their desire to fit in with the rest of the group members.
       d)   they are not especially motivated to be accurate in their judgments.
       Ans: b   LO: 3   Page: 259-260   Type: A

33.   Normative influence tends to produce _____, whereas informational influence leads to _____.
       a)   compliance; obedience
       b)   conversion; compliance
       c)   public conformity; private conformity
       d)   pluralistic ignorance; pluralistic knowledge
       Ans: c   LO: 3   Page: 257-260   Type: F

34.   We can conclude that participants in Sherif's study exhibited private conformity rather than public
       conformity because
       a)   when retested without their fellow group members, participants reverted to their original estimates.
       b)   they would report their group's normative estimate when asked to respond aloud, but not when asked
             to respond in writing.
       c)   they continued to use their group estimates when retested alone one year later.
       d)   the task was too easy for people to demonstrate public conformity.
       Ans: c   LO: 3   Page: 259-260   Type: C

35.   Laverne conforms because of informational influence and Shirley conforms because of normative influence.
       Laverne is more likely than Shirley to
       a)   internalize the conforming behavior.
       b)   exhibit superficial behavioral changes.
       c)   be rejected by her group.
       d)   conform publicly but not privately.
       Ans: a   LO: 3   Page: 257-260   Type: A

36.   Baron and others (1996) found that participants' levels of conformity depended on how motivated they were
       to do well. When offered a financial incentive
       a)   conformity went down when the task was difficult and up when the task was easy.
       b)   conformity went up in both conditions.
       c)   conformity went down in both conditions.
       d)   conformity went up when the task was difficult and down when the task was easy..
       Ans: d   LO: 3   Page: 260   Type: F

37.   The experience of being ostracized has been found to be
       a)   fleeting and relatively harmless.
       b)   more disturbing for women than for men.
       c)   similar in brain activation to the experience of physical pain.
       d)   likely to lead to gun use and other forms of violence.
       Ans: c   LO: 4   Page: 258   Type: F

38.   Research examining ostracism and the Internet has found that
       a)   lonely people spend more time on-line than non-lonely people.
       b)   spending time on-line often leads to increases in perceived loneliness.
       c)   unlike in-person interactions, being left out of a chat room conversation has little effect on people's
             self-esteem and emotional state.
       d)   None of these.
       Ans: d   LO: 4   Page: 258   Type: F

39.   The concepts of ostracism and conformity are related in that
       a)   failure to conform can lead to ostracism.
       b)   being ostracized typically reduces future conformity.
       c)   ostracism always comes before conformity.
       d)   when people do not conform, they typically tend to ostracize.
       Ans: a   LO: 4   Page: 258-259   Type: C

40.   In a study by Baron et al. (1996) in which groups of three participants were asked to act as eyewitnesses, the
       greatest level of conformity occurred when participants were motivated to be _____ and the task was quite
       _____.
       a)   accurate; easy
       b)   accurate; difficult
       c)   accepted by their partners; easy
       d)   accepted by their partners; difficult
       Ans: b   LO: 5   Page: 260   Type: F

41.   Conan participates in an experiment where he and three other participants are asked to judge the quality of a series of abstract paintings. Conan is *least* likely to exhibit informational influence if
    a)   each painting is shown for only a few seconds.
    b)   he is motivated to be very accurate in his judgments.
    c)   there are no objective criteria by which to make such judgments.
    d)   there is a clear and unambiguous response for each painting.
    Ans: d   LO: 5   Page: 259-260   Type: A

42.   Three witnesses observe a crime that takes place in a very short amount of time. Paris and Lindsay are both suspects. The first two witnesses indicate that it was Paris who committed the crime. The third witness is *most* likely to conform with the other two if
    a)   she stands to receive a reward if it turns out that Paris did commit the crime.
    b)   it is a very minor crime.
    c)   she is the first person to be asked to identify the culprit.
    d)   she is shown a videotape of the crime that happens to be available.
    Ans: a   LO: 5   Page: 259-260   Type: A

43.   Conformity levels do *not* continue to increase dramatically as the group size gets bigger and bigger because additions to the group are subject to
    a)   the law of diminishing returns.
    b)   low-balling.
    c)   the silence of norms.
    d)   perceptual contrast.
    Ans: a   LO: 5   Page: 261   Type: C

44.   According to the law of diminishing returns, the 9th person to offer public agreement with a group's position exerts _____ social influence on individual group members compared to the 3rd person to agree with the group position.
    a)   less
    b)   more
    c)   the same amount of
    d)   None of these; it depends on the nature of the issue being debated.
    Ans: a   LO: 5   Page: 261   Type: C

45.   Horatio is asked what main dish was served for lunch at the cafeteria yesterday. He knows that it was roast beef, but before responding, he observes six other students who say the main dish was pizza. Horatio is *most* likely to say the main dish was pizza if he hears the response from
    a)   the six other students in three pairs of two.
    b)   all the students at once.
    c)   the six students at six different times in six different places.
    d)   the six other students in two pairs of three.
    Ans: c   LO: 5   Page: 261   Type: A

46.   As group size increases, conformity will
    a)   increase.
    b)   decrease.
    c)   increase as long as each additional member of the group is perceived as an independent source of influence.
    d)   decrease as long as each additional member of the group is perceived as an independent source of influence.
    Ans: c   LO: 5   Page: 261   Type: C

47.   With respect to the impact of group size on conformity, Asch found
    a)   greater conformity with ten confederates than with five confederates.
    b)   that conformity increases as an exponential function of group size.
    c)   that one group of six confederates produced more conformity than two groups of three confederates.
    d)   negligible increases in conformity after three or four confederates.
    Ans: d   LO: 5   Page: 261   Type: F

48.   Reuben notices one group of eight people littering in the park. Rachel sees four different pairs of people littering in the park. Which of the following is *true*?
      a)   Reuben is more likely to conform to the behavior of the litterbugs than is Rachel.
      b)   Rachel is more likely to conform to the behavior of the litterbugs than is Reuben.
      c)   Reuben and Rachel are equally likely to conform to the behavior of the litterbugs.
      d)   Reuben is more likely to conform because of informational influence, but Rachel is more likely to conform because of normative influence.
      Ans: b   LO: 5   Page: 261   Type: A

49.   Prentice and Miller (1996) found that *most* college students overestimate how comfortable their peers are with alcohol on campus. This misperception is an example of
      a)   pluralistic ignorance.
      b)   psychological reactance.
      c)   mass psychogenic illness.
      d)   the chameleon effect.
      Ans: a   LO: 5   Page: 261-262   Type: C

50.   Research by Prentice and Miller (1996) found that college students are likely to have more positive attitudes toward drinking on campus and consume more alcohol if they
      a)   attend colleges that strictly forbid drinking on campus.
      b)   participate in workshops designed to increase their personal responsibility for drinking.
      c)   overestimate the favorability of their peers' attitudes toward drinking.
      d)   believe such attitudes and behavior are inconsistent with social norms.
      Ans: c   LO: 5   Page: 261-262   Type: C

51.   Pluralistic ignorance about alcohol use on college campuses is a good example of a psychological process affected by
      a)   compliance.
      b)   accurate perception of social norms.
      c)   diminishing marginal returns.
      d)   None of these.
      Ans: c   LO: 5   Page: 261-262   Type: C

52.   Cialdini et al. (1991) observed participants in a clean or cluttered parking garage and found that participants were *most* likely to litter when they observed a confederate
      a)   litter in the cluttered garage.
      b)   litter in the clean garage.
      c)   place trash in the proper receptacle in a cluttered garage.
      d)   place trash in the proper receptacle in a clean garage.
      Ans: a   LO: 5   Page: 261-262   Type: C

53.   Social norms are *most* likely to lead to conformity when they are
      a)   behavioral.
      b)   salient.
      c)   complex.
      d)   subtle.
      Ans: b   LO: 5   Page: 261-262   Type: C

54.   Stuart works for an energy company. He thinks the company's money should be invested in developing solar energy. However, in a meeting of his co-workers, it becomes evident to Stuart that his co-workers support the company's continued investment in fossil fuel, the typical source of energy for residents in their community. Which of the following would make Stuart *less* likely to conform to the opinion of his co-workers?
      a)   If the group decreases in size from fifteen to ten
      b)   If supporting continued investments is consistent with the norms of the company
      c)   If Joyce, one of his co-workers, voices her support for investing the company's money in developing nuclear energy
      d)   If Stuart is younger than his co-workers
      Ans: c   LO: 5   Page: 262   Type: A

55. Mary has just heard five friends say that Massachusetts is the largest state in New England, when she knows it is Maine. Rob, the next friend in line, says that New Hampshire is the largest state in New England. In this situation, Mary is now *less* likely to conform with the first five friends than if Rob had said that
    a)   Maine is the largest state.
    b)   Massachusetts is the largest state.
    c)   he isn't familiar with New England.
    d)   Vermont is the largest state.
    Ans: b   LO: 5   Page: 262   Type: A

56. The fact that the presence of an ally, regardless of her competence, reduces conformity indicates that
    a)   informational social influence typically wins out over normative social influence in the long run.
    b)   it is exceedingly difficult to hold out against the pressure to conform without one supporter in the group.
    c)   conformity does not occur for high-stakes decisions with important repercussions.
    d)   men conform less in private than they do in public.
    Ans: b   LO: 5   Page: 262   Type: C

57. The normative pressure to conform to a majority is *reduced* by
    a)   allies who are articulate and intelligent, but not by less persuasive allies.
    b)   only allies who are credible.
    c)   only same-sex allies.
    d)   any ally.
    Ans: d   LO: 5   Page: 262   Type: F

58. Lily is interested in conducting an experiment to demonstrate that there are some situations in which men are more likely to conform than women. Which of the following strategies should Lily adopt in designing her study?
    a)   She should have participants engage in a discussion about politics.
    b)   She should have participants engage in a discussion about fashion.
    c)   She should tell participants that they are being observed throughout the study.
    d)   She should tell participants that their primary goal in the study should be to appear attractive towards group members of the opposite sex.
    Ans: b   LO: 5   Page: 263   Type: A

59. Research has shown that a factor affecting whether men conform more than women, or vice versa, is
    a)   whether the individuals have earned idiosyncrasy credits.
    b)   whether the individuals think they are being observed.
    c)   whether the individuals are familiar with the topic being discussed.
    d)   Two of the above are correct
    Ans: b   LO: 5   Page: 263   Type: F

60. Which of the following concerning the relationship between gender and conformity is *true*?
    a)   Men exhibit greater conformity than women in face-to-face interactions.
    b)   Men exhibit greater conformity than women regardless of the situation.
    c)   Women exhibit greater conformity than men in face-to-face interactions.
    d)   Women exhibit greater conformity than men regardless of the situation.
    Ans: c   LO: 5   Page: 263   Type: C

61. Women conform more and men conform less when they believe they are being observed. Eagly (1987) argues that this occurs because
    a)   being watched makes people self-aware, which brings out their underlying personalities.
    b)   women are easier to manipulate, whereas men tend to be more independent.
    c)   women and men tend to be knowledgeable about different kinds of topics.
    d)   people feel greater pressure in public to behave in ways consistent with their gender-role.
    Ans: d   LO: 5   Page: 263   Type: C

62. Pat attends a pre-screening of a new romantic comedy with a group of four people and then participates in a focus group where the group is asked several questions about the film. The group is asked, "How funny is the film?" Each member of the group responds to the question. Pat responds last, after hearing the rest of the group say that the movie was very funny. Pat is more likely to agree with them if
    a) Pat is female.
    b) Pat is from an individualistic culture.
    c) Pat is elderly.
    d) Pat's group had seven people instead of four.
    Ans: a   LO: 5   Page: 263   Type: A

63. Often overlooked in Asch's conformity study is the fact that participants refused to conform _____ of the time.
    a) 25%
    b) 37%
    c) 63%
    d) 75%
    Ans: c   LO: 6   Page: 263-264   Type: F

64. According to Moscovici, majorities derive their power to influence others by virtue of their _____, whereas minorities derive their power to influence others from their _____.
    a) social connections; sheer number
    b) informational connections; social standing
    c) sheer number; style of behavior
    d) informational influence; normative influence
    Ans: c   LO: 6   Page: 263-264   Type: F

65. Professor Hildebrand just gave back to his students their first exam. Many in the class are convinced that one of the questions he asked had more than one correct answer. In fact, 13 students from the class show up to his office hours to protest the question. Professor Hildebrand is convinced that there is only one correct answer, and so he tries to convince the larger group of students that he is right. He will be most likely to convince this group of his point of view if he
    a) presents his arguments forcefully and consistently.
    b) tries to exert normative social influence on the group of students.
    c) presents himself as an outgroup member rather than as part of their ingroup.
    d) makes salient the norms of the group.
    Ans: a   LO: 6   Page: 264-265   Type: A

66. Keith is a member of a jury trying to decide whether the accused is guilty of the heinous murder for which she has been charged. All of the members of the jury wish to convict except Keith who believes she is innocent. Keith will have the *best* chance at having the others seriously consider his position if he
    a) appears confident in his view that she is innocent.
    b) only considers evidence that supports his point of view.
    c) stands up while presenting his view to the group.
    d) presents his view after all the other members have stated their views.
    Ans: a   LO: 6   Page: 264-265   Type: A

67. All of the following could explain why a consistent behavioral style increases minority influence *except*
    a) a consistent minority draws more attention to its position.
    b) a consistent minority puts increased pressure on the majority to compromise.
    c) the position advocated by a consistent minority is more likely to be perceived as valid.
    d) a consistent minority is more likely to exert normative social influence on the group.
    Ans: d   LO: 6   Page: 264-265   Type: C

68. The "minority slowness effect" refers to the finding that
    a) members of minority groups are often slow to change their minds during group discussion.
    b) it takes longer for minority group members to change the minds of majority group members than vice versa.
    c) people with minority opinions are slower to respond to questions about the topic than people with majority opinions.
    d) All of these.
    Ans: c   LO: 6   Page: 264   Type: F

69. Hiroko is usually very agreeable and goes along with his friends' plans. Tonight, however, he tells his friends that even though they all want to go out for Mexican food, he has a strong preference for Italian food. Even though he is the only person who initially votes for Italian, Hiroko's friends eventually come to agree with him because he usually does go along with the group. This best epitomizes which of the following phenomena associated with minority influence?
    a) Consensus attribution
    b) Idiosyncrasy credits
    c) Door-in-the-face technique
    d) Graduated and reciprocated initiative in tension-reduction (GRIT)
    Ans: b   LO: 6   Page: 264-265   Type: A

70. The residents on Northgate Road have convened to discuss whether their private road should be paved. The majority are in favor of having the road paved. However Nicholas, a long-time resident, expresses his opposition. Which of the following is *unlikely*?
    a) The residents will think more carefully about the issue of paving the road because Nicholas presented a dissenting opinion.
    b) Nicholas's status of being a long-time resident and its accompanying idiosyncrasy credits will help him influence the group.
    c) Nicholas will not gain private conformity to his opinion, only public conformity.
    d) Nicholas will be more influential if he repeatedly expresses his opposition as the group discusses the benefits of paving the road.
    Ans: c   LO: 6   Page: 264-265   Type: A

71. According to Hollander's (1958) work on idiosyncrasy credits, which of the following people would be *most* effective in convincing a majority to change their opinion?
    a) A person who has just joined the group, because such a person has no history of antagonism with any of the majority group members
    b) A person who does not belong to the group at all, because such a person would be perceived as the most objective
    c) A person who has been in the group for quite a while, but consistently disagrees with the group
    d) A person who has been in the group for a long time, and usually goes along with the majority of the group
    Ans: d   LO: 6   Page: 265   Type: C

72. The idea that minority influence works in the same way that majority influence does is *most* consistent with
    a) the interpersonal relations model.
    b) research comparing normative and informational influence.
    c) the single-process approach.
    d) research comparing private and public conformity.
    Ans: c   LO: 6   Page: 265-266   Type: C

73. According to the dual-process approach to understanding minority influence
    a) majority and minority influence occur for similar reasons and through similar psychological processes.
    b) group majorities and minorities exert their influence in very different ways.
    c) majority influence is likely to produce private conformity for ambiguous situations and public conformity for unambiguous situations.
    d) minority influence occurs through different psychological processes in collectivist versus individualistic cultures.
    Ans: b   LO: 6   Page: 265-266   Type: F

74. According to the dual-process approach, majorities exert influence by producing _____, whereas minorities
     exert influence by producing _____.
     a)   informational influence; normative influence
     b)   public conformity; private conformity
     c)   reactance; obedience
     d)   conversion; compliance
     Ans: b   LO: 6   Page: 265-266   Type: C

75. At a student council meeting, the officers representing the second-, third-, and fourth-year students all
     supported a particular policy concerning alcohol at parties. Only those officers representing the first-year
     students were opposed to this policy. According to the relevant research, the majority in this case would be
     most likely to influence the minority by producing
     a)   private conformity.
     b)   reciprocation wariness.
     c)   long-lasting conformity.
     d)   normative pressures.
     Ans: d   LO: 6   Page: 265-266   Type: A

76. At a campaign meeting, the majority of the staff argues that they should use negative ads to attack their
     opponent. Despite their strong feelings on this matter, Stefan argues successfully for positive ads.
     According to the dual-process approach, Stefan's influence has probably resulted in
     a)   defiance.
     b)   conversion.
     c)   public conformity.
     d)   collusion.
     Ans: b   LO: 6   Page: 265-266   Type: A

77. Research on majority and minority influence suggests all of the following *except*
     a)   majorities are more influential than minorities on subjective questions.
     b)   majorities exert normative influence, whereas minorities exert informational influence.
     c)   majorities are more influential than minorities on questions of fact.
     d)   majority influence is greater on public measures of conformity, whereas minority influence is greater
            on private measures of conformity.
     Ans: a   LO: 6   Page: 265-266   Type: C

78. According to work by Nemeth (1986), minority viewpoints
     a)   can dramatically impair the functioning of a group.
     b)   are valuable because they can improve the quality of the groups' decision making.
     c)   are likely to make members of the majority more close-minded and defensive.
     d)   can only effectively produce a change in the majority if supported by normative pressures.
     Ans: b   LO: 6   Page: 265-266   Type: C

79. Individualistic cultures tend to exhibit all of the following *except*
     a)   greater complexity.
     b)   greater affluence.
     c)   greater cultural diversity.
     d)   greater conformity.
     Ans: d   LO: 5   Page: 266-268   Type: F

80. According to work by Triandis (1995), collectivist cultures are characterized by a pattern of
     a)   low complexity, low affluence, and cultural homogeneity.
     b)   low complexity, high affluence, and cultural heterogeneity.
     c)   high complexity, low affluence, and cultural homogeneity.
     d)   high complexity, high affluence, and cultural heterogeneity.
     Ans: a   LO: 5   Page: 267   Type: F

81. Some researchers are planning to go around the world and put participants in a version of the Asch study in which they are asked to make judgments about the lengths of lines. Cross-cultural research suggests that the least amount of conformity should be observed in cultures
    a) characterized by financial independence and prosperity.
    b) where the majority of the people in positions of power are men.
    c) where the people live a simple life, as in an isolated farming community.
    d) with very little cultural diversity.
    Ans: a   LO: 5   Page: 266-268   Type: A

82. Individuals from Eastern cultures are more likely than those from Western cultures to
    a) have an independent orientation.
    b) conform to a public norm.
    c) disobey an authority.
    d) possess greater heterogeneity.
    Ans: b   LO: 5   Page: 266-268   Type: C

83. If American and Chinese children were placed in the same classroom, which of the following would probably be *true*?
    a) The American children would never demonstrate conformity, and the Chinese children would always conform.
    b) The American children would demonstrate less conformity than the Chinese children.
    c) The American children would demonstrate less private conformity, but more public conformity than the Chinese children.
    d) The two groups of children would conform to the same extent and degree.
    Ans: b   LO: 5   Page: 266-268   Type: A

84. Psychologists tend to refer to a culture that values the virtues of interdependence and social harmony as
    a) conformist.
    b) collectivist.
    c) communist.
    d) cooperative.
    Ans: b   LO: 5   Page: 266-268   Type: F

85. As compared to conformity, compliance occurs
    a) only after careful deliberation.
    b) in response to a direct request.
    c) publicly, but not privately.
    d) as a result of less direct pressure from others.
    Ans: b   LO: 7   Page: 268   Type: C

86. Research has found that when people are presented with a request accompanied by a reason that does *not* offer a real justification for the request, they often respond
    a) with skeptical reactance.
    b) by asking for a more complete explanation.
    c) with surprise followed by caution.
    d) by complying mindlessly.
    Ans: d   LO: 7   Page: 268-269   Type: F

87. Mara needs to borrow James's pen and is pondering how to ask him. She considers three options—asking for the pen outright without any reasoning, telling him that she needs the pen "to write something," or telling him that she needs it "to sign a letter." Which of the following is *true*?
    a) James is more likely to comply with the outright request than the "letter" plea.
    b) James is equally likely to comply with the "letter" plea and the outright request.
    c) James is less likely to comply with the "write something" plea than the outright request.
    d) James is equally likely to comply with the "letter" plea and the "write something" plea.
    Ans: d   LO: 7   Page: 269   Type: A

88. Delfina says to Polly, "I would appreciate it if you could give me a cracker because I am hungry." Which of the following alternative requests would *not* affect the likelihood that Polly will help Delfina?
    a) "I would appreciate it if you could give me a cracker."
    b) "I would appreciate it if you could give me a cracker, but any type of snack will do."
    c) "I would appreciate it if you could give me a cracker, because I need it."
    d) "I would appreciate it if you could give me a cracker, but please do not expect me to return the favor later."

    Ans: c   LO: 7   Page: 269   Type: A

89. The unspoken rule dictating that we should treat others as they have treated us is called the
    a) social impact theory.
    b) norm of reciprocity.
    c) dual-process approach.
    d) equity principle.

    Ans: b   LO: 8   Page: 269-270   Type: F

90. In order to convince people to buy lunch from their restaurant in the food court, employees at the Chinese restaurant gave out free samples of chicken teriyaki to everyone who walked by. The restaurant employees are hoping to take advantage of the
    a) door-in-the-face technique.
    b) that's-not-all technique.
    c) norm of reciprocity.
    d) chameleon effect.

    Ans: c   LO: 8   Page: 269-270   Type: A

91. People who are especially likely to exploit the norm of reciprocity for personal gain can be identified by questionnaires that measure their
    a) social impact.
    b) vulnerability.to informational influence.
    c) idiosyncrasy credits.
    d) reciprocation ideology.

    Ans: d   LO: 8   Page: 269-270   Type: F

92. Nomar is trying to get Trot to buy a set of encyclopedias. If Nomar wants to use the foot-in-the-door technique properly and successfully, he should be careful to make sure that
    a) Trot attributes his compliance with the first request to external reasons.
    b) the first request is more cumbersome than the second request.
    c) he gets someone else to make the second request.
    d) he minimizes the contrast between the first and second request.

    Ans: d   LO: 8   Page: 270-271   Type: A

93. The compliance technique in which compliance to a desired request is increased by first gaining compliance to a smaller, but related, request is called
    a) low-balling.
    b) the that's-not-all technique.
    c) the foot-in-the-door technique.
    d) the door-in-the-face technique.

    Ans: c   LO: 8   Page: 270-271   Type: F

94. The foot-in-the-door technique takes particular advantage of the
    a) desire to maintain consistent self-perceptions.
    b) norm of reciprocity.
    c) effect of mindlessness.
    d) perceived contrast between small and large requests.

    Ans: a   LO: 8   Page: 270-271   Type: C

95. As he was about to enter the mall, Evan was approached by someone and asked to wear a small green ribbon on his shirt to show his support for the "Save the Squirrels" campaign. Evan wasn't quite sure that squirrels were actually endangered, but he agreed to wear the ribbon. A week later, Evan was approached again and asked to contribute $10 to help save the squirrels. Though he would have rather spent his money elsewhere, he agreed. Evan has been the victim of
    a) low-balling.
    b) the foot-in-the-door technique.
    c) the door-in-the-face technique.
    d) the that's-not-all technique.
    Ans: b   LO: 8   Page: 270-271   Type: A

96. The technique of getting a commitment from a potential customer and then changing the terms of the agreement is *best* described as
    a) reciprocal concession.
    b) cognitive dissonance.
    c) the foot-in-the-door technique.
    d) low-balling.
    Ans: d   LO: 8   Page: 272   Type: F

97. One important similarity between the foot-in-the-door technique and the door-in-the-face technique is that they both
    a) require a substantial delay between the two requests.
    b) take advantage of people's desire to avoid cognitive dissonance.
    c) work best between people who already know each other well.
    d) only work when used in a building with doors.
    Ans: b   LO: 8   Page: 270-273   Type: C

98. Imogene calls potential research participants and asks if they would be willing to participate in her psychology experiment. Once they have agreed to participate, she informs them that the experiment is at 7:00 in the morning on a Saturday. Though most participants are not happy to hear this information, almost all of them do show up for the experiment. Imogene has taken advantage of
    a) low-balling.
    b) the foot-in-the-door technique.
    c) the door-in-the-face technique.
    d) psychological reactance.
    Ans: a   LO: 8   Page: 272   Type: A

99. Jamie wants an extra day to write a paper for class. Jamie first asks the professor for a one-week extension for the paper assignment. The professor refuses. Jamie then asks for a one-day extension. The professor agrees. Jamie's behavior *best* illustrates
    a) the door-in-the-face technique.
    b) the foot-in-the-door technique.
    c) reactance.
    d) the dual-process approach.
    Ans: a   LO: 8   Page: 272-273   Type: A

100. All of the following can help to explain why the door-in-the-face technique can increase compliance *except*
    a) feelings of guilt.
    b) psychological commitment.
    c) perceptual contrast.
    d) reciprocal concessions.
    Ans: b   LO: 8   Page: 272-273   Type: F

101. The _____ technique often elicits compliance even though the recipient of the request knows she is being misled, and often resents the person making the request as a result.
    a) that's-not-all
    b) door-in-the-face
    c) low-balling
    d) foot-in-the door
    Ans: a   LO: 8   Page: 273-274   Type: C

102. Natasha convinces Joel to take her to the airport by first asking him to loan her his car for a week. Her attempt to get Joel to do her a favor is *most* likely based on the principles of
      a)   commitment and reciprocity.
      b)   perceptual contrast and self-perception.
      c)   reciprocal concessions and perceptual contrast.
      d)   self-perception and commitment.
      Ans: c   LO: 8   Page: 273   Type: A

103. When trying to close a car sale, Jerry often tries to sweeten the deal by telling the customer that he will throw in 6 free oil changes as well. This sales technique is best described as
      a)   low-balling.
      b)   the that's-not-all technique.
      c)   the foot-in-the-door technique.
      d)   the door-in-the-face technique.
      Ans: b   LO: 8   Page: 273-274   Type: A

104. Resistance to the requests of others can be encouraged by all of the following *except*
      a)   mindfulness.
      b)   reciprocal wariness.
      c)   following the norm of reciprocity.
      d)   knowledge that the other person is trying to get you to comply.
      Ans: c   LO: 8   Page: 274-275   Type: C

105. Milgram's research on obedience
      a)   has stirred controversy regarding its ethics.
      b)   revealed that far fewer people would deliver maximum shocks than was predicted by psychiatrists.
      c)   was conducted to better understand the war in Vietnam.
      d)   had disturbed individuals serve as participants.
      Ans: a   LO: 9   Page: 276-278   Type: F

106. Which of the following was *not* part of the procedure in Milgram's research on destructive obedience?
      a)   Participants were ordered to administer electric shocks that were apparently so intense that it caused the learner to scream in pain.
      b)   Participants playing the role of teachers were ordered to increase the electric shocks in increments of 15 volts for every wrong answer the learner gave.
      c)   Participants playing the role of learners were ordered to give shocks to the teacher who was trying to complete the task.
      d)   The experimenter told participants who wanted to leave that they had no choice but to continue with the study.
      Ans: c   LO: 9   Page: 276-278   Type: F

107. What percentage of the participants in Milgram's study of destructive obedience demonstrated complete obedience to the experimenter?
      a)   10%
      b)   35%
      c)   65%
      d)   90%
      Ans: c   LO: 9   Page: 278   Type: F

108. One factor that did *not* seem related to the amount of obedience exhibited in the Milgram obedience study was the
      a)   participant's sex.
      b)   proximity of the learner to the teacher.
      c)   location of the study.
      d)   physical presence of the experimenter.
      Ans: a   LO: 9   Page: 278-279   Type: F

109. When Cheryl is with her supervisors, she obeys their decisions without question. But when she is with employees under her supervision, she is aggressive and demanding. Cheryl is likely to be described by social psychologists as having
    a)   idiosyncrasy credits.
    b)   an introverted character.
    c)   reciprocation wariness.
    d)   an authoritarian personality.
    Ans: d   LO: 9   Page: 279   Type: A

110. The questionnaire measure used to assess an individual's authoritarian personality is referred to as the
    a)   A-scale.
    b)   F-scale.
    c)   Asch-scale.
    d)   Milgram-scale.
    Ans: b   LO: 9   Page: 279   Type: F

111. The Milgram study demonstrated
    a)   the specific personality traits that predict destructive obedience to authority.
    b)   that people will typically harm another individual with little to no social pressure to do so.
    c)   obedience to authority is most destructive when the authority figure is particularly harsh and demanding.
    d)   the potential for situational influences to lead ordinary people to commit extraordinarily destructive acts.
    Ans: d   LO: 9   Page: 279   Type: C

112. Who of the following is *most* likely to obey in Milgram's study?
    a)   A man participating in a run-down office building with an experimenter in a lab coat
    b)   A man who has to physically place the learner's hand down on a shock plate
    c)   A woman participating at Yale University with an experimenter in a lab coat
    d)   A man participating at Yale University with an experimenter dressed casually
    Ans: c   LO: 9   Page: 279-280   Type: C

113. All of the following reduced the level of obedience in the Milgram experiment *except*
    a)   lowering the prestige of the institution where the experiment was conducted.
    b)   having the experimenter in a different location.
    c)   informing the participants that the experimenter assumed responsibility for the learner's welfare.
    d)   having the learner be in the same room as the participant.
    Ans: c   LO: 9   Page: 279-281   Type: F

114. Those participants in Milgram's study who went to the very end of the shock meter were
    a)   diagnosed as abnormal by a team of psychiatrists.
    b)   in the minority among participants in the study.
    c)   not told that the learner had a previous heart condition.
    d)   None of these.
    Ans: d   LO: 9   Page: 279-281   Type: F

115. Which of the following is *true* of Milgram's obedience study?
    a)   When participants were required to manually force the victim's hand onto a shock plate, obedience completely disappeared.
    b)   The experimenter informed participants that he took complete responsibility for any consequences of the participant's actions.
    c)   Participants obeyed to the same extent whether the experimenter gave directions in person or over the telephone.
    d)   The percentage of participants who obeyed to the end was the same as the percentage of participants who conformed in the Asch study.
    Ans: b   LO: 9   Page: 280-281   Type: F

116. The original Milgram obedience study
    a)   demonstrates the personality characteristics associated with obedience to authority.
    b)   has been followed up by a number of additional studies that have varied specific aspects of the research situation.
    c)   confirms that conformity results from both informational and normative social pressures.
    d)   randomly assigned participants to one of two experimental conditions.
    Ans: b   LO: 9   Page: 281-283   Type: F

117. Though this was certainly not Milgram's intent,
    a)   many theorists use the results of his studies to try to explain the behavior of Nazi guards and others during the Holocaust.
    b)   some scholars suggest that his findings indicate that *anyone* is capable of destructive obedience if placed in the right situation.
    c)   raising people's awareness of the explanations for someone else's wrongdoing also tends to render people more forgiving of this wrongdoing.
    d)   subsequent researchers have extended his findings to other cultures and time periods.
    Ans: c   LO: 10   Page: 282-283   Type: C

118. Recent research, in which Burger (2009) conducted a partial replication of Milgram's study
    a)   suggests that people would be less likely to obey in the Milgram paradigm in the present day.
    b)   fails to replicate Milgram's findings regarding the importance of the experimenter's presence.
    c)   revealed that, like in Milgram's study, 70 percent of participants continued past 150 volts.
    d)   cannot be compared to the Milgram study because the task was not distasteful.
    Ans: c   LO: 11   Page: 282-283   Type: C

119. Twenge's 2006 book *Generation of Me* argues that Burger's findings are all of the following *except*?
    a)   statistically comparable to the increase in U.S. obesity rates during this same time period.
    b)   demonstrative of a significant decline in rates of obedience since Milgram's original study.
    c)   actually more significant than Burger concluded.
    d)   actually less significant than Burger concluded.
    Ans: d   LO: 11   Page: 283   Type: C

120. Research regarding group size and obedience suggests that
    a)   disobedience to authority is much more likely in the presence of other allies who will also disagree.
    b)   the presence of an ally has very different results for obedience than it does for conformity.
    c)   participants in the Milgram studies would have been even more likely to obey had there been another participant seated at the shock panel with them.
    d)   the presence of a group of people is a guaranteed safeguard against destructive obedience.
    Ans: a   LO: 11   Page: 283-284   Type: C

121. According to social impact theory, the source's proximity in time and space determines its
    a)   strength.
    b)   immediacy.
    c)   number.
    d)   popularity.
    Ans: b   LO: 12   Page: 285-287   Type: F

122. Which of the following would *not* be predicted by social impact theory?
    a)   A person is more likely to obey a nearby authority than one who is far away.
    b)   Each person in a group of ten contributes less money to a tip for their waitperson than each person in a group of three.
    c)   A teacher can exert more control over a large class than a small class.
    d)   Patients are more likely to follow advice given by doctors than advice given by nurses.
    Ans: c   LO: 12   Page: 285-287   Type: C

123 Recent approaches to social impact theory suggest that
   a)   the effect of immediacy does not necessitate physical proximity.
   b)   it is more relevant to understanding conformity than to understanding obedience.
   c)   source strength is less important than the number of sources.
   d)   the strength of a source depends more on prestige than intelligence.
Ans: a   LO: 12   Page: 285-287   Type: C

124. Stan is a new student in his sixth-grade class. The other students exert normative pressure on him to conform to their opinion on some issue. According to social impact theory, Stan will be more likely to *resist* this influence if
   a)   there are twenty rather than eleven students in the class.
   b)   he perceives the other students as having high status.
   c)   there are three other new students in the class who are receiving the same pressures.
   d)   he comes from a culture that values a collectivist orientation.
Ans: c   LO: 12   Page: 285-287   Type: A

125. According to social impact theory, resistance to social pressure is most likely to occur when social impact is
   _____
   a)   divided among many strong and distant targets.
   b)   divided among many weak and immediate targets.
   c)   consolidated within one distant target.
   d)   consolidated within one immediate target.
Ans: a   LO: 12   Page: 285-287   Type: C

ESSAY

126. Compare and contrast normative influence and informational social influence. Which of these types of social influence played a bigger role in Sherif's study (in which participants estimated how far a dot of light appeared to move)? And which played a bigger role in Asch's study (in which participants made judgments involving the lengths of lines)? Explain your answers.
   Ans: Normative social influence leads people to conform out of fear of the negative consequences of appearing deviant. Indeed, to avoid standing out from the rest of the group and risking embarrassment, individuals will often conform to the majority even if they think the majority is wrong. Alternatively, informational social influence leads people to conform when they believe others are correct in their judgments. In this case, they conform to the majority because they assume that the relatively large number of people holding a particular opinion or behaving in a particular way suggests that these people are correct. The primary influence found in Sherif's study was informational because the situation was rather ambiguous for the participants. They could not be sure how far the dot of light really moved, so they looked to the other participants to provide information about the correct answers. Even when participants in Sherif's study were later asked to make the same judgments alone (where there would be little pressure against deviating from a group norm), they continued to make judgments consistent with the group norm; this suggests that the participants conformed to the group norm because of the information provided earlier. In Asch's study, however, normative influence played the bigger role. Here, the situation was not ambiguous; the correct answers were obvious to the participants. Not needing the other people in the group to provide them with answers that they already knew, the participants were not particularly vulnerable to informational influence. Rather, Asch's participants were concerned about deviating from the opinions expressed by a unanimous majority. Indeed, when these participants were asked to write down their answers privately, their levels of conformity dropped sharply.   Page: 255-257

127. A council meeting has produced heated debate about an issue. Most of the members of the council hold one opinion, but a few hold another. During a break in the meeting, the members of the council who have the minority opinion call you for advice as to the best way to influence the majority of the council. Based on social psychological research, particularly concerning the dual-process approach, what should you advise them to do?
   Ans: According to the dual-process approach, minorities and majorities exert influence in different ways. You should advise the council members to take advantage of factors that enhance minority influence rather than trying to manipulate factors that enhance majority influence. One such factor is style of behavior. The research of Moscovici and others has suggested that consistency is very important for a group minority.

That is, the people in the minority should be forceful, persistent, and unwavering in support of their view, while appearing to be open-minded and flexible. Hollander recommends a different approach, however. Hollander argues that those in the minority should first conform to the majority opinions in order to establish themselves as competent insiders, and only then dissent from the majority. Thus, you should advise the council members that they initially show their support for the majority's opinion and then suggest their own opinion, and further, that they present their arguments for this latter position in a forceful, persistent, and unwavering style. In addition, the council members should also call for an anonymous, private vote on the issue, as minorities exert stronger influence on private measures of conformity than on public measures. Page: 265-266

128. Describe the door-in-the-face technique, and explain why this is an effective compliance strategy. What evidence is there to support your explanation of why this technique is effective?
Ans: The door-in-the-face technique is a two-step technique. It begins with a ridiculous request, which, once denied by the target, is followed up with a more reasonable request. This strategy is effective because it draws on the norm of reciprocity (i.e., the reduction leads the target to reciprocate and accede to the second request) and on perceptual contrast (i.e., the second request does not look so arduous as compared with the first one). In one study, college students were more likely to agree to escort a group of juvenile delinquents on a one-day trip to the zoo if they had been first asked to volunteer time over many weeks to work with these children.   Page: 272-273

129. Specific variables concerning the victim in Milgram's research on destructive obedience affected participants' levels of obedience. Identify one such variable, and describe the nature of its effect.
Ans: One variable in question was the proximity of the victim in relation to participants. The less physically separated they were, the less willing participants were to obey the experimenter and administer the maximum shock voltage. When the victim was in the same room as the participants, 40% of the participants fully obeyed, compared to 65% in the baseline condition where the victim was in an adjacent room. When participants were required to physically grasp the victim's hand and force it onto a metal shock plate, full obedience dropped to 30%. Physical separation from the victim allowed participants to distance themselves emotionally from the consequences of their actions, enabling them to obey the experimenter's orders. But the closer the victim was to the participants, the more difficult it was for them to achieve this emotional distance, and, therefore, the negative consequences of their actions were impossible to ignore. Social impact theory offers a related explanation, one that accounts for the effects of proximity in terms of the immediacy of the sources of influence. Just as the experimenter is a source of influence on the participants, so, too, is the victim a source of influence, albeit in an opposite manner. That is, the experimenter influences the participants to obey, and the victim, by protesting and crying out in pain, influences the participants to defy the experimenter's orders. The more distant the victim is from the participant, the less immediate is this source of influence, and, therefore, the less social impact it exerts.   Page: 276-281

130. In Asch's study, in which participants made judgments involving the lengths of lines in the context of a group of people (actually confederates), a surprisingly high level of conformity was observed among the participants. By contrast, in a study conducted by Gamson et al. in which an experimenter ordered groups of participants to make videotaped statements supporting an oil company, most of the participants defied the orders of the experimenter. From the perspective of social impact theory, explain why so many of the participants in Asch's study conformed, while so many in Gamson et al.'s study were defiant.
Ans: Social impact theory maintains that social influence depends on the strength, immediacy, and number of source persons relative to target persons. It is this third component—the number of source persons relative to target persons—that is particularly relevant in explaining the difference between the two studies. Although the participants in both studies participated in groups, the groups exerted different influences on the participants. In Asch's study, the groups consisted of a number of confederates, each of whom was a source of influence operating on the one naive participant. These confederates all gave the same wrong answers, creating normative pressure on the naive participant to not deviate from the unanimous majority. In contrast, the groups in Gamson et al.'s study consisted of naive participants, all of whom were targets of the one source of social influence in the study. According to social impact theory, the social impact of a source person is weakened when it is divided across a number of target persons. This was the case in the study by Gamson and colleagues. Thus, whereas the presence of other people in the Asch study created more sources of social influence, thereby increasing the pressure on participants to conform, the presence of other people in the study by Gamson et al. diluted the impact of the one source of social influence, thereby making it easier for the participants to resist this influence.   Page: 283-284

CHAPTER 8

Group Processes

MULTIPLE CHOICE

1. Which of the following is *true* of groups?
    a) Groups differ from the sum of their parts.
    b) Groups make better decisions than individuals.
    c) People work harder in groups than they do alone.
    d) Discussion moderates group opinions.
    Ans: a   LO: 1   Page: 294-296   Type: F

2. Three people in the same place at the same time, but not interacting with one another are best described as a
    a) social group.
    b) minimal group.
    c) collective.
    d) conjunctive group.
    Ans: c   LO: 1   Page: 294-296   Type: C

3. Groups differ from collectives in that
    a) groups, but not collectives, engage in common activities.
    b) collectives, but not groups, engage in common activities.
    c) groups have more direct interaction with one another than collectives.
    d) collectives have more direct interaction with one another than groups.
    Ans: c   LO: 1   Page: 294-296   Type: C

4. Which of the following would *most* likely be described as a collective?
    a) Students in a small, discussion-focused seminar
    b) Members of a sports team
    c) Passengers on a plane
    d) A boy scout troop
    Ans: c   LO: 1   Page: 294-296   Type: C

5. The extent to which group members think, act, and feel like a single entity is known as
    a) social integration.
    b) social facilitation.
    c) need for affiliation.
    d) groupthink.
    Ans: a   LO: 1   Page: 294-296   Type: F

6. People join groups for all of the following reasons *except* to
    a) be protected from threat.
    b) fulfill the need to belong.
    c) reduce superordinate identities.
    d) facilitate interactions with liked others.
    Ans: c   LO: 1   Page: 295-296   Type: F

7. Madeline has recently been accepted into a sorority at her college. She is likely to
    a) look to the other new members of the group to determine appropriate group behavior.
    b) resist the norms created by established members of the group.
    c) social loaf until she feels like an accepted member of the group.
    d) model her behavior on that of long-standing group members.
    Ans: d   LO: 1   Page: 296-297   Type: A

8.   Nita has just joined the outing club, an organization that has been low in members for the last several years.
      It is likely that Nita will
      a)   assimilate into the club making whatever changes are necessary to fit in, while the club will make
            little accommodation.
      b)   become committed to the group if the group members accept each other and the group.
      c)   make few changes to fit in, hoping the group will accept her as she is.
      d)   rarely rely on her relationships with established members of the club.
      Ans: b   LO: 1   Page: 296-297   Type: A

9.   Tuckman and Jensen propose that groups develop through which order of stages (from beginning to end)?
      a)   forming, storming, norming, performing, adjourning
      b)   forming, norming, storming, performing, adjourning
      c)   forming, performing, storming, norming, adjourning
      d)   forming, norming, performing, storming, adjourning
      Ans: a   LO: 1   Page: 296-297   Type: F

10.   Compared to Tuckman and Jensen's (1977) stages of group development, Gersick (1988) suggests that
      a)   groups develop gradually through a series of stages.
      b)   groups adopt problem-solving strategies relatively quickly in their development.
      c)   groups progress through the first stage of development rather quickly, but relatively slowly through
            the latter stages.
      d)   there is little variability between groups in the course of development.
      Ans: b   LO: 1   Page: 296-297   Type: C

11.   Groups include all of the following essential components *except*
      a)   roles.
      b)   norms.
      c)   cohesiveness.
      d)   status.
      Ans: d   LO: 1   Page: 297-299   Type: F

12.   Roles are
      a)   the rules of conduct for group members.
      b)   dissimilar to norms in that only roles can be formal or informal.
      c)   similar to norms in that both must be present for group cohesiveness.
      d)   beneficial to a group if clear, but can create stress if ambiguous.
      Ans: d   LO: 1   Page: 297-298   Type: F

13.   Deborah has just joined a sorority at her school. She is unsure what she should wear when she goes to eat at
      the sorority's dining hall. Her concern reflects Deborah's uncertainty of the
      a)   informal role.
      b)   formal role.
      c)   informal norm.
      d)   formal norm.
      Ans: c   LO: 1   Page: 298-299   Type: A

14.   A leader who focuses his or her group on the task(s) it needs to achieve is playing a(n)
      a)   facilitator role.
      b)   instrumental role.
      c)   normative role.
      d)   expressive role.
      Ans: b   LO: 1   Page: 297-298   Type: F

15.   In her group, Melanie is always the one who breaks the tension with a funny story and provides a shoulder
      to cry on when things go wrong. She can be described as playing a(n)
      a)   expressive role.
      b)   facilitator role.
      c)   instrumental role.
      d)   normative role.
      Ans: a   LO: 1   Page: 297-298   Type: A

16. Loss of productivity is *least* likely to occur in which of the following scenarios?
     a)   Daphne isn't quite sure what her role in the group is.
     b)   Fred must play both an instrumental and an expressive role in the group.
     c)   Velma's role in the group seems to be constantly changing.
     d)   Shaggy assumes a clearly defined instrumental role in the group.
     Ans: d   LO: 1   Page: 297-298   Type: A

17. A group's cohesiveness and its performance have been found to be positively related. This is particularly the case
     a)   in larger groups.
     b)   for tasks involving interdependence.
     c)   for all-male groups.
     d)   when groups spend a good deal of time worrying about cohesiveness.
     Ans: b   LO: 1   Page: 299   Type: F

18. Group cohesiveness is decreased by
     a)   threats from within the group.
     b)   commitment to the group cause.
     c)   high costs associated with leaving the group.
     d)   a dangerous environment.
     Ans: a   LO: 1   Page: 299   Type: F

19. The fact that members of an organization who blow the whistle on problematic practices are often treated harshly by the rest of the group illustrates the power of group
     a)   roles.
     b)   norms.
     c)   storming.
     d)   development.
     Ans: b   LO: 1   Page: 298-299   Type: C

20. Research concerning the relationship between group cohesiveness and performance suggests that
     a)   cohesiveness has a greater effect on performance than vice versa.
     b)   performance has a greater effect on cohesiveness than vice versa.
     c)   the relationship is negative.
     d)   the relationship is stronger among men than among women.
     Ans: b   LO: 1   Page: 299   Type: C

21. According to research by Nibler and Harris (2003), which of the following groups is most likely to experience better performance when group members feel free to disagree with one another?
     a)   A group of friends in China
     b)   A group of friends in the U.S.
     c)   A group of strangers in China.
     d)   A group of strangers in the U.S.
     Ans: b   LO: 1   Page: 300   Type: F

22. Cross-cultural research suggests that when individuals fail to carry their own share of the weight for the group
     a)   cohesiveness suffers less in groups from collectivistic cultures because other people are quick to pick up the slack.
     b)   collectivist groups are more likely to kick out these individuals than are more individualistic groups.
     c)   cohesiveness suffers more in groups from collectivistic cultures.
     d)   collectivistic groups are more likely to seek increases in task complexity.
     Ans: c   LO: 1   Page: 300   Type: F

23. In one of the earliest social psychological experiments, Triplett (1898) had children wind fishing reels as quickly as they could. He found that
     a)   the children were fastest when observed by the experimenter.
     b)   winding times were faster without an audience than with an audience.
     c)   the children were faster when working next to another child rather than alone.
     d)   the children were faster working alone than with a partner.
     Ans: c   LO: 2   Page: 300-301   Type: F

24. The tendency for the presence of other people to increase performance on easy tasks and impair performance on difficult tasks is known as
a)   social loafing.
b)   social facilitation.
c)   group polarization.
d)   groupthink.
Ans: b   LO: 2   Page: 300-301   Type: C

25. Vladimir, a basketball novice, makes about 60 percent of his free throws when practicing alone. However, when playing with his friends, he only makes about 30 percent of his free throws. This decrease is *most* likely the result of
a)   social facilitation.
b)   deindividuation.
c)   group polarization.
d)   social security.
Ans: a   LO: 2   Page: 300-301   Type: A

26. The facilitation of the dominant response from increased arousal will tend to
a)   make easy tasks easier, but difficult tasks more challenging.
b)   make both easy and difficult tasks easier.
c)   have no effect on easy tasks, but will make difficult tasks more challenging.
d)   have no effect on challenging tasks, but will make easy tasks easier.
Ans: a   LO: 2   Page: 300-301   Type: C

27. According to Zajonc's model of social facilitation, the three steps in determining the influence of the presence of others on performance are
a)   arousal, dominant response, and task difficulty.
b)   relaxation, elimination of apprehension, and task difficulty.
c)   construal, arousal, and attribution.
d)   social comparison, attribution, and justification.
Ans: a   LO: 2   Page: 301-302   Type: F

28. Zajonc's model for how the presence of others influences individual performance is known as social facilitation. "Facilitation" refers to the fact that the presence of others *facilitates* a performer's
a)   ability to focus on the task at hand.
b)   task performance.
c)   evaluation apprehension.
d)   dominant response.
Ans: d   LO: 2   Page: 301-302   Type: C

29. According to the theory of social facilitation, the presence of others should lead to all *except for* which of the following?
a)   Improved performance on an easy task
b)   Physiological arousal
c)   A dominant response
d)   More carefully deliberated behavior
Ans: d   LO: 2   Page: 300-302   Type: C

30. Your psychology professor calls you in front of the class and asks you to answer practice exam questions in front of everyone. You find the questions to be easy. According to the model of social _____, you should perform _____ than you would if you had worked on the questions alone.
a)   loafing; better
b)   loafing; worse
c)   facilitation; better
d)   facilitation; worse
Ans: c   LO: 2   Page: 300-302   Type: A

31. Research by Zajonc et al. (1969) in which cockroaches run in simple or complex mazes either alone, in pairs, or with an audience provides support for which explanation of social facilitation?
     a)   The evaluation apprehension theory
     b)   The distraction-conflict theory
     c)   The persuasive arguments theory
     d)   The mere presence theory
     Ans: d   LO: 2   Page: 301-302   Type: C

32. According to Zajonc, social facilitation
     a)   occurs because of concerns about being evaluated by others.
     b)   results from the physical immediacy of others.
     c)   occurs in humans, but not in less intelligent animals.
     d)   can be explained by considering attentional processes.
     Ans: b   LO: 2   Page: 301-302   . Type: C

33. Cottrell et al. (1968) found that dominant responses were no more frequent among people working in the presence of blindfolded others than among people working alone. This finding is consistent with which theory of social facilitation?
     a)   The evaluation apprehension theory
     b)   The distraction-conflict theory
     c)   The persuasive arguments theory
     d)   The mere presence theory
     Ans: a   LO: 2   Page: 303-304   Type: C

34. Gardner and Knowles (2008) asked participants to complete tasks in front of a picture of a favorite TV character and found that
     a)   social facilitation occurs in such a situation, even though no other actual people are present.
     b)   social facilitation could still occur, but only when the character was a human one.
     c)   social facilitation effects are dependent on the presence of real people in a situation.
     d)   participants became less apprehensive regarding their performance.
     Ans: a   LO: 2   Page: 302-303   Type: C

35. All of the following accounts have been proposed to explain social facilitation *except*
     a)   the mere presence of others.
     b)   apprehension about being evaluated.
     c)   distraction, which can create attentional conflict.
     d)   a tendency for people to feel less accountable in a group context.
     Ans: d   LO: 2   Page: 303-304   Type: C

36. The distraction-conflict explanation for social facilitation suggests that
     a)   the "tunnel vision" brought about by the presence of others always leads to decreased performance.
     b)   concern about being evaluated by others can distract people who perform in front of others.
     c)   loud noises and bright lights can lead to the same social facilitation effects as can the presence of other people.
     d)   performance in the presence of others actually *improves* for a difficult task.
     Ans: c   LO: 2   Page: 303   Type: C

37. Better performance by an individual on difficult tasks in the presence of others can be encouraged the *most* when the individual's arousal level is _____ and evaluation pressure on the individual is _____.
     a)   high; high
     b)   low; low
     c)   high; low
     d)   low; high
     Ans: b   LO: 2   Page: 300-303   Type: C

38. According to the model of _____, when the presence of others is physiologically arousing, a person's performance tends to _____ on a task that is difficult.
     a)   social loafing; decline
     b)   social loafing; improve
     c)   social facilitation; decline
     d)   social facilitation; improve
     Ans: c   LO: 3   Page: 300-303   Type: C

39.   Ringelmann's research in the 1880s demonstrated that
     a)   people exert less effort in simple group tasks than they would if working alone.
     b)   the presence of other people improves performance on simple group tasks.
     c)   groups tend to make more extreme decisions than individuals.
     d)   individual performance is impaired by the distraction of an audience.
     Ans: a   LO: 3   Page: 304-305   Type: F

40. Ingham (1974) asked participants to pull on a rope and found that participants pulled almost 20% harder when they thought they were pulling alone than when they thought they were part of a group. This finding *best* illustrates
     a)   social loafing.
     b)   a social dilemma.
     c)   groupthink.
     d)   social facilitation.
     Ans: a   LO: 3   Page: 304-305   Type: C

41. An employee is working with a group of co-workers to finish a project at work. The employee will be more likely to engage in social loafing if the employee
     a)   is high in need for cognition.
     b)   is from a collectivist culture.
     c)   perceives the project outcome to be personally important.
     d)   is male.
     Ans: d   LO: 3   Page: 304-305   Type: A

42. Which of the following conditions makes social loafing *more* likely to occur?
     a)   When people believe that their own performance can be identified and evaluated by others
     b)   When people believe that the task in question is not important
     c)   When the group in question is small
     d)   When group members expect to be punished if the group performs poorly
     Ans: b   LO: 3   Page: 304-305   Type: C

43. Lynn needs to get her subordinates to all invest considerable time and energy into the development of a new design for the company's fall clothing line. If she wants to reduce the likelihood of social loafing she should
     a)   bring together a large group of diverse individuals.
     b)   tell the subordinates how important the project is to her.
     c)   bring together a group of men rather than a group of women.
     d)   communicate to them how success of the project will benefit each of them personally.
     Ans: d   LO: 3   Page: 306   Type: A

44. Aggarwal and O'Brien (2008) studied hundreds of college students and identified several keys to reducing social loafing. All of the following are examples of the strategies they suggest *except*
     a)   breaking down complex projects into smaller components.
     b)   keeping groups small.
     c)   selecting group members low in achievement motivation.
     d)   using peer evaluations.
     Ans: c   LO: 3   Page: 305-306   Type: C

45. Esteban's work group has been assigned a new project by management. Before deciding how much effort to exert on this new assignment, Esteban considers how important the group goals are to him and whether his input will help the group reach its goals. Esteban's thinking is *most* consistent with
    a) distraction-conflict theory.
    b) the collective effort model.
    c) the social identity model of deindividuation.
    d) persuasive arguments theory.
    Ans: b   LO: 3   Page: 306   Type: A

46. Mr. Belding notices that his students seem to put more effort into their individual assignments than into their group projects. This is *most* likely the result of
    a) social loafing.
    b) group facilitation.
    c) groupthink.
    d) group polarization.
    Ans: a   LO: 3   Page: 304-306   Type: A

47. According to the collective effort model, social loafing is more likely when people
    a) see the group outcome as personally important.
    b) believe the group outcome is important to other group members.
    c) believe that their efforts will lead to the desired outcome.
    d) feel that their input will not compensate for social loafing by others.
    Ans: d   LO: 3   Page: 306   Type: C

48. Henderson suspects that the other members of his work group may slack off, so he works late and puts in extra time on their proposal. Henderson is engaging in
    a) social compensation.
    b) social facilitation.
    c) social loafing.
    d) deindividuation.
    Ans: a   LO: 3   Page: 306   Type: A

49. Research suggests that which of the following people would be *most* likely to engage in social loafing?
    a) A woman from a collectivist culture
    b) A man from a collectivist culture
    c) A woman from an individualistic culture
    d) A man from an individualistic culture
    Ans: d   LO: 3   Page: 306-307   Type: C

50. All of the following individual differences are described by your textbook as predicting social loafing tendencies *except*
    a) gender.
    b) cultural background.
    c) achievement motivation.
    d) attachment style.
    Ans: d   LO: 3   Page: 306-307   Type: C

51. Individuals from collectivist cultures are more likely to engage in social loafing
    a) when a group norm of low effort has already been established.
    b) when tasks are difficult.
    c) in groups with a majority of female members.
    d) when task orientation is high.
    Ans: a   LO: 3   Page: 306-307   Type: C

52. All of the following factors have been suggested to contribute to deindividuation *except*
    a) the presence of others.
    b) reduced feelings of responsibility.
    c) low arousal.
    d) anonymity.
    Ans: c   LO: 4   Page: 307-308   Type: F

53. Deindividuation refers to the
    a) loss of individuality and reduction of constraints against deviant behavior.
    b) decrease in individual effort on simple group tasks.
    c) tendency for group decisions to be more extreme than the decisions of the individuals comprising the group.
    d) impairment in group decision making that results from a concern with unanimity.
    Ans: a   LO: 4   Page: 307-308   Type: F

54. Attentional cues that decrease self-awareness should increase
    a) deindividuated behavior.
    b) social facilitation on an easy task.
    c) cooperation in a prisoner's dilemma.
    d) groupthink in a decision-making process.
    Ans: a   LO: 4   Page: 307-308   Type: C

55. The fact that many assaults are committed by people wearing disguises—and that these disguised assaults are often the most vicious ones—illustrates the concept of
    a) social loafing.
    b) entrapment.
    c) deindividuation.
    d) distraction-conflict.
    Ans: c   LO: 4   Page: 307-308   Type: C

56. Deindividuation is more likely when
    a) accountability for behavior is high.
    b) accountability for behavior is low.
    c) the group is engaged in a conjunctive task.
    d) the group is engaged in a disjunctive task.
    Ans: b   LO: 4   Page: 307-308   Type: C

57. Sheila and Peter are invited to a masquerade party. At the party, people start insulting and pushing around Parker, another guest at the party. Given the research on deindividuation, which of the following is most likely *false*?
    a) If Sheila was dressed as a nun and Peter was dressed as a priest, their costumes would decrease the likelihood that they would behave aggressively toward Parker.
    b) If there was a loud band playing that made the floor shake, Sheila and Peter would be more likely to behave aggressively toward Parker.
    c) If Sheila and Peter were dressed in costumes in which they could not be recognized, Peter would likely behave more aggressively toward Parker than Sheila would.
    d) If Sheila and Peter believed that at the end of the party all the guests would have to reveal their true identities, they would be less likely to behave aggressively toward Parker.
    Ans: c   LO: 4   Page: 307-309   Type: A

58. Various phenomena commonly occur when people are relatively anonymous and their performance cannot be evaluated. Which of the following is/are more likely to occur in conditions when an actor feels anonymous and free from evaluation apprehension? I. social facilitation, II. social loafing, III. deindividuation
    a) I and II only
    b) II and III only
    c) III only
    d) I, II, and III
    Ans: b   LO: 4   Page: 303; 307-309   Type: F

59. At crowded parties, Amy loses her sense of self and, as a result, often behaves in ways that she later regrets. These parties seem to create in Amy a state of
    a) deindividuation.
    b) cohesiveness.
    c) groupthink.
    d) entrapment.
    Ans: a   LO: 4   Page: 307-308   Type: A

60. It seems that every Halloween night in Gotham is marred by violence and vandalism. In order to reduce the likelihood of such behavior, the leaders of Gotham should
   a) increase self-awareness by making sure everyone who goes out wears a name tag.
   b) increase anonymity by making sure that everyone who goes out wears a mask.
   c) make sure that people only venture outside in groups.
   d) create a highly stimulating environment by playing loud Halloween music over all public address systems.
   Ans: a   LO: 4   Page: 308-309   Type: A

61. Harriett goes trick-or-treating on Halloween. She arrives at her neighbor's door just as the phone is ringing. Her neighbor puts the candy on the table and says, "I need to get the phone, so help yourself to whatever kind of candy you want, but please take only one piece." Which of the following would *most* encourage Harriett to take only one piece of candy?
   a) If Harriet's costume prevented the neighbor from recognizing her
   b) If Harriett was dressed up as a pirate
   c) If the candy was placed in front of a mirror
   d) If Harriett was high in need for cognition
   Ans: c   LO: 4   Page: 308-309   Type: A

62. Johnson and Downing (1979) found that participants wearing nurses' uniforms delivered lower levels of shock when they were anonymous than when they were identifiable. This finding suggests that deindividuation causes people to
   a) feel that the normative standards of the group do not apply to them.
   b) engage in destructive behavior when they are anonymous.
   c) rely more heavily on personal standards of behavior when they are anonymous.
   d) act in ways that are consistent with the norms of the most salient group.
   Ans: d   LO: 4   Page: 309   Type: C

63. In many anonymous online communities, accountability is _____ and attentional cues are _____.
   a) low; low
   b) low; high
   c) high; low
   d) high; high
   Ans: a   LO: 4   Page: 308   Type: F

64. According to the _____, whether deindividuation affects people for better or for worse depends on a group's characteristics and norms.
   a) process loss model
   b) social identity model of dendividuation effects
   c) emotional reciprocation model
   d) conflict-distraction model of deindividuation
   Ans: b   LO: 4   Page: 309   Type: F

65. In conjunctive tasks, group performance is determined by the
   a) sum of the performance of each individual in the group.
   b) ratio of individual performance to group performance.
   c) performance of the weakest group member.
   d) performance of the strongest group member.
   Ans: c   LO: 5   Page: 310-311   Type: F

66. Sam, Diane, and Frasier are members of a team competing in a test of general knowledge. Any team member can answer the moderator's questions. The team's task can be described as
   a) additive.
   b) conjunctive.
   c) disjunctive.
   d) collective.
   Ans: c   LO: 5   Page: 310-311   Type: A

67. Tendencies that interfere with a group's ability to live up to its full potential are referred to as examples of
     a)   disjunctive tasks.
     b)   process loss.
     c)   sample biases.
     d)   nonadditive effects.
     Ans: b   LO: 5   Page: 310-311   Type: C

68. Groups tend to outperform individuals on
     a)   additive tasks, but not disjunctive tasks.
     b)   disjunctive tasks, but not conjunctive tasks.
     c)   conjunctive tasks, but not additive tasks.
     d)   additive, conjunctive, and disjunctive tasks.
     Ans: a   LO: 5   Page: 310-311   Type: C

69. Which of the following concerning process loss is *false*?
     a)   Lack of motivation can contribute to process loss.
     b)   Lack of coordination among group members can contribute to process loss.
     c)   Process loss contributes to social loafing.
     d)   Process loss is restricted to disjunctive tasks.
     Ans: d   LO: 5   Page: 310-311   Type: F

70. Research on brainstorming in groups demonstrates that
     a)   people brainstorming together produce fewer and lower-quality ideas than those brainstorming
          individually.
     b)   people believe that the ideas generated in group brainstorming sessions are not as good as those
          generated by individuals.
     c)   group brainstorming can be enhanced by production blocking.
     d)   people feel more comfortable expressing unusual ideas in group brainstorming sessions.
     Ans: a   LO: 5   Page: 311-312   Type: C

71. Farooq and his co-workers are trying to develop a creative direct mail campaign that will increase sales of
     their new snowboard. Which of the following strategies is *least* likely to yield high-quality ideas?
     a)   Hold a brainstorming session with a facilitator trained in group brainstorming.
     b)   Form an interactive group employing electronic brainstorming.
     c)   Hold a brainstorming session using Osborn's ground rules for brainstorming.
     d)   Create "nominal groups" and work independently.
     Ans: c   LO: 5   Page: 311-312   Type: A

72. Research on brainstorming suggests that
     a)   it is typically an effective practice, even though people often dislike doing it.
     b)   it is typically an ineffective practice, even though people often enjoy doing it.
     c)   it works better among very large groups than among smaller groups.
     d)   it works better for disjunctive tasks than for conjunctive tasks.
     Ans: b   LO: 5   Page: 311-312   Type: C

73. All of the following appear to reduce the effectiveness of group brainstorming *except*
     a)   production blocking.
     b)   social compensation.
     c)   evaluation apprehension.
     d)   performance matching.
     Ans: b   LO: 5   Page: 311-312   Type: F

74. The tendency for groups to become more extreme in their positions following discussion is called
     a)   group polarization.
     b)   social loafing.
     c)   a social dilemma.
     d)   social facilitation.
     Ans: a   LO: 6   Page: 312-314   Type: F

75. Following group discussion, group decisions tend to _____ the positions of the individuals comprising the group.
    a) be more conservative than
    b) be more risky than
    c) reflect the average of
    d) be more extreme than
    Ans: d   LO: 6   Page: 312-314   Type: F

76. Before a meeting, each of several city council members was tentatively considering an air pollution ordinance. After a meeting, they expressed strong support of the ordinance. This outcome is an example of
    a) group polarization.
    b) social loafing.
    c) a social dilemma.
    d) social facilitation.
    Ans: a   LO: 6   Page: 312-314   Type: A

77. A group of students is discussing whether same-sex couples should be allowed to marry. The students begin the discussion with opinions that are somewhat in favor of gay marriage. If group polarization occurs
    a) students will be more strongly supportive of gay marriage after the discussion.
    b) students will be more strongly opposed to gay marriage after the discussion.
    c) students' attitudes will not change as a result of the discussion.
    d) a great deal of disagreement and conflict will occur during the discussion.
    Ans: a   LO: 6   Page: 312-314   Type: A

78. The phenomenon of group polarization depends on the assumption that
    a) most people are risk-averse.
    b) people tend to join groups with others who have similar attitudes.
    c) group disagreement impedes positive group performance.
    d) group members are from an individualistic culture.
    Ans: b   LO: 6   Page: 312-314   Type: C

79. Consider a study in which researchers created groups of relatively prejudiced and unprejudiced high school students and asked them to respond to issues concerning racial attitudes, both before and after discussion of these issues. Following the group discussions, you would expect that
    a) both groups would become more prejudiced.
    b) both groups would become less prejudiced.
    c) those who were relatively unprejudiced would become less prejudiced and those who were relatively prejudiced would become more prejudiced.
    d) those who were relatively unprejudiced would become more prejudiced and those who were relatively prejudiced would become less prejudiced.
    Ans: c   LO: 6   Page: 312-314   Type: F

80. Group polarization is *most* likely to occur
    a) on important issues.
    b) on unimportant issues.
    c) when group members know one another.
    d) when group members do not know one another.
    Ans: a   LO: 6   Page: 312-314   Type: F

81. Group polarization may, in part, stem from
    a) an increase in dominant responses under conditions of high arousal.
    b) lack of group cohesiveness.
    c) deindividuation of group members.
    d) the desire to distinguish one's group from other groups.
    Ans: d   LO: 6   Page: 312-314   Type: C

82. Based on the social comparison explanation of group polarization, group members' attitudes toward an issue should be *most* influenced by
     a)   how different their attitudes are from those of an outgroup.
     b)   those in the ingroup who favor a cautious approach.
     c)   the number of people in their group who share that attitude.
     d)   those in the ingroup who offer the most arguments relevant to the issue.
     Ans: c   LO: 6   Page: 312-314   Type: C

83. Latasha joined a campus group called "Young Republicans." Which of these outcomes is most consistent with the *persuasive-arguments* explanation for group polarization?
     a)   In the attempt to fit in, Latasha adjusts her attitudes to be even more conservative.
     b)   Latasha self-categorizes as a Republican, and her political beliefs become more extreme as a result.
     c)   After exposure to ideas she has not thought of before, Latasha comes to possess even more conservative beliefs.
     d)   In an attempt to convince others she is a "good" Republican, Latasha persuades herself to be more conservative.
     Ans: c   LO: 6   Page: 312-314   Type: A

84. Which of the following is a strictly informational social influence explanation for group polarization?
     a)   Social comparison theory
     b)   Self perception theory
     c)   Persuasive arguments theory
     d)   None of these.
     Ans: c   LO: 6   Page: 312-314   Type: C

85. An informational social influence explanation for group polarization is _____; a normative explanation for the phenomenon is _____.
     a)   mindless conformity; biased sampling
     b)   persuasive-arguments; social comparison
     c)   social comparison; biased sampling
     d)   mindless conformity; persuasive-arguments
     Ans: b   LO: 6   Page: 312-314   Type: C

86. In which of the following situations is group polarization *least* likely to occur?
     a)   In deciding the best way to recruit new members, the members of Alpha Beta Fraternity are concerned that their fraternity is distinct from the other fraternities on campus.
     b)   While discussing the possibility of offering more outpatient services, the members of the hospital board are surprised that so many members favor the proposal.
     c)   The Senator's re-election committee discusses both the potential advantages and disadvantages of leaking negative information about the opposing candidate.
     d)   In one of the most important decisions it has ever faced, the prosecution team must decide whether to press criminal charges against a high ranking public official.
     Ans: c   LO: 6   Page: 312-314   Type: C

87. Groupthink emerges when
     a)   the need for agreement takes priority over the desire to obtain correct information.
     b)   group members feel that they will be unable to compensate for social loafing.
     c)   individual benefits are in conflict with the needs of the group.
     d)   group norms overwhelm individual identities.
     Ans: a   LO: 7   Page: 314-316   Type: F

88. Groupthink is more likely to occur
     a)   when groups have systematic decision-making procedures.
     b)   if the group lacks a strong directive leader.
     c)   in low-stress situations.
     d)   in highly cohesive groups.
     Ans: d   LO: 7   Page: 314-316   Type: C

89. The characteristics of groups that contribute to groupthink include all of the following *except*
     a)   group cohesiveness.
     b)   group structure.
     c)   group size.
     d)   group stress.
     Ans: c   LO: 7   Page: 314-316   Type: F

90. Hendrika owns a small aerospace company and wants to make sure that she recognizes the signs of groupthink if it crops up in her group meetings. She should be especially concerned that groupthink may be occurring if the group exhibits
     a)   coalition formation.
     b)   social loafing.
     c)   divergent thinking.
     d)   closed-mindedness.
     Ans: d   LO: 7   Page: 314-316   Type: A

91. Four groups—a, b, c, and d—are meeting separately. Each is making an important decision. Below is one quotation overheard from each group's meeting. Based on these quotations, which group seems *least* likely to fall victim to groupthink?
     a)   "The good Lord is on our side."
     b)   "This is not the time nor the place to bring up worst-case scenarios."
     c)   "This has to be done right even if it takes us all day to decide."
     d)   "The threat is very real and we must act decisively and unanimously."
     Ans: c   LO: 7   Page: 314-316   Type: F

92. John, George, Paul, and Richard are air traffic controllers. They encounter a stressful, anxious situation in which two planes might soon collide. Which of the following conditions would *most* encourage this group of air traffic controllers to display groupthink when pondering their next step?
     a)   A majority decision is more acceptable than a unanimous decision.
     b)   There are systematic procedures in place to handle such situations.
     c)   None of them is considered to be a supervisor of any of the others.
     d)   They are a cohesive group.
     Ans: d   LO: 7   Page: 314-316   Type: A

93. Which of the following would be an effective way for a leader to reduce the possibility of groupthink?
     a)   Express her opinion only after other group members have voiced their opinions.
     b)   Emphasize that the group decision must be a unanimous one.
     c)   Take a more directive role in the group discussion.
     d)   Appoint a few people in the group to act as "mindguards."
     Ans: a   LO: 7   Page: 316-317   Type: A

94. Computerized group support systems help to minimize the potential for groupthink by
     a)   providing more power to the leader of the group.
     b)   allowing group members to raise concerns anonymously.
     c)   focusing the attention of group members on their relationships with one another.
     d)   increasing the cohesiveness of the group.
     Ans: b   LO: 7   Page: 316-317   Type: F

95. Which of the following historical events is *not* cited by your book as a potential example of groupthink?
     a)   NASA's decision to launch the space shuttle *Challenger* in 1986.
     b)   The decision by the U.S. and Britain to invade Iraq in 2003.
     c)   The behavior of Nazi concentration camp guards during World War II.
     d)   John Kennedy's decision to invade Cuba in 1961.
     Ans: c   LO: 7   Page: 315-317   Type: F

96.   _____ is referred to as when a group increases its commitment to a failing course of action in order to
       justify previous investments.
       a)   The escalation effect
       b)   Mindguarding
       c)   Graduated and reciprocated initiatives in tension-reduction
       d)   Biased sampling
       Ans: a   LO: 7   Page: 317   Type: F

97.   Though the new mentoring program doesn't seem to be working very well, Principal McVickers argues that
       the school should continue to invest in it because they have already committed so many resources to it. This
       illustrates
       a)   social loafing.
       b)   groupthink.
       c)   the escalation effect.
       d)   the sucker effect.
       Ans: c   LO: 7   Page: 317   Type: A

98.   A group is likely to optimize its potential performance when
       a)   tasks can be divided into subtasks and assigned to individual members.
       b)   specific roles are avoided and group members are left to choose their own tasks and responsibilities.
       c)   there is an absence of competition from other groups.
       d)   the task in question is difficult and has no clear solution.
       Ans: a   LO: 8   Page: 318-319   Type: C

99.   Three students form a study group for their social psychology course. Which of the following possibilities
       would be the best indication than the group is experiencing biased sampling?
       a)   The students focus on the information they all already know instead of reviewing the unique
             knowledge that each person brings to the group.
       b)   The students assign specific roles and tasks to each other.
       c)   In the effort to categorize themselves as "good" group members, the students conform to each other's
             opinions about the quality of the course instruction thus far.
       d)   The students refuse to utilize the strategy of brainstorming.
       Ans: a   LO: 8   Page: 318-319   Type: A

100.   Biased sampling is *least* likely to reduce group effectiveness when group members have _____ experience
       with each other, and unique information is known by _____.
       a)   a lot of; only one group member
       b)   a lot of; more than one group member
       c)   very little; only one group member
       d)   very little; more than one group member
       Ans: b   LO: 8   Page: 318-319   Type: C

101.   Biased sampling is an example of
       a)   process loss.
       b)   process gain.
       c)   the risky shift.
       d)   deindividuation.
       Ans: a   LO: 8   Page: 318-319   Type: C

102.   Research on information processing in groups suggests that
       a)   if the individuals who comprise the group are prone to rely on a particular heuristic, the group will be
             even less likely to use this heuristic.
       b)   if the individuals who comprise the group are prone to rely on a particular heuristic, the group will be
             even more likely to use this heuristic.
       c)   regardless of the information-processing propensities of individual group members, groups are less
             likely than individuals to rely on heuristics.
       d)   regardless of the information-processing propensities of individual group members, groups are more
             likely than individuals to rely on heuristics.
       Ans: b   LO: 8   Page: 319   Type: C

103. Biased sampling in groups is the process whereby
    a) people tend to choose those they know well to be in a group.
    b) information that is known by many group members tends to enter into the discussion more than information known only by a few.
    c) people tend to discuss negative information more than positive information in their discussion about an important decision.
    d) sharing information in a group can be impeded by the gender composition of the group.
    Ans: b   LO: 8   Page: 318-319   Type: F

104. A shared system for remembering information that allows groups to demonstrate more efficient memory than individuals is known as
    a) semantic memory.
    b) transactive memory.
    c) process loss.
    d) facilitative memory.
    Ans: b   LO: 8   Page: 319   Type: F

105. Coach Valentine does not think that his team is playing up to its full potential. To increase the performance of the team, the coach should
    a) build the team's confidence by setting goals that are not challenging and easy to attain.
    b) urge each team member to try to do his or her best.
    c) set specific, challenging, and reachable goals for the team.
    d) avoid giving the team any particular goals to minimize the pressure on the team.
    Ans: c   LO: 9   Page: 319-320   Type: A

106. Research on goal setting in groups demonstrates that
    a) groups tend to set less ambitious goals than individuals.
    b) groups tend to set more ambitious goals than individuals.
    c) groups are more likely to set goals for disjunctive tasks, but not conjunctive tasks.
    d) groups are more likely to set goals for conjunctive tasks, but not disjunctive tasks.
    Ans: a   LO: 9   Page: 319-320   Type: C

107. Rashid is considering employing a computerized group decision support system to increase the quality of decision-making in his company. This may work because
    a) the anonymity of computer mediated discussions increases reliance on information processing heuristics.
    b) there is no risk of evaluation apprehension in computer mediated discussions.
    c) the probability of process loss will be increased as multiple people attempt to speak at the same time.
    d) computer mediated discussions tend to reduce biased information sampling.
    Ans: d   LO: 9   Page: 321   Type: A

108. Research by Woolley and colleagues (2008) suggest that when it comes to expertise and planning
    a) groups with experts can typically get away with not planning their strategy ahead of time, with little adverse effect on performance.
    b) groups that create a clear plan for how to address a problem don't enjoy any extra benefits from having experts as members.
    c) expertise is much more important than planning when it comes to group performance.
    d) None of these
    Ans: d   LO: 9   Page: 320-321   Type: F

109. Research on diversity suggests that
    a) even the mere expectation of being part of a diverse group can impact performance.
    b) the benefits of diversity for group performance tend to be much greater in collectivist versus individualistic cultures.
    c) diversity is often associated with positive group dynamics.
    d) diversity often has negative effects when it comes to outcomes like market share and profits.
    Ans: a   LO: 9   Page: 322   Type: F

110. Viviana lives in an ethnically diverse community. She is attending a PTA meeting concerning how to provide a complete and fair history curriculum. It is likely that
    a)   the members of the PTA will judge their own work more positively than will members of PTAs in ethnically homogenous communities.
    b)   the PTA will come up with more creative solutions than will PTAs in ethnically homogenous communities.
    c)   misunderstandings will be less likely among her PTA members than among PTA members from ethnically homogenous communities.
    d)   cliques will be less likely to form in her PTA than in PTAs from ethnically homogenous communities.
    Ans: b   LO: 9   Page: 322   Type: A

111. Research on diversity and group performance suggests that
    a)   people often think that diversity has had a negative impact on their group, even when it has not.
    b)   diverse groups always outperform non-diverse groups.
    c)   racial diversity has stronger effects on group performance more than gender diversity.
    d)   diversity has its most positive effects when it leads group members to assert their own individuality within the group.
    Ans: a   LO: 9   Page: 322   Type: C

112. Research on the prisoner's dilemma has shown that people respond to mixed-motive situations with
    a)   depression.
    b)   reciprocity.
    c)   duplicity.
    d)   confusion.
    Ans: b   LO: 10   Page: 323-324   Type: F

113. Consider the prisoner's dilemma. You will receive the worst possible outcome in such a scenario if you decide to be _____ and your partner decides to be _____.
    a)   selfish; selfish
    b)   selfish; cooperative
    c)   cooperative; selfish
    d)   cooperative; cooperative
    Ans: c   LO: 10   Page: 323-324   Type: F

114. Jean-Paul works for National Public Radio. He has been assigned to run the fund drive necessary to keep NPR on the air in various communities. Suppose that keeping NPR on the air in a given community is contingent upon the percentage of people in the community that donate money. It is likely that
    a)   Jean-Paul will get more donations from people who have a collectivist orientation than from those who have an individualist orientation.
    b)   Jean-Paul will be likely to get a greater percentage of donations from people living in the city than from people living in smaller close-knit communities.
    c)   whether the people Jean-Paul speaks with are in a good mood or a bad mood will have no influence on their willingness to donate.
    d)   if Jean-Paul is truthful and tells people that many others have already donated, people will be less likely to donate their own money.
    Ans: a   LO: 10   Page: 324-326   Type: A

115. Five students—Jalen, Chris, Juwan, Jimmy, and Ray—move into a house together and discover they share the odd habit of drinking milk with ice in it every night before bed. They own several ice trays and make a pact to always refill the trays when they are emptied so that the supply of ice will never run out. But the five often do not have the time or energy to refill the trays, and after a few weeks it becomes quite common for them to meet in the kitchen and discover that they have no ice. This would best be characterized as what type of dilemma?
    a)   Prisoner's dilemma
    b)   Normative dilemma
    c)   Tit-for-tat dilemma
    d)   Resource dilemma
    Ans: d   LO: 10   Page: 324-326   Type: A

116. Two competing companies in a small individualistic town are hooked up to the Internet through the same wiring. Each has the capacity to sever the connection, which would reduce the ability of both companies to communicate via e-mail with their clients, and thus impede their work. Of the following choices, research on dilemmas suggests that the two companies
    a) will be negatively affected if they are unaware of their ability to sever the connection.
    b) will probably each sever the connection, leading to the worst outcome for both companies.
    c) would be affected more negatively if only one company could sever the connection.
    d) are less likely to sever the connection than if they were in a collectivist culture.
    Ans: b   LO: 11   Page: 324-325   Type: A

117. Chinese-American college students primed with Chinese images before playing a Prisoner's Dilemma game
    a) cooperated more when playing with strangers than when playing with friends.
    b) cooperated more than did Chinese-Americans primed with American images.
    c) endorsed collectivist ideals during the game, but tended to play in a rather competitive manner.
    d) endorsed individualistic ideals during the game, but tended to play in a rather cooperative manner.
    Ans: b   LO: 10   Page: 326-327   Type: C

118. With regard to behavior during social dilemmas, groups tend to be more _____ than individuals.
    a) cooperative
    b) averse to risk
    c) gullible
    d) competitive
    Ans: d   LO: 10   Page: 325-326   Type: F

119. The leaders of the Republic of Heavyhandedness believe that, because they can punish anyone who disagrees with their policies, residents will not dare to challenge those policies. The Republic of Heavyhandedness thus believes in the efficacy of
    a) social loafing.
    b) social comparison.
    c) entrapment.
    d) threat capacity.
    Ans: d   LO: 11   Page: 327-328   Type: A

120. Conflict between groups is *least* likely to be exacerbated by
    a) the ability to carry out a threat against the other side.
    b) a mismatch in the perceptions each side has of the other.
    c) dehumanization of individuals on the other side.
    d) holding the other side to a different standard.
    Ans: b   LO: 11   Page: 328-329   Type: F

121. At Verbal High, the football players and cheerleaders do not get along at all. The cheerleaders think the football players are vain and superficial. The football players feel the same way about the cheerleaders. The football players and the cheerleaders seem to suffer from
    a) a resource dilemma.
    b) superordinate identities.
    c) mirror image perceptions.
    d) groupthink.
    Ans: c   LO: 11   Page: 328-329   Type: A

122. Bart hopes to employ the GRIT strategy with his opponent, Homer. In order for the strategy to work, it is necessary that
    a) Homer like Bart.
    b) Homer has a cooperative orientation.
    c) Bart retaliate equally if Homer acts competitively.
    d) Bart carry out an initiative only after the previous one has been reciprocated.
    Ans: c   LO: 11   Page: 329   Type: A

123. A negotiated reduction to a conflict in which all parties obtain outcomes that are superior to those they would have obtained from an equal division of contested resources is called a(n)
    a)   social dilemma.
    b)   superordinate identity.
    c)   integrative agreement.
    d)   prisoner's dilemma.
    Ans: c   LO: 11   Page: 329-330   Type: F

124. The perception that members of different groups belong to a larger whole that encompasses both groups is called
    a)   group polarization.
    b)   an integrative agreement.
    c)   a superordinate identity.
    d)   social facilitation.
    Ans: c   LO: 11   Page: 332-333   Type: C

125. Hans and Frans are cousins who grew up in the same town in Michigan. Hans goes to the University of Michigan to major in biology. Frans, who is two years younger, still lives at home, but hopes to one day major in psychology. Which of the following is presently a superordinate identity for the cousins?
    a)   Resident of Michigan
    b)   College student
    c)   Psychologist
    d)   None of these.
    Ans: a   LO: 11   Page: 332-333   Type: C

ESSAY

126. Explain how the presence of others affects performance on easy and hard tasks, and give three explanations to account for these effects.
    Ans: The presence of others facilitates performance on easy tasks and impedes performance on hard tasks. Three mechanisms have been proposed to account for this phenomenon, often referred to as social facilitation: (1) the mere presence theory suggests that the mere presence of others is arousing and it is this general arousal that is responsible for the effects of social facilitation; (2) the evaluation apprehension model suggests that it is the fear of being evaluated by others that is responsible for social facilitation effects; and (3) the distraction-conflict theory suggests that other people are distracting and it is simply the distraction provided by their presence that enhances performance on an easy task and impedes performance on a difficult task.   Page: 300-304

127. Describe how being in a crowd can lead people to engage in destructive behaviors.
    Ans: Being in a crowd can cause people to lose their sense of individuality and self-awareness, leading to a loosening of normal restraints against deviant behavior. This state is called deindividuation. Once the normal restraints on deviant behavior have been removed, violent and destructive behaviors often ensue. Page: 307-308

128. Explain how discussion of a topic with like-minded others can lead people to hold their views with greater conviction, and why this happens.
    Ans: When people discuss a topic with like-minded others, they often experience an exaggeration of the initial tendencies in their thinking. For example, individuals who enter a discussion with a slight preference for a risky course of action often leave that discussion endorsing an even riskier position. This phenomenon is called group polarization, for which at least two explanations have been proposed. (1) Persuasive arguments theory suggests that people in a group discussion with like-minded others hear novel informational arguments to support their initial views that then intensify these views. (2) Social comparison theory suggests that once people get in a group they compare themselves with others and then adjust their own attitudes to be even more typical of the group norm so that they appear to be "good" group members. Page: 312-314

129. Define groupthink, and identify antecedents that contribute to the phenomenon as well as strategies for preventing it.

Ans: Groupthink is the tendency to prioritize agreement among group members over the motivation to get accurate information and make appropriate decisions. In Janis's model of groupthink, there are three primary antecedents to groupthink: (1) group cohesiveness, (2) group structure (e.g., unsystematic procedures, isolation, etc.), and (3) stressful situations. It should be noted, however, that recent work indicates that high cohesiveness may not by itself encourage groupthink. Rather, high cohesiveness in conjunction with other conditions conducive to groupthink can encourage this tendency. Janis has offered several strategies for preventing groupthink, including consulting with outsiders, having leaders encourage open debate and refrain from taking a strong position, assigning an individual in the group the role of challenging the group's ideas, and meeting for a second time after a decision has been reached before implementing a chosen action. Recent research suggests some additional strategies, including holding members of the group personally accountable for the decision, having a member of the group assigned the role of "reminder," having leaders encourage information seeking and independent thinking and discourage seeking agreement, and using computerized group support systems.   Page: 314-317

130. Discuss how GRIT can lead to the reduction of group conflict.

Ans: GRIT (graduated and reciprocated initiatives in tension-reduction) is a unilateral strategy aimed at reducing conflict between groups. When using GRIT an individual or group issues a general statement of intention to reduce conflict and proposes an initiative aimed at reducing tension. The individual or group then carries out the initiative as proposed. If the other party makes a cooperative move, the initiator reciprocates with a more cooperative move, and so on. The initiator maintains a retaliatory capability to avoid exploitation at the hands of an uncooperative partner. This tit-for-tat strategy has been shown to have promise for conflict reduction.   Page: 329

CHAPTER 9

Attraction and Close Relationships

MULTIPLE CHOICE

1. Baumeister and Leary (1996) suggest that humans have a fundamental drive to have positive and meaningful interpersonal relationships with others. They refer to this as the
   a) need to belong.
   b) need for affiliation.
   c) "sociostat."
   d) need to love.
   Ans: a   LO: 1   Page: 340   Type: F

2. Individuals who suffer from social anxiety are likely to
   a) have an unusually high need for affiliation.
   b) experience feelings of discomfort in the presence of others.
   c) be very concerned with the overall balance of their relationships.
   d) be very popular with other people and yet not realize that they are popular.
   Ans: b   LO: 1   Page: 340   Type: C

3. Support for the idea of the "sociostat" (social thermostat) is provided by the finding that rats
   a) tend to prefer to remain on their own once a period of isolation ends.
   b) are less likely to approach other rats after a period of prolonged contact.
   c) aggress against other rats when a shared resource is scarce.
   d) always prefer the company of other rats to being alone.
   Ans: b   LO: 1   Page: 340-341   Type: C

4. Which of the following is most accurate regarding the human need for affiliation?
   a) People tend to prefer as much social contact with others as possible.
   b) There is little variation between individuals when it comes to desired level of social contact.
   c) People are motivated to maintain an optimum balance of time alone and social contact.
   d) On average, men in individualistic cultures desire more social contact than do women, but in collectivist cultures women prefer more than men.
   Ans: c   LO: 1   Page: 340-342   Type: C

5. Timo has a network of close social ties. In comparison to individuals lacking such a network, research suggests that he will
   a) be more likely to suffer from social anxiety.
   b) be more likely to die a premature death.
   c) have worse physical health.
   d) have higher self-esteem.
   Ans: d   LO: 1   Page: 340-342   Type: A

6. Rita has a strong desire to establish and maintain social contact with others. Rita has
   a) a low need to belong.
   b) severe social anxiety.
   c) a high need for affiliation.
   d) a broken social thermostat.
   Ans: c   LO: 1   Page: 340-342   Type: A

7. Participants in a study by O'Connor and Rosenblood (1996) indicated about every hour whether they were alone or with others and whether they wanted to be alone or with others. The results of this study revealed that
    a) most of the time participants wanted to be with others, but were alone.
    b) most of the time participants wanted to be alone, but were with others.
    c) regardless of whether they wanted to be alone or with others, most of the time participants were not in their desired social state.
    d) regardless of whether they wanted to be alone or with others, most of the time participants were in their desired social state.
    Ans: d   LO: 1   Page: 340-342   Type: C

8. Derek is informed that as part of his fraternity initiation he must sing the school fight song as loudly as he can while standing on the roof of the fraternity house in his underwear. He is then given the choice to await his turn alone or with the girls from the neighboring sorority. Which of the following is *most* likely?
    a) Derek will choose to wait alone in order to achieve cognitive clarity.
    b) Derek will choose to wait alone as waiting with the sorority members will likely increase his stress.
    c) Derek will choose to wait with the sorority members in order to reduce his level of stress.
    d) Derek will choose to wait with the sorority members because they will be able to offer him a different perspective.
    Ans: b   LO: 1   Page: 340-342   Type: A

9. Rofe (1984) argued that stress increases the desire to affiliate only when
    a) being with others has the potential to reduce the negative impact of the situation.
    b) the stress is embarrassing in nature.
    c) in collectivist cultures.
    d) with people who are experiencing the same type of stressful situation, but not with people who have successfully overcome the same stressful situation.
    Ans: a   LO: 1   Page: 341-342   Type: C

10. Though they had all been together on the transcontinental flight for three hours, the passengers didn't start to talk to one another until the plane ran into some serious turbulence. This behavior is *best* explained by the
    a) tendency for external threat to increase affiliation.
    b) matching hypothesis.
    c) proximity effect.
    d) evolutionary perspective on the sociostat.
    Ans: a   LO: 1   Page: 340-342   Type: A

11. Whether stress produces increased or decreased affiliation depends on the
    a) norm of reciprocity.
    b) ambiguity of the situation.
    c) familiarity of the stimulus in the situation.
    d) perceived utility of affiliation in the situation.
    Ans: d   LO: 1   Page: 340-342   Type: C

12. Kulik and Mahler (1989) found that patients waiting for heart surgery preferred to have roommates who were post-operative rather than pre-operative. This finding supports the hypothesis that
    a) people have great difficulty regulating their need for affiliation.
    b) external threat reduces affiliation tendencies in order to reduce embarrassment.
    c) having a close network of social support increases physical health.
    d) affiliation in response to threat can provide cognitive clarity.
    Ans: d   LO: 1   Page: 341-342   Type: C

13. Ollie is about to undergo a painful and risky surgical procedure. Research suggests that Ollie could *most* effectively cope with this threat if he did which of the following?
     a)   Prior to his surgery, speak with someone who has gone through the same procedure to gain insight about the experience.
     b)   Prior to his surgery, spend some time by himself in order to clear his mind.
     c)   Prior to his surgery, speak with someone who is about to have the same procedure so that they can share their concerns with one another.
     d)   After his surgery, speak with someone who has had the same procedure so that they can share their experiences.
     Ans: a   LO: 1   Page: 340-342   Type: A

14. With regard to shyness, all but one of the following have been revealed. Which is the *exception*?
     a)   Shyness may be an inborn trait, but may also develop in response to failed social interactions.
     b)   In different countries, people describing themselves as shy typically constitute about 20 percent of the population.
     c)   Many shy people isolate themselves, resulting in feelings of loneliness.
     d)   Shy people blame themselves when they experience failure in social interactions.
     Ans: b   LO: 2   Page: 342-343   Type: F

15. Using fMRI techniques, researchers have observed that shy people exhibit
     a)   less activity in the amygdala than those who are bold.
     b)   greater activity in the hippocampus than those who are bold.
     c)   greater activity in the amygdala than those who are bold.
     d)   less activity in the hippocampus than those who are bold.
     Ans: c   LO: 2   Page: 342-343   Type: F

16. According to the relevant research, who of the following is likely to be the loneliest?
     a)   José, who is an adolescent
     b)   Hector, who is forty years old and has never been married
     c)   Selena, who is sixty years old and is married
     d)   Marble, who is sixty years old and has never been married
     Ans: a   LO: 2   Page: 342-343   Type: A

17. Miranda is in her first semester of college and is feeling quite lonely. If she is like most other college students, which strategy is she *least* likely to use to cope with her loneliness?
     a)   Invest effort in trying to do well in her courses
     b)   Distract herself by reading and watching television
     c)   Isolate herself from the other students on campus
     d)   Improve her physical appearance
     Ans: c   LO: 2   Page: 342-343   Type: A

18. An evolutionary perspective on attraction suggests that people prefer mates who will
     a)   provide a boost to their social reputation and status.
     b)   favor the conception and birth of their offspring.
     c)   make them laugh.
     d)   are close in proximity to them.
     Ans: b   LO: 3   Page: 343-344   Type: F

19. Which of the following is *most* consistent with the idea that we are attracted to others with whom a relationship is rewarding?
     a)   Tina likes Tony because he is playing hard to get.
     b)   Tina likes Tony because they are about equally attractive.
     c)   Tina likes Tony because they live in the same apartment building.
     d)   Tina likes Tony because he smiles at her and compliments her.
     Ans: d   LO: 3   Page: 343-344   Type: C

20. Someone who argues that attraction is simply a function of wanting to have healthy offspring probably endorses
    a) the belief that situational variables influence attraction.
    b) social exchange theory.
    c) the matching hypothesis of attraction.
    d) the approach of evolutionary psychology.
    Ans: d   LO: 3   Page: 343-344   Type: C

21. According to your textbook, the single best predictor of whether two people will get together is
    a) complementarity.
    b) matching levels of physical attractiveness.
    c) physical proximity.
    d) similarity.
    Ans: c   LO: 3   Page: 344   Type: F

22. Festinger's (1950) research of college student housing found that
    a) students were more likely to become friends with people who lived nearby than those who lived farther away.
    b) married college students were not as affected by proximity effects in forming friendships as were single college students.
    c) mere exposure had a greater effect on platonic friendships versus romantic relationships.
    d) All of these
    Ans: a   LO: 3   Page: 344   Type: F

23. Which of the following is consistent with the mere exposure effect?
    a) The more new dating partners talk to each other, the more they realize they differ in important ways.
    b) The more we see someone, the greater the attraction.
    c) A couple falls in love at first sight.
    d) The old saying "Birds of a feather flock together."
    Ans: b   LO: 3   Page: 344-345   Type: C

24. Dr. Green is conducting an experiment on mere exposure effects. To produce the maximal levels of liking, Dr. Green should
    a) present his stimuli too quickly to be consciously perceived.
    b) select stimuli toward which participants are likely to have initial attitudes that are negative.
    c) present each stimulus at least 100 times to ensure overexposure.
    d) prescreen participants and select only those who are easily bored.
    Ans: a   LO: 3   Page: 344-345   Type: A

25. Mita et al. (1977) found that female college students preferred their own mirror image to their actual appearance. This finding is consistent with
    a) the matching hypothesis.
    b) mere exposure effects.
    c) social exchange theory.
    d) excitation transfer.
    Ans: b   LO: 3   Page: 345   Type: C

26. All of the following have been demonstrated in research on physical attractiveness *except*
    a) attractive students were able to solicit more signatures on a petition than unattractive students.
    b) unattractive defendants received larger court fines than attractive defendants.
    c) teachers expect attractive children to be smarter and achieve more than unattractive children.
    d) attractive employees earn approximately the same salaries as unattractive employees.
    Ans: d   LO: 4   Page: 345-346   Type: C

27. The idea that some faces are inherently more attractive than others is supported by research demonstrating that
    a) people prefer averaged composite faces to individual faces.
    b) standards of beauty change over time.
    c) people from different cultures enhance their appearance in different ways.
    d) people we like seem more attractive to us.
    Ans: a   LO: 4   Page: 346-348   Type: C

28. Lee (2008) and colleagues ran a study in which they examined people's ratings of photos on the website hotornot.com. They found that participants' own level of attractiveness
     a)   were positive predictors of how attractive they rated the photos.
     b)   were negative predictors of how attractive they rated the photos.
     c)   did not predict their ratings of the photos.
     d)   predicted their ratings of male but not female photos.
     Ans: c   LO: 4   Page: 346-347   Type: F

29. The finding that infants spend more time looking at attractive, as compared to unattractive, faces supports the hypothesis that
     a)   beauty is objective.
     b)   beauty is subjective.
     c)   familiarity increases physical attractiveness.
     d)   physical attractiveness increases familiarity.
     Ans: a   LO: 4   Page: 347-348   Type: C

30. The idea that physical attractiveness is inherently subjective is supported by research demonstrating that
     a)   specific facial features tend to be associated with physical attractiveness.
     b)   there is a high degree of cross-cultural consistency in ratings of attractiveness.
     c)   liking someone increases their perceived physical attractiveness.
     d)   averaged faces are judged more attractive than individual faces.
     Ans: c   LO: 4   Page: 348-349   Type: C

31. Which of the following is *not* a reason why we seem to be attracted to averaged faces?
     a)   They are prototypically face-like.
     b)   They are symmetrical.
     c)   They look unusual.
     d)   They seem more familiar to us.
     Ans: c   LO: 4   Page: 347-348   Type: F

32. An evolutionary explanation for the relationship between a face's symmetry and its perceived attractiveness is that
     a)   asymmetrical faces are less familiar and therefore more distinctive in memory.
     b)   facial symmetry is associated with physical health and fitness.
     c)   biological factors have very little to do with facial symmetry.
     d)   parents devote more resources to caring for offspring with symmetrical faces.
     Ans: b   LO: 4   Page: 347-348   Type: F

33. Anderson et al. (1992) found that heavy women are perceived as more attractive than slender women in countries where food is often in short supply. This finding is consistent with the idea that
     a)   certain body types are inherently more attractive than others.
     b)   beauty is subjective.
     c)   symmetry is an important component of attractiveness.
     d)   beauty is objective.
     Ans: b   LO: 4   Page: 348   Type: C

34. Women with an "hourglass" figure are rated as most attractive by men in European cultures. This phenomenon is best explained by the fact that this waist to hip ratio signals
     a)   hunger.
     b)   overall health
     c)   reproductive fertility.
     d)   None of these
     Ans: c   LO: 4   Page: 348   Type: C

35. Research on students' teaching ratings on the website www.ratemyprofessor.com indicate that
     a)   female professors who are rated as strong teachers tended to be seen as less attractive.
     b)   both male and female professors who are rated as "hot" are also given high teaching ratings.
     c)   teachers' non-physical qualities have nothing to do with their likeability.
     d)   for male teachers, perceptions of attraction and teaching skill were unrelated.
     Ans: b   LO: 4   Page: 349   Type: C

36. Eliot and Niesta (2008) found that what color increased the attractiveness ratings of female photos?
    a) White
    b) Red
    c) Gray
    d) Blue
    Ans: b   LO: 4   Page: 349   Type: C

37. The belief that physically attractive individuals also possess desirable personality characteristics is called the
    a) matching phenomenon.
    b) what-is-beautiful-is-good stereotype.
    c) aesthetic appeal of beauty.
    d) reinforcement-affect principle.
    Ans: b   LO: 5   Page: 350   Type: F

38. Research concerning the what-is-beautiful-is-good stereotype demonstrates all of the following *except*
    a) attractive characters in Hollywood movies are also portrayed as virtuous and successful.
    b) students who watched a film depicting the beautiful-is-good stereotype were more likely to be influenced by physical attractiveness in subsequent judgments.
    c) physically attractive people tend to be more intelligent and have higher self-esteem.
    d) physically attractive people tend to have more friends and better social skills.
    Ans: c   LO: 5   Page: 350   Type: C

39. Which of the following statements regarding physically attractive people is *false*?
    a) Attractive people tend to have more sexual experience than unattractive people.
    b) Attractive people tend to be more popular than unattractive people.
    c) Attractive people tend to have higher self-esteem than unattractive people.
    d) Attractive people, when told that a judge who has just given them praise has seen what they look like, often come to have doubts about the true quality of their work.
    Ans: c   LO: 5   Page: 350   Type: F

40. Snyder and colleagues (1977) ran a study in which mixed-gender pairs had a phone conversation. Male participants were given either an attractive or unattractive photo of their conversation partner. Which of the following statements about the study findings is *false*?
    a) Men were friendlier towards the partners who they believed to be attractive.
    b) The outcome of the conversation was more influenced by the women's actual level of attractiveness than by how attractive the men believed the women to be.
    c) Men formed more positive impressions of the personality of women who they believed to be attractive.
    d) Women talking with men who believed they were attractive were actually warmer and more confident during the conversation.
    Ans: b   LO: 5   Page: 350-351   Type: C

41. Interactions with physically attractive others are often rewarding because
    a) physically attractive people tend to have higher self-esteem.
    b) physically attractive people are likely to experience attributional ambiguity during the interaction.
    c) we perceive physically attractive others to be similar to ourselves.
    d) we expect interactions with physically attractive others to be positive.
    Ans: d   LO: 5   Page: 350-351   Type: C

42.   Snyder and colleagues (1977) ran a study in which mixed-gender pairs had a phone conversation. Male participants were given either an attractive or unattractive photo of their conversation partner. Imagine that researchers are interested in extending the results of this study. These new researchers hope to examine the variables of competence and weight because they are interested in studying the stereotype that people who are overweight are perceived to be less competent. In this new study, participants are shown a picture of someone who is either overweight or average weight. They are then told to conduct a phone interview of the person shown in photograph. In fact, they actually conduct a phone interview of another participant (the interviewee), who is not the person in the photo; in reality the photos shown to the participants are assigned at random. The interviewee's responses are tape-recorded for later rating by judges blind to experimental condition. Based on the et al. (1977) findings, we would expect that
       a)   participants conducting the phone interviews would rate "overweight" interviewees as less competent than "average" weight interviewees, but the blind judges would not be affected by weight.
       b)   the blind judges would rate "overweight" interviewees as less competent than "average" weight interviewees, but the participants conducting the interviews would not be affected by weight.
       c)   both the blind judges and the participants would rate "overweight" interviewees as less competent than "average" weight interviewees.
       d)   participants conducting the interviews would rate "overweight" interviewees as most competent, but blind judges would rate "average" weight interviewees as most competent.
       Ans: c   LO: 5   Page: 350-351   Type: A

43.   Which of the following *best* reflects the benefits and cost of being attractive?
       a)   While attractiveness often brings a social advantage to attractive individuals, it can cause them to doubt the sincerity of others' praise for their work.
       b)   While attractiveness often brings heightened self-esteem to attractive individuals, it can lead them to doubt others' praise of their attractiveness.
       c)   While attractiveness often brings greater popularity to attractive individuals, it can increase mental health difficulties.
       d)   While attractiveness often brings lifetime happiness to attractive individuals, it can put pressure on them to maintain their appearance.
       Ans: a   LO: 5   Page: 351-352   Type: C

44.   Keira knows that she is very physically attractive. Her physical appearance has biased her employer to think that her work is better than it really is. The employer therefore frequently compliments her work. The relevant research suggests, however, that Keira will *not* benefit psychologically from these compliments because she
       a)   is too conceited to be affected by the opinions of others.
       b)   lacks the social skills that more average-looking people tend to have.
       c)   suffers from social anxiety.
       d)   does not believe the sincerity of the compliments.
       Ans: d   LO: 5   Page: 351-352   Type: A

45.   Traci is used to people telling her how attractive she is. Research suggests that if she receives positive feedback on a paper she writes for class, she will be most likely to believe that the feedback is genuine and feel good about it if
       a)   the person who graded the paper has never seen her before.
       b)   she has considered herself to be fairly unattractive when she was much younger.
       c)   it is given to her in person.
       d)   her friends do not get good grades on the same assignment.
       Ans: a   LO: 5   Page: 351-352   Type: A

46.   Newcomb's (1961) classic study on attraction in which he set up an experimental college dormitory revealed that
       a)   students' friendships with members of the opposite sex tended to turn into romantic relationships.
       b)   students who had similar backgrounds tended to like each other.
       c)   students who held dissimilar attitudes were more likely to form romantic relationships.
       d)   friendships were more likely than romantic relationships to be based on proximity.
       Ans: b   LO: 6   Page: 352-355   Type: F

47. Similarity leads to attraction for all of the following reasons *except*
    a) similar others provide confirmation of our beliefs and attitudes.
    b) we expect positive interactions with similar others.
    c) similarity implies physical attractiveness, which leads to attraction.
    d) we assume that similar others will like us.
    Ans: c   LO: 6   Page: 352-355   Type: C

48. Popular wisdom is often contradictory, as with the following two sayings: 1) "opposites attract," 2) "birds of a feather flock together." Research on the relationship between similarity and liking suggests that
    a) #1 is more accurate; people tend to be more attracted to those who are dissimilar from themselves.
    b) #2 is more accurate; people tend to be more attracted to those who are similar to themselves.
    c) both are right for different people; heterosexual men tend to be attracted to similar others whereas gay men tend to be attracted to dissimilar others.
    d) both are right in different conditions; people are attracted to similar others when they are interested in long-term relationships, but they prefer dissimilar others for less serious relationships without commitment.
    Ans: b   LO: 6   Page: 352-355   Type: F

49. Rosenbaum (1986) argues that social psychologists overestimate the role of attitudinal similarity in attraction, and suggests that it is not that similarity creates attraction but that
    a) dissimilarity produces interpersonal repulsion.
    b) opposites attract.
    c) similarity in physical appearance is the only form of similarity that affects attraction.
    d) the evidence for the role of complementarity processes is much stronger.
    Ans: a   LO: 6   Page: 354-355   Type: C

50. According to the two-stage model of attraction proposed by Byrne et al. (1986), people
    a) seek partners who are similar with respect to physical attractiveness, but dissimilar with respect to attitudes.
    b) seek partners who are similar with respect to attitudes, but dissimilar with respect to personality.
    c) first approach similar others and then weed out those who are least similar.
    d) first avoid dissimilar others and then approach those remaining who are most similar.
    Ans: d   LO: 6   Page: 354-355   Type: F

51. Walster et al. (1966) randomly matched students for a dance. At the end of the evening, students indicated how satisfied they were with their dates. The strongest predictor of satisfaction was
    a) physical attractiveness.
    b) attitudinal similarity.
    c) proximity of dorm rooms.
    d) complementary personalities.
    Ans: a   LO: 6   Page: 354-355   Type: F

52. Pinel and colleagues (2006) refer to "I-sharing" as an important form of similarity whereby individuals share
    a) a subjective experience.
    b) a level of physical attractiveness.
    c) political ideologies.
    d) technological expertise.
    Ans: a   LO: 6   Page: 354-355   Type: F

53. Furio believes that people desire and form relationships with others who are similar in terms of attitudes, values, physical attractiveness, and so on. Furio subscribes to
    a) equity theory.
    b) the matching hypothesis.
    c) social penetration theory.
    d) social exchange theory.
    Ans: b   LO: 6   Page: 354-355   Type: A

54. According to research by Aronson and Linder (1965), which of the following patterns of comments about us would lead us to like the speaker the most?
     a)   Critical comments followed by flattering comments
     b)   Critical comments followed by more critical comments
     c)   Flattering comments followed by more flattering comments
     d)   Flattering comments followed by critical comments
     Ans: a   LO: 6   Page: 356-357   Type: C

55. Spike likes L.J., but Spike doesn't like Reggie. The relationship among these three individuals would be balanced if
     a)   L.J. likes Reggie.
     b)   L.J. doesn't like Reggie.
     c)   Reggie likes Spike.
     d)   Reggie likes L.J.
     Ans: b   LO: 6   Page: 356-357   Type: A

56. The hard-to-get effect can be hard to get because
     a)   we are turned.off by those who reject us because they are committed to someone else.
     b)   we prefer individuals who are moderately selective over those who are nonselective.
     c)   we like dates who selectively desire us more than they desire others.
     d)   All of these
     Ans: d   LO: 6   Page: 356-357   Type: C

57. Wegner and colleagues (1994) conducted a study in which mixed-gender foursomes played a card game. Some couples were instructed to play "footsie" secretly under the table, some were instructed to do so out in the open, and others were not told to do anything at all. Findings indicated that participants reported being most attracted to their partner when
     a)   they had not been asked to play "footsie."
     b)   they played "footsie" in secret.
     c)   they played "footsie" so that the other pair knew they were doing it.
     d)   they played either type of "footsie."
     Ans: b   LO: 6   Page: 357   Type: C

58. Matthew is considering going on a blind date. According to the evolutionary perspective, he will be *most* concerned with
     a)   the social status of his date.
     b)   the physical attractiveness of his date.
     c)   whether he and his date have similar attitudes.
     d)   whether he and his date are equally intelligent.
     Ans: b   LO: 7   Page: 358-360   Type: A

59. According to the evolutionary perspective, women prefer
     a)   wealthy men because wealth is the criterion they use to estimate their best chances for reproductive success.
     b)   physically attractive men because of the social benefits that come from being associated with such men.
     c)   wealthy men because wealth gives them the freedom to pursue the lifestyle they have been socialized to desire.
     d)   men who play hard to get because such men bring about psychological reactance, which can lead to the misattribution of arousal.
     Ans: a   LO: 7   Page: 358-360   Type: C

60. According to evolutionary psychologists, Tom would feel the *most* upset if his girlfriend Julie
     a)   had been sexually unfaithful to him.
     b)   had become very attracted to a close friend of his.
     c)   spent all her time with friends.
     d)   had committed emotional infidelity.
     Ans: a   LO: 7   Page: 358-360   Type: A

61. Which of the following is consistent with the evolutionary account of mate selection?
    a)   Women of all ages prefer partners who are similar in age.
    b)   Men are more disturbed by emotional infidelity and women are more disturbed by sexual infidelity.
    c)   Both men and women seek partners who are kind and dependable.
    d)   In personal ads, women tend to offer beauty and men offer wealth.
    Ans: d   LO: 7   Page: 358-360   Type: C

62. Consider Buss's study in which he examined what people from 37 different cultures around the world prefer in a romantic partner. Which of the following statements about the results of this study is accurate?
    a)   In most countries, men rated physical attractiveness to be more important than women did, while women rated good financial prospects as more important than men did.
    b)   Before the age of 30, men tended to report having more sexual partners than did women, but that difference disappeared among older participants.
    c)   Women rated kindness, dependability, and sense of humor as more important than men did.
    d)   All of these.
    Ans: a   LO: 7   Page: 358-360   Type: C

63. An analysis of Yahoo personal ads demonstrated that
    a)   men of all ages were more likely to seek younger women.
    b)   women of all ages were more likely to seek income status information.
    c)   women were more likely to seek men who were older, but only up until age 75.
    d)   All of these
    Ans: d   LO: 7   Page: 360   Type: F

64. Which of the following *most* accurately represents differences in mating preferences?
    a)   Men's preferences for young fertile women overcome their interest in other attributes.
    b)   Men's preferences for young fertile women and women's preferences for economically secure men are less pronounced as they age.
    c)   Physical attractiveness is only important to men's mating preferences.
    d)   Differences found between the sexes regarding mating preferences are small compared to the similarities in their mating preferences.
    Ans: d   LO: 7   Page: 361-362   Type: C

65. Eastwick and Finkel (2008) examined men's and women's preferences during a speed dating event. They found significant gender differences in what men and women reported as important mate characteristics before the event began—differences that _____ once they actually started interacting with the potential mates at the event.
    a)   increased
    b)   stayed constant
    c)   disappeared
    d)   became more subtle
    Ans: c   LO: 8   Page: 361   Type: F

66. Joshua is attracted to Daniel because of his warm eyes and great smile. Daniel is attracted to Joshua because of his muscular body. Joshua and Daniel are in Murstein's
    a)   stimulus stage.
    b)   value stage.
    c)   role stage.
    d)   norm stage.
    Ans: a   LO: 8   Page: 363-364   Type: A

67. Roshumba is conducting a study of married couples. She interviews a number of couples about how their relationships developed. It is likely that she will find that
    a)   all relationships developed through a fixed sequence of stages.
    b)   there is considerable variability in how the couples' relationships developed.
    c)   the couples generally went through the value stage before the role stage.
    d)   relationship rewards were unrelated to couples' feelings of being in love.
    Ans: b   LO: 8   Page: 363-364   Type: A

68.   According to social exchange theory, an individual's primary motive in establishing and maintaining relationships is
       a)   maximizing rewards and minimizing costs.
       b)   achieving an equitable balance of inputs and outputs.
       c)   maintaining reciprocal levels of self-disclosure.
       d)   the reproductive fitness of a potential partner.
       Ans: a   LO: 8   Page: 364-366   Type: F

69.   Bruce and Pam have just started dating. According to social exchange theory, their relationship is likely to last longer and be more satisfying if they each feel that
       a)   the rewards gained from the relationship are shared equally between them.
       b)   the costs of maintaining the relationship are shared equally between them.
       c)   the rewards gained from the relationship are equal to the costs of maintaining the relationship.
       d)   the rewards gained from the relationship are greater than the costs of maintaining the relationship.
       Ans: d   LO: 8   Page: 364-366   Type: A

70.   The average, general outcome that an individual expects in a relationship is called the
       a)   intimacy level.
       b)   investment level.
       c)   comparison level.
       d)   self-disclosure level.
       Ans: c   LO: 8   Page: 364-366   Type: F

71.   According to social exchange theory, an outcome from a relationship will produce satisfaction if it falls above a person's
       a)   self-disclosure level.
       b)   level of similarity to the partner.
       c)   intimacy level.
       d)   comparison level.
       Ans: d   LO: 8   Page: 364-366   Type: C

72.   Although she cheats on him, Abdul stays with his girlfriend because he doesn't think he would be able to find anyone better. Abdul has a(n)
       a)   low comparison level for alternatives.
       b)   high comparison level for alternatives.
       c)   secure attachment style.
       d)   avoidant attachment style.
       Ans: a   LO: 8   Page: 364-366   Type: A

73.   Within the framework of social exchange theory, satisfaction in relationships is a function of all of the following *except*
       a)   rewards.
       b)   costs.
       c)   investments.
       d)   comparison levels.
       Ans: c   LO: 8   Page: 364-366   Type: F

74.   Marcie and Karl have been married for several years. Marcie is unhappy in her marriage and is trying to decide whether or not to leave Karl. Which of the following would encourage her the *most* to leave the marriage?
       a)   Her comparison level for alternatives is low.
       b)   Her comparison level is low.
       c)   Her comparison level for alternatives is high.
       d)   Her comparison level is high.
       Ans: c   LO: 8   Page: 364-366   Type: A

75. Zachary is unhappy in his relationship and is trying to decide whether to break up with his girlfriend. Which of the following factors might encourage him to stay?
    a)   If his comparison level for alternatives is high
    b)   If his comparison level is high
    c)   If his investment is high
    d)   If his costs for staying are high
    Ans: c   LO: 8   Page: 364-366   Type: A

76. Benedict is very committed to his relationship with Beatrice. Given this, it is likely that
    a)   Benedict will have a very high comparison level for alternatives.
    b)   Benedict will engage in behaviors that enhance Beatrice's trust in him.
    c)   Benedict will feel over-benefited in relation to Beatrice.
    d)   Benedict and Beatrice will keep investments in their relationship to a minimum.
    Ans: b   LO: 8   Page: 364-366   Type: A

77. Unlike social exchange theory, equity theory suggests that
    a)   people keep track of benefits and contributions to a relationship.
    b)   people are not always out to simply maximize personal reward in a relationship.
    c)   examining relationships in terms of costs and benefits is too economical for something as social and subjective as intimate relationships.
    d)   childhood attachment styles can impact intimate relationships in adulthood.
    Ans: b   LO: 8   Page: 366-367   Type: C

78. Equity theory predicts that people are *most* satisfied in their relationships when the
    a)   perceived rewards of the relationship are equal to the perceived costs of the relationship.
    b)   perceived rewards of the relationship outweigh the perceived costs of the relationship.
    c)   rewards and costs one partner experiences are roughly equal to those of the other partner.
    d)   actual rewards and costs of the relationship exceed the expected rewards and costs of the relationship.
    Ans: c   LO: 8   Page: 366-367   Type: C

79. A "trust-insurance system" in a relationship is when
    a)   both partners lack trust toward the other.
    b)   one partner is overbenefited.
    c)   both partners keep an unconscious tally of the relationship's costs and benefits in order to maintain equity.
    d)   one partner has a low comparison level for alternatives.
    Ans: c   LO: 8   Page: 366-367   Type: C

80. Jon feels like he isn't a good enough husband to his wife, Kate. According to the trust-insurance system, he is likely to
    a)   go out of his way to benefit her through restorative actions..
    b)   withdraw emotionally from the relationship, thereby contributing to a downward cycle.
    c)   become more jealous of her than he was previously.
    d)   feel underbenefited in the relationship.
    Ans: a   LO: 8   Page: 366-367   Type: A

81. Jack and Diane have been dating and living together for two years. Jack always puts Diane's needs before his own, is very supportive of Diane, and devotes a great deal of time and energy to the relationship. Diane, on the other hand, focuses on her own needs and problems and does not exert a great deal of effort when it comes to the relationship. According to equity theorists
    a)   Jack should feel underbenefited and upset about the nature of the relationship, whereas Diane will be content because her needs are being met at minimal cost to her.
    b)   Jack and Diane should be content with the relationship because people in an equity relationship do not keep track of costs and benefits.
    c)   Jack should feel underbenefited and upset about the nature of the relationship and Diane should feel overbenefited and guilty.
    d)   None of these
    Ans: c   LO: 8   Page: 366-367   Type: A

82. Peter offers to help Liza whenever she needs help. In return, however, Peter expects Liza to drop what she is doing to help Peter immediately when he needs help. His understanding of the relationship is *most* likely to be that it is
    a)   an equitable relationship.
    b)   an exchange relationship.
    c)   a communal relationship.
    d)   an intimate relationship.
    Ans: b   LO: 9   Page: 367   Type: A

83. In their relationship, Clyde is concerned with maintaining an equal ratio of rewards and costs, whereas Bonnie is concerned with being responsive to Clyde's needs. Clyde views their relationship as a(n) _____ relationship, whereas Bonnie views it as a(n) _____ relationship.
    a)   reciprocal; exchange
    b)   exchange; communal
    c)   communal; passionate
    d)   passionate; companionate
    Ans: b   LO: 9   Page: 367   Type: A

84. Ben goes out of his way to help Jennifer whenever he can. However, Jennifer has been busy lately and unable to reciprocate. Ben doesn't seem upset because he knows she is sensitive to his needs overall. Which of the following best describes their relationship?
    a)   Equitable relationship
    b)   Exchange relationship
    c)   Communal relationship
    d)   Companionate relationship
    Ans: c   LO: 9   Page: 367   Type: C

85. Keith and David are most likely to have a communal relationship if they are _____ and most likely to have an exchange relationship if they are _____.
    a)   business partners; friends
    b)   romantic partners; strangers
    c)   teammates; brothers
    d)   classmates; business competitors
    Ans: b   LO: 9   Page: 367   Type: A

86. Conchita has good relationships with her boyfriend and with her parents. She is also able to form caring and supportive friendships. Conchita probably has a(n)
    a)   anxious/ambivalent attachment style.
    b)   multiple attachment style.
    c)   secure attachment style.
    d)   avoidant attachment style.
    Ans: c   LO: 9   Page: 367-369   Type: A

87. Everyone doted on Ann when she was a child, and in high school all of the boys wanted to date her. Now, as an adult, Ann expects a lot of attention from her spouse. Ann's expectation can be described as
    a)   an intimacy need.
    b)   an attachment style.
    c)   a comparison level.
    d)   self-disclosure reciprocity.
    Ans: c   LO: 9   Page: 367-369   Type: A

88. Which of the following people sounds most like he has an anxious attachment style?
    a)   Wayne relies heavily on others for support and acceptance.
    b)   Keyshawn very much wants to be close to his partner, but fears that his affections won't be returned.
    c)   Vinny values intimacy, finds it easy to get close to others, and trusts his partner.
    d)   Curtis finds it difficult to trust others and often feels his partners want to be closer than he would like.
    Ans: b   LO: 9   Page: 367-369   Type: A

89. Which attachment style best characterizes the passage that follows: "It makes me uncomfortable to be close to other people. I tend to distrust others, and getting close to people makes me nervous. Most of my partners have wanted me to be more open and intimate with them than I was comfortable with."
a)   Secure attachment style
b)   Anxious attachment style
c)   Avoidant attachment style
d)   Companionate attachment style
Ans: c   LO: 9   Page: 367-369   Type: C

90. Which of the following has been demonstrated in research on attachment style?
a)   People's attachment styles relate to the type of romantic relationships they have.
b)   Attachment styles are relatively fixed throughout the life course.
c)   The distribution of attachment styles varies depending on geographical location.
d)   People classified as securely attached often have lower comparison levels.
Ans: a   LO: 9   Page: 367-369   Type: C

91. Mark has been dating Dierdra for some time. He never lets her go out with her friends or talk to other men. He is demanding and possessive of her. His love for Dierdra could *best* be categorized as
a)   agape.
b)   ludus.
c)   storge.
d)   mania.
Ans: d   LO: 10   Page: 369-370   Type: A

92. Which of the following *best* describes existing gender differences with respect to Lee's (1988) styles of love?
a)   Men and women score about the same on storge and mania styles of love.
b)   Women tend to score higher on ludus love, but men score higher on eros love.
c)   Men tend to score higher on eros love, but women score higher on agape love.
d)   Men tend to score higher on ludus love, but women score higher on pragma love.
Ans: d   LO: 10   Page: 369-370   Type: F

93. Considering the love taxonomies of Lee, Sternberg, and Hatfield, which of the following classifications all seem to reflect a similar type of love?
a)   Lee's storge, Sternberg's intimacy, and Hatfield's passionate love
b)   Lee's eros, Sternberg's passion, and Hatfield's companionate love
c)   Lee's ludus, Sternberg's commitment, and Hatfield's companionate love
d)   Lee's storge, Sternberg's intimacy, and Hatfield's companionate love
Ans: d   LO: 10   Page: 369-370   Type: C

94. According to Sternberg's triangular theory of love, the basic components of love are
a)   intimacy, passion, and commitment.
b)   rewards, costs, and investments.
c)   romance, companionship, and reciprocity.
d)   ludus, eros, and storge.
Ans: a   LO: 10   Page: 369-370   Type: F

95. In Sternberg's triangular theory of love, _____ is the emotional component and _____ is the cognitive component.
a)   intimacy; commitment
b)   passion; intimacy
c)   commitment; intimacy
d)   passion; commitment
Ans: a   LO: 10   Page: 369-370   Type: F

96. Eileen says she loves Jesse, even though they met very recently and both of them are still dating other
     people. When her best friend asks her what she means by "love," Eileen says, "I feel like even though we
     just met, I could tell him anything in the world. And he's so sexy—I get butterflies just thinking about him."
     According to the triangular theory of love, Eileen's feelings towards Jesse would best be labeled
     a)   consummate love.
     b)   companionate love.
     c)   fatuous love.
     d)   romantic love.
     Ans: d   LO: 10 . Page: 369-370   Type: A

97. After a two-week whirlwind romance, Barbie and Ken fly to Vegas to marry. In the framework of the
     triangular theory of love, Barbie and Ken's love would be categorized as
     a)   companionate.
     b)   romantic.
     c)   fatuous.
     d)   storge.
     Ans: c   LO: 10   Page: 369-370   Type: A

98. Herman and Flora have been married for 40 years. They still have a strong relationship and say they are
     each other's best friends. Their relationship seems to be an example of
     a)   exchange love.
     b)   passionate love.
     c)   communal love.
     d)   companionate love.
     Ans: d   LO: 10   Page: 369-370   Type: A

99. Romantic love characterized by high arousal, intense attraction, and fear of rejection is called
     a)   companionate love.
     b)   storge love.
     c)   passionate love.
     d)   agape love.
     Ans: c   LO: 11   Page: 370-372   Type: F

100. Bruno just finished working out at the gym. On his way to the locker room, he passes Charmaigne, a very
     pretty woman. Bruno feels his heart pounding and is convinced that he must be in love with Charmaigne.
     Bruno's feelings are *best* explained by
     a)   negative affect reciprocity.
     b)   excitation transfer.
     c)   psychological reactance.
     d)   social penetration.
     Ans: b   LO: 11   Page: 370-371   Type: A

101. Dutton and Aron (1974) examined the effects of arousal on attraction by conducting a study in which a
     female approached and asked survey questions of men on a rickety suspension bridge. Which of the
     following scenarios is most analogous to the results of this study?
     a)   After swerving to avoid an oncoming car, your heart races and your mind is flooded with images of
          how much you care about your significant other.
     b)   Ten minutes after you've begun a strenuous workout, the person next to you strikes up a conversation
          and you immediately feel attracted to him/her.
     c)   When a classmate that you find particularly attractive happens to sit down next to you, you feel your
          pulse quicken and you stutter as you try to make conversation.
     d)   You are still agitated after a heated phone conversation with your mother, and when you run into
          someone you had a crush on several years ago, you are surprised to realize you don't find him/her that
          attractive in your current state of arousal.
     Ans: b   LO: 11   Page: 371-372   Type: A

102. In Dutton and Aron's (1974) bridge study, how did the researchers assess the extent to which male participants were attracted to a female participant?
    a)   By measuring their heart rate
    b)   By asking them to complete a questionnaire
    c)   By seeing how close to the experimenter they stood after crossing the bridge
    d)   None of these.
    Ans: d   LO: 11   Page: 371-372   Type: F

103. Bonita and Helga are asked to list people they "love," people they are "in love with," and people they are "sexually attracted to." It is likely that the names on
    a)   all three lists will overlap considerably.
    b)   the "love" and "in love" lists will overlap considerably.
    c)   the "in love" and "sexually attracted to" lists will overlap considerably.
    d)   all three lists will be fairly different.
    Ans: c   LO: 11   Page: 371-372   Type: A

104. If people are asked to characterize romantic love, which of the following attributes will over two-thirds of the people list?
    a)   Happiness
    b)   Sexual desire
    c)   Commitment
    d)   Communication
    Ans: b   LO: 11   Page: 371-372   Type: F

105. The idea that relationships progress from superficial exchanges to relatively deeper ones is known as
    a)   social penetration theory.
    b)   social exchange theory.
    c)   the mere exposure effect.
    d)   the matching hypothesis.
    Ans: a   LO: 12   Page: 373-374   Type: F

106. When they first started dating, Norma and Nathan didn't share much about themselves with one another, but as their relationship developed they began to talk more about personal issues and reveal more about themselves to each other. Their behavior is *most* consistent with the predictions of
    a)   the matching hypothesis.
    b)   equity theory.
    c)   the triangular theory of love.
    d)   social penetration theory.
    Ans: d   LO: 12   Page: 373-374   Type: A

107. Which of the following statements best captures the relationship between lying and relationship intimacy?
    a)   The more intimate a relationship becomes, the more tempted people are to lie to their partner.
    b)   The more intimate a relationship, the less likely people are to lie to their partner.
    c)   People lie to strangers more than close friends, but they lie to close friends more than mere acquaintances.
    d)   Once a relationship progresses to marriage, lying becomes more frequent.
    Ans: b   LO: 12   Page: 372-373   Type: F

108. Research suggests that self-disclosure reciprocity is more important
    a)   in the early stages of a relationship.
    b)   when interacting with a man.
    c)   among couples sharing companionate love.
    d)   in opposite-sex interactions.
    Ans: a   LO: 12   Page: 372-373   Type: A

109. Cross-cultural research suggests that passionate love
    a)   is uncommon in cultures that value chastity in a potential mate.
    b)   is widespread across nations.
    c)   is more detectable in countries with higher divorce rates.
    d)   None of these.
    Ans: b   LO: 13   Page: 374-375   Type: F

110. In India and China, love is
    a)   essential for marriage.
    b)   emphasized more among females than males.
    c)   not a sufficient basis for marriage.
    d)   viewed in more dispositionl terms than it is in America.
    Ans: c   LO: 13   Page: 374-375   Type: F

111. Members of cultures having an individualistic orientation seem to
    a)   exhibit lower levels of passionate love.
    b)   give priority in marital decisions to their own feelings.
    c)   be especially concerned about social approval.
    d)   find loveless marriages to be more palatable.
    Ans: b   LO: 13   Page: 374-375   Type: F

112. Which of the following conclusions is *not* supported by data?
    a)   Men often tend to see the world in "sexualized" terms.
    b)   Men are more likely to fantasize about sex with multiple partners.
    c)   Men tend to be more sexually permissive than women.
    d)   Women do not engage in casual sex without emotional commitment.
    Ans: d   LO: 13   Page: 375-377   Type: C

113. Denise and Brandon are just getting to know each other. Each compliments how the other one looks. Given the research on men, women, and sexuality, which of the outcomes is *most* likely?
    a)   Denise will interpret Brandon's compliment as a sexual come-on.
    b)   Brandon will interpret Denise's compliment as a sexual come-on.
    c)   Both Denise and Brandon will interpret each other's compliments as a sexual come-on.
    d)   Neither Denise nor Brandon will interpret each other's compliments as a sexual come-on.
    Ans: b   LO: 13   Page: 375-377   Type: A

114. Homosexual behaviors
    a)   are more common than an exclusive homosexual orientation.
    b)   have been observed in more than 450 animal species.
    c)   vary in incidence by culture.
    d)   All of these.
    Ans: d   LO: 13   Page: 377-380   Type: F

115. Survey research regarding adults' life histories reveals that homosexuals are more likely than heterosexuals to have been
    a)   overattached to their same-sex parents as children.
    b)   sexually abused as children.
    c)   relatively late in the development of puberty.
    d)   None of these.
    Ans: d   LO: 13   Page: 377-380   Type: F

116. LeVay's (1991) examination of the human brain found that
    a)   the hypothalamus of homosexual and heterosexual men did not differ.
    b)   the hypothalamus of men who died of AIDS differed from that of men who did not have AIDS.
    c)   the hypothalamus of homosexual men was similar in many respects to that of heterosexual women.
    d)   differences in the hypothalamus were more pronounced for homosexual and heterosexual men than they were between homosexual and heterosexual women.
    Ans: c   LO: 13   Page: 377-380   Type: F

117. Baumeister and colleagues use the phrase *erotic plasticity* to suggest that
    a) women are more likely to change sexual preference over time than men.
    b) men are turned on by a wider range of stimuli than women are.
    c) men are more likely to have multiple sexual partners than women are.
    d) women are more accepting of "alternative" sexual preferences than men are.
    Ans: a   LO: 13   Page: 378-379   Type: C

118. Which of the following statements regarding marital satisfaction is *false*?
    a) There is typically a honeymoon period in which both partners are satisfied with the marriage.
    b) Heterosexual couples with one child report a faster decline in marital satisfaction than homosexual couples do.
    c) There is a positive association between the degree of initial decline in satisfaction and the likelihood a couple will break up.
    d) The decline following the honeymoon period typically stabilizes by the second year.
    Ans: d   LO: 14   Page: 380-383   Type: C

119. Research on the marital trajectory suggests that once a couple's children have grown up and left the home
    a) married couples actually wind up spending less time together than they did before..
    b) marital satisfaction tends to increase.
    c) sexual infidelity rates increase.
    d) both members of the couple typically adhere even more strongly to gender roles.
    Ans: b   LO: 14   Page: 380-383   Type: F

120. Research concerning the marital trajectory demonstrates that
    a) the longer couples are married, the more satisfied they become.
    b) wives are significantly more satisfied in their marriages than are husbands.
    c) husbands are significantly more satisfied in their marriages than are wives.
    d) the more new experiences married couples share, the greater their satisfaction.
    Ans: d   LO: 14   Page: 380-383   Type: C

121. Carly hurls an insult right back at James when James expresses his negative feelings toward her. Such a pattern illustrates
    a) social penetration.
    b) a demand/withdraw interaction pattern.
    c) negative affect reciprocity.
    d) distress-maintaining attributions.
    Ans: c   LO: 14   Page: 382-383   Type: A

122. When in conflict in close relationships, women often try to get their husbands to talk about the problem and men retreat. This communication pattern
    a) leads exchange relationships to become more communal.
    b) reflects negative affect reciprocity.
    c) illustrates the demand/withdraw interaction pattern.
    d) fosters social penetration.
    Ans: c   LO: 14   Page: 382-383   Type: F

123. Your significant other has just been short-tempered and impatient with you. Your reaction is to think, "well, s/he's had a very stressful week, so I'll just forget that it happened." Your reaction would be best described as an example of
    a) affect reciprocity.
    b) a relationship-enhancing attribution.
    c) a demand/withdraw interaction pattern.
    d) a depressive explanatory style.
    Ans: b   LO: 14   Page: 382-383   Type: A

124.   Research concerning coping with divorce suggests that
       a)   several years after divorce, people tend to be just as satisfied with their lives as are married people.
       b)   immediately after a divorce, life satisfaction ratings tend to increase somewhat.
       c)   men have an easier time bouncing back from divorce than do women.
       d)   None of these.
       Ans: b   LO: 14   Page: 383-384   Type: F

125.   Samantha and David had no close friends outside of their marriage but instead relied on each other for
       everything. When the marriage failed, they were both extremely distressed, *most* likely as a result of their
       a)   identities.
       b)   comparison level alternatives.
       c)   misattribution.
       d)   interdependence.
       Ans: d   LO: 14   Page: 383-384   Type: A

ESSAY

126.   What is the phenomenon known as mere exposure, and how can it affect attraction? What is the role of
       awareness in this effect?
       *Ans: The mere exposure effect is the phenomenon whereby the more often people are exposed to a stimulus,
       the more positively they tend to evaluate it. Through mere exposure, repeated contact with an individual
       can heighten one's attraction to that individual. This effect may occur even if the individual is unaware that
       he or she has been repeatedly exposed to this individual. For example, we tend to prefer our own mirror
       images, whereas others prefer actual photos of us. One caveat to this tendency is that when our initial
       reaction to a person or stimulus is negative, repeated exposures often serve to exaggerate that negative
       impression   Page: 344-345*

127.   What are the benefits of being beautiful? What are the drawbacks?
       *Ans: It has been shown that good-looking people have more friends, better social skills, and a more active
       sex life. Beauty can give the attractive individual an advantage. For example, research by Downs and Lyons
       (1991) showed that Texas judges set lower bail and imposed smaller fines on suspects rated as attractive
       rather than as unattractive. However, beauty also has its pitfalls. When one is attractive, it is hard to tell
       whether attention received is for one's good looks or for actual performance. A second disadvantage is that
       there is pressure to maintain appearance, pressures that could contribute, for example, to disordered eating
       such as bulimia and anorexia nervosa.   Page: 350-352*

128.   How are mating preferences explained from an evolutionary perspective?
       *Ans: From an evolutionary perspective, optimal mating strategies are those that best promote the
       conception, birth, and subsequent reproduction of offspring. Although the goal is the same for men and
       women—to ensure the survival of their genes in future generations—the optimal strategies for achieving
       this goal are different. Because men are potentially able to produce a large number of offspring, their
       optimal strategy is to inseminate many different women selected for their reproductive capacity. And
       because women who are young and healthy are perceived as having the highest reproductive capacity, it is
       in the best interest of men to be concerned about the age and health of women. From an evolutionary
       perspective, this is why men are particularly interested in women's physical appearance. Women, in
       contrast, are biologically more limited in terms of the number of offspring they can produce. The optimal
       strategy for women, therefore, is to maximize the chances that the offspring they do have will survive and
       have offspring of their own. And these chances are improved when women select mates who can provide the
       resources necessary to ensure both their well-being and that of their children. According to the
       evolutionary perspective, this is why women value the socioeconomic status of men.   Page: 358-360*

129. Explain the basic premise of social exchange theory and describe one prediction about intimate
      relationships derived from this theory.
      *Ans: Social exchange theory suggests that people interact with each other in an attempt to maximize their
      own rewards and minimize their costs. One prediction derived from social exchange theory is that people
      who have invested in a relationship are likely to stay in that relationship.*   Page: 364-366

130. Compare and contrast passionate and companionate love.
      *Ans: Both passionate love and companionate love involve feelings of deep concern for and intimacy with
      another individual. However, passionate love is characterized by intense emotional experiences, typically
      occurs early in a relationship, and is unencumbered by costs to a relationship. Companionate love, on the
      other hand, entails deep commitment and trust and exists between friends as well as lovers.*   Page: 370-374

CHAPTER 10

Helping Others

MULTIPLE CHOICE

1. Helping behavior is adaptive from an evolutionary standpoint if
    a)   it contributes to the survival of the fittest individual.
    b)   the economic rewards of helping are greater than the costs.
    c)   it helps to secure propagation of an individual's genes.
    d)   it is performed for altruistic rather than egoistic motives.
    Ans: c   LO: 1   Page: 391-392   Type: C

2. The evolutionary principle of kin selection dictates that we are more likely to help someone who is
    a)   a potential mate.
    b)   likely to return the favor.
    c)   physically attractive.
    d)   genetically similar to us.
    Ans: d   LO: 1   Page: 391-392   Type: C

3. Evolutionary perspectives on helping behavior suggest that individuals
    a)   sometimes offer assistance to others even when doing so puts their own survival at great risk.
    b)   are more likely to offer help to attractive others who seem to be good potential mates.
    c)   are more likely to offer help to distant versus close relatives.
    d)   who only look out for themselves tend to be most successful from a reproductive standpoint.
    Ans: a   LO: 1   Page: 391-392   Type: C

4. Abigail ran back into the burning house to rescue her sister, Sophia, but when she found out that her neighbor, Mitchell, was also in the house, she just waited for the firemen to arrive. According to the study by Fitzgerald (2009), which of the following best explains Abigail's actions?
    a)   In high-risk scenarios, we are motivated to help anyone.
    b)   In low-risk scenarios, we are wiling to help friends and relatives
    c)   In all scenarios, we are unlikely to help someone not genetically related to us.
    d)   In high-risk scenarios, we are more willing to help only our closest relatives.
    Ans: d   LO: 1   Page: 392   Type: A

5. Madsen et al. (2007) found that participants showed a greater willingness to suffer longer for a close relative than for a distant relative. This finding is consistent with
    a)   kin selection.
    b)   the bystander effect.
    c)   pluralistic ignorance.
    d)   the negative-state relief model.
    Ans: a   LO: 1   Page: 391-392   Type: C

6. Which of the following is *not* consistent with the predictions of evolutionary psychology and kin selection?
    a)   Children indicate a greater willingness to help a sibling as compared to a friend.
    b)   Adults indicate a greater willingness to help healthy relatives than those in poor health.
    c)   Adults indicate a greater willingness to help older as compared to younger relatives.
    d)   Adults indicate a greater willingness to help siblings as compared to cousins.
    Ans: c   LO: 1   Page: 391-392   Type: F

7. Which of the following *cannot* be explained from an evolutionary perspective?
    a)   Group members helping a retarded member of the group
    b)   People helping their siblings
    c)   People helping an injured animal
    d)   People helping their friends, knowing that in turn these friends will help them
    Ans: c   LO: 1   Page: 391-392   Type: C

8. The principle of kin selection is based on the assumption that
    a) although it is sometimes beneficial to help our kin, we must focus primarily on helping ourselves if we are to survive danger.
    b) it is the survival of genes that matters most from an evolutionary perspective.
    c) we will help those who are likely to reciprocate that help regardless of whether or not they are genetically related to us.
    d) those who have the greatest reproductive fitness share more genes with their kin.
    Ans: b   LO: 1   Page: 391-392   Type: C

9. Joey and Chandler are not related to each other, yet Chandler goes out of his way to leave work early so he can give Joey a ride to the airport. Ross, who is a scientist, suggests that he can account for Chandler's helping behavior using an evolutionary perspective. Which concept could he cite in doing so in this case?
    a) Kin selection
    b) Reciprocal altruism
    c) The arousal: cost-reward model
    d) Moral hypocrisy
    Ans: b   LO: 1   Page: 392-394   Type: A

10. Online file-sharing web sites depend on the idea of
    a) reciprocal altruism.
    b) kin selection.
    c) audience inhibition.
    d) the arousal: cost-reward model.
    Ans: a   LO: 1   Page: 392-394   Type: A

11. Warneken and Tomasello (2006) studied the helping behavior of 18-month old infants with an adult experimenter. They found that
    a) infants this young didn't demonstrate empathy or helping of any kind.
    b) infants this young understood when the experimenter needed help and, in the majority of cases, attempted to help.
    c) infants this young didn't seem to sense when the experimenter needed help.
    d) infants this young understood when the experimenter needed help but did not know how to offer help.
    Ans: b   LO: 1   Page: 396   Type: F

12. Non-human animals have been observed to demonstrate behaviors indicating
    a) kin selection.
    b) reciprocal altruism.
    c) group selection.
    d) All of these.
    Ans: d   LO: 1   Page: 392-396   Type: F

13. The idea that "I help you and somebody else helps me" is best described as an example of
    a) indirect reciprocity.
    b) vicarious altruism.
    c) sociocultural modeling
    d) signaling
    Ans: a   LO: 1   Page: 394-395   Type: C

14. The concept of empathy is defined by all of the following *except*
    a) may not be uniquely human.
    b) involves an emotional component known as empathic concern.
    c) feeling sympathy and compassion for another individual.
    d) does not include a cognitive component.
    Ans: d   LO: 2   Page: 396-397   Type: C

15.   When Jo witnessed a serious plane crash, she felt compassion, sympathy, and tenderness for the victims. Her feelings are indicative of
      a)   anxious introspection.
      b)   perspective taking.
      c)   personal distress.
      d)   empathic concern.
      Ans: d   LO: 2   Page: 395-396   Type: A

16.   The cognitive component of empathy that involves seeing the world through someone else's eyes is called
      a)   anxious introspection.
      b)   personal distress.
      c)   perspective taking.
      d)   empathic affect.
      Ans: c   LO: 2   Page: 395-396   Type: F

17.   As compared to feelings of personal distress, empathic concern
      a)   is more likely in emergency situations.
      b)   does not directly impact helping behavior.
      c)   is more cognitive in nature.
      d)   is other-oriented rather than self-oriented.
      Ans: d   LO: 2   Page: 395-396   Type: C

18.   Which of the following would be *most* consistent with the negative state relief model?
      a)   Shoppers who are given a free gift are more likely to donate money to a solicitor as they leave the store.
      b)   Students who feel guilty about falling asleep in class are more likely to volunteer to help a professor by completing a questionnaire.
      c)   Professional athletes are more likely to sign autographs for fans following a win than following a loss.
      d)   People who win the lottery are more likely to give money to charity than those who have not won the lottery.
      Ans: b   LO: 2   Page: 397-398   Type: A

19.   The negative state relief model of helping behavior
      a)   supports the existence of altruism in the real world.
      b)   applies more to emergencies than to non-emergency situations.
      c)   identifies yet another way in which helping can be egoistic.
      d)   All of these.
      Ans: c   LO: 2   Page: 397-398   Type: C

20.   Kirk passes a homeless person on the street. Kirk is *most* likely to help this person if the costs of
      a)   not helping are small and Kirk will gain nothing from helping.
      b)   not helping are small and Kirk will feel better about himself by helping.
      c)   helping are large and Kirk will feel better about himself by helping.
      d)   helping are small and Kirk will feel better about himself by helping.
      Ans: d   LO: 2   Page: 397-398   Type: A

21.   The idea that people respond to emergency situations by acting to reduce their personal distress in the most cost-effective way is *most* consistent with the
      a)   negative state relief model.
      b)   attribution-affect-action model.
      c)   norm of social responsibility.
      d)   arousal: cost-reward model.
      Ans: d   LO: 2   Page: 397-398   Type: F

23.   Research conducted by Wayment (2004) in the wake of the 9/11 terrorist attacks reveals that
      a)   people derive more satisfaction from helping strangers than from helping close others.
      b)   giving help to others often leads to increase in mental and physical well-being.
      c)   in an emergency, bystanders often do not have the time to weigh the costs and benefits of helping.
      d)   women are more likely to help strangers than are men.
      Ans: b   LO: 2   Page: 397-398   Type: F

22. Arianna notices that her neighbor's house is on fire. According to the arousal: cost-reward model, her initial reaction should be
    a) feelings of personal distress.
    b) feelings of empathic concern.
    c) a consideration of the rewards of helping.
    d) a consideration of the costs of helping.
    Ans: a   LO: 2   Page: 397-398   Type: A

24. Research by Rilling et al. (2003) suggests that _____ behavior is linked to activation of the brain in areas associated with processing rewards.
    a) selfish
    b) dangerous
    c) evolutionarily adaptive
    d) mutually cooperative
    Ans: d   LO: 2   Page: 397-398   Type: F

25. "Good Samaritan" laws
    a) encourage bystanders to intervene in emergencies.
    b) increase the cost of failing to help.
    c) are fairly rare in the United States.
    d) All of these.
    Ans: d   LO: 2   Page: 399   Type: F

26. When Christine sees how upset Jim is about his father's death, she too becomes upset. As a result, she goes out of her way to console Jim. Christine's actions are consistent with the
    a) empathy-altruism hypothesis.
    b) mood maintenance model.
    c) norm of reciprocity.
    d) threat to self-esteem model.
    Ans: a   LO: 2   Page: 400-402   Type: A

27. The empathy-altruism hypothesis maintains that, regardless of how easy it is to escape from a situation, people will help someone else if their motives are
    a) altruistic.
    b) simplistic.
    c) idiosyncratic.
    d) egoistic.
    Ans: a   LO: 2   Page: 400-402   Type: C

28. According to the empathy-altruism hypothesis, altruistic behavior is primarily the result of
    a) taking another's perspective.
    b) rewards and costs.
    c) personal distress.
    d) evolution.
    Ans: a   LO: 2   Page: 400-402   Type: C

29. Research on the empathy-altruism model has demonstrated that individuals _____ in empathic concern offer help _____.
    a) high; when escape from the situation is difficult, but not when escape is easy
    b) low; if they can easily escape from the situation, but not if escape is difficult
    c) high; regardless of the ease of escape from a situation
    d) low; regardless of the ease of escape from a situation
    Ans: c   LO: 2   Page: 400-402   Type: F

30. The empathy-altruism model suggests that when escape from a situation is easy, people will
    a) offer help only when they have empathic concern.
    b) offer help only when they are in a good mood.
    c) almost always exhibit altruism.
    d) be likely to experience empathic concern.
    Ans: a   LO: 2   Page: 400-402   Type: C

31. Research by Batson and colleagues (2007) on perspective taking and emotional warmth in helping behavior indicates that
     a)   perspective taking is far more powerful than feelings of emotional warmth when it comes to whether or not you help someone else.
     b)   feelings of emotional warmth are far more powerful than perspective taking when it comes to whether or not you help someone else.
     c)   helping behavior is most likely when you both assume the perspective of someone else and feel emotional warmth towards them.
     d)   None of these
     Ans: c   LO: 2   Page: 400-402   Type: F

32. Batson et al. (2003) asked participants to assign two tasks—one desirable and one less desirable—to themselves and a laboratory partner. Compared to participants who were told to imagine how their partner will feel in this situation, participants who were told to imagine how they themselves would feel if they were assigned a task by a partner
     a)   demonstrated more altruism.
     b)   were more likely to claim that they had flipped a coin to decide which task to assign to which person.
     c)   were more likely to assign the desirable task to their partner.
     d)   were able to avoid exhibiting moral hypocrisy.
     Ans: b   LO: 2   Page: 400-402   Type: C

33. Sandhya missed class because she is sick, but Luis did attend the lecture. Sandhya asks Luis if she can borrow his notes. If Luis considers Sandhya's situation from her point of view and decides to offer help, he is most likely
     a)   invoking the norm of reciprocal altruism.
     b)   operating under an altruistic motive.
     c)   operating under an egoistic motive.
     d)   following the negative state relief model.
     Ans: b   LO: 2   Page: 400-402   Type: A

34. Research on egoistic and altruistic motives for helping behavior suggests that
     a)   it does not really matter which motivation underlies helping since the real-life outcome is the same either way.
     b)   those who help out of altruism are likely to continue to help for a longer period of time than those who volunteer help for egoistic reasons.
     c)   altruism is far more likely to occur in collectivist than in individualistic cultures.
     d)   None of these.
     Ans: d   LO: 2   Page: 402-404   Type: F

35. Which of the following statements regarding egoistic helping behavior is *true*?
     a)   It is a form of prosocial behavior.
     b)   It occurs when people offer help for totally selfless reasons.
     c)   It is far less common than altruistic helping behavior.
     d)   It is not susceptible to the bystander effect.
     Ans: a   LO: 2   Page: 402-404   Type: C

36. Giles volunteers his time to his local community center because he thinks it will look good on his college applications. Giles's behavior would *best* be described as
     a)   democratic.
     b)   egoistic.
     c)   altruistic.
     d)   realistic.
     Ans: b   LO: 2   Page: 400-402   Type: A

37. The primary distinction between altruistic and egoistic helping concerns the
     a)   motivations of the helper.
     b)   ratio of rewards to costs.
     c)   number of bystanders present.
     d)   mood of the helper.
     Ans: a   LO: 2   Page: 400-403   Type: C

38. Charlene volunteers one afternoon each week at the local soup kitchen because she is genuinely concerned about the welfare of the less fortunate citizens in her community. Charlene's behavior would *best* be characterized as
    a) egoistic.
    b) altruistic.
    c) affective.
    d) evolutionary.
    Ans: b   LO: 2   Page: 400-402   Type: A

39. Ferguson and others (2008) found that _____ rewards were the best motivator to convince students to give blood.
    a) egoistic.
    b) selfish.
    c) altruistic.
    d) selfless.
    Ans: a   LO: 2   Page: 402-403   Type: C

40. The bystander effect refers to the tendency for
    a) a greater number of bystanders to increase the probability that a victim will receive help.
    b) a greater number of bystanders to reduce the probability that a victim will receive help.
    c) bystander helping to be motivated more by egoistic concerns than altruistic ones.
    d) bystander helping to be motivated more by altruistic concerns than egoistic ones.
    Ans: b   LO: 3   Page: 405-406   Type: F

41. Benny has a heart attack while riding a crowded city bus and nobody on the bus attempts to help him. This exemplifies
    a) the bystander effect.
    b) the good mood effect.
    c) moral hypocrisy.
    d) the norm of social responsibility.
    Ans: a   LO: 3   Page: 405-406   Type: A

42. The bystander effect does *not* occur when
    a) the bystanders are all friends.
    b) the bystanders are all strangers.
    c) the bystanders are only in one's mind.
    d) the bystanders are on the internet.
    Ans: a   LO: 3   Page: 405-406   Type: C

43. Many different factors contribute to the bystander effect. Which of the following is *not* one of them?
    a) Audience inhibition
    b) Time pressure
    c) Pluralistic ignorance
    d) Diffusion of responsibility
    Ans: b   LO: 3   Page: 405-406   Type: F

44. Kramer was on the subway during rush hour and failed to offer assistance to a woman who fell down and lost consciousness. One explanation for why he might not have noticed the emergency would be
    a) audience inhibition.
    b) pluralistic ignorance.
    c) diffusion of responsibility.
    d) stimulus overload.
    Ans: d   LO: 3   Page: 406   Type: A

45. Which of the following factors will lead to greater helping in an emergency situation?
    a) A large group of bystanders witnesses the emergency
    b) The emergency occurs in a busy environment
    c) The emergency involves two people who are clearly related
    d) The situation is clearly an emergency
    Ans: d   LO: 3   Page: 406-407   Type: C

46. Having struggled with panhandlers on the subway, hassles at the office, and telephone calls at dinner, Allison retreats to her bedroom rather than noticing that her daughter needs help with a homework assignment. She is probably reacting to
     a)   social norms.
     b)   bystander calculus.
     c)   stimulus overload.
     d)   reactance.
     Ans: c   LO: 4   Page: 406   Type: A

47. Which of the following is *not* one of the five steps to helping proposed by Latané and Darley (1970)?
     a)   Interpret the event as an emergency
     b)   Invoke the norm of reciprocity
     c)   Take responsibility for providing help
     d)   Notice that something is happening
     Ans: b   LO: 3   Page: 406-407   Type: F

48. Which of the following situational changes would *not* have made it more likely that someone would've acted to help Kitty Genovese during her attack?
     a)   If some of her neighbors had been police officers
     b)   If there had been 76 witnesses instead of 38
     c)   If it had been 3:20 p.m. instead of 3:20 a.m.
     d)   If some of the witnesses had just heard a lecture on the situational influences on helping behavior
     Ans: b   LO: 3   Page: 405-408   Type: A

49. The belief that one's own thoughts and feelings differ from those of others, even though everyone is behaving in the same way, is called
     a)   stimulus overload.
     b)   pluralistic ignorance.
     c)   courageous resistance.
     d)   diffusion of responsibility.
     Ans: b   LO: 3   Page: 407-408   Type: F

50. Newman notices that the passenger seated across from him on the subway has his eyes closed and hasn't moved in a while. But he looks around and sees that no one else, including those passengers who were on the train when he boarded, seems too concerned about this man. He decides that this probably means there isn't an emergency and the man is not in need of help. This line of thinking epitomizes which of the following concepts?
     a)   stimulus overload.
     b)   pluralistic ignorance.
     c)   audience inhibition.
     d)   diffusion of responsibility.
     Ans: b   LO: 3   Page: 407-408   Type: A

51. Cosmo is walking home on a busy downtown street when he notices a woman lying on the sidewalk who appears to have lost consciousness. Which of the following obstacles to helping would best explain why he did not interpret the event as an emergency?
     a)   Audience inhibition
     b)   Pluralistic ignorance
     c)   Diffusion of responsibility
     d)   Stimulus overload
     Ans: b   LO: 3   Page: 407-408   Type: A

52. Dewanto hears what sounds like gunshots coming from the school parking lot. None of his classmates appears concerned, so Dewanto assumes that they know the sound was only a car backfiring or someone playing with firecrackers. Dewanto's beliefs illustrate
     a)   diffusion of responsibility.
     b)   empathic concern.
     c)   audience inhibition.
     d)   pluralistic ignorance.
     Ans: d   LO: 3   Page: 407-408   Type: A

53. During his statistics class this morning, Stuart was completely confused. He considered asking questions during the lecture, but because nobody else asked questions, he did not want to raise his hand and make a fool of himself in front of everyone. Stuart's failure to ask questions *most* likely stems from
    a)   diffusion of responsibility.
    b)   stimulus overload.
    c)   pluralistic ignorance.
    d)   audience inhibition.
    Ans: c   LO: 3   Page: 407-408   Type: A

54. Asuni hears her neighbor's burglar alarm go off in the middle of the night, but she doesn't call the police because she assumes that one of the other neighbors will do so. Asuni's failure to call the police is the result of
    a)   pluralistic ignorance.
    b)   audience inhibition.
    c)   diffusion of responsibility.
    d)   stimulus overload.
    Ans: c   LO: 3   Page: 408-409   Type: A

55. Research by Garcia and colleagues (2002) suggests that imagining you are in a group with other people
    a)   makes you more likely to engage in helping behavior.
    b)   makes you less likely to engage in helping behavior.
    c)   only influences altruistic helping behavior.
    d)   does not affect helping behavior.
    Ans: b   LO: 3   Page: 408-409   Type: F

56. Diffusion of responsibility can be reduced if
    a)   a bystander's training is relevant to the emergency at hand.
    b)   there are many bystanders.
    c)   the bystanders do not know each other.
    d)   the bystanders do not know the victim.
    Ans: a   LO: 3   Page: 408-409   Type: C

57. Ginny thinks she hears a husband physically abusing his wife. However, she does *not* call the police because she is afraid that her neighbors will ostracize her if she is wrong. Ginny's failure to act is a case of
    a)   negative state relief.
    b)   audience inhibition.
    c)   empathic concern.
    d)   pluralistic ignorance.
    Ans: b   LO: 3   Page: 410   Type: A

58. According to Latané and Darley's (1970) five-step model of helping, analysis of costs and rewards occurs at what step?
    a)   Noticing the event
    b)   Interpreting the event as an emergency
    c)   Taking responsibility to help
    d)   Providing help
    Ans: d   LO: 3   Page: 410   Type: F

59. Stimulus overload would interfere with potential helping behavior at which step of Latané and Darley's (1970) five-step model of helping?
    a)   Noticing the event
    b)   Interpreting the event as an emergency
    c)   Taking responsibility to help
    d)   Providing help
    Ans: a   LO: 3   Page: 410   Type: C

60.   Which of the following would be the *most* effective way for a person to secure help in an emergency situation?
      a)   Make a very loud general plea for help.
      b)   Ask a specific individual for help.
      c)   Request help from those who are more psychologically distant from the situation.
      d)   Appear to have the situation entirely under control.
      Ans: b   LO: 3   Page: 412   Type: C

61.   Research suggests that the bystander effect
      a)   has become much less pronounced in our modern, technology-driven era.
      b)   is more common among women than men.
      c)   happens more often among friends than among strangers.
      d)   can occur with on-line and virtual groups as well as in-person groups.
      Ans: d   LO: 3   Page: 410-412   Type: C

62.   Research on cyberhelping indicates that
      a)   the bystander effect is much less pronounced in anonymous internet and virtual settings.
      b)   even direct appeals for help that include mention of a fellow chat room member's name are not enough to overcome the power of the bystander effect.
      c)   individuals who spend a good deal of their free time on-line actually tend to be more helpful people overall than other individuals.
      d)   None of these
      Ans: d   LO: 3   Page: 410-412   Type: C

63.   As Stalder (2008) points out, one reason why an individual in need may still be more likely to receive help from a large group of witnesses than from a lone witness is that
      a)   the odds of any one witness avoiding the obstacles to helping behavior are increased in a larger group.
      b)   reciprocity norms are not as strong in large groups.
      c)   egoistic concerns trump empathic concern in large groups.
      d)   All of these
      Ans: a   LO: 4   Page: 410-412   Type: C

64.   Fiona needs to get people to fill out her survey. The likelihood that people will help Fiona will increase if she approaches all of the following people *except* those who
      a)   live in the country rather than the city.
      b)   seem to be in a good mood.
      c)   just passed by a bakery.
      d)   are in a hurry.
      Ans: d   LO: 4   Page: 412-413   Type: A

65.   People are *less* likely to notice an emergency if they
      a)   display empathic concern for others.
      b)   are aware of their surroundings.
      c)   are in a good mood.
      d)   are under time pressure.
      Ans: d   LO: 4   Page: 412-413   Type: F

66.   Darley and Batson (1973) found that the helping behavior of seminary students was *best* predicted by
      a)   how religious they were.
      b)   the type of speech they were about to give.
      c)   how much time they had.
      d)   the sex of the person being helped.
      Ans: c   LO: 4   Page: 412-413   Type: F

67. In their famous Good Samaritan study, Darley and Batson (1973) found that
    a) students studying to become ministers were more likely to offer assistance to a stranger than college students.
    b) seminary students on their way to give a sermon involving the Good Samaritan parable were more likely to offer assistance to a stranger than students preparing sermons on other topics.
    c) the more religious seminary students were, the more likely they were to stop to offer assistance to a stranger as they walked across campus.
    d) None of these
    Ans: d   LO: 4   Page: 412-413   Type: C

68. Research on situational factors that influence helping demonstrates that
    a) the lower the overall population, the more likely people are to help.
    b) the higher the cost of living, the more likely people are to help.
    c) the greater the population density, the more likely people are to help.
    d) the lower the time pressure, the less likely people are to help.
    Ans: a   LO: 4   Page: 413-414   Type: F

69. The tendency for people in urban areas to help less than those in rural areas can be explained by all of the following *except*
    a) stimulus overload is more likely in urban areas than in rural areas.
    b) residents of urban areas represent more diverse populations than those in rural areas.
    c) urban residents tend to be wealthier than rural residents.
    d) people feel more anonymous in urban areas than rural areas.
    Ans: c   LO: 4   Page: 413-414   Type: C

70. Kemmelmeier and colleagues (2006) found that residents of more individualistic states in the United States are _____ than residents of more collectivist states.
    a) less likely to offer assistance in an emergency
    b) more likely to give to charity
    c) more susceptible to the bystander effect
    d) less generous
    Ans: b   LO: 4   Page: 415-416   Type: F

71. While outside enjoying the sunshine, Claudia happily gives directions to a lost tourist. Claudia's willingness to help a stranger is *most* likely due to
    a) the good mood effect.
    b) reciprocity norms.
    c) pluralistic ignorance.
    d) negative state relief.
    Ans: a   LO: 4   Page: 416-417   Type: A

72. Research suggests that if you are soliciting the help of strangers at the mall, you are most likely to be successful if you
    a) stand in front of a bakery.
    b) approach older adults as opposed to younger people.
    c) position yourself by the exit of a movie theater that is showing a sad film.
    d) appear to be angry.
    Ans: a   LO: 4   Page: 416-417   Type: A

73. Muriel, who is generally a happy person, becomes quite sad to find out that she failed her psychology exam. When her roommate asks Muriel for a ride to the airport, Muriel should
    a) be more likely to help.
    b) be less likely to help.
    c) focus more on the costs of helping rather than the rewards.
    d) be more concerned with the potential for reciprocity.
    Ans: a   LO: 4   Page: 416-417   Type: A

74. Forgas and others (2006) conducted a study on whether the mood of salespeople would affect their tendency
     to help. The results indicated that
     a)   the mood manipulation had the strongest effect on the least experienced staff.
     b)   the mood manipulation had no effect.
     c)   the mood manipulation had the strongest effect on the most experienced staff.
     d)   the mood manipulation had the same effect on both more experienced and less experienced staff.
     Ans: a   LO: 4   Page: 416-417   Type: F

75. Feeling good can lead to increased helping behavior because
     a)   people want to stay in a good mood.
     b)   people in a good mood have a higher level of mental arousal.
     c)   people in a good mood are more likely to avoid pluralistic ignorance and notice an individual in need
           of help.
     d)   there is a positive correlation between good mood and an altruistic personality.
     Ans: a   LO: 4   Page: 416-417   Type: F

76. As she is about to walk into the grocery store, Melissa sees a woman struggling with her groceries. Melissa
     is *most* likely to help this woman if
     a)   the woman is obviously drunk.
     b)   the store is located in an urban environment.
     c)   Melissa only has five minutes to purchase her donuts and beer, and get to work on time.
     d)   Melissa feels guilty about having parked in the handicapped space.
     Ans: d   LO: 4   Page: 417-418   Type: A

77. Suppose Barbara is feeling sad and she sees Mort struggling to move a piece of furniture. She would be
     most likely to help Mort if Barbara
     a)   felt personally responsible for her bad mood.
     b)   and Mort were young children.
     c)   was self-focused on her own concerns.
     d)   blamed someone else for her bad mood.
     Ans: a   LO: 4   Page: 417-418   Type: A

78. Research suggests that negative moods tend to enhance helping
     a)   almost never.
     b)   when responsibility for the negative mood is placed elsewhere.
     c)   when helping values are salient.
     d)   when helping is thought to repair mood.
     Ans: d   LO: 4   Page: 417-418   Type: C

79. Which social norm suggests that people who are fairly well-off in life should use their position to help those
     who are in need?
     a)   Norm of social responsibility
     b)   Norm of reciprocity
     c)   Norm of equity
     d)   Norm of justice
     Ans: c   LO: 4   Page: 419-420   Type: C

80. Jake spends countless hours in front of the television. It is likely that
     a)   the violence Jake sees on television will be more influential on his behavior than the prosocial
           behavior he sees.
     b)   the prosocial behavior Jake sees on television is more likely to be reflected in his behavior than the
           violence he sees.
     c)   the aggressive and prosocial behaviors that Jake sees on television are equally likely to be imitated.
     d)   neither the aggressive nor prosocial behavior that Jake sees on television will have an effect on his
           behavior.
     Ans: b   LO: 4   Page: 419-420   Type: A

81. Helpful models increase prosocial behavior for all of the following reasons *except*
     a)   helpful models provide an example of behaviors that others can imitate.
     b)   helpful models demonstrate that helping others is rewarding.
     c)   helpful models make social norms governing helping salient.
     d)   helpful models make perspective taking more likely to occur.
     Ans: d   LO: 4   Page: 419-420   Type: C

82. Simon's decision whether or not to help someone is based primarily on whether that person seems to deserve assistance. Simon is motivated by concerns about
     a)   administrative rules.
     b)   equity.
     c)   social responsibility.
     d)   justice.
     Ans: d   LO: 4   Page: 419-420   Type: A

83. Kevin asks Winnie to drive him to the airport. Though Winnie doesn't really want to, she agrees because Kevin loaned her money last week. Winnie agreed to help because of the norm of
     a)   equity.
     b)   reciprocity.
     c)   justice.
     d)   cooperation.
     Ans: b   LO: 4   Page: 419-420   Type: A

84. A study by Burger and others (2009) about the norm of reciprocity demonstrated that
     a)   people will reciprocate only if they expect to receive recognition.
     b)   people will reciprocate even if their reciprocation will be unknown.
     c)   people will reciprocate only with close friends.
     d)   people will reciprocate only with strangers.
     Ans: b   LO: 4   Page: 420   Type: C

85. Which of the following observations best illustrates the conclusion that the norm of reciprocity can influence helping behavior?
     a)   If someone has the opportunity to help you but chooses not to, you are less likely to offer them assistance when they need it in the future.
     b)   Individuals are more likely to offer assistance to others who are perceived to be "deserving" of help.
     c)   When people are in a situation in which they feel that they have received more benefits than they really have earned, they are eager to help those who are underbenefited.
     d)   Instead of helping others out of concern for their well-being, sometimes we offer assistance simply to avoid looking bad.
     Ans: a   LO: 4   Page: 419-420   Type: C

86. The norm of equity prescribes that when people are in a situation in which they feel _____, they should help those who are _____.
     a)   overbenefited; underbenefited.
     b)   underbenefited; overbenefited.
     c)   understimulated; overstimulated.
     d)   overstimulated; understimulated.
     Ans: a   LO: 4   Page: 419-420   Type: C

87. Even though he feels that drug addicts often deserve their plight, Steven donates clothes to a rehabilitation center because he believes he has an obligation to help those who need assistance, whatever the reasons behind their condition. Steven's thoughts regarding his actions are *most* consistent with the norm of
     a)   reciprocity.
     b)   justice.
     c)   equity.
     d)   social responsibility.
     Ans: d   LO: 4   Page: 419-420   Type: A

88. Helene spends a few weeks helping the victims of a tornado because she believes that people should help others, especially those who deserve assistance. Helene's thoughts regarding her actions are consistent with the norm of
    a)   reciprocity.
    b)   justice.
    c)   equity.
    d)   social responsibility.
    Ans: b   LO: 4   Page: 419-420   Type: A

89. Cross-cultural research suggests that college students in India apply the norm of social responsibility _____ than students in the U.S.
    a)   less selectively
    b)   less often
    c)   less automatically
    d)   None of these.
    Ans: a   LO: 4   Page: 420-421   Type: C

90. Miller et al. (1990) compared the perception of social norms governing helping in India and the United States. This research demonstrated that
    a)   children in India regard helping as more of a social obligation than do children in the United States, but there were no differences among adults.
    b)   adults in the United States regard helping as more of a social obligation than do adults in India, but there were no differences among children.
    c)   both adults and children in India regard helping as more of a social obligation than do adults and children in the United States.
    d)   both adults and children in the United States regard helping as more of a social obligation than do adults and children in India.
    Ans: c   LO: 4   Page: 420-421   Type: F

91. Social norms fail to produce helping behavior when they are too
    a)   cognitive.
    b)   sophisticated.
    c)   general.
    d)   personal.
    Ans: c   LO: 4   Page: 419-420   Type: F

92. Yablo and Field (2007) found that Thai students appeared more altruistic and helpful than American students. Which of the following reasons did they cite as the most important one to explain this phenomenon?
    a)   Religion.
    b)   Collectivism.
    c)   Kindness.
    d)   Responsibility.
    Ans: a   LO: 4   Page: 421   Type: C

93. Eisenberg and others (2002) found that the extent to which preschool children exhibited spontaneous helping behavior predicted how helpful they would be in later childhood and early adulthood. This finding is consistent with the hypothesis that
    a)   there are stable individual differences in helping.
    b)   situational factors can overwhelm personality differences in helping.
    c)   the altruistic personality is genetically based.
    d)   individuals high in empathy tend to be more helpful than those low in empathy.
    Ans: a   LO: 5   Page: 421   Type: C

94. Research on helping behavior has shown all of the following about personal influences on helping behavior *except* that
   a)   personal influences are more powerful than situational influences.
   b)   helping tendencies may be inherited.
   c)   people who help in emergencies tend to differ from those who help in non-emergencies.
   d)   extroversion is positively correlated with helping behavior.
   Ans: a   LO: 5   Page: 421-423   Type: C

95. Which of the following combinations of traits has been shown to be essential to helping?
   a)   Extroversion and conscientiousness
   b)   Empathy and advanced moral reasoning
   c)   Empathy and introversion
   d)   Independence and conscientiousness
   Ans: b   LO: 5   Page: 421-423   Type: F

96. People seem to be more likely to help an individual who has all of the following characteristics *except*
   a)   good looks.
   b)   charisma.
   c)   friendliness.
   d)   intelligence.
   Ans: d   LO: 6   Page: 423-424   Type: F

97. Lydia needs people to help her by signing a petition. She can increase her chances of receiving help by
   a)   making herself look more attractive.
   b)   invoking empathy by noting she is in a bind because she waited until the last minute.
   c)   first putting potential helpers in a self-focused negative mood.
   d)   making her requests over the telephone rather than in person.
   Ans: a   LO: 6   Page: 423-424   Type: F

98. Research on attractiveness and helping indicates that
   a)   we are more likely to help attractive people than unattractive people.
   b)   attractive people are more helpful than unattractive people.
   c)   both a. and b. are correct.
   d)   None of these.
   Ans: a   LO: 6   Page: 423-424   Type: F

99. Male motorists in France were more likely to offer a ride to a female hitchhiker who
   a)   had a small bust, but was smiling.
   b)   had an enhanced bust size and was smiling.
   c)   had an enhanced bust size and who was not smiling
   d)   None of these
   Ans: b   LO: 6   Page: 424   Type: F

100. Research on people's willingness to help individuals with AIDS indicates that we tend to be more likely to offer assistance
   a)   to people we believe are deserving of help.
   b)   to people who are gravely ill.
   c)   when we are in a good mood.
   d)   when we are in a bad mood.
   Ans: a   LO: 6   Page: 424   Type: C

101. Peggy feels sorry for smokers who have lung cancer because she believes they were duped by tobacco companies to develop a deadly addiction and are therefore not responsible for their disease. When asked to donate money to support lung cancer research, Peggy gives generously. Peggy's prosocial behavior can *best* be explained by
   a)   the negative state relief model.
   b)   attributions of responsibility.
   c)   the arousal: cost-reward model.
   d)   a norm of equity.
   Ans: b   LO: 6   Page: 424   Type: A

102. Renaldo is driving out of a beautiful national park that is having some financial trouble. There is a box for donations by the park exit, and no one around. Which of the following would *most* likely encourage Renaldo to leave a donation?
    a)   If he believed that the norm was not to donate money
    b)   If he was thinking about his breakup with his girlfriend
    c)   If he observed that the person in the car in front of him did not leave a donation
    d)   If he had heard that a wealthy benefactor had just rescinded funds for the park due to losses in the stock market
    Ans: d   LO: 6   Page: 424   Type: A

103. Jerry, a devout Mets fan, stops to help a stranded motorist wearing a Mets jersey, but passes by the stranded motorist in the Yankees jersey. Which of the following could account for Jerry's behavior?
    a)   Having already helped one person, Jerry was in a good mood and therefore less likely to help a second person.
    b)   Jerry felt more empathy for the Mets fan than the Yankees fan.
    c)   Audience inhibition is greater when the person in need of help is similar.
    d)   Pluralistic ignorance is reduced when the person in need of help is dissimilar.
    Ans: b   LO: 6   Page: 425-426   Type: A

104. Some cross-racial helping is *not* truly altruistic because it can be a sign of
    a)   kin selection.
    b)   utility.
    c)   self-support.
    d)   feelings of superiority over the person being helped.
    Ans: d   LO: 6   Page: 425-426   Type: F

105. Manny needs help and Pedro is capable of giving it. Pedro is more likely to help if he
    a)   perceives Manny as responsible for his predicament.
    b)   is of lower status than Manny.
    c)   endorses the norm of justice more than the norm of social responsibility.
    d)   has a shared identity with Manny.
    Ans: d   LO: 6   Page: 425-426   Type: A

106. The finding that people often help similar others who are unrelated to them can be explained by the tendency to
    a)   more easily empathize with such individuals.
    b)   exhibit kin selection.
    c)   avoid stimulus overload.
    d)   resist social norms.
    Ans: a   LO: 6   Page: 425-426   Type: C

107. People in exchange relationships are more likely than those in communal relationships to
    a)   exhibit pure altruism towards one another.
    b)   get angry at violations of the reciprocity norm.
    c)   feel good about helping one another.
    d)   demonstrate helping behavior in an effort to alleviate negative mood.
    Ans: b   LO: 6   Page: 426   Type: F

108. Tex and his brother Slim are both trying to get into medical school. When Tex asks Slim for help with his application materials, Slim begrudgingly agrees, but then fails to point out several typing errors on Tex's application. This behavior is *best* explained by the
    a)   empathy-altruism hypothesis.
    b)   negative state relief model.
    c)   attribution-affect-action theory.
    d)   self-evaluation maintenance model.
    Ans: d   LO: 6   Page: 426   Type: A

109. Grady asks Joe for some coaching tips. According to the self-evaluation maintenance model, Joe will be less helpful to Grady in which of the following situations?
    a) Grady is an acquaintance. Joe is feeling confident about his own abilities and Grady is performing well. Coaching ability is core to Joe's self-concept.
    b) Grady is an acquaintance. Joe is not feeling confident about his own abilities and Grady is performing well. Coaching ability is not core to Joe's self-concept.
    c) Grady is a good friend. Joe is not feeling confident about his own abilities and Grady is performing well. Coaching ability is core to Joe's self-concept.
    d) Grady is a good friend. Joe is feeling confident about his own abilities and Grady is performing well. Coaching ability is not core to Joe's self-concept.
    Ans: c   LO: 6   Page: 426   Type: A

110. Women are more likely than men to help others in situations involving
    a) physical danger and an audience.
    b) anonymous circumstances.
    c) another man.
    d) emotional support.
    Ans: d   LO: 6   Page: 426-427   Type: F

111. Men are more likely than women to help others in situations involving
    a) physical danger and an audience.
    b) anonymous circumstances.
    c) another man.
    d) emotional support.
    Ans: a   LO: 6   Page: 426-427   Type: F

112. According to your textbook, which of the following statements regarding gender and helping behavior is *false*?
    a) Men, unlike women, often feel that their self-esteem is threatened by needing to ask for help from someone else .
    b) Men are more likely than women to offer help in a situation involving potential physical danger.
    c) Men, unlike women, are more likely to offer help in situations where they can do so anonymously.
    d) Men are less likely than women to receive help in an emergency situation.
    Ans: c   LO: 6   Page: 426-427   Type: F

113. Karen and Rob are talking to a mutual friend who suddenly breaks down and asks if one of them can stay and talk about an important problem. Who is probably more likely to help?
    a) Karen is more likely to help.
    b) Rob is more likely to help.
    c) Both are equally likely to help.
    d) Whether Karen or Rob is more likely to help depends on the gender of the friend.
    Ans: a   LO: 6   Page: 426-427   Type: A

114. The threat-to-self-esteem model suggests that receiving help is experienced as _____ when the recipient feels appreciated and cared for, but is experienced as _____ when the recipient feels inferior and overly dependent.
    a) self-supportive; self-threatening
    b) self-enhancing; self-handicapping
    c) self-promoting; self-conscious
    d) self-aggrandizing; self-demoralizing
    Ans: a   LO: 7   Page: 427-428   Type: F

115. While Sue was temporarily unemployed, her mother called regularly just to make sure she was okay and to cheer her up. The help Sue's mother gave her can be described as
    a) kindred.
    b) calculating.
    c) self-supportive.
    d) self-directed.
    Ans: c   LO: 7   Page: 427-428   Type: C

116. Brad decides to help his younger brother with his basketball skills. This help is likely to be self-threatening if
    a)   Brad's brother has low self-esteem.
    b)   Brad is dissimilar to his brother.
    c)   basketball is ego-relevant to Brad's brother.
    d)   Brad's motives for helping are egoistic.
    Ans: c   LO: 7   Page: 427-428   Type: A

117. People are less likely to react negatively to receiving help if they
    a)   are high in self-esteem.
    b)   are in an interdependent relationship with the helper.
    c)   are adults rather than young children.
    d)   belong to a group that tends to be stigmatized.
    Ans: b   LO: 7   Page: 427-428   Type: C

118. Members of traditionally disadvantaged or stigmatized groups tend to feel worse about themselves when receiving help that is both
    a)   unsolicited and from an ingroup member.
    b)   emotional in nature and from an outgroup member.
    c)   unsolicited and from an outgroup member.
    d)   solicited and from an anonymous source.
    Ans: c   LO: 7   Page: 427-428   Type: F

119. People who have _____ are most likely to be threatened by offers of help.
    a)   doubts about their own competence
    b)   high self-esteem
    c)   a high need for affiliation
    d)   None of these.
    Ans: b   LO: 7   Page: 427-428   Type: F

120. Whether or not someone seems responsible for her own predicament is more influential on helping behavior
    a)   in individualistic cultures..
    b)   when the target in need of help is male.
    c)   when the person in need of help is a family member.
    d)   None of these
    Ans: a   LO: 6   Page: 429-430   Type: C

121. People are less likely to help if they think the person is responsible for his plight
    a)   in both collectivist and individualist cultures
    b)   in collectivist cultures
    c)   in individualist cultures
    d)   in neither collectivist nor individualist cultures
    Ans: a   LO: 7   Page: 429-430   Type: C

122. One way for the social connection of a community to increase is to
    a)   experience a natural disaster.
    b)   become wealthier.
    c)   increase its ratio of men to women.
    d)   None of these.
    Ans: a   LO: 7   Page: 429-430   Type: A

123. Eleanor is asked to help the people who live on the other side of the city restore their block after it was burned down in a fire. It is *most* probable that she will help if _____ the people on the other side of the city.
    a)   her personality is similar to that of
    b)   her values are similar to those of
    c)   she has the same social status as
    d)   she feels a meaningful connection with
    Ans: d   LO: 7   Page: 429-430   Type: A

124. One reason that perceived similarity may increase helping is that it
   a)   causes people to think about their values.
   b)   enables people to see the power of the situation.
   c)   breaks down dispositional inferences.
   d)   provides a meaningful connection between the helper and the person being helped.
   Ans: d   LO: 7   Page: 429-430   Type: C

125. We help our family and our friends more than strangers. We tend to be more helpful when we are empathic toward the plight of others. Diffusion of responsibility is reduced if we anticipate making the acquaintance of someone who needs help. All of these examples illustrate
   a)   the influence of social norms on behavior.
   b)   the underlying human need for social connections.
   c)   the predisposition for people to help others.
   d)   the conflict between altruistic and egocentric motives.
   Ans: b   LO: 7   Page: 429-430   Type: C

ESSAY

126. Explain how empathy affects helping.
   Ans: The empathy-altruism hypothesis proposes that people are more likely to help someone altruistically if they take his or her perspective. Doing so creates an emotional response or concern for this other person, which in turn creates a motive to help that is satisfied when his or her distress is reduced. This hypothesis suggests, then, that helping is sometimes altruistic, not egoistic. Some would argue, however, that there is no such thing as pure altruism, and that all helping behavior includes an egoistic component.
   Page: 400-402

127. Describe how the presence of bystanders affects helping.
   Ans: When bystanders are present, a victim is less likely to receive help. Bystanders impede helping by reducing the likelihood that potential helpers will (1) notice that the victim needs help, (2) interpret the situation as an emergency, (3) take responsibility for helping, and (4) decide to offer help. These factors together make it less likely that a victim will be helped by someone in a crowd than by a single individual.
   Page: 405-409

128. Describe how moods, both good and bad, affect helping.
   Ans: Both good and bad moods can lead to increased helping. When in good moods, positive thoughts become more accessible, leading to more consideration of helping others. In addition, people in good moods may help more in order to maintain these moods. Alternatively, people in bad moods may help more in order to remove their guilt or to rid themselves of the bad moods. It should be noted, however, that bad moods only tend to increase helping in adults and older children.   Page: 416-418

129. Identify two characteristics of a person in need that might affect the likelihood that the person is helped.
   Ans: Attractive people tend to be helped more than unattractive people, as do individuals who are not considered to be responsible for their predicament. We are also more likely to help those who are similar and those who share family or group ties with us.   Page: 423-424

130. Describe how feeling connected to others affects the likelihood that we will help them.
   Ans: When we feel connected to others, we are more likely to help them. Research on kin selection indicates that we are more likely to help our blood relatives than strangers or unrelated friends. Cognitive and emotional connections such as empathy increase helping, as does similarity. In emergencies, bystanders who know the victims are more likely to help. And people in close relationships usually find it easier and more comfortable to receive help from each other. Together these findings suggest that helping has a profound social element—we are more likely to help those to whom we feel connected.
   Page: 429-430

CHAPTER 11

Aggression

MULTIPLE CHOICE

1. The defining characteristic of aggression is that the aggressor
   a) intends to injure another living being.
   b) actually causes physical or psychological harm.
   c) is angry or otherwise emotionally aroused during the aggressive act.
   d) derives enjoyment from the aggressive act.
   Ans: a   LO: 1   Page: 436-437   Type: F

2. Which of the following *best* illustrates aggression?
   a) Felix and Oscar engage in a heated debate concerning the merits of the Big Mac versus the Whopper.
   b) Maude trips over the scooter her son absentmindedly left in the driveway.
   c) In his attempt to save Samantha from drowning, Darin breaks three of her ribs.
   d) Ginger kicks MaryAnn in the shins to keep her from eating the last coconut pie.
   Ans: d   LO: 1   Page: 436-437   Type: A

3. A negative, antagonistic attitude toward another person or group is called
   a) emotional aggression.
   b) hostility.
   c) anger.
   d) instrumental aggression.
   Ans: b   LO: 1   Page: 436-437   Type: F

4. Whitley feels that Lena deliberately left the tuna fish sandwich sitting out in the sun so that Whitley would get food poisoning after she ate it. Whitley's emotional response would *best* be described as
   a) instrumental aggression.
   b) hostility.
   c) anger.
   d) displacement.
   Ans: c   LO: 1   Page: 436-437   Type: A

5. The difference between aggression and violence is best described as one of
   a) extremity.
   b) intent.
   c) affect.
   d) hostility.
   Ans: a   LO: 1   Page: 436-437   Type: F

6. Which of the following situations *best* illustrates instrumental aggression?
   a) When Buster finds out that his favorite television show has been preempted by the presidential debates, he kicks Gob, who just happens to be standing nearby.
   b) After getting fired from his job at the nuclear power plant, Homer pulls out his semi-automatic machine gun and shoots at the squirrels.
   c) Karen pinches Grace until Grace finally moves out of the way so that Karen can get to the liquor cabinet.
   d) Edith stabs Archie with a fork when she finds out that he forgot her birthday.
   Ans: c   LO: 1   Page: 436-437   Type: A

7. When Katie found out that her brother Matt had pulled the heads off all of her Barbie dolls, she threw her Easy Bake oven at him. Katie's behavior illustrates
    a) instrumental aggression.
    b) proactive aggression.
    c) incompatible responses.
    d) reactive aggression.
    Ans: d   LO: 1   Page: 436-437   Type: A

8. Mugging someone who is well-dressed because you need money is an example of
    a) instrumental aggression.
    b) emotional aggression.
    c) relational aggression.
    d) institutional aggression.
    Ans: a   LO: 1   Page: 436-437   Type: C

9. Forbes and others (2009) examined how levels of aggression differed in individualist vs. collectivist cultures. They found that
    a) aggression levels were highest in the U.S., a highly individualist culture.
    b) aggression levels were highest in China, a highly collectivist culture.
    c) aggression levels were lowest in the U.S., a highly collectivist culture.
    d) Both the U.S. and China had equally high levels of aggression.
    Ans: a   LO: 1   Page: 438-439   Type: A

10. United States citizens tend to be more likely than those of other nations to engage in
    a) politically motivated violence directed toward groups.
    b) mob violence at sporting events.
    c) violence against young girls.
    d) gun-related violence against individuals.
    Ans: d   LO: 2   Page: 438-439   Type: F

11. United States citizens tend to be more likely than those of other nations to disapprove of
    a) violence against young girls.
    b) gun violence.
    c) a husband slapping his wife.
    d) bullying.
    Ans: c   LO: 2   Page: 438-439   Type: F

12. One form of violence that seems to be fairly consistent across cultures is
    a) violence against young girls.
    b) gun violence.
    c) domestic violence.
    d) bullying.
    Ans: d   LO: 2   Page: 440   Type: F

13. Based on Bonta's (1977) research on nonviolent societies, a powerful way to reduce violence within a society would be to
    a) emphasize a strict division of labor by gender.
    b) promote cooperation.
    c) harshly punish all acts of aggression.
    d) separate subcultures within the society.
    Ans: b   LO: 2   Page: 440-441   Type: C

14. Which of the following would decrease the likelihood that Chris would behave aggressively?
    a) If Chris is a teenager
    b) If Chris is male
    c) If Chris is drunk
    d) none of the above
    Ans: d   LO: 2   Page: 441-442   Type: A

15. The fact that the American population has been aging in recent years has been offered as an explanation for the
    a)   decrease in violent crimes.
    b)   increase in gun-related violence.
    c)   greater availability of violent pornography.
    d)   current overcrowded conditions in prisons.
    Ans: a   LO: 2   Page: 441-442   Type: C

16. Which of the following concerning violent crime in America is *true*?
    a)   Teens are more likely to commit violent crimes, whereas older adults are more likely to be the victim of such crimes.
    b)   Older adults are more likely to commit violent crimes, whereas younger adults are more likely to be the victim of such crimes.
    c)   Older adults are more likely to both commit violent crimes and be the victims of such crimes.
    d)   Teens are more likely to both commit violent crimes and be the victims of such crimes.
    Ans: d   LO: 2   Page: 441-442   Type: F

17. A murder has been committed. Given the research on homicide, which of the following is *most* likely?
    a)   The murderer was of a different race than the victim.
    b)   The murder occurred in the eastern United States.
    c)   The murderer was thirty-five years old.
    d)   The murderer and victim were both African-American.
    Ans: d   LO: 2   Page: 441-442   Type: C

18. According to FBI statistics, who of the following is *least* likely to be the victim of a homicide?
    a)   A Black man
    b)   A Black woman
    c)   A White man
    d)   A White woman
    Ans: d   LO: 2   Page: 441-442   Type: F

19. The relatively greater violence rates in the southern United States has been attributed to
    a)   greater variability of temperature in the South than in the North.
    b)   the manner in which residents of the South respond to status threats.
    c)   the ratio of males to females living in the South.
    d)   the age demographics of the South.
    Ans: b   LO: 2   Page: 441-442   Type: C

20. Which of the following statements regarding human gender differences and aggression is *false*?
    a)   In virtually every culture, males are more violent than females.
    b)   Studies of 3–6 year-olds suggest that boys are more likely than girls to play games that involve or mimic aggression.
    c)   Males are more likely to engage in risky, self-destructive behavior than females.
    d)   Boys demonstrate more overt and relational forms of aggression than do girls.
    Ans: d   LO: 3   Page: 442-443   Type: F

21. Women are more likely than men to
    a)   exhibit overt forms of aggression.
    b)   be victims of murder.
    c)   engage in bullying.
    d)   none of the above.
    Ans: d   LO: 3   Page: 442-443   Type: F

22. Carmen, an 8-year-old girl, is angry with her brother, so she tells their mother that he was playing video games when he was supposed to be doing his homework; she then tells all his friends that he is afraid of the dark. Carmen's behavior illustrates
    a)   indirect aggression.
    b)   hostile aggression.
    c)   physical aggression.
    d)   overt aggression.
    Ans: a   LO: 3   Page: 442-443   Type: A

23. Which of the following concerning gender differences in aggression is *true*?
a) Men use more relational aggression than verbal aggression.
b) Women use relational aggression more than men.
c) When there is a clear provocation, men use much more overt aggression than women.
d) Women use more verbal aggression than indirect aggression.
Ans: b   LO: 3   Page: 442-443   Type: C

24. Regarding self-esteem and aggression, which of the following is *false*?
a) Narcissism is a good predictor of aggression.
b) Low self-esteem is a good predictor of aggression.
c) Narcissism is correlated with aggression in response to provocation.
d) High self-esteem is predictive of aggression when combined with narcissism and provocation.
Ans: b   LO: 3   Page: 443-444   Type: C

25. Markus is extremely impulsive. Research suggests that he will tend to
a) be more aggressive than most people across situations.
b) rely more on verbal versus physical aggression.
c) be more aggressive than other people when provoked.
d) exhibit more relational than overt forms of aggression.
Ans: c   LO: 3   Page: 443-444   Type: A

26. According to Smith's (2007) book about the evolutionary origins of human warfare
a) pacifists have a greater chance for reproductive success.
b) pacifism is likely to become part of human nature.
c) warriors have a greater chance for reproductive success.
d) warriors are least likely to be accepted as part of the group
Ans: c   LO: 4   Page: 444-445   Type: F

27. The theory that emphasizes genetic (rather than individual) survival is referred to as
a) catharsis.
b) evolutionary social psychology.
c) reproductive success.
d) instrumental aggression.
Ans: b   LO: 4   Page: 444-446   Type: C

28. Evolutionary accounts of aggression emphasize the
a) role of aggression in securing food and land.
b) contribution of genetics and hormones to aggressive behavior.
c) importance of intrapsychic conflict in aggressive behavior.
d) role of aggression in securing a mate.
Ans: d   LO: 4   Page: 444-446   Type: C

29. Which of the following is *most* consistent with evolutionary explanations of aggression?
a) Children are more likely to be abused by their biological parents than by stepparents.
b) Male-to-female violence is predominantly triggered by sexual jealousy.
c) Male-to-male violence is triggered by a rise in testosterone.
d) Different cultures demonstrate different levels of aggressiveness.
Ans: b   LO: 4   Page: 444-446   Type: C

30. According to an evolutionary perspective, males are competitive with each other because
a) males are predisposed to sexual jealousy.
b) females select high-status males for mating.
c) aggression enhances the male's confidence in the paternity of his offspring.
d) All of the above.
Ans: d   LO: 4   Page: 444-446   Type: C

31. Women are more likely than men to use relational aggression because women
a) lack direct access to wealth.
b) have lower levels of testosterone.
c) place more of a value on their own lives and therefore avoid risky behaviors.
d) do not want to risk physically harming the father of their offspring.
Ans: c   LO: 4   Page: 444-446   Type: C

32. The finding that male-to-male violence occurs primarily in response to status challenges, but male-to-female violence occurs primarily in response to sexual jealousy supports the
     a)   instinct view of aggression.
     b)   evolutionary perspective on aggression.
     c)   learning theory account of aggression.
     d)   socio-cultural perspective on aggression.
     Ans: b   LO: 4   Page: 444-446   Type: C

33. Finnegan notices his wife talking to another man and flies into a jealous rage. According to the evolutionary perspective, Finnegan's behavior is designed to
     a)   assert his social power.
     b)   increase his confidence in the paternity of his offspring.
     c)   deflect the death instinct outward instead of inward.
     d)   increase the level of serotonin in his brain.
     Ans: b   LO: 4   Page: 444-446   Type: A

34. Belligeria is an extremely violent society, whereas Harmonia is entirely nonviolent. These cultural variations suggest that aggression is
     a)   an evolutionarily adaptive strategy.
     b)   an inborn tendency.
     c)   the result of hormonal fluctuations.
     d)   determined primarily by social factors.
     Ans: d   LO: 4   Page: 444-446   Type: C

35. In a study about status (to successfully compete for mates), Vladas Griskevicius and others (2009) found that
     a)   women do not use aggression of any type to boost their status.
     b)   men are more likely to boost their status through indirect aggression.
     c)   women are more likely to boost their status through direct aggression.
     d)   men are more likely to boost their status through direct aggression
     Ans: d   LO: 4   Page: 445-446   Type: C

36. Which of the following research results would provide evidence that aggression is a heritable trait?
     a)   Identical twins reared together are more similar in their levels of aggressiveness than identical twins reared apart.
     b)   Adopted children are more similar in levels of aggressiveness to their adoptive parents than to their biological parents.
     c)   Fraternal twins are more similar in levels of aggressiveness than non-twin siblings.
     d)   Identical twins are more similar in levels of aggressiveness than fraternal twins.
     Ans: d   LO: 4   Page: 446   Type: C

37. Twin research indicates that _____ is more heritable than _____.
     a)   overt aggression; relational aggression
     b)   instrumental aggression; emotional aggression
     c)   verbal aggression; physical aggression
     d)   none of the above.
     Ans: a   LO: 4   Page: 446   Type: F

38. Anglelina is interested in whether the teenager she is preparing to adopt is likely to be aggressive as an adult. Research suggests that she would be wise to consider whether he
     a)   is a twin.
     b)   was aggressive as an 8-year-old.
     c)   has long fingers.
     d)   was born in a nation with a warm climate.
     Ans: b   LO: 4   Page: 446   Type: A

39. Research on testosterone and aggression indicates that
     a)   it is surprising that women ever aggress given that they have no testosterone.
     b)   their relationship is stronger among non-human animals than it is among humans.
     c)   very little regarding aggressive behavior is actually heritable.
     d)   their relationship disappears when you examine samples of elderly adults.
     Ans: b   LO: 4   Page: 446-447   Type: F

40. The strong positive correlation between testosterone levels and aggressive behavior could reflect all of the following *except*
    a) testosterone and aggression are unrelated.
    b) testosterone increases aggression.
    c) aggression increases testosterone.
    d) stress may increase both aggression and testosterone.
    Ans: a   LO: 4   Page: 446-447   Type: C

41. Research concerning the role of testosterone in aggression has demonstrated that
    a) acts of aggression may increase levels of testosterone.
    b) testosterone levels drop after successful aggressive episodes.
    c) the relationship between testosterone and aggression is stronger among fraternity members than college males who do not belong to fraternities.
    d) individuals with low testosterone levels tend to smile less.
    Ans: a   LO: 4   Page: 446-447   Type: F

42. Several studies have found that finger length ratio is associated with higher levels of _____ aggression in _____ and _____ aggression in _____.
    a) direct, men; indirect, women.
    b) indirect, men; direct women.
    c) positive men; negative, women.
    d) negative, women; positive, men.
    Ans: a   LO: 5   Page: 446-447   Type: F

43. Research on aggression with transsexual participants
    a) indicates that gender differences in aggressive tendencies have been greatly exaggerated by previous researchers.
    b) conclusively identifies a link between biology and aggression.
    c) provides a rare means of ethically studying the causal effects of testosterone on human aggression.
    d) All of the above
    Ans: c   LO: 4   Page: 447   Type: F

44. According to research on the role of the brain and executive function in predicting aggressive tendencies, when very aggressive teenagers witnessed a situation in which someone intentionally inflicted pain on another person, they exhibited brain activity associated with
    a) being part of a group.
    b) empathy.
    c) experiencing rewards
    d) None of the above.
    Ans: c   LO: 4   Page: 448   Type: F

45. The only way that Britney can get her husband to stop leaving his dirty socks on the kitchen table is to pinch him every time he does it. Britney is using aggression as a
    a) positive reinforcement.
    b) negative reinforcement.
    c) positive punishment.
    d) negative punishment.
    Ans: b   LO: 5   Page: 448-449   Type: A

46. Consider a mother who slaps her son whenever he engages in aggression. The behavior of the mother is an example of
    a) instrumental aggression.
    b) corporal punishment.
    c) positive punishment.
    d) all of the above.
    Ans: d   LO: 5   Page: 448-449   Type: A

47. Each of the following people behaved aggressively, and each was punished for his or her aggression. For which of these people should the indicated punishment have the *best* chance of successfully reducing aggression?
    a)   Jake, who was punished immediately following his act of aggression
    b)   Keifer, who was extremely angry when punished after committing an act of emotional aggression
    c)   Lakeesha, who was punished in a very angry, hostile manner by her parents after committing an act of instrumental aggression
    d)   Danielle, who was punished for some of her aggressive acts but not for others, and cannot discern a pattern in the incidence of punishment
    Ans: a   LO: 5   Page: 448-449   Type: A

48. Which of the following has *not* been offered as a criticism of the use of punishment to decrease aggression?
    a)   It is only effective when a number of stringent conditions have been satisfied.
    b)   When perceived as arbitrary, it can provoke retaliatory aggression.
    c)   It fails to allow the recipient to safely reduce aggressive intent through catharsis.
    d)   It provides a model of aggressive behavior that can actually lead to more aggression in the future.
    Ans: d   LO: 5   Page: 448-449   Type: F

49. Gershoff's (2002) analysis of studies with over 36,000 participants indicates a positive correlation between corporal punishment and
    a)   aggression as a child.
    b)   aggression as an adult.
    c)   criminal behavior.
    d)   all of the above.
    Ans: d   LO: 5   Page: 449   Type: F

50. Mario and Luigi are trying to decide whether to spank their child when she does something undesirable. Research suggests that this type of punishment
    a)   will be most effective if she perceives her parents to be warm and supportive.
    b)   is very unlikely to lead their daughter to engage in serious aggression later in life.
    c)   is not used by many of their friends, if they are representative of U.S. citizens.
    d)   all of the above.
    Ans: a   LO: 5   Page: 448-449   Type: A

51. Ira believes that aggression is an acquired tendency picked up by observing others and by experience with rewards and punishments. Ira's beliefs are *most* consistent with
    a)   social learning theory.
    b)   the evolutionary perspective.
    c)   instinct theory.
    d)   negative affect escape model.
    Ans: a   LO: 5   Page: 449-451   Type: A

52. Bandura's (1961) study of aggressive behavior in children
    a)   demonstrated that children will follow an adult model's lead in terms of degree and nature of aggression demonstrated.
    b)   identified the specific antisocial personality characteristics associated with highly aggressive children.
    c)   demonstrated that violent TV has little effect on children's own aggressive tendencies.
    d)   illustrated the ability of punishment to curtail the aggressive tendencies of children.
    Ans: a   LO: 5   Page: 449-451   Type: C

53. Jamie's parents occasionally use corporal punishment when she breaks their rules. They believe that spanking will act as a negative reinforcement for her bad behavior. Which of the following concepts explains why spanking may actually backfire and lead Jamie to demonstrate increased aggression?
    a)   The arousal-affect model
    b)   Social learning theory
    c)   Cultivation
    d)   Culture of honor
    Ans: b   LO: 5   Page: 449-451   Type: A

54. Deion is *least* likely to imitate the aggressive behaviors of Darcy if Darcy
    a)   is a cartoon character.
    b)   is punished for behaving aggressively.
    c)   is rewarded for behaving aggressively.
    d)   experiences catharsis following the aggressive behavior.
    Ans: b   LO: 5   Page: 449-451   Type: A

55. Aggressive models teach aggressive behavior by all of the following *except*
    a)   teaching observers how to perform the aggressive act.
    b)   fostering positive attitudes toward aggression.
    c)   allowing observers to construct aggressive scripts.
    d)   increasing the frustration experienced by observers.
    Ans: d   LO: 5   Page: 449-451   Type: C

56. Gee and Leith (2007) analyzed aggressive behavior in the National Hockey League (NHL). They concluded that players born in North America were more likely to resort to fighting to deal with their frustration because
    a)   hockey players generally have aggressive personalities.
    b)   they were always punished severely when they acted aggressively.
    c)   the sport of hockey makes people act aggressively.
    d)   they had been exposed to models of aggression in hockey from a young age.
    Ans: d   LO: 5   Page: 450-451   Type: C

57. Nonie gets a new Barbie doll for her sixth birthday and she immediately begins to punch, kick, and throw the doll around the house. Which of the following is likely to have contributed to this behavior?
    a)   Nonie saw Uncle Floyd yell at Auntie Mame when she threw her Barbie doll.
    b)   Nonie saw her cousin Brucie hug and kiss his Barbie doll.
    c)   Nonie just finished watching the new Barney beat up Barbie in a cartoon on television.
    d)   Nonie has been socialized in a stereotypical female role.
    Ans: c   LO: 5   Page: 450-451   Type: A

58. Marty watches his older brother act non-aggressively after being provoked. According to social learning theory, Marty is subsequently likely to
    a)   act less aggressively and experience stronger restraints against aggression.
    b)   refrain from acting aggressively because he believes that he will be punished for aggressing.
    c)   experience catharsis and displace his aggression onto safer, more acceptable targets.
    d)   find more socially acceptable outlets for his impulses, such as rough sports.
    Ans: a   LO: 5   Page: 449-451   Type: A

59. Based on the principles of social learning theory, which of the following measures is *most* likely to be successful in teaching a child to act nonviolently?
    a)   Punishing the child physically for acting aggressively
    b)   Exposing the child to older models who are punished harshly for acting aggressively
    c)   Exposing the child to older models who act non-aggressively in response to provoking situations
    d)   Teaching the child how to displace frustrations and anger in safe, socially acceptable ways, such as by hitting a punching bag or role-playing a desired outcome
    Ans: c   LO: 5   Page: 449-451   Type: C

60. A socialization explanation for gender differences in aggressive tendencies
    a)   would focus on differences between men and women in levels of hormones and neurotransmitters.
    b)   might consider ways in which parents react differently to the aggressive actions of young boys versus girls.
    c)   would suggest that such differences should be identical across different cultures.
    d)   none of the above.
    Ans: b   LO: 5   Page: 451-452   Type: C

61. Which of the following concerning a culture of honor is *true*?
    a)   It is more prevalent among women than men.
    b)   It is more prevalent in the northern United States than in the southern United States.
    c)   It is a product of socialization that can influence the tendency to aggress.
    d)   It is produced by differences in testosterone and serotonin levels.
    Ans: c   LO: 5   Page: 452-454   Type: C

62. Research has shown that argument-related murders committed by White males occur at much higher rates in the South and Southwest than in other regions in the United States, whereas felony-related murders exhibit much smaller or even reversed regional differences. This set of findings is *best* explained by which of the following statements?
    a)   Greater interracial tensions and frustrations are experienced in the South and Southwest than in other regions.
    b)   Economic frustrations are likely to be greater in the South and Southwest.
    c)   The prevalent culture of the South and Southwest places a higher premium than that of other regions on protecting one's honor by retaliating aggressively to others' insults.
    d)   Due to different socialization practices, children in the South and Southwest are less likely to be rewarded for distinguishing between instrumental and emotional aggression.
    Ans: c   LO: 5   Page: 452-454   Type: C

63. Vandello, Cohen and Ransom (2008) found that white men from the southern part of the U.S. were more likely than white northern men to
    a)   respond to frustration with aggression.
    b)   show negative attitudes toward aggression.
    c)   overestimate the aggressiveness of their peers.
    d)   underestimate the aggressiveness of their peers.
    Ans: c   LO: 5   Page: 452-454   Type: C

64. Ethan has been released from jail in the United States and is applying for jobs in the South and the Northeast. Ethan is probably more likely to land interviews in the South than in the Northeast if he was in jail for
    a)   murdering a person who taunted him in public about an affair with his wife.
    b)   committing fraud on a million dollar insurance claim.
    c)   illegally importing cocaine across the border.
    d)   robbing a jewelry store owned by a member of a racial minority group.
    Ans: a   LO: 5   Page: 452-454   Type: A

65. Which of the following conclusions is *least* consistent with the original formulation of the frustration-aggression hypothesis?
    a)   The need to aggress in response to frustration can be reduced if the frustrated individual behaves in an aggressive but relatively harmless way toward an object that is not related to the source of the frustration.
    b)   The need to aggress in response to frustration is taught directly by reinforcement, important models, and the media, and can be "unlearned" if the reinforcements and models change.
    c)   The need to aggress in response to frustration is a psychological drive that resembles the physiological drive of seeking food in response to hunger.
    d)   The need to aggress in response to frustration can lead to nonviolent acts of aggression such as spreading rumors about someone or telling hostile jokes.
    Ans: b   LO: 6   Page: 455-457   Type: C

66. When his wife tells him that he cannot go out bowling with the guys, Homer gets mad and throttles his son, Bart. Homer's behavior is an example of
    a)   instrumental aggression.
    b)   catharsis.
    c)   displacement.
    d)   vicarious aggression.
    Ans: c   LO: 6   Page: 455   Type: A

67. Betty, an anti-war activist, is mad at the President for leading the country to war. Because she cannot go straight to the source of her frustration, she takes out her aggression on her next-door neighbor, Wilma, instead. This situation sounds most like an example of
    a)   excitation transfer.
    b)   displacement.
    c)   arousal substitution.
    d)   hostile attribution bias.
    Ans: b   LO: 6   Page: 455   Type: A

68. Of the following, the frustration-aggression hypothesis would probably be *least* effective as an explanation for
    a)   instrumental aggression.
    b)   emotional aggression.
    c)   a strong correlation between economic conditions and prejudice toward minority groups.
    d)   examples of "road rage."
    Ans: a   LO: 6   Page: 455-457   Type: C

69. Which of the following terms provides an example of the concept of displacement?
    a)   Catharsis
    b)   Habituation
    c)   Scapegoating
    d)   Diffusion of blame
    Ans: c   LO: 6   Page: 455-457   Type: C

70. Some people believe that they can reduce their likelihood of aggressing against others by engaging in aggressive sports, such as boxing and ice hockey. This belief is *least* consistent with
    a)   social learning theory.
    b)   the frustration-aggression hypothesis.
    c)   the original notion of catharsis.
    d)   the negative affect escape model.
    Ans: a   LO: 6   Page: 456-457   Type: C

71. Research suggests that we're most likely to displace aggression
    a)   towards others who are members of an outgroup.
    b)   towards those who are biologically related to us.
    c)   in the absence of provocation.
    d)   when opportunities for catharsis are unavailable to us.
    Ans: a   LO: 6   Page: 455-457   Type: F

72. Research on catharsis demonstrates that
    a)   observing aggressive models reduces arousal.
    b)   aggressive behavior that makes people feel good is likely to occur again.
    c)   responding to frustrations with aggression is more effective than simply letting the frustration dissipate on its own.
    d)   venting frustrations reduces feelings of hostility and anger.
    Ans: b   LO: 6   Page: 456-457   Type: C

73. The concept of catharsis has been undermined by findings suggesting that engaging in or witnessing aggression often
    a)   reduces the likelihood of cultivation.
    b)   produces displacement.
    c)   causes habituation.
    d)   slowly weakens restraints against aggression.
    Ans: d   LO: 6   Page: 456-457   Type: C

74. As described by Dollard, the original notion of catharsis included two steps. What are those steps?
    a)   Reduction of physiological arousal; decrease in anger and aggression
    b)   Freeing up of intrapsychic energy; greater ability to distract oneself from a frustrating stimulus
    c)   Increase of physiological arousal; displacement of aggression onto weaker targets
    d)   none of the above.
    Ans: a   LO: 6   Page: 456-457   Type: C

75. Shawna has just gone through a break-up with her arrogant and selfish boyfriend. While hitting the
     punching bag in her kickboxing class, she imagines that she is punching her boyfriend's head. Shawna
     believes that engaging in the relatively harmless pursuit of hitting the punching bag will drain the energy
     from her more violent tendencies (like her temptation to slit the tires of his car or to break his legs).
     Research on the idea of catharsis suggests that
     a) hitting the punching bag will reduce Shawna's "hot-blooded" aggressive intent.
     b) the good feelings Shawna derives from hitting the punching bag will be replaced by feelings of guilt
         and shame which will make her less likely to engage in aggression in the future.
     c) hitting the punching bag will be a more successful technique for Shawna's attempt to reduce future
         aggression than would distracting herself by going out and having fun with other friends.
     d) hitting the punching bag will act as a positive reinforcement of Shawna's aggressive feelings and
         hostility.
     Ans: d   LO: 6   Page: 456-457   Type: A

76. According to Berkowitz's (1989) revision of frustration-aggression theory, aggression is a response to
     a) only moderate, not extreme or mild, frustrations.
     b) previously displaced aggression.
     c) negative emotions.
     d) catharsis.
     Ans: c   LO: 6   Page: 456-457   Type: F

77. Exposure to all of the following increases aggression *except*
     a) testosterone.
     b) cigarette smoke.
     c) novel odors.
     d) uncomfortably cold temperatures.
     Ans: c   LO: 7   Page: 457   Type: F

78. Reifman et al. (1991) found that as temperatures rise, major league baseball pitchers are more likely to hit
     batters with a pitch. This finding is consistent with
     a) social learning theory.
     b) the cognitive neoassociation model.
     c) the revised frustration-aggression hypothesis.
     d) scapegoating.
     Ans: c   LO: 7   Page: 457-458   Type: C

79. Which of the following is *most* likely to increase a person's aggressive response?
     a) Embarassment
     b) Anger
     c) Social rejection
     d) Kindness
     Ans: c   LO: 7   Page: 458   Type: A

80. On his way back from work, Orin nearly collided head-on with another car. After swerving out of the way
     at the last minute, Orin could feel his heart racing and his hands shaking. A few minutes later he arrived
     home and, just as he walked in, received a phone call from a salesperson. Orin then became verbally
     abusive toward the salesperson. This outcome is *most* consistent with the concept of
     a) instrumental aggression.
     b) excitation transfer.
     c) the death instinct.
     d) incompatible responses.
     Ans: b   LO: 7   Page: 458-459   Type: A

81. Men who engaged in vigorous exercise were _____ attracted to an attractive female.
     a) less
     b) equally
     c) more
     d) none of the above
     Ans: c   LO: 7   Page: 458-459   Type: C

82. The idea that arousal created by one stimulus can intensify an individual's emotional response to another stimulus is called
    a) social learning theory.
    b) the negative affect escape model.
    c) excitation transfer.
    d) aggression cultivation.
    Ans: c   LO: 7   Page: 458-459   Type: F

83. The scope of excitation transfer is not limited to physical arousal. Which of the following other stimuli have also been shown to increase aggression?
    a) noise.
    b) violent movies.
    c) music.
    d) all of the above.
    Ans: d   LO: 7   Page: 458-459   Type: F

84. Two people are placed in a room and are provoked to behave aggressively toward one another. Which of the following is *most* likely to happen if there is a weapon in the room?
    a) There is a greater likelihood that they will behave aggressively toward one another than if there was no weapon.
    b) There is a greater likelihood that they will engage in higher-order cognition and subsequently behave less aggressively toward one another than if there was no weapon.
    c) The weapon will increase the likelihood that they will behave aggressively toward one another, but only if the two people are male.
    d) The weapon will have no effect on whether or not they behave aggressively toward one another.
    Ans: a   LO: 7   Page: 459-460   Type: A

85. Which of the following *most* closely represents the weapons effect?
    a) The presence of weapons deters individuals from performing aggressive acts, but not from learning the positive reinforcements that are associated with violence.
    b) The presence of weapons can act as an aggression cue that suggests a way to release anger.
    c) Although the presence of weapons does not make aggression more likely, it does tend to increase the severity of aggression.
    d) Exposure to weapons in the media desensitizes individuals to violence, thus reducing their inhibitions against aggression.
    Ans: b   LO: 7   Page: 459-460   Type: C

86. When exposed to situational cues, such as the presence of a gun, people tend to
    a) demonstrate decreases in aggression.
    b) feel socially rejected.
    c) experience a decrease in testosterone.
    d) have automatic cognitions regarding aggression.
    Ans: d   LO: 7   Page: 459-460   Type: C

87. Which of the following theories explains the deliberate, thoughtful consideration that we give to stimuli before reacting to it?
    a) arousal-affect model
    b) higher-order cognitive processing
    c) frustration-aggression hypothesis (original version)
    d) relational association theory
    Ans: b   LO: 7   Page: 461   Type: C

88. The tendency to perceive hostile intent in the actions of others is called
    a) aggression cultivation.
    b) emotional aggression.
    c) excitation transfer.
    d) the hostile attribution bias.
    Ans: d   LO: 7   Page: 461   Type: F

89. When Paulie accidentally bumps into Christopher causing Christopher to spill his coffee, Christopher
     assumes that Paulie's behavior was deliberately intended to make him spill his coffee. He responds by
     yelling obscenities at Paulie. Christopher could be described as
     a)   having a hostile attribution bias.
     b)   suffering from catharsis.
     c)   displaying instrumental aggression.
     d)   displaying relational aggression.
     Ans: a   LO: 7   Page: 461   Type: A

90. A set of experiments about social rejection by DeWall and others (2009) demonstrated that
     a)   the more socially rejected participants made hostile attributions, the more aggressive was their
           subsequent behavior.
     b)   the less socially rejected participants made hostile attributions, the more aggressive was their
           subsequent behavior.
     c)   the more socially rejected participants made hostile attributions, the less aggressive was their
           subsequent behavior.
     d)   hostile attributions did not have any affect on whether or not participants' subsequent behavior was
           aggressive.
     Ans: a   LO: 7   Page: 461   Type: C

91. Research investigating the relationship between alcohol and aggression has shown that
     a)   intoxicated people are likely to base their aggressive responses on initial, salient information about a
           situation and fail to recognize later, subtle cues.
     b)   small and large amounts of alcohol tend to increase aggression, whereas moderate amounts tend to
           decrease it.
     c)   alcohol makes men more likely to aggress, but it makes women less likely to aggress.
     d)   intoxicated people are more likely to be influenced by the weapons effect, whereas sober people are
           more likely to be affected by factors relevant to the cognitive neoassociation analysis.
     Ans: a   LO: 7   Page: 461-462   Type: C

92. Jim thinks it would be funny to replace Dwight's regular after-work pitcher of beer with non-alcoholic brew
     without telling him. Research suggests that after drinking this pitcher, Dwight would
     a)   be much less aggressive than he usually is after drinking alcoholic beer.
     b)   exhibit a severe form of alcohol myopia.
     c)   potentially be just as aggressive as usual given his expectation that he has consumed alcohol.
     d)   be less likely than usual to engage is displacement.
     Ans: c   LO: 7   Page: 461-462   Type: A

93. Aleta gets extremely drunk. Given the research on alcohol and aggression, which of the following is
     unlikely to happen?
     a)   She will be more aggressive if she tends to be high in aggressiveness than if she tends to be generally
           non-aggressive.
     b)   She will be more aggressive under the influence of alcohol than she is sober.
     c)   She will fail to be as attentive to mitigating information when she is drunk.
     d)   She will feel less anxious and thus will feel less inhibited about behaving aggressively.
     Ans: a   LO: 7   Page: 461-462   Type: A

94. Alcohol narrows people's focus of attention. This phenomenon is called
     a)   alcohol myopia.
     b)   alcohol hostility.
     c)   alcohol aggression.
     d)   alcohol blindness.
     Ans: a   LO: 7   Page: 461-462   Type: F

95. Research on the link between media violence and aggression has demonstrated that
    a) exposure to violent films increases aggressive behavior in the lab, but decreases aggressive behavior in the field.
    b) violent films increase aggressiveness, but violent music videos and song lyrics do not increase aggressiveness.
    c) all media violence ultimately reduces aggression by providing a cathartic outlet.
    d) all forms of media violence appear to increase aggressive behavior.
    Ans: d   LO: 8   Page: 464-468   Type: F

96. Many researchers maintain that there is a positive relationship between exposure to violent media and real-life aggressive behavior. The claim that exposure to violence actually *causes* an increase in aggression would be best supported by which of the following?
    a) A study in which the variable "number of hours of violent television watched per week" is used to predict the likelihood that participants will be convicted of a violent crime in the future.
    b) A study in which participants who are randomly assigned to play violent video games later administer greater levels of electric shock to a confederate than participants who are assigned to play neutral games.
    c) Real-world examples where young people have committed crimes intended to mimic behaviors they have seen in violent movies.
    d) A study in which men who have been accused of sexually aggressive behavior in the past report high levels of exposure to violent media.
    Ans: b   LO: 8   Page: 464-468   Type: C

97. Studying aggression in the lab can be difficult because of practical and ethical considerations. Which of the following is *not* a way in which a contemporary social psychologist might assess aggression in the lab?
    a) Seeing how much hot sauce a participant places in another person's drinking glass
    b) Recording how much aversive noise a participant chooses to blast in a partner's headphones
    c) Measuring the voltage of a dangerous electrical shock that a participant elects to administer to another person
    d) Assessing how aggressively a participant "behaves" during the course of a violent video game
    Ans: c   LO: 8   Page: 464-468   Type: C

98. Research on violent media suggests that depictions of indirect, relational forms of aggression on TV targeted towards adolescents are
    a) not particularly common.
    b) more likely to be demonstrated by male than female characters.
    c) often portrayed as eliciting a clear reward.
    d) do not influence the immediate behavior of adolescent viewers.
    Ans: c   LO: 8   Page: 467-468   Type: F

99. Research on violent media suggests compared to watching a violent video game, actually playing a violent game
    a) has less on an impact of subsequent aggressive behavior in the real world.
    b) is more likely to lead to the calming effects of catharsis.
    c) has more on an impact of subsequent aggressive behavior in the real world
    d) can actually make participants more helpful by habituating them to suffering.
    Ans: c   LO: 8   Page: 467   Type: F

100. When Mina first started playing the new Blood Bath Beach Party video game, the extremely violent images made her cringe. Now she has played the game so many times that she barely even notices such images. This illustrates
    a) displacement.
    b) cultivation.
    c) habituation.
    d) catharsis.
    Ans: c   LO: 8   Page: 468-469   Type: A

101. An attorney has a copy of a videotape that shows her client being beaten very violently by two men. Her client is suing these men. The jury has already seen this video several times during the trial, and the attorney is considering showing it many more times. However, an expert social psychologist should warn the attorney that replaying the videotaped beating many more times may reduce the likelihood of winning a large amount of money because the jurors might
    a)   become habituated to the beatings and thus grant less significance to the video in their final judgment.
    b)   engage in higher-order cognitive processing and thus feel less sympathy for the client.
    c)   become cultivated by the beatings and thus try to avoid thinking about them when making their final judgment.
    d)   be vulnerable to the weapons effect and thus be less likely to award a high settlement.
    Ans: a   LO: 8   Page: 468-469   Type: A

102. Nikki, who watches a lot of violent television shows as well as horror movies, thinks that the world is much more violent than it really is. Her overestimate is likely to be due to
    a)   habituation.
    b)   displacement.
    c)   dehumanization.
    d)   cultivation.
    Ans: d   LO: 8   Page: 468-469   Type: A

103. Ophelia has seen so many violent movies that she has become habituated to them. This means that she
    a)   believes the world is a much more violent place than it is in reality.
    b)   believes the world is a much less violent place than it is in reality.
    c)   experiences more physiological arousal in response to new images of violence.
    d)   experiences less physiological arousal in response to new images of violence.
    Ans: d   LO: 8   Page: 468-469   Type: A

104. In summary, an investigation by Gentile (2009) and others about the effects of prosocial video games found that those who played prosocial games
    a)   were significantly more helpful than those who played neutral games.
    b)   experienced the same symptoms of physiological arousal that those who played violent games did.
    c)   were significantly less helpful than those who played neutral games.
    d)   showed no increase in prosocial behavior.
    Ans: a   LO: 8   Page: 470   Type: F

105. Charles plays a lot of violent video games. The concept of desensitization suggests that he would
    a)   be likely to prefer violent movies as well.
    b)   be more likely to respond to a public insult with aggression than would someone who did not play violent video games.
    c)   become very aroused by witnessing an act of real-life violence.
    d)   show muted symptoms of arousal when shown a violent film clip as compared to someone who did not play violent video games.
    Ans: d   LO: 8   Page: 468-469   Type: A

106. The consumption of nonviolent pornography seems to lead to
    a)   sexual aggression but not other types of aggression.
    b)   positive emotional responses.
    c)   habituation over time with no ill effects.
    d)   increased aggression toward a same-sex other.
    Ans: d   LO: 9   Page: 471   Type: C

107. Rudolph is viewing some nonviolent pornography. In which of the following conditions is Rudolph *most* likely to show greater subsequent levels of aggression?
    a)   When he is angry
    b)   When the pornography portrays nude women
    c)   When Rudolph is sexually aroused by the pornography
    d)   When Rudolph has not viewed pornography before
    Ans: a   LO: 9   Page: 471   Type: A

108. Jay has just been exposed to highly arousing violent pornography, whereas Dave has just been exposed to equally arousing but nonviolent pornography. The research on pornography and aggression suggests that, compared to Dave, Jay should subsequently be
    a) less aggressive toward both women and men.
    b) more aggressive toward both women and men.
    c) less aggressive toward women but no different in his level of aggression toward men.
    d) more aggressive toward women but no different in his level of aggression toward men.
    Ans: d   LO: 9   Page: 471-472   Type: A

109. Violent pornography involving rape increases aggression *especially* when
    a) the viewers are male and are provoked.
    b) the woman is portrayed as an unwilling participant, and the viewers are made angry.
    c) the woman is portrayed as an unwilling participant, and opportunities to aggress against a same-sex other are readily available.
    d) the viewers are provoked, and do not find rape to be acceptable behavior.
    Ans: a   LO: 9   Page: 471-472   Type: F

110. In experiments, male participants who view violent erotic material
    a) administer lower levels of shock to female confederates.
    b) are more accepting of interpersonal violence against women.
    c) are equally aggressive toward male and female confederates.
    d) are less likely to endorse false beliefs about rape.
    Ans: b   LO: 9   Page: 471-472   Type: F

111. Research suggests that men's attitudes toward violence against women as well as their beliefs about rape myths
    a) are primarily influence by nonviolent pornography rather than violent pornography.
    b) are stable personality traits that are not influenced by exposure to violent pornography unless the exposure is very frequent and the material is extremely violent.
    c) tend to be affected by the men's *own* arousal-based aggressive behaviors, but are not likely to be affected by observation of the aggressive behavior depicted in a movie.
    d) can influence the extent of their aggressive behavior in response to violent pornographic material.
    Ans: d   LO: 9   Page: 471-472   Type: C

112. Daniel fits a rapist's profile. This means that he probably exhibits _____ in response to violent pornography and tends to have _____ attitudes toward violence against women.
    a) increased arousal; negative
    b) increased arousal; positive
    c) decreased arousal; negative
    d) decreased arousal; positive
    Ans: b   LO: 9   Page: 472   Type: A

113. Among the following, which conclusion has *not* been drawn based on laboratory experiments studying pornography and aggression?
    a) Exposure to nonviolent pornography decreases subsequent aggression in the lab.
    b) Exposure to violent pornography increases subsequent aggression in the lab.
    c) Exposure to dehumanizing, nonviolent pornographic images of women affects men's attitudes regarding sexual aggression toward women.
    d) Exposure to violent pornography decreases subsequent aggression in the lab if the women in the pornography are depicted as passive.
    Ans: d   LO: 9   Page: 471-472   Type: F

114. Sexually coercive behavior is *least* likely to be exhibited by someone who
    a) is highly sexually aroused by violent pornography.
    b) indicates greater acceptance of interpersonal violence against women.
    c) thinks he or she has consumed alcohol.
    d) indicates strong rejection of rape myths.
    Ans: d   LO: 10   Page: 472   Type: F

115. Which of the following concerning sexual aggression is *true*?
   a)   Women are more likely than men to engage in both physical and psychological coercion to obtain sex.
   b)   Men are more likely than woman to engage in both physical and psychological coercion to obtain sex.
   c)   Women are more likely than men to engage in physical coercion to obtain sex, but men are more likely than women to engage in psychological coercion to obtain sex.
   d)   Men are more likely than women to engage in physical coercion to obtain sex, but women are more likely than men to engage in psychological coercion to obtain sex.
   Ans: b   LO: 10   Page: 472   Type: F

116. Marx et al. (1999) had male college students listen to an audiotape designed to sound like date rape. They found that alcohol consumption
   a)   had no influence on participants' perceptions of the incident.
   b)   made it impossible for participants to accurately judge the incident.
   c)   led participants to take longer to decide that the man on the tape should stop pursuing sexual contact with the woman.
   d)   made participants more hostile in their evaluations of the woman on the tape.
   Ans: c   LO: 10   Page: 473-474   Type: F

117. The link between alcohol and aggression
   a)   is only seen among men.
   b)   can be seen among women in terms of their failure to effectively recognize danger
   c)   applies principally to relational forms of aggression as opposed to direct physical aggression.
   d)   is not as strong as the media typically depicts it to be.
   Ans: b   LO: 10   Page: 473-474   Type: C

118. Which of the following concerning violence in intimate relationships is *false*?
   a)   Women are more likely than men to use violence in self-defense.
   b)   Men are more likely than women to use violence to intimidate.
   c)   Women are more likely than men to be killed in instances of domestic violence.
   d)   Husband-to-wife violence is more common than wife-to-husband violence.
   Ans: d   LO: 10   Page: 474-475   Type: C

119. Though women are more likely than men to aggress in an intimate relationship, men's aggression in such relationships differs in that it typically
   a)   emerges in the face of provocation.
   b)   has more severe consequences.
   c)   results from alcohol abuse.
   d)   is sexual in nature.
   Ans: b   LO: 10   Page: 474-475   Type: F

120. Which of the following concerning child abuse is *true*?
   a)   Girls suffer more sexual abuse and boys suffer more physical abuse.
   b)   Girls suffer both more sexual abuse and physical abuse.
   c)   Boys suffer more sexual abuse and girls suffer more physical abuse.
   d)   Boys suffer both more sexual abuse and physical abuse.
   Ans: a   LO: 10   Page: 475   Type: F

121. Maureen was abused as a child. She is now married to a man who abuses her and she is physically abusive toward her child. This pattern of behavior is consistent with
   a)   the negative affect escape model.
   b)   the arousal affect model.
   c)   aggression cultivation.
   d)   the cycle of family violence.
   Ans: d   LO: 10   Page: 475   Type: A

122. Rowell believes that the best way to treat violent juvenile offenders is to address the needs of these children as well as the many contexts in which they are embedded. This approach is called
    a)   aggression cultivation.
    b)   the negative affect escape model.
    c)   multisystemic therapy.
    d)   the arousal affect model.
    Ans: c   LO: 10   Page: 475-476   Type: A

123. An improved economy and healthier living conditions can help reduce aggression by
    a)   reducing negative affect.
    b)   changing the cost-reward payoffs associated with aggression.
    c)   reducing aggression anxiety.
    d)   increasing attention to salient cues.
    Ans: a   LO: 3   Page: 476   Type: C

124. The key to reducing intimate violence is
    a)   more forceful prosecution of intimate violence cases.
    b)   more effective communication.
    c)   harsher prison sentences for those convicted of intimate violence.
    d)   self-esteem workshops.
    Ans: b   LO: 10   Page: 477-478   Type: C

125. A local community is committed to reducing violence among its residents. The community leaders have come up with four proposals whose potential success is to be evaluated by a social psychologist. According to social psychological research on aggression, which of the following proposals should be rejected because it would be the *least* likely to reduce violence?
    a)   Rewarding non-aggressive behavior
    b)   Providing air-conditioned shelters when it is hot outside
    c)   Opening to public viewing executions and other physical punishments of criminals
    d)   Reduction of the display of weapons in the community
    Ans: c   LO: 10   Page: 478-479   Type: A

ESSAY

126. To what extent does culture affect the type and amount of violence one observes in a society?
    Ans: Culture exerts a number of different effects on aggression. Aggression against individuals tends to be higher in the United States, and aggression against groups tends to be higher in the Middle East, Africa, and Eastern Europe. Moreover, overt sexual aggression is less acceptable in the United States than in many other countries. Aggression tends to be higher in cultures where one's status and family afford a feeling of "honor," as is true in the southern United States. In general, it appears that aggression is lower in cultures that emphasize cooperation and strongly oppose competition.   Page: 437-442

127. Under what conditions should punishment be most and least effective in reducing aggression? From the perspective of social learning theory, explain why punishment might increase rather than decrease aggression.
    Ans: Punishment is most likely to be effective in decreasing aggression when it immediately follows the aggressive behavior, when it is strong enough to be perceived by the aggressor as a real deterrent, when it is applied consistently, and when it is perceived by the aggressor as fair and legitimate. In the absence of these conditions, punishment is less likely to be effective and may even be counterproductive. Punishment is also less likely to be effective if the aggressor is engaged in instrumental aggression and thus cannot see any way of obtaining a desired goal other than through aggression, or if the aggressor is engaged in an act of emotional aggression and continues to be very angry. Finally, the person being punished may perceive the punishment itself (particularly if it is delivered in a hostile manner) as a model of aggression, leading the person to imitate the behavior and thus act aggressively. This latter point is consistent with social learning theory, which maintains that behavior is learned through imitation of others as well as through direct experience of rewards and punishments. For example, a parent who uses aggression to punish a child may act as a model for the child, unintentionally teaching the child that aggression is an accepted way of dealing with problems or conflicts.   Page: 448-451

128. Discuss the role played by arousal and affect in aggression.
Ans: Independently, both negative affect and high arousal tend to increase aggression. But in combination, arousal and affect can lead to either more or less aggression. For example, among people who are experiencing negative affect, those who are highly aroused are particularly likely to be aggressive. High arousal also tends to increase aggression among people who are experiencing neutral affect. Among people who are experiencing positive affect, however, high arousal can either increase aggression (through excitation transfer) or decrease aggression (given the incompatibility of strong positive feelings and unpleasant angry feelings). Page: 457-459

129. Give two examples of research that illustrates the important role of thought in aggressive behavior. Explain both examples.
Ans: The research of Leonard Berkowitz's and colleagues clarifies the process by which thoughts and feelings interact. One example is research on the weapons effect, which indicates that there mere presence of weapons can increase people's thoughts about aggression and, therefore, their aggressive tendencies. A study on the effects of alcohol also illustrates the role of thought in aggression (Steele & Josephs, 1990). According to this study, intoxicated people who are made angry may fail to take into account mitigating information that would have otherwise led them to not aggress. In short, alcohol reduces one's ability to engage in thoughtful, higher-order processing, rendering the person more likely to respond aggressively despite cues present in the situation that would ordinarily signal the inappropriateness of aggressive behavior.   Page: 460-462

130. A neighborhood group is debating whether or not to put pressure on the local movie theater to discourage the showing of violent films. Knowing that you are taking a social psychology course, the group has asked you to summarize for them social psychological theories regarding the effects of violent films on aggression. Focusing on the frustration-aggression hypothesis and the social learning model, how would you answer this question?
Ans: The frustration-aggression hypothesis, particularly in its original formulation, would predict that the observation of violence in film produces catharsis, thus reducing the observers' aggression. According to this view, any frustrations that the filmgoers already have will be released through observation of aggression, thereby making them less likely to need to aggress to release their frustrations. However, research typically does not support the theory's prediction regarding aggression, and, moreover, if the film elicits reactions of frustration or negative affect, then the filmgoers' aggression might increase. Social learning theory would predict that observation of violent films increases aggression, particularly if the aggression in the films is perceived by the observers to be rewarded in some way. According to social learning theory, then, the filmgoers will become more likely to imitate the aggression they see in the film and to behave aggressively themselves. Indeed, they will do so even if the aggression is not rewarded on screen. In sharp contrast to the frustration-aggression hypothesis, social learning theory does not accept the notion of catharsis.   Page: 464-470

CHAPTER 12

Law

MULTIPLE CHOICE

1. Waleska is a social psychologist who studies the legal system. Which of the following objectives would she be *least* likely to pursue in her research?
    a) Improving the ability of police officers to determine when a criminal suspect is lying
    b) Determining under what circumstances jurors are best able to understand and follow a judge's instructions
    c) Assessing how judges apply sentencing guidelines to complex cases
    d) Identifying the types of psychological disorders most likely to lead people to engage in criminal behavior
    Ans: d   LO: 1   Page: 486-487   Type: A

2. Which of the following is *not* a component of jury selection?
    a) Compiling a list of potential jurors from sources such as voter registration lists
    b) Using random selection to obtain a representative sample of community members who will be summoned for jury duty
    c) Making sure that every single 12-person jury is representative of the community from which it is drawn
    d) Subjecting those individuals who appear for jury duty to a pretrial interview to exclude those who might be biased
    Ans: c   LO: 1   Page: 487-488   Type: F

3. The pretrial interview of prospective jurors conducted by the judge and lawyers is called
    a) decision control.
    b) jury nullification.
    c) scientific jury selection.
    d) voir dire.
    Ans: d   LO: 1   Page: 488   Type: F

4. The defense attorney asks Melinda, a prospective juror, if she has ever been the victim of a violent crime or if she knows the prosecuting attorney personally. This illustrates
    a) the voir dire process.
    b) sentencing disparity.
    c) informational influence.
    d) jury nullification.
    Ans: a   LO: 1   Page: 488   Type: A

5. From the court's perspective, the voir dire process is intended to
    a) allow the lawyers to present evidence to the judge without the jurors present.
    b) identify and dismiss prospective jurors who may be biased.
    c) familiarize prospective jurors with one another before they begin deliberation.
    d) familiarize prospective jurors with the facts of the case prior to the actual trial.
    Ans: b   LO: 1   Page: 488   Type: C

6. Lawyers may dismiss prospective jurors without having to justify their dismissal by using
    a) jury nullification.
    b) sentencing disparity.
    c) peremptory challenges.
    d) normative influence.
    Ans: c   LO: 1   Page: 488-489   Type: F

7.   Litigants at trial may remove prospective jurors from their jury through the use of peremptory challenges. Traditionally, no explanation has to be given for the use of a peremptory, but within the past few decades the U.S. Supreme Court has ruled that peremptories may not be based on a juror's...
      a)   education level.
      b)   race.
      c)   physical appearance.
      d)   All of these
      Ans: b   LO: 1   Page: 488-489   Type: F

8.   Claire, a district attorney, believes that elderly women are likely to be sympathetic to criminal defendants. She, therefore, summarily dismisses elderly prospective jurors during voir dire. This exemplifies the
      a)   use of peremptory challenges.
      b)   advantages of scientific jury selection.
      c)   process of jury nullification.
      d)   power of informational influence.
      Ans: a   LO: 1   Page: 488-489   Type: A

9.   Research by Sommers and Norton (2007) on the impact of race on the use of peremptory challenges indicates that attorneys
      a)   are equally likely to remove from the jury Black and White individuals.
      b)   do not always give accurate explanations when asked to justify a peremptory challenge.
      c)   are impacted by prospective jurors' gender more so than their race.
      d)   are influenced by race moreso in civil trials as opposed to criminal trials.
      Ans: b   LO: 1   Page: 488-489   Type: C

10.   Research by Sommers and Norton (2007) found that a prospective juror's race influenced the jury selection judgments of
      a)   college students.
      b)   law students.
      c)   practicing attorneys.
      d)   All of these
      Ans: d   LO: 1   Page: 437-438   Type: C

11.   Jonnie is a defense attorney representing a client charged with drug offenses. He conducts a survey in the community and discovers that residents with conservative politics are particularly unsympathetic to defendants in drug cases. He therefore decides to use his peremptory challenges during jury selection to remove from the panel prospective jurors with a history of voting for conservative political candidates. Jonnie is making use of
      a)   scientific jury selection.
      b)   an implicit personality theory.
      c)   trial attorney intuition.
      d)   jury consultants.
      Ans: a   LO: 1   Page: 489-491   Type: A

12.   One criticism of scientific jury selection is that it
      a)   focuses jury selection on the question of whether or not a juror will be able to be impartial in evaluating the case.
      b)   does not make use of empirical data.
      c)   can only be afforded by the wealthiest of defendants and plaintiffs.
      d)   is used in civil trials, but not in criminal cases.
      Ans: c   LO: 1   Page: 489-491   Type: C

13.   The use of community surveys to identify correlations between demographics and attitudes relevant to the trial is called
      a)   scientific jury selection.
      b)   implicit personality theories.
      c)   jury nullification.
      d)   the leniency bias.
      Ans: a   LO: 1   Page: 489-491   Type: F

14.   Miguel will be using scientific jury selection in an upcoming trial. The first step of this process will be to
    a)   ask prospective jurors personal questions during the voir dire.
    b)   assess demographic characteristics and trial-relevant attitudes of the community in which the trial will take place.
    c)   submit a motion to the judge to allow an independent consulting firm to interview prospective jurors.
    d)   meet with the judge and opposing counsel to discuss the range of questions that will be permitted during the voir dire.
    Ans: b   LO: 1   Page: 489-491   Type: F

15.   An attorney would like to identify potential jurors who are likely to vote for conviction. The attorney should look for jurors who
    a)   are highly educated.
    b)   are of low socioeconomic status.
    c)   have an extroverted personality.
    d)   have an authoritarian personality.
    Ans: d   LO: 2   Page: 489-491   Type: A

16.   Research on race and jury decision making indicates that jurors are
    a)   always more lenient towards defendants of their same race.
    b)   more likely to discriminate by race when race is a prominent issue during the trial.
    c)   not influenced by race when evidence in a case is strong.
    d)   None of these.
    Ans: d   LO: 2   Page: 491-492   Type: C

17.   Henry is a White male and the foreman of a criminal jury. The defendant in the trial is also a White male, and the evidence against him is quite strong. Research suggests that Henry is likely to be
    a)   harsher in his judgments than he would have been if the defendant were not White.
    b)   more lenient in his judgments than he would have been if the defendant were not White.
    c)   more forceful than the other jurors in making his arguments about the case.
    d)   less concerned with procedural aspects of the deliberations than other jurors.
    Ans: a   LO: 2   Page: 491-492   Type: A

18.   Sommers and Ellsworth (2001) found that when a crime involves race, White jurors
    a)   discriminated against a Black defendant.
    b)   avoided discrimination against a Black defendant.
    c)   were particularly motivated to be elected foreperson of the jury.
    d)   processed trial evidence less carefully than when the crime was race-neutral.
    Ans: b   LO: 2   Page: 491-492   Type: C

19.   As described in your book, Sommers's (2006) study examining the influence of a jury's racial composition indicates that
    a)   White and Black jurors are often equally likely to vote to convict a Black defendant.
    b)   Black jurors often successfully convince White jurors to change their votes during deliberations, particularly when they offer multiple arguments for doing so.
    c)   White jurors often evaluate a trial differently when their jury is diverse versus all-White.
    d)   diverse juries have a harder time coming to a unanimous decision than do all-White juries.
    Ans: c   LO: 2   Page: 491-492   Type: C

20.   Franklin, a Black male, is on trial for attempted murder. The study conducted by Sommers (2006) regarding jury racial composition suggests which of the following jurors would be most likely to vote to convict Franklin?
    a)   Jerry, a White male on an all-White jury
    b)   Robin, a White male on a racially-diverse jury
    c)   Eddie, a Black male on an all-Black jury
    d)   Dave, a Black male on a racially-diverse jury
    Ans: a   LO: 2   Page: 491-492   Type: A

21.   Death qualification refers to
       a)   pretrial hearings that are conducted to determine whether a defendant should receive the death penalty.
       b)   a procedure used during voir dire to ensure that jurors are prepared for potentially graphic testimony concerning violence, usually involving murder.
       c)   a jury selection procedure that permits judges to exclude from capital cases all prospective jurors who say they would refuse to vote for the death penalty under any circumstance.
       d)   jurors' decision to recommend the death penalty even if the prosecution has not asked for it.
       Ans: c   LO: 3   Page: 492-493   Type: C

22.   Prospective jurors who indicate a willingness to vote for the death penalty typically exhibit all of the following *except*
       a)   a greater concern with crime.
       b)   more negative attitudes toward defense attorneys.
       c)   a greater suspiciousness of police officers.
       d)   a greater tendency to convict.
       Ans: c   LO: 3   Page: 492-493   Type: C

23.   According to research findings, which of the following individuals is most likely to be an opponent of the death penalty?
       a)   Michael, who scores low on a self-report measure of authoritarianism.
       b)   Buster, who holds fundamentalist religious beliefs.
       c)   Lindsey, who believes that the world is a fair place in which you get what you deserve.
       d)   Gob, who believes in the deterrent potential of capital punishment.
       Ans: a   LO: 3   Page: 492-493   Type: A

24.   Tyson sits on a jury. Tyson is more likely to believe the defendant is guilty if
       a)   Tyson has an authoritarian personality.
       b)   the defendant is of the same race as Tyson and the evidence is weak.
       c)   Tyson has principled objections to the death penalty.
       d)   Tyson is a young adult.
       Ans: a   LO: 2   Page: 492-493   Type: A

25.   Saul is a prospective juror in a mass murder case who, when asked by an attorney, says that he opposes the death penalty. The presiding judge then excludes him from the jury. This is an example of
       a)   leniency bias.
       b)   death qualification.
       c)   scientific jury selection.
       d)   jury nullification.
       Ans: b   LO: 3   Page: 492-493   Type: A

26.   In a murder trial, Eugenia was selected to serve on a death-qualified jury. Given her attitude toward the death penalty, she is probably _____ than the average U.S. citizen.
       a)   more likely to vote for acquittal
       b)   less likely to recommend the death penalty
       c)   less sympathetic toward victims of violence
       d)   less tolerant of procedures that protect the accused
       Ans: d   LO: 3   Page: 492-493   Type: A

27.   Death qualification has been criticized on all but one of the following grounds. Which is the *exception*?
       a)   Death-qualified juries are overly skeptical of prosecutorial procedures.
       b)   Death-qualified jurors are more likely to vote for conviction.
       c)   The questions used to assess death qualification bias jurors.
       d)   Death qualification excludes jurors who would be willing to vote for the death penalty in some situations but not others.
       Ans: a   LO: 3   Page: 492-493   Type: C

28. Police interrogators often use minimizing techniques to secure confessions. One such tactic is to
    a)   express certainty in the suspect's guilt.
    b)   claim to have an eyewitness to the crime.
    c)   blame the victim of the crime.
    d)   use physical force.
    Ans: c   LO: 4   Page: 494-495   Type: F

29. When a police interrogator lies and tells a suspect that they have fingerprint evidence that ties him to the scene of a crime, this is an example of the strategy known as
    a)   maximization.
    b)   learned helplessness.
    c)   minimization.
    d)   internalization.
    Ans: a   LO: 4   Page: 494-495   Type: F

30. Police interrogations are often conducted in small, bare, soundproof rooms so that
    a)   distractions will be minimized and the suspect will be better able to focus on the interrogation.
    b)   suspects feel socially isolated and powerless.
    c)   police operating costs will be kept to a minimum.
    d)   other police officers will not become biased against particular suspects.
    Ans: b   LO: 4   Page: 494-495   Type: C

31. After a 36-hour interrogation, Liz just wanted to make it end so she confessed to the kidnapping even though she knew she had not committed the crime. Liz's confession would be labeled as
    a)   internalized.
    b)   compliant.
    c)   reactive.
    d)   misinformed.
    Ans: b   LO: 4   Page: 495-497   Type: F

32. With respect to social influence processes in interrogations, internalization refers to the process in which
    a)   innocent suspects come to believe that they have committed the crimes for which they are being interrogated.
    b)   suspects confess to crimes that they did not commit in order to escape aversive interrogations.
    c)   accused suspects are offered lighter sentences in exchange for important information.
    d)   juries are able to disregard confession testimony that was extracted through coercion.
    Ans: a   LO: 4   Page: 495-497   Type: F

33. Which of the following conclusions is *not* consistent with the results of Kassin and Kiechel's (1996) study?
    a)   Suspects are more likely to make a false confession when they are led to believe that evidence links them to the crime, even if this so-called evidence does not really exist.
    b)   People often make false confessions to crimes, but they rarely come to internalize the belief that they are actually guilty.
    c)   You are more likely to falsely confess to a crime if you were under the influence of alcohol or drugs at the time of the event.
    d)   Beyond individual difference predictors, there are numerous situational factors that increase the likelihood of a suspect making a false confession.
    Ans: b   LO: 4   Page: 496   Type: C

34. Which of the following *best* describes the conclusions reached by Kassin and Kiechel (1996) concerning false confessions?
    a)   People are highly unlikely to confess to crimes they did not commit.
    b)   Internalized false confessions are most likely to occur when a suspect is intimidated with bright lights and physical threats.
    c)   Compliant false confessions are most likely to occur when a friendly interrogator offers sympathy and advice to a suspect.
    d)   Internalized false confessions are most likely to occur when false evidence of guilt is presented.
    Ans: d   LO: 4   Page: 496   Type: F

35. A police officer testifies that the defendant in a murder trial confessed to the crime. Under cross-examination, the officer reveals details of the interrogation that suggest it is likely that the defendant was coerced into confessing. How are jurors likely to react to the confession evidence?
    a) Jurors will discount the confession because it was coerced.
    b) Jurors will accept the confession because as a general rule jurors don't believe that people would confess to a crime that they did not commit.
    c) Jurors will believe that they have discounted the confession, but will vote to convict anyway.
    d) If the judge instructs jurors to disregard the confession evidence, then they will discount it, but otherwise, they will not.
    Ans: c   LO: 4   Page: 497-498   Type: A

36. Jurors often fail to adequately discount coerced confessions because of
    a) the positive coercion bias.
    b) the fundamental attribution error.
    c) a sentencing disparity.
    d) reconstructive memory.
    Ans: b   LO: 4   Page: 497-498   Type: C

37. Among the following, which conclusion is *not* consistent with research on confessions?
    a) Confessions are discounted more by jurors who see a videotape that focuses on the interrogator instead of the defendant.
    b) When false evidence is presented by an interrogator, suspects are not only more likely to confess to a crime they did not commit but also to believe this confession.
    c) Jurors often fully discount a defendant's confession if they learn that the confession was obtained while the defendant was being physically threatened by police.
    d) Police detectives use an average of five to six tactics when trying to obtain a confession.
    Ans: c   LO: 4   Page: 497-498   Type: C

38. Jurors in criminal trials often fail to fully discount coerced confessions. In what sense can the fundamental attribution error explain this tendency?
    a) People often overlook the situational factors that lead others to commit criminal acts.
    b) We tend to think that no situational influences could be strong enough to lead someone to confess to something they did not do.
    c) Jurors usually think that false confessions result from certain personality characteristics, such as passivity or lack of education.
    d) Few people think that they themselves would ever admit to a crime they did not commit.
    Ans: b   LO: 4   Page: 497-498   Type: C

39. Harwin is hooked up to a mechanical instrument that records his heart rate, blood pressure, breathing, and sweat gland activity. Harwin is being subjected to
    a) a polygraph test.
    b) an internalized interrogation.
    c) the voir dire process.
    d) a show up.
    Ans: a   LO: 5   Page: 498-499   Type: A

40. Polygraph tests
    a) are extremely effective in detecting guilt in those who are guilty, and innocence in those who are innocent.
    b) are difficult to fake.
    c) can be fairly accurate when the suspect is naive and the examiner is competent.
    d) can be admitted into evidence in all district courts throughout the United States.
    Ans: c   LO: 5   Page: 498-499   Type: F

41. Martha is accused of insider trading. During a polygraph test, she is asked if she ever littered as a child. This question is an example of a
    a) control question.
    b) crime-relevant question.
    c) peremptory challenge.
    d) reconstructive memory.
    Ans: a   LO: 5   Page: 498-499   Type: A

42. In theory, when innocent suspects are subjected to a polygraph test, they
    a) are more aroused by crime-relevant questions than control questions.
    b) are more aroused by control questions than crime-relevant questions.
    c) exhibit overall lower levels of arousal than guilty suspects.
    d) exhibit overall higher levels of arousal than guilty suspects.
    Ans: b   LO: 5   Page: 498-499   Type: C

43. Guilty suspects can fool a polygraph test if they
    a) simply deny any and all involvement in the crime for which they are being questioned.
    b) meditate prior to the administration of the test.
    c) lie in response to any crime-relevant questions, but tell the truth in response to the control questions.
    d) artificially inflate their arousal to control questions by tensing their muscles.
    Ans: d   LO: 5   Page: 498-499   Type: C

44. A major problem with using the polygraph as a lie detector is that
    a) truthful persons often fail the test.
    b) arousal cannot be measured with the polygraph.
    c) it measures only the vocal channel, ignoring all other channels.
    d) control questions do not evoke arousal in innocent people.
    Ans: a   LO: 5   Page: 498-499   Type: C

45. Intentional efforts to "beat" a lie polygraph exam are known as
    a) countermeasures.
    b) counterbalances.
    c) bogus pipeline.
    d) manipulation.
    Ans: a   LO: 5   Page: 498-499   Type: F

46. Which of the following is *not* currently being investigated by researchers as a potential alternative to traditional polygraph tests?
    a) Hypnosis
    b) fMRI assessment of blood oxygen in the brain
    c) Examination of involuntary facial muscle movement
    d) Pupil dilation
    Ans: a   LO: 5   Page: 498-499   Type: F

47. Which of the following seems to be *true* when an eyewitness positively identifies a defendant?
    a) The defendant is more likely to be found guilty and, in almost all cases, this is the correct verdict.
    b) The defendant is less likely to be found guilty, though he or she usually is.
    c) The defendant is more likely to be found guilty, though in many cases he or she has been misidentified.
    d) The defendant is less likely to be found guilty and, in most cases, this is the correct verdict.
    Ans: c   LO: 6   Page: 499-500   Type: F

48. Recent DNA exoneration cases have revealed the most common cause of mistaken convictions to be
    a) a coerced confession.
    b) false alibis.
    c) racially biased juries.
    d) inaccurate eyewitnesses.
    Ans: d   LO: 6   Page: 499-500   Type: F

49. Research concerning eyewitness testimony has demonstrated that
    a) confident eyewitnesses are more accurate.
    b) while some eyewitnesses are better than others, eyewitness identifications are generally not susceptible to situational biases.
    c) juries are not well-informed about many of the factors that influence eyewitness accuracy.
    d) judges and lawyers are well aware of the limitations of eyewitness testimony.
    Ans: c   LO: 6   Page: 499-500   Type: F

50. Jesse has just witnessed a brutal assault. In his highly aroused state, Jesse is likely to focus on all of the following *except* the
    a) weapon.
    b) culprit.
    c) setting.
    d) victim.
    Ans: c   LO: 6   Page: 500-501   Type: A

51. Which of the following *best* illustrates the acquisition stage of memory?
    a) When the terrorists entered the building, Petra noticed that they were heavily armed.
    b) After witnessing a hit and run, Vera repeats the license plate of the car over and over so that she can give it to the police.
    c) When interviewed by the police, Marlon told them everything he could remember about the bar brawl.
    d) When asked to identify her attacker from a lineup, Coral wasn't sure which suspect had attacked her.
    Ans: a   LO: 6   Page: 500-501   Type: A

52. A witness's consumption of alcohol is most likely to pose problems for the _____ of memory.
    a) acquisition
    b) storage
    c) retrieval
    d) All of these are equally likely.
    Ans: a   LO: 6   Page: 500-501   Type: F

53. After Natalie testifies in court that she witnessed the defendant committing the crime in question, a memory expert is called to testify on behalf of the defense. The expert testifies that Natalie's ability to acquire the information accurately was probably impaired. Which of the following circumstances did the expert *most* likely have in mind when he questioned Natalie's ability to acquire the information accurately?
    a) The weapon-focus effect
    b) Reconstructive memory
    c) Misleading questions
    d) Leniency bias
    Ans: a   LO: 6   Page: 500-501   Type: A

54. The presence of a weapon reduces eyewitness accuracy because
    a) weapons interfere with the retrieval of events.
    b) witnesses have less sympathy for someone holding a weapon.
    c) the sight of a weapon causes witnesses to become more self-aware.
    d) witnesses tend to focus attention on the weapon to the exclusion of other cues.
    Ans: d   LO: 6   Page: 500-501   Type: C

55. Prida has witnessed a violent crime involving a knife. Research suggests that he will be less likely to identify the culprit than in a situation where no knife was present because Prida will
    a) be less aroused.
    b) focus more on the victim.
    c) spend more time looking at the knife.
    d) be too afraid to remember anything accurately.
    Ans: c   LO: 6   Page: 500-501   Type: A

56. Tony, Silvio, Paulie, and Christopher were all in the convenience store when it was robbed. Who is likely to be the *most* reliable eyewitness?
   a)   Tony, who was the only one to notice that the thief was brandishing a gun
   b)   Silvio, who was extremely aroused by the whole incident
   c)   Paulie, who was drunk at the time of the crime
   d)   Christopher, who is the same race as the thief
   Ans: d   LO: 6   Page: 501   Type: A

57. The cross-racial identification bias
   a)   results primarily from problems with the retrieval stage of memory.
   b)   is consistent in many ways with the concept of outgroup homogeneity.
   c)   has been observed among White, but not non-White eyewitnesses.
   d)   is alleviated by the presence of a weapon during the crime in question.
   Ans: b   LO: 6   Page: 501   Type: C

58. Eyewitnesses' reports of crime details can be altered by exposure to post-event information. This results from
   a)   the reliance on peremptory challenges.
   b)   the reconstructive nature of memory.
   c)   normative influence pressures.
   d)   the positive coercion bias.
   Ans: b   LO: 6   Page: 501-503   Type: C

59. Loftus and Palmer (1974) manipulated the wording of questions posed to participants who witness a filmed traffic accident. Their findings suggest that
   a)   post-event information becomes integrated into a witness's actual memory for an event.
   b)   once a memory enters into storage, it will emerge unchanged at retrieval.
   c)   witnesses often store multiple, contradictory memories for a single event.
   d)   most eyewitness errors have to do with problems that arise during acquisition.
   Ans: a   LO: 6   Page: 501-503   Type: C

60. The tendency for false post-event information to become integrated into a person's memory for the event is called the
   a)   misinformation effect.
   b)   familiarity induced bias.
   c)   leniency bias.
   d)   positive coercion bias.
   Ans: a   LO: 6   Page: 502-503   Type: F

61. Among the following, which *most* accurately summarizes an important point of controversy that has been debated among researchers who study reconstructive memory?
   a)   Some believe that post-event information actually alters a witness's real memory, whereas others believe it affects only the reporting of the memory.
   b)   Some believe that post-event information can bias an eyewitness's reporting of an event, whereas others believe that only information that is learned during acquisition can bias an eyewitness's reporting.
   c)   Some believe that scientific jury selection is an effective way to reduce the chances that jurors will be biased by reconstructive memory, whereas others believe that this strategy is unethical.
   d)   Some believe that the use of peremptory challenges leads to false memories, whereas others believe it helps ensure accurate memories.
   Ans: a   LO: 6   Page: 501-503   Type: C

62. Kirk is going to be called to the witness stand to give his eyewitness testimony regarding a murder. It is likely that if Kirk first hears other eyewitness accounts it will
   a)   make his testimony less accurate.
   b)   counteract the misinformation effect.
   c)   encourage him to be more accurate if the other eyewitnesses agree among themselves as to who the assailant was.
   d)   encourage him to be less accurate if the other eyewitnesses disagree among themselves as to who the assailant was.
   Ans: a   LO: 6   Page: 501-503   Type: A

63.   Research on children's memory for events demonstrates that
      a)   they may be especially susceptible to the effects of repetitive questions.
      b)   they are particularly resistant to the effects of suggestive questions and misinformation.
      c)   children witnesses often completely fabricate events in order to deceive adults.
      d)   children usually make better witnesses because they are more honest than adults.
      Ans: a   LO: 6   Page: 502-503   Type: C

64.   Maxwell witnesses a man assault a woman with a silver hammer. A few days later, he is called to the police
      station to identify the culprit from a lineup. Maxwell is *most* likely to be accurate if
      a)   the police tell him that the culprit is in the lineup.
      b)   one of the men in the lineup resembles the description that Maxwell had given the police, while the
           other men in the lineup look very different from that description.
      c)   he is first presented with some mug shots and then views a lineup containing one of the men whose
           mug shot he has seen.
      d)   he observes the suspects and foils one at a time rather than together in a single lineup.
      Ans: d   LO: 6   Page: 504-506   Type: A

65.   Manisha witnesses a crime and is brought to the police station for an interview about what she saw. She is
      given a face construction booklet and asked to pick which of the 100 hairstyles looks most like the culprit's.
      Then she does the same for eyes, nose, mouth, ears, etc. Research suggests that this process is likely to lead
      Manisha to
      a)   perform more accurately if she is shown a lineup including the culprit several days later.
      b)   perform less accurately if she is shown a lineup including the culprit several days later.
      c)   become more confident in her ability to identify the culprit.
      d)   become less confident in her ability to identify the culprit.
      Ans: b   LO: 6   Page: 504-506   Type: A

66.   With respect to lineup identification, eyewitnesses tend to be less accurate when
      a)   there are six foils present in the lineup.
      b)   the suspect is of the same race as the witness.
      c)   the witness is informed that the suspect may be in the lineup.
      d)   the suspect and the foils are viewed one at a time.
      Ans: c   LO: 6   Page: 504-506   Type: C

67.   Kobayashi describes to police the man who attacked him as follows: 6' tall, White, gray hair, close to 200
      pounds. The lineup that the police put together to present to Kobayashi includes 8 individuals, 4 with
      brown hair and 2 who are bald. In this instance the police have done a poor job
      a)   selecting the foils for the lineup.
      b)   guarding against the misinformation effect.
      c)   avoiding bias in their lineup instructions to the witness.
      d)   All of these
      Ans: a   LO: 6   Page: 504-506   Type: A

68.   An eyewitness identified Ashtok from a lineup as the man who robbed the bookstore. As an employee of the
      store, Ashtok was present during the crime but was not the person who committed the crime. The
      eyewitness's false identification was *most* likely the result of
      a)   the leniency bias.
      b)   the misinformation effect.
      c)   a familiarity induced bias.
      d)   the fundamental attribution error.
      Ans: c   LO: 6   Page: 504-506   Type: A

69.   Brandon is a juror in a murder trial in which both the prosecution and defense are relying on eyewitnesses.
      It is likely that Brandon will
      a)   be able to distinguish those eyewitnesses who are accurate from those who are not.
      b)   judge eyewitnesses who appear confident to be more accurate than those who appear less confident.
      c)   underestimate the accuracy of all of the eyewitnesses.
      d)   understand the factors that influence eyewitness accuracy enough to determine whether an eyewitness
           is biased.
      Ans: b   LO: 7   Page: 506-508   Type: A

70. Research on eyewitness accuracy has demonstrated that eyewitness confidence
     a)   predicts accuracy for adults, but not for children.
     b)   predicts accuracy for children, but not for adults.
     c)   predicts accuracy for both adults and children.
     d)   does not predict accuracy for either adults or children.
     Ans: d   LO: 7 ·   Page: 506-508   Type: C

71. Which of the following statements concerning eyewitness testimony is *false*?
     a)   Eyewitnesses who remember trivial details of a crime scene are more likely to correctly identify the culprit.
     b)   After suggestive questioning, witnesses may believe that a red light was green or that a yield sign was a stop sign.
     c)   Eyewitness confidence is not related to eyewitness accuracy.
     d)   Retelling events commits people to their recollections, regardless of whether or not those recollections are accurate.
     Ans: a   LO: 7   Page: 506-508   Type: C

72. Being repeatedly questioned about their observations is likely to
     a)   increase eyewitness accuracy as well as confidence.
     b)   increase eyewitness accuracy, but not confidence.
     c)   increase eyewitness confidence, but not accuracy.
     d)   neither increase eyewitness accuracy nor confidence.
     Ans: c   LO: 7   Page: 506-508

73. Research by Wells and Bradfield suggests that feedback can influence an eyewitness's confidence and memory only when
     a)   they make an accurate identification.
     b)   the feedback is positive.
     c)   when the suspect is of a different race.
     d)   None of these.
     Ans: d   LO: 7   Page: 507-508   Type: C

74. Wells and Bradfield found that eyewitnesses who were told "good, you identified the suspect" tended to
     a)   show an increase in subsequent identification accuracy.
     b)   be more accurate in sequential but not simultaneous lineup presentations.
     c)   overestimate how good a view they were able to get of the culprit during the incident in question.
     d)   be particularly susceptible to familiarity induced biases.
     Ans: c   LO: 7   Page: 507-508   Type: C

75. Research on lineup administration by Greathouse and Kovera (2009) suggests that the police officer who conducts a lineup
     a)   can affect the actual identification that a witness makes.
     b)   can impact how confident an eyewitness is.
     c)   will not unduly bias an eyewitness as s/he makes a conscious effort not to.
     d)   None of these
     Ans: a   LO: 7   Page: 508   Type: C

76. Kwame, a noted psychologist, has been called as an expert witness in a trial. Kwame is likely to provide testimony concerning all of the following *except*
     a)   alcoholic intoxication can impair ability to recall events.
     b)   police instructions can influence an eyewitness's confidence.
     c)   eyewitness confidence is not a good predictor of accuracy.
     d)   hypnosis increases the accuracy of eyewitness memory.
     Ans: d   LO: 7   Page: 508-509   Type: A

77.   One way in which expert testimony may increase the competence of jurors is by
      a)   facilitating judges' use of scientific jury selection.
      b)   leading jurors to be more critical of eyewitness testimony.
      c)   eliciting sentencing disparity.
      d)   modeling confidence, thus providing the jurors with a standard against which they can assess the
            confidence of non-expert witnesses.
      Ans: b   LO: 7   Page: 508-509   Type: C

78.   Which of the following is an example of a source of nonevidentiary influence?
      a)   Pre-trial publicity
      b)   The testimony of expert witnesses
      c)   Fingerprint evidence
      d)   Eyewitness testimony
      Ans: a   LO: 7   Page: 509-510   Type: C

79.   Research on pretrial publicity has demonstrated that it typically produces a bias
      a)   in favor of the defendant, and people will be well aware of this bias.
      b)   in favor of the defendant, though people will not realize they are biased.
      c)   against the defendant, and people will be well aware of this bias.
      d)   against the defendant, though people will not realize they are biased.
      Ans: d   LO: 8   Page: 509-510   Type: C

80.   Pretrial publicity tends to produce a bias against defendants because
      a)   people assume that defendants are guilty until proven innocent.
      b)   information in news reports usually comes from police or district attorneys.
      c)   most people charged with crimes really are guilty.
      d)   the publicity makes the defendant seem more familiar, resulting in a familiarity induced bias.
      Ans: b   LO: 8   Page: 509-510   Type: C

81.   Kara sees a news story on television about an upcoming criminal defendant who was previously charged
      with similar crimes. If Kara is selected to serve as a juror for this defendant's trial, it is likely that
      a)   the information concerning the defendant's prior criminal activity will have no impact on her verdict
            as long as she agrees to be objective and impartial.
      b)   the information concerning the defendant's prior criminal record may bias her impression of the
            defendant, but instructions from the judge can counteract such a bias.
      c)   Kara will interpret the facts of the case in a way that is consistent with the information about the
            defendant's prior criminal record.
      d)   the pretrial publicity will make the defendant seem more familiar to Kara and so she will be less
            likely to convict.
      Ans: c   LO: 8   Page: 509-510   Type: A

82.   Research on inadmissible evidence suggests that, contrary to the judge's instructions, juries often pay
      attention to such information
      a)   even when it is unreliable.
      b)   when it is reliable but inadmissible because of a legal "technicality."
      c)   when it is emotional in content.
      d)   All of these
      Ans: b   LO: 8   Page: 510-511   Type: C

83.   All of the following are potential explanations for the finding that jurors often fail to comply with a judge's
      instruction to disregard inadmissible evidence *except*
      a)   they do not like being told what they can and cannot pay attention to.
      b)   the judge's instruction often draws greater attention to the evidence in question.
      c)   jurors are primarily motivated to reach the "right" decision.
      d)   judicial instructions do not make it clear precisely which information should be disregarded and
            which should not.
      Ans: d   LO: 8   Page: 510-511   Type: C

84. During a trial, the prosecution refers to an illegally obtained tape recording of a phone call that makes the defendant appear guilty. Research suggests that after hearing this information, jurors are *most* likely to
    a) disregard the information if the defense attorney objects, even if the judge rules that the information is admissible.
    b) vote guilty, unless the judge rules that the information is inadmissible.
    c) vote guilty, even if the judge rules that the information is inadmissible.
    d) vote guilty if the judge rules the information is admissible, but vote not guilty if the judge rules that the information is inadmissible.
    Ans: c   LO: 8   Page: 510-511   Type: A

85. During a trial, the judge admonishes Baruch and his fellow jurors to ignore a damaging letter written by the defendant. Baruch will be *most* likely to do so if the
    a) letter was obtained illegally, and is not very emotionally charged.
    b) letter is not very emotionally charged, and is hard to read.
    c) judge is particularly forceful in this admonition.
    d) pre-trial publicity surrounding the case made explicit mention of the letter.
    Ans: b   LO: 8   Page: 511-512   Type: A

86. One reason judges' instructions tend to have little impact on jurors is that
    a) the instructions typically come before the evidence is presented, increasing the likelihood that the jurors will forget them.
    b) the jurors often find the instructions incomprehensible, leading to misunderstandings and confusion.
    c) the jurors frequently consider the instructions to be irrelevant to the trial, leading them to experience reactance.
    d) jurors usually try to avoid jury nullification.
    Ans: b   LO: 8   Page: 511-512   Type: C

87. Research with mock jurors suggests that jurors comprehend judges' conventional instructions relatively well when these instructions are
    a) accompanied by graphs.
    b) presented by the attorneys rather than by the judge.
    c) given first to the jury foreperson, who then passes them along to the rest of the jury.
    d) rewritten in plain language.
    Ans: d   LO: 8   Page: 511-512   Type: F

88. Judges' instructions often have little impact on jurors for all of the following reasons *except*
    a) the language is too confusing.
    b) the jurors disagree with the law.
    c) they are delivered too late in the trial.
    d) the jurors are afraid of the judge.
    Ans: d   LO: 8   Page: 511-512   Type: F

89. Jurors' power to disregard the law when it conflicts with their personal conceptions of justice is called
    a) the inquisitorial model of justice.
    b) jury nullification.
    c) sentencing disparity.
    d) the process of peremptory challenges.
    Ans: b   LO: 8   Page: 512   Type: F

90. Eighteen-year-old André has been accused of statutory rape because he had sex with his seventeen-year-old girlfriend, who is considered a minor. When the case goes to trial, the prosecution presents evidence confirming that André broke the law; yet the jurors vote not guilty because they feel the law is outdated. The jury's action illustrates
    a) the positive coercion bias.
    b) internalization.
    c) sentencing disparity.
    d) jury nullification.
    Ans: d   LO: 8   Page: 512   Type: A

91.   All of the following are *true* about jury forepersons *except* that they
      a)   tend to be the individuals who speak first in the jury room.
      b)   usually spend more time discussing procedural matters than indicating their opinion about the trial.
      c)   are usually chosen after a careful, deliberate discussion among jury members.
      d)   tend to moderate jury discussions more than dominate them.
      Ans: c   LO: 9   Page: 513-514   Type: F

92.   A juror is more likely to be chosen as foreperson if the juror is
      a)   male as opposed to female.
      b)   of higher rather than lower occupational status.
      c)   vocal during the initial stages of deliberations as opposed to quiet.
      d)   All of these
      Ans: d   LO: 9   Page: 513-514   Type: F

93.   Shaquille has been selected to be the foreperson of his jury. It is likely that Shaquille
      a)   will exert more influence over the jury's decision than other members of the jury.
      b)   will spend more time than other jurors discussing procedural items.
      c)   was selected because he had never served on a jury before.
      d)   will spend more time than other jurors expressing his opinion.
      Ans: b   LO: 9   Page: 513-514   Type: A

94.   Based on the relevant research, which of the following people is *most* likely to be chosen as foreperson of a jury?
      a)   Monica, who works on an assembly line similar to the one the defendant has worked on
      b)   Joey, who sits in a chair situated on the long side of the jury table, close to the middle
      c)   Rachel, who is one of only three jurors who does not say anything during the first few minutes of the deliberations.
      d)   Ross, who is chief of surgery at a local hospital
      Ans: d   LO: 9   Page: 513-514   Type: A

95.   Norbert is selected as the foreperson of the jury. Assuming that a *typical* selection process occurred, he was probably chosen
      a)   very quickly.
      b)   after a long, heated, often irrational debate.
      c)   after very careful, rational consideration of the candidates.
      d)   by the judge at some point during the course of the trial.
      Ans: a   LO: 9   Page: 513-514   Type: A

96.   The stage of deliberation during which jurors set an agenda, talk in open terms, raise questions, and explore the facts is called
      a)   orientation.
      b)   open conflict.
      c)   reconciliation.
      d)   nullification.
      Ans: a   LO: 9   Page: 514-515   Type: F

97.   The members of a jury have been deliberating for several weeks. As they begin to converge on a verdict, disagreement is smoothed over and satisfaction with the verdict is affirmed. This stage of deliberation is called the period of
      a)   retrieval.
      b)   orientation.
      c)   reconciliation.
      d)   nullification.
      Ans: c   LO: 9   Page: 514-515   Type: F

98. The members of a jury are at the point in their deliberations where they are scrutinizing the evidence, constructing stories to account for the evidence, and discussing the judge's instructions. This jury is at what stage of deliberation?
    a) Open conflict
    b) Orientation
    c) Reconciliation
    d) Nullification
    Ans: a   LO: 9   Page: 514-515   Type: F

99. In a jury deliberation context, the "leniency bias" refers to
    a) jurors' tendency to go easier on ingroup defendants versus outgroup defendants.
    b) the impact of judicial instructions on jurors..
    c) the tendency of individual jurors to be more likely to vote guilty on their own than in a group.
    d) the finding that judges are harsher on defendants than are juries.
    Ans: c   LO: 8   Page: 515   Type: C

100. The tendency for jury deliberations to produce a tilt toward acquittal is called
    a) the misinformation effect.
    b) sentencing disparity.
    c) the leniency bias.
    d) jury nullification.
    Ans: c   LO: 9   Page: 515   Type: F

101. Phoebe suggests that jury deliberations rarely include any surprises since the first rule of juries is that "majority rules." Which of the following phenomena provides the strongest exception to her conclusion?
    a) Jury nullification
    b) The leniency bias
    c) Misinformation effect
    d) The peremptory challenge
    Ans: b   LO: 9   Page: 515   Type: C

102. Research shows that a jury's final verdict can often be predicted accurately if which of the following is known?
    a) Nonverbal behaviors of the jurors during the trial
    b) Thoughts of the individual jurors just before deliberation begins
    c) Initial vote of the foreperson
    d) Proportion of men to women on the jury
    Ans: b   LO: 9   Page: 514-515   Type: C

103. If there is a majority opinion in a jury's initial vote, then
    a) the deliberations will be marked by informational rather than normative influence.
    b) the leniency bias is less likely to play a role in the final verdict delivered.
    c) the ultimate verdict will usually be consistent with the vote taken during the orientation stage.
    d) jury nullification becomes less likely to affect the outcome of the deliberations.
    Ans: c   LO: 9   Page: 514-515   Type: F

104. Research suggests that it is easier to
    a) create a reasonable doubt in the minds of your fellow jurors than it is to convince them that they have no reasonable doubt.
    b) convince fellow jurors to change their votes from not guilty to guilty than it is to convince them to change from guilty to not guilty.
    c) persuade a fellow juror using normative social influence than it is to do so using informational social influence.
    d) change the minds of fellow jurors when deliberating on a civil trial versus a criminal trial.
    Ans: a   LO: 9   Page: 515   Type: C

105. Research on the leniency bias and jury deliberations suggests that which of the following juries will have the easiest time reaching a unanimous decision?
    a)   A jury in which 10 jurors vote "not guilty" and 2 jurors vote "guilty" to start with
    b)   A jury in which 10 jurors vote "guilty" and 2 jurors vote "not guilty" to start with
    c)   A jury that is evenly split at 6-6 to start with
    d)   A jury that has paid close attention to the judge's final instructions
    Ans: a   LO: 9   Page: 514-515   Type: A

106. If a jury is evenly split on their initial vote, then
    a)   the final verdict is more likely to be acquittal.
    b)   the final verdict is more likely to be conviction.
    c)   they will most likely end as hung jury.
    d)   there is equal probability of acquittal, conviction, or hung jury.
    Ans: a   LO: 9   Page: 514-515   Type: C

107. As deliberation begins, nine jurors think that the defendant is guilty. At first, the three jurors who think otherwise are resistant to changing their minds, but after hearing what the others have to say, they are genuinely persuaded and decide to vote guilty. The factor *most* likely to have led these three jurors to change their verdict is
    a)   the leniency bias.
    b)   the influence of peremptory challenges.
    c)   normative influence.
    d)   informational influence.
    Ans: d   LO: 9   Page: 515   Type: A

108. Which of the following is *not* a reason why many psychologists believe that allowing smaller jury sizes is a bad idea?
    a)   Tension and interpersonal conflict are more likely in small groups as opposed to large ones.
    b)   Smaller juries are less representative of the communities from which they are drawn.
    c)   Smaller juries spend less time discussing the case.
    d)   It is harder for a dissenting juror to hold out for her position when she does not have a single ally.
    Ans: a   LO: 9   Page: 515-516   Type: F

109. Research suggests that small juries are more likely than large juries to
    a)   produce non-unanimous decisions.
    b)   resist normative pressures within the group.
    c)   deliberate for a shorter period of time.
    d)   be representative of the larger population.
    Ans: c   LO: 9   Page: 515-516   Type: F

110. Relative to large juries, smaller juries may spend less time deliberating mostly because they are
    a)   less conducive to the emergence of minority allies.
    b)   more likely to have a male foreperson.
    c)   less inclined to reach a unanimous verdict.
    d)   not used in trials involving complex decisions.
    Ans: a   LO: 9   Page: 515-516   Type: C

111. Relative to deliberations in which the jury must reach a unanimous verdict, deliberations in which the jury can use a non-unanimous decision rule tend to
    a)   encourage open conflict among jurors.
    b)   breed closed-mindedness among jurors.
    c)   increase the influence of jurors in the minority.
    d)   increase jurors' confidence.
    Ans: b   LO: 9   Page: 516-517   Type: F

112. In a murder case involving a six-person jury, five of the jurors think the defendant is guilty and one thinks the defendant is not guilty. In another murder case involving a twelve-person jury, ten think the defendant is guilty and two think the defendant is not guilty. Based on Asch's research on conformity, and all other things being equal, what predictions can be made about the likelihood that the jurors in the minority in these two trials will resist the pressures exerted by those in the majority to change their verdicts?
    a) The minority in the smaller jury should be less likely to maintain his or her independence because the minority in the smaller jury has no allies in dissent.
    b) The minority in the larger jury should be less likely to maintain their independence because the majority in the larger jury is comprised of more people.
    c) Because the proportion of majority to minority jurors is equivalent in these two juries, the minorities should be equally likely to maintain their independence.
    d) If the evidence in both cases is ambiguous, the minority in the smaller jury should be less likely to maintain his or her independence; but if the evidence in both cases is unambiguous, there should be no difference between the juries.
    Ans: a   LO: 9   Page: 515-516   Type: A

113. Pilar is serving on a jury that is required to reach a 10-2 decision. Relative to juries that are required to reach unanimous decisions, Pilar and the other jurors will
    a) spend more time discussing the case.
    b) be more likely to marginalize jurors with dissenting opinions.
    c) be more confident in their final verdict.
    d) be more persuaded by information influence.
    Ans: b   LO: 9   Page: 516-517   Type: A

114. In which of the following juries will jurors spend the *most* time discussing the case?
    a) A twelve-person jury that must reach a unanimous decision
    b) A twelve-person jury that must reach a majority decision
    c) A six-person jury that must reach a unanimous decision
    d) A six-person jury that must reach a majority decision
    Ans: a   LO: 9   Page: 516-517   Type: C

115. One reason for controversy surrounding sentencing decisions in this country is that Americans often
    a) disagree about the adversarial model.
    b) believe that juries are inept.
    c) resist the inquisitorial model of justice.
    d) disagree about the goals of imprisonment.
    Ans: d   LO: 10   Page: 517-519   Type: F

116. All of the following are potential motivations that underlie punishment in the criminal justice system *except*
    a) retribution.
    b) incapacitation.
    c) nullification.
    d) deterrence.
    Ans: c   LO: 10   Page: 517-519   Type: F

117. Sentencing disparity refers to the
    a) tendency for different judges to apply different sentences for the same offense.
    b) fact that judges believe that the purpose of sentencing the convicted is deterrence, but the general public believes the purpose is retribution.
    c) tendency for judges to give harsher sentences for harsher crimes despite differences in the recidivism rates of the crimes.
    d) difference between the sentence given by a judge and the amount of time a convicted offender actually serves.
    Ans: a   LO: 10   Page: 518-519   Type: F

118. Research concerning race and capital punishment indicates that
    a) for judgments of such serious repercussion, judges and juries are rarely if ever influenced by race.
    b) the more "stereotypically Black" a defendant appears, the more likely he is to be sentenced to death.
    c) defendants are most likely to be sentenced to death when they murder a same-race victim.
    d) None of these.
    Ans: b   LO: 10   Page: 518-519   Type: C

119. Which of the following is *not* a reasonable criticism of the Stanford University prison study?
    a) All of the participants were younger than 30 years old.
    b) Lack of random assignment made it possible that the individuals assigned to be guards were generally more sadistic.
    c) Participants were not real prisoners and guards, so their behavior may not be representative.
    d) Some of the participants endured pain and suffering, making the study ethically questionable.
    Ans: b   LO: 10   Page: 519-521   Type: C

120. The Stanford University prison simulation teaches us that
    a) sentencing disparity is much more pervasive than was previously believed.
    b) the conditions at privately-run prisons are far superior to those at state-run prisons.
    c) demographic profiles play a very important role in determining the degree to which the prisoners will use their prison time in a constructive manner.
    d) even normal people can be dehumanized by institutional roles and practices.
    Ans: d   LO: 10   Page: 519-521   Type: C

121. Carnahan and McFarland (2007) conducted a study to determine whether a particular type of person is likely to sign up for a study like the Stanford University prison study. They found that advertisements for a study on "prison life" attracted potential participants higher-than-average in _____ and lower-than-average in _____.
    a) authoritarianism; aggression.
    b) self-monitoring; altruism
    c) need for cognition; need for closure.
    d) narcissism; empathy
    Ans: d   LO: 10   Page: 520-521   Type: F

122. Ming was involved in a civil dispute that came to trial. Though unhappy with the judge's decision, he felt that he truly had the chance to express his views and present his case completely. Ming apparently was *most* satisfied with
    a) the sentencing disparity.
    b) the voir dire.
    c) his process control.
    d) the deliberation stage.
    Ans: c   LO: 11   Page: 521-522   Type: A

123. A newly developing country hopes to maximize its citizens' satisfaction with its new legal system. The new leaders of this country must be sure to
    a) afford high levels of process control.
    b) put the decisions in the hands of neutral experts who collect information on both sides of the issue.
    c) endorse a competitive orientation.
    d) limit decision control to those who are charged.
    Ans: a   LO: 11   Page: 521-522   Type: A

124. In comparison to the inquisitorial system of justice, the adversarial system
    a) is higher in decision control.
    b) provides less satisfaction for participants.
    c) is higher in process control.
    d) is far more common.
    Ans: c   LO: 11   Page: 521-522   Type: C

125. Emmett has been arrested for drug trafficking. He hires a lawyer who puts together a defense against the case created by the prosecuting attorney. Each side then presents its case in court. This scenario is an example of the
    a)   deliberation process.
    b)   adversarial model.
    c)   reconciliation phase.
    d)   inquisitorial model.
    Ans: b   LO: 11   Page: 521-522   Type: A

ESSAY

126. Describe death qualification in the context of jury selection. Explain the controversy surrounding the practice.
    *Ans: Death qualification is a jury selection procedure used in capital cases that excludes prospective jurors who say they would refuse to vote for the death penalty under any circumstance. Although excluding such jurors from only the sentencing decisions in capital cases would not be controversial (because these jurors admit that they are not willing to endorse one of the sentencing options), death qualification is very controversial because it also excludes these jurors from serving on the juries that determine verdicts in the first place. The procedure is controversial because research suggests that people who support the death penalty are not only more prosecution-minded on a host of issues but also more likely to vote guilty in a trial compared to those who oppose the death penalty. The implication, then, is that using the practice of death qualification biases juries against defendants, such that they are more likely to be found guilty by a death-qualified jury than by one consisting of a mix of proponents and opponents of capital punishment.
    Page: 492-493*

127. Describe two tactics other than physical violence, or the threat of physical violence, that police use to extract confessions from suspects. Also explain the conditions under which people are most likely to internalize a false confession.
    Ans: There are many strategies that police use to extract confessions. One approach is to minimize the offense by making excuses on behalf of the suspect. By doing so, the police can sometimes lull suspects into a false sense of security, such that they expect leniency and thus become more likely to confess. Another approach is to inform the suspects that the police have incriminating evidence against them. Through this tactic, the police try to make suspects believe that it is futile to deny the charges or launch a defense in court, so they again are more likely to confess. Sometimes, however, suspects confess to crimes they did not commit. In such cases, these suspects may have internalized their confessions; that is, they come to believe that they are indeed guilty of the crime. Research suggests that people can be induced to falsely confess, and to internalize the confession, when they are presented with false evidence that incriminates them or when they lack a strong memory for the events in question.   Page: 494-496

128. Summarize the means by which the polygraph works as a lie detector. What two major problems call its accuracy into question?
    Ans: A polygraph is an instrument that records physiological arousal from multiple channels. The assumption underlying its use is that when a suspect lies, he or she becomes anxious in ways that can be measured—specifically, through changes in breathing, blood pressure, and perspiration. First, the suspect's baseline level of arousal is established. Then, the examiner asks a series of yes-no questions and compares the suspect's reactions to emotionally arousing crime-relevant questions with his or her reactions to control questions that are arousing but not relevant to the crime. In theory, suspects whose denials about the crime are truthful should be more aroused by the control questions, whereas suspects whose denials are false should be more aroused by the crime-relevant questions. One problem with the use of the polygraph as a lie detector is that truthful people often fail the test. A second problem is that the test can be faked. To avoid being aroused by crime-relevant questions, some guilty individuals are able to use countermeasures such as distraction or an artificial inflation of their arousal responses to control questions (by, for example, clenching their toes so that the arousal observed in their responses to crime-relevant questions does not seem high in comparison).   Page: 498-499

129. Summarize the theory of reconstructive memory as it relates to eyewitness testimony. What does the research suggest about the use of such testimony from children?

Ans: Reconstructive memory is a concept underlying the theory that eyewitness testimony can be altered by exposure to post-event information. According to this theory, first proposed by Elizabeth Loftus, even false information about an event we have earlier observed can influence and be incorporated into our memory of that event. For example, Loftus and Palmer (1974) demonstrated that when participants who viewed a film of a traffic accident were later asked questions about the accident, the wording of these questions significantly influenced their recollections. By implication, the accuracy of eyewitnesses' testimony can be reduced by post-event information to which the eyewitnesses were exposed—a particular concern when the eyewitnesses are children. Indeed, children have a difficult time distinguishing between their real memories and the post-event suggestions to which they are later exposed. Laboratory experiments indicate that preschool-age children are more likely than older children or adults to incorporate such post-event suggestions into their memories.   Page: 501-503

130. Identify three structural factors that can affect the process and outcome of jury deliberations.

Ans: Among the several factors that can affect the process of jury deliberation are (1) the size of the jury, (2) the type of verdict required, and (3) the initial vote split of the jurors. Research has demonstrated that, in general, smaller juries (where allies are less available) and juries that must only come to a majority (nonunanimous) verdict tend to spend less time deliberating, though this does not necessarily change the actual verdict in all cases. Research suggests that the best predictor of a jury's final verdict is the predeliberation vote split of its jurors. One exception to this rule, however, is known as the leniency bias—a tendency to acquit defendants when the jury is split at the outset of deliberations. Finally, juries that are death-qualified tend to be more prosecution-minded.   Page: 513-517

CHAPTER 13

Business

MULTIPLE CHOICE

1. When Americans were asked what they would do if they won a state lottery, *most*
    a) say they would still work.
    b) say they would quit their jobs immediately and never work again.
    c) men say they would continue to work, whereas most women say they would never work again.
    d) people in high-status jobs say they would continue to work, whereas most in low-status jobs say they would never work again.
    Ans: a   LO: 1   Page: 529-530   Type: F

2. As of 2009, the current unemployment rate in the United States is
    a) 10%
    b) 4%
    c) 8%
    d) 2%
    Ans: a   LO: 1   Page: 529-530   Type: F

3. The study of human behavior in the workplace defines the field of
    a) clinical psychology.
    b) experimental psychology.
    c) economic/applied psychology.
    d) industrial/organizational psychology.
    Ans: d   LO: 1   Page: 529-530   Type: F

4. Dr. Price is a psychologist who studies practical issues concerning job interviewing, leadership, and employee motivation. She is *most* likely a(n)
    a) clinical psychologist.
    b) experimental psychologist.
    c) economic/applied psychologist.
    d) industrial/organizational psychologist.
    Ans: d   LO: 1   Page: 529-530   Type: A

5. Which of the following questions would an industrial/organizational psychologist be *least* likely to study?
    a) Do employer expectations influence job performance?
    b) What personality characteristics are associated with effective leaders?
    c) Are people more or less satisfied with their current romantic partner?
    d) How do financial incentives affect worker motivation?
    Ans: c   LO: 1   Page: 529-530   Type: C

6. The Hawthorne effect
    a) describes the relationship between working conditions and job satisfaction.
    b) refers to the tendency for observation of employees to increase productivity.
    c) suggests that employees become so engaged in their work that they are immune to environmental manipulations.
    d) is the tendency for bright levels of illumination to decrease worker productivity.
    Ans: b   LO: 1   Page: 530-531   Type: F

7. The Hawthorne effect is named after
    a) a social psychologist.
    b) an industrial/organizational psychologist.
    c) a factory.
    d) a city in Illinois.
    Ans: c   LO: 1   Page: 530-531   Type: F

8.   The discovery of the Hawthorne effect laid the foundation for industrial/organizational psychology because
     it illustrated the role of
     a)   social influences in the workplace.
     b)   job interviewing techniques in the creation of a homogenous workforce.
     c)   equity motivation in worker loyalty.
     d)   personality variables in economic decision making.
     Ans: a   LO: 1   Page: 530-531   Type: C

9.   Lorissa, a teacher, is attempting to improve the performance of her students by making the classroom more
     learning-friendly. She rearranges the desks, purchases lighter window shades, and adds more color to the
     bulletin boards. Her students do in fact improve. If this improvement stemmed from a Hawthorne effect,
     then it can be *best* attributed to
     a)   the students' knowledge that she was attempting to improve their performance.
     b)   the students' feeling that their classroom is better than those of friends in other classes.
     c)   Lorissa's positive attitude toward education.
     d)   the effect of physical setting on academic performance.
     Ans: a   LO: 1   Page: 530-531   Type: A

10. The original intent of the managers at the Hawthorne plant was to see if they could make their factory
     workers more productive by changing light levels in the factory. To do this, they increased the lighting for
     one group of workers in a special test room and kept the lights the same in the control room. They found that
     a)   workers in the special test room came to outperform workers in the control room.
     b)   workers in the control room actually and unexpectedly outperformed workers in the special test room.
     c)   neither group of workers showed an increase in productivity.
     d)   both groups of workers showed an increase in productivity.
     Ans: d   LO: 1   Page: 530-531   Type: F

11. The tendency of students in working groups to exert more effort on their project when their teacher is
     standing within earshot is an example of
     a)   social comparison
     b)   the Hawthorne effect
     c)   counterfactual thinking
     d)   self-fulfilling prophecy
     Ans: b   LO: 1   Page: 530-531   Type: A

12. Hal has narrowed the field of potential job applicants down to just two people, a man and a woman with
     very similar résumés. Research suggests that he is more likely to hire
     a)   the woman.
     b)   the man.
     c)   whichever applicant is younger.
     d)   whichever applicant is older.
     Ans: b   LO: 2   Page: 531-533   Type: A

13. Gender effects on ratings of job applicants seem to decrease when
     a)   applicants are around the same age.
     b)   decisions are based only on written materials.
     c)   the employer and the job applicant are of the same gender.
     d)   greater amounts of information about the applicants are available.
     Ans: d   LO: 2   Page: 531-533   Type: C

14. Cathy applied for a job as a mechanical engineer. In addition to being evaluated based on her résumé and
     other written materials, Cathy participated in a live, face-to-face interview during which she was asked a set
     of standardized questions put to all the candidates for this job. This interview *most* likely
     a)   decreased the chances that she would be hired.
     b)   diminished the likelihood that stereotyped judgments would be made of her.
     c)   produced the Hawthorne effect in the interviewer's behavior.
     d)   elicited responses from Cathy concerning her leadership skills.
     Ans: b   LO: 2   Page: 531-533   Type: A

15. Face-to-face interviews are believed to reduce all of the following types of bias *except*
    a) preference for male candidates.
    b) preference for White candidates.
    c) preference for physically attractive candidates.
    d) preference for young candidates.
    Ans: c   LO: 2   Page: 531-533   Type: F

16. Research suggests that face-to-face interviews
    a) increase the probability of stereotyped judgments.
    b) exacerbate gender preferences in hiring decisions.
    c) reduce, but do not eliminate, racial preferences in hiring decisions.
    d) produce hiring decisions that are perceived to be more open-minded, but are no different from decisions based on evaluations of written materials.
    Ans: c   LO: 2   Page: 531-533   Type: C

17. Research on physical attractiveness and job hiring suggests that attractiveness influences
    a) perceptions of female applicants, but not perceptions of male applicants.
    b) perceptions of both female and male applicants.
    c) evaluations made by male interviewers, but not female interviewers.
    d) evaluations made by both male and female interviewers.
    Ans: b   LO: 2   Page: 531-533   Type: F

18. Which of the following has been demonstrated in research on traditional employment interviews?
    a) Interviews tend to be very high in predictive validity.
    b) Applicants who exhibit the least amount of self-promotion are likely to be hired.
    c) Interviews eliminate biases toward physically attractive applicants.
    d) An employer's expectations can distort the interview process.
    Ans: d   LO: 2   Page: 532-533   Type: F

19. Amanda is trying to get hired by the Up and Coming Company. All of the following will help her cause *except*
    a) being physically attractive.
    b) securing a personal interview.
    c) engaging in self-promotion.
    d) an interviewer who has low expectations of her.
    Ans: d   LO: 2   Page: 532-533   Type: A

20. Marilyn is the director of human resources for a small financial services company. The CEO of the company, Phil, asks her to interview three candidates for an open position in the billing department. Phil is particularly excited about candidate A, and tells Marilyn this. Research suggests that when interviewing candidate A, Marilyn will
    a) be somewhat more outgoing and cheerful than when she interviews the other candidates.
    b) scrutinize every response more carefully in the effort to disconfirm Phil's expectations.
    c) engage in self-promotion.
    d) hold off on making any judgments about the candidate until she completes the other two interviews as well.
    Ans: a   LO: 2   Page: 532-533   Type: A

21. Cecil is competing with Pete for the same position. Cecil is concerned because Pete is perceived as more attractive than he. To minimize the effect of attractiveness on ratings of applicants, Cecil should hope that
    a) the interviewer is female.
    b) Pete is interviewed by someone of the same gender.
    c) the interviewer is very experienced.
    d) his interviewer is a transactional leader.
    Ans: c   LO: 2   Page: 531-533   Type: A

22. Because applicants try to present themselves in the *best* light, traditional employment interviews often lack
    a)   reliability.
    b)   predictive validity.
    c)   construct validity.
    d)   standardization.
    Ans: b   LO: 2   Page: 531-533   Type: C

23. Which of the following behaviors did college students in the Levashina and Campion (2007) study exhibit as forms of "faking" in job interviews?
    a)   ingratiation
    b)   exaggeration
    c)   outright lying
    d)   All of these
    Ans: d   LO: 2   Page: 532-533   Type: F

24. The concern about a self-fulfilling prophecy with regard to the interview process is that
    a)   interviewers may tend to discount information learned in an interview if it is counter to the interviewer's expectations.
    b)   interviewers will be predisposed to like applicants who are similar to themselves, regardless of the applicant's credentials.
    c)   interviewers who are trying to promote the company to an applicant will evaluate that particular candidate with more scrutiny.
    d)   interviewers will be predisposed to evaluate less attractive candidates more favorably.
    Ans: a   LO: 2   Page: 532-533   Type: C

25. Barney, an admissions officer, is interviewing a college applicant about whom he has very high positive expectations. Barney is outgoing and cheerful during the interview, spends considerable time recruiting the applicant, and asks the applicant questions that solicit positive information. As a result, Barney is pleased with the applicant's performance and admits her to the school. This interview process demonstrates an example of
    a)   the Hawthorne effect.
    b)   a self-fulfilling prophecy.
    c)   a contrast effect.
    d)   entrapment.
    Ans: b   LO: 2   Page: 532-533   Type: A

26. Phyllis, based upon her written application materials, is perceived as the best candidate for a position with Conglomerate Company. It is likely that her interviewer will
    a)   elicit negative information from Phyllis in order to make sure that his positive expectations are not wrong.
    b)   hold Phyllis to a higher standard than usual in order to offset any personal bias.
    c)   spend more time assessing Phyllis's fitness as a worker than really getting to know her.
    d)   provide Phyllis with more information about the company and the job than other candidates would receive.
    Ans: d   LO: 2   Page: 532-533   Type: A

27. All of the following personnel selection procedures are used legally by employers regardless of profession *except*
    a)   polygraph testing.
    b)   integrity tests.
    c)   assessment centers.
    d)   personality tests.
    Ans: a   LO: 2   Page: 533   Type: F

28. Darlene is in charge of hiring new police officers. Which of the following is *true*?
    a)   It would be legal for her to use a polygraph during the hiring process.
    b)   Her expectations about particular candidates will not influence her hiring decisions.
    c)   A graphology assessment would yield useful information.
    d)   If she has lots of experience at her job, then she will be biased to hire physically attractive applicants over unattractive ones.
    Ans: a   LO: 2   Page: 533-534   Type: A

29. Research that examines workers' personality characteristics has concluded that
    a) people who score high in conscientiousness tend to be too timid and cautious to be highly-productive workers.
    b) low self-monitors are more likely to become organizational leaders.
    c) extraverts are more likely than introverts to succeed as managers.
    d) self-esteem has little ability to predict job productivity or satisfaction.
    Ans: c   LO: 2   Page: 534   Type: F

30. The three general types of standardized written tests in the employee selection process include all of the following *except* tests that measure
    a) cognitive abilities.
    b) personality traits related to work-related outcomes.
    c) a potential employee's integrity.
    d) an employee's overall level of mental health.
    Ans: d   LO: 2   Page: 534   Type: F

31. Murphy's (2003) survey of over 700 professionals indicated that most
    a) relied extensively on standardized tests of intelligence in personnel selection.
    b) had never heard of the use of standardized tests of intelligence in personnel selection.
    c) agreed that intelligence is difficult to measure with standardized tests.
    d) believed that integrity tests were more important than standardized tests of intelligence.
    Ans: c   LO: 2   Page: 534   Type: F

32. Lenny is viewed as outgoing by his many friends and he is often the center of attention because of his talkativeness. Based on research on personality traits relevant to desired work outcomes, Lenny would probably be *most* successful as
    a) an accountant.
    b) a librarian.
    c) a salesperson.
    d) a medical records clerk.
    Ans: c   LO: 2   Page: 534   Type: A

33. A major concern when it comes to the effort to assess a future employee's character is that applicants tend to present themselves in overly positive ways. One form of assessment that avoids this problem is
    a) face-to-face interviews.
    b) overt integrity tests.
    c) covert integrity tests.
    d) non-structured interviews.
    Ans: c   LO: 2   Page: 535-536   Type: F

34. Melanie completed an integrity test and was told that she scored the highest of all the applicants who took the test. Melanie should feel good about her results because
    a) the test proves she is a good person.
    b) according to the research, integrity is the most important attribute of an employee.
    c) scores on integrity scales are predictive of job performance.
    d) integrity is not at all related to job performance.
    Ans: c   LO: 2   Page: 535-536   Type: A

35. When Kinard applied for a job at a new firm, they gave him a paper-and-pencil questionnaire that asked questions about whether or not he had been involved in any of several transgressions, such as illegal drug use and shoplifting. Kinard took a(n)
    a) situational judgment test.
    b) polygraph test.
    c) integrity test.
    d) personality test.
    Ans: c   LO: 2   Page: 535-536   Type: A

36. A test measuring broad personality characteristics unrelated to the workplace is known as a(n)
     a)   overt integrity test.
     b)   covert integrity test.
     c)   standardized test.
     d)   None of these.
     Ans: b   LO: 2   Page: 535-536   Type: F

37. Which of the following has been demonstrated in research on integrity tests?
     a)   Such tests are predictive of job performance and behaviors such as theft or disciplinary problems.
     b)   Both overt and covert integrity tests can be easily faked by motivated or knowledgeable test-takers.
     c)   While covert tests can be easily faked, overt tests are too obvious to fake.
     d)   Such tests are no more predictive of job performance than the flip of a coin.
     Ans: a   LO: 2   Page: 535-536   Type: C

38. Compared to a paper-and-pencil personality test, a structured interview is
     a)   more difficult to fake.
     b)   less predictive of future performance.
     c)   too expensive for most companies to utilize.
     d)   All of these.
     Ans: a   LO: 2   Page: 536   Type: C

39. A structured interview is similar to a standardized test in that both
     a)   require applicants to first pass rigorous pre-screening procedures before they can be administered.
     b)   involve collecting the same information in the same way from all applicants.
     c)   maximize an employer's impact on potential applicants.
     d)   are potentially compromised by subjective judgments of the interviewer.
     Ans: b   LO: 2   Page: 534-536   Type: C

40. Neve will be using a structured interview to hire her new assistant. One of the applicants for the position has requested a phone interview because she lives far from the job site. Based on the existing research, Neve
     a)   should be concerned because structured interviews are only effective when administered in person.
     b)   has no reason to worry because she can focus more intently on the applicant's responses during a phone interview.
     c)   should feel reassured because structured phone interviews have been shown to be predictive of future productivity.
     d)   will have to use a written integrity test rather than a structured interview in this situation.
     Ans: c   LO: 2   Page: 536   Type: A

41. The advantage of structured rather than traditional interviews when screening applicants is that an employer
     a)   can avoid conducting biased interviews.
     b)   can use integrity tests and/or polygraph tests as part of the interview procedure.
     c)   can get a better implicit understanding of each applicant.
     d)   has more flexibility to pursue interesting lines of questioning in the interview.
     Ans: a   LO: 2   Page: 536   Type: C

42. When job applicants are evaluated by multiple methods and multiple evaluators, they can be described as participating in a(n)
     a)   assessment center.
     b)   contingency model.
     c)   structured interview.
     d)   polygraph.
     Ans: a   LO: 2   Page: 536   Type: F

43. Compared to an in-person interview, interviews done via teleconferencing or computer tend to be
     a)   more predictive of future employee performance.
     b)   less susceptible to self-fulfilling prophecy.
     c)   viewed as less fair by applicants.
     d)   harder for applicants to "fake."
     Ans: c   LO: 2   Page: 536-537   Type: F

44. Genie is considering using various evaluation techniques to help her hire a new employee. In trying to choose between general assessments of attributes versus job-specific tests, she should
     a)   be aware that general assessments are more effective predictors of future work success.
     b)   be aware that job-specific tests lack the predictive validity of other instruments.
     c)   be aware that potential applicants see job-specific tests as most fair.
     d)   realize that each assessment has significant weaknesses.
     Ans: c   LO: 2   Page: 536-537   Type: A

45. A company's attempt to conduct targeted employment recruitment in neighborhoods in which they haven't successfully recruited employees before is known as a _____ form of affirmative action.
     a)   blind
     b)   hard
     c)   soft
     d)   loose
     Ans: c   LO: 3   Page: 537-540   Type: F

46. Concerning the issue of affirmative action, surveys tend to show that Americans are
     a)   strongly in favor of it, regardless of their race or sex.
     b)   strongly opposed to it, regardless of their race or sex.
     c)   divided on the issue, with African-Americans more supportive of it than Whites.
     d)   divided on the issue, with men more supportive of it than women.
     Ans: c   LO: 3   Page: 537-540   Type: F

47. Which of the following employees of Corporation X is most likely to believe that their company is very supportive of affirmative action policies?
     a)   A White female employee
     b)   A White male employee
     c)   An African-American male employee
     d)   A Hispanic female employee
     Ans: b   LO: 3   Page: 537-540   Type: C

48. Nacoste (1996) argues that affirmative action affects everyone involved in the hiring and promotion process and that procedural reverberations within the system are likely to occur when
     a)   all interested parties have a chance to express their views.
     b)   group issues are considered more important than individual issues.
     c)   policy is determined out in the open rather than behind closed doors.
     d)   minorities are hired based on their merits.
     Ans: b   LO: 3   Page: 537-540   Type: F

49. Which of the following would be an example of a "soft" form of affirmative action?
     a)   Giving preference to job applicants of color, but not considering gender in evaluating applications
     b)   Taking into consideration the socioeconomic status of college applicants, but not their racial background
     c)   Outreach programs intended to recruit applicants from underrepresented groups
     d)   A firm quota that stated that 50% of all new employees at a firm must be female
     Ans: c   LO: 3   Page: 538-539   Type: C

50. Madeline, Joe, and Ian have all applied for the same promotion. Madeline is chosen but may be particularly likely to devalue the promotion if she believes that
     a)   it was based on equity considerations.
     b)   the decision was made on the basis of an assessment center.
     c)   her intrinsic motivation, not her ability, determined the decision.
     d)   she got it because of her gender.
     Ans: d   LO: 3   Page: 539-540   Type: A

51. Chapter 13 reviews studies which suggest that preferential-selection processes (often referred to as affirmative action) can undermine the performance of those individuals they are supposed to benefit. What is the applicability of this conclusion to college and university admissions policies?
     a)   It would only be relevant if colleges and universities admitted students based on race without considering other merit-based factors.
     b)   It would only be relevant if colleges and universities considered race but not gender in their admissions practices.
     c)   It would only be applicable if students were able to find out whether they were admitted due to affirmative action considerations.
     d)   It is not applicable to college and university admissions because the studies on which these conclusions are based are only correlational in nature.
     Ans: a   LO: 3   Page: 537-540   Type: A

52. Heilman et al. (1998) had pairs of men and women work on two-person tasks in which the woman was always assigned a leadership role. The women in the study were
     a)   more confident in their leadership ability when they felt they had, at least in part, earned the position on merit than when they were assigned to it based on their gender.
     b)   less satisfied with their performance on the task when they felt they had been appointed leader based on merit than when they were assigned to it based on gender.
     c)   more negative in their appraisals of their performance than their male partners when gender was in any way part of the decisional process for assigning leaders.
     d)   likely to perceive the leadership selection process as unfair to the extent that their gender contributed in any way to their leadership position.
     Ans: a   LO: 3   Page: 539-540   Type: F

53. An employer, in implementing an affirmative action policy, should do all of the following *except*
     a)   set and communicate clear and explicit qualifications criteria.
     b)   emphasize the target applicant's unique contributions to the organization.
     c)   clearly inform employees that the use of a quota in certain cases is justifiable.
     d)   provide the target applicant and co-workers with feedback about the target's qualifications.
     Ans: c   LO: 3   Page: 537-540   Type: C

54. Chao and Moon (2005) refer to the idea that every worker has a multidimensional identity as constituting an organizational
     a)   melting pot.
     b)   cultural mosaic.
     c)   quilt of demography.
     d)   diversity profile.
     Ans: b   LO: 3   Page: 540-541   Type: F

55. Plaut and colleagues (2009) found that companies with White supervisors who endorsed a multicultural perspective on diversity
     a)   employed more minority employees.
     b)   employed minority employees who reported being more engaged in their work.
     c)   paid their minority employees more money than did other companies.
     d)   reported lower earnings than did other companies.
     Ans: b   LO: 3   Page: 541-542   Type: F

56. When Purdie Vaughns and others (2008) presented African-American corporate professionals with a brochure for a fictitious management consulting firm, they found that
     a)   If the brochure depicted a low level of minority representation, they were uncomfortable with the idea that the firm was colorblind.
     b)   If the brochure depicted a low level of minority representation, they were comfortable with the idea that the firm was colorblind.
     c)   If the brochure depicted a high level of minority representation, they were uncomfortable with the idea that the firm was colorblind.
     d)   The professionals were uncomfortable with the colorblind firm regardless of what was depicted in the brochure.
     Ans: a   LO: 3   Page: 541-542   Type: F

57. An optimistic take on the effects of diversity for an organization's performance would suggest that diversity
    a) leads to stronger ingroup/outgroup categorization processes.
    b) increases the breadth of perspectives and skills made available for solving any particular problem.
    c) renders unnecessary the continued use of affirmative action in the business world.
    d) eliminates the problems posed by superordinate identities.
    Ans: b   LO: 3   Page: 540-542   Type: C

58. Two changes in the world that have led organizational psychologists to begin to consider cultural issues in the workplace are
    a) the U.S Civil Rights movement and affirmative action.
    b) affirmative action and a worldwide trend towards globalization.
    c) an increase in the number of workplace discrimination lawsuits and a worldwide trend towards globalization.
    d) the U.S. Civil Rights movement and an increase in the number of workplace discrimination lawsuits.
    Ans: b   LO: 3   Page: 540-542   Type: C

59. Fegapessa is required to evaluate all of her employees and then communicate the results of these evaluations to the employees. Fegapessa is conducting
    a) performance appraisals.
    b) integrity tests.
    c) participative decision making.
    d) preferential selection.
    Ans: a   LO: 4   Page: 542   Type: A

60. Dwight is a salesman for a paper company. His performance is assessed by determining how many boxes of paper he sells each month, which means that he is being appraised in terms of
    a) psychographic criteria.
    b) preferential absolute criteria.
    c) objective performance criteria.
    d) subjective performance criteria.
    Ans: c   LO: 4   Page: 542   Type: A

61. Performance standards based on the perceptions of employees reported by their supervisors, co-workers, or clients are considered
    a) concrete appraisals.
    b) integrity tests.
    c) quantitative criteria.
    d) subjective measures.
    Ans: d   LO: 4   Page: 542   Type: F

2. Supervisor appraisals of an employee seem to be *least* influenced by
    a) technical proficiency.
    b) friendliness.
    c) job knowledge.
    d) dependability.
    Ans: b   LO: 4   Page: 542-543   Type: F

63. Jane, an accountant, is evaluated based primarily on the number of errors she makes while doing her job. According to the relevant research, these ratings are likely to be
    a) less accurate than ratings based on subjective criteria.
    b) influenced less by Jane's dependability than by her friendliness.
    c) limited by their failure to take into account the quality of her work.
    d) particularly susceptible to social perception biases.
    Ans: c   LO: 4   Page: 542-543   Type: A

64. Michael, the regional manager of his company, believes that Jim is a personable and productive individual. When asked to rate Jim's leadership skills, Michael does not have much to go on and therefore assumes he is also a good leader. This is an example of a(n)
     a)   contrast effect.
     b)   halo effect.
     c)   escalation effect.
     d)   Hawthorne effect.
     Ans: b   LO: 4   Page: 543   Type: A

65. Halo effects are *most* likely to be caused by
     a)   reliance on implicit personality theories.
     b)   the tendency to perceive women as having a nurturing role.
     c)   biases in the graphology process.
     d)   the use of structured interviews in personnel selection.
     Ans: a   LO: 4   Page: 543   Type: C

66. Tyler is a company supervisor who oversees more than 35 employees. Halo effects are likely to be *most* pronounced in his performance appraisals of
     a)   employees he knows very well.
     b)   employees he does not know well.
     c)   masculine employees.
     d)   feminine employees.
     Ans: b   LO: 4   Page: 543   Type: A

67. Jacques is required to evaluate several of his employees this year. To avoid problems associated with the halo effect, he should
     a)   make sure he is familiar with each of his employees.
     b)   request that he evaluate only workers he has not evaluated before.
     c)   make sure his ratings are not uniform.
     d)   try to use both subjective and objective criteria in his evaluations.
     Ans: a   LO: 4   Page: 543   Type: A

68. Derek is a fantastic baseball player. A variety of scouts come to watch him play and evaluate him on three separate occasions. He plays great in the first two games they see, but his performance in the third game is fairly unremarkable. If the scouts fall victim to a contrast effect, they will rate Derek's performance in the third game
     a)   as being better than it actually was.
     b)   as being worse than it actually was.
     c)   differently in public than they will in private.
     d)   more quickly than they did his performance in the first two games.
     Ans: b   LO: 4   Page: 543   Type: A

69. Angus is accused of having a restriction of range problem in his evaluations of co-workers. What is *most* likely to be true about Angus?
     a)   His ratings fluctuate dramatically over time.
     b)   He tends to believe that friendly subordinates are also competent.
     c)   He rates a negative performance more negatively after a succession of positive performances.
     d)   He probably fails to make adequate distinctions among subordinates.
     Ans: d   LO: 4   Page: 543   Type: A

70. Mara performs very well at her job. All other things being equal, it is likely that Mara will be appraised positively by all of the following evaluators *except* one who
     a)   is in a position of power.
     b)   exhibits a restriction of range problem.
     c)   uses objective rather than subjective criteria.
     d)   shows halo effects when rating others.
     Ans: a   LO: 4   Page: 542-543   Type: A

71. Jerry is a comedian, who is scheduled to appear after a set by his friend Larry. Larry has a great set and receives roars of approval and laughter from the audience. Based upon the contrast effect, Jerry should
   a) be concerned that the audience will be less impressed with his performance than if Larry had not been so funny.
   b) feel confident that the audience will respond positively to his act because they are already in a good mood.
   c) be concerned that the audience will be too distracted by the previous performance to pay much attention to his jokes.
   d) increase his credibility by pointing out to the audience just how funny Larry was.
   Ans: a   LO: 4   Page: 543   Type: A

72. As managers, Homer is viewed as easygoing and agreeable, while Marge is seen as very conscientious. Which of the following is *most* likely to occur?
   a) Homer will be more lenient than Marge in evaluating employees.
   b) Homer will be harsher than Marge in evaluating employees.
   c) Marge will be more likely than Homer to use objective measures of appraisal.
   d) Marge will be more likely than Homer to use subjective measures of appraisal.
   Ans: a   LO: 4   Page: 543   Type: A

73. Aloysius, a cashier in a department store, has been asked by store management to evaluate his shift supervisor. Aloysius is being asked to provide
   a) situational judgments.
   b) upward feedback.
   c) preferential absolute information.
   d) due process.
   Ans: b   LO: 4   Page: 543-544   Type: A

74. Anson asks an industrial/organizational psychologist for advice concerning whether he should ask his employees to complete self-evaluations. Which of the following is the psychologist *least* likely to indicate?
   a) Self-evaluations tend to be more positive than supervisor evaluations.
   b) Self-evaluations tend to be less predictive of job performance than supervisor evaluations.
   c) Individuals who have more power in the company will give themselves more positive evaluations than those who have less power.
   d) Female employees will give more positive evaluations of themselves than will male employees.
   Ans: d   LO: 4   Page: 543-544   Type: A

75. Compared to supervisor ratings, self-evaluations are likely to be
   a) more positive and more predictive of job performance.
   b) more positive but less predictive of job performance.
   c) more negative and more predictive of job performance.
   d) more negative and less predictive of job performance.
   Ans: b   LO: 4   Page: 543-544   Type: F

76. To increase the accuracy of performance appraisals, it is recommended that managers
   a) maintain at least a two-week delay between performance and evaluations.
   b) use a single rater rather than multiple raters so as to avoid discrepancies.
   c) educate evaluators about the biases of social perception.
   d) train evaluators to focus their ratings on the middle of rating scales.
   Ans: c   LO: 4   Page: 544-545   Type: C

77. Gretel wants to be as accurate and fair as she can when evaluating her subordinates. Which of the following would help her be both accurate and fair in her evaluations?
   a) Gretel has her employees evaluate themselves and then observes them on repeated occasions, rating their performance on a numerical scale.
   b) Gretel receives training on the biases of social perception and gives her subordinates clear performance standards.
   c) Gretel remains detached from her employees and is the sole evaluator.
   d) Gretel has several raters assess her subordinates and then gives the employees feedback without using due process in her appraisal.
   Ans: b   LO: 4   Page: 544-545   Type: A

78. The practice of obtaining multiple evaluations of an individual worker from supervisors, peers, and
     subordinates is known as a _____ appraisal.
     a)   circular
     b)   360-degree
     c)   multidirectional
     d)   recombinant
     Ans: b   LO: 4   Page: 544-545   Type: F

79. Izzy is a surgical resident. The hospital wants to conduct a 360-degree appraisal of her performance, which
     required obtaining evaluations from
     a)   patients.
     b)   her fellow residents.
     c)   the chief resident and supervising attending physicians.
     d)   All of these.
     Ans: d   LO: 4   Page: 544-545   Type: A

80. Linda wants her managers to be better evaluators of her employees. Towards this end, she can do all of the
     following *except*
     a)   rely on one evaluator who is shown to be objective for all her employees.
     b)   reward her managers for being accurate in their evaluations.
     c)   provide her managers with training to improve their evaluation skills.
     d)   minimize the time between employee performance and performance evaluation.
     Ans: a   LO: 4   Page: 544-545   Type: A

81. Vito, the owner of a new company, believes that all appraisals in his company should be based on *evidence*
     of job performance rather than other considerations. In order for Vito to operate according to the due
     process model of appraisal, he must also
     a)   make his performance standards clear and encourage workers to evaluate themselves.
     b)   give employees useful and timely feedback, and make sure they are rated several times by one
           supervisor.
     c)   make his performance standards clear, and give employees useful and timely feedback.
     d)   encourage workers to evaluate themselves, and make sure they are rated several times by one
           supervisor.
     Ans: c   LO: 4   Page: 545   Type: A

82. All of the following are aspects of the due process model of performance appraisal *except*
     a)   adequate notice.
     b)   fair hearing.
     c)   integrity tests.
     d)   evidence of job performance.
     Ans: c   LO: 4   Page: 545   Type: F

83. Eunice is upset because she believes that the only reason she received a poor evaluation at work was
     because she did not really understand what was expected of her or what criteria would be used to evaluate
     her. Eunice would probably say that her company lacks what principle of the due process model?
     a)   Adequate notice
     b)   Fair hearing
     c)   A multiple-rater system
     d)   Situational control
     Ans: a   LO: 4   Page: 545   Type: A

84. The principle of the due process model that dictates that employees have the right to be evaluated by a
     supervisor familiar with their work as well as receive timely feedback about their evaluation is called
     a)   adequate notice.
     b)   procedural fairness.
     c)   fair hearing.
     d)   situational control.
     Ans: c   LO: 4   Page: 545   Type: F

85. Bobby, Peter, Greg, and Mike are all very effective leaders. Although their leadership styles vary, they are particularly likely to have in common
    a)   an emphasis on smoothing over potentially tense relationships.
    b)   the ability to negotiate deals efficiently and to their own advantage.
    c)   an engaging way of speaking.
    d)   the ability to use social influence effectively.
    Ans: d   LO: 5   Page: 545-546   Type: A

86. Grant, a chief executive officer for more than two decades, has observed the rise of many people to positions of leadership in his company. In retrospect, he realizes that most of these people have exhibited a particular set of traits, including intelligence, ambition, a need for power, and an ability to adapt to changing circumstances. Grant's observations are consistent with the
    a)   Great Person Theory.
    b)   interactionist approach.
    c)   transactional approach.
    d)   contingency model.
    Ans: a   LO: 5   Page: 546-547   Type: A

87. According to Kirkpatrick and Locke (1991), effective leaders have all of the following attributes *except*
    a)   inner drive.
    b)   creativity.
    c)   self-confidence.
    d)   single-mindedness.
    Ans: d   LO: 5   Page: 546-547   Type: F

88. "Great leadership emerges out of time, place, and circumstances." Such a statement is *best* reflected in
    a)   the classic trait approach.
    b)   the contingency model of leadership.
    c)   "top-down" views of leadership.
    d)   the transactional model of leadership.
    Ans: b   LO: 5   Page: 547-548   Type: C

89. The idea that leadership effectiveness is determined both by the personal characteristics of leaders and the control afforded by the situation is *most* consistent with the
    a)   contingency model.
    b)   transformational model.
    c)   expectancy theory.
    d)   Great Person Theory.
    Ans: a   LO: 5   Page: 547-548   Type: C

90. The contingency model of leadership suggests that for a task in which there is low situational control
    a)   a relations-oriented leader often offers too little guidance.
    b)   a task-oriented leader is unlikely to be successful.
    c)   a transactional leader will usually fail to set clear goals.
    d)   a transformational leader will often rub subordinates the wrong way.
    Ans: a   LO: 5   Page: 547-548   Type: C

91. Nicola has good relations with her subordinates, exerts considerable power over them, and is faced with clearly structured tasks within the organization. According to the contingency model, Nicola is *most* likely to be an effective leader if she
    a)   concentrates on making sure that her subordinates' feelings remain positive.
    b)   appears to individualize her attention.
    c)   explicitly endorses due process considerations.
    d)   is very task-oriented.
    Ans: d   LO: 5   Page: 547-548   Type: A

92. Paige is elected the leader of a group requiring a moderate degree of situational control. According to the contingency model, she is *most* likely to be an effective leader if she
     a) is relations-oriented.
     b) is single-minded in her focus on job performance.
     c) makes most decisions herself and does not ask for guidance.
     d) is task-oriented.
     Ans: a   LO: 5   Page: 547-548   Type: A

93. Mismatches between a leader's personal style and the demands of the situation are *most* likely to lead to
     a) high situational control.
     b) low rates of employee absenteeism.
     c) increased leader competence.
     d) increased job stress.
     Ans: d   LO: 5   Page: 547-548   Type: C

94. Aretha is trying to determine the extent to which she should include her subordinates in a decision she is making regarding a company problem that has arisen. According to the normative model of leadership, which of the following factors should she consider?
     a) The clarity of the problem
     b) The magnitude of the problem
     c) The immediacy of the problem
     d) The consequences of the problem
     Ans: a   LO: 5   Page: 548   Type: A

95. A leader who sets clear goals for her followers, rewarding those who live up to their end of the bargain and correcting those who do not, is known as a(n) _____ leader.
     a) transformational
     b) normative
     c) transactional
     d) autocratic
     Ans: c   LO: 5   Page: 548-549   Type: A

96. Isaac, a well-respected man with charisma, wants to preserve some uninhabited islands from development. He carries out a "Save the Islands" campaign by focusing on people's love for nature, addressing their concern about what they believe is becoming an overdeveloped world. He also presents a strategy for preserving the islands forever. Such leadership *best* reflects
     a) the classic trait approach to leadership.
     b) a normative model of leadership.
     c) transformational leadership.
     d) task-oriented leadership.
     Ans: c   LO: 5   Page: 549-551   Type: A

97. Jordan, a successful CEO, is asked in an interview to explain her success. She replies, "To lead, you must inspire." Given her response, she can *best* be described as a
     a) transactional leader.
     b) relations-oriented leader.
     c) transformational leader.
     d) task-oriented leader.
     Ans: c   LO: 5   Page: 549-551   Type: A

98. According to research on leadership, which of the following seems to be *true*?
     a) Transformational leaders are more effective than transactional leaders.
     b) Transformational leaders are less effective than transactional leaders.
     c) Transformational leaders and transactional leaders are equally effective.
     d) Transformational leaders are more effective in their use of rewards than are transactional leaders.
     Ans: a   LO: 5   Page: 548-551   Type: F

99. Lyness and Thompson's (2000) survey of corporate executives indicated that, compared to their male counterparts, female executives are more likely to have
    a)   greater access to role models and mentors.
    b)   a more task-oriented leadership style.
    c)   sought competitive, hierarchical positions.
    d)   been passed over for jobs requiring relocation.
    Ans: d   LO: 5   Page: 551-552   Type: F

100. Research regarding gender and leadership indicates that
    a)   men are typically more effective leaders than women.
    b)   women are typically more effective leaders than men.
    c)   male leaders are more task-oriented than female leaders and females are more relations-oriented than males.
    d)   male leaders are more controlling in their approach than are female leaders, and females are more democratic than males.
    Ans: d   LO: 5   Page: 551-552   Type: F

101. Research on race and corporate leadership indicates that
    a)   while minority individuals are underrepresented in entry-level positions, minority leaders and CEOs are well-represented.
    b)   there is a disproportionately low number of racial minority CEOs.
    c)   male leaders are more task-oriented than female leaders and females are more relations-oriented gender, but not racial underrepresentation is observed among leaders of Fortune 500 companies.
    d)   race, but not gender underrepresentation is observed among leaders of Fortune 500 companies
    Ans: b   LO: 5   Page: 551-552   Type: F

102. Bernard is an African-American professional. Research suggests fairly clearly that he will be more likely than a White professional to
    a)   respond positively to a task-oriented leader.
    b)   receive more negative employee evaluations.
    c)   establish a mentoring relationship with a supervisor.
    d)   feel excluded socially from informal work groups.
    Ans: d   LO: 5   Page: 551-552   Type: A

103. One race-related difference in employment experiences is that young employees of color are less likely than White employees to
    a)   be assigned to work with a transformational leader.
    b)   develop mentoring relationships with influential White men in their companies.
    c)   be evaluated using a 360-degree appraisal.
    d)   receive the benefits of the sunk cost principle.
    Ans: b   LO: 5   Page: 551-552   Type: F

104. In considering whether or not she is satisfied with the compensation she receives from her job, Imelda is likely to consider all of the following *except*
    a)   benefits such as health care and stock options.
    b)   how raises are determined.
    c)   salary differences within the company.
    d)   the procedural interdependence of the company.
    Ans: d   LO: 6   Page: 553-554   Type: A

105. Fredi believes that the best way to motivate his employees is to remind employees how valuable their contributions are to the company and to reward them for excellent performance. Fredi's beliefs are *most* consistent with
    a)   expectancy theory.
    b)   the normative model of leadership.
    c)   escalation effects.
    d)   equity theory.
    Ans: a   LO: 6   Page: 553-554   Type: A

106. According to expectancy theory, worker motivation depends on all of the following *except*
   a)   valued rewards.
   b)   high intrinsic motivation.
   c)   performance recognition.
   d)   a belief that extra effort will be effective.
   Ans: b   LO: 6   Page: 553-554   Type: F

107. Lancelot would like to increase employee motivation and productivity. According to expectancy theory, which of the following would be *most* effective?
   a)   Continually urging employees to do their best
   b)   Providing equal rewards to all employees regardless of effort or outcomes
   c)   Using only mildly positive symbolic rewards rather than monetary ones
   d)   Instituting a profit-sharing plan based on job performance
   Ans: d   LO: 6   Page: 553-554   Type: A

108. Carmelo is an extremely talented basketball player, and professional teams keep offering him lots of money to play for them. Though he doesn't particularly enjoy playing basketball, he continues to do so because of the money. In this situation, Carmelo is
   a)   relations-oriented.
   b)   task-oriented.
   c)   intrinsically motivated.
   d)   extrinsically motivated.
   Ans: d   LO: 6   Page: 554-555   Type: A

109. Thor would like to get his son to read more without compromising the child's intrinsic motivation to read. Which of the following could *best* achieve this?
   a)   Give the child a strict deadline by which time he must have read a set number of books.
   b)   Set up a competition with other kids in the neighborhood to see who can read the most books.
   c)   Create a schedule of how many hours the child should be reading each day and then closely supervise him to make sure he sticks to the schedule.
   d)   Give the child a new book for every book that he reads and make it clear that he is doing a good job of reading the books.
   Ans: d   LO: 6   Page: 554-555   Type: A

110. Cleon has always enjoyed making ceramic figurines for his colleagues. In return for a particular piece, a colleague gives him $100. Cleon's intrinsic motivation for making ceramic figurines is particularly likely to be undermined if he
   a)   perceives the payment as having informational value.
   b)   did not expect to receive any money.
   c)   perceives the money as controlling his behavior.
   d)   believes in contingency models.
   Ans: c   LO: 6   Page: 554-555   Type: A

111. People often try to relieve the distress of being underpaid or overpaid by
   a)   convincing themselves that equity already exists.
   b)   escalating commitment.
   c)   using assessment centers.
   d)   perceiving rewards as having informational value.
   Ans: a   LO: 6   Page: 555-558   Type: F

112. Terrell is concerned because he feels that he is working harder and performing better than most of the other wide receivers in the NFL, yet he is not being paid more than many of them. His concerns are consistent with
   a)   contrast effects.
   b)   equity theory.
   c)   halo effects.
   d)   360-degree appraisals.
   Ans: b   LO: 6   Page: 555-558   Type: A

113. Greenberg (1988) found that workers assigned to higher-status offices improve their job performance, whereas those assigned to lower-status offices slow their performance. This finding supports the predictions of
    a)   the transformational model.
    b)   equity theory.
    c)   the contingency model.
    d)   intrinsic motivation.
    Ans: b   LO: 6   Page: 555-558   Type: C

114. Summer, the owner of a music box company, subscribes to equity theory. It is likely that she will be especially concerned that
    a)   she maximizes employees' participation in the making of company decisions.
    b)   individuals who put the most into the company earn the highest salaries.
    c)   she provides for a variety of different kinds of rewards.
    d)   salaries are based on objective measures of performance.
    Ans: b   LO: 6   Page: 555-558   Type: A

115. In 2006, American women were paid 81 cents for every dollar men were paid. All of the following are explanations provided by the book for this gender-based wage disparity *except*
    a)   consistent with the history of gender discrimination in this country, women have simply come to expect lower salaries than men do.
    b)   even when they perform well, women's self-ratings tend to be less positive than men's.
    c)   in making social comparisons, women tend to compare themselves with other women, not with men.
    d)   women tend to exhibit an interdependent or collectivist self-view, whereas men are more likely to value independence or individualism in the workplace.
    Ans: d   LO: 6   Page: 557-558   Type: F

116. Research by Vohs and colleagues (2006) demonstrates the effects of leading participants to think about money. Which of the following is *not* one of those effects?
    a)   People tend to prefer to work alone as opposed to in groups.
    b)   People tend to fail to ask for help with a problem they are having trouble solving.
    c)   People tend to encroach on the personal space of other people, standing too close to them or engaging in unwanted physical touching.
    d)   People tend to offer less help to others who are clearly in need of assistance.
    Ans: c   LO: 7   Page: 558-559   Type: F

117. According to research by Zhou and colleagues (2009), social rejection
    a)   leads people to give up pleasures such as chocolate and sunshine.
    b)   leads people to value money less.
    c)   leads people to value money more.
    d)   leads people to strive harder for social acceptance.
    Ans: c   LO: 7   Page: 559   Type: F

118. Shefrin (2000) suggests that stock market decisions are heavily influenced by
    a)   social psychological variables.
    b)   purely economic factors.
    c)   random fluctuations.
    d)   insider trading.
    Ans: a   LO: 7   Page: 559-562   Type: F

119. Researchers suggest that investors are more influenced by news and stock market tips during periods of rising and falling prices than during periods of relative stability. This is consistent with social psychological research concerning
    a)   social exchange theory and equity theory.
    b)   normative influence and social comparison processes.
    c)   cognitive dissonance and self-perception theories.
    d)   contrast effects and excitation transfer.
    Ans: b   LO: 7   Page: 559-562   Type: C

120. Being able to make attributions for a dip in a stock makes investors
   a)   more likely to sell the stock, regardless of the credibility of the rumors.
   b)   more likely to sell the stock, but only if the rumors are deemed credible.
   c)   less likely to sell the stock, regardless of the credibility of the rumors.
   d)   less likely to sell the stock, but only if the rumors are deemed credible.
   Ans: a   LO: 7   Page: 559-562   Type: C

121. Andreasson (1987) found that investors tend to buy low and sell high in the absence of potential
   explanations for market fluctuations, but follow the flow of the market when given newspaper explanations
   for market fluctuations. This finding is consistent with the hypothesis that investor decisions are often based
   on
   a)   the maximum amount of money they are willing to lose.
   b)   the minimum amount of profit they wish to make.
   c)   whether the market has been stable.
   d)   their attributions for the rise or fall of stock prices.
   Ans: d   LO: 7   Page: 561-562   Type: C

122. One difficulty that homeowners often run into when they attempt to sell is that they tend to value their own
   property much higher than do other people, including real estate agents and potential buyers. This tendency
   is consistent with the
   a)   sunk cost principle.
   b)   endowment effect.
   c)   escalation effect.
   d)   concept of entrapment.
   Ans: b   LO: 7   Page: 562   Type: C

123. The behavior of the second highest bidder in Teger's (1980) dollar auction demonstrates
   a)   effective use of the sunk cost principle.
   b)   that people do not handle money as carefully as professionals do.
   c)   escalation of a counterproductive endeavor.
   d)   the fact that people take greater risks when gains are at stake.
   Ans: c   LO: 7   Page: 562-563   Type: C

124. Less than 30 minutes into the four-hour film, Sanford could tell he was going to hate the movie. He
   considered getting up and walking out but felt compelled to sit through the whole movie because he had
   already spent his money on the ticket. This illustrates
   a)   the sunk cost principle.
   b)   the normative model.
   c)   the due process model.
   d)   equity theory.
   Ans: a   LO: 7   Page: 563   Type: A

125. People who violate the sunk cost principle often
   a)   attribute random fluctuations in the stock market to predictable causes, thereby increasing the
         likelihood that self-fulfilling prophecies will occur.
   b)   feel entrapped by their own initial commitments to some failing course of action but continue to
         pursue it in an effort to justify their prior decisions.
   c)   wait too long before making their investment decisions, thereby passing up the opportunity to buy
         stocks when they are least expensive.
   d)   base their decisions purely on economic rules, and ignore the psychological implications of their
         actions.
   Ans: b   LO: 7   Page: 563   Type: C

ESSAY

126. Name two factors that affect *both* supervisor ratings of employees and employee self-ratings.
    Ans: Restriction of range problems and power are two factors common to both types of rating. A restriction of range results when supervisor ratings are clustered around one part of the scale, leading to very weak distinctions between employees. Similarly, self-ratings show a restriction of range in that most ratings cluster in the positive end of the scale. Power can also affect both rating types. Supervisors with power, compared to those without power, tend to give lower performance ratings to subordinate others, whereas individuals with high levels of power rate themselves exceptionally favorably.   Page: 542-544

127. Describe the characteristics of an effective leader according to the transactional model of leadership. Is this type of leader more consistent with the trait approach or the interactional models? Why?
    Ans: According to Hollander's transactional model, leaders are effective only if they respond to the concerns and needs of the people who follow their lead. An effective leader in the workplace, for example, listens to the concerns and ideas of the workers, fulfills their needs, and provides tangible rewards in exchange for expected levels of job performance. This type of leader is consistent with interactional models, which emphasize the interaction between personal and situational factors. The transactional model emphasizes this interaction by focusing on the relationship between the leader and the workers. By contrast, the trait approach focuses on the characteristics that make a good leader.   Page: 545-549

128. Compare and contrast men and women in terms of style and effectiveness as leaders.
    Ans: Research has suggested that female leaders in the workplace are as task oriented as their male counterparts, and have similar aspirations, abilities, values, and job-related skills. The only difference is that men tend to be more controlling and thus are more effective leaders in positions that require a directive style, whereas women tend to be more democratic and thus are more effective as leaders in positions that require cooperation and openness. In short, female leaders interact more with subordinates, inviting them to participate in decision-making processes and to share information and power. Research has also shown that female leaders are devalued relative to male leaders when they adopt a "masculine" style of leadership or work in "masculine" positions. But overall, both men and women have equal potential for effective leadership in most situations.   Page: 551-553

129. How do rewards affect intrinsic motivation?
    Ans: People are intrinsically motivated to pursue a particular activity when they do so purely out of interest, challenge, or sheer enjoyment. The receipt of rewards for engaging in that activity can thus undermine their intrinsic motivation. Indeed, people who start getting paid for a task that they already enjoy and used to do for free sometimes lose interest in the task and continue it only because of the money they are earning. Rewards are particularly likely to undermine intrinsic motivation when they are perceived as controlling such behavior. For example, if people who enjoy sculpting begin to get paid for this activity, they will likely lose intrinsic motivation to the extent that they perceive the money to be the primary reason for continuing to sculpt. If, instead, the money is perceived as having informational value in that it offers positive feedback about the quality of the art, and the artists believe that the money is not an important reason for sculpting, then their intrinsic motivation should not be undermined and may even be increased.   Page: 554-555

130. Explain how investors are influenced by attributions about fluctuations in the stock market.
    Ans: When stock prices increase and decrease, the attributions that people make about these fluctuations play an important role in their investment decisions. If they attribute these increases and decreases to general causes that are likely to persist, rather than to specific causes for which they have clear explanations, they are more likely to follow the flow of the marketplace and buy stocks when they are rising and sell them when they are falling (thereby violating the conventional wisdom of trying to buy low and sell high). For example, a person with money invested in Stock X who learns that its price has dropped for three consecutive days is more likely to sell stock if he or she attributes the drop to some world event. Indeed, when many people make the same attributions, self-fulfilling prophecies begin to emerge. Let's say that a large number of investors believe that Stock X's decline has resulted not from the typical fluctuations of the stock market but instead from some new technology that has been developed or some war that is brewing; these investors are likely to sell their stock, causing the price to drop further, which in turn seems to confirm their original belief about the stock. If, in contrast, they attribute the decrease to a less serious matter, they are more likely to avoid panic and to rely on the more economically sound principle of buying low and selling high.   Page: 559-562

CHAPTER 14

Health

MULTIPLE CHOICE

1. Health psychology
   a) is one of the oldest subfields in all of psychology.
   b) recognizes the clear distinction between biological and psychological factors.
   c) is the application of psychology to the promotion of physical health.
   d) focuses primarily on mental health and psychological well-being.
   Ans: c   LO: 1   Page: 569-570   Type: F

2. Which of the following research questions would a health psychologist be *least* likely to study?
   a) How does social support affect the subjective well-being of nursing-home residents?
   b) What is the efficacy of various strategies for coping with stress?
   c) What is the role of attributions in discrimination against the mentally ill?
   d) How can high-risk individuals be persuaded to receive testing for AIDS?
   Ans: c   LO: 1   Page: 569-570   Type: A

3. Marla studies the link between psychological stress and physical health. Marla is *most* likely a(n)
   a) forensic psychologist.
   b) health psychologist.
   c) industrial/organizational psychologist.
   d) social worker.
   Ans: b   LO: 1   Page: 570   Type: A

4. Compared to life in the year 1900, Americans are more likely to die from
   a) infectious diseases, such as pneumonia.
   b) preventable diseases, such as heart attacks and strokes.
   c) natural disasters, such as hurricanes and floods.
   d) All of these.
   Ans: b   LO: 1   Page: 569-570   Type: F

5. By definition, stress is
   a) a state of arousal.
   b) anxiety-producing.
   c) permanent.
   d) inescapable.
   Ans: a   LO: 1   Page: 570   Type: F

6. The process by which we make judgments about the demands of potentially stressful events is called
   a) coping.
   b) subjective well-being.
   c) appraisal.
   d) stress-and-coping process.
   Ans: c   LO: 1   Page: 570   Type: F

7. The APA conducted a nationwide survey in 2008 in which they asked men and women to indicate the sources of stress in their lives. Four out of five cited which of the following?
   a) love
   b) illness
   c) money
   d) work
   Ans: c   LO: 1   Page: 570   Type: F

8. According to Lazarus and Folkman (1984), the way in which stress is experienced and the particular coping strategies that are used depend primarily on
    a) a person's amount of social support.
    b) the health of the immune system.
    c) a subjective appraisal of the situation.
    d) the general adaptation syndrome.
    Ans: c   LO: 1   Page: 570   Type: C

9. The distressing effects of a natural disaster are most likely to emerge among an individual who
    a) was least distressed before the event.
    b) is high in self-efficacy.
    c) experienced the most danger during the event.
    d) relies on emotion-focused coping.
    Ans: c   LO: 1   Page: 571-573   Type: C

10. Paradise City was just hit by a severe hurricane. Which of the following outcomes is most likely?
    a) Those who were relatively more stressed before the hurricane will be less affected by it than those who were relatively less stressed.
    b) Everyone will experience primarily physical symptoms, rather than psychological ones.
    c) Those who were in greater danger during the hurricane will experience greater psychological stress.
    d) There will be a greater rate of suicide compared to cities hit by earthquakes.
    Ans: c   LO: 1   Page: 571-573   Type: A

11. Nancy was already having difficulty coping with multiple challenges in her life when her home was destroyed by a flood. Compared to other people, she will probably be
    a) more distressed by the flood.
    b) less distressed by the flood.
    c) able to ignore the flood.
    d) no more or less distressed by the flood.
    Ans: a   LO: 1   Page: 571-573   Type: A

12. Imagine that an earthquake occurs in Missouri soon after a hurricane strikes Florida and a flood strikes South Dakota. Jorge, a psychiatrist with a specialty in dealing with suicidal individuals, is ready to be dispatched to one of these locations to offer assistance. Based on the suicide rates that follow major disasters, Jorge will be
    a) equally needed in all locations.
    b) most needed in Missouri and Florida.
    c) most needed in Florida and South Dakota.
    d) most needed in Missouri and South Dakota.
    Ans: b   LO: 1   Page: 571-573   Type: A

13. Following a terrible car accident, Ruby is anxious, socially withdrawn, has difficulty sleeping, and experiences flashbacks of the crash. Ruby is *most* likely suffering from
    a) the illusion of invulnerability.
    b) posttraumatic stress disorder.
    c) a depressive explanatory style.
    d) Type A behavior.
    Ans: b   LO: 1   Page: 573   Type: A

14. Posttraumatic stress disorder (PTSD)
    a) rarely afflicts people for a long time following the trauma they experienced.
    b) is found exclusively in people who have been in traumatic war circumstances.
    c) is more likely in people who perceive having no control over the trauma.
    d) will afflict over 40% of people at some point during their lifetime.
    Ans: c   LO: 1   Page: 573   Type: C

15.   Posttraumatic stress disorder (PTSD)
       a)   is most likely to occur when an individual feels personally responsible for the outcome of a traumatic event.
       b)   is more prevalent among men versus women.
       c)   is observed among military personnel, but not the general citizenry.
       d)   often occurs 3 to 6 months after a soldier's return rather than immediately afterward.
       Ans: d   LO: 1   Page: 573   Type: F

16.   In interviews with hospital patients, Holmes and Rahe (1967) found that illness was often preceded by either a positive or negative major life event. This finding is consistent with the hypothesis that
       a)   stress is caused by change.
       b)   childhood trauma can exacerbate stress, especially among those who are ill.
       c)   negative events are experienced as more stressful than positive events.
       d)   life itself, rather than stress, produces physical illness.
       Ans: a   LO: 1   Page: 573-574   Type: C

17.   Which of the following appears to be *true*?
       a)   The stress caused by positive events can be as long-lasting as the stress caused by negative events.
       b)   People can experience positive and negative emotions simultaneously.
       c)   A positive major life event usually offsets the stress that is caused by several negative microstressors.
       d)   Negative events produce more antibodies than do positive events.
       Ans: b   LO: 1   Page: 573-574   Type: F

18.   Major positive and negative life events
       a)   result in similar levels of distress and physical illness.
       b)   are a more common source of stress than everyday hassles.
       c)   have different effects on physical illness.
       d)   are related to psychological, but not physical, illness.
       Ans: c   LO: 1   Page: 573-574   Type: C

19.   All of the following are examples of microstressors *except*
       a)   traffic.
       b)   noisy neighbors.
       c)   natural disasters.
       d)   waiting in a long line.
       Ans: c   LO: 1   Page: 574-575   Type: F

20.   Elaine is a college student. Which of the following does research suggest will be the *most* stressful for Elaine?
       a)   She and her boyfriend are constantly fighting.
       b)   She lives in a suite in her college dormitory.
       c)   It is the beginning of her junior year.
       d)   Her parents are selling their home.
       Ans: a   LO: 1   Page: 574-575   Type: A

21.   Research on burnout suggests it is more likely when workers lack
       a)   support from their supervisors.
       b)   cordial relationships with their co-workers.
       c)   opportunity for promotion.
       d)   All of these.
       Ans: d   LO: 1   Page: 574-575   Type: A

22.   Married couples who are financially strained are more likely to experience
       a)   high levels of satisfaction, but low levels of commitment.
       b)   high levels of commitment, but low levels of satisfaction.
       c)   illusions of invulnerability in their relationship.
       d)   conflict in their relationship.
       Ans: d   LO: 1   Page: 575   Type: A

23. Selye's (1936) general adaptation syndrome includes all of the following stages *except*
    a) alarm.
    b) exhaustion.
    c) recovery.
    d) resistance.
    Ans: c   LO: 2   Page: 575-577   Type: F

24. While walking home alone late at night, Winona suddenly hears footsteps behind her. She can feel her heart pounding, her breathing quicken, and the adrenaline racing through her body. Within the framework of the general adaptation syndrome, Winona is in the _____ stage.
    a) alarm
    b) exhaustion
    c) recovery
    d) resistance
    Ans: a   LO: 2   Page: 575-577   Type: A

25. Bernie is about to be attacked by the class bully, and thus is under stress. According to general adaptation syndrome, Bernie can expect
    a) his digestive functions to accelerate.
    b) his stress to impede his ability to defend himself.
    c) higher levels of adrenaline in his bloodstream.
    d) local immunological defenses to be activated immediately.
    Ans: c   LO: 2   Page: 575-577   Type: A

26. From an evolutionary perspective, stress is a(n)
    a) "recent invention."
    b) "adaptive benefit."
    c) "long-term selection advantage."
    d) "nuisance variable."
    Ans: a   LO: 2   Page: 576-577   Type: C

27. Which of the following has been demonstrated in research concerning the impact of gender on responses to stress?
    a) Men and women exhibit the fight-or-flight response to the same degree.
    b) Women become more nurturing and affiliative than do men.
    c) Women react more aggressively than men.
    d) Men are less likely than women to suffer negative health consequences following prolonged stress.
    Ans: b   LO: 2   Page: 576-577   Type: F

28. Gurjit is easily angered when threatened and hates it when his co-workers are not prepared. In addition, he is always in a rush and feels that he has to be the best employee in the company. Gurjit's personality is *most* consistent with
    a) optimism.
    b) hardiness.
    c) self-focused depression.
    d) the Type A behavior pattern.
    Ans: d   LO: 2   Page: 577-579   Type: A

29. Which of the following concerning personality and coronary heart disease is *true*?
    a) Individuals with a Type B personality are more likely to have coronary heart disease than those with Type A personalities.
    b) Observations of a person's behavior are a better indicator of Type A personality than self-reports.
    c) An estimated 5 million Americans suffer from coronary heart disease.
    d) The most toxic personality ingredient associated with coronary heart disease is competitiveness.
    Ans: b   LO: 2   Page: 577-579   Type: F

30. Caleb has a Type A personality. The aspect of his behavior that is likely to place Caleb at *greatest* risk for coronary heart disease is his
    a) mistrust of other people.
    b) competitive orientation.
    c) impatience.
    d) workaholism.
    Ans: a   LO: 2   Page: 577-579   Type: A

31. All of the following are characteristics associated with coronary-prone behavior *except*
    a) time consciousness.
    b) competitiveness.
    c) creativity.
    d) strong drive.
    Ans: c   LO: 2   Page: 577-579   Type: F

32. Bernd gets annoyed when others criticize him, frequently mutters at the television during the news, and counts the items in the baskets of those ahead of him in the express checkout lane to be sure they are not over the limit. These behaviors are consistent with
    a) high levels of hostility.
    b) a competitive orientation.
    c) the Type B personality.
    d) high levels of neuroticism.
    Ans: a   LO: 2   Page: 578-579   Type: A

33. High levels of hostility have been found to predict
    a) decreased use of alcohol and cigarettes.
    b) greater use of emotion-focused coping.
    c) more intense cardiovascular responses to events.
    d) risky behaviors.
    Ans: c   LO: 2   Page: 578-579   Type: C

34. Jack learns that hostility and anger are factors in the development of high blood pressure, so he now tries to suppress his anger. How will this behavior likely affect his body over time?
    a) His blood pressure will probably decrease.
    b) His blood pressure will probably increase.
    c) His blood pressure will remain stable at its current level.
    d) His blood pressure will decrease, but only if he believes that suppression can have such an effect.
    Ans: b   LO: 2   Page: 578-579   Type: A

35. Penelope tends to be hostile and angry much of the time. She recently had an argument with her best friend Daisy. Daisy, who is more easygoing, is loath to bring up the debated subject again, even after a significant period of time has elapsed. Daisy probably recognizes that
    a) Penelope has a strong fight-or-flight response.
    b) Penelope, because of her hostile nature, will exhibit intense reactions long after the argument by just being reminded of it.
    c) people who are high in hostility are also likely to remember events in ways that minimize their feelings of anger.
    d) Penelope has the three most important risk factors for coronary heart disease.
    Ans: b   LO: 2   Page: 578-579   Type: A

36. An emerging subfield that examines the link between the mind and heart is known as
    a) psychoneuroimmunology.
    b) psychocardiology.
    c) somatic cardiology
    d) thoracic psychology
    Ans: b   LO: 2   Page: 579   Type: F

37. Psychological stress has been implicated as a factor in a wide variety of illnesses. This can be explained by the fact that stress
    a) can be experienced as either positive or negative.
    b) compromises the body's immune system.
    c) is both a cause and effect of illness.
    d) promotes an illusion of invulnerability to disease.
    Ans: b   LO: 2   Page: 579-581   Type: C

38. After an extraordinarily stressful week at work, Mahmoud spends the weekend in bed with the flu. Which of the following *best* explains why Mahmoud became ill?
    a) Mahmoud depleted his body's stress-fighting resources, thus increasing his susceptibility to illness.
    b) Prolonged activity of Mahmoud's stress-fighting resources caused other bodily systems to break down, increasing his susceptibility to illness.
    c) Mahmoud's natural stress-fighting resources weakened with prolonged use, making his body more susceptible to illness.
    d) Mahmoud has a Type B, rather than a Type A, personality.
    Ans: b   LO: 2   Page: 579-581   Type: A

39. Psychoneuroimmunology is the study of the relationship between psychological factors,
    a) the nervous system, and the brain.
    b) the heart, and the nervous system.
    c) the immune system, and the brain.
    d) the immune system, and the heart.
    Ans: c   LO: 2   Page: 579-581   Type: F

40. Which of the following has been demonstrated in research concerning the impact of stress on the immune system?
    a) Individuals deprived of sleep for long periods of time exhibit a weakened immune system.
    b) Recently divorced or widowed individuals show increased functioning of their immune systems.
    c) Both positive and negative events weaken the immune system.
    d) Stress weakens the immune systems of rats, but not humans.
    Ans: a   LO: 2   Page: 579-581   Type: F

41. Stress may weaken the immune system in part by increasing
    a) the number of lymphocytes in the bloodstream.
    b) blood pressure.
    c) unhealthy behaviors.
    d) physical exertion and rest.
    Ans: c   LO: 4   Page: 579-581   Type: C

42. Which of the following *best* characterizes the relationship between stress and illness?
    a) Stress increases the number of lymphocytes in the bloodstream, which diminishes the body's ability to fight off disease.
    b) Stress increases levels of adrenaline and other hormones that suppress immune cell activity and increase susceptibility to illness.
    c) Stress increases the negative attributions that people make, and negative attributions can become self-fulfilling prophecies.
    d) Under high levels of stress, people tend to sleep too much which weakens the immune system and makes illness more likely.
    Ans: b   LO: 2   Page: 581-582   Type: C

43. Based on research concerning the link between stress and illness, which of the following people is *most* likely to actually contract a cold if exposed to a cold virus?
    a) Carrie, who has a Type B personality
    b) Charlotte, who is happily married, but just had an argument with her husband
    c) Samantha, who has been unemployed for two months
    d) Miranda, who got a speeding ticket on her way home from work
    Ans: c   LO: 2   Page: 581-582   Type: A

44. Which of the following concerning the link between stress and illness is *true*?
   a)   Stress can increase vulnerability to short-term illnesses, like colds, but does not affect the course of more serious long-term diseases like cancer.
   b)   Stress can influence whether or not a person contracts a particular illness, but not the time course or outcome of that illness.
   c)   Stress increases susceptibility to coronary heart disease, but not colds or cancer.
   d)   Stress can influence both short-term and long-term illnesses, including colds, coronary heart disease, and cancer.
   Ans: d   LO: 2   Page: 581-582   Type: C

45. In an experiment that tested the effects of negative emotions on the immune system, experimenters gave each participant a blister using a vacuum pump. Which were the participants that took the longest to heal?
   a)   Participants who had financial problems.
   b)   Participants who had recently undergone a major life stressor.
   c)   Participants who ate an unhealthy diet.
   d)   Participants who had anger-control problems.
   Ans: d   LO: 2   Page: 580-581   Type: C

46. Arthur takes a protein pill every day for weeks. Research suggests that the more positive events in Arthur's life, the
   a)   fewer antibodies his body will create in response to the pill.
   b)   more antibodies his body will create in response to the pill.
   c)   more pills he will need to take in order to achieve his desired results.
   d)   less resistant his body will be to the effects of the pill.
   Ans: b   LO: 2   Page: 580-582   Type: A

47. Monty signs up for an experiment in which he is supposed to learn a series of word pairs. When he is later tested on his memory for these words, Monty is given a shock after every answer he gives, even when he gets the answer correct. In a different memory task the following week, Monty does not even try to study the photos he is given, even though he is told that he will receive shocks for every incorrect response he makes. Monty is demonstrating
   a)   problem-focused coping.
   b)   hardiness.
   c)   learned helplessness.
   d)   self-efficacy.
   Ans: c   LO: 3   Page: 583-584   Type: A

48. According to Seligman (1975), depression results primarily from
   a)   proactive coping.
   b)   learned helplessness.
   c)   high self-complexity.
   d)   specific external attributions.
   Ans: b   LO: 3   Page: 583-584   Type: F

49. Ralph has had a stressful month. His girlfriend dumped him, he failed three exams, and someone stole his car. According to Abramson et al.'s (1989) notion of hopelessness, Ralph's reactions to these events depend on his
   a)   upbringing.
   b)   achievements.
   c)   attributions.
   d)   self-esteem.
   Ans: c   LO: 3   Page: 583-584   Type: A

50. The habitual tendency to attribute negative events to causes that are stable, global, and internal is characteristic of
   a)   hardiness.
   b)   optimism.
   c)   Type A behavior.
   d)   a depressive explanatory style.
   Ans: d   LO: 3   Page: 583-584   Type: C

51. Waylon was just fired from his job. If he is depressed, then he is likely to believe that
    a)   his boss simply didn't recognize how hard Waylon was working.
    b)   his co-workers must have been plotting against him.
    c)   though it won't be easy to get another job, he'll find an even better one eventually.
    d)   his wife will leave him, the bank will repossess his car, and his life is totally ruined.
    Ans: d   LO: 3   Page: 583-584   Type: A

52. If Maurice has a depressive explanatory style, then he is likely to attribute his failures to
    a)   stable, global, and internal factors.
    b)   stable, global, and external factors.
    c)   unstable, situational, and internal factors
    d)   unstable, situational, and external factors.
    Ans: a   LO: 3   Page: 583-584   Type: A

53. Percival loses his job. As he thinks about getting laid off, he considers how he has been rejected in other areas of his life. He focuses on his previous girlfriend and remembers that she was the one to end the relationship. He begins to blame himself for getting fired and feels lousy about himself. This example illustrates how attributions to negative events that are _____ can contribute to learned helplessness.
    a)   stable and specific
    b)   unstable and external
    c)   specific and external
    d)   global and internal
    Ans: d   LO: 3   Page: 583-584   Type: A

54. A depressive explanatory style is marked by attributions for negative events that are
    a)   internal, stable, and global.
    b)   external, unstable, and global.
    c)   external, stable, specific.
    d)   internal, unstable, and specific.
    Ans: a   LO: 3   Page: 583-584   Type: F

55. Research in Israel on resilience in the face of terrorism and violence indicates that _____ tend to be more resilient than _____ .
    a)   Arabs; Jews
    b)   women; men.
    c)   more educated people; less educated people.
    d)   single people; married people
    Ans: c   LO: 4   Page: 584-585   Type: F

56. Marsha, an advertising executive, believes that her outcomes are controlled by her actions. She also perceives change as normal and life as meaningful. Marsha has the attribute of
    a)   externality.
    b)   hardiness.
    c)   self-complexity.
    d)   vulnerability.
    Ans: b   LO: 4   Page: 584-585   Type: A

57. Lucille lives in a nursing home where she gets to choose her daily activities. Peggy Sue lives in a nursing home where the staff schedules all activities. Research suggests that compared to Peggy Sue, Lucille will be
    a)   happier, but not healthier.
    b)   healthier, but not happier.
    c)   happier and healthier.
    d)   just as happy and healthy.
    Ans: c   LO: 4   Page: 585-586   Type: A

58.   When Don passes an exam, he thinks his success is due to his hard work. When he fails an exam, he thinks
       his failure is due to a lack of hard work. These perceptions reflect a sense of _____ and make it _____ likely
       that Don will get sick.
       a)   self-efficacy; less
       b)   optimism; more
       c)   pessimism; more
       d)   control; less
       Ans: d   LO: 4   Page: 585-586   Type: A

59.   The expectation that our behaviors can produce satisfying outcomes is referred to as
       a)   self-efficacy.
       b)   control.
       c)   hardiness.
       d)   internal explanatory style.
       Ans: a   LO: 4   Page: 585-586   Type: F

60.   Although Helloise would like to quit smoking, she is convinced that she is addicted and will never be able
       to stop. With respect to smoking, Helloise is
       a)   high in self-efficacy.
       b)   low in self-efficacy.
       c)   high in self-complexity.
       d)   low in self-complexity.
       Ans: b   LO: 4   Page: 585-586   Type: A

61.   Which of the following has been demonstrated in research on self-efficacy?
       a)   Individuals who have high self-efficacy with respect to coping with stress are likely to give up more
             quickly in the face of failure.
       b)   Individuals who have high self-efficacy tend to have higher self-esteem.
       c)   Individuals who have high self-efficacy with respect to coping with stress exhibit enhanced immune
             system functioning.
       d)   Individuals who have high self-efficacy with respect to coping with stress may try harder to cope, but
             they are no more likely to succeed.
       Ans: c   LO: 4   Page: 585-586   Type: C

62.   According to Sarkar and colleagues (2009), heart disease patients were more likely to survive
       hospitalization, when they
       a)   were confident in their ability to maintain their usual activities.
       b)   had low ratings of self-efficacy.
       c)   had depressive explanatory styles.
       d)   made stable, global attributions.
       Ans: a   LO: 4   Page: 585-586   Type: C

63.   Sue Ellen typically explains negative events using unstable, specific, external attributions. According to
       Seligman (1991), Sue Ellen could *best* be described as possessing
       a)   a Type B personality.
       b)   hardiness.
       c)   learned helplessness.
       d)   optimism.
       Ans: d   LO: 4   Page: 586-587   Type: A

64.   According to Seligman (1991), a non-depressive explanatory style is characteristic of
       a)   Type B personality.
       b)   optimism.
       c)   learned helplessness.
       d)   low self-efficacy.
       Ans: b   LO: 4   Page: 586-587   Type: F

65. A 2001 study of 1,306 adult men from the Boston area found that optimism was
    a) positively correlated with emotion-focused coping.
    b) positively correlated with problem-focused coping.
    c) negatively correlated with coronary heart disease 10 years later.
    d) negatively correlated with self-serving appraisal styles.
    Ans: c   LO: 4   Page: 586-587   Type: F

66. Which of the following has *not* been revealed by research on the relationship between optimism and health?
    a) Optimists are more likely than pessimists to make a quicker and fuller recovery from coronary artery bypass surgery.
    b) A positive correlation exists between hopelessness and mortality.
    c) Optimism can have negative consequences when it leads people to believe that they have control over uncontrollable events.
    d) Optimists are more likely than pessimists to take an emotion-focused approach to dealing with stress.
    Ans: d   LO: 4   Page: 586-587   Type: F

67. The biological explanation for the correlation between optimism and physical health focuses on
    a) risky behaviors and adrenaline.
    b) alcohol consumption.
    c) the immune system.
    d) genetic heritability.
    Ans: c   LO: 4   Page: 586-587   Type: F

68. Sean believes that he has a high sense of control over his own health, so when his kidney transplant unexpectedly fails, he is likely to
    a) avoid feeling depressed.
    b) feel particularly depressed.
    c) seek out the company of more pessimistic patients in the same situation.
    d) exhibit a particularly strong immune response.
    Ans: b   LO: 4   Page: 588   Type: A

69. One limitation to the positive relationship between a sense of control and resiliency is that
    a) setting control expectations too high can be harmful when outcomes are negative.
    b) a personal sense of control often predicts oversensitivity to the needs and feelings of others.
    c) it is much stronger in collectivist cultures than in individualistic cultures.
    d) it tends to disappear when a person opts for emotion-focused coping rather than problem-focused coping.
    Ans: a   LO: 4   Page: 588   Type: A

70. "The biology of hope (described by Norman Cousins, 1989) says that
    a) positive expectations can be self-fulfilling
    b) positive expectations lead to optimism.
    c) negative expectations are inevitable.
    d) when there's hope there's life.
    Ans: a   LO: 4   Page: 587-588   Type: C

71. Within Carver et al.'s (1989) multidimensional framework, individuals who cope with stressful events by trying to find the good in the situation are relying on
    a) mental disengagement.
    b) restraint coping.
    c) active coping.
    d) positive reinterpretation.
    Ans: d   LO: 5   Page: 588-590   Type: F

72. According to Carver et al.'s (1989) multidimensional framework, which of the following coping strategies is *least* commonly used?
    a) Acceptance
    b) Seeking social support
    c) Venting emotions
    d) Denial
    Ans: d   LO: 5   Page: 588-590   Type: F

73. In their study of procrastination, Tice and Baumeister (1997) found that, compared to non-procrastinators, procrastinators tended to report
    a) lower levels of stress throughout the semester.
    b) higher levels of stress throughout the semester.
    c) lower levels of stress early in the semester and higher levels late in the semester.
    d) higher levels of stress early in the semester and lower levels late in the semester.
    Ans: c   LO: 5   Page: 590-592   Type: F

74. Research suggests that procrastination is problematic. Nonetheless, a more controlling orientation epitomized by tackling tasks head-on can be problematic too in that it can
    a) prevent problem-focused coping.
    b) lead to development of a Type B personality.
    c) lead to decrements in attention.
    d) be physiologically taxing.
    Ans: d   LO: 5   Page: 590-592   Type: C

75. Frazier's (2003) research on blame, control, and coping among rape victims indicates that
    a) assigning blame leads to less stress.
    b) self-blame is only adaptive when it leads to feelings of future safety.
    c) blaming the assailant is the best way to recover from the trauma.
    d) past control is more important that present control.
    Ans: b   LO: 5   Page: 590-592   Type: C

76. Janoff-Bulman's research indicates that self-blame is adaptive in the long-term when it is directed at _____ as opposed to _____.
    a) one's behavior; oneself as a person
    b) one's past behavior; one's present behavior
    c) emotion; behavior
    d) one's character; one's behavior
    Ans: a   LO: 5   Page: 590-592   Type: C

77. Upon discovering that she has lung cancer, Mary blames the illness on her stupidity and lack of willpower. The blame she assigns herself is _____ and it is likely to _____ her sense of future control.
    a) situational; increase
    b) behavioral; increase
    c) characterological; decrease
    d) cathartic; decrease
    Ans: c   LO: 5   Page: 590-592   Type: A

78. Characterological self-blame reduces future control because it is a(n)
    a) unstable, internal attribution.
    b) stable, internal attribution.
    c) unstable, external attribution.
    d) stable, external attribution.
    Ans: b   LO: 5   Page: 590-592   Type: C

79. Emo lost three fingers in a machinery accident. If he engages in behavioral self-blame, there is a chance that he will cope successfully because the attribution is
    a) unstable and internal.
    b) stable and internal.
    c) unstable and external.
    d) stable and external.
    Ans: a   LO: 5   Page: 590-592   Type: A

80. Positive emotions such as joy help people cope with adversity by
    a) increasing blood pressure.
    b) allowing for proactive coping.
    c) distracting them from the stressor.
    d) narrowing their focus of attention.
    Ans: c   LO: 5   Page: 592   Type: C

81. Fredrickson's (2009) "broaden and build" theory highlights the importance of _____ to coping with challenging events in life.
    a) social support
    b) positive emotions
    c) good nutrition and eating habits
    d) religious belief
    Ans: b   LO: 5   Page: 592   Type: C

82. Cedric has been under a great deal of stress at work for the past year (he is an entertainer) and doesn't think he has any control over the situation. Cedric would be most likely to try to deal with this stress by engaging in
    a) proactive coping.
    b) subjective coping.
    c) emotion-focused coping.
    d) problem-focused coping.
    Ans: c   LO: 5   Page: 592-596   Type: A

83. When people make efforts directed at reducing anxiety, fear, and other internal signs of psychological stress, they are engaging in
    a) negativity appraisals.
    b) learned helplessness.
    c) emotion-focused coping.
    d) self-efficacy.
    Ans: c   LO: 5   Page: 592-596   Type: F

84. Katarina is on a plane that has been hijacked. Assuming she will be in this situation for an extended period of time, which of the following coping strategies to alleviate her stress would probably be *least* effective?
    a) Distracting herself
    b) Helping other passengers
    c) Deep breathing exercises
    d) Muscle relaxation
    Ans: b   LO: 5   Page: 593-594   Type: A

85. Which of the following statements about the coping strategies of distraction and suppression is *false*?
    a) Distraction tends to be a better way to manage stress than suppression.
    b) Suppression is more physically taxing than distraction.
    c) In the face of stressful stimuli, people practicing distraction will exhibit a greater cardiovascular response than people practicing suppression.
    d) People who try suppression take longer to recover from physical pain than do people who try distraction.
    Ans: c   LO: 5   Page: 592-595   Type: C

86. The rebound effect in thought suppression disappears when people
    a) try to think positively.
    b) receive social support.
    c) engage in focused distraction.
    d) are high in self-complexity.
    Ans: c   LO: 5   Page: 593   Type: F

87. When uncontrollable life events are especially traumatic, it tends to be healthier to
    a) make global attributions than specific attributions.
    b) raise perceptions of control to an extremely high level than to simply acknowledge a total lack of controllability.
    c) engage in problem-focused coping than in emotion-focused coping.
    d) open up to trusted others than to keep things to oneself.
    Ans: d   LO: 5   Page: 594-595   Type: F

88.   Opening up to others makes the problem at hand seem
      a)   more complicated, but doing so decreases blood pressure.
      b)   more complicated, and doing so increases blood pressure.
      c)   clearer, and doing so decreases blood pressure.
      d)   clearer, but doing so increases blood pressure.
      Ans: c   LO: 5   Page: 594-595   Type: C

89.   The principal cognitive benefit of opening up and sharing stressful experiences with others is known as
      a)   venting.
      b)   insight.
      c)   self-focus.
      d)   discharge.
      Ans: b   LO: 5   Page: 594-595   Type: F

90.   Albert, a child prodigy in mathematics is devastated to learn that he is unable to juggle. He dwells on the
belief that he has failed terribly and then falls into a deep depression. This outcome is *most* consistent with
      a)   the learned helplessness model.
      b)   catharsis.
      c)   adaptation level theory.
      d)   the self-focusing model.
      Ans: d   LO: 5   Page: 595-596   Type: A

91.   Self-awareness theory suggests that
      a)   self-focus brings out our personal shortcomings.
      b)   we spend too much time thinking about ourselves.
      c)   self-focus is triggered more by negative moods than positive moods.
      d)   self-focus is a central part of problem-focused coping.
      Ans: a   LO: 5   Page: 595-596   Type: C

92.   Kelley spends a lot of time focusing on herself. Her psychological health could be threatened if this self-
focus leads to
      a)   attempts at getting attention.
      b)   rumination about problems.
      c)   attributions to situations.
      d)   bids for social support.
      Ans: b   LO: 5   Page: 595-596   Type: A

93.   Walter and Helen are both recently divorced and trying to cope with the stress of their failed relationships.
      Compared to Walter, Helen is more likely to cope by
      a)   ruminating about her negative feelings.
      b)   using physical activity as a distraction.
      c)   engaging in anti-social behavior.
      d)   using alcohol or drugs to escape her feelings.
      Ans: a   LO: 5   Page: 595-596   Type: A

94.   Yvonne has a choice of activities for this evening. She can paint, at which she is accomplished, or go
      rollerblading, at which she struggles. If Yvonne is in a bad mood and wants to feel better, then she should
      a)   go rollerblading.
      b)   paint.
      c)   stay home and do nothing.
      d)   either paint or go rollerblading as both will make her feel equally good.
      Ans: a   LO: 5   Page: 595-596   Type: A

95.   Proactive coping
      a)   is an up-front effort to modify the onset of a stressful event.
      b)   is much more effective than social support.
      c)   only works for less traumatic events.
      d)   cannot prevent a stressor from occurring.
      Ans: a   LO: 6   Page: 596-597   Type: C

96. The major difference between proactive coping and other forms of coping (such as problem-based and emotion-based) is that proactive coping
     a)   occurs before a stressful event takes place.
     b)   is principally a cognitive strategy.
     c)   has no reported physiological effects.
     d)   is effective for events low in controllability.
     Ans: a   LO: 6   Page: 596-597   Type: C

97. Sophia is anxious about her first day in school. Her mother assures her that everything is fine, walks her to the classroom door, and waits until she seems comfortable in her new surroundings. Sophia's mother has provided
     a)   social support.
     b)   role modeling.
     c)   self-focused attention.
     d)   normative influence.
     Ans: a   LO: 6   Page: 597-599   Type: A

98. Social support accomplishes all of the following *except*
     a)   prolonging a cancer victim's life.
     b)   lowering a person's blood pressure.
     c)   suppressing the immune system's response to stress.
     d)   reducing suicidal intent among individuals infected with HIV.
     Ans: c   LO: 6   Page: 597-599   Type: F

99. Research on marriage and stress suggests that
     a)   being married leads to decreases in stress.
     b)   being married leads to increases in stress.
     c)   the relationship between the two depends on the level of marital conflict.
     d)   the relationship between the two becomes weaker as people age.
     Ans: c   LO: 6   Page: 598   Type: F

100. Arlene believes that she has lots of social support in her life because she has a large family and lots of friends. Arlene's views are consistent with the _____ model of social support.
     a)   intimacy
     b)   social contact
     c)   adaptation level
     d)   self-focused
     Ans: b   LO: 6   Page: 599   Type: A

101. Defining social support as the "number of social contacts" is problematic because
     a)   women who have many intimate friends exhibit lower levels of depression than women with fewer intimate friends.
     b)   people who have no social contacts at all often have lower mortality rates.
     c)   people immersed in several poor relationships may be more distressed.
     d)   None of these.
     Ans: b   LO: 6   Page: 599   Type: C

102. The idea that social support can be defined in terms of the availability of a close, confiding relationship with a significant other is *most* consistent with the
     a)   self-focus model.
     b)   intimacy model.
     c)   social contact model.
     d)   perceived availability model
     Ans: b   LO: 6   Page: 599   Type: C

103. Hamrick et al. (2002) examined the relationship between stress and social contact when it comes to developing illnesses. They found that for people under low stress _____, whereas for people under high stress _____.
    a) social contact did not matter; high levels of social contact led to increases in illness
    b) social contact did not matter; high levels of social contact led to decreases in illness
    c) high levels of social contact led to increases in illness; social contact did not matter
    d) high levels of social contact led to decreases in illness; social contact did not matter
    Ans: a   LO: 6   Page: 598-599   Type: C

104. Joshua has a caring, affectionate relationship with his wife but few other social ties. Among the following, which model of social support would predict good psychological health for Joshua?
    a) The intimacy model
    b) The self-focus model
    c) The perceived availability model
    d) The social contact model
    Ans: a   LO: 6   Page: 599   Type: A

105. The book describes several different models for assessing social support, including
    a) number, diversity, quality, and availability of social contacts.
    b) integrated, independent, and collectivist mentalities.
    c) efficacious, non-efficacious, direct, and indirect social ties.
    d) communal, exchange, and equity relationships.
    Ans: a   LO: 6   Page: 599   Type: F

106. Strawbridge (2001) found that attending religious services is correlated with
    a) increases in emotion-focused coping.
    b) increases in smoking.
    c) decreases in exercise.
    d) None of these.
    Ans: d   LO: 6   Page: 599-600   Type: F

107. Compared to European Americans, Asians are
    a) less likely to seek out sociall support in times of stress.
    b) more likely to cope with stress by turning to others for social support.
    c) more likely to experience microstressors.
    d) more likely to experience major life stressors.
    Ans: b   LO: 6   Page: 600-601   Type: F

108. Explicit social support is
    a) disclosing one's distress to others and seeking their advice, aid and comfort.
    b) thinking about others without asking for help.
    c) likely to lead European Americans to react with more stress.
    d) typically a collectivist coping style.
    Ans: a   LO: 6   Page: 600-601   Type: C

109. What seems to matter the *least* when it comes to determining whether a therapy will be successful or not?
    a) The intensity of social support provided
    b) The school of thought on which the therapy is based
    c) The amount of choice patients have in how the therapy proceeds
    d) Whether it communicates a positive expectation
    Ans: b   LO: 7   Page: 601-602   Type: C

110. All of the following contribute to successful therapeutic treatment *except*
    a) the communication of positive expectations.
    b) being able to make meaningful choices.
    c) exerting effort.
    d) having a few treatment options rather than many.
    Ans: d   LO: 7   Page: 601-602   Type: F

111. If preventive programs are to be effective, they must combine the use of fear-arousing tactics with
    a)   personal testimonials.
    b)   defensive denial.
    c)   advice regarding how to avoid the feared outcome.
    d)   emotion-focused rather than problem-focused coping.
    Ans: c   LO: 7   Page: 603-605   Type: F

112. Adele would like to start a TV campaign to reduce risky sexual behaviors and HIV rates at the community high school. Research suggests that which of the following spokespersons would Adele be wisest to recruit in order to promote behavioral change among the students?
    a)   Local physicians
    b)   Celebrity athletes
    c)   Community leaders
    d)   Fellow students
    Ans: a   LO: 7   Page: 603-605   Type: A

113. Research has systematically linked all of the following to fewer risky sexual behaviors *except*
    a)   vocal leaders within the gay community.
    b)   upward rather than downward social comparisons.
    c)   high self-efficacy with respect to safe sex behaviors.
    d)   pressure by significant others to decrease risk.
    Ans: b   LO: 7   Page: 603-605   Type: C

114. In Ephraim's favorite movies, which date back to the 1950s, most of the actors smoke. As models, these actors are likely to provide Ephraim with
    a)   subjective norms.
    b)   problem-focused coping.
    c)   a sense of invulnerability.
    d)   fear arousal.
    Ans: a   LO: 7   Page: 603-605   Type: A

115. Research by Prentice and Miller (1996) suggests that college students may abuse alcohol
    a)   in order to stand out among their peers and to gain attention.
    b)   because they lack knowledge about the effects of alcohol.
    c)   because they overestimate the amount of alcohol use on campus.
    d)   in order to enjoy the thrill of taking a risk.
    Ans: c   LO: 7   Page: 604-605   Type: C

116. One reason why subjective norms often sustain unhealthy behaviors is that
    a)   people violate the subjective norms in the effort to appear independent.
    b)   people overestimate the rate of such behaviors among their peers.
    c)   individuals engaged in unhealthy behaviors lack sufficient social support.
    d)   subjective norms tend to exaggerate the incidence of healthy behaviors.
    Ans: b   LO: 7   Page: 604-605   Type: C

117. One issue with AIDS prevention strategies is that
    a)   people who were most informed, motivated and skilled at using condoms are most likely to participate in the program to begin with.
    b)   the highest risk individuals are least likely to attend prevention programs.
    c)   for any HIV prevention program to work, it needs to bring in members of the community who need it most.
    d)   All of these.
    Ans: d   LO: 8   Page: 604-605   Type: F

118. Many social psychologists refer to the concept of happiness using the phrase
    a)   "self-efficacy."
    b)   "subjective well-being."
    c)   "relative privation."
    d)   "temporary disposition."
    Ans: b   LO: 8   Page: 605-609   Type: F

119. Research on subjective well-being demonstrates that
    a)   the majority of Americans describe themselves as unhappy.
    b)   happy people tend to be less intelligent than unhappy individuals.
    c)   happiness levels fluctuate randomly throughout the day.
    d)   happy people enjoy better physical health than unhappy individuals.
    Ans: d   LO: 8   Page: 605-609   Type: F

120. Which of the following people is likely to report the *highest* level of subjective well-being?
    a)   Tino, who has lost touch with his family and friends since starting graduate school
    b)   Mariano, who works as a college librarian
    c)   Paul, who has had a cold for two weeks
    d)   Derek, who is very physically attractive
    Ans: b   LO: 8   Page: 605-609   Type: A

121. Research on the relationship between money and happiness suggests that
    a)   upward comparisons tend to increase feelings of subjective well-being.
    b)   within a particular country, the wealthier citizens report significantly greater levels of happiness.
    c)   as the wealth of a particular country increases, the subjective well-being of its citizens increases.
    d)   in general, citizens of wealthier nations report greater levels of happiness.
    Ans: d   LO: 8   Page: 605-609   Type: C

122. Which of the following has *not* been offered as an explanation for the modest relationship between income and happiness?
    a)   People engage in both upward and downward social comparisons.
    b)   Subjective well-being depends on self-efficacy.
    c)   Satisfaction is based upon the level of success to which one is accustomed.
    d)   Everyone has a different baseline level of happiness.
    Ans: b   LO: 8   Page: 605-609   Type: C

123. Adaptation-level theory suggests that
    a)   our present satisfaction depends on the level of success to which we are accustomed.
    b)   the more money we have, the less we need to feel happy.
    c)   we will make upward comparisons more than we make downward comparisons.
    d)   high-impact events will have long-lasting effects on happiness levels.
    Ans: a   LO: 8   Page: 608-609   Type: C

124. Which of the following best illustrates the adaptation-level theory of happiness?
    a)   People who lose a limb are just as happy with their lives 10 years later as people who do not have accidents.
    b)   Individuals who win $1 million in the lottery tend to express greater happiness than individuals who win less money than that.
    c)   Tourists who leave cold climates for vacations in the sun report greater happiness during their trip than they do before they depart.
    d)   College transfer students usually show an increase in life satisfaction in their first semester at their new school.
    Ans: a   LO: 8   Page: 608-609   Type: A

125. Yoshiko won $500,000 in a lottery. After the initial excitement wears off, research suggests that her overall level of happiness will
    a)   increase as will the pleasure she derives from routine activities.
    b)   increase though she will derive less pleasure from routine activities.
    c)   decrease as will the pleasure she derives from routine activities.
    d)   decrease though she will derive greater pleasure from routine activities.
    Ans: c   LO: 8   Page: 608-609   Type: A

ESSAY

126. Distinguish between negative and positive life changes in terms of the amount of stress they produce.
    Ans: Contrary to Holmes and Rahe's prediction that all life changes result in stress and, potentially, health problems, research has shown that some changes are more stressful than others. In particular, negative changes such as divorce produce more stress than do positive changes such as marriage. In addition, positive changes are less likely to have negative health consequences.   Page: 573-574

127. Discuss how attributions may be related to health.
    Ans: Learned helplessness results from the tendency to make global, stable, internal attributions for the negative events in one's life. This attributional pattern characterizes the depressive explanatory style, and is associated with depression and decreased physical health. For example, one study showed that people with depressive explanatory styles exhibited a weaker immune response, though admittedly these data are only correlational. In contrast, individuals who make specific, unstable, and external attributions for negative life events tend to be healthier and recover from surgery more quickly.   Page: 583-588

128. Explain how self-focus may exacerbate the negative effects of stress, and how this may be avoided.
    Ans: The self-focus model of depression suggests that people often become depressed because they ruminate about how their behavior fails to measure up to their standards. In a self-perpetuating feedback loop, this depressive mood and negative self-evaluation is heightened by the self-focus that a stressful event brings. This leads to an increase in depressive mood and negative self-evaluation, which then leads to the further heightening of self-focus, and so on. A healthy alternative is to become engaged in activities that remove attention from the self.   Page: 595-596

129. Define social support and discuss the four models that have been proposed to measure it.
    Ans: Social support refers to the coping resources provided by friends and others. Researchers have proposed four models to measure the degree to which social support influences health: (1) The social contact model posits that social support should be defined as the number of social contacts a person has. Although there is some evidence to support this definition, it is also the case that bad social relationships can be health-endangering, as can crowded living environments. (2) The diversity model suggests that a network consisting of, for example, a spouse, close family members, friends, co-workers, and neighbors is more beneficial than a similarly sized social network comprised almost entirely of close friends. Being socially "integrated" through connections to different types of people in different types of relationships has been found to predict positive health outcomes. (3) The intimacy model emphasizes a close relationship with a significant other, and is supported by studies such as one showing that suicide likelihood is lower among individuals with a history of close relationships. (4) The perceived availability model argues that simply perceiving social resources to be available is what matters. Again, there is evidence for this model, particularly showing that people who are optimistic about social resources are high on other positive attributes such as self-esteem.   Page: 597-599

130. Physicians at a new AIDS clinic hope to promote less risky sexual behavior among their clients. Suggest three strategies they should consider adopting.
    Ans: To promote less risky behavior, there are several approaches physicians can take. One is to expose clients to fear-related information via film and other media, though the information needs to be strong and accompanied by additional material about how these clients can reduce their own risk of getting AIDS. Another tactic is to contact opinion leaders and encourage them to speak out in favor of (and practice) safe sex, relying on the power of modeling and subjective norms. Third, the physicians should train clients regarding how they might engage in safe sex in order to increase their self-efficacy (a significant predictor of precaution adoption). And finally, the physicians should consider putting together discussion groups of several clients, who then might model the safe sex behavior of fellow discussants. Such discussions might also elicit revisions in potentially distorted estimates of how often the clients' peers engage in risky sexual behavior.   Page: 603-605